Contents

UNIT FIVE: INDUSTRIALIZATION AND GLOBAL INTEGRATION (1750–1900) / 241

As you review the content in this book to work toward earning that **5** on your AP World History exam, here are five essential points you should focus on.

Barron's Essential 5

1 **Know the course themes.** As important as factual knowledge is, you can't and won't be able to know every detail about the history of the world, nor will the exam focus on fact memorization. You need to think about how the facts fit into the wider contexts addressed by the themes. Not only will the multiple-choice questions be geared in this way, the essay questions will be theme-inspired. As a reminder, the official course themes are: interaction between humans and the environment, development and interaction of cultures, state-building, expansion, and conflict, creation, expansion, and interaction of economic systems, and development and transformation of social structures.

2 **Understand historiography.** Historiography, the study of how historians think and write about history, is a topic of importance. What topics do historians choose to focus on? What sources and documents do they use as evidence, and how do they evaluate the strengths, weaknesses, and biases of that evidence? How do historians determine what causes a major event or development? How do they decide when historical eras begin and end? A number of multiple-choice questions will ask you to analyze images, quotations, and excerpts from historical writing. The document-based question (DBQ) is designed expressly to make you think like a historian.

3 **Know and understand the method of periodization chosen by the course.** One of the most basic historiographic skills is periodization: identifying key dates in the history of a country or region, or in the history of a topic or theme, and using those dates to define historical periods that make logical sense and organize facts and details in a way that makes them easier for students to learn. It is helpful to know major dates when they serve as key dividing points. It is even more helpful to know why such dates are considered important. The periodization chosen by the AP World History course is (were chosen carefully) meant to help you organize your studies. Understanding this will help you both on multiple-choice questions and all essays.

4 **"How" and "why" (and "how are they alike?") are more important than "who" and "when."** Names, dates, and other such details are never unimportant in the study of history. Mastery of facts can earn you extra points on essay questions and increase your chances of answering multiple-choice questions correctly. However, the exam is far more likely to emphasize how things were done, or why they happened, rather than who did them or when. Causes and effects matter greatly as well. Also, as you study any topic, always consider how it *compares* with similar topics in other times and places.

5 **Focus on interactions.** Note the number of times the word "interaction" appears in the course themes and historical periods. This is a topic of major interest, and you should concentrate on it throughout your studies. Note that interaction can take place on several levels—local, regional, interregional, and global—and in many forms.

INTRODUCTION

How to Use This Book

TO TEACHERS AND STUDENTS

This book can be a useful supplement to classwork and study materials. For readers who are not taking—or have never taken—a course in world history, it can serve as an independent study aid. Ideally, however, it will be used in conjunction with an actual academic course in world history, or by students who have taken such a course and are attempting to review.

This unit offers strategies for approaching the various types of questions encountered on the AP World History exam. These include multiple-choice questions, the document-based essay question, the continuity and change over time essay question, and the comparative essay question.

Units One through Six contain review chapters. Each unit is dedicated to one of the major historical periods covered by the exam and contains three to four chapters dealing with key concepts emphasized by the Advanced Placement course in world history. Each unit is preceded by a historical overview. A review section, consisting of 20 multiple-choice questions and four essay questions, follows each of these six units.

TO THE TEACHER

This book's review chapters can be used as supplements to summarize or reinforce particular teaching units and classroom or homework assignments. Unit overviews and chapter introductions assist students in looking at historical events from a broad perspective. The unit overviews also strive to place historical events and developments in the comparative context that the World History exam emphasizes.

The sample examinations in Unit Seven can be used near the end of the academic year as a culmination of a world history course. The sample exams also serve as good practice for the actual AP exam.

This introductory unit should be covered with students at the beginning of a world history course and then at several points afterward. The sooner students are familiar with the structure and procedures of the AP World History exam, the more comfortable they will be with the exam process itself.

TO THE STUDENT

This book can be used as an independent review device, whether or not you are taking an AP course in world history. Even for those who have never taken an academic or AP course in world history, this book can prove helpful. It is optimal, however, if you are using it while taking a course in world history, or if you have taken a world history course in the past and are using this book as a refresher.

It is best to use this book over a long period of time, rather than trying to cram at the last minute. You will want to absorb information and ideas thoroughly.

At the beginning, read this introductory unit on the structure of the Advanced Placement exam and the types of questions asked by it. To do well on the exam, it is crucial to know the procedure and follow directions closely. The sooner you acquaint yourself with the rules and procedures, the more natural they will feel when you take the actual test.

Pay special attention to unit overviews and chapter introductions. These will help you to see world history from a "big picture" perspective. They place trends and facts in a comparative context. Your ability to compare and contrast different eras and parts of the world will be tested extensively by the Advanced Placement exam.

SUGGESTED TIMELINES

How you use this book will largely depend on how much time you have to prepare. The more time, the better. Three possible timelines are provided; adapt as necessary to your own situation and abilities.

7-DAY TIMELINE

With such limited time, it is best to concentrate on test-taking methods and big-picture issues.

Day 1: Read all sections of this unit carefully. Take one of the model exams to get a sense of how ready you are.

Day 2: Read Units One and Two. Read ALL the overviews for Units One through Six.

Day 3: Read Unit Three. Again, read all the unit overviews.

Day 4: Read Unit Four. Read all unit overviews.

Day 5: Read Unit Five. Read all unit overviews.

Day 6: Read Unit Six. Read all unit overviews.

Day 7: Review the introductory unit. Take the second model exam.

4-WEEK TIMELINE

Having roughly a month to prepare will allow you some time to examine topics in depth, in addition to focusing on essentials.

Week 1: Read all of this introductory unit to get a sense of how the AP exam works. Move on to study Units One and Two.

Week 2: Study Units Three and Four.

Week 3: Study Units Five and Six.

Week 4: Take the model exams. Review this introductory unit about the exam itself, as well as the overviews for Units One through Six.

SCHOOL-YEAR (9-MONTH) TIMELINE

This is the ideal scenario. Here, you are likely using this book as a supplement to a world history course. If so, you should proceed at the same pace and in the same order as your teacher and classmates. Otherwise, the following will give you a good grounding.

Month 1: Read this introductory unit. Study Units One and Two.

Month 2: Review Units One and Two. Study Unit Three.

Month 3: Review Unit Three. Study Unit Four.

Month 4: Review Unit Four. Study Unit Five.

Month 5: Review Unit Five. Study Unit Six.

Month 6: Review Unit Six. Take the model exams. Assess your strengths and weaknesses.

Month 7: Skim Units One through Six, focusing on weak points. Use the unit overviews to help you think about comparisons.

Month 8: Continue reviewing the unit overviews. Reread the introductory unit carefully.

Month 9: Review as needed. Skim unit overviews and the introductory unit a final time.

GENERAL NOTES

Dates are given according to the standard Western calendar, with one exception. The abbreviations B.C.E. ("before common era") and C.E. ("common era") are used, rather than the traditional B.C. ("before Christ") and A.D. (*anno domini,* or "year of our Lord"). This usage shows more respect to those world cultures whose traditions are not based on Christianity. The Western calendar is only one of many systems used for measuring time. According to the Hebrew calendar, for example, year 1 is the equivalent of 3760 B.C.E. Year 1 of the Muslim calendar, by contrast, is 622 C.E.

Dates with no designation—those that appear simply as numerals—are assumed to be C.E.

Names and terms from a variety of languages are used throughout this book. Many, such as Russian, Chinese, Arabic, Japanese, and Hebrew, use different alphabets, rather than the Latin script used by English speakers. There is no single way of transliterating, or converting, one alphabet to another.

When referring to people or terms transliterated from non-Latin scripts, this book will try to use versions that are both linguistically accurate and easily recognizable. Be aware that certain well-known names and terms have several variants. For example, Genghis Khan versus Chinggis Khan (or Jenghiz Khan), Mao Tse-tung versus Mao Zedong, Mohammed versus Muhammad, or Sundiata versus Son-Jara. Students may encounter some or all of these different versions in different textbooks and readings.

The Advanced Placement Examination in World History: An Overview

FORMAT

The Advanced Placement exam lasts a total of 3 hours and 5 minutes.

Students are allowed 55 minutes to complete 70 multiple-choice questions.

For the completion of the free-response, or essay, section of the examination, 130 minutes are allotted. This section of the test consists of the following types of questions:

- *Document-based question (DBQ):* Roughly 50 minutes, including a mandatory period of 10 minutes to read documents.
- *Continuity and change-over-time essay question (CCOT):* Roughly 40 minutes, devoted to a thematic essay touching on at least one of the time periods covered in the exam.
- *Comparative essay question:* Roughly 40 minutes given to a question focusing on broad issues and dealing with at least two societies.

The free-response portion of the exam begins with a 10-minute document-reading period. During this time, students may make notes on the document sheets, but they are not allowed to work on actual essays. Once the document-reading period is over, it is recommended that students spend 5 or so minutes planning answers for each essay question.

GRADING

Grades for the exam are calculated as follows:

- The 70 multiple-choice questions: one half of the total raw score (60 out of 120 possible points).
- The 3 free-response questions: one half of the total raw score. Each essay receives a grade of 0 (the worst) to 9 (the best). A complex formula converts the total of 0 to 27 to a raw score of 0 to 60. This is added to the raw multiple-choice score, for a total of 0 to 120.

Another calculation converts the 0–120 raw score to a standard score of 1 through 5. This is the number students will see at the end. Scores can be interpreted as follows:

5: Extremely well qualified. Accepted by the majority of colleges and universities for some kind of academic credit or benefit. Earned by roughly 10 percent of students.

4: Well qualified. Accepted by many colleges and universities for some kind of academic credit or benefit. Earned by roughly 15 percent of students.

3: Qualified. Accepted by many colleges and universities for some kind of academic credit or benefit, but often of a limited nature. Earned by roughly 25 percent of students.

2: Possibly qualified. Accepted by a few colleges and universities for credit or benefit, generally quite limited. Earned by roughly 25 percent of students.

1: No recommendation. Not accepted anywhere. Earned by roughly 25 percent of students.

Universities and colleges have different policies regarding AP exams. Students should contact the school of their choice to determine what benefit, if any, a particular score will give them.

TIME FRAME

The AP World History exam focuses on global developments between humankind's origins and the present. The percentage of multiple-choice questions pertaining to each era is approximately as follows:

- ca. 8000 B.C.E. to 600 B.C.E.: 5 percent of questions
- 600 B.C.E. to 600 C.E.: 15 percent of questions
- 600 to 1450: 20 percent of questions
- 1450 to 1750: 20 percent of questions
- 1750 to 1900: 20 percent of questions
- 1900 to present: 20 percent of questions

THEMES

The Advanced Placement World History exam is broad in scope and seeks to test critical and interpretive skills, not just the mastery of facts and data. The study of world history challenges students to examine questions from a "big-picture" perspective, and questions will emphasize social, economic, and intellectual-cultural trends; issues of gender and ethnic identity; interrelationships among various civilizations and between humanity and the environment; and the ability to compare historical eras and societies.

Topics such as battles, the lives of political leaders, and the careers of individual "great figures" will receive less coverage than on traditional history exams. It will be necessary to place such events, lives, and careers in their broader political, economic, cultural, and social contexts.

No more than 20 percent of multiple-choice questions will cover topics in European history. The United States will be included only as part of global or comparative topics,

such as colonization, foreign affairs, and the globalization of trade and culture. There will be no coverage of the internal politics of the United States.

Five overarching themes form the heart of the Advanced Placement World History course and are intended to assist students in analyzing broad trends and insightfully comparing different times and places.

- *Interaction between humans and the environment.* How has the natural world shaped the development of human societies, and how have human societies, using different forms of technology, shaped the natural world? How, where, and why have human groups migrated and settled? How have diseases, epidemics, and other medical phenomena affected the course of world history?

- *Development and interaction of cultures.* How do belief systems—such as religions, philosophies, and political ideologies—arise? How do they affect social and intellectual development, or the interaction between states and societies? To what extent do art and architecture reflect the values of the societies producing them? How are scientific ideas and technological innovations developed? How do societies exchange cultural and scientific ideas and concepts?

- *State-building, expansion, and conflict.* What political forms do various societies take, and how do these change over time? How do uprisings and revolutions affect a nation's history or world history as a whole? What are empires and nation-states, and what structures and organizations other than these—such as regional associations or international bodies like the United Nations—give political shape to larger parts of the globe? What forms of conflict arise between political units, and how do war and diplomacy affect world history?

- *Creation, expansion, and interaction of economic systems.* What stages of economic development tend to be common among most societies? What distinguishes hunter-gatherer, pastoral, and agricultural societies from each other? How do trade and commerce affect societies and the way they interact? What systems, including slavery, serfdom, indentured servitude, and prison labor, have societies used to organize labor throughout history? How are industrialization, capitalism, and socialism interrelated, and how have they shaped the modern era?

- *Development and transformation of social structures.* How does specialization of labor lead to the creation of class structures, and how hierarchical or flexible are those structures within a given society? Who has power and status within a society, and why? What roles do cities play in social and economic development? How do family and kinship ties affect social development, and how are they affected in turn by various historical changes? What role does gender difference play in a society, and how are gender relations governed? How is ethnic or racial identity defined, and how are ethnic and racial minorities treated in a given society?

HISTORICAL THINKING SKILLS

A key purpose of the AP World History course is to foster certain skills used by professional historians and emphasized in college and university courses in history. Many of these are related to the subfield known as "historiography": the study of how historical research is conducted, how historical consensus is argued over and arrived at, and how history itself is written by historians. Four such skills are especially important.

- *Crafting historical arguments from historical evidence.* Can you identify the thesis of a historical argument and develop a thesis of your own when writing about history? Do you know about different types of historical evidence (primary sources vs. secondary sources, for example, or a visual document vs. oral testimony) and how to assess them—and whatever points of view or biases they may have?

- *Chronological reasoning.* Can you place historical events and developments in their proper sequence? Do you understand how (or whether) one factor affects or causes another, or how most major changes are generally due to many causes rather than just one? Do you understand the difference between long-term and short-term or immediate causes? Can you identify major changes or continuities over time? Do you understand how historians define major historical periods, and how periodization may change depending on what country or region one studies, or what type of history one is interested in (gender history vs. military history, for example), or even based on the emergence of new evidence or major rethinking within a historical subfield?

- *Comparison and contextualization.* Do you have the factual knowledge to place a specific document or piece of information in its proper context? Can you compare multiple developments within one society at a particular point of time (gender relations vs. political trends vs. economic developments in one country during one time period, for instance)? Can you compare the ways that one major issue plays out between one time period and another, or is dealt with in one society as opposed to another?

- *Historical interpretation and synthesis.* Going full circle to the first skill listed above, are you able to read and analyze various forms of historical evidence, including myths and oral traditions, art and architecture, graphs and charts, diaries and autobiographies, government documents, and other sources? Can you determine point of view and possible bias? Can you combine, or synthesize, pieces of evidence—even if they sometimes contradict each other—to arrive at a comprehensive understanding of a historical question? Are you aware of how insights from disciplines, such as archaeology, paleontology, statistics, and the environmental sciences, can aid historians in their research? Do you have a sense of how historical consensus and standard wisdom change over time or from country to country?

Multiple-Choice Question Strategies

The AP Examination in World History will require you to answer 70 multiple-choice questions. Each question will have four answer choices. Your goal is to pick the one answer that BEST responds to the question.

You will be given 55 minutes to complete this section of the test.

The percentage of questions devoted to each historical period will be the same as described earlier (origins to 600 B.C.E., 5 percent; 600 B.C.E. to 600 C.E., 15 percent; 600–1450, 20 percent; 1450–1750, 20 percent; 1750–1900, 20 percent; 1900 to present, 20 percent).

Assuming that you complete the free-response (essay) parts of the exam acceptably, you must answer 50 percent of the multiple-choice questions correctly in order to qualify for an overall score of 3. For a 4 or 5, you should aim for at least 70 percent. You receive a point for each correct answer and nothing for a question left blank. Incorrect responses will not be penalized, so it is in your interest to answer EVERY question.

TIPS FOR THE MULTIPLE-CHOICE QUESTIONS

Here are some guidelines to keep in mind when taking the multiple-choice section of the exam:

- *Look for the BEST answer.* Read the question's key words carefully. Is it calling for the "most important"? The "best explanation"? Does it qualify the issue some other way? A question asking you to identify the IMMEDIATE cause of World War I might give you a choice among "the assassination of Archduke Francis Ferdinand," "the Anglo-German naval race," and "competition over colonies in Africa." All three helped cause World War I. But because the question asks for the most immediate cause, the BEST answer is "the assassination of Archduke Francis Ferdinand." The other responses deal with long-term causes.

- *Watch out for "except" and "which of these is not true" questions.* These reverse the normal logic by asking what is NOT true. If you are told that "the Columbian Exchange brought all of the following to the Americas EXCEPT...," the list might include "smallpox," "horses," "the potato," and "coffee." Here, you must avoid the three "correct" choices in favor of the "incorrect" one (in this case, "the potato"), which is actually the right response.

- *Answer every question.* With no penalty for incorrect responses, there is no reason to leave any question blank. Answering 70 questions in 55 minutes requires a pace of 45 seconds per question. If you cannot work that quickly, skip the questions that seem like they will take too long for you to think through, aiming instead to answer 70 to 75 percent of them quickly and confidently—in other words, without guessing. (Topping 50 percent correct is generally enough to earn an overall score of 3; 70 to 75 percent will typically put you in a position to earn a 4, perhaps even a 5, depending on the quality of your essays.) In the last 10 or so minutes, return to the questions you've skipped. Guess carefully where possible,

but make sure that, by the end of 55 minutes, you've left nothing blank, even if that calls for some random choices in the end.

- *Save time by eliminating obviously incorrect answers.* This is the first and most effective part of the narrowing process. As you read through the question and the answers, strike out any answer that is obviously false. Answers containing absolute statements (such as "never," "always," "none of," or "all of") are almost always incorrect. Ideally your first read-through will eliminate at least one or two answers, leaving you with two or three to think about more carefully.

- *Trust your intuition—to a point.* Most teachers and exam-preparation specialists say that your first choice is generally the correct one, *if* you have read the question and the answers carefully. Unless you have a concrete reason for changing your mind (for example, you remember a crucial piece of information or notice something in the question that you missed when you skimmed through it), you should probably stick with your first choice. On the other hand, this should not be an excuse for lazy reading or sloppy thinking. Don't make that first choice until you have closely read and thought about the question.

SAMPLE MULTIPLE-CHOICE QUESTIONS

Advanced Placement multiple-choice questions test the historical skills referred to earlier. All questions will require you to think about historical **context**, to understand **cause and effect**, to **compare and contrast** effectively, and to ponder abstract issues such as **argumentation**, handling of **evidence**, **change and continuity**, and **synthesis** of knowledge.

A portion of the multiple-choice questions will call upon you to interpret **maps**, **images** (artwork, cartoons, photographs of architecture or artifacts), **quotations**, and **graphs** and **charts**.

Below are examples of possible multiple-choice questions, along with answers and explanations.

1. Which of the following religions or philosophies did Qing emperors such as Kangxi encourage in their attempt to increase public respect for political authority in China?

   (A) Stoicism
   (B) Taoism
   (C) Christianity
   (D) Confucianism

ANSWER: **D**

Because they are principally Western, A and C can be readily eliminated. You might decide between B and D based on knowledge of the Qing emperors, but you might also recall that Taoism is more about living in the moment, whereas Confucianism places stress on proper social relations and hierarchy, making it more suitable for a ruler hoping to encourage political obedience.

2. This city became one of West Africa's greatest centers of trade and Islamic scholarship from the thirteenth to the fifteenth centuries.

   (A) Timbuktu
   (B) Zimbabwe
   (C) Zanzibar
   (D) Alexandria

ANSWER: **A**

This may seem to be a straightforward identification question: You either know the answer or you don't. Still, basic geographic context can assist your process of elimination. Zanzibar is on Africa's east coast. Alexandria is in Egypt, to the north, and flourished most as a cultural center before the emergence of Islam. Zimbabwe is far to the south and experienced its peak as a civilization in the pre-Islamic period.

3. Which of the following is NOT true of most human societies during the Stone Age?

   (A) Despite technological limitations, Stone Age humans designed many innovative tools.
   (B) Biological differences between men and women often gave rise to a gendered division of labor.
   (C) Human beings tended to be more aggressive during the Stone Age than during later periods.
   (D) Human beings settled the Americas later than they did Africa, Asia, and Europe.

ANSWER: **C**

This question requires you to choose the one INCORRECT answer. Answer A reminds us that societies are not necessarily "primitive" just because they lack metal-based technology. Although labor was not as specialized during the Stone Age as it would be in more advanced societies, specific gender roles were common from the start, making B correct as well. Academic consensus has it that human beings appeared first in Africa, then spread throughout Eurasia, so D is also correct. Given the catastrophic nature of wars in recent history, C is clearly incorrect, making it the "right" choice in this case.

4. How did the storming of the Bastille affect the course of the French Revolution?

   (A) It led directly to the imprisonment and execution of Louis XVI.
   (B) It ended the Third Estate's attempt to negotiate a reformist solution to France's financial crisis.
   (C) Louis XVI agreed soon afterward to call the Estates General to Versailles.
   (D) Women were granted the vote as a reward for their role in the uprising.

ANSWER: **B**

Proper understanding of causality and chronology allows you to ignore A and C, because A took place many months after the Bastille uprising, whereas C took place beforehand. Despite their grand ideals, the Revolution's leaders did not extend suffrage to women, making D incorrect. Answer B correctly identifies how Bastille Day marked the shift from negotiation to revolution.

5. Which of the following best summarizes the beliefs of a practicing Buddhist?

   (A) Conversion of nonbelievers by force is justified by God's will.
   (B) At the end of the world, God will judge all sinners and condemn them to eternal torment.
   (C) Justice should be based on the principle of an eye for an eye, a tooth for a tooth.
   (D) People are born and reborn into lives of suffering but can escape this cycle by attaining enlightenment.

ANSWER: **D**

Basic knowledge of religious tenets is necessary here. Answer C is associated with the retributive justice of Hammurabi's law code and Judaic scripture. Answers A and B are more characteristic of monotheistic religions like Islam, Judaism, and Christianity (even though the history of Buddhism has not been without violence). Although there are many forms of Buddhism that differ on key questions, answer D captures the core belief that one transcends the karmic cycle of birth, death, and rebirth by gaining enlightenment.

6. Which of the following did World War II help to bring about?

   (A) Women in Great Britain and the United States received the vote partly as recognition for their homefront labor efforts.
   (B) The war concentrated strategic might and economic power in the hands of the United States and the Soviet Union.
   (C) The Ottoman Empire collapsed, paving the way for Mustafa Kemal's modernization of Turkey.
   (D) Spain's Latin American colonies took advantage of the monarchy's weakness and declared independence.

ANSWER: **B**

All these changes resulted from various wars, but only B, the creation of the Cold War superpowers, has to do with World War II. Answers A and C are the products of World War I, and the Latin American wars of independence alluded to in D followed the wars of Napoleon. This question tests causation and context.

7. "Although the empire was conquered on horseback, it could not be governed from there."

The quotation above, adapted from Sun Tzu's *Art of War* by the thirteenth-century Chinese official Yeh-lü Ch'u-ts'ai, most likely refers to which conquering force?

(A) the Hun armies led by Attila
(B) the Mongol Empire created by Genghis Khan
(C) the Aryan forces thought to have invaded India around 1500 B.C.E.
(D) the infantry of the Roman Republic

ANSWER: **B**

Although this proverb dates back to centuries before Genghis Khan's invasions, it is most commonly cited to describe the Mongols' dilemma: that although they conquered vast stretches of territory, they did not have the capability to control them for very long. A Chinese speaker during the 1200s would most likely be referring to the army most relevant to him in terms of time and geography, making it safe to eliminate A, C, and D.

8. The sculpture pictured below is most likely

(A) a personal likeness commissioned by a wealthy patron.
(B) an example of Asian influence on Western art.
(C) a ritual object with religious significance crafted in Africa.
(D) an artistic protest against wage inequality suffered by women in the workplace.

ANSWER: **C**

Image-based questions may ask you to interpret the image—especially if there is accompanying text, as in a poster or cartoon—or identify it, using context. As in this case, you will often have to be familiar with the basic characteristics of different artistic and architectural traditions. Based on logic, you can feel safe in discarding A and D; only in a nontraditional sense can this be considered a portrait, and it would need more context to make the sort of comment referred to in D. Left to decide between B and C, you will ideally have a sense of how Asian and African art differ—but even if you don't, it would be worth guessing, with the number of possible answers whittled down to two.

9. What historical development does this map depict?

(A) the expansion of Chinese trade routes
(B) James Cook's voyages of discovery
(C) Japan's military assault on the South Pacific
(D) the migration of Polynesian peoples

ANSWER: **D**

A close look at the dates referred to on the map is all it takes to reject B and C, which took place in the 1700s or the 1900s. Premodern China did not trade so far to the east (and the lines do not go back and forth to China, as one would expect with trade routes), making A incorrect.

10. What is the most likely explanation for the population rise experienced by the cities included on the chart below?

Year	Cities (Pop. in thousands)				
	London	Paris	Antwerp	Berlin	Moscow
1800	960	600	60	170	250
1850	2,700	1,400	90	500	360
1900	6,500	3,700	280	2,700	1,000

(A) industrialization
(B) foreign immigration
(C) the elimination of diseases such as tuberculosis and polio
(D) more advanced forms of birth control

ANSWER: **A**

Answer D can be eliminated right away, because birth control slows population growth. Although some chart- and graph-interpretation questions focus more on interpreting the data contained in the chart and graph, others, like this one, require you to apply context and background knowledge. The nineteenth century was a time of emigration *away from* Europe, not into it, so B does not fit. Western societies did not eliminate TB and polio until the twentieth century (and have not *completely* eradicated them even now), allowing us to strike C. Even a basic grasp of industrialization should allow you to remember that industrialization and urban growth almost always go hand in hand, and that Europe industrialized during the years covered by this chart.

Free-Response (Essay) Questions: General Tips

The free-response section of the AP exam in World History lasts 130 minutes. During this time, you will be required to write three essays: a document-based question (DBQ), a continuity and change-over-time question (CCOT), and a comparative essay.

Once the 10-minute document-reading period is over, you can write the essays in whichever order you like, and you can use the 120 minutes however you please—no one will tell you when to finish one essay or start another. You SHOULD spend roughly 40 minutes on each essay, and the one you SHOULD write first is the DBQ. The documents will be fresh in your mind, and the DBQ is the most complicated essay, so it will be good to have it out of the way. Time management is crucial. Students often fail to complete the third essay because they have not practiced writing essays in 40 minutes or less. Make sure you try doing so at least once or twice.

APPROACHING THE ESSAYS

Unlike the multiple-choice questions, which are graded by machine, the written portions of AP examinations are evaluated by high-school teachers, university professors, and other specialists. For each subject area, several hundred of these evaluators gather together for about a week.

In that time, an AP reader is likely to mark several hundred essays. He or she is careful and well-trained. Still, because your reader will be looking over so many essays in such a short time, it is up to you to make the quality of your work stand out.

Each of your essays will receive a score of 1 through 9 (later, these numbers are plugged into a complicated formula to determine your overall free-response score). In each case, the AP grader will check to see if your essay meets five or six elementary requirements (the *basic core*); you can earn up to 7 points this way. If you fulfill ALL the requirements of the basic core, the grader will check your essay against a list of advanced criteria (the *expanded core*). Here, you can earn an additional 1 or 2 points.

The requirements for fulfilling the basic core and moving on to the expanded core are different for each essay. However, one thing is the same for all three: you CANNOT earn ANY of the expanded-core points unless you earn ALL the basic-core points. Think of this as opening a gate with five or six locks. Until you open them all, you cannot go any farther. The happy news is that, if you do a good job on each part of the basic core, you will already be doing some of the things necessary to score well on the expanded core.

Here are some ways to impress your readers:

- *Open your essay with a clear thesis statement.* You must make an argument or draw a concrete conclusion, and you must let your reader know you are doing it. No matter how good the rest of your essay is, you will lose many points if you fail to do this, because you cannot get through the gateway from the *basic core* to the *expanded core* without "a clear, analytical, and comprehensive thesis." Your thesis should be BRIEF, ACCURATE, and STRAIGHTFORWARD. It should mention the time period(s) in question, but should NOT restate the question. Do not make this first paragraph too elaborate; save context, evidence, and supporting material for the essay's main body—which is where you earn your main credit, and which you want to get to as quickly as possible.
- *Read the directions and follow them closely.* You are writing three different essays, each with its own set of rules. AP readers are trained to judge your work based on how well you follow those rules. Even if your essay is beautifully written, you will lose points if you do not follow the directions.
- *Read the question carefully.* This may seem obvious, but many students fail to do it. Read the question more than once. Underline or circle key words. Make sure you understand WHAT the question wants you to do (pay special attention to KEY VERBS, such as "compare and contrast," or "analyze") and what its MAIN FOCUS is. If the question wants you to discuss the reasons for an empire's collapse, don't spend time talking about what the empire was like at its peak. If it asks you about the long-term consequences of a war, don't describe the conduct

of the war itself. You want to work quickly, but making sure you understand the question fully is an excellent investment of your time.

- *Provide analysis.* All three questions require you to do this. Explanation and insight, not simple listing of facts, will earn you points. You must demonstrate an awareness of HOW and WHY things happen, or how they are related or affect each other. You want to demonstrate that you can comprehend a complex issue and construct an argument (meaning a logical assertion, not a quarrelsome or aggressive rant) about it.

- *Show balance and "big-picture" awareness.* Issues and debates have more than one side, and events generally have more than one cause. Acknowledge different or opposing points of view, even if you favor a particular argument or interpretation. Also try to link the specific question with its larger historical context and with broader historical developments. This will strengthen your analysis and impress your readers.

- *Write neatly and clearly.* Your readers will be marking hundreds of essays and will not enjoy having to struggle to understand what you are saying. Guidelines state that "substance takes precedence over neatness," but neatness helps the reader appreciate the substance more fully.

- *Divide your essay into paragraphs.* Effective use of paragraphs shows the reader that you know how to think and write in an organized fashion. They should be clearly indented.

- *Give an answer of an appropriate length.* There is no hard-and-fast rule as to how long your essay should be. Length may depend on how large your handwriting is or whether you skip lines. Also, quantity does not always mean quality: A good argument can be made concisely, and a bad essay can ramble on for pages. However, an essay less than two pages long will be regarded with suspicion. If your handwriting is of normal size and you do not skip lines, a MINIMUM length to aim for is two FULL pages. Three or four is optimal.

- *If you have time, reread your essay.* If necessary, revise it. Cross out mistakes or awkward phrasings. If new information or a good idea occurs to you, add it. Make corrections neatly.

Document-Based Question Strategies

You should spend 50 minutes on the DBQ. This includes the 10 minutes you will be given to read the documents (during which time you will not be allowed to write).

As noted earlier, the DBQ should be the first essay you write (although you can choose differently). The DBQ is the essay with the most elaborate rules, and it is extremely important to be familiar with the procedure.

APPROACHING THE DOCUMENT-BASED QUESTION (DBQ)

You will be provided with four to ten documents. Many will be traditional written texts: excerpts from books, memoirs, and essays; transcriptions of speeches or radio and television addresses; government papers; and so on. In other cases, song lyrics, poetry, or images will be included. The authors cited may or may not be famous.

The DBQ's purpose is to assess your ability to evaluate and comment on primary documents. Therefore, you must not only write a good essay with a clear thesis but actively incorporate all, or all but one, of the documents. You must also comment on at least one OTHER type of document, NOT included, that might shed light on the question.

Following is the official AP scoring guide for the DBQ.

Generic Scoring Guide for AP World History Document-Based Question

Basic Core	Points
1. Has an acceptable thesis.	1
2. Addresses and shows understanding of all (or all but one) of the documents.	1
3. Thesis is supported by evidence from all documents or all but one. (Supported by all but two documents.)	2 (1)
4. Analyzes point of view in two or more documents.	1
5. Analyzes documents by clustering them in two or three ways.	1
6. Identifies one type of additional document and explains why it is needed.	1
Subtotal	**7**

Expanded Core	Points
Expands beyond the basic core of 1–7 points. A student must earn **7** points in this core area before earning points in the expanded-core area.	0–2
Examples:	
• Has an analytical, clear, comprehensive thesis.	
• Demonstrates careful and insightful analysis.	
• Makes convincing use of documents as evidence.	
• Discusses point of view in most or all documents.	
• Compares, groups, and synthesizes the documents in additional ways.	
• Employs useful external historical content.	
• Identifies and explains the need for two or more additional document types.	
Subtotal	**2**

TOTAL   9

A few of these items deserve additional attention because they must be done in specific ways to avoid losing points.

Using and analyzing documents, and adding "outside" content. You must use ALL the documents (misinterpretation of one is allowed, although you should avoid this). "Careful and insightful analysis" will follow if you group the documents effectively, discuss point of view well, and present interesting comparisons and contrasts. Demonstrating external knowledge—by providing information about the

author of a document or a document's historical context—is a good way to earn expanded-core points, and it can be done in combination with attribution.

Attribution. The best way to refer to documents is simply by number (for example, "doc. 3"). You do not have to identify the author and title.

Point of view. Simply attributing the documents is not sufficient. You must also comment on point of view. What is the bias or perspective of the author, speaker, or artist? This may be clear from nationality, ethnicity, gender, social class, religion, or political affiliation. Especially important is whether the document's point of view affects its RELIABILITY, and how. For partial credit, you must analyze the point of view of two or three documents. For full credit, especially if there are fewer than five or six documents, you must do this for all or most of the documents.

Grouping documents. One of the skills you MUST demonstrate is an ability to group documents into useful and meaningful categories. Can the documents be grouped by national origin or chronology (generally weak approaches)? From a class perspective? According to a political philosophy or outlook? By purpose? By gender? According to cultural attitudes? There is no single right way to group. However, your groupings must make sense, and the DBQ will be designed in such a way that some methods of grouping will be more appropriate than others. Also, the NUMBER of groups is typically two or (generally more preferable) three. More may be too complicated or, with a small set of documents, not feasible.

Identifying additional documents. The DBQ asks you to demonstrate your judgment about how historical evidence is used by commenting on what is missing from the picture presented to you. If OTHER documents could be provided to you, what types would you find useful? Explain and analyze WHY these extra documents are needed. This must be done at least once. Doing it more than once is a way to earn expanded-core points.

Thesis. Don't forget your thesis. Most often, your thesis will determine how you group your documents. Conveniently, each category—especially if you have three—can be used as a main point in the body of your essay.

SAMPLE QUESTION

1. In the modern world, major political and social changes have been brought about by different means. Using the documents presented below, discuss the various methods of political and social transformation that they advocate. Be sure to explain the need for at least one additional type of document.

Document 1

Source: Vladimir Lenin, Russian revolutionary leader and head of the Soviet state, *What Is to Be Done?* (1902).

A small, compact core of the most reliable, experienced, and hardened workers, with responsible representatives in the principal districts and connected by all the rules of strict secrecy with the organization of revolutionaries, can . . . perform all the functions of a trade union organization.

I assert: 1) that no revolutionary movement can endure without a stable organization of leaders that maintains continuity . . . 3) that such an organization must consist chiefly of people professionally engaged in revolutionary activity; 4) that in an autocratic state, the more we confine the membership of such an organization to people who are professionally engaged in revolutionary activity and have been professionally trained in the art of combatting the political police, the more difficult it will be to wipe out such an organization. . . .

Only a gross failure to understand Marxism . . . could prompt the opinion that the rise of a mass, spontaneous working-class movement relieves us of the duty of creating a good organization of revolutionaries. On the contrary, this movement imposes this duty upon us, because the spontaneous struggle of the proletariat will not become its genuine "class struggle" until this struggle is led by a strong organization of revolutionaries.

Document 2

Source: Gamal Abdel Nasser, Arab nationalist and president of Egypt, "The Philosophy of the Revolution" (1959).

As I often sit in my study and think quietly of this subject, I ask myself: "What is our positive role in this troubled world, and where is the scene in which we can play that role?"

Can we ignore that there is a Muslim world to which we are tied by bonds which are not only forged by religious faith, but also tightened by the facts of history? . . . It is not in vain that our country lies to the southwest of Asia, close to the Arab world, whose life is intermingled with ours. . . . It is not in vain that Islamic civilization and Islamic heritage, which the Mongols ravaged in their conquest of the old Islamic capitals, retreated and found refuge in Egypt, where they found shelter and safety as a result of the counterattack with which Egypt repelled the invasion of these Tartars at Ein Galout.

All these are fundamental facts, whose roots lie deeply in our life. Whatever we do, we cannot forget them or run away from them.

Document 3

Source: Mikhail Bakunin, nineteenth-century anarchist, "Principles of Revolution" (1869).

We recognize no other activity but the work of extermination, but we admit that the forms in which this activity will show itself will be extremely varied— poison, the knife, the rope, etc. In this struggle, revolution sanctifies everything alike.

Document 4

Source: Kwame Nkrumah, leader of Ghana's independence movement, "The African Personality," speech delivered to a conference of independent African states (April 13, 1958).

Africa is the last remaining stronghold of colonialism. Unlike Asia, there are on the continent of Africa more dependent territories than independent sovereign nations. Therefore we, the free independent states of Africa, have a responsibility to hasten the total liberation of Africa . . .

We, the delegates of this conference, in promoting our foreign relations, must endeavor to seek the friendship of all and the enmity of none. We must stand for international peace and security, in conformity with the United Nations charter.

This will enable us to assert our own African personality and to develop our own ways of life, our own customs, traditions, and cultures. . . .

If we can as independent African states show by our own efforts that we can settle our own problems in Africa, then we shall be setting an example to others. . . . For this reason it may be necessary for this conference to examine the possibility of setting up some sort of machinery to maintain the links we shall forge here and to implement the decisions we shall reach. . . .

Today we are one. . . . An injury to one is an injury to all of us. From this conference must go out a new message: "Hands off Africa! Africa must be free!"

Document 5

Source: Gloria Steinem, American feminist, "Far from the Opposite Shore" (1978).

Even the late suffragists, the ones who are most often labeled reformers because of their concentration on the vote, used radical tactics. Yes, they lobbied politely, sometimes, and took tea with their friends in Congress, but they also picketed the White House and engaged in the civil disobedience that those same congressmen abhorred. . . .

Chaining themselves to the White House fence, going to jail, declaring a hunger strike, being cruelly force-fed: those events are now famous. But the range of tactics [also] included humor, theatrics, passive resistance, [and] persuasion.

Document 6

Source: Mao Tse-tung, leader of the Chinese Communist Party, "The Peasant Movement in Hunan" (1926).

In a very short time, . . . several hundred million peasants will rise like a mighty storm. . . . There are three alternatives. To march at their head and lead them? To trail behind them, gesticulating and criticizing? Or to stand in their way and oppose them?

Every revolutionary comrade should know that the national revolution requires a great change in the countryside. The Revolution of 1911 did not bring about this change, hence its failure. This change is now taking place, and it is an important factor for the completion of the revolution. Every revolutionary comrade must support it, or he will be taking the stand of counterrevolution.

Document 7

Source: Henry David Thoreau, American philosopher and activist, *On the Duty of Civil Disobedience* (1848).

How does it become a man to behave toward this American government today? I answer that he cannot without disgrace be associated with it. I cannot for an instant recognize that political organization as *my* government which is the *slave's* government also.

All men recognize the right of revolution; that is, the right to refuse allegiance to and to resist the government, when its tyranny or its inefficiency are great and unendurable . . . those who call themselves abolitionists should at once effectually withdraw their support, both in person and property, from the government of Massachusetts. . . . Under a government which imprisons any unjustly, the true place for a just man is also a prison. . . . A minority is powerless while it conforms to the majority . . . but it is irresistible when it clogs by its whole weight.

Document 8

Source: Mohandas K. Gandhi, member of the Indian National Congress and leader of the Indian independence movement, letter to Russian novelist Leo Tolstoy (1909).

These Indians [living in South Africa] have for several years labored under various legal disabilities. The prejudice against color and in some respect against Asiatics is intense in that colony. . . . The climax was reached three years ago, with a law which I and many others considered to be degrading and calculated to unman those to whom it was applicable. I felt that submission to a law of this nature was inconsistent with the spirit of true religion. I and some of my friends were and still are firm believers in the doctrine of non-resistance to evil. The result has been that nearly one-half of the Indian population [of Transvaal], that was unable to stand the heat of the struggle, to suffer the hardships of imprisonment, have withdrawn from the Transvaal rather than submit to a law which they have considered degrading. Of the other half, nearly 2,500 have for conscience's sake allowed themselves to be imprisoned, some as many as five times. . . . The struggle still continues, and one does not know when the end will come. This, however, some of us at least have seen most clearly, that passive resistance will and can succeed where brute force must fail.

Sample Answer

Many times throughout history, legal means of political and social change have failed to bring about desired results. On such occasions, there are frequently calls for radical or drastic forms of transformation. As the documents discussed in this essay demonstrate, these include national liberation, revolution, and civil disobedience. As a rule, when any of these options—as opposed to reform or gradual

change—is seen as necessary, it is a sign that the existing system has failed in some fundamental way.

[The thesis paragraph correctly identifies the nature of the documents and tells the reader how they will be categorized. A simple but acceptable thesis results from the grouping of the documents into three categories of political and social change. The last sentence adds an insightful observation—even a secondary thesis—about how radical forms of change tend to be caused by general social or political failure.]

Documents 2 (Nasser's "The Philosophy of the Revolution") and 4 (Nkrumah's "The African Personality") have to do with decolonization in Africa and Asia after World War II. Like Sukarno in Indonesia, Nasser, president of Egypt, was one of several modernizing strongmen who led successful national liberation movements, then encouraged the so-called Third World to assert its global power and defy the West. Nkrumah came to power in Ghana, the first British colony in sub-Saharan Africa to gain freedom. Both appeal not just to their own people but to larger cultural units: the Muslim world in Nasser's case, all of Africa in Nkrumah's. Both are politicians, and this is a way to boost their international influence (but it also reflects the fact that boundaries in Africa and the Mideast had been artificially imposed by Western colonizers). Such appeals stirred up pride, but had limits. Nasser's pan-Arab nationalism did not catch on, and his patriotic appeal at home has to be balanced against his authoritarianism. Nkrumah's pan-Africanism was too unrealistic to succeed in a region of such extreme ethnic and linguistic diversity.

[Two documents are grouped here. They are attributed by number, title, and author. There is historical context about postwar decolonization, including an outside reference to a similar political leader. The documents are not just listed; their political purpose is discussed, as is the question of whether the ideals they express were met. Point of view—that of politicians trying to increase their stature—is touched on. So far, there has been no discussion of what other documents might be helpful. (One possibility would have been to suggest diaries, newspaper editorials, or other materials to indicate whether ordinary people found pan-Arabism or pan-Africanism appealing.) Another option to be aware of: Document 8 (Gandhi) could have been included here, but this essay uses it differently. There will generally be more than one "right" way to group documents.]

Revolutionary ideologies are a hallmark of modern history, as shown by Documents 3 (Bakunin's "Principles of Revolution"), 1 (Lenin's *What Is to Be Done?*), and 6 (Mao's "The Peasant Movement in Hunan"). Bakunin, founder of the anarchist movement, is the most extreme: in declaring that "revolution sanctifies everything alike," he restates the age-old argument that the ends justify the means. Lenin, leader of the Soviet Union, subscribes to the same idea in *What Is to Be Done?*, written while he was still a young Marxist, plotting to overthrow the tsar. Lenin discourages working-class democracy on the grounds that absolute secrecy is necessary for revolution to succeed. This stance can be explained partly by Lenin's point of view: he was leader of an illegal party in a repressive country with a powerful secret police. Unfortunately, Lenin's antidemocratic approach was one of many

things that later turned the USSR, a state founded on utopian ideals, into a dictatorship. In #6, Mao, years before communist victory in China, appears more committed to open mass movements as he describes the revolutionary power of the peasantry (an unusual position for a Marxist, because Marxism puts more stress on the industrial working class). After coming to power, however, Mao proved just as much a dictator as Lenin did in the USSR. All three documents propose that the potential benefits of revolution are worth any price, but they say nothing about actual costs. For the sake of balance, it would be useful to have statistics or first-hand accounts related to the mass arrests, persecutions, and famines that resulted from revolution in Soviet Russia and Maoist China.

[This paragraph provides a second effective grouping, dealing with revolution. Transition from the previous paragraph is clear, and the attribution of documents remains explicit. Historical information is included for the sake of context. Detailed point of view is provided in Lenin's case. (Also, a reader might give point-of-view credit for mentioning the unorthodoxy of Mao's Marxist views.) This paragraph fulfills the basic core by making a suggestion about possibly useful additional documents.]

Another way to bring about change is nonviolent resistance. The American thinker Henry David Thoreau argues in *On the Duty of Civil Disobedience* (#7) that even democratic governments can do wrong. An idealist philosopher angry about the Mexican-American War and slavery, Thoreau asks whether a good person acting in a good cause is justified in violating his or her country's laws. His answer is "yes." In her essay "Far from the Opposite Shore" (#5), American feminist Gloria Steinem describes how nineteenth-century suffragettes used civil disobedience, not just lawful reform, to fight for the vote. (She seems to be encouraging similar action in her own day, and the fact that she is writing about history to a modern audience for political purposes should be noted.) Perhaps the most admired advocate of civil disobedience is Gandhi, spiritual father of India's freedom movement. In a 1909 letter (#8) to Russian author Leo Tolstoy—also known for his activism and pacifism—Gandhi explains his strategy of passive resistance in South Africa, where Indians, like blacks, were racially discriminated against. Later, Gandhi's method of *satyagraha*, which combined Hindu faith with nonviolent political action, was an effective tool in persuading the British to grant India its independence. As effective as civil disobedience has been, however, it works only under certain circumstances. Gandhi's confident assertion that "passive resistance will and can succeed where brute force must fail" applies only in liberal or democratic societies, where the use of brute force is seen as embarrassing or shameful. It is hard to imagine civil disobedience bringing about change in a truly dictatorial regime such as Hitler's, Stalin's, or Mao's.

[A third and final grouping appears in this paragraph. Attribution is complete, and Steinem's point of view is noted. So are Thoreau's and Gandhi's, to a lesser extent. (Many readers would assign an expanded-core point to this essay for analyzing the point of view of "all or most" of the documents.) Much historical information is provided, as well as an evaluation of civil disobedience as a political strategy.]

None of the documents discuss what is perhaps the fairest and most desirable means of social and political change: the proper functioning of democratic government. Also, while the documents provide examples of one extremist form of change, communist revolution, they do not mention fascism, another common form of extremism. Memoirs or newspaper reports demonstrating fascist excess and the effective operation of democracy would have been useful.

[This brief conclusion caps off the essay, even though time is running out. It also raises a general analytical point about democratic change. Most important, it earns an expanded-core point by making a second suggestion about potentially useful documents.]

Continuity and Change-Over-Time Essay Question Strategies

Another type of essay the World History exam will ask you to write is the continuity and change-over-time (CCOT) question. This exercise tests your ability to trace a broad trend or development over a long period of time. Topics may include cultural interchange, global trade, the movement and migration of peoples, the role of minorities in a given society, the status of women, environmental issues, biological developments, changes in technology, artistic and cultural attitudes, and scientific innovations.

The CCOT lends itself to a topical approach. In order to follow how a particular issue changed or stayed the same through long periods of time, consult the overviews at the beginning of Units One through Six. These track "big-picture" issues as they played out over different eras.

Moreover, as you read through the material covered in Units One through Six, keep in mind how long-term trends develop, not just within geographical areas but across borders.

APPROACHING THE CONTINUITY AND CHANGE-OVER-TIME ESSAY

As with all essays, follow the General Tips provided earlier in this unit.

It is recommended that you take 40 minutes to complete the CCOT. Spend 5 or so minutes (no more than 10) looking over the question and organizing and outlining your thoughts.

The CCOT will request that you analyze the evolution of a trend or phenomenon over a long period of time. You will be asked to focus on a particular nation or region, although you may be given a choice. On the next page is the official AP scoring guide for the CCOT.

The CCOT's requirements are more straightforward than the DBQ's. Aside from following the general essay-writing tips, concentrate on showing that you understand what changed, and how and what did NOT change. Start by establishing a baseline: what were things like at the beginning of the period you have been

assigned? What changed? How and why? What were things like at the end of the period in question? What differences did those changes make? What remained the same? A common error is to neglect continuity and focus too much on change. Be sure to explain and analyze BOTH.

To create a thesis, focus on the cause(s) and/or effect(s) of the change(s) or continuity(ies) you are writing about. While you discuss whether change outweighed continuity or vice versa you should not base your thesis simply on this.

Generic Scoring Guide for AP World History Continuity and Change-Over-Time Essay

Basic Core	Points	Expanded Core	Points
1. Thesis deals acceptably with the global issues and time period(s) in question.	1	Goes beyond the basic core of 1–7 points. A score of **7** must be earned before a student can gain expanded-core points.	**0–2**
2. Deals with all parts of the question, though not necessarily evenly or completely.	2	Examples:	
(Deals with most parts of the question; for instance, change but not continuity.)	(1)	• Begins with an explicit, analytical, and comprehensive thesis.	
3. Backs up the thesis with appropriate historical evidence.	2	• Deals with all aspects of the question: global issues, chronology, causation, change, continuity, content.	
(Partially backs up thesis with appropriate historical evidence.)	(1)	• Gives ample historical evidence to back up thesis.	
4. Uses historical context to illustrate continuity and change over time.	1	• Creatively links topic to relevant ideas, trends, and events.	
5. Analyzes the process of change and continuity.	1		
Subtotal	**7**	**Subtotal**	**2**
		TOTAL 9	

SAMPLE QUESTION

2. Choose one of the following regions. Discuss the changes and continuities in how women were treated—socially, economically, and politically—between 1000 C.E. and 1750 C.E. If a woman's social class factored into the way she was treated, discuss that in your answer.

the Middle East
China and Japan
sub-Saharan Africa

Sample Answer

In most times and places, women have occupied a secondary status in society, whether because of gender division of labor, cultural and religious bias, or simple sexism. However, the type of discrimination a woman experienced and how bad it was varied greatly, depending on where and when she lived, as well as her social class. Neither China nor Japan between 1000 and 1750 is an exception. In both places, women remained subservient to men. There were also changes, and, in both cases, they tended to go from bad to worse.

[This introduction refers to all key elements in the question. It tells the reader what region the essay will focus on. It recognizes that change and continuity are both relevant. Most important, it clearly states a complex thesis by discussing the secondary status of women generally and asserting that, both in China and Japan, the situation of women worsened over time.]

Around 1000 C.E., women in Song China and Heian Japan enjoyed some rights and privileges, although their situation was still secondary. As in many societies, they could own and inherit property, and they had informal influence over the management of households. Women of the upper classes could exercise indirect power through their husbands or personal connections at the imperial court. Japanese women were luckier: the Heian aristocracy placed a great emphasis on cultural brilliance, and the literary achievements of women like Lady Murasaki, author of *The Tale of Genji*, gained them some prestige. Also, Confucianism, which did nothing to improve the status of women, was not yet as prevalent as it was in China, where it had been part of tradition for centuries. One woman, Wu Zhao, actually ruled China as empress, but hers was an extremely rare case that says little about the lives of most women there.

[This paragraph establishes a baseline by describing the situation as it was at the beginning of the time period in question. It provides much outside historical knowledge. It shows analytical awareness by noting that generalizing from one unusual case (Wu Zhao's) is risky.]

In China, conditions worsened for women mainly because of religious and cultural reasons. Since the 400s B.C.E., Confucianism, with its strict sense of hierarchy, had done much to lower the status of Chinese women, but its influence had waxed and

waned over time. Starting in the 600s C.E., though, Confucianism revived more permanently in the form of Neo-Confucianism. The Song, Yuan, and Ming dynasties were increasingly drawn to Neo-Confucianism, and the place of women lessened as a result. Brides' families now paid dowries to the groom; earlier, it had been the other way around. This change in custom made it expensive to marry off daughters, and families came to want girl children less. The most infamous means of subjugating women was foot binding. Tiny feet were considered to be more attractive, but observing this fashion had the effect of crippling women and turning them into little more than beautiful objects. Foot binding gradually gained in popularity, spreading from the upper classes downward. It was widely practiced by 1200 and continued till the 1900s.

[This paragraph discusses change in China. It identifies a primary agent of change and provides concrete historical information.]

Political events were more important in changing the role of women in Japan. The transition from the culturally refined Heian regime to the feudal shogunates in the late 1100s led to a steep decline in the status of women. During the first shogunates and the disunity of the 1400s and 1500s, prestige belonged to the samurai class, and their warrior ethic left little room for the accomplishments or abilities of women. Also, unlike European chivalry, which at least required knights to respect and cherish women (however condescending this was), the Japanese code of Bushido did nothing to encourage samurai to treat women well. Things got even worse as Japan reunited in the late 1500s and early 1600s. Society became tremendously stratified, and under the Tokugawa shoguns, women were required to obey their husbands without question—if they did not, they could be put to death.

[Like the previous paragraph, this one discusses change, this time in Japan. It identifies the principal reason for change and provides specific details and information.]

It should be noted that all these changes were less pronounced among the lower classes, as was often the case in most societies. In China, lower-class families were less likely than upper-class families to follow Confucian rules closely. Foot binding was for the aristocracy: A peasant woman with bound feet would be useless for farm or household work. In Japan, samurai ideals were irrelevant to the lives of people farther down in society. Even among the lower classes, though, the question of who paid dowries for marriage was important, and in both countries, regardless of class, the overall desirability of girl children decreased. (This is still a cultural problem today in much of Asia, especially in China.) During the premodern era, female infanticide was not uncommon.

[This supplemental paragraph addresses the question of social class, talking about likenesses AND differences. Links with the present ("still a cultural problem today") are a way of earning expanded-core points.]

To sum up, the condition of women tended to worsen, both in China and Japan, between 1000 and 1750. The increased role of Neo-Confucian beliefs was mainly responsible for change in China, while the rise of warrior government was the

primary cause in Japan. Feminism and equal rights took a long time to come to both countries—not until late in the twentieth century—and one could argue that the influence of this traditional sexism is still felt today.

[This short conclusion recaps the thesis and its main points. It gives a sense of what followed the historical period in question and also comments on the present (one way to get an expanded-core point).]

Comparative Essay Question Strategies

Yet another exercise you will complete on the World History exam is the comparative essay, which will ask you to compare and contrast the ways different societies deal with major issues and phenomena. These may include technological innovation and interaction with the environment; the social and economic impact of warfare; the treatment of minorities and women; the evolution of political systems; international economic exchange; and systems of labor organization.

The organizers of the AP World History course consider the comparative approach especially important. The overviews preceding Units One through Six provide lists of issues that lend themselves well to comparative questions. Read them carefully. In addition, as you study the material covered in these units, think about broad patterns and see if you can come up with examples of major developments that most, if not all, societies undergo as they evolve historically.

APPROACHING THE COMPARATIVE ESSAY

As with all essays, follow the General Tips provided.

You should devote 40 minutes to complete the comparative essay. Spend 5 or so minutes (no more than 10) looking over the question, thinking about it, then organizing and outlining your thoughts.

The comparative essay will require you to compare and contrast how at least two civilizations, regions, or nations have undergone or responded to a historical event, trend, or experience, which will relate to one of the AP course's five major themes. Give equal weight to both (or all) civilizations or nations specified in the question. Also be sure to address similarities AND differences, although you may decide that one is more important than the other.

The official AP scoring guide for the comparative essay is on the next page.

In constructing a thesis for the comparative essay, it is not enough to assert that likenesses outweigh differences or vice versa. You may discuss this point, and doing so may make your thesis stronger or more complex, but it cannot serve as the thesis itself. Base your thesis on the *reasons* for the likenesses or differences in question.

SAMPLE QUESTION

3. Compare and contrast the degree to which TWO of the following regions modernized between the end of the First World War and the beginning of the Second World War.

South Asia
Latin America
the Middle East

Generic Scoring Guide for AP World History Comparative Essay

Basic Core (Competence)	Points	Expanded Core (Excellence)	Points
1. Opens with acceptable thesis. (Compares the issues or themes specified.)	1	Goes beyond the basic core of 1–6 points. The basic core score of **7** must be earned before a student can gain expanded core points.	0–2
2. Deals with all parts of the question, perhaps not evenly or thoroughly.	2	Examples:	
(Deals with most parts of question.)	(1)	• Opens with an analytical, clear, comprehensive thesis.	
3. Backs up thesis with appropriate historical evidence.	2	• Deals with all relevant parts of the question: comparisons, chronology, causation, connections, themes, interactions, content.	
(Partly backs up thesis with appropriate historical evidence.)	(1)	• Gives ample historical evidence to back up thesis.	
4. Provides one or two relevant, direct comparisons between or among societies.	1	• Links comparisons to larger global context.	
		• Draws several direct comparisons between or among societies.	
5. Analyzes one or more reasons for a difference or similarity discussed in a direct comparison.	1	• Regularly examines the reasons for and the resullts of key similarities and differences.	
Subtotal	7	**Subtotal**	2
		TOTAL 9	

Sample Answer

The two decades that followed World War I brought immense changes to most parts of the globe. Among the regions affected were the Middle East and Latin America, each of which modernized during the 1920s and 1930s. Both had several things in common, such as relative backwardness, heavy influence from outside powers, and not much success with representative government. However, there were also key differences that, arguably, outweigh the similarities: Latin American states were already more modern and more independent, traditional Islam was more an obstacle to change than Catholicism, and events like WWI and the Depression affected both areas differently.

[This introductory paragraph addresses the question's key elements and identifies the regions to be compared. It acknowledges that there are similarities and differences, and it tackles the basic core by starting the process of comparison right away. It lays out a thesis about why differences in the two countries' experiences will outweigh the similarities.]

Prior to WWI, the Middle East was backward in comparison to the West, and it was dominated by outside powers. Egypt was under British control, and Persia, while technically free, was divided into British and Russian spheres of influence. The one major independent state, the Ottoman Empire, was in decline and widely known as the "sick man of Europe." The Ottomans attempted some changes, the Tanzimat reforms, in the nineteenth century, and there was some social modernization and industrialization—but not enough to prevent the Young Turks from taking over in 1908 and attempting even faster change. Unfortunately for the Ottomans, the Young Turks sided with the Germans in WWI. Therefore, more so than Latin America, the Middle East was directly involved in the war. The Ottomans were among the losers, and their empire was broken up.

[This paragraph sets the stage by describing the existing state of modernization in the Middle East before and during World War I. This essay is about comparing two processes of change, so a starting point has to be established in both cases. One comparative note—the Middle East's greater involvement in World War I—has already been included.]

At first, the end of WWI brought greater foreign domination to the Middle East. Egypt and Persia remained under British influence. Arabs, who had rebelled against Ottoman rule and sided with the Allies, hoping to gain a united, independent Arab state, were disappointed. The English and French imposed a mandate system over Arab regions such as Iraq, Syria, Lebanon, Jordan, and Palestine. These were not technically colonies, but were dominated by the French and British. (Britain's Balfour Declaration, which guaranteed a Jewish homeland in Palestine, also alienated the Arabs.) In 1932, Ibn Said created the state of Saudi Arabia, but it remained very traditionalist. Economic modernization came only after the discovery of oil in 1938, and even then, it benefitted only the Saudi elite and foreign investors.

Real modernization in the Middle East occurred in Turkey and Persia, in both cases as a result of bold action by strong-willed and authoritarian leaders. In 1923, Mustafa Kemal took over the Turkish government and renamed himself Ataturk ("father of all Turks"). In 1925, Reza Khan Pahlavi rose to power in Persia, threw out the British, and crowned himself shah. Both were Westernizers who industrialized their economies and encouraged Western ideas and education (Ataturk even gave women the vote). Both saw Islam as a backward force standing in the way of change, and both sought to reduce, even eliminate, Islam's role in law and politics. Middle Eastern modernization took place only in a handful of countries, and it was imposed from above.

[These two paragraphs describe where and how modernization in the Middle East occurred. Good historical detail is provided, and several examples are analyzed in order to demonstrate a general pattern.]

Like the Middle East, Latin America before and during WWI was relatively backward and heavily influenced by outside powers, especially the United States. On the other hand, most nations in Latin America had been free since the early 1800s, thanks to the Latin American wars of independence, and foreign domination was economic, not directly colonial. There was also more industrialization in Latin America—although most Latin American economies were based on the exploitation of one or two commodities, such as an agricultural crop (coffee or bananas) or a natural resource (copper, fertilizer, or steel), and foreign investors had great control over those economies. One more difference is that Latin American nations had almost no direct involvement with WWI.

[Just as the second paragraph did for the Middle East, this paragraph establishes a starting point for Latin America. It also continues the process of comparing the Middle East with Latin America directly.]

After WWI, American economic influence over Latin America increased, because countries like Britain and France were in such bad economic shape that they pulled out many of their investments. During the 1920s, the U.S. backed up its business interests with political pressure and military force. This lessened only when President Franklin Roosevelt started his Good Neighbor Policy. By that point, though, the Great Depression had begun, and because Latin American economies were so dependent on U.S. investment, the Depression hurt Latin America badly and slowed down modernization. (The Middle East was less affected by the Depression, another important difference.)

Industrialization and modernization took place in Latin America during the 1920s and 1930s but not, as in the Middle East, because of one ruler's will. Instead, the economic interests of a larger elite—and foreign investors—stimulated growth. Dictatorial governments, some mild (like Mexico's PRI party), some severe, were common. This authoritarianism grew worse in the 1930s, largely because of economic stress caused by the Depression, partly because of the influence of European fascism. A military government seized control of Argentina in 1930, and that same

year, the right-wing dictator Vargas took power in Brazil and created one of the continent's most brutal regimes.

[These two paragraphs describe change in Latin America during the 1920s and 1930s. They provide concrete details but also discuss general trends. There are direct comparisons to the Middle East.]

During the interwar period, both Latin America and the Middle East modernized and industrialized despite lingering backwardness from the 1800s, outside interference, and, on the whole, undemocratic government. Latin America started from a more advanced position, however, with politically independent countries and partially industrialized economies and societies. In the Middle East, modernization was rarer and, when it happened, was pushed through by westernizing politicians opposed to Muslim traditionalism.

[This conclusion restates key similarities and differences. It is somewhat rough and rushed, but when time is running out, it is more important to get points across than to worry about style.]

UNIT ONE

TECHNOLOGICAL AND ENVIRONMENTAL TRANSFORMATIONS
(8000 B.C.E.–600 B.C.E.)

Unit Overview

GENERAL REMARKS

Humanlike, or hominid, creatures emerged on earth approximately 3 to 4 million years ago. Modern humans (*Homo sapiens sapiens*) developed sometime between 100,000 and 250,000 years ago. According to most scholars, humanity's birthplace was Africa. From there, humans spread to the rest of the globe, starting around 100,000 years ago.

The period from approximately 2.5 million years ago to 5,000 or 6,000 years ago is referred to as the Stone Age. During this time, human communities took shape, but remained at a relatively primitive state of development, socially and technologically. After around 10,000 years ago, during the Neolithic revolution, human societies gradually became more advanced. Various peoples learned how to domesticate plants and animals. They developed what are generally considered to be the basic attributes of civilized society. They practiced agriculture, invented systems of recordkeeping (especially writing), and made metal (rather than stone) tools. They developed complex forms of social and political organization, and sophisticated modes of economic exchange.

The earliest "civilized" societies appeared between 3500 and 2000 B.C.E. All four were born along the banks of major river systems. They were

- The Sumerian-Babylonian civilization of Mesopotamia (the Tigris and Euphrates rivers)
- Egypt (the Nile River)
- The Indus valley civilization (the Indus River)
- Early China (the Yellow River, or Huang He)

Also among the world's oldest civilizations were the Olmec, who arose in Central America around 1200 B.C.E., and the Chavín, who appeared in the Andes Mountains after 900 B.C.E.

Quickly, other developed societies appeared throughout the world. By 600 B.C.E., civilizations had emerged in Asia, Europe, North Africa, sub-Saharan Africa, North America, and Central and South America. Many were connected by trade, warfare, and other forms of interaction. Several of the world's major religions had been born.

BROAD TRENDS

Humans and the Environment

- Migration took *Homo sapiens* out of Africa sometime around 100,000 years ago, first to the Middle East and the southern parts of Asia. By 40,000 years ago, humans had moved into Europe and the northern parts of Asia, and they are believed to have crossed the Bering land bridge into the Americas around 15,000 years ago.
- During the Stone Age, humans learned to make tools and shape their environment with them. They also learned how to use fire.
- How early societies developed was heavily conditioned by their physical environment.
- Even the earliest and least advanced forms of social organization had an impact on the environment, in the form of pollution, resource consumption, and resource extraction.
- The Neolithic Revolution changed many societies' relationship with their environment by encouraging agricultural production and permanent settlement.
- Advanced societies altered their environment radically by farming, mining, irrigating, building roads and cities, and clearing forests.
- On occasion, societies damaged or altered their environments severely enough that they died out or had to move elsewhere.
- Migration continued to play a role in spreading human populations across the globe. Key examples that began during this period include the movement of Indo-Europeans across Eurasia, the Bantu migrations in sub-Saharan Africa, and the Polynesian voyages from Southeast Asia across the Pacific.

Development and Interaction of Cultures

- Even during the Stone Age, human beings expressed themselves artistically, by means of painting and music. They developed oral traditions.
- Prehistoric societies buried their dead, worshipped gods, and practiced religious rituals. Early forms of religion included ancestor worship, animism, and shamanism.
- Writing and other forms of recordkeeping emerged in most civilized societies, starting around 3000 B.C.E.
- Many of the world's major religions were born, including Judaism, Zoroastrianism, and Vedism, the precursor to Hinduism.
- In a process called cultural diffusion, societies exchanged ideas, artistic practices, and religious beliefs with each other.
- With the disappearance of the Bering land bridge, the peoples of the Americas were physically and culturally isolated from those living on the rest of the continents.
- The peoples of Europe, North Africa, the Middle East, South Asia, and East Asia were linked by a large system of exchange that involved war, conquest, trade, travel, and cultural-religious interaction.

State-Building, Expansion, and Conflict

- The first states grew out of core civilizations in the Middle East, China, Mesoamerica, and South America's Andes Mountains.
- With the development of agriculture and fixed settlements, complex forms of political organization began to appear, including the formation of elite classes and bureaucracies.
- Most governments were monarchies (rule by a single leader) or oligarchies (rule by a small elite). Representative forms of government were all but nonexistent.
- Organized warfare became more common as states formed. Many states built empires by means of military conquest.
- Attacks by nomads and mobile pastoralists caused civilized societies to react by building stronger city walls, adopting weapons like the recurve bow, and learning the arts of cavalry warfare and charioteering.

Economic Systems

- The earliest social groups tended to be hunting and foraging societies, living at subsistence, possessing few goods, and with little specialization of labor. Trade tended to be limited, and based on simple barter.
- The development of agriculture allowed the accumulation of food surpluses, which enabled some members of society to make a living by means other than growing food. The results were specialization of labor, class distinction, and social stratification.
- The switch from nomadism to sedentary, or settled, life led to the accumulation of wealth and the concept of private property.
- Cities served as centers of governance, cultural exchange, and trade.
- As settled civilizations encountered each other, they tended to trade—one of the most important forms of interaction between civilizations. Trade networks tended to follow waterways for ease of transport. Trade routes were especially wide-ranging in Eurasia and parts of Africa.

Social Structures

- The ability of humans to mate when and with whom they chose gave rise to family units during the prehistoric era. Early social units, such as clans, were based on kinship systems.
- Basic physical differences between the sexes led to a gender division of labor in most Stone Age societies. The emergence of agriculture deepened the gender division of labor.
- Gender division tended to give rise to patriarchalism and gender inequality. In most places, women were relegated to a secondary role, although the degree to which this happened depended on the society. In some cultures, women were decidedly subservient. In others, they had at least some rights (divorce, inheritance, ownership of property). They might also exercise informal influence within their societies or over their families.

- Specialization of labor led to social stratification and the emergence of socio-economic classes (upper-class aristocracies, middle-class merchants and artisans, lower-class urban dwellers and peasants).
- Slavery and other forms of coerced labor were common.

QUESTIONS AND COMPARISONS TO CONSIDER

- What roles do geography, climate, and environment play in shaping human societies? How have different societies affected their environments? What practices have put most strain on the environment?
- What features make a society "primitive" or "civilized"? What technologies and innovations appear to have been crucial for the development of advanced societies?
- How do agricultural and urban societies compare with pastoral and nomadic ones? How do these different types interact? How did military threats from pastoral nomads influence civilized societies?
- How did the appearance of cities affect the development of ancient societies?
- What is the importance of cultural interaction and diffusion versus that of independent innovation in changing societies technologically, scientifically, or culturally?
- Compare how different religions and philosophical traditions have supported political regimes. Also, how have they been used to justify class systems, hierarchies, and gender and ethnic discrimination?
- Examine and compare various forms of social inequality (slavery and other forms of coerced labor, caste systems, patriarchy, gender or ethnic discrimination) in different cultures.
- How have different societies organized themselves economically? What role did trade play in the prehistoric and ancient world? Describe the characteristics of interregional trade networks (between Egypt and Nubia, for example, or between Mesopotamia and the Indus Valley).
- What roles did large-scale migrations play in various parts of the world during this period? Consider the passage of Asiatic peoples to the Americas over the Bering land bridge, the Pacific-wide migration of the Polynesians, the Bantu migrations throughout Africa, and the spread of Aryans and Indo-Europeans.

Big Geography and the Peopling of the Earth

- Prehistory
- Major continents and bodies of water
- Hominid development and the "Out of Africa" thesis
- The Stone Age (Paleolithic and Neolithic)
- Hunter-forager societies
- Gender division of labor

Hominid, or humanlike, life has existed on earth for 3 million to 4 million years. Humans and their immediate ancestors appeared 100,000 to 200,000 years ago, but the history of human civilization stretches back only a little more than 5,000 years. The vast expanse of time preceding the birth of civilized societies is called **prehistory**. Because written sources from this period are rare to nonexistent, much of the knowledge historians have of the prehistoric period comes from the work of other scholars, including paleontologists (who study the remains of ancient plants and animals), paleoclimatologists (who study the ancient environment), anthropologists (who study the physical, social, and cultural characteristics of human beings), and archaeologists (who study the objects and buildings left behind by humans). These scholars constantly make new discoveries and form new theories, and so the ways historians understand the prehistoric age frequently change.

Coverage of the prehistoric era by the AP World History exam is limited, but knowing the basics is important. In addition, familiarity with basic geography is indispensable no matter what time period one studies, as is an understanding of how human societies have migrated throughout the world and interacted with their environments, whether in ancient or modern times.

GEOGRAPHIC ORIENTATION

To get a sense of the labels preferred by the AP World History course for various world regions, consult the map in the Appendix at the end of this book.

Of the world's seven continents, Antarctica, covering the south polar region, has no native human population. Australia, the smallest continent, is home to the earth's oldest surviving ethnic group (the Aborigines) but remained largely isolated for most of its history. The thousands of islands sprinkled throughout the Pacific form no continent but are often referred to, along with Australia, as **Oceania**.

Africa is considered by most scholars to be the birthplace of humanity. Its northern third is home to the world's largest desert, the **Sahara**. **Asia** is the largest and most

populous continent on earth, ranging from the **Middle East** to the Indian subcontinent and, farther east, China and Japan. The island chains that make up Indonesia, Malaysia, and the Philippines are also considered part of Asia. Thanks to its size, Asia contains the world's most diverse mix of climates, geographical features, ethnicities, languages, and cultures. In addition to the Middle East, the continent contains several distinct subregions: **Central Asia**, **South Asia**, **Southeast Asia**, and **East Asia**. **Europe**, a relatively small continent with a large population, is resource-rich and, on the whole, mild and temperate in climate. Europe is physically joined to Asia, and the two continents together are referred to as **Eurasia**. From humanity's earliest days, there was constant interaction among the populations of Africa and Eurasia, and the AP World History course frequently uses the term **Afro-Eurasian** to describe trends spanning all three continents.

North and **South America** were originally settled by migrating peoples from Asia, who crossed a land bridge that existed only temporarily. Until the late 1400s C.E., the Americas developed in social and environmental isolation from the other three major continents. Abundant in resources and, in most places, agriculturally fertile, the Americas became home to many advanced cultures. From 1492 C.E. onward, contact with European societies changed the Americas dramatically.

For thousands of years, **water transport** remained cheaper, easier, and more efficient than overland travel. Although large bodies of water were formidable barriers, many early societies were capable of coastline and river navigation. Oceans, seas, lakes, and rivers not only provided food and other resources, but enabled the transfer of people, goods, ideas, technology, religious beliefs, and cultural practices. Of the world's four oceans, the **Atlantic**, **Indian**, and **Pacific** have been particularly important in this respect (the Arctic Ocean still remains difficult to navigate), as have seas like the **Caribbean**, the **Mediterranean**, the Black and Red seas, and the seas of Japan, East China, and South China. Major river systems include the **Nile**, the Congo, the **Tigris** and **Euphrates**, the **Indus**, the Ganges, the **Huang He** (**Yellow**), the **Yangzi** (Yangtze), the Volga, the **Danube**, the **Rhine**, the **Mississippi-Missouri**, and the **Amazon**.

Human societies and their physical environments mutually influence each other. Especially with technology to help them adapt to different geographical conditions, human beings have created societies in all but the harshest environments on earth. Still, as a general rule, societies were most prone to develop into advanced civilizations if the local geography featured one or more of the following:

- a climate that was not extremely hot, cold, dry, or wet
- a suitable amount of fertile land, preferably flat
- a reliable source of water
- topography (the shape of the land) that permitted reasonably easy movement
- access to a river, seacoast, or both, for the sake of transport and food supply
- the presence of one or more desirable natural resources
- proximity to one or more trade routes

Not all these conditions had to prevail. Think of the monsoons of India (extreme weather) or the terraced fields of the Andean civilizations (little or no flat land for agriculture). However, an advanced society is unlikely to develop without at least some of them working in its favor.

NOTE

An older school of historical thought, **geographic determinism**, used to argue that geography was the paramount force behind a society's development, but few subscribe to that view now.

HUMAN ORIGINS AND THE FIRST MIGRATIONS

The earliest hominids, or humanlike creatures, emerged in southern and east Africa around 3 million to 4 million years ago. They were part of the zoological order called primates, which includes apes and monkeys. Between 2 million and 3 million years ago, the earliest members of the genus *Homo*, to which humanity belongs, also appeared in Africa. Later species within genus *Homo* made basic stone and wooden tools and clothed themselves in skins and furs.

Much debate continues as to where the dividing line lies between anatomically modern humans (*Homo sapiens*) and earlier species of *Homo*. Also uncertain is what interactions, if any, *Homo sapiens* may have had with variant species of *Homo*, such as the Neanderthals, who coexisted with *Homo sapiens* for thousands of years. What seems clear is that *Homo sapiens* evolved sometime around 150,000 years ago in the vicinity of East Africa's Rift Valley and then migrated outward. This theory is informally referred to as the **"Out of Africa" thesis**. An opposing model held by a minority of scholars, the multiregional thesis, proposes that modern humans, descending from earlier hominid groups that had already left Africa, appeared independently in different places throughout the world.

Homo sapiens spread throughout Africa between 150,000 and 100,000 years ago. Beyond that, the **peopling of the earth** most likely resulted from a pattern of migration that took humans from Africa to the Middle East around 100,000 years ago. From there, human populations spread throughout the southern parts of Asia, reaching places like India and Southeast Asia around 70,000 years ago, and China at about 67,000 years ago. Around 50,000 years ago, settlers crossed from Southeast Asia to Australia and other parts of Oceania. It took longer for people to move northward into Europe, Central Asia, and Siberia, because of cooler climates caused by the periodic **ice ages** of the Pleistocene epoch (a geological time period lasting approximately 2.5 million to 12,000 years ago). Still, by about 40,000 years ago, numerous human communities had pushed into these places.

The question of how humans moved into the Americas remains contentious. Most believe that, sometime around 15,000 years ago, settlers from Eurasia crossed the **Bering land bridge** that spanned Siberia and Alaska during periods of heavy glaciation. Others have argued for an earlier crossing date, while others have speculated that at least some of the earliest Americans arrived by boat, whether across the Pacific or Atlantic, but none of these theories has gained wide acceptance. By 8000 B.C.E., humans had settled in all but the most inhospitable parts of the globe.

HUNTER-FORAGER SOCIETIES DURING THE EARLY AND MIDDLE STONE AGES

The earliest humans made tools out of many materials, such as wood, bone, and animal skins and sinews. The most important, and the most numerous today, because they have survived best over time, were made of stone. Consequently, the first period of hominid history is known as the **Stone Age**, which lasted roughly from 2.5 million to 5,000 or 6,000 years ago. The Stone Age is typically subdivided into the Paleolithic (the "early Stone Age," ending approximately 12,000 years ago), the Mesolithic (a transitional period lasting from about 12,000 to 10,000 years ago), and the

Neolithic (the "new Stone Age," beginning around 8000 B.C.E.). The Paleolithic overlapped with the Pleistocene epoch and its recurring ice ages. The last of these lasted roughly between 28,000 and 10,000 years ago—with the glaciers reaching their largest extent and causing the global climate to reach its coolest between 22,000 and 18,000 years ago.

Tools helped Stone Age hunter-foragers adapt to a variety of climates and terrains, from jungles and rain forests to deserts, mountains, and tundra. The most favored habitats tended to be grasslands, such as savannas and steppes, which supported large numbers of game animals and enough plant life to supplement the meat gained by hunting.

Stone Age humans lived in natural dwellings, such as caves and canyons, but also built tents, huts, and structures of wood and stone (and even bone, such as the mammoth-tusk constructions found in paleolithic Eastern Europe) that demanded advanced carpentry and construction skills. They used **fire** to heat their dwellings (allowing them to expand into colder regions), cook their food, and safeguard themselves from predators. At what point organized warfare began to be practiced is unknown, but Stone Age humans had to protect themselves against dangers of many sorts. The first weapons included rocks and clubs.

When Stone Age humans designed **tools**, their greatest concerns were to ensure a steady and plentiful food supply, to manufacture clothing appropriate to the climate, and to provide themselves with adequate shelter. Multipurpose devices such as knives and axes were especially useful. Spears (often propelled by throwing sticks called atlatls), slings, fishhooks, and harpoons were used for fishing and hunting. Some archaeologists believe that the bow and arrow first appeared during the late Paleolithic or Mesolithic, but if it did, it was not widespread until later. Certain tools meant for hunting and food preparation could also be used for self-protection and in combat. There were wooden implements to dig roots from the ground, as well as mats and baskets to carry nuts, berries, and other foodstuffs. Clay pots were used for cooking as early as 12,500 years ago. The earliest clothes were made from furs and animal hides, sewn with bone needles. As time passed, Stone Age humans began to use plant fibers, and, by 26,000 years ago, at least some were weaving cloth and dyeing it to add color.

Social organization during the Stone Age was based on **kinship groups**. Extended families tended to cluster together, forming clans and larger groups such as bands and tribes. Almost universally, these social groups sustained themselves by **hunting and foraging** (also known as hunting and gathering). Rather than produce food themselves, these societies lived off the resources taken directly from the land, including birds and animals. They fished lakes, rivers, and seashores. They gathered nuts, berries, and roots. They often practiced **nomadism**, following their favorite game animals on seasonal rounds of migration—or abandoning old hunting grounds for new ones if resources grew scarce.

Hunter-forager social structures tended to be relatively free of hierarchy. Chieftains or councils of elders provided leadership, and most groups appointed one or more figures to exercise spiritual authority. But most members of hunter-forager groups performed similar functions and had similar skills (although labor was divided by gender). Private property was scarce and ownership of land unheard of,

and so few if any distinctions were made between classes or between "rich" and "poor." Even without a complex class structure, the organization of Stone Age clans and tribes could be quite sophisticated. A high level of teamwork was necessary to hunt large creatures, and many believe that such complex coordination of effort helped ancient peoples to develop effective means of waging war. Stone Age groups did not develop in isolation but are known to have traded and interacted with each other over great distances, exchanging goods, ideas, and religious beliefs.

Stone Age peoples enjoyed a rich artistic and religious life. They expressed themselves by means of music as early as 30,000 years ago (flutes from that time are the oldest known instruments), and also by their cave paintings, the earliest of which date back to 32,000 years ago. Whether such paintings served an artistic or a religious purpose is unclear, and the same is true of the figurines sculpted during the Paleolithic and Mesolithic, which often seem to be pregnant women or goddesses. Stone Age peoples practiced a variety of religious rituals, including the burial of their dead and the offering of sacrifices to deities, departed ancestors, and spirits. Most hunter-forager peoples followed some form of **animism** or **totemism**, belief systems in which all things in the natural world, including beasts, trees, and even mountains and rivers, possess some form of spirit. Religious leaders in such societies are generally called **shamans** (a term originating among the Tungus peoples of Siberia), who were believed to be able to speak to spirits and heal the sick.

The **gender division of labor** made itself felt as early as the hunter-forager stage, with various tasks assigned by sex because of basic physical differences. Men, who were on average stronger and larger, hunted large animals, fought, and performed heavy labor. Women gathered plants and hunted small game, hauled back food that men had hunted and prepared it, maintained the home, and tended children. Some historians believe that, during the Stone Age, division of labor did not necessarily mean that men's roles were seen as superior to women's, although this assumption is open to debate. The division of labor by gender continued long after the Stone Age and gave rise to a long-standing **gender inequality** that most commonly favored men and disadvantaged women. Traces of this inequality are still found today, in even the most advanced societies, despite technological advances that have made the genders' differences in physical strength less important.

The Neolithic Revolution and Early Agricultural Societies

- The Neolithic Revolution
- Pastoralism and herding societies
- Agriculture
- Specialization of labor
- Social stratification
- Patriarchalism
- Metallurgy and the Bronze Age
- Writing and recordkeeping

After peaking at about 20,000 years ago, the last of the Pleistocene's ice ages ended 12,000 years ago, causing milder conditions, warmer temperatures, and higher ocean levels. Vast expanses of tundra were transformed into grassland, and former grasslands became forest. These and other environmental changes profoundly altered the lives of Stone Age people. Human population increased rapidly. Fewer than 2 million humans had been alive at any given time during the last ice age. By 5000 B.C.E., the world population was at least 10 million, and grew to somewhere between 50 million and 100 million by 1000 B.C.E.

Aside from the more congenial climate, the primary cause of this population growth was a key transformation in how human societies provided themselves with food. Although many groups continued hunting and foraging, certain peoples in various parts of the world, starting around 12,000 years ago, began to produce their own food. This practice involved the domestication of animals and plants, new skills that gave birth to pastoral and agricultural modes of production. Each allowed humans to manipulate their environment to a greater degree than before.

The earthshaking importance of this change has made it traditional to refer to a **Neolithic revolution**. A few scholars question the validity of this label on the grounds that the "revolution" took place over a long period of time and that, in some parts of the world, the changes began in the Mesolithic. But the concept is accepted by most, and the changes, whether revolutionary or gradual, were immense.

PASTORALISM AND HERDING SOCIETIES

Humankind's **domestication of animals** began during the Stone Age. First to be tamed was the dog, which provided companionship, security, and help in hunting. Next, goats, sheep, and pigs were domesticated for meat and milk.

47

As the Neolithic era progressed, more animals were domesticated. Horses, water buffalo, oxen, camels, and (in the Americas) llamas provided transport and labor. For groups involved in agriculture, animal droppings were useful as fertilizer. Many animals were raised for wool or hides, in order to make clothing. Most important, animals provided a steady source of food. Like sheep, goats, and pigs, cattle and poultry yielded meat, milk, eggs, and other edibles.

Groups that domesticated animals but not plants developed **pastoralist**, or **herding**, societies. These emerged most commonly in grassland regions, particularly in Eurasia and Africa. Although not to the degree that agricultural societies did, pastoralists accumulated wealth and experienced some **social stratification**. Warrior elites arose more frequently than among hunter-foragers, and the gender division of labor tended to deepen.

Because livestock consumed huge quantities of grass or fodder, pastoralists lived **nomadic** lifestyles, migrating constantly, generally according to seasonal patterns. Highly mobile, they were often expert **horseback riders**, and many invented or made use of **wheeled vehicles** such as carts and **chariots**, pulled by horses, oxen, or donkeys. This sort of wandering made it harder for herding groups to develop into settled societies, but they often traded or warred with such societies. As a result, pastoralists played a key role in the process of **cultural diffusion**, helping to spread new technologies (especially military-related ones, such as the chariot, the **compound bow and arrow**, and **iron weapons**) and new religious beliefs.

Pastoralism had a considerable impact on the environment. The domestication of animals led to an artificial selection of certain species over others, and the grazing of large numbers of herbivores taxed the growing capacity of grasslands, sometimes severely. Overgrazing led to erosion and, on occasion, caused the transformation of grassland to desert.

The Practice of Agriculture, ca. 8000 B.C.E.
During the transition from the Paleolithic Era to the Neolithic, communities in the Middle East and northern China began to practice agriculture systematically.

AGRICULTURE

The **domestication of plants**, or **agriculture**, became known in many parts of the world about 10,000 years ago. In the Middle East, wheat and barley cultivation began around 8000 B.C.E. From there, it spread to the Balkans (6500 B.C.E.), the Nile valley (6000 B.C.E.), other parts of northeast Africa (5500 B.C.E.), and continental Europe (4000 B.C.E.). Sub-Saharan Africa developed its own agricultural tradition, growing plantains, dates, and yams. Isolated from the other continents, the peoples of the Americas, starting in the Andes, developed agriculture sometime between 10,000 B.C.E. and 5000 B.C.E. Early crops here included quinoa, potatoes, maize (corn), beans, and squash. Taro was cultivated in New Guinea 9,000 years ago, while millet and rice were grown in India as early as 6000 to 5000 B.C.E. Probably on their own, the people of China's river valleys learned to grow millet by 6000 B.C.E. Rice cultivation began in Southeast Asia around 5000 B.C.E. and seems to have spread from there to southern China.

It was a combination of **independent innovation** and **cultural diffusion** that led agriculture to be adopted throughout these and other parts of the world. As time went on, diffusion played an increasingly important role. As more societies began to domesticate plants, certain techniques were borrowed and handed on. Seeds and crops were exchanged as well. Most scholars agree that women, already responsible for food collection in most hunter-forager societies, played an important role in stimulating the transition to agriculture.

Agriculture's greatest advantage was that it provided a more dependable supply of food. In exchange, agriculture required intensive labor, a great deal of cooperative effort, and a long-term commitment to a particular place, all of which encouraged a **sedentary**, or settled, lifestyle. Agriculturalists began to live in larger communities such as **villages** and, in some cases, cities. The concepts of **private property** (in the form of land, tools, and livestock, and then luxury goods) and the accumulation of wealth came to seem more natural. These, combined with food surpluses (which allowed people not directly involved in food production to be fed and to develop other skills) promoted the **specialization of labor**, causing social structures to become more complex and more hierarchical. **Patriarchalism**, or male dominance, tended to be the norm, with gender inequities and the gender division of labor more pronounced than among hunter-foragers or pastoralists.

The environmental impact of agriculture was likewise far heavier than that of hunting-foraging or pastoralism. Plant and animal species selected artificially by humans came to dominate regions where agriculture was the chief mode of production. Practices such as **forest clearing** and **irrigation** vastly increased humanity's "ecological footprint" on the land. The same is true for **mining**, as well as engineering projects such as swamp dredging, dam building, and canal digging—all more common as agricultural communities grew larger and more advanced.

FROM STONE AGE TO THE AGES OF METAL: TRANSITIONS TO CIVILIZATION

Because it required greater effort and organization, agriculture encouraged closer ties and the formation of long-lasting settlements. The permanence and stability associated with agriculture proved crucial in **civilizing** early societies. This involved more elaborate forms of social organization, as well as a corresponding increase in technological innovation and religious and cultural sophistication.

In certain places, the increased social complexity of the Neolithic era led to the emergence of **cities**. Cities offered protection and defense for large numbers of people. They served as points of trade and economic activity, and as centers for political leadership. They enabled the exchange of ideas, information, religious beliefs, and cultural values. As did villages, but on a greater scale, cities permitted people with different skills and talents to gather in a single area, allowing greater **specialization of labor** and **social stratification**. Classes typically found in these more hierarchical societies include political elites, religious clergy, professional soldiers, artisans and craftspeople, traders and merchants, and farmers. The first cities date back as far as 8000 to 7000 B.C.E. They include Jericho, on the west bank of the Jordan River, and Çatal Hüyük, in what is today Turkey. An urban center, Danpo, appeared in China between 5000 B.C.E and 4000 B.C.E.

All during the Neolithic, technological aptitude improved. Tools invented during the Paleolithic and Mesolithic became more refined. Newer devices, such as hoes, shovels, chisels, and saws, appeared. The peoples of the Middle East invented the **wheel**, permitting the invention of a number of vehicles, including carts and chariots. The art of **weaving** made clothing and textiles more easily available. Many groups taught themselves the multipurpose craft of **pottery**. The **plow** extended the amount of land under cultivation and increased labor productivity. The result was **surplus production**, which gave rise to further specialization of labor and social stratification.

Nearer the end of the Neolithic, many societies were on the brink of discovering how to smelt and shape metals. As a tool-making material, metal is stronger and more versatile than stone. However, **metallurgy** (the science of extracting and refining metal from raw ore) and **metalworking** (the craft of shaping metal into tools) are highly advanced skills that took thousands of years to discover and perfect.

Large-scale metallurgy first began in the Middle East and China, sometime between 4000 B.C.E and 3000 B.C.E. In both areas, toolmakers hit upon the idea of mixing copper and tin to create a harder alloy, bronze. The Neolithic era ended, and the **Bronze Age** (ca. 3500–1200 B.C.E.) began. With the development of **iron**, a metal of even greater strength and usefulness, the Bronze Age came to a close.

One innovation almost always associated with the transition to civilization is **writing**. Ancient societies developed rich **oral traditions**, but the written word enabled them to keep records, pass on learning, and transfer information more effectively than before. Perhaps the earliest form of writing was developed in the ancient Middle East, by the Sumerians, between 3500 B.C.E and 3000 B.C.E., followed by the Egyptians at about 3000 B.C.E., the Indus River people around 2200 B.C.E., and the Chinese before 2000 B.C.E. A handful of cultures, including

the Incas, reached a civilized state without the benefit of a written script, but this happened rarely.

Religious practices grew more advanced as well. Animism, totemism, and shamanism, the faiths of most hunter-foragers, held less appeal to those living in more settled societies. Rituals became more complicated, and worshippers turned to more formal **polytheistic** pantheons of deities, who tended to be more anthropomorphic, or humanlike. The veneration of ancestors was common as well. Permanent sites of worship and ritual were constructed, including shrines, temples, great burial mounds (like the kurgan tumulus tombs of prehistoric Russia and Central Asia), and megaliths (large standing stones, such as those used for calendrical purposes in the 4000s B.C.E. at Nabta Playa, in the Nubian Desert, as well as the Carnac, Newgrange, and Stonehenge constructions in France, Ireland, and England, all dating to the 3000s B.C.E.).

The Development and Interactions of Early Agricultural, Pastoral, and Urban Societies

- Civilization
- The river valley civilizations
- The Olmecs
- Andean cultures
- Monarchies, oligarchies, and other elites
- Forms of coerced labor
- Trade
- Writing and recordkeeping
- Key works of art, architecture, and literature
- Shamanism, ancestor veneration, and polytheism
- Vedism
- Hebrew monotheism
- Zoroastrianism

The first **civilizations** are considered to have come into being around 5,500 to 5,000 years ago. How one should define "civilized" (especially as opposed to less flattering terms like "primitive" and "barbaric") has long been a matter of debate, with criteria changing over time. Still, most agree that civilized societies—defined by Webster's Dictionary as "social organizations of a high order, marked by advancements in the arts and sciences"—have certain basic features in common, such as the following:

- An economic system, based at least partly on trade, capable of producing food surpluses and permitting the specialization of labor
- A government that provides political and military leadership and enforces laws
- A social system that is hierarchical, class-based, and to some degree urbanized
- A moral or ethical code, generally in the form of a shared religion
- An intellectual tradition that typically includes a written language and encourages the pursuit of knowledge, science, and the arts

CORE/FOUNDATIONAL CIVILIZATIONS AND THE FIRST STATES

Between 3500 B.C.E and 2000 B.C.E., river systems in the Middle East, India, and China gave birth to the world's oldest civilizations: Mesopotamia, Egypt, the Indus River Valley, and Shang China. These, along with the Olmecs and the Chavín, two civilizations that arose in the Americas between 1200 B.C.E and 850 B.C.E., are considered core, or foundational, civilizations by the AP World History course. The first **states** and **empires** (states which expand by means of military conquest) had their origins in these core/foundational civilizations.

Mesopotamia

One of the world's two oldest civilizations, if not the oldest, was the Sumerian-Babylonian culture that arose in the region of **Mesopotamia** (a Greek term meaning "land between the waters"). The rivers giving life to this so-called Fertile Crescent were the **Tigris** and **Euphrates**. Settlement began in this area as early as 8000 B.C.E., and large-scale agriculture was practiced by 5000 B.C.E. Between 3500 B.C.E and 2350 B.C.E., the first true civilization here was begun by the **Sumerians**. As time passed, a variety of other local groups, especially the Akkadians, the **Babylonians** (1900–1600 B.C.E.), and **Assyrians** (911–612 B.C.E.), achieved political dominance. Still, the Sumerians' culture and religious traditions influenced the later peoples of Mesopotamia for centuries to come.

The Mesopotamians built many cities (including **Babylon**) and were governed by a small ruling class of priests and a kinglike figure known as the *lugal* (literally, "big man"). Mesopotamia was not always politically centralized; at times, individual city-states enjoyed much autonomy. The region's first empire was formed by the Akkadian conqueror Sargon, who proclaimed himself "King of Sumer and Akkad" sometime around 2200 B.C.E.

The Ancient Middle East, ca. 1200 B.C.E.
Note the importance of bodies of water in giving birth to ancient civilizations. The Fertile Crescent, between the Tigris and Euphrates rivers, encouraged the formation of advanced societies in Mesopotamia. The Nile did the same in Egypt. The Mediterranean Sea was crucial for the movement of people and trade goods.

In the Western tradition, if not worldwide, the Sumerians were the first to develop a written script: **cuneiform** (ca. 3300 B.C.E.). Sumerian poems gave rise sometime around 2000 B.C.E. to the **Gilgamesh epic**, one of the world's oldest literary works. One of the world's first law codes was compiled in Mesopotamia, by the Babylonian king Hammurabi (1792–1750 B.C.E.). Although **Hammurabi's law code** was quite harsh (death and mutilation were common punishments) and favored the upper classes, the idea that a consistent set of regulations, rather than the arbitrary will of a ruler, should govern society was an important innovation.

The Mesopotamians were skilled builders and craftspeople. Using clay, they erected dozens of large cities and, to honor their gods and goddesses, pyramid-like temples called **ziggurats**. They built canals and dams, and were accomplished at pottery and metalworking (bronzeworking began here around 3000 B.C.E.). Skilled astronomers, the Mesopotamians developed a high level of mathematical knowledge, originating the **base-60 number system** still used today to measure time and navigational calculations. The Mesopotamian peoples were great traders, and their economic network extended not just throughout the Middle East and North Africa, but through the Indian Ocean to present-day Pakistan and Afghanistan.

During the 1300s B.C.E. and 1200s B.C.E., the **Hittites**, from nearby Anatolia in the north, came to rule much of Mesopotamia. Skilled at chariot warfare, they are also notable for being among the first groups to make systematic use of **iron weapons**. Even more powerful were the **Assyrians**, who, between 911 B.C.E. and 612 B.C.E., formed one of the largest of the world's early empires. Armed with iron weapons and making good use of **cavalry** (horseback) warfare, the Assyrians conquered sizable parts of the Middle East, including Mesopotamia and Egypt, holding their empire together by means of a deliberate policy of cruelty.

Egypt

The other earliest civilization of the Middle East appeared in **Egypt**, on the banks of the **Nile**. Surrounded by desert, Egypt depended for survival on the Nile's waters. Agricultural settlements emerged there as early as 5500 B.C.E.

Egypt's history as a civilization is considered to have begun in 3100 B.C.E., when Upper (southern) and Lower (northern) Egypt were united. Its ancient history is divided into several long periods. During the Early Dynastic (ca. 3100–2575 B.C.E.) and Old Kingdom (2575–2134 B.C.E.) periods, basic social and political features took shape. Civil war tore Egypt apart during the First Intermediate Period (ca. 2134–2040 B.C.E.), but a more powerful and culturally dynamic Middle Kingdom arose around 2040 B.C.E., conquering the Nubian lands farther south on the Nile. The Middle Kingdom lasted until approximately 1640 B.C.E., when outside invaders called the Hyksos, armed with chariots and powerful compound bows, ushered in a Second Intermediate Period (ca. 1640–1532 B.C.E.). Rebelling against Hyksos rule around 1532 B.C.E., the Egyptians formed a New Kingdom that lasted until 1070 B.C.E. Under vigorous leaders, especially Rameses II (ca. 1304–1237 B.C.E.), New Kingdom Egypt conquered a great deal of territory in northern Africa and the Middle East. Eventually, the New Kingdom collapsed, due to internal disorder and foreign invasions. By the 900s B.C.E., most of Egypt had lost its independence.

Even more so than the Mesopotamians, the Egyptians developed a centralized society presided over by a monarch and a small caste of priests. The monarch, or **pharoah**, was considered the living incarnation of the sun god. Although their society was less urban than that of the Mesopotamians, and although they did not trade as widely, the Egyptians still built many cities and were part of a sizable economic network.

Egyptian women, while secondary to men in terms of power and status, enjoyed certain privileges. They managed household finances and the education of children. They had the right to divorce their husbands and could receive alimony. They could own property. Some managed businesses, and upper-class women could serve as priestesses. One queen, Hatshepsut, became pharoah of Egypt in her own right.

The Egyptians had an elaborate religion and many gods. Their chief deity was Ra, the sun god, and their principal religious text the **Egyptian Book of the Dead**. Concern about life after death gave rise to mummification (the art of preserving bodies after death) and the building of gigantic tombs, including the famous **pyramids**, which provided resting places for pharaohs after they died.

The cultural and scientific attainments of the Egyptians were many. Around 3100 B.C.E., they developed the written characters known as **hieroglyphs**. Using the fiber of reeds called **papyrus**, they invented the craft of papermaking. The Egyptians were skilled engineers and architects. From the beginning, they knew how to irrigate their fields, extending the reach of the Nile's waters far from the river valley itself. They began to construct pyramids around 2630 B.C.E., and their other monuments were impressive. They were talented makers of bronze tools and weapons and possessed a great knowledge of medicine, mathematics, and astronomy. They devised the **365-day calendar** that, with only minor modifications, is still in use today.

The Indus River Valley

Far to the east was a third civilization, growing up on the coast of the Arabian Sea and farther inland, in what is today Pakistan and northwestern India. This was the **Indus River civilization**, which arose around 2600 B.C.E. and lasted approximately seven centuries. Although the people here had a written language, it has not been deciphered by modern scholars, and even though some of their sculptures are still intact, they left behind little pictorial art. As a result, much about their civilization remains unclear, especially their origins, their culture, and the reasons for their decline and disappearance.

The Indus River civilization was quite large, about the size of present-day France, and heavily urbanized. Like the Nile in Egypt, the river itself, rich with silt, flooded regularly, allowing the widespread practice of agriculture. The Indus River people built several hundred cities, the largest of which, **Harappa** and **Mohenjo-Daro**, had populations of 35,000 and perhaps 100,000, respectively. (These are the cities' modern names, because the original ones are unknown to us.) Mohenjo-Daro sat on the Indus floodplain, while Harappa, about 500 miles to the northeast, appears to have been a gateway into the less settled but resource-rich frontier.

Because the layout of most Indus River cities is virtually identical, with streets laid out in extremely straight grids, it is thought that the society was unified and highly centralized. It also appears to have been prosperous, based on the fact that most cities

feature large baths (whether public or private is not known), warehouses for food storage, and covered drainpipes for disposing of sewage. The Indus River civilization produced metal tools and objects of high quality, as well as precious stones. It traded not only with its neighbors, but far beyond its borders, even with Mesopotamia.

The Indus River civilization lasted until approximately 1900 B.C.E. How it met its end is a matter of contention. It used to be thought that invasion by outside enemies, the Aryans, destroyed the Indus River cities. However, a majority of scholars now believe that environmental factors—most likely the drying up or diversion of rivers secondary to the Indus—led to the downfall.

Early China and the Shang Dynasty

The fourth river valley civilization emerged in China, along the **Yellow River** (or **Huang He**) in the north. The western reaches of China border on desert, and much of China's interior is hilly or mountainous. This makes the two east-west rivers, the Yellow and Yangzi (Yangtze), exceptionally important in supporting agriculture, allowing movement, and fostering social and political unity. Around 8000 B.C.E., small neolithic societies formed along the Yellow River, which takes its name from the dust carried by west winds from Central Asia, and which forms fertile loess soil when combined with water. By no later than 6000 B.C.E., wheat and millet were being grown in the north. Only in the south, along the Yangzi and below it, could rice be cultivated. In both cases, immense amounts of cooperative labor were required. In the north, forests had to be cleared and dams built. In the south, the planting of rice is among the world's most labor-intensive forms of agricultural production. By 2000 B.C.E., the Chinese had discovered the craft of bronzeworking.

Most of China's long history as a civilization, from the 1700s B.C.E. to 1911 C.E., is measured in dynasties, or successions of emperors. Tradition speaks of a dynasty called the Xia arising around 2000 B.C.E., but most scholars consider it mythical. The first historically verifiable dynasty, and the bedrock of Chinese civilization, is the **Shang dynasty**, which emerged on the banks of the Huang He and established a rapidly growing state around 1750 B.C.E. Led by a warrior aristocracy and able to feed and equip an army of tens of thousands, the Shang fought its northern and western neighbors, whom it considered to be barbarians, and expanded its boundaries by conquest. Shang armies used chariots, which they may have come to know about via contact with the Middle East, and they learned cavalry warfare from the steppe nomads they fought in the north. Prisoners of war were typically enslaved.

The Shang traded extensively, and many believe that its economic network may have stretched as far as the Middle East. Principal commodities included jade and ivory carvings, as well as **silk,** on which the Chinese enjoyed an unbroken monopoly for many hundreds of years. The Chinese system of writing, **pictograms**, originated with the Shang. So did two of the most important aspects of early Chinese religion: divination (or fortune-telling) and **ancestor veneration** (a tradition that reinforced a strong sense of patriarchalism). The Shang also considered themselves to be at the center of the world, an idea giving rise to the long-standing tradition of viewing China as a superior "Middle Kingdom." Shang rulers were religious authorities as well as political ones, acting as intercessors with the gods by performing sacrifices and rituals of divination.

China's second dynasty, and its longest-lasting, was the **Zhou** (**Chou**), founded by a herding society from the west that rebelled against Shang rule. Traditionally, the dynasty's beginnings date to the battle of Muye ("Shepherd's Wild"), fought in 1046 or 1045 B.C.E. The Zhou lasted until 221 B.C.E., although it was in serious decline long before that, from around 800 B.C.E. The internal collapse and civil wars that plagued the Zhou are reflected in the name given to the last phase of its history: the "Warring States" period (480–221 B.C.E.).

The Zhou preserved much of the knowledge of the Shang but added innovations of its own. Around 600 B.C.E., the Chinese learned to make iron tools and weapons. Political sophistication increased: A central principle of the Zhou was the **Mandate of Heaven**, the idea that, as long as a leader governed wisely and fairly, he could claim a divine right to rule.

The Olmecs

A great variety of advanced civilizations appeared in the Americas during and after the 2000s B.C.E. In Central America, also known as Mesoamerica, and Mexico, a succession of agricultural societies emerged, some of them deeply influencing the ones that followed. Among the oldest and most significant were the **Olmecs** (arising between 1400 B.C.E. and 1200 B.C.E. and lasting until 400 B.C.E.), considered by many to be a "mother civilization" in Mesoamerica in much the same way that the Sumerians were in Mesopotamia.

The chief Olmec cities—San Lorenzo, La Venta, and Tres Zapotes—were located in south-central Mexico, near present-day Tabasco and Veracruz. Unlike

One of the carved stone heads characteristic of the Olmec cultural style (ca. 1200–400 B.C.E.). Because the Olmec written script has never been deciphered, it is unclear whether these massive sculptures represent deities, political leaders, or some other kind of figure unknown to us.

most other early civilizations, such as Mesopotamia, Egypt, Shang China, and the Indus River culture, the Olmecs arose without the benefit of a large river system nearby. Their written language remains a mystery to scholars, but their art, monumental architecture, and religion clearly had an impact on peoples within a large radius, as well as on the civilizations that came after them. The presence of jade and obsidian from faraway places indicates a large trading network, and they were skilled potters and canal-builders. As with most peoples in the region, their diet consisted of corn, beans, and squash. They are most famous for carving huge stone heads, weighing up to 40 tons, and they constructed tall mounds and platforms which seem to be prototypes of the pyramids that later appeared in the region. They appear to have passed on a fascination with astronomy, a complicated ball game played for ritual purposes, and several deities, including their jaguar god. They very likely practiced **human sacrifice**, like the peoples who emerged later in the region.

Andean Cultures and the Chavín

In the northwestern part of South America, several civilizations rose up in the peaks and valleys of the Andes. Recent discoveries indicate that the first city in the Americas, Caral, was probably founded along the Supe River, in central Peru, around 2600 B.C.E. Most **Andean cultures** were skilled at weaving, pottery, and metalworking. It is thought that in the Americas, metallurgy originated here and then spread northward. Andean cultures formed heavily urban, class-stratifed societies. Their most important domesticated animal was the **llama**. Like the Olmecs in Mesoamerica, they created advanced cultures without growing up on the banks of a major river. Written languages did not develop here, but a system of recordkeeping later called **quipu** evolved, using knots tied into strings.

The most noteworthy of these civilizations was the **Chavín**, who emerged around 1000 B.C.E. and dominated the coastal plain and Andean foothills of what is today Peru. Their chief city, Chavín de Huántar, was located more than 10,000 feet above sea level. Individual clans took responsibility for maintaining roads, bridges, and irrigation systems in the difficult mountain terrain. Trade was conducted between the seacoast and the mountain valleys, and the Chavín subsisted on a diet of fish, shellfish, corn, quinoa, and potatoes. They worshipped a variety of gods, including a jaguar deity and a fierce-looking figure identified by archaeologists as the Walking Sticks God. The Chavín people are particularly known for their elaborate textiles.

The South American plains gave rise to nomadic herders. The rain forests of the Amazon basin were home to innumerable tribes. However, in neither place did large, settled civilizations appear before 1000 C.E.

Other Cultures and Civilizations

Other peoples from this period with distinctive features to be aware of include the inhabitants of **Nubia**, located to the south of Egypt along the Nile River and settled around 3000 B.C.E. An important corridor of exchange between north and south,

Nubia traded with Egypt and sub-Saharan Africa, although Egypt conquered the Nubian kingdom of Kush around 1500 B.C.E. The **Hebrews** of the Middle East emerged around 2000 B.C.E., gained a homeland in Israel around 1000 B.C.E., and developed the first major **monotheistic** religion, Judaism.

In the Mediterranean, the bull-worshipping Minoan civilization took shape on the island of Crete between 2000 B.C.E and 1450 B.C.E., powerfully influencing the Greeks who later emerged on the nearby islands and mainland. More directly ancestral to the Greeks were the Mycenaeans, who reached their peak between 1600 B.C.E and 1200 B.C.E. and fought the real-life version of the **Trojan War** (ca. 1250 B.C.E.) immortalized in the Homeric epics. **Greek culture** grew more cohesive during the Greek Dark Ages (ca. 1150–800 B.C.E) and the Archaic Period (ca. 800–500 B.C.E.). In Italy, the city of **Rome** is traditionally considered to have been founded in 753 B.C.E.

Another Mediterranean people to make note of are the **Phoenicians** (the Greek name for the group known as Canaanites in the Christian bible), a maritime culture that traded and colonized widely throughout the Mediterranean between 1550 B.C.E and 300 B.C.E. From their main cities of Byblos, Tyre, and Sidon in Syria and Lebanon, they harvested cedar and manufactured a famous purple dye from shellfish. Their greatest legacy is the **alphabet**, a written script in which each sign represents a sound rather than a concept or object, and which was adopted in modified form by the Greeks and Romans.

Even if they did not form civilizations themselves, **migrating pastoralists** influenced those who did in many ways. These include the **Indo-Europeans**, thought to have spread throughout Eurasia from Central Asia during the 1000s B.C.E. One

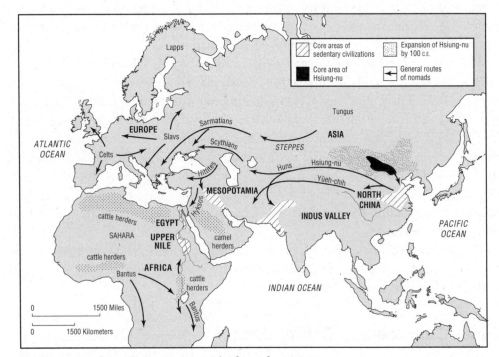

The Movement of Peoples in Eurasia and Africa after 2000 B.C.E.
Migration played a major role in the formation and development of early civilizations. Migrations often led to war and conquest, but they also facilitated cultural interaction and the spread of technology, science, languages, and religions.

Indo-European group, the **Aryans**, also called the Aryas, is considered by many to have played a foundational role in Indian prehistory by invading from the north around 1500 B.C.E. (Famously and tragically, Adolf Hitler and the Nazis misinterpreted the Aryans as the Europeans' "purest" ancestors and used this concept to justify their genocidal policies.) It was around 1500 B.C.E. that **Bantu** herders began their long migrations from the Niger River basin throughout most of sub-Saharan Africa. Egypt was conquered by the **Hyksos** people (a Greek term for "shepherd king") during the 1600s B.C.E, and the Shang and Zhou dynasties were constantly threatened by steppe nomads from Central Asia. Such pressures typically caused settled civilizations to become more effective at building walls and other city defenses, and also to adopt new military techniques like horseback riding, chariot warfare, and the use of bows and arrows. Conflicts between cities gave rise to increasingly organized and professional armies, as well as the art of siege warfare.

SOCIETY, TRADE, AND ECONOMICS

All societies exhibit some form of **class distinction**, according to which people are defined by wealth, ancestry, or occupation. Such distinctions are minor in hunter-forager societies and only somewhat more noticeable among pastoralists, but far more important in agricultural and settled societies characterized by **specialization of labor**. Examples of specialized occupations in early societies include soldiers, priests, craftspeople, artisans, scribes, and accountants.

The most common form of government in ancient civilizations (and throughout most of history) was **monarchy**, or rule by a single individual. In premodern eras, the monarch's power was often justified in religious terms: He or she was considered an embodiment of a god or said to rule by the gods' will. Most monarchs governed with the assistance of a small upper class, or **nobility** (or **aristocracy**). Also prominent in the ancient world was **oligarchy**, or rule by the few, in which a small group, typically made up of wealthy aristocrats, wields power. A government dominated by a religious elite is known as a **theocracy**.

Certain roles, such as political, military, and religious leadership, are inherently more powerful or more valued than others, causing the phenomenon of **social stratification**. A culture's system of ranking social classes is known as a **hierarchy**, and each culture has its own way of determining how classes interact with each other, how difficult it is for an individual to move from one class to another (the concept of **social mobility**), and what benefits or disadvantages each class possesses. In earlier periods of history, status was almost always hereditary, and religion often played a role in justifying social hierarchies. In most early societies, the privileged, or **elite**, classes were quite small, and social stratification tended to be rigid. Certain cultures devised extremely strict arrangements called **caste systems**, in which movement from one class to another was impossible. Upper classes typically enjoyed many legal and financial advantages, such as more lenient treatment before the law and immunity from taxation. At most times and in most parts of the world, political power, religious leadership, and important social functions have been controlled mainly by men, especially since the rise of settled agricultural and urban cultures. Societies in which male domination prevails are referred to as **patriarchal**. Examples of matriarchal societies are extremely rare.

At the bottom of any social hierarchy are those whose labor is coerced. **Slavery**, the most common form of forced labor, was widespread until recent times and still exists in some parts of the world today. Most ancient civilizations made use of slaves or enriched themselves by means of **slave trades**. People fell into slavery in many ways. Some were prisoners of war or captives taken by raids into enemy territory. Some slaves were owned directly by the state. **Debt slavery** and **indentured servitude** put people to work for owners who had paid money or taxes they owed. In some societies, slave status was hereditary. The severity of slaves' treatment, the length of their service, and the degree to which they had legal rights or protections depended on the laws and customs of each society. An institution similar to slavery, called **serfdom**, bound peasants to the land they lived on. Although they were not technically slaves, they owed labor to their landowner. **Prison labor**, common to most societies, often involved especially backbreaking tasks, such as rowing in galleys, clearing forests, building roads, or working on large construction or architectural projects.

The exchange of goods and services, or **trade**, took place on an individual level (**barter**), but also on local, regional, and transregional levels. Within societies, trade led to the creation of **marketplaces** and brought villages, cities, and rural communities into closer contact. When societies traded with other societies, they created connections and interdependencies throughout large parts of the world. Trade facilitated the exchange of ideas, beliefs, and technology, and it also motivated societies to develop more effective means of **water transport** and **overland transport**, including **caravan routes**. Until the invention of railroads and modern highways, water transport remained far easier than land transport, meaning that trade tended to flourish along rivers, lakeshores, and the coastlines of seas and oceans.

Key transregional routes during this era include the Nile, which connected **Egypt and Nubia**, a land rich in gold, ebony, and ivory, and was a conduit for goods from even farther south. This was not a wholly friendly relationship: Even during peacetime, Egyptian traders had to negotiate carefully with Nubian chiefs, and on other occasions, the Egyptians invaded Nubia, captured slaves there, or conquered it outright. The **eastern Mediterranean** supported a vast network of trade, connecting Egypt with the Levant (home to modern Israel, Lebanon, and Syria), Mesopotamia, Anatolia (present-day Turkey), and the Balkans. Boats were used for trade here as early as the 4000s B.C.E. Boats also connected the Middle East with the Indian Ocean basin, with trade flourishing between **Mesopotamia and the Indus River people**. The Indus River people exchanged tin and precious stones for wool, cloth, barley, and oil from Mesopotamia. Some believe that China became involved with this trade network, but evidence for this is slender.

CULTURE, THOUGHT, AND RELIGION

From earliest times, humans produced art and culture both for individual enjoyment and for social purposes. The formation of civilizations allowed works of great complexity and sophistication to be created. Much of the art and architecture in the ancient world was created for political purposes—as a way to impress populations and foreign visitors with the grandeur of kings and monarchs—or for religious reasons.

Most prominent are works of **monumental architecture**, which required enormous expenditures of resources and labor, often provided by slaves and prisoners. Motivations for these mammoth investments include religion, defense, entertainment, and the public display of political power. Examples from this era include tombs like the Egyptian **pyramids**; temples and ritual centers, such as Mesopotamia's **ziggurats**, the **Abu Simbel** complex constructed by Egypt's Rameses II to celebrate victory at the battle of Kadesh, and the platformed mounds built by the Olmecs; and palaces like those at Babylon, the Egyptian capital of Memphis, and David's palace in Jerusalem. They also include city walls, paved streets and roads, and sewage and water systems like the ones found in Mohenjo-Daro and Harappa. All cities are the product of **urban planning**, although some (again, like Mohenjo-Daro and Harappa) are planned in a more controlled fashion than others.

TIP

Common forms of art include carving and sculpture, painting, wall decorations, and the weaving of textiles. Familiarize yourself with representative samples of different cultures' artworks, such as the elaborate textiles of the Chavín culture and the purple cloth dyed by the Phoenicians, or the winged bulls carved to decorate the walls and guard the gates of Assyrian palaces, and the masterful bronze artifacts manufactured by China's Shang dynasty.

Most, but not all, civilizations devise systems of **writing**, which allow for complex recordkeeping and the efficient storage and transfer of ideas, information, and knowledge. The earliest approach to writing was to use symbols mainly to represent concepts and objects, as in the **cuneiform** script devised by the Sumerians around 3300 B.C.E., in which wedge-shaped characters were pressed into clay tablets with a stylus. This was the same logic behind Egyptian **hieroglyphs** and Chinese **pictographs**. The difficulty with such forms of writing is that they require the memorization of thousands of characters. Sometime after 1200 B.C.E., the Phoenicians created the **alphabet**, which represented sounds, not concepts, and allowed the formation of any word from a small set of symbols. The Phoenician alphabet was the forerunner of the Aramaic alphabet, which in turn influenced the Hebrew and Arabic scripts. It was also adopted with only slight modification by the Greeks and Romans, who transformed it into the Latin alphabet used by many languages today, including English. In the Andes, no form of writing emerged until after the conquest of the Incas by the Spanish in the 1500s C.E. But an interesting form of recordkeeping arose there known as **quipu**, or "talking knots." Most famously associated with the Incas, the quipu was in existence long before them, and used knots tied in strings, and the combination of various colors, to record information.

The first literary works appeared during this period of early civilizations. Among the world's oldest is Mesopotamia's **Gilgamesh epic**, compiled around 1800 B.C.E., but based on Sumerian poems that date back to before 2000 B.C.E. The epic is a fictionalized account of a king who actually existed in the city-state of Uruk. He begins the story as an oppressor of his people whom the gods send on a series of quests to atone for his wrongdoing. He gains wisdom during his adventures and eventually searches for the secret of immortality. Another key text from the Middle East is the **Egyptian Book of the Dead**, which describes how souls are judged after death and advises readers on what to do to ensure a happy afterlife. This involves not just good behavior while one is alive, but the proper mummification and entombment of one's remains. India's *Rig Veda*, a collection of Vedic hymns composed in Sanskrit sometime between 1700 B.C.E and 1100 B.C.E., is one of the world's oldest Indo-European

texts and one of the earliest Hindu scriptures. It describes the origin of the world and contains over a thousand hymns to the Vedic gods. From the world of the early Greeks, most likely from around 850 B.C.E., come the Homeric epic, the *Iliad* and *Odyssey*—which, contrary to popular belief, were not composed by a single poet named Homer. The first is a fictionalized account of the Trojan War (ca. 1250 B.C.E.), complete with roles for the Greek gods, while the second describes the many adventures of the warrior Odysseus as he returns home from the war to his family.

NOTE

Mesopotamian and Greek myths both contain accounts of a catastrophic flood, much like the one described in the Christian bible's tale of Noah. Egyptian legends of the god Osiris, husband of the goddess Isis, speak of how he was murdered by his evil brother Set but brought back to life, a story of resurrection that many historians of religion believe may have influenced the New Testament depiction of Jesus. The Indo-European deities of the Vedic pantheon bear a strong resemblance to the gods of the Greco-Roman and Norse traditions, and are thought by most scholars to have been absorbed and adapted by these cultures, despite the great distances between them. All of these are classic examples of how far-reaching **religious borrowing** can be.

Religions, developed by all societies to address questions of ethics and morality, the possibility of an afterlife, and humanity's place in the universe, grew more complex with the advent of civilization. Religious beliefs crossed borders quite easily: sometimes peacefully through trade, **proselytizing**, and **missionary activity**, sometimes by **forced conversion**. Older forms of worship, such as **shamanism** and **animism**, remained common among hunter-foragers. **Ancestor veneration**, an equally ancient practice, was popular even in many settled communities, especially in China. Most common in advanced societies was **polytheism**, the veneration of elaborate pantheons of gods, each with a distinct personality or function. Among the best-known of these are the Sumerian-Babylonian deities, shared by many people of the ancient Middle East; the Egyptian gods; the Olympian deities worshipped by the Greeks (and, in modified form, by the Romans); the Vedic gods of ancient India; the Teutonic and Norse gods worshipped in northern Europe; and the "celestial bureaucracy" of deities venerated in China.

Of the new religions appearing during this era, the most influential over the long term were Vedism, the precursor to Hinduism; the Hebrew monotheism that evolved into Judaism; and Zoroastrianism. **Vedism** is thought to have been brought to India by Indo-European invaders from the north around 1500 B.C.E. Its sacred texts are four scriptures called Vedas, meaning "knowledge," the oldest and best-known being the *Rig Veda*. Vedism set into place a rigid **caste system** later adopted by Hinduism. At the top were priest-scholars called **brahmins**, followed by warriors and political rulers, then traders and artisans, and finally the lower classes, including servants and peasants. The brahmin class controlled worship of the Vedic pantheon, which included Indra (the thunder deity and king of the gods), Agni (the god of fire who accepted sacrifices made to the gods), and Varuna (god of justice and the sky). They taught that all creatures possessed a soul, or atman, which yearned to be reunited with the World Soul, or Brahman, in spiritual perfection. This perfection was achieved by undergoing a cycle of life, death, and **reincarnation**. According to the law of deeds (**karma**), a person's actions in one life determined how one would be reborn in the next. Vedism placed great value on elaborate rituals, obedience to the brahmin class, and accepting one's lot in life—a perfect example of religious justification of social hierarchy. After about 700 B.C.E., the brahmins' authority and the inflexibility of Vedic doctrine were challenged by new ideas, a development that eventually gave birth to Buddhism and Hinduism.

According to Judaic tradition, the **Hebrews** entered into a covenant as the "chosen people" of the god YHWH (often rendered as Yahweh or Jehovah) during the time of the patriarch **Abraham**, believed to be sometime around 2000 B.C.E. The resulting religion, **Judaism** (even though the terms "Jews" and "Jewish" were not used commonly until after the 900s B.C.E.), is considered to be the birth of the first **monotheistic** faith—the first to devote itself to the worship of one deity alone. To the extent one can match Hebrew scriptures (the Tanakh) with historical chronology, the Hebrews migrated to Egypt around 1700 B.C.E., became slaves, and then escaped under the leadership of the prophet **Moses** around 1300 to 1200 B.C.E—the exodus celebrated during the **Passover** holiday. Moses led the Hebrews to the "promised land" of Canaan (present-day Israel) and is said to have handed down from YHWH the principles of Jewish law, including the **Ten Commandments**, and to have authored the **Torah** ("teaching"), the first five books of the **Tanakh**, or Hebrew scripture. Having conquered Canaan, the Hebrews were ruled at first by judges, then by kings. The Hebrew kingdom reached its zenith under **David** (ca. 1000–961 B.C.E.) and his son **Solomon** (ca. 961–922 B.C.E.), the two of whom united the kingdom, established a capital at Jerusalem, and built the **First Temple** to YHWH there. After Solomon's death, the Hebrew kingdom split into two lands, Israel and Judah, and then suffered conquest by a number of invaders, starting with the Assyrians in 722 B.C.E. and followed by the Babylonian Empire of Nebuchadnezzar in 587 B.C.E. By this stage, many of Judaism's doctrines, and many of the Jewish customs that derived from Hebrew practice, were already in place—but much of the formalization of scripture and the faith of Judaism itself would be completed in the 500s and 400s B.C.E.

The origins of **Zoroastrianism** are extremely difficult to uncover, with the dates given for the life of **Zoroaster** (Zarathustra) ranging from 1700 to 500 B.C.E., and his birthplace uncertain. Most believe that he lived around 1000 B.C.E., probably in eastern Iran, and that the earliest Zoroastrian texts, the hymns known as the Gathas, were written by him at this time. The larger body of Zoroastrian scripture, the **Avesta** (which includes the Gathas and is also known as the *Zend-Avesta*), was compiled over the course of many centuries, and Zoroastrianism emerged as a major faith in Persia by the 500s B.C.E., when it was adopted by Darius the Great to justify his rule as king of kings. Like the Hebrew religion, Zoroastrianism was monotheistic, venerating a single god: **Ahura Mazda**, the world's creator and "wise lord." If worshippers lead virtuous lives, their good deeds combat chaos and assist Ahura Mazda in his cosmic struggle against the evil spirit Ahriman (Angra Mainyu). An end time of judgment will come, and an afterlife is promised to those who are found worthy. Although it is kept alive by only a few followers today—the Parsi sect found in parts of Iran, Pakistan, and India—Zoroastrianism profoundly influenced much of the Middle East for centuries, and many of its core elements are thought to have found their way into Judeo-Christian doctrines as they evolved.

Unit One: Review Questions

SAMPLE ESSAY QUESTIONS (CCOT AND COMPARATIVE)

CCOT 1

Analyze changes and continuities in state-building ONE of the following regions before 600 B.C.E.

China
Mesopotamia

CCOT 2

Analyze the changes and continuities in the organization of labor between the Stone Age and the emergence of the first civilizations.

COMP 1

Analyze similarities and differences in the way TWO of the following civilizations used monumental architecture.

Mesopotamia
The Indus Valley
The Olmecs

COMP 2

Analyze differences and similarities in how environmental factors affected the development of TWO of the following civilizations before 600 B.C.E.

Egypt
China
The Chavín

MULTIPLE-CHOICE QUESTIONS

1. Which of the following is least likely to encourage the growth of an advanced civilization?

   (A) the presence of a nearby river
   (B) surroundings dominated by steep mountains
   (C) temperate climate
   (D) rich metal deposits in the neighboring hills

2. Of the following environmental impacts, which is an example of resource extraction?

   (A) sowing crop seed
   (B) building a dam
   (C) mining for iron ore
   (D) digging a canal

3. Shamanism differs most from Vedism in that

   (A) it renounces the possibility of reincarnation.
   (B) it tends to be monotheistic.
   (C) it does not rely on a body of written scripture.
   (D) it advocates the practice of human sacrifice.

4. How were women treated in most Stone Age societies?

   (A) They were revered and given positions of superiority.
   (B) Equal treatment of both genders was typical.
   (C) Women were forbidden to take any role in hunting.
   (D) Labor tended to be divided along gender lines.

5. A key result of the Neolithic Revolution was

   (A) a quick transition to the manufacture of iron tools.
   (B) the widespread growth of literacy.
   (C) a greater proliferation of settled communities.
   (D) a general improvement in the status of women.

6. Which of the following inaccurately describes agricultural societies?

   (A) Agriculture allowed humans to manipulate their environment as never before.
   (B) Women are thought to have played a key role in the transition to agriculture.
   (C) Agriculture promoted the formation of permanent settlements.
   (D) Agricultural societies were less socially stratified than hunter-forager societies.

7. Ancient pastoralists would have been most likely to spread which of the following innovations to villages and cities in Bronze Age Eurasia?

   (A) the chariot
   (B) weaving
   (C) the stirrup
   (D) pottery

8. Which of the following would best serve as evidence of social stratification in an ancient society?

   (A) human skeletal remains with damage indicating blows to the skull
   (B) the burial of beads, jewelry, and fine attire in the tombs of a few out of many graves
   (C) the presence of spears and daggers in the graves of a community's males
   (D) the placement of some graves closer to a community's center, and of others farther from it

9. Specialization of labor tends to result from

    (A) the pressures of war forcing more of a society's men to become soldiers.
    (B) development of better educational systems following the invention of writing.
    (C) surpluses allowing some members of a society to develop skills unrelated to food production.
    (D) the direct orders of a centralizing monarch seeking to diversify his society.

10. Which of the following best describes ancient Egypt's relationship with Nubia?

    (A) It traded with Nubia for gold and conquered it when it could.
    (B) It had little interaction with Nubia despite its proximity.
    (C) It was constantly threatened by Nubian attempts to expand north along the Nile.
    (D) It allied with Nubia against invading powers like the Hyksos.

11. Which of the following is NOT true of the Gilgamesh epic and the *Iliad*?

    (A) They reflect the ideals of kingship and heroism held by the societies that created them.
    (B) They depict human beings in direct contact with the gods.
    (C) They are each attributable to a single author.
    (D) They are both based at least partly on real-life figures or events.

12. Shang China and ancient Egypt were most alike in that

    (A) both preserved bodies as a way to prepare the dead for a happy afterlife.
    (B) both developed phonetically based written scripts.
    (C) both collapsed primarily due to environmental causes.
    (D) both were governed by rulers claiming to embody or communicate with the divine.

13. What is diffusion, in the context of early societal development?

    (A) the assimilation of minority ethnic groups by a larger population
    (B) the conquest of one civilization by a more powerful one
    (C) the gradual demise of a society because of environmental factors
    (D) the spread of goods, ideas, and inventions from one people to another

14. In what way did the Olmecs and the first Andean civilizations develop along similar lines?

    (A) Both invented the wheel without outside influence.
    (B) Both arose without the advantage of a major river nearby.
    (C) Both built advanced societies in the midst of thick jungle.
    (D) Both domesticated llamas as a source of wool.

15. How do the endings of the Shang dynasty and Indus River civilization compare?

    (A) The Shang were overthrown by rebellion, whereas the shifting of rivers destroyed the Indus civilization.
    (B) Steppe nomads invaded Shang China, whereas interethnic strife undermined the Indus civilization.
    (C) A plague struck down the Shang dynasty, whereas barbarian warriors overwhelmed the Indus valley.
    (D) Shang China exhausted itself in wars of conquest, whereas economic crisis weakened the Indus civilization.

16. Trade between Mesopotamia and the Indus River civilization

    (A) was conducted mainly overland.
    (B) was forcefully imposed on the former by the latter.
    (C) required traders to cross long distances by sea.
    (D) involved the exchange of Mesopotamian ivory for spice from the Indus.

17. The architectural feature pictured above is most likely

    (A) an expression of political might.
    (B) the depiction of a ritual honoring a leading deity.
    (C) décor for a privately owned residence.
    (D) ornamentation for an arena or amphitheater.

18. In its key doctrines, Zoroastrianism most resembles which other religion?

    (A) Buddhism
    (B) Christianity
    (C) Hinduism
    (D) Daoism

19. Which of the following best illustrates religious support for social hierarchy?

    (A) a shaman conducting a healing ritual for a tribal chieftain
    (B) King Solomon's building of the First Temple in Jerusalem
    (C) the Vedic division of all people into four castes
    (D) Zoroaster's call for worshippers to strengthen Ahura Mazda by performing virtuous acts

20. Which of the following was NOT among the ways the Shang dynasty projected power?

    (A) the taking of slaves
    (B) military conquest
    (C) proclaiming the "mandate of heaven"
    (D) large construction projects

ANSWERS

1. **(B)** Although civilizations can form in nearly any climatic or topographical conditions, nearby bodies of water provide easier transport, food, and irrigation. Natural resources and temperate climates are helpful. Mountain settings have not prevented civilizations such as the Inca from forming, but they are the least advantageous of the choices available here.

2. **(C)** All of these answers provide examples of human impact on the environment. Only mining, however, involves taking resources from the earth.

3. **(C)** Shamanism, common among hunter-forager societies around the world—although the name comes from the Tungus people of Siberia and Central Asia—involves rituals performed by an individual believed to have

the ability to travel to the realm of spirits and communicate with them. It is a preliterate form of worship and not monotheistic, and human sacrifice tended to be performed by more organized societies, such as the Maya.

4. **(D)** Although gender division of labor was more pronounced in agricultural and urban societies, biological differences gave rise to some forms of it from the beginning. Equal treatment of women has been rare throughout history and is a recent phenomenon, and in almost no cases were women systematically treated as superior. Stone Age women hunted small game and helped to process the larger game killed by men.

5. **(C)** The domestication of plants, an innovation of the Neolithic Revolution, caused larger numbers of people to settle permanently. Answers A and B reflect changes that would come with time, but long after the Stone Age was over, and the sharper gender division of labor that resulted from the creation of settled societies makes D incorrect.

6. **(D)** As agricultural societies produced food surpluses, a greater number of individuals were able to develop skills not directly related to food production. This specialization of labor gradually led to social stratification, as some skills were valued more than others.

7. **(A)** Pastoralist societies were highly mobile, and they played a key role in transmitting ideas and technologies over wide areas. The technologies they would be most likely to transfer would have to do with mobility, making B and D less likely. The stirrup, however, was not invented until long after the Bronze Age, making A the only probable answer.

8. **(B)** This question requires you to assess evidence as a historian (or archaeologist, in this case) would. Answer A indicates nothing more than a violent death, whereas C implies only that most males owned tools useful for hunting and fighting, and both would have been common among stratified and unstratified societies alike. Placement of burial sites, as in

D, sometimes indicates social status, but B, which shows clear signs of wealth as opposed to poverty, is the better answer.

9. **(C)** In hunter-forager societies, and only somewhat less so in pastoral societies, most members possess similar skills and perform similar functions, mainly related to hunting and herding. Once food surpluses allow some members of society to devote time to becoming expert in various skills, specialization of labor is possible. Building a large army, as in A, does not by itself cause social stratification, and stratification does not emerge as the conscious decision of a leader, as in D. The sort of educational system described in B would be a very long time in coming.

10. **(A)** In times of peace, the Egyptians traded with the Nubians for gold, ivory, ebony, and other items. It was via Nubia, an important corridor, that Egypt enjoyed access to trades from sub-Saharan Africa. However, at times, Egypt raided Nubia for slaves and, as during its conquest of the kingdom of Kush ca. 1500 B.C.E., sometimes occupied it militarily.

11. **(C)** The Gilgamesh epic is a compilation of Sumerian poems composed and gathered over many centuries, and therefore has no single author. Tradition has it that the blind poet Homer composed the *Iliad* and *Odyssey* sometime around 850 B.C.E., about four centuries after the real-life Trojan War took place, but there is no evidence that any such individual ever lived, and the poems were most likely compiled over time. Many ancient works of literature were created this way.

12. **(D)** The Egyptian pharaohs claimed to be incarnations of the sun god, whereas the Shang rulers performed a number of rituals that supposedly proved their connection with the gods. Answer A applies only to Egypt, and B and C apply to neither.

13. **(D)** Discoveries and new cultural developments can arise because of independent innovation or because of cultural diffusion, which

means the exchange of ideas and practices between different societies.

14. **(B)** The wheel never appeared in the ancient Andes, and the llama was unknown in Mesoamerica. While jungle is common in Mesoamerica, it is not in the Andes, leaving only B as a possible answer.

15. **(A)** All of the answers given are plausible causes for the destruction of empires and civilizations. In these cases, though, the Shang were toppled by the Zhou rebellion, and environmental factors are now thought to have been responsible for the downfall of the Indus River civilization—which was once believed to have been caused by the invasion of Indo-European invaders from the north.

16. **(C)** Although overland trade was not unknown in the ancient world, it was comparatively rare over long distances, making it reasonably safe to eliminate A. Knowledge of geography should allow you to remember that Mesopotamia is unlikely to be the home of ivory-producing animals, eliminating D. Mesopotamia and the Indus River people are not known to have fought each other, especially at such a great distance, leaving C as the most logical answer.

17. **(A)** Without any accompanying text, the meaning of this image—one of the famous winged bulls of Assyria—is open to interpretation. Its size and monumentality make it unlikely to be privately owned, excluding C.

Answer D is possible, but the purpose seems more solemn than an entertainment facility would call for. Without any knowledge of ancient Middle Eastern architecture, you could still narrow the plausible choices to a fifty-fifty guess, although with no ritual activity evident, the safer answer would be A.

18. **(B)** Not only is Zoroastrianism monotheistic, excluding A, C, and D, but its resemblance to Christianity is even closer, thanks to its doctrines of last judgment and heavenly afterlife in the company of a supreme deity. Many historians of religion in fact believe that Zoroastrian ideas, widely known throughout the Middle East, helped to shape early Christian doctrine.

19. **(C)** While A and B speak to political involvement with religion, they do not comment specifically on how society is structured; the shaman would presumably perform the same service for any member of the social group. Answer D is even more generalized. The Vedic-Hindu caste system is one of the classic examples of how religious doctrine reinforces the concept of social hierarchy, making C clearly the best answer.

20. **(C)** The Shang famously carried out the policies detailed in answers A, B, and D. The concept of the mandate of heaven, while central to Chinese political thought, did not come into being until the Zhou dynasty—which used it to justify the rebellion that overthrew the Shang.

UNIT TWO

ORGANIZATION AND REORGANIZATION OF HUMAN SOCIETIES
(600 B.C.E.–600 C.E.)

Unit Overview

GENERAL REMARKS

The period between 600 B.C.E. and 600 C.E. can be thought of as a time of increased political consolidation, technological aptitude, and social and cultural sophistication. World population continued to rise, and **networks** of **interregional communication and exchange** widened. Humankind's ability to affect its environment, and often to strain it, steadily grew.

Although less-advanced societies continued to exist in all parts of the globe, this era saw in many places the emergence of the most powerful and most highly **centralized states and empires** ever seen in the world to that date. Thanks to effective bureaucracies and improved communications, these states were capable of governing large and diverse populations. They regulated systems of **trade**, economic exchange, tax collection, and food supply over great distances. **Cities** played a larger role than ever in concentrating political leadership, economic activity, and cultural and artistic dynamism. **Law codes** and increasingly **organized religions** helped societies function more smoothly, and religions, along with common languages and **shared artistic and cultural traditions**, helped to foster social cohesion and a stronger sense of cultural identity. In certain parts of the world, the civilizations of this era were **classical**, in that after they faded, they left behind important cultural-intellectual and linguistic legacies and golden-age memories of political unity and socioeconomic stability.

Not that instability was a thing of the past. Even the most powerful states broke apart due to **overextension** of their political capacities. As this unit will show, there were many ways to do this, and most empires, as they declined and fell, experienced at least one of these problems, and generally some combination of them. Large-scale **migrations** continued to redistribute the world's population over vast distances, and war remained a constant reality.

BROAD TRENDS

Humans and the Environment

- Societies in the Americas remained isolated from those in Africa and Eurasia.
- Certain large-scale migrations that began before 600 B.C.E. continued during this era, including the movement of the Bantu through sub-Saharan Africa and the voyages of the Polynesian peoples through the Pacific.

- Eurasia was swept by a centuries-long wave of migrations, consisting mainly of Asiatic and Germanic peoples moving east to west, starting shortly after 0 C.E. and lasting till around 1000 C.E.
- More societies developed the city-building and construction skills to affect their environment in major ways. Monumental architecture, canal-building, pollution, the expansion of farming, and other practices made humanity's "ecological footprint" even heavier than before.
- Innovations in overland and maritime transport allowed for easier and wider travel.
- Diseases and new foods spread more quickly and more widely than before. Some historians argue that this was the case more in Eurasia than in the Americas or Africa, because east-west movement (along the same parallel and thus within similar climate zones) was easier there.

Development and Interaction of Cultures

- Existing religions, such as Judaism and Vedism, underwent reform and further codification.
- Major belief systems arising during this time were Hinduism, Buddhism, Confucianism, Daoism, and Christianity.
- Successful religions spread widely across regions and cultures, due to trade and missionary activity. As they changed the societies that adopted them, the religions themselves sometimes underwent change, as their new practitioners modified doctrines or rituals.
- Certain languages, such as Sanskrit, Mandarin Chinese, and Latin, became trans-regionally influential because they were sacred to major religions or the official tongues of large and enduring empires.
- In some cases, people adopted a new religion but retained some of their older beliefs and practices. Or they fused elements of more than one religion. This phenomenon is known as syncretism. Examples include the interplay of Buddhism, Confucianism, and Daoism in China and neighboring areas; the dual observance of Shinto and Buddhism in Japan; and the persistence of pagan folklore and ritual in newly Christianized parts of Europe.
- Literature and art were produced on a greater scale, often by clearly identifiable authors and artists.
- Systematic scientific observation and experimentation emerged, especially in China, the Middle East, and the Greco-Roman world.

State-Building, Expansion, and Conflict

- Most states were still governed by monarchies and oligarchies.
- The expansion of states into empires by means of conquest remained common.
- A few civilizations developed representative forms of government, such as republics and democracies, but these were rare.
- Many states grew extremely adept at centralizing authority, building complex bureaucracies, and other means of projecting political power.

- Armies grew larger, more skilled, and equipped with better technology. Effective empires drew on their subject peoples to provide soldiers and specialized military skills.
- Many states and empires from this era eventually overextended themselves politically, economically, or territorially (becoming victims of their own success) and collapsed as a result.

Economic Systems

- Transregional trade was practiced on a larger scale than before.
- Centralized states ensured (or attempted to ensure) a steady supply of food for its citizenry.
- States created the infrastructure to support local, regional, and transregional trade. This included the building and maintenance of markets, roads, harbors, and other facilities.
- Systems of tax collection and rent-gathering grew more efficient and intrusive.
- Currency was invented in a number of places and greatly facilitated economic exchange.

Social Structures

- Social structures in centralized states grew more complex, and a greater variety of social classes appeared.
- Society tended to remain highly hierarchical. Elite classes remained small and generally hereditary.
- Patriarchalism continued to be the norm, with women still generally occupying a secondary status and remaining on the disadvantaged side of the gender division of labor.
- Shared religions, political allegiances, and cultural traditions tended to make a society more cohesive and stable.
- Law codes appeared in more societies. Even though they were not always fair by today's standards or perfectly observed, they lent stability to the societies creating them.
- Slavery and other forms of coerced labor were common to the point of being almost universal.

QUESTIONS AND COMPARISONS TO CONSIDER

- What are "classical" civilizations? What does that concept mean? Be able to compare major civilizations—India, China, Persia, Greece, or Rome—during their classical phases.
- How and why do empires and major civilizations decline and collapse? Good comparisons might include Han China and the Roman Empire, or Persia and India. Did imperial collapse prove more devastating in western Europe than it did farther to the east? If so, why?
- How did agricultural practice change and expand during these years?

- Compare the movement of Eurasian nomads into the territory of more settled civilizations such as Rome, Han China, and India's Gupta Empire.
- What positive changes did communication and exchange bring to various societies? What negative changes resulted?
- What role did disease play in the history of this period? What about the exchange of new crops and foodstuffs?
- What technologies and techniques, old and new, enabled the freer movement of people over greater distances? Compare land transport versus sea transport.
- Examine the operation of one or all of the following avenues of trade: Mediterranean sea routes, the silk roads leading across Eurasia, caravan routes across the Sahara, and the Indian Ocean basin.
- What roles did religion play in supporting or challenging the status quo? Consider the crisis of Vedism in India, or the reasons for Christianity's rapid spread throughout the Roman Empire. Also examine the role of Confucianism in Chinese society or Judaism in shaping social norms.
- What was religious syncretism? How and where did it manifest itself?
- Compare the emergence of scientific thinking in the Greco-Roman world with intellectual trends elsewhere.
- In what ways did the larger and more centralized states of the era affect their physical environment? In what ways did environmental problems affect states and empires? Consider phenomena such as desertification, erosion, and deforestation.
- How did the role of women change from the preceding era? How did women's experience vary from society to society? To what degree did this depend on social class?

The Development and Codification of Religious and Cultural Traditions

- Classical civilizations
- Judaism
- Hinduism
- Buddhism
- Confucianism
- Daoism
- Christianity
- The scientific method
- Cultural developments and interactions
- Syncretism

Integral to the growth of any civilization is the development of belief systems that address questions of ethics, morality, and spirituality. Religions provide societies with a sense of unity and pride, and they inspire great works of art and architecture. They exert enormous political and social influence, legitimating governments and justifying hierarchies and gender norms. They have also caused tension in many forms. Religious institutions have at times opposed scientific and technological innovation or social progress. Clashes between different faiths, or different denominations within faiths, have led to social tension, bigotry, persecution, and war. During the period between 600 B.C.E. and 600 C.E., several religions experienced major change, formally codifying their scriptures and practices or reforming themselves significantly. Many new religions appeared as well.

Also during this period, artistic and literary traditions flourished. Like religions, these provided a sense of shared cultural identity. The literature, art, and architecture produced by **classical** civilizations, as well as the languages used by them, was often much longer-lived in its influence than the states that produced them.

THE PERSISTENCE OF OLDER FORMS OF WORSHIP

Forms of worship remained diverse during this period. Especially in less-advanced societies, belief systems based on the veneration of spirits, such as **shamanism** and **animism**, remained popular. Among the functions performed by shamans (who were called by various names depending on the society from which they came) were healing of the sick, the telling of fortunes, the prediction of weather, praying to the

spirits for success in hunting, and the enforcement of **taboos**, or forbidden behaviors. A prominent example of animism is the "dreamtime" concept peculiar to the Australian aborigines. An interesting instance of an animist tradition practiced by a more advanced society is **Shinto**, a religion indigenous to Japan, and one that survives even today, alongside Buddhism.

Another practice carried over from earlier times by many civilizations was **ancestor veneration**, also known commonly as ancestor worship. Although details varied from society to society, this practice was rooted in the belief that the spirits of departed ancestors lived on and could influence the well-being of those still alive. Showing proper respect brought good fortune; failure to do so could call down the ancestors' wrath. Observing correct funeral practices and mourning periods was important, as was the offering of sacrifices, such as food, wine, or, as in the Chinese tradition, "spirit money." In China, the veneration of ancestors, especially male ones, was practiced during the Shang dynasty and spread throughout East Asia thanks to Chinese influence. The emergence of Confucian thought, with its emphasis on **filial piety**, reinforced the custom. In the Andes, peoples such as the Inca mummified their ancestors and placed them in special chambers, where they could be consulted for oracular advice on important questions; proper treatment of them was thought to ensure a steady supply of water. Most African peoples placed ancestor veneration at the heart of their religious practice, as did many societies of the Mediterranean. Proper burial of the dead was exceptionally important to the Hebrews and Greeks, among others. In ancient Rome, families built household shrines to ancestral spirits (variously called lares, penates, and manes) and performed regular rituals in their honor to keep them from turning spiteful and destructive. They also celebrated the yearly festival of Parentalia, or "ancestral days."

In many societies, the blending of old and new religious beliefs was common, as was the fusing or simultaneous observation of practices from more than one religion. This phenomenon is called **syncretism**. The absorption of ancestor veneration into Buddhist or Confucian worship is one example, as is the dual practice of Shinto and Buddhism in Japan. In India, Vedic concepts were incorporated into the newer religion of Hinduism. The persistence of pagan practices and folk beliefs among newly Christianized peoples—as in the morphing of local deities into minor saints, or the conversion of pagan holidays like the winter and summer solstices into Christian ones like Christmas and St. John's Eve—also illustrates how syncretism works.

REFORMED FAITHS AND NEW RELIGIONS

Judaism

During this era, the **monotheistic** faith of the **Hebrews** took more solid shape in the form of **Judaism**. Starting in the 700s B.C.E., the Hebrew kingdoms were conquered by a succession of overlords, including the Assyrians (722 B.C.E.), Nebuchadnezzar's Neo-Babylonian empire (587 B.C.E.), the Persians (539 B.C.E.), Alexander the Great (333–331 B.C.E.), and the Romans (66–64 B.C.E.). Both under the Assyrians and Nebuchadnezzar, the Hebrews were uprooted from their lands, and the latter had the First Temple built by Solomon torn down. The Persians allowed Hebrews to return to Jerusalem, where a second temple was restored, but

many chose to remain in their new homes, beginning the **Jewish diaspora**. This regional, then worldwide, scattering of the Jewish population went many steps further during Roman rule, when rebellions and the Jewish Wars of 70–73 C.E. caused the Romans to destroy the second temple and disband the Jewish kingdom.

In the face of exile and adversity, religious adherence helped Jews preserve their sense of identity. They renounced the polytheistic gods of their conquerers by maintaining their monotheistic compact with YHWH. They turned to rabbis ("teachers") for guidance and, in gathering places that came to be known as synagogues, they worshipped and organized schools. It was also during this period, especially in the 400s B.C.E. and afterward, that Jewish doctrines and customs were formalized. Scripture, or **Tanakh**, was codified (including the **Torah**, the Hebrew bible's first five books), as were Jewish laws, spelled out by the Torah's Deuteronomic code and elaborated further in the **Talmud** ("Instruction"), which contains rabbinic commentary on scripture. The Jewish code of conduct was strict and placed a high premium on righteous behavior. Law operated on a retributive principle—an eye for an eye, a tooth for a tooth—that was common throughout the ancient Middle East, and the **Code of Hammurabi** in particular is thought to have influenced texts like the **Ten Commandments** said to have been revealed to Moses by YHWH on Mount Sinai. Dietary restrictions were strict, as were rules governing sexual practice, with marriage outside the Jewish community strongly forbidden. Although women were respected in the home, Hebrew society as a whole was patriarchal. As did most people of the eastern Mediterranean, the Hebrews practiced slavery, but Jewish scripture also insisted on charity, social responsibility, and concern for the poor. Jews also came to believe that a savior, or messiah ("anointed one"), would appear someday to free them from oppression.

From Vedism to Hinduism

In India, where **Vedism** had dominated since around 1500 B.C.E., a religious crisis arose after 700 B.C.E. This resulted from growing discontent with the brahmin, or priestly, class, which insisted that the only chance for one to be reincarnated into a better state in one's next life was to obey the brahmins unquestioningly and to observe the complex rituals that only they could perform. Several hundred essays and poems called the **Upanishads** (set down in written form between 900 B.C.E. and 500 B.C.E.), began raising the possibility that people could take greater responsibility for liberating themselves from the cycle of life, death, and rebirth without relying on the brahmins and their rituals. Similarly, new teachers encouraged dietary and meditative discipline (**yoga**) to achieve liberation. The new faith of Buddhism, as discussed below, emerged in the 500s B.C.E. as a result of these debates. For the majority of people in India, however, Vedism was not rejected outright, but subsumed into the larger set of beliefs known as **Hinduism**. This process unfolded over a long period of time, but was essentially complete by the 300s B.C.E.

Hinduism recognizes thousands of gods and goddesses—330 million by one count—making it the most polytheistic religion in the world. In syncretic fashion, the Vedic gods have their place, but three deities in particular enjoyed the largest followings by the 200s B.C.E. **Brahma** is the masculine personification of the World

Soul, or Brahman (a concept retained from Vedism). **Vishnu** the Preserver is a savior figure, a great friend to humanity who appears in various avatars, or alternative incarnations, in literary works like the Ramayana and the **Bhagavad-Gita. Shiva** the Destroyer is the god of creation and destruction, reflecting the duality of life and death. He is depicted in paintings and sculptures as a dancer. Hinduism's many female deities are considered incarnations of the great mother goddess **Shakti**. Her most famous avatars are Parvati (wife of Shiva), Durga (a warrior goddess), Lakshmi (Vishnu's wife), and Kali (goddess of death).

From Vedism, Hinduism inherited the concepts of **karma** and **reincarnation**. Another legacy was the **caste system**, which is thought to have originated after 1500 B.C.E., when Indo-European invaders from the north relegated menial tasks and manual labor to the darker-skinned natives. Between the 800s B.C.E. and 600s B.C.E., this scheme had grown into a rigid system of social stratification involving four distinct classes: priests (brahmins), warriors and rulers (kshatriyas), farmers and artisans (vaishyas), and servants and serfs (shudras). Over time, the system grew increasingly complex and came to include a category of **untouchables**, who performed degrading and impurifying tasks like the handling of human waste and burial of the dead. The **Law of Manu** (compiled between 200 B.C.E. and 200 C.E.) put forward the most famous arguments in favor of the caste system. Acceptance of one's social situation was considered an essential part of dharma, or moral duty, and good behavior as a member of a lower caste would result in good karma, increasing the likelihood of being reborn into a higher caste. Hindu society was highly patriarchal, although Hindu codes of behavior required that women, who played a vital role within the family, be treated with respect. Men performed family rituals and had a monopoly on education and the ownership of property. Women were considered legal minors even as adults; many married in childhood, and divorce was rare. The most extreme form of female subservience was the **sati ritual** (also known as suttee), in which women of certain castes were required to throw themselves on the funeral pyres of their deceased husbands. This practice was discouraged by

The Practice of Sati.
The ritual of sati (or suttee) was a long-standing Hindu tradition. When a man of high caste died, his widow was expected to be burned to death on her husband's funeral pyre. Only in the twentieth century was this practice fully abolished.

India's colonial masters, the British, during the nineteenth century, and outlawed by the Indians themselves in the twentieth. Today, the vast majority of people in India are Hindu. Sizable Hindu populations live elsewhere in South and Southeast Asia, and in emigration throughout the world.

Buddhism

Several movements besides Hinduism arose in India during the spiritual ferment that caused the transition away from traditional Vedism. One of these was **Buddhism**, based on the teachings of **Siddhartha Gautama** (ca. 563–483 B.C.E.), a nobleman from northern India. Appalled by the pain and poverty suffered by the common people, Buddha abandoned his aristocratic life to seek an answer to the question of human suffering. Having been born into one spiritual extreme—a love of worldly luxuries—Gautama turned first to the opposite extreme: fasting and self-deprivation. Deciding that path did not lead to salvation, he chose instead a "middle way" of moderation and peace. This discovery is said to have brought him **enlightenment**, after which he took the name Buddha, "the awakened one," and began to preach. A community of followers spread his teachings. Long after Gautama's death, the Mauryan emperor **Ashoka** (269–231 B.C.E.) became a great supporter of Buddhism, spreading it throughout India and beyond its borders. Its influence is felt throughout all of South, Southeast, and East Asia.

Although Buddhism originated with the teachings of one person, the variety of beliefs and practices that came to fall into the category "Buddhist" is staggering. In its earliest form, Buddhism was less a religion and more a philosophy whose purposes were to correct what Gautama saw as the worst features of Vedism. Like Hinduism, Buddhism postulates that souls evolve toward spiritual perfection by means of birth, death, and **reincarnation**, and according to the law of **karma**. However, Gautama rejected the caste system and argued that anyone could achieve liberation from the wheel of life, or **nirvana**, without the aid of priests or rituals. All that was necessary to attain enlightenment was to realize the Four Noble Truths and to follow the Eightfold Path of good conduct and the Five Moral Rules. At no time did the Buddha claim to be divine.

After the Buddha's death, the tradition he founded split into various denominations, roughly divided into two major schools. The older is **Theravada** Buddhism ("way of the elders"), also referred to as Hinayana ("lesser vehicle"). Prominent in South and Southeast Asia, Theravada remains closer to the Buddha's actual teachings. It emphasizes simplicity, meditation, and an interpretation of nirvana as a dissolution of one's self into the all-encompassing spirit that transcends time and place. The newer school, **Mahayana** ("greater vehicle") Buddhism, caught on farther

NOTE

One religious path that emerged in India during the debates arising over Vedism might have grown into a larger faith if not for the simultaneous appearance of Buddhism. This was Jainism, established by Mahavira (ca. 540–468 B.C.E.), who preached a doctrine of non-violence and self-denial.

TIP

The Four Noble Truths are as follows:
(1) human existence is inseparable from suffering;
(2) the cause of suffering is desire;
(3) suffering is extinguished by extinguishing desire;
(4) desire may be extinguished by following the Eightfold Path (know the truth; resist evil; do nothing to hurt others; respect all forms of life; work for the well-being of others; free your mind of evil; control your thoughts; practice meditation). In addition to the Eightfold Path, the Buddha described Five Moral Rules (do not kill any living being; do not take what is not given to you; do not speak falsely; do not drink intoxicating drinks; do not be unchaste).

to the north, especially in Japan, Korea, Tibet, and parts of China. Mahayana forms of Buddhism involve more ritual and symbology than the Buddha intended. Part of this was the result of **syncretism**: Upon reaching new lands, Buddhism was often blended with local beliefs. Moreover, many later Buddhists found the original teachings to be too austere for comfort and began to argue for means of salvation that the Buddha himself had not spoken of. In some Mahayana denominations, the concept of nirvana came to resemble a heavenly afterlife. Concepts of hell appeared, as did complex pantheons of gods and bodhisattvas (souls who had achieved nirvana but chose to remain in the earthly realm to help living humans), and the Buddha came to be seen as divine. Worshippers came to rely on a myriad of new ceremonies and scriptures (sutras).

Confucianism

Like Buddhism, **Confucianism** arose from a philosophy articulated by an individual who made no claim to divinity. Its founder, a government official named K'ung Fu-tzu and better known as **Confucius** (ca. 551–479 B.C.E.), lived in China during the politically chaotic Zhou dynasty and during an intellectually fertile age known in Chinese history as the "Hundred Schools of Thought" era (roughly 700–200 B.C.E.). Upon retiring from state service, he pondered the proper relationship between society and the individual, and his followers captured his thoughts on paper. Although Confucius is traditionally credited with authoring many works, what survives is the transcription of conversations he is said to have held with his students, and even these *Analects* were compiled long after his death. The figure most responsible for codifying Confucianism's key doctrines is Meng-tzu, or Mencius (371–289 B.C.E.).

Confucianism took for granted the existence of the **celestial bureaucracy** of traditional Chinese gods, but was most concerned with wise and ethical conduct in this world. Confucius proposed that a harmonious society could be created by a combination of benevolent rulership from above and good behavior from below. Order and **hierarchy** are paramount, and the well-being of the group comes before that of the individual. Good government is the responsibility of the ruler, and as long as the ruler performs his duties well, his people have an obligation to obey him. Confucianism thus squared well with the **mandate of heaven** ideology that emerged during the Zhou period and remained central to Chinese political thought. Above all, Confucianism emphasized **filial piety** and envisioned society as operating like a model family, with junior members paying respect to their elders. It therefore dovetailed well with China's longstanding tradition of **ancestor veneration**. Confucianism, a highly **patriarchal** system, firmly established females as the subservient sex. Men ruled society, fought wars, and received educations. They could keep more than one wife, as well as concubines, and could divorce any woman who failed to produce an heir. Women were exclusively homemakers and mothers. Laws prohibited them from owning property, and they were not provided financial security through a dowry system, although they were allowed a limited education.

TIP

Confucius described five relationships as most important to social tranquility: The ruler should be just, those who are ruled should be loyal. The father should be loving, the son respectful. The husband should be righteous, the wife obedient. The older brother should be genteel, the younger brother humble. The older friend should be considerate; the younger friend, deferent.

Implicit in these hierarchical relationships were the concepts of reciprocity and mutual respect. Central of Confucian thought was a "golden rule" similar to the one found in Christianity: In the *Analects*, Confucius declares, "Never do to others what you would not like them to do to you." Confucius's assumption that people are inherently good and remain so if treated well contrasted with the logic behind a rival doctrine in China, **Legalism**, which viewed people as innately immoral, and advocated harsh punishments as the only way to control them. Confucianism coexisted with, and at times competed against, Daoism and Buddhism. Several times, it gained, lost, and regained its status as a state-sanctioned code of conduct. By the 600s C.E., a newer variation of the creed, **Neo-Confucianism**, appeared. Even when it was not in official favor, Confucianism's influence persisted. China's traditional emphasis on filial piety, social hierarchy, and respect for authority stems in large part from Confucianism and has lasted into the modern era, even under the communist regime.

Daoism

Like Confucianism, **Daoism**, a more mystical strain of thought, took shape in China during and after the 500s B.C.E. Another product of the "Hundred Schools of Thought" era, its founder is considered to be **Laozi** or Lao-tse (ca. 600 B.C.E.), who may or may not have been an actual historical figure, and who came to be venerated as a deity by the 100s B.C.E. The religion's central text, the **Tao-te Ching**, traditionally attributed to Laozi, was most likely written in the 300s or 200s B.C.E., at around the time of Zhuangzi (Chuang-tse), the second-most important figure in the development of Daoism.

Daoist belief maintains that the universe is governed by the **dao** (the "way" or "path"), an invisible yet irresistible force. Daoism is deliberately antirational, training the worshipper through parables to perceive the world in non-logical ways. The most famous of these paradoxes was voiced by Zhuangzi, who asked whether he was a man just awakening from a dream in which he had been a butterfly, or a butterfly dreaming that he was a man. The "three jewels of the dao" are compassion, moderation, and humility: The Daoist seeks harmony with the universe by attuning himself or herself with the dao and is unconcerned with politics and material possessions, which are illusory and meaningless.

A flexible and individualistic belief system, unlike Confucianism, Daoism was easily reconciled with **ancestor veneration** and respect for the **celestial bureaucracy** of Chinese gods. It became associated with many cultural practices, including traditional medicine (both in China and beyond its borders) and martial arts. Its embrace of alchemy and astrology had an impact on the sciences of metallurgy and astronomy. Fortune-telling, with its deep roots in China, was crucial to Daoism, one of whose key texts, the **I-Ching** ("Book of Changes"), was used to read the future. Daoism's influence on poetry was profound, especially during the Tang dynasty, which produced some of the most beautiful verse in China's history. Daoist ritual became interwoven with the architectural art of **feng shui**, or harmonious placement, which orients buildings and the items inside them in ways that ensure good fortune. Daoism's most famous symbol is the **yin-yang**, a circle whose dark and light halves are divided by a double-curved line, illustrating that nothing is

absolute, and that opposites flow into each other. Daoism spread throughout China, and elements of it were transported to the many parts of Asia where China had a strong cultural influence. In all these places, it became common for people to blend Daoist, Buddhist, and Confucian practices **syncretically**.

Christianity

A child of Judaism, with which it has had a long relationship, sometimes troubled and always intimate, **Christianity** was founded by **Jesus of Nazareth** (ca. 4 B.C.E.– 29 C.E.)—later known as the Christ, from the Greek translation of the Jewish term "messiah." Details about Jesus come from the Gospels, the first four books of the Christian bible's New Testament. Leaving aside the question of his divinity, the degree to which the Gospels' account of the *historical* aspects of Jesus's life can be considered accurate has been a matter of debate for centuries.

According to Christian tradition, Jesus was born into a Jewish family of humble background, becoming a wandering teacher as an adult and gathering an inner circle of disciples. He spoke of upholding Jewish laws and traditions, but he also sought to reform them. To him, obeying rabbis and observing customs were not enough to please YHWH (God, in later Christian usage). Charity, compassion, and forgiveness were more important, a message reinforced in the **Sermon on the Mount** ("Blessed are the poor in spirit . . .") and in what came to be known as the **Golden Rule** ("Do unto others as you would have them do unto you"). During his ministry, Jesus claimed to be the Christ, or the messiah foretold by Hebrew prophecy. Although many Jews expected the messiah to restore the Hebrew state politically, Jesus spoke of a heavenly kingdom instead, calling himself the "Son of God," whose teachings would redeem those who followed him.

These teachings proved immensely popular, especially among the common people and the poor. On the other hand, his claims to be the messiah and his questioning of tradition angered conservatives within the Jewish religious establishment. Also, rumors that Jesus had assumed the title "king of the Jews" (a misinterpretation of what he meant by being the messiah) aroused the suspicions of the Jews' Roman overlords. When Jesus came to preach in Jerusalem during the Passover season, Jewish religious authorities demanded that the Roman procurator, Pontius Pilate, arrest him. Pilate, fearing the political repercussions of Jesus's ministry, found him guilty of treason and sentenced him to death by crucifixion, a common punishment in the ancient world. The instrument of Jesus's death, the cross, is the Christian faith's central symbol.

Before his arrest, Jesus had claimed that he would return from the dead before returning to God in heaven. After the crucifixion, his disciples began to preach that he had indeed been resurrected, the event celebrated by the Easter holiday. Veneration of the risen Jesus, soon known as Christianity, was carried on by his closest followers, including **Peter** (considered the first pope) and the four authors of the Gospels. These and other **apostles** spread the story of the Crucifixion and Resurrection, foretelling as well a Second Coming, when all souls would be subjected to a Day of Judgment—with virtuous Christians to live in heaven with God and Christ, and nonbelievers to be damned to hell.

Roman law made Christianity illegal, and yet it gained a large following over the next three centuries, first in the Middle East and then throughout the Roman Empire. Crucial to the organization of the early church was the apostle **Paul**, who began as a persecutor of Christians named Saul, but suddenly converted to the new faith. With Peter, Paul worked approximately from 45 to 64 C.E. to establish new centers of worship. His greatest contribution was to widen Christianity's appeal beyond its original community of Jewish followers. By decreeing that Christians did not have to observe Jewish law—particularly dietary restrictions and the circumcision of male believers—Paul made it easier to convert Greeks, Romans, and others, allowing the new religion to expand faster.

Christianity caught on among many groups, especially those who felt powerless in Roman society: noncitizens, slaves, the poor, commoners, and women. The new religion was open to all, and it held out the hope of a happy afterlife to those whose present lives were drab or miserable. The early church gave women a sense of belonging and influential roles within apostolic communities. But as it grew older and more hierarchical, the church adhered more to a strict interpretation of the story of Adam and Eve, assigning women the blame for humanity's "**original sin.**" Paul's writings in particular put women in a secondary position: They were to obey men, and they were not allowed to occupy positions of leadership within the church, including priesthood. Cultures that adopted Christianity were affected by this worldview for centuries to come.

In 313 C.E., three centuries of persecution ended when the Roman emperor **Constantine** legalized Christianity by means of the **Edict of Milan**. In 380 C.E., Christianity became the empire's official religion, and in 392 C.E., was proclaimed its only legal faith. The church formalized its hierarchy of priests and bishops, with the pope at the top, and with men only as priests. It also established a body of dogma, an officially agreed-upon set of beliefs, to decide on the nature of Christ (at once fully human and fully divine) and to establish the doctrine of the **trinity** (the belief that God exists in the three persons of God the Father, Christ the Son, and the Holy Spirit). Beliefs not included as dogma were condemned as heresy. Another task was to compile the books of the **Bible**, which consisted of the Old Testament (parts of the Hebrew Bible) and the New Testament (the four Gospels, plus letters written by the apostles and other texts). These tasks were completed during a series of councils held during the 300s C.E. and afterward, and those who took part are referred to as the church fathers. Among the most famous are Jerome (347–420), who completed the first Latin translation of the Bible, and **Augustine** (354–430), whose *City of God* laid the foundation for further Christian doctrine.

After the collapse of Rome in the 400s C.E., the Christian church drifted apart in terms of leadership and doctrine. In the west, Roman Catholicism remained dominant and provided much of Europe with a badly needed force for cultural unity. In the eastern Mediterranean and Middle East, the church, based in centers such as Alexandria, Antioch, and especially Constantinople, evolved into **Eastern Orthodoxy**. The split between the two became formal in the Great Schism of 1054 C.E. Despite this rupture, the **Judeo-Christian tradition** was and remained for centuries the bedrock of Western culture.

THOUGHT AND CULTURE

Many peoples from this era developed an excellent working knowledge of mathematics, astronomy, anatomy, and engineering and were adept at learning **empirically**, or by means of observation. Most, however, attributed the workings of the world to cosmic forces or the will of the gods, and it took far longer for ancient societies to gain a theoretical comprehension of science and its **underlying principles**. The first place this is thought to have occurred is among the Greeks, approximately between 600 B.C.E. and 200 B.C.E. Heavily influenced by Egyptian learning, Greek thinkers, beginning with the so-called "Ionian scientists" (including Pythagoras) and continuing with individuals like Euclid and Archimedes, outlined many of the basic laws of geometry, physics, astronomy, medicine, and natural history. Most important, they combined empirical observation with logic and experimentation to create the **scientific method**. The Greeks' findings and conclusions were not always correct, and this was no straightforward shift from religious to secular thinking, for most Greek scholars continued to believe in the gods to some degree. But there was a definite jump forward in understanding how the world works. Centuries later, the **decimal system**, the misnamed "**Arabic numerals**," and the concepts of *pi* and **zero** were all created by scholars from Gupta India.

The Greeks, followed by the Romans, also pioneered the systematic mode of rational thought known as **philosophy**. Generations of Greek thinkers, culminating in Socrates (470–399 B.C.E.), Plato (428–347 B.C.E.), and Aristotle (384–322 B.C.E.), created the intellectual foundation on which all of Western thought rests. All three asked fundamental questions about the nature of reality, moral behavior, and, especially in Plato's *Republic*, the best way to govern a society. Among the Romans, the emperor Marcus Aurelius gave powerful voice to the Stoic point of view, which called for courage and virtuous behavior even in the hardest of circumstances. The Greco-Roman blossoming in philosophy can be compared to the explosion of ideas caused in India by the religious debates over Vedism, and in China during the "Hundred Schools of Thought" era.

Scientifically-minded or not, all major civilizations made great strides in the cultural sphere during this time period. Enduring works of literature appeared, forming the foundation of the literary traditions in their regions. In India, for example, famous texts included the Ramayana (ca. 350 B.C.E.), a tale describing the adventures of Rama, the seventh incarnation of the god Vishnu. Even more important is the **Mahabharata**, composed between 200 B.C.E. and 200 C.E., a grand epic of 90,000 stanzas, making it perhaps the longest poem in the world. The Mahabharata depicts a great war between two royal houses. Its most renowned section is the **Bhagavad-Gita** ("Song of the Lord"), a poetic dialogue between the young prince Arjuna and the demigod Krishna—another of Vishnu's avatars—who lectures Arjuna on the concept of moral duty, or the dharma. Early Chinese literature included little fiction, but the Confucian and Daoist classics, including the *Analects*, the *Tao-te Ching*, and the *I-Ching*, are considered key works, as is *The Art of War* (500s B.C.E.), by **Sun Tzu**, one of world history's most renowned works on strategy and diplomacy. In ancient Greece, which already had a tradition of great epic poetry, such as the *Iliad* and *Odyssey*, the practice of theatrical performance grew out of religious festivals. **Greek dramas** such as Aeschylus's *Oresteia* trilogy,

Sophocles's Oedipus trilogy, and the bitter plays of Euripides commented on the darker side of human nature, the role played in the universe by gods versus free will, and the rights of the individual balanced against the obligations of belonging to a larger society. The *Aeneid*, an epic poem by Virgil, serves as a foundation myth for ancient Rome, which is depicted as having been founded by refugees from the Trojan War. Certain literary languages, especially if they were also the languages of widespread religions, powerful empires, or **classical** civilizations with long-lasting cultural legacies, became historically and transregionally influential. Among these were **Sanskrit**, **Mandarin Chinese**, **Greek**, and **Latin**.

Regionally distinct forms of architecture took shape during this era, typically for religious and political purposes, although military defense was important as well, and some structures now served more public purposes. Large building projects continued in the Middle East, including the **Great Library of Alexandria** in Egypt and the **Hanging Gardens of Babylon** created by Nebuchadnezzar. Greco-Roman architecture, influenced by earlier Mediterranean styles, made distinctive use of columns and facades, with the Romans adding archways and domes—which required advanced engineering skills—to the repertoire. Key works include the **Parthenon** (the temple of Athena on Athens's Acropolis), Rome's **Pantheon** (a temple to all Roman gods) and **Colosseum**, as well as the Church of St. Sophia built in Constantinople in the 500s C.E. The cultures of Mesoamerica, especially the Maya and Aztecs, remain famous for their large **pyramids**, which were used not as tombs, as in Egypt, but as places of human sacrifice. Representative works from this period

The Buddha Guarded by the Greek Demigod Herakles (Hercules)
This architectural feature, created during the 100s C.E. in the Kingdom of Gandhara, located on the border of present-day Pakistan and Afghanistan, illustrates the unique fusion of Greco-Roman and Buddhist culture that followed the far-ranging military conquests launched by Alexander the Great.

of Indian history include huge **cave temples**, built in honor of Buddhist and Hindu deities—sometime both at the same complex—at places like Ajanta and Ellora. The walls and towers guarding the Mauryan capital of Pataliputra rank as another Indian masterpiece, and numerous **Pillars of Ashoka**, inscribed with Buddhist teachings and Ashoka's own commentary about society and morality, were erected at sites throughout Mauryan India.

One style unique to this era is the **Greco-Buddhist architecture and sculpture** that resulted from the campaigns of **Alexander the Great** in the 300s B.C.E. and the establishment of Greek colonies and Indo-Greek kingdoms in Central Asia and present-day Pakistan, Afghanistan, and India for centuries afterward. A striking example of **cultural borrowing**, this fusion of two styles is thought by some to have led to the first artistic depictions of the Buddha in human form—a great strength of Greek sculpture.

The Development of States and Empires

- Persia
- Qin and Han China
- Aryans and Dravidians
- The Mauryan and Gupta empires
- The Phoenicians and Carthage
- The Greeks and Athens
- Alexander the Great and Hellenistic culture
- The Roman Republic and Empire
- Teotihuacan and the Maya
- The Moche
- Administrative institutions and bureaucracies
- Ways of projecting power
- Forms of organizing labor
- Imperial overreach

State-building during this era reached new levels of complexity and sophistication. Fielding better-armed and better-organized military forces, and with stronger bureaucratic and recordkeeping mechanisms and their administrative disposal, **key states and empires** brought political, economic, and social unity to wide-ranging territories in a number of places. Many of these became the **classical** civilization in their part of the world, bestowing a long-lived cultural inheritance to the societies that succeeded it.

In a process often referred to as **imperial overreach**, empires typically overextended themselves in one or more of several ways, leading to downfall in one form or another.

KEY STATES

Among the most centralized and most influential states of this period are those listed below. In studying them, be sure to think about patterns in the way they governed themselves and organized their societies.

The Persian Empires (Southwest Asia)

In a very short time, the **Persians** (550–331 B.C.E.) of present-day Iran came to dominate the Middle East, building one of the largest empires in world history. Their first dynasty, the **Achaemenid**, was founded by Cyrus, who overthrew the Median kingdom that had ruled the region since the 700s B.C.E. The Persians quickly conquered the **Lydians** (who are said to have invented **metal coinage** around 600–500 B.C.E.),

the Neo-Babylonians, the Egyptians, and others, until, by the end of the reign of the third ruler, Darius the Great (522–486 B.C.E.), the empire stretched from Turkey and Libya to India, measuring more than 2 million square miles, the largest state seen in the world to that date. From two capitals—Susa for administrative affairs and **Persepolis** built by Darius in the Mesopotamian style to impress citizens with his power—the Persians ruled with the help of an advanced postal system, an excellent network of roads, a single currency, and a highly developed form of **provincial government** that divided the empire into twenty or so regions and delegated authority over them to officials called **satraps**. Under the Achaemenids, Persia was patriarchal and rigidly stratified, with the population divided into warriors, priests called magi, and peasants. The ruler was known as "king of kings" (*shahan-shah*) and referred to all subjects as "my slaves." Darius embraced the Zoroastrian religion, but the Persians remained relatively tolerant of other faiths.

The Achaemenid Persians fought several wars with their Greek neighbors to the west in the 500s and 400s B.C.E. In 331 B.C.E., they fell to the Hellenistic conqueror Alexander the Great. A new dynasty, the Parthians (247 B.C.E.–224 C.E.) arose by rebelling against the kingdom that had been founded in Persia by Alexander's generals. Somewhat more decentralized than the previous states, Parthian Persia combined elements of Greek and Persian culture and grew wealthy from trade along the **Silk Road**. They were powerful enemies of the Roman Empire as it expanded eastward. Rising up in the Parthians' place was the **Sassanid Empire** (224–651 C.E.), another great rival of Rome and the Byzantine Empire that followed it. The Sassanid shahs derived their riches from the Silk Road, but also from the commerce generated by **Arab traders**. Like earlier Persian rulers, they practiced Zoroastrianism, but made it an official state faith and were much less tolerant than their Achaemenid predecessors. The Sassanid Empire was swept away suddenly by the rapid military expansion of **Islam** out of the Arabian Peninsula.

The Qin and Han Empires (East Asia)

From the 200s B.C.E. to about 600 C.E., a united and steadily growing China was ruled by several major dynasties. The most notable were the Qin, or Ch'in (221–206 B.C.E.), and the Han (206 B.C.E.–220 C.E.).

Although short-lived, the **Qin dynasty** was important because of its founder, Shi Huangdi, who ended the "Warring States" period and united northern China with the Yangzi valley in the south—the first ever to do so. Shi Huangdi turned the Qin state, which many historians believe gave the country its name of "China," into a dictatorial, centralized nation governed by a large and effective **bureaucracy**. He standardized weights and measures and modernized the Chinese army by introducing iron weapons, crossbows, and cavalry warfare. He used forced labor to build thousands of miles of roads and canals, as well as the first of the structures that collectively came to be known as the **Great Wall of China**. The Qin government ended slavery and serfdom, not out of kindness, but because free peasants had to pay taxes and serve in the army. The Qin taxed so heavily that, shortly after Shi Huangdi's death, rebellions broke out and destroyed the dynasty.

The **Han dynasty**, brought to power by these uprisings, became one of China's strongest and longest lasting. It built on the foundations of the Qin state to create a

The Great Wall of China.
The so-called Great Wall was actually a network of many walls. Construction began as early as the
200s B.C.E., under the emperor Shi Huangdi, and took centuries. Thousands of the workers, many of
them prisoners, died. As impressive a feat of engineering as the Great Wall is, it failed to defend
China from attack. Note the state of disrepair depicted in this engraving.

centralized, efficient empire. Its armies expanded hundreds of miles to the west,
north, and south, absorbing all of Inner China, much of Outer China, and parts of
Vietnam, Korea, Manchuria, and inner Mongolia. Where they did not take over
directly, the Han rulers established a **tributary system**, exacting payment from
neighboring states. **Cavalry warfare** and the **crossbow** gave them an advantage over
their neighbors and allowed them to oppose **steppe nomads** on their frontiers (especially the Turkic Xiongnu) effectively.

From their capital at **Chang'an**, the Han rulers, like the Qin before them, put into
place an efficient bureaucracy, postal service, and tax-collecting system. They built
roads, defensive fortifications (enlarging the Great Wall), and canals to link the country's major rivers. However, they governed less ruthlessly than the Qin, reviving the
Zhou ideal of the **Mandate of Heaven**, which stated that only virtuous rulers
deserved to rule. Similarly, the Han favored **Confucianism**, with its argument that
superiors owed kindness and good treatment to their inferiors, whereas the Qin had
followed the doctrine of Legalism, which emphasized the absolute power of the ruler.
The Han rulers expanded China's **law code** from three volumes to twenty-seven, providing the foundation for the code used by later dynasties.

During most of the Han period, China's economy was strong, spurred by
improved agricultural techniques (including better irrigation and the invention of
the **horse collar**, which allowed horses to pull heavier loads) and the country's
monopoly on **silk production**, which made it a dominant player in **Silk Road** trade.
By 200 C.E., though, the Han state was in decline. A downturn in agricultural production and an overall economic slump sapped its strength, as did governmental corruption and weak leadership. Bandits, rebels, and nomadic invaders, particularly the
Xiongnu, made it difficult for the Han to protect their borders. The **epidemic** spread

of what appears to have been smallpox in the late 100s C.E. had also weakened the country. In 220 C.E., the dynasty collapsed. Over the next three and a half centuries, several minor dynasties rose and fell, which China itself was mired in anarchy. Not until 589 C.E. did a strong dynasty, the Sui (589–618 C.E.), reestablish order.

The Maurya and Gupta Empires (South Asia)

To what degree the Indus River valley civilization can be considered "Indian" is unclear, and the true foundations of Indian culture remain unknown. Conventionally, it is said to have taken shape around 1500 B.C.E., when northern India was invaded by the **Indo-Europeans** known as **Aryans**. These lighter-skinned warriors conquered India's darker-skinned natives (collectively known as the **Dravidians**), expanding from north to south, and the two groups fused to form a truly Indian culture. However, variety within this cultural tradition was great, with dozens of ethnicities, languages, and traditions evolving throughout the subcontinent.

India's size and diversity meant that it was rarely unified as a single state during its ancient and classical periods. The first to bring most of the region together was the **Mauryan Empire** (ca. 324–184 B.C.E.), founded by Chandragupta Maurya (324–301 B.C.E.), who ruled from his capital of **Pataliputra** on the eastern Ganges. The empire, which included all but India's southernmost tip, developed an elaborate **bureaucracy** that collected a 25 percent tax on all agricultural production and maintained a network of informers to spy on its own people and make sure they remained obedient. They had a powerful army that used elephants in addition to chariots and cavalry, and their trade network was extensive. The Mauryans used a unified currency and traded not just with East and Southeast Asia, but as far away as Mesopotamia and the eastern parts of the Roman Empire. Key goods included salt, iron, and cotton cloth. The best known of the Mauryan emperors was **Ashoka** (269–232 B.C.E.). A great warrior as a youth, Ashoka became sickened by war after one of his greatest victories. He converted to Buddhism and advocated peace and tolerance, spreading those ideals by means of the **Pillars of Ashoka**, stone monuments placed throughout the country. He encouraged trade with China, especially for its silk, and opened trade routes to the north. He was admired for his justice and wisdom, and he remains famous for his efforts to create harmony between Buddhists, Hindus, and the followers of India's other religions. His efforts to spread Buddhism throughout India and elsewhere played a key role in its establishment as a formal religion.

In 184 B.C.E., the Mauryan Empire collapsed due to attacks from outside enemies, and for the next five hundred years, India reverted to a state of political disunity. Not until 320 C.E. did another large empire rise up, also along the eastern Ganges: the **Gupta Empire**, which controlled most of north-central India, with vassal states to the east and northwest. The Gupta rulers consciously imitated the Mauryan Empire. The first of them, Chandra Gupta, borrowed the name of the first Mauryan emperor, and they governed from Pataliputra. The Gupta Empire was smaller and less centralized than the Mauryan, and it depended more on diplomacy to maintain its authority. Although the Gupta rulers were Hindu, they practiced religious toleration. Gupta India traded by boat with Malaysia and Indonesia, exchanging cotton,

worked metal, and salt for spices, and also with China for silk. Their network also included the Arabian Sea and eastern Mediterranean. Gupta scholars created the **decimal system** (and the wrongly named "Arabic numerals") and the concepts of *pi* and **zero**. As did the Mauryans, the Gupta imposed a 25 percent tax on agricultural products. They were more patriarchal than the Gupta, and the status of women declined. Women lost the right to property, they were obligated to be more obedient to male members of their family, and the **sati** ritual of burning oneself alive with one's dead husband became more common.

Like the Mauryans before them, the Gupta emperors fell mainly as a result of outside pressure, especially from attacks by the nomadic **White Huns** on the northwestern frontier. From then until after 1000 C.E., India would remain decentralized. Muslim invaders then moved into the subcontinent, doing much to shape Indian politics and culture.

Phoenicia, Greece, Alexander the Great, and Rome (The Mediterranean)

In the Mediterranean, the **Phoenicians** reached their peak as a civilization during this era. Originators of the **alphabet** and great seafarers and traders, the Phoenicians spread out from present-day Syria and Lebanon to establish **city-states** throughout the Mediterranean. Their westward expansion began around the 800s B.C.E., taking them to North Africa, where they founded the great port of **Carthage**, as well as southern Spain and islands like Sicily and Sardinia. City-states in this decentralized society were mainly autonomous, and social mobility was greater than in most civilizations. Carthage was governed by a Senate and two judges, elected from a merchant aristocracy that was not restricted by birth. The Phoenicians worshipped a polytheistic pantheon headed by the storm god Baal, and they are known to have sacrificed children to their deities. Carthage possessed a large and technologically advanced navy, relying on mercenaries or soldiers recruited from subject peoples to fill their armies. Carthage proved a powerful foe to Rome in the 200s B.C.E., and the **Punic Wars** between the two cities determined the destiny of the Mediterranean world for centuries.

The ancient **Greeks** (or **Hellenes**) formed a distinct culture, united by a common language and the worship of the Olympian gods, between 1150 and 800 B.C.E. During the centuries that followed, and especially during the classical period (ca. 500–338 B.C.E.), they organized themselves into a society of **city-states and colonies** (the Greek term for "city-state," *polis*, is the root of our word "politics"), not just in Greece itself, but on islands and shorelines throughout the eastern Mediterranean, between Italy and the Turkish coast. Each city-state governed itself and the land surrounding it, and in a variety of ways. Some were monarchies, but most were **oligarchies** ("rule by the few"), in which a narrow elite made up of rich, powerful families ruled. The most influential city-states of the classical period were Sparta and Athens. **Sparta** was a rigid, slave-holding dictatorship that created the Greek world's most effective and most feared army. **Athens** became a culturally and politically advanced city that gained wealth through trade, and power thanks to its naval strength. Slavery was common in all city-states, but it was most prevalent in Sparta.

Greek women were treated as social and political inferiors. Ancient Greece's most significant political innovation came from the city of Athens. This was **democracy**, or rule by the people, which began in 508 B.C.E. and reached its peak under the statesman Pericles (ca. 461–429 B.C.E.). As in other Greek city-states, women and slaves were excluded from Athenian political life.

Hellenic culture, described in the previous chapter, gave rise to **philosophy**, the **scientific method**, **Greek dramas**, and some of the world's finest architecture and most lifelike sculpture. Politically, the Greeks remained highly decentralized, although most city-states joined together under Spartan and Athenian leadership to resist Persian conquest in two wars fought between 492 B.C.E and 479 B.C.E. A generation later, competition between Sparta and Athens led to a devastating civil conflict known as the **Peloponnesian War** (431–404 B.C.E.). Although Sparta and its allies triumphed, the war left both sides exhausted. By 338 B.C.E., that weakness opened Greece to conquest by its neighbor to the north, Macedonia, whose people were ethnically related to the Greeks but not as culturally advanced.

It was from this Greek-Macedonian kingdom that the ancient world's most skilled general, **Alexander the Great** (356–323 B.C.E.), launched one of the most successful military campaigns of all time. Alexander crossed into Asia, took over the Achaemenid Persian Empire, and conquered territory all the way to the borderlands of India. Before dying at the age of thirty-three, he had led his army on a journey lasting almost ten years and covering more than 20,000 miles. His generals split his empire among them, preserving Greek-Macedonian rule for many years in places like Egypt, Persia, and Central Asia. Alexander's greatest accomplishment, even more important than his battle victories, was the preservation of Greek art and learning and the fusing of it with other societies' traditions to create **Hellenistic ("Greek-like") culture**. Hellenistic influences spread across a huge portion of Eurasia, from North Africa and the Mediterranean to India's northwest frontier, where the Greco-Buddhist culture mentioned in the last chapter flourished. His grand capital, the Egyptian city of **Alexandria**, with its **Great Library**, became one of the ancient world's greatest centers of trade, learning, and culture.

As the Greeks' political power faded, a new force emerged in Europe: the city of **Rome**, said to have been founded in 753 B.C.E. From their homeland on the Italian peninsula, the **Romans** spread outward to dominate the Mediterranean and the regions bordering it, creating one of the largest and longest-lasting empires in history. For several centuries, Rome remained a monarchy, until rebellion created the **Roman Republic** (509–31 B.C.E.). From the Latin term *res publica*, meaning "public thing," a **republic** is a state in which all or most adult citizens (in premodern cases, only males) play some role—although not necessarily equal roles—in government. During this period, Roman society experienced tensions between the lower (**plebeian**) and upper (**patrician**) classes. Through a long process of compromise and negotiation, the former gained greater, but never complete, social and political equality. The latter controlled the Senate and the consuls, two officials elected from the patrician class who provided executive leadership. It was during the republican period that Rome expanded into a Mediterranean empire, first conquering the Italian peninsula, by about 270 B.C.E., and then fighting three bitter conflicts, the **Punic Wars** (264–146 B.C.E.), against the Phoenician city of Carthage. Victory over

Carthage made Rome the strongest state in the western Mediterranean. It then turned east, taking Greece and parts of Turkey, setting the stage for future conquests in Egypt and Asia.

Such rapid expansion caused the **collapse of the Roman Republic** during the first century B.C.E. In particular, small farmers, the closest Rome had to a middle class, went bankrupt, thanks to falling grain prices and the increased use of slave labor by larger landowners. Poverty worsened, and many of the urban poor joined violent mobs. Rome was shaken by a series of civil wars from 91 to 30 B.C.E., and political power began to fall into the hands of a single ruler. The most famous of the late republican politicians was the great general Julius Caesar, who assumed dictatorial powers during the civil war of 49–45 B.C.E. and was assassinated in 44 B.C.E. by republicans who feared he wished to become a king. More war followed, until the republic's end in 31 B.C.E.

A new regime, the **Roman Empire** (31 B.C.E.-476 C.E.), was founded by Caesar's adopted son, who renamed himself Caesar Augustus, restored order, revived Rome's strength and wealth, and created the position of emperor. Over time, Rome's emperors became more despotic, although some used their power more wisely than others. Despite occasional episodes of political violence, Rome between the reign of Augustus and the mid-200s C.E. experienced a golden age of peak power and prosperity known as the *pax Romana* ("Roman peace"). Its economic and military might increased, and its huge territory extended from Spain in the west to Asia Minor in the east, from northern Africa in the south to the British Isles in the north. The Romans were master administrators, dividing the empire into provinces governed by regional officials called **proconsuls**, and building a tremendous network of roads, sea lanes, aqueducts (to carry water over long distances), and fortifications, including city walls and frontier defense barriers such as Hadrian's Wall in Scotland.

After the early 200s C.E., Rome found itself in crisis. During the 300s C.E., the eastern half of the empire was split off from the western half, becoming the **Eastern Roman** (or **Byzantine**) **Empire**, headquartered in the city of **Constantinople** (Byzantium). Overextension of military and political strength made it difficult to govern what remained of the western empire, and the army gained a large degree of control over the government. With the empire deprived of the east's wealth, and forced to pay the army ever-larger amounts of money, the economy experienced severe downturns. Migrating waves of **Germanic** and **Asiatic nomads**, ("**barbarians**" to the Romans) attacked Roman lands from the east and the north for more than four centuries. Although some settled in Rome and adopted its civilized ways, others did not. By the 400s C.E., the empire's heartland lay open to barbarian invasion. The city of Rome was sacked by Germanic Goths in 410 C.E. Another wave of Goths took over completely in 476 C.E., the year Rome's western empire is considered to have fallen.

Roman society was sharply divided into citizens and noncitizens, who were subject peoples with no civil rights. Among citizens, the primary social distinction was between patrician and plebeian. Slavery was widely practiced, with occasional slave revolts (like that of Spartacus in the 70s B.C.E.) disturbing the order of things. The role of women changed over time. During the republican period, Roman society was strictly patriarchal, and the male family head (**paterfamilias**) had absolute power over

his wife and children. By the late republican period and early empire, women gained more freedom to divorce, more economic rights, and greater influence over family financial affairs. They still had no vote.

As with Greece, Rome's cultural heritage is immense. The Romans, who greatly admired Hellenic culture, to the point of adopting the Olympian pantheon (with some name changes), preserved much of the Greeks' Hellenic philosophy, literature, and scientific learning. In their own right, the Romans were master builders and engineers. Many of the roads, aqueducts, cities, and fortifications they constructed were of use to the people who came after them for centuries to come, in some cases up to the present. They were the first to use large arches and domes on a regular basis. In terms of politics, the monarchs of medieval Europe would long attempt to live up to the ideal of imperial Roman unity. Roman political thinking guided the formation of many of Europe's nations, and Roman law remains one of the keystones of Western legal thought. The concept of "innocent until proven guilty" derives from early Roman law as codified in the **Twelve Tables**. Finally, it was at the eastern edge of the Roman Empire that the religion of Christianity was born, during the first century C.E. By **legalizing Christianity** in the 300s C.E., and then adopting it as their official faith, the Romans ensured that the new religion would remain a major intellectual and cultural force long after the empire itself was gone.

Teotihuacan, the Maya, and the Moche (Mesoamerica and the Andes)

In Mesoamerica, many societies built upon the religious and cultural foundation left behind by the Olmecs, who faded around 400 B.C.E. These tended not to be unified nations, but city-states that shared a common culture, interacted economically, and warred with each other frequently. Most tended to be hierarchical dictatorships ruled by kings and priests. Women were subject to rigidly defined gender roles. A few upper-class women gained status as priestesses or used noble status to exert informal influence, and at least two Mayan kingdoms were ruled by women. Like the Olmecs before them, many Mesoamerican peoples practiced **human sacrifice**. They built **pyramids** that symbolized sacred mountains with roots in the underworld, but reaching to the heavens as well.

Among these societies was the one centered on the city of **Teotihuacan** (ca. 100 B.C.E.–750 C.E.), located near present-day Mexico City and, with a population of approximately 200,000, one of the world's largest cities at the time. Ruled by an oligarchy rather than a monarchy, the Teotihuacan people practiced human sacrifice and built temples to the sun and moon, as well as to the god Quetzalcoatl, a bird-serpent worshipped by other Mesoamericans, including the Mayans. The people of Teotihuacan engaged in **intensive farming**, with elaborate irrigation of fields, draining of swamps, and terracing of hillsides. In shallow lakes, they built *chinampas*, or "floating islands," which created more space for growing crops. They manufactured pottery and obsidian carvings and traded widely, including with the Maya. Teotihuacan entered into decline around 650 C.E. An older view blamed the downfall on an external war, but it is now thought by most that elite overspending caused social tensions that led to violent and crippling revolts.

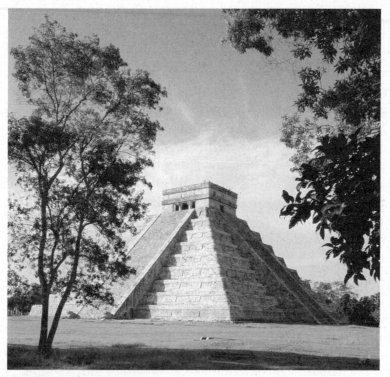

Mayan Pyramid of Chichén Itzá.
The Maya founded the city of Chichén Itzá around 250 C.E. It remains a treasure trove of archaeological evidence of how the Maya lived.

Overlapping with Teotihuacan's peak was the rise of the **Maya** (ca. 250–900 C.E.), whose culture emerged in present-day Guatemala and spread to Honduras, Belize, and southern Mexico. The Mayan lands were governed by approximately forty city-states and rival kingdoms, such as Tikal and Uxmal. At its height, the Mayan population reached three million.

The Mayan kings served a priestly function as well. Like others in the region, the Maya built pyramids and satisfied their polytheistic gods—which included jaguar deities and the winged serpent Quetzalcoatl—by means of human sacrifice. The Maya devised an elaborate **hieroglyphic** script, the most advanced system of writing in the pre-Columbian Americas. Superb astronomers and mathematicians, they understood the concept of **zero** and invented an intricate and accurate **calendar**. The reasons for their collapse, indicated by the abandonment of most Mayan cities between 800 and 900 C.E., remain a mystery. Theories include environmental degradation caused by overuse of the land or overpopulation, nearby volcanic activity, disease, and intercity warfare.

As noted in the previous unit, the other site of advanced societies in the Americas was South America's **Andes Mountains**. Several advanced cultures arose around this time in what is now Peru, including the Nazca (ca. 100–800 C.E.) and Huari (ca. 500–800 C.E.). Most powerful were the **Moche** (ca. 200–700 C.E.). Like other societies in the region, the Moche used the **quipu**, or knot-tying, system of recordkeeping, and they lived in clans called **ayllu**, who owned land communally.

As political elites in Andean societies grew more powerful, as the warrior-priests who governed the Moche did, they compelled ayllu to perform labor according to the **mit'a** system, a form of obligation that combined elements of serfdom and *corvée* labor. Members of an ayllu would typically farm land owned by the elite, tend llama and alpaca herds, or build roads, bridges, or hillside terraces for farming. Those living in the valleys grew quinoa, corn, and potatoes, while coastal settlements fished, and trade with the Amazon provided fruit. The Moche produced excellent ceramics. The society was highly stratified, but not politically unified into a single state. With no written script available, historians speculate as to what caused the end of the Moche, theorizing that it was a combination of environmental factors (an earthquake's shifting of the Moche River, plus natural erosion caused by heavy rains) and pressure placed by a military rival on its major trade routes.

METHODS OF RULE

Governing large states and empires required a complicated mix of political skill, military strength, and good economic judgment. In studying the societies described above, pay attention to how different regimes dealt with the key aspects of rulership and be able to compare and contrast the techniques they used.

Administrative institutions were crucial to rulership in all states. **Centralized government** was the goal of many kings and emperors. Among the most successful centralizers were Persia, Qin and Han China, Mauryan India, and Rome. Societies organized on a **city-state** basis, such as Phoenicia, ancient Greece, and the Maya, tended to be culturally unified but politically decentralized. **Law codes** and **courts** provided societies with structure and a way of enforcing rules, although in most premodern states they did not guarantee equal treatment of all classes; those of elite status received more rights and privileges and were generally punished more lightly for most crimes. **Bureaucracies** enabled rulers to exercise their will over large areas: among the tasks they performed were **tax collection**, **law enforcement**, **military defense**, the **regulation of trade** (including the creation of **currencies** and standard weights and measures), and the construction and maintenance of **infrastructure** (including roads, canals, postal systems, and so on). Most rulers created **regional** and **local levels of government** and delegated authority to officials at those levels. Persia was subdivided into provinces governed by **satraps**, and large units in Rome were administered by **proconsuls**. In Qin and Han China, the empire was organized into units called *jun*, run jointly by three people—a civilian governor, a military commander, and an imperial inspector—and then into smaller counties, overseen by a magistrate. Mauryan and Gupta India likewise maintained several levels of government.

Other techniques of rule included **religious justification** (the Mandate of Heaven in the case of Han China, the priestly functions claimed by leaders like the Mayan and Moche rulers, the notion in most societies that the ruler was somehow blessed by the gods), **claiming the legacy** of an earlier state (as the Gupta did in India by emulating the Mauryan Empire), and creating a **secret police** or **network of informants** to monitor one's own people. **Official religions** were one way to strengthen

feelings of social unity, but they could also create resentments in states with diverse populations. Some empires forced their official religion on all subjects, while others, such as the early Persians and India under the Mauryans and Guptas, practiced **religious toleration** to one degree or another. Because it made the task of governing easier, Rome's imperial policy was to allow the people it conquered to worship as they pleased, as long as they obeyed Roman law and respected Rome's gods along with their own. Alexander the Great followed a similar policy.

The **projection of power** involved the effective use of **military force**. The most successful states and empires had versatile armies capable of fighting in several ways: on foot, from horseback, using missile weapons, and perhaps using chariots or animals such as elephants. China, Rome, the Greek city-state of Sparta, and the Mayans are known for their powerful **land armies**. **Naval warfare** was an effective way to project force, but took great skill and much money, and is often associated with societies whose economies were based mainly on trade rather than agriculture. The Phoenicians and the Greek city-state of Athens were famous for their naval aptitude. **Siegecraft**, the art of capturing enemy cities, required knowledge of engineering and was a particular strength of the Romans, Indians, and Chinese. Many states **hired mercenaries** and **recruited soldiers from conquered peoples**. Not only did the latter technique save money and humanpower, it allowed armies to recruit troops who were familiar with a certain region or especially skilled in a particular form of combat, such as archery, cavalry warfare, or naval warfare.

War, typically very costly, could be avoided or made easier by means of **diplomacy**. States sought allies, ended or sidestepped quarrels by negotiating treaties, and sought to keep their foes and rivals fighting each other. Mauryan political advisers coined the famous phrase "the enemy of my enemy is my friend," and the Romans originated the term "divide and conquer," but all the states described above used these techniques. **Divide and conquer** was particularly useful for empires facing different nomadic tribes, many of whom disliked each other as much as they did the imperial power. China dealt with steppe nomads in this fashion, and Rome did the same with the barbarian peoples on its frontiers. Sometimes states turned their neighbors into **vassal** or **tributary states**. This saved the expense of outright conquest and typically involved collecting money from or dictating policy to one's neighbor. Han China and Gupta India relied on this technique.

The effective projection of force demanded that armies and navies be fed and equipped properly, and that they be able to move efficiently. Organized states laid out **supply lines** to make sure that their forces were not without food or gear. They gained control of **sea lanes**, especially in the Mediterranean, the Indian Ocean, and China's coastal waters. They also built **roads**, which not only permitted the rapid movement of troops, but facilitated trade. Persia's 1,600-mile Great Royal Road could be traveled in less than a week, and the networks built by Han China and Rome were masterpieces of engineering. Road-building was harder in Mesoamerica and extremely difficult in the Andes. **Fortifications** in the form of **city walls** protected population centers. They were also used to defend frontiers, with two familiar examples being the **Great Wall of China** and **Hadrian's Wall**, built by the Romans on the borderline between England and Scotland.

SOCIAL STRUCTURES

The greatest hallmark of civilized societies, as opposed to less advanced ones, was the presence of **cities**. Cities served as hubs for trade, both within and between regions, especially if they happened to be **seaports** or **river ports**. They were often the site of the major temples and monasteries, and the places where key religious rituals were enacted. They acted as garrisons, barracks, and navy yards for military forces. They also provided the seat of government in most societies.

Be able to locate and describe the characteristics of the era's major cities. These include **Persepolis** (the ceremonial capital of the first Persian Empire), **Chang'an** (capital of Han China and a key point on the **Silk Road**), **Pataliputra** (the chief city of the Mauryan and Gupta empires), **Athens** (the commercial and naval power of the Greek city-states), **Carthage** (a trading center and naval power founded by the Phoenicans on the North African coast and an early enemy of Rome), **Rome** (in west-central Italy and home to perhaps the most efficiently centralized state of the ancient world), **Alexandria** (the Egyptian port founded by Alexander the Great as his capital, and the Mediterranean world's most cosmopolitan center of learning), **Constantinople** (the eastern headquarters of the Roman Empire and the Byzantine Empire that followed it, situated on the crossroads between Europe and Asia in present-day Turkey), and **Teotihuacan** (present-day Mexico City).

Class structures and **social hierarchies** grew more complex during this time. Most places were characterized by **low social mobility**, and the most rigid, as in India, maintained **caste systems**. Social classes included political elites (rulers and their families and closest advisors), aristocracies (families of high birth who typically had a hand in running the government), religious elites (high-ranking members of priesthoods), merchants and traders, artisans and craftspeople, unskilled laborers, servants, and cultivators (farmers, peasants, and other growers of food). Elite status was typically **hereditary**, and even when **merit** played a role in gaining jobs within a **bureaucracy** (as it was beginning to in places like Han China), **literacy**, which was available to very few in any given society, was typically required. The wealth of aristocratic classes tended to be based on **land ownership** (often inherited), whereas merchants generated wealth through **commerce and trade**. The presence of a strong merchant class generally meant a higher degree of social mobility, as in Athens and Phoenicia.

Each society had to choose how to organize **labor** and **food production**. **Slaves** and **serfs** were used commonly, both as servants to carry out household tasks and, most importantly, to grow food. Free members of the lower classes had to pay rents to landowners or the state, or **taxes**, or **tribute** in the form of food or other goods. They could also be mobilized against their will by states or landlords to provide **corvée labor**, which typically involved large-scale projects such as cutting forests, draining swamps, irrigating fields, or building roads or major architectural projects. The **mit'a** system of labor obligation found in the Andes involved elements of serfdom and corvée labor. Members of the lower classes were also frequently **conscripted**, or drafted to serve as soldiers, sailors, or rowers of galleys. Whether or not a slave or serf owed taxes depended on the society in question. Most societies maintained some system of **food storage and distribution**, whether for emergencies or for everyday use. Rome's rulers, for example, kept social order by providing grain, much

of it from the breadbasket of Egypt, for its common people. (They created lavish entertainments for the same purpose, leading some to speak of **bread and circuses** as a crude way to keep societies under control.)

Without exception, major societies from during this era were **patriarchal**, although how much so varied from place to place and sometimes over time.

POLITICAL AND IMPERIAL OVERREACH

States collapsed for a variety of reasons and in a variety of ways. The end could come suddenly or gradually, and it could be due primarily to **internal** or **external factors**. Especially in the case of empires, the problem stemmed from **overreach**: the state simply assumed too many responsibilities or expenses, conquered too much territory, or caused itself too many social problems for its rulers, bureaucracies, and armies to handle.

Pay attention to how each of the states described above met its end. Typically, a combination of factors, and not just one cause, brings about the downfall. Challenges commonly faced by states in decline or crisis include:

- unwise or corrupt political leadership
- rebellions and social upheavals caused by overtaxation or elite injustice
- civil wars
- conquest of more territory than one can effectively govern
- economic downturns and disruptions of regional trade patterns
- neglect of infrastructure, such as roads
- war with one or more advanced states or the sudden appearance of a powerful enemy
- constant, long-term frontier harassment by raiding or migrating nomads (classic examples including the attacks on Rome by Germanic barbarians, on Gupta India by the White Huns, and on Han China by the Xiongnu)
- external environmental factors, such as climate change, natural disasters, or the appearance of new diseases (such as smallpox, measles, or bubonic plague)
- self-inflicted environmental problems, such as overpopulation, overuse of wood (deforestation), overuse of water (desertification), or the silting of rivers and the erosion of soil caused by large construction projects or overfarming

Emerging Transregional Networks of Communication and Exchange

- Transregional trade
- Mediterranean sea lanes
- The Indian Ocean basin
- Trans-Saharan caravan routes
- The Silk Road
- Domestication of pack animals
- Coastal versus open-water navigation
- Intensive agriculture
- The spread of diseases

New technologies and greater familiarity with larger parts of the world facilitated the movement of peoples throughout Afro-Eurasia and throughout the Americas. (For the time being, these two large geographical units continued to exist in isolation from each other.) Such movement gave rise to greater transregional interaction among states, or between states and nomadic societies. **Networks** of communication and exchange increased in number and breadth.

Alongside **war** and **migration**, the most powerful force driving this process was **trade**. Whatever motivated the spinning of these new and more extensive networks, the consequences, both positive and negative, were many and profound. These include the transfer of technology and knowledge, the diffusion and intermingling of religious beliefs, the redistribution of plants and animals, the ability to wage war over longer distances, and the spread of disease pathogens.

TRANSREGIONAL TRADE ROUTES

In many places, trade operated mainly on the local level, within communities or between closely neighboring communities, and on the regional level. This was especially the case in areas where the climate or terrain varied widely, because very different foods and resources could be obtained from not very far away. This was especially the case among the islands of Oceania, and also in the Americas. An array of goods were exchanged among the societies of Mesoamerica, a relatively small space. In the Andes, trade took place fairly locally between people living on the coast

Principal African-Eurasian Trade Routes, ca. 200 B.C.E.–200 C.E.
During this time, merchants sold goods along a vast trade network that spanned from England in the northwest, to western Africa, Central Asia, and as far east as the Han Empire.

and those living nearby in the mountain valleys, and more regionally with the tribes of the Amazon River basin. There were no horses in the Americas as of yet, and so the principal pack animal in the Andes was the **llama**.

Transregional trade, which spanned greater distances, required more effort, but was typically more lucrative. During this era, four major transregional trade routes came into being, thanks to technological innovations and improved geographical knowledge.

The Mediterranean

Geographically the smallest of the major trading zones, the **Mediterranean Sea** facilitated communication all along the southern coast of Europe, the shores of present-day Turkey and the Levant, and the entirety of North Africa, including Egypt. The fact that the Mediterranean is studded with many islands also made navigation here easier.

Societies that took special advantage of Mediterranean trade during this era were the Persians, the Greeks (who colonized widely between Italy and Turkey), the Phoenicians (based in the Levant, but also colonists of southern Spain and the North African metropolis of Carthage), and the Romans. At the peak of their power, the Romans had quite literally turned the Mediterranean into their private lake, using it to move goods, passengers, and armies over long distances with relative ease. Of crucial importance was the maritime connection between Italy and Egypt, a source of wheat and key breadbasket for the Roman Empire.

Mediterranean peoples relied on ships with square sails and rowed ships, and rarely ventured far from the coast. Because of the short distances involved, war was common, and traders tended to maintain closer ties with their home societies. Via the Turkish straits, Mediterranean sea lanes connected with the Black Sea to the north. Via Egypt and the Suez isthmus, they connected with the Red Sea to the southeast, and eventually to the Arabian Sea and Indian Ocean. The ports of the eastern Mediterranean were tied directly into the Eurasian Silk Road.

The Indian Ocean Basin

Far more extensive than those of the Mediterranean, the sea lanes of the **Indian Ocean maritime network** connected East Africa, the Middle East, South Asia, and Southeast Asia with China and Japan.

A journey from west to east could begin in one of several places: the Red Sea (between Egypt and the Arabian Peninsula), the ports of East Africa (including Zanzibar), or the Persian Gulf (between northwest Arabia and southern Persia). It could then proceed to India's west coast along the southern coast of Persia or, farther to the south, directly across open water from East Africa. Sailing around the tip of India and Ceylon (Sri Lanka), traders came to India's east coast, the Malay Peninsula, and Indonesia. Continuing on, they entered the South China Sea, part of the Pacific, and could sail to the ports of China's east coast (such as Canton)—even connecting with the Pacific end of the overland Silk Road. Arab and Persian traders tended to dominate in the western part of the basin, Indians and Malays in eastern India and the islands of Southeast Asia, and Chinese and Malays in the South China Sea.

The volume of trade carried by this network appears to have been lower than in the Mediterranean, but it was still of value. Wood and ivory came from Africa. Copper, myrrh, and frankincense came from Arabia. Spices came from India and Southeast Asia, and China sold pottery and silk. The ability to sail over open water, which required special ships and sails, was unusual and is a key difference between the way trade worked here and the way it worked in the Mediterranean. Because of the long distances, sailors and traders were often less connected with their home societies. Instead, small **diasporic communities** of foreign traders began to live in port cities, including Chinese traders in the Malay lands, or Arabs in the Chinese city of Canton. The lack of islands and ports, compared with the Mediterranean, meant fewer assets to fight over, and therefore less war, although violence and piracy were not unknown.

Trans-Saharan Caravan Routes

Ever since becoming desert around 2500 B.C.E., the expanse of the Sahara has been a large obstacle to movement and trade between sub-Saharan Africa and the Mediterranean. Animals capable of carrying large loads over long distances through such arid conditions are rare, and specialized knowledge of **oases**, or sources of water, was crucial.

Prior to this era, one of the few avenues of north-south trade was the region of **Nubia**, on the southern Nile and therefore able to connect Egypt with the south. Between the 300s B.C.E. and the 100s C.E., a Nubian kingdom, with the prosperous

iron-producing city of Meroë as its capital, revived this trade until topsoil erosion caused by deforestation caused its decline.

The fortunes of the Roman Empire had a certain effect on trade in this region. While the Roman Empire thrived, societies in North Africa, often under Roman control, directed their economic efforts to the north. And although Rome had some interest in goods from farther south in Africa, this traffic was not large. With Rome in decline, there was more incentive for the peoples of North Africa and the Middle East to look south.

Major caravan routes, traveled by **camels**, linked the central Sahara to Egypt and the Middle East. In northwest Africa, the Berbers of the north traded with **Ghana**, a kingdom taking shape in the 500s C.E. Among the commodities going south were salt and manufactured goods. Coming up from the forests of the south were nuts, oil, exotic foods, and gold. Slavery was common and would become even more so over time.

Eurasia's Silk Roads

The most famous overland route of premodern times, the **Silk Road**, actually existed twice: first during this era, between 100 B.C.E. and 900 C.E. and again between the 1200s and 1600s C.E. It came into being gradually, although its "discovery" is commonly attributed to the Chinese general and explorer Zhang Jian, who crossed the barren regions north of Tibet and came into the lush Ferghana Valley in 128 B.C.E.

In the west, the Silk Road, more than 4,000 miles long, began in the ports of the eastern Mediterranean. From there it crossed through the Persian empire of the Parthians, the Central Asian cities of Bukhara and Samarkand, the western reaches of China, and then to China itself. Passing through the Chinese city of Chang'an, it continued to the Pacific coast. By extension, it was linked on both ends to all of the networks discussed above: in the west, the sea lanes of the Mediterranean and the caravan routes through the Sahara, and, in the east, the Indian Ocean sea lanes.

Although overland transport was far more difficult and took far longer than water transport, it was cheaper. And in this case it was the only way to reach the Central Asian interior, which had its own goods to sell. Spices went west from India and Southeast Asia, as did paper, pottery, and especially silk from China. Jewels, glassware, perfumes, and slaves were transported as well. The impact of the Silk Road on the transfer of technology and cultural and religious borrowing was astounding.

INNOVATIONS IN TRANSPORT

Trade and travel are made easier by improvements in geographical knowledge, which results in more reliable maps and charts, and better understanding of weather patterns in a given region. They are also assisted by changes in technology, several of which widened the ability of people to move between regions during this era, both by land and by sea.

Overland transport during the premodern era required more effort and time and was more subject to political disruption. It was, however, less expensive, and the only way to reach places far from rivers and coastlines. Moving large amounts of cargo depended on **domesticated pack animals**. Sometimes **wheeled vehicles** such as carts

and wagons were helpful, but rough terrain could make them useless, meaning that the animals would have to carry the loads themselves. One of the earliest pack animals in Eurasia was the **horse**, although it was not as strong as **oxen**, which could haul far heavier loads. In the Americas, where there were no horses, the most common pack animal was the **llama**, excellently suited to the mountainous conditions of the Andes. **Camels**, which came in two major species, but could also be interbred, were vital to trade in the Sahara, the Middle East, and along the Silk Road. The one-humped dromedary was better suited to desert conditions, while the two-humped Bactrian camel withstood the arid but often cooler climate of Central Asia. Hybrids, able to tolerate a wide range of weather conditions, were ideal for long-distance travel along the Silk Road. Large processions of pack animals and/or vehicles were called **caravans**. The larger the caravan, the larger the profit, and there was more safety in traveling in larger numbers.

Several technologies from this era heightened the usefulness of pack animals. The **stirrup**, which emerged in Central Asia at some point around the first century C.E., added greater stability for those riding camels or horses. (They also transformed warfare by making hand-to-hand combat—especially the wearing of heavy armor and the use of swords, axes, and lances—from the saddle more feasible.) **Yokes** and **collars** allowed animals to pull heavier loads without choking. More specialized **pack saddles**, such as those devised by horsemen in Central Asia or the camel riders of Arabia and the Sahara, enabled pack animals to carry more cargo on their own backs rather than haul vehicles—an indispensible function in mountains, deserts, and rough ground that did not allow wheeled vehicles to pass.

Where possible, **water transport** was easier and preferable to land transport, although it generally cost more to outfit ships than to organize caravans. During this period, changes in **maritime technology** made overseas trade more efficient. Beforehand, most traders and navies were restricted to **coastal navigation**, meaning that they could not go far from land. In most of the Mediterranean, for example, the principal vessel was the **galley**, an oared ship that also carried a square sail. The galley was too unsteady for **open-water navigation**, and its square sail did not permit heading into the wind. In the Red and Arabian seas, however, mariners developed the **dhow**, a large vessel whose planks were not nailed together, as in the Mediterranean, but drilled, tied together with ropes or fibers, and then sealed together. In addition to being sturdier, dhows also used **lateen sails**, which were tall and peaked sharply, and could handle stronger winds than the square sails used on galleys. The dhow style of shipbuilding caught on throughout the Indian Ocean, and it is known as the uru in some parts of India. Indian Ocean sailors also knew how to take advantage of the **monsoon** winds to cross the open water more quickly.

TRANSMISSIONS: THE EFFECTS OF COMMUNICATION AND EXCHANGE

Common consequences of trade include **technology transfer, environmental** and **medical impact**, and **religious** and **cultural borrowing**.

The exchange of crops and foodstuffs over long distances changed people's dietary habits, as well as their farming and irrigation techniques. The cultivation of rice and

cotton, for example, spread from South Asia to East Asia and the Middle East. The Silk Road brought new foods, such as spinach, pistachios, sesame, and walnuts, to China. Spices went west from East and South Asia. The Bantu, as they migrated through sub-Saharan Africa, spread new crops all over the continent.

Both to handle growing populations, as well as to grow new foods where doing so was possible, many societies turned to **intensive agriculture**, or the use of technology to maximize the productive capacity of every square foot of a given area. Beforehand, the most primitive form of agricultural production, practiced widely, had been **swidden** (or **slash-and-burn**) agriculture, in which trees and bushes were chopped down and burned, fertilizing the soil for a while. Once the soil's nutrients were used up, the farmers would move elsewhere. The method was easy, but not an efficient use of space. More sophisticated and more intensive farming and irrigation techniques include the **terracing of hillsides** common in Mesoamericas and the Andes, the laborious **rice-paddy cultivation** that originated in Southeast Asia, the **draining of swamps** and **wetlands**, the building of **elevated fields** and "**floating islands**" (such as the *chinampas* constructed at Teotihuacan), the construction of **aqueducts** (most famous in the Roman case, but also done in India and the Middle East), and the **qanat**, originating in Persia but used widely throughout Eurasia (this involved sinking vertical shafts in the ground that connected to an underground channel, collected rainwater, and carried it horizontally, but at a gentle downward slope, toward the area one wished to irrigate). The Chinese pioneered the use of the **horse collar**, which made plowing easier.

The **spread of disease** paralleled the movement of humans, whether caused by trade, warfare, religious missionizing, or migration. In premodern times, populations were exceptionally vulnerable to diseases to which they had not built up immunities, and so new encounters often caused mass deaths due to epidemic. Certain diseases recurred periodically, breaking out in epidemic waves. Eurasia in particular was a huge alleyway for the spread of diseases, which over time tended to make people there more resistant to illnesses than those in Africa and especially the Americas. During this era, **bubonic plague** appears to have spread from India to Southeast Asia and China by the 600s C.E., and even earlier to the Eastern Roman, or Byzantine, Empire in the 500s. **Smallpox** and measles affected both the Roman and Han Empires. Nomadic warriors infected Han soldiers with what appears to have been smallbox in 162 C.E., and the spread of the disease to the general population may have contributed to the collapse of the empire. The same diseases were borne westward to the Roman Empire by Asiatic peoples such as the Huns, with similar effect. Smallpox and measles were carried to tiny, isolated Japan from mainland Asia by Buddhist missionaries.

Religions spread as well, sometimes due to gradual cultural contact, sometimes due to peaceful **proselytizing** and **missionary activity**, and sometimes due to war and **forced conversion**. Most key religions traveled far from their original birthplaces. Hinduism spread throughout Southeast Asia; Buddhism spread from India to much of Southeast and Central Asia and all of East Asia. Confucianism and Daoism influenced religious and philosophical thinking in many other parts of Asia besides their native China. Judaism and Christianity (and, soon enough, Islam) came out of the Middle East to affect all of Eurasia.

In spreading, the religions themselves often changed, thanks to the phenomenon of **syncretism**, or the fusing and blending of religious traditions. Hinduism as adopted in various parts of India, and especially by the cultures of Southeast Asia, absorbed local gods and rituals. Many parts of Southeast Asia adopted both Hinduism and Buddhism, and the lines between the two were sometimes blurred. As monks and pilgrims took Buddhism from India along the Silk Road and to places like China, Korea, and Japan (where it arrived in 522 C.E., via Korea), it also evolved. As noted in Chapter 4, the split between Theravada and Mahayana forms of Buddhism had much to do with how local populations adopted the Buddha's original teachings and made them their own. Early Christianity changed as well in order to widen its appeal, ending its insistence on the observance of Jewish dietary and circumcision laws and thereby attracting converts from Greeks and other non-Jewish residents of the Roman Empire. Doctrinal and ritual differences between major branches such as Roman Catholicism and Eastern Orthodoxy (and smaller denominations such as the Armenian, Ethiopian, and Coptic Christian churches) reflect how the religion adapted to the needs and preferences of local converts. As it spread to the east, into Central Asia, certain forms of Christianity, such as Nestorianism, blended in unique ways with elements of Zoroastrianism, Manicheanism (a dualistic variant of Zoroastrianism that perceives the supreme deity and the evil spirit as equal in power), Buddhism, and other faiths.

Unit Two: Review Questions

SAMPLE ESSAY QUESTIONS (CCOT AND COMPARATIVE)

CCOT 1

Analyze continuities and changes in the status of women in ONE of the following regions between 600 B.C.E. and 600 C.E.

India
China

CCOT 2

Analyze continuities and changes in the functioning of ONE of the following trade routes between 600 B.C.E. and 600 C.E.

trans-Saharan caravan routes
the Eurasian Silk Roads

COMP 1

Analyze similarities and differences in how religion justified social hierarchies in TWO of the following regions between 600 B.C.E. and 600 C.E.

India
the Andes
Rome

COMP 2

Analyze similarities and differences in the techniques of political and military administration used by rulers in TWO of the following places between 600 B.C.E. and 600 C.E.

Han China
Persia
Mesoamerica

MULTIPLE-CHOICE QUESTIONS

1. The Ten Commandments' injunction to "honor thy mother and father" gives Judaism the greatest degree of commonality with which of the following belief systems?

    (A) Confucianism
    (B) shamanism
    (C) Hinduism
    (D) Zoroastrianism

2. Ashoka and Constantine are MOST alike in that

    (A) they are each remembered as great lawgivers.
    (B) they each provided crucial support for a major religion.
    (C) they each radically reformed their empire's administration.
    (D) they each expanded their empire's boundaries considerably.

3. Phoenician and Mesoamerican religious practices had which of the following in common?

    (A) ancestor worship
    (B) veneration of sea gods
    (C) human sacrifice
    (D) pyramid construction

"By the side of the stupa of Ashoka, there has been made a Mahayana monastery, very grand and beautiful. There is also a Theravada one; the two together containing 600 or 700 monks. The rules of demeanor and the scholastic arrangements in them are worthy of observation."

4. The author of this statement, the fifth-century Chinese monk Faxian, most likely

    (A) feels regret at the split of Buddhism into competing denominations.
    (B) disapproves of the favoritism shown to Theravada Buddhists by Ashoka.
    (C) prefers Mahayana Buddhism aesthetically to Theravada.
    (D) respects all forms of Buddhist worship and scholarship.

5. How was the Greeks' cultural tradition MOST different from those of other advanced societies between 600 B.C.E. and 0 C.E.?

    (A) They turned away from their polytheistic gods in favor of monotheistic worship.
    (B) They preferred abstract paintings and sculptures of the human form to realistic ones.
    (C) They gained the mathematical proficiency to complete the world's earliest engineering projects.
    (D) They became the first to embrace a scientific method of thinking.

6. What change to early Christian doctrine did the MOST to make it more appealing to people throughout the Roman Empire?

    (A) eliminating the need to observe Jewish dietary restrictions and circumcision
    (B) allowing women to serve alongside men as clergy
    (C) including the Holy Spirit as part of the Trinity
    (D) calling attention to its conceptual similarities to Zoroastrianism

7. Which of the following is MOST true of Roman law?

    (A) It derived mainly from religious principles.
    (B) It operated on the retributive principle of "an eye for an eye."
    (C) It guaranteed equal treatment of all classes before the law.
    (D) It assumed innocence until guilt was proven.

8. Sanskrit and Latin are most alike in that both were

    (A) used exclusively by the political and religious elites in their respective cultures.
    (B) helpful in allowing communication among traders on the Silk Road.
    (C) written in a pictographic script that made them extremely difficult to learn.
    (D) culturally important long after the societies that first used them had passed.

9. Which of the following would be the most effective administrative means by which an advanced state ca. 300 B.C.E. might regulate trade?

    (A) taking a thorough census of the population
    (B) devising a civil law code
    (C) standardizing weights and measures
    (D) forming a network of police informants

10. The Roman Empire's legacy does NOT include

    (A) preserving the influence of Greek culture
    (B) roads and fortifications that have lasted for centuries
    (C) the adoption of Zoroastrianism as an official faith
    (D) a legal code whose impact persists today

11. Which of the following presents a correct sequence of developments?

    (A) the Han expansion of China's tributary system; the epidemic spread of smallpox in China; the weakening of China's state by Xiongnu raiders; the Qin centralization of the Chinese state
    (B) the Qin centralization of the Chinese state; the Han expansion of China's tributary system; the epidemic spread of smallpox in China; the weakening of China's state by Xiongnu raiders
    (C) the epidemic spread of smallpox in China; the Han expansion of China's tributary system; the Qin centralization of the Chinese state; the weakening of China's state by Xiongnu raiders
    (D) the weakening of China's state by Xiongnu raiders; the Qin centralization of the Chinese state; the Han expansion of China's tributary system; the epidemic spread of smallpox in China

12. Persian satraps can be BEST equated to

    (A) Roman proconsuls.
    (B) Chinese generals.
    (C) Mauryan scholars.
    (D) Mayan chieftains.

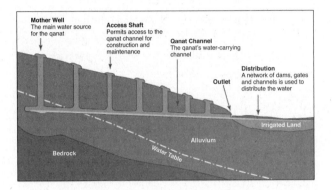

13. The illustration above most likely depicts

    (A) a system of hydraulic engineering inspired by the Roman aqueduct.
    (B) a device intended to irrigate fields owned by a free farmer.
    (C) a piece of infrastructure constructed by a centralized authority.
    (D) a project intended to reduce the environmental impact of local agriculture.

14. Carthage and Athens were most alike in that they both

    (A) resisted conquest by the Assyrian Empire.
    (B) practiced human sacrifice.
    (C) traded directly with Gupta India.
    (D) maintained powerful navies.

15. Which of the following best characterizes Andean methods of organizing labor at around 500 C.E.?

    (A) The economy was based primarily on maritime commerce.
    (B) Slavery was the dominant means of producing food.
    (C) Clan-based groups grew crops and tended herds for the elite.
    (D) Coastal fishing was the main occupation for most.

16. Which of the following accurately reflects the spread of diseases between 600 B.C.E. and 600 C.E.?

    (A) A disease thought to be smallpox crippled Han China shortly before its downfall.
    (B) Bubonic plague arriving from the Roman Empire proved deadly to the population of Gupta India.
    (C) The peoples of the Americas were exposed to most of the same pathogens as the societies of Afro-Eurasia.
    (D) Sexually transmitted diseases are believed to have played a role in the collapse of the Mayan civilization.

17. Intensive farming would most likely NOT include which of the following methods?

    (A) the terracing of hillsides
    (B) slash-and-burn farming
    (C) construction of "floating islands" like *chinampas*
    (D) rice-paddy farming

18. The significance of the dhow ship is that it

    (A) conferred naval superiority upon the peoples of the Middle East.
    (B) enabled Indian Ocean traders to cross wide expanses of open water.
    (C) rendered the oared galley obsolete in the Mediterranean.
    (D) facilitated Chinese trade with the islands of Oceania.

19. Which of the following did the most to facilitate trade along the Silk Road?

    (A) the construction of stone highways
    (B) the universal acceptance of a single currency
    (C) the domestication of the camel
    (D) the invention of the lodestone compass

20. Which of the following cities would have been most directly involved with trans-Saharan caravan trade between 600 B.C.E. and 600 C.E.?

    (A) Chang'an
    (B) Persepolis
    (C) Alexandria
    (D) Rome

ANSWERS

1. (A) Although many religions stress proper conduct toward one's parents, Confucian's special emphasis on filial piety makes it the best match for this particular part of Jewish—and Christian—scripture.

2. (B) Both rulers are remembered as effective administrators and lawmakers, making A plausible. Constantine was associated with C, but Ashoka was not, and neither was involved with D (in Constantine's time, the empire was actually shrinking). Constantine adopted Christianity and made it legal, and Ashoka was a passionate supporter of Buddhism.

3. (C) The Phoenicians did not build pyramids, and neither civilization laid particular emphasis on the worship of sea gods, although the Phoenicians were expert at maritime travel. Both are known to have practiced human sacrifice, although the scale in Mesoamerica was far greater.

4. (D) Faxian's statement shows no signs of prejudice toward or against either school of Buddhism, making B and C obviously incorrect. If there is any sadness about the split, he hides it, making A wrong as well. Faxian clearly speaks approvingly of both.

5. (D) The ancient Greeks were masters at the lifelike sculpture of human figures, and many civilizations before them had been accomplished mathematicians and engineers, making B and C wrong. The Greeks, like the Romans who adopted the Greek gods, remained polytheistic during the time in question. Already by 600 B.C.E., Greek thinkers were applying logic and experimentation to arrive at underlying causes for physical phenomena.

6. (A) Official Christianity moved in the exact opposite direction from B, and even though there are definite similarities between Christianity and Zoroastrianism, Christians would hardly have made a selling point of that fact. Answer B is based on fact, but would not have widened the new faith's appeal in the way that loosening rules of conduct did. This is a good example of how the spread of a religion often changes the nature of the religion itself.

7. (D) Answer B is more typical of ancient Middle Eastern law, and few if any premodern law codes spoke to C. Although the Romans were highly religious, their law code was mainly secular. The principle expressed in D comes from the Twelve Tables.

8. (D) Neither language would have been spoken very widely on the Silk Road, and Latin, based on the Phoenician alphabet, is far from pictographic, making B and C incorrect. Although both were indeed used by elites, they were used more widely as well, eliminating A.

9. **(C)** All these answers are examples of how states administered themselves in the ancient world. Only C, however, would do anything to facilitate trade.

10. **(C)** The Romans accomplished all these things except C. It was Christianity, of course, that they adopted as their official religion in the 300s C.E.

11. **(B)** The Qin preceded the Han, making A and C automatically incorrect. Although smallpox epidemics struck near the end of the Han dynasty, the attack of the Xiongnu also came later and is one of the prime causes of the Han downfall. This eliminates D.

12. **(A)** Satraps and proconsuls are excellent examples of the provincial officials who allowed emperors to govern more efficiently. Effective bureaucracies and forms of regional government are among the techniques of rule used by such states.

13. **(C)** Examples of *qanat* irrigation have been found in Persia long before the Romans built aqueducts, so A is wrong. Costly and difficult to build, *qanats* would have far likelier been constructed by somebody with great financial means, making B unlikely (even though it contains the leading word "irrigate"). Few ancient societies devoted much attention to limiting their ecological "footprint," making D improbable.

14. **(D)** Answer B applies to Carthage, but not to Athens, and while Athens resisted Persia, neither fought Assyria. They were both great naval powers, making D correct. Gupta India emerged long after Athens's peak.

15. **(C)** Although the Andeans harvested food from the sea, they were not sea traders nor were the majority—who lived in the mountains or mountain valleys—fishermen, and so A and D are wrong. Outright slavery was not widespread, but the mit'a system, especially with the passage of time, obliged ayllu clans to labor on behalf of the upper classes.

16. **(A)** Many factors may have played a role in the Mayan collapse, but D is not thought to be among them, and B reverses the direction of the bubonic plague's spread. The Americas' geographic isolation kept C from being true, with the tragic result being that indigenous Americans were devastated upon their first encounter with Eurasian diseases. Smallpox may have some role in causing Han China's downfall.

17. **(B)** Slash-and-burn farming is one of the most primitive methods known to early agriculturalists. All other answers list intensive methods, which seek to maximize crop yield within a given area.

18. **(B)** Emerging in the Middle East, the dhow was sturdy enough and carried a sail of the right shape (lateen) to cross open ocean water. It was a vessel of commerce, not of war, and it was used primarily in the Indian Ocean, not the Pacific—or at least not far out. Galleys continued to be used in the Mediterranean and elsewhere for centuries after the dhow emerged. Each ship was useful in its own context.

19. **(C)** No society had the means to build Roman- or Persian-like roads across the entire expanse of Eurasia, making A wrong. Answer D applies more to maritime travel, and no state or institution had the wherewithal to impose a single currency over such a wide expanse. The versatile camel was able to carry large loads over different terrains and in a wide variety of weather conditions, making it ideal for most sections of the Silk Road.

20. **(C)** As the only city located in Africa, Alexandria would have been the most directly connected with the trade coming up from beyond the Sahara.

UNIT THREE

REGIONAL AND TRANSREGIONAL INTERACTIONS (600–1450)

Unit Overview

GENERAL REMARKS

Between 600 and 1450, newer world civilizations matured, largely on the foundations of older cultures that had collapsed or faded away. This was also an age when world civilizations came into ever-increasing contact with each other.

Many of the world's **classical civilizations** failed or fell into decline between the 200s and 600s C.E., including the Roman Empire (with the Greek influence it had kept alive), Han China, and India's Mauryan and Gupta empires. The same process continued up to about 1000 C.E., as other societies considered "classical"—such as Tang China, Heian Japan, and the Abbasid Caliphate—weakened or collapsed.

New civilizations were created on the foundations of these classical cultures. In some cases, as in Europe after the fall of Rome, a lengthy period of backwardness, decentralization, and chaos followed the collapse of a classical civilization. In others, as in China, the transition was less traumatic or lasted a shorter time. Whatever the case, sophisticated, advanced cultures—many of them building on the legacy left behind by classical predecessors—appeared throughout the world during the period between 600 and 1450.

One important historical question is whether these civilizations are best studied as **nation-states** (countries as formally defined political entities, in the modern sense of the word) or **cultural units** (defined less by political boundaries, and more by shared traditions, religion, ethnicity, government by a larger imperial or regional authority, and sometimes language). Examples of the latter include the Islamic world, European Christendom, sub-Saharan Africa, and Mesoamerica.

In many parts of the world, **increased productive capacity** became the economic norm. Another general trend was the continued growth of **networks of communication and exchange** between world cultures. Although the Americas remained isolated, vibrant systems of interaction appeared among the civilizations of Africa, Europe, the Middle East, Central Asia, Southeast Asia, and the Far East. Trade, religious influence, technological, and cultural exchange all marked this era. **Diaspora communities**, **migration**, and the **movement of nomadic peoples**, such as the Vikings, Bantu, Polynesians, and Mongols, greatly affected settled societies. (A key question is how nomadic movement as a cause of historical change compares to the importance of cities during this period.) Even though the world was not as joined together as it would later become—with the Europeans' encounter with the Americas and greater improvements in communications and transport technology—extensive systems of global interaction were emerging between 1000 and 1450.

BROAD TRENDS

Humans and the Environment

- The Americas remained cut off environmentally and culturally from Afro-Eurasia.
- Nomadic and migratory populations (especially the Vikings, Mongols, Bantu, and Polynesians) continued to have a profound impact on large parts of the world.
- Massive epidemics (pandemics) struck Eurasia. Most famous was the wave of bubonic plague that swept China, the Middle East, and Europe (the "black death") in the 1300s.
- Human impact on the environment increased dramatically as a result of population growth and the greater capacity of advanced societies to carry out large-scale engineering projects.
- The increased scale of agriculture heightened the risks of soil erosion, deforestation, and other forms of major environmental damage.
- Increased trade activity spread plants and foodstuffs, including bananas, rice, cotton, sugar, and fruits, far from their point of origin.
- A global warming trend, often called the medieval climatic optimum, lasted between 800 and 1300, greatly affecting the patterns of migration, agricultural life, and interregional trade.
- Between the late 1200s and the early 1500s, a cooling trend began, leading to the so-called Little Ice Age, which persisted until the early- to mid-1800s.

Development and Interaction of Cultures

- The societies of Afro-Eurasia expanded and intensified their networks of communications and exchange.
- Distinct artistic and cultural traditions developed in each major region of the world. They often drew from and/or influenced neighboring traditions.
- A new religion, Islam, was born in the Middle East and rapidly spread throughout Afro-Eurasia.
- The civilizations possessing the greatest degree of scientific knowledge and cultural sophistication were China, the Middle East, Japan, and Muslim Spain.
- Europe underwent great cultural development, especially during the Renaissance.
- China and India exerted tremendous cultural and religious influence over their neighbors. Buddhism, Hinduism, and art and architectural styles spread from these countries to Southeast Asia, Korea, Japan, Tibet, and elsewhere.
- The Middle East played a large role in spreading knowledge, scholarship, music, art, and architecture to North Africa and Europe. Middle Eastern cultural influence on medieval and Renaissance Europe was considerable.
- Travelers and explorers created links between societies and increased geographical and cultural awareness. Examples include Zheng He, Marco Polo, and Ibn Battuta.

- Certain languages attained regional status, either because of their cultural preeminence, their usefulness as languages of learning, or their suitability as a lingua franca for trade.
- The invention of block printing in China (perhaps in Korea) began to alter cultural life not only in Asia, but elsewhere, as this new innovation spread.
- Even more dramatically, the invention of the movable-type printing press in Europe during the 1430s led to an information explosion, the rapid spread of knowledge and ideas, and a revolution in intellectual life.

State-Building, Expansion, and Conflict

- Most forms of government remained non-representative. Monarchies and oligarchies were the most common. A few nations placed formal restrictions on the power of the monarch—concrete legal systems or lawmaking bodies that shared governmental authority—and still remained centralized. England, with its Magna Carta and Parliament, is a prime example.
- Many states were not nations in the modern sense of the word. Many were decentralized. Others were multicultural empires joined only by the fact that a single authority had conquered them all. Feudalism became a common form of political (and economic) organization in decentralized areas. Well-known examples are medieval Europe and the Japanese shogunates.
- Cities played a larger role in the political life of most cultures.
- The most politically advanced and influential civilizations during these years were China and the Ottoman Empire. Nations of medieval Europe, particularly in the west, gained in power and sophistication. Some major states, such as Mali, Ghana, Great Zimbabwe, the Delhi Sultanate, the Aztecs, and the Incas, flourished, but for a comparatively short time.
- During the 1200s and 1300s, the Mongols radically altered the power equation in Eurasia. Their empire, one of the largest in history, brought together vast portions of Europe and Asia. For a time, the Mongols imposed not just political unity but a measure of economic and cultural connectedness not seen since the days of ancient Rome or Han China.
- The invention and diffusion of gunpowder technology started to change the balance of world power.

Economic Systems

- Transregional trade was practiced on a massive scale. The most important trade networks centered on the Mediterranean, the cities of the Hanseatic League, the Silk Road, trans-Saharan caravan routes, the gold-rich Niger River, the Indo-Persian sphere, the Indian Ocean, and the Pacific.
- Along far-reaching trade routes, diasporic communities and foreign enclaves formed in many towns and ports.
- More state institutions, such as mints and customs agencies, emerged to regulate trade and commerce.
- Commerce and banking developed to support trade and the general economic life of advanced societies.

- Certain cities became important centers for interregional trade. They include Venice, Cairo, Mombasa, Zanzibar, Samarkand, Canton (Guangzhou), Malacca (Melaka), Timbuktu, and Calicut.
- Interregional trade was facilitated by the warmer weather of the medieval climatic optimum and then affected by the global cooling that led to the Little Ice Age.

Social Structures

- Most societies remained fundamentally agricultural. The vast majority of people resided in the countryside and made their living by farming.
- Artisanry and craftsmanship, however, were becoming increasingly important. Many in these professions formed guilds or similar societies.
- Urbanization, or the growth of cities, became a slow but steady trend.
- The growing importance of trade and commerce made merchant classes larger and more influential.
- Places that were more urbanized, and whose economies were based more on trade and commerce, tended to enjoy less stratification and more social mobility.
- Many forms of coerced labor, such as slavery and serfdom, persisted, and new ones emerged.
- Unrest caused by unfair treatment of workers or peasants became more common in various parts of the world.
- Patriarchalism continued to be the norm, but women's roles came to vary more from society to society. Women's political rights were minimal or nonexistent, and they had sharply defined occupational roles, confined to childbearing, homemaking, and low-status jobs such as weaving, food gathering, farm chores, and domestic servitude.
- In most places, however, women had at least some freedoms and rights (which might include the right to divorce abusive husbands, the right to a dowry, or the right to inherit and own property). They also tended to play informal but important roles as they managed households and family finances, supervised the education of children, and influenced their husbands.
- In most societies, upper-class women lived easier lives but found themselves more constrained by religious and cultural restrictions on their behavior. Lower-class women, whose lives were much harder, were often less bound by such restrictions because the rules of "proper" behavior applied less to them.

QUESTIONS AND COMPARISONS TO CONSIDER

- Differences and likenesses of various global and interregional trading networks.
- Differences and likenesses among systems of labor organization, both free and coerced.
- What roles did environmental factors, such as the medieval climatic optimum and the Little Ice Age, play in social and economic development? What about diseases?

- Intellectual and cultural developments in different societies, and the ways in which societies influence each other. Good examples include the Middle Eastern influence on medieval Europe (both during the Crusades and at other times, like the Renaissance), India's influence on Southeast Asia, the mutual influence between Tang China and the Abbasid Caliphate (or between China and its neighbors), and the transfer of technology and knowledge throughout the Mongol Empire during the "pax Mongolica."
- Pay attention to explorers, travelers, and diasporic communities as agents of cultural diffusion and change.
- The methods and techniques that powerful states and empires used to administer their lands and project power effectively. How did they legitimate their power?
- How did new technology affect warfare during these years? Travel? Agriculture? Other aspects of life?
- How important is the nation-state, as opposed to larger cultural units, as an object of study during this historical period?
- Consider the role of nomadic movement as a cause of change (environmental, social, political) during these years. Do the same for the growth of cities.
- Examine major migratory movements during this period and their various effects.
- What roles did religions play in political development? Especially in areas that attempted to create large, multinational civilizations united by religion, such as Christendom or the Islamic caliphates.

Europe During the Middle Ages and the Renaissance

- The medieval period (Middle Ages)
- Feudalism and serfdom
- Roman Catholicism and the ideal of Christendom
- Formation of European states
- The Crusades
- Trade, commerce, and urbanization
- The Black Death (bubonic plague)
- Aristotle and Greco-Latin learning
- Scholasticism
- The movable-type (Gutenberg) printing press
- The Renaissance (classicism and humanism)

The medieval period of European history, also known as the **Middle Ages**, lasted from approximately 500 to 1500. The question of periodization is complicated by the fact that from the 1200s onward, certain parts of Europe—particularly Italy—began to experience the famous cultural rebirth known as the **Renaissance**.

The years from 500 to 1000 were a time of political decentralization and overall backwardness. From 1000 to 1300, Europe enjoyed a general revival. Nations became better defined, the economy grew healthier, and the level of technological and cultural knowledge improved. The concept of Europe as a single civilization joined by a common cultural heritage and the Christian religion took greater shape during these years.

The period between 1300 and 1500 was a complex one, marked by crisis and advancement. On one hand, Europe was struck by social unrest, constant warfare, and, in the form of the so-called Black Death, one of the worst epidemics in world history. On the other hand, the Renaissance began, ushering in a period of artistic and intellectual achievement.

FEUDALISM AND THE MANOR SYSTEM

The Origins of Feudalism

In the aftermath of Rome's fall, Europe became politically decentralized. No single ruler was strong enough to provide Europe with central authority, and monarchs typically did not have the power, money, or military strength to govern their lands effectively. The solution was the system of **feudalism**, in which lords and monarchs awarded land to loyal followers. In exchange, these followers guaranteed that their

parcels of land (fiefs) would be governed, that law and justice would be dispensed, that crops would be grown, and that the land itself would be protected. Feudalism remained at the heart of medieval European politics for centuries.

Feudal Nobility, the Manor System, and Serfdom

The retainers to whom monarchs gave large land grants developed into Europe's **noble** (or **aristocratic**) **class**. The feudal nobility were supposed to help provide political leadership.

The feudal nobility also served a military function. One of feudalism's goals was to provide an army of foot soldiers (recruited by nobles) and an elite force of armored cavalry (**knights**) formed by the nobles themselves. According to the code of **chivalry**, the knight was to be a virtuous, Christian warrior. Songs and legends, such as those of King Arthur's Round Table, provided examples of how real-life knights were supposed to conduct themselves. Chivalry did restrain the knight's most violent behavior, but in actuality, the code was often broken.

Economically, the feudal system relied on the labor of peasants. Most peasants in Europe during the Middle Ages were **serfs**. Although serfs were not technically slaves, they were legally unfree. They were not allowed to change residence or profession without permission. A portion of their own crops and livestock had to be given to the lord. In addition, serfs had to spend a certain number of days per month fulfilling various labor obligations. Overall, living conditions were harsh.

A Medieval Tournament.
The military and political backbone of medieval Europe's feudal system was the knight. High-born and trained from youth in cavalry warfare, the knight was the state-of-the-art warrior of his era. Knights also made up Europe's noble class. Knights honed their military skills—and cultivated the arts of chivalry—at tournaments such as the one portrayed here.

THE IDEAL OF CHRISTENDOM

The Unifying Influence of Christianity

One of the few things binding European nations together following the fall of Rome was the Christian faith, which acted as a unifying force throughout the continent, both culturally and politically.

Rome itself was one of the two major headquarters of Christian worship. The other was Constantinople, capital of the Byzantine Empire. By 1054, doctrinal differences and geographical distance led to the Great Schism, which separated Christians into two churches: **Roman Catholicism** and **Eastern Orthodoxy**. The former was dominant in central and western Europe; the latter was prominent in the Middle East and the Greek and Slavic parts of eastern Europe.

The Catholic Church shaped medieval society in key ways. Its monasteries preserved Latin and Greek manuscripts, containing a wealth of information, left over from the Roman era. The church also provided the people of Europe with a sense that, despite national and linguistic differences, they were linked by a single faith. This gave a much-needed feeling of cultural cohesion at a time of extreme decentralization.

The Medieval Papacy and the Political Power of the Catholic Church

The leader of the Catholic Church was the pope. At the lowest level was the priest, who served the needs of an individual community. Only men could become priests. Above the priest were bishops, archbishops, and cardinals. Also part of the church hierarchy were monks and nuns.

After 1000, the Catholic Church became immensely powerful politically. The pope governed a sizable territory in central Italy, the Papal States. The popes had moral authority and the right to determine what was **heresy**, exclude worshippers from the Catholic Church (**excommunication**), and issue calls for holy wars (**crusades**). The ultimate goal of medieval popes was to join the nations of Europe into a single Christian community. Referred to as **Christendom**, this community was to be governed by the pope, with kings and emperors subject to his rule. The Catholic Church never realized this ideal, but for several hundred years, the popes heavily influenced how European monarchs ruled their countries.

The Catholic Church owned vast amounts of land. Combined with its right to collect tithes from the general population, this made the church very wealthy. Another way the church exercised worldly power was control over education, thought, and culture. In 1231, the **Holy Inquisition**, a set of special courts with wide-ranging powers, was established to hunt out and punish heresy and religious nonconformity.

THE WESTERN MONARCHIES AND THE EASTERN FRONTIER

Early Kingdoms and the Carolingian Empire

It took several centuries after the fall of Rome for stable nations to form. Short-lived kingdoms, founded by warlords and barbarian chiefs, rose and fell frequently during the 500s and 600s. Internally, decentralization kept states weak, as did external threats such as Viking raids and Muslim invasions.

One of the earliest European nations was the Frankish kingdom, which, by the 700s, grew into the Carolingian Empire. The Frankish military leader Charles

NOTE

Most institutions of learning were connected in one way or another with the Catholic Church. It was dangerous for any scholar or artist to write, say, or produce anything counter to Catholic doctrine.

Martel successfully turned back Muslim invaders at the **Battle of Tours** (732), one of the most influential battles of the medieval era. Charles Martel established the Carolingian dynasty, and his son Pepin strengthened the kingdom's ties with the Catholic Church.

Even more successful as a nation-building monarch was Pepin's son **Charlemagne** (768–814), whose name means "Charles the Great." Charlemagne defended Frankish territory against Viking, barbarian, and Muslim attacks. He greatly expanded the kingdom, becoming the Holy Roman Emperor in 800. He actively supported education and culture, much of which he entrusted to the church.

Other early nations emerged in the late 800s and 900s. Saxon kings united large parts of England. The Capetian dynasty came to rule the area around Paris and gradually gained control over more of France. The eastern, Germanic portion of Charlemagne's realm reformed itself as the Holy Roman Empire, which ruled most of central Europe for centuries to come.

The Vikings

NOTE

By forcing nations such as England, France, and the Holy Roman Empire to defend against their attacks, the Vikings (though not on purpose) prompted those nations to centralize more than they had during the early medieval period.

An important factor shaping the development of early medieval European nations was the appearance of the **Vikings**, expert sailors and fierce warriors from Scandinavia. Owing mainly to overcrowding in their homelands, large numbers of Vikings poured out of the north from the 800s through the 1100s. One of the few peoples of this era who could navigate on the open ocean, the Vikings, in their long-boats, raided and conquered land throughout most of coastal Europe, as far south as the Mediterranean.

The Vikings colonized Iceland and Greenland. Around 1000 C.E., voyagers led by Leif Eriksson reached what is today Canada. The Vikings also settled in parts of England, Scotland, and Ireland. They created long-lasting kingdoms in northwestern France and Sicily. A group of Vikings established a trade route from Scandinavia to Byzantium, through Russia. In the process, they created the first Russian state.

England and France

In the west, the most stable states were England and France. For four centuries, the political leadership of both countries was intertwined. In 1066, Normans (descendants of Vikings who had settled in France) led by William the Conqueror, invaded England, defeated the Saxon king, and established their rule there. Because William and his successors were connected to the French throne by blood ties and feudal obligations, there was much competition between England and France over land and political legitimacy until the middle of the 1400s.

The **Norman Conquest** brought French-style feudalism to England and helped create a rich cultural fusion, not only Celtic and Anglo-Saxon but also Latin-based, in the British Isles. By medieval standards, England became quite centralized, and it did so despite the fact that significant checks were put on the power of the king. (Normally, the less powerful the monarch, the less centralized the state.) In 1215, the **Magna Carta**, imposed on the king by his barons, guaranteed the nobility certain rights and privileges, limiting the monarch's might. Later in the 1200s, the English nobility won the right to form a **Parliament**, which eventually became a

representative lawmaking body that governed in conjunction with the king. In the 1200s and 1300s, English monarchs extended their rule to Wales and Scotland. Ireland would follow later.

In France, the Capetian kings centralized their nation by increasing their own power (the typical route to premodern nation building). Originally, the Capetians ruled only a tiny part of France. England controlled large territories, such as Aquitaine and Brittany, while large and economically important regions such as Flanders and Burgundy remained independent. Generations of Capetian monarchs expanded the size of the French kingdom, beat the English in a number of wars (including the Hundred Years' War), and gained control over Burgundy and other stubborn regions. By the mid-to-late 1400s, France was large and centralized, and the French kings were among the most powerful in Europe. Unlike their English counterparts, French monarchs were not limited or obligated to share power in any legally meaningful way.

The political event that most affected England and France during the fourteenth and fifteenth centuries was the **Hundred Years' War** (1337–1453). The war's first years coincided with the onset of other European crises, including social uprisings and the Black Death. Until the early 1400s, the English won a number of victories, gaining control over more than half of France. Only after the 1420s did the French king, helped by the warrior maid Joan of Arc, drive the English out. The war ended most of the awkward connections between the French and English royal families.

The Holy Roman Empire and Italian States: Decentralization

Important states formed in central and southern Europe, but they were less centralized. Dominating the middle of Europe was the Holy Roman Empire, a multicultural monarchy founded in the 900s by the heirs of Charlemagne. Its name was inspired by the theoretical ideal of a state that was large and powerful ("Roman") and brought a variety of peoples into a single Catholic ("holy") community. The emperor was supposed to work in partnership with the pope, but in real life, the two clashed more than they cooperated.

The Holy Roman Empire was large, but the emperor's powers were comparatively weak. His position was not hereditary—he was chosen by the empire's most powerful noble families. The empire's population was ethnically diverse (German, Italian, Hungarian, Slavic, and more), and the empire itself consisted of dozens of duchies, kingdoms, and principalities (almost 200 in the mid-1300s). A key centralizing factor was the rise of the **Habsburg** family, which gained permanent control over the imperial throne from 1438 until 1918.

Even more decentralized than the Holy Roman Empire was Italy, not an actual country at this time. Most of northern Italy was under the Holy Roman Empire's control, and many southern areas passed in and out of the hands of other foreigners, including the French, Spanish, Muslims, and Byzantines. The parts of Italy that remained free were governed by dozens of city-states; Italy was one of the most urbanized parts of Europe, with a high cultural level that made it the birthplace of the Renaissance. Italy's position in the Mediterranean—which enabled trade with the

NOTE

Victory over the English helped the French kings to centralize their power at home.

NOTE

From the 1300s onward, the Holy Roman Empire served as Europe's military bulwark against the long wave of Turkish attacks from the east.

Middle East and Egypt (and, by extension, the Far East, China, and the Indian Ocean)—allowed its cities to develop strong commercial economies. The chief city-states of medieval and Renaissance Italy were Florence, Milan, and Venice in the north, and Naples in the south. Also important was Rome, the heart of the Papal States.

Spain and Portugal

The medieval development of Spain and Portugal was shaped above all by the fact that they had been taken over by Muslim invaders, known as the Moors, during the 700s. From 1031 onward, the people of Spain and Portugal fought the Moors in a long struggle known as the **Reconquista**. By the end of the 1200s, the Spanish had pushed the Moors into Granada, the southernmost part of the country. For the next 200 years, the Moors held out there, until they were expelled completely in 1492, by the armies of Ferdinand and Isabella.

The effects of the Moors and the war against them were many. Spanish territory was liberated gradually, and each newly freed region remained independent, delaying centralization. By the 1400s, there were about half a dozen Spanish kingdoms, not counting Portugal. Only late in the 1400s, when the rulers of the two largest kingdoms, **Ferdinand of Aragón** and **Isabella of Castile**, married and joined their lands together, did Spain take shape as a single country. Another result of the Reconquista was intense religious intolerance. The war caused Catholic authorities in Spain to be extremely rigid in terms of doctrine and hostile to nonbelievers. Muslims and Jews (whom the Moors had welcomed to Spain) were persecuted, and, by the end of the 1400s, forced to convert to Catholicism or leave the country.

The Moorish presence brought benefits as well. Islamic culture was more advanced than that of medieval Europe, so Spain was able to take advantage of the medical, scientific, and technological knowledge brought there by the Muslim conquerors (as well as the Jewish scholars and professionals who came with them). The Spanish city of **Córdoba** was one of Europe's greatest centers of learning and science, thanks to the long-standing Muslim presence there.

Portugal, an independent principality, began its tradition of world exploration during the 1400s, starting a trend that would sweep the globe. (For more, see Chapter 15.)

NOTE

Spanish art and architecture were also affected by the Moorish style, elements of which still persist today.

Byzantium and Eastern Europe

The farther east, the less centralized European nations became, with the exception of the Byzantine Empire, the crossroads between Christian Europe and the Islamic Middle East. **Constantinople** was a tremendously important trading center, linking Mediterranean Europe with the Middle East and, by extension, the overland routes (such as the Silk Road) and sea lanes that joined the Middle East with China, India, and the East Indies.

Although Byzantium was superior to the rest of Europe in terms of economic and cultural advancement, it entered a long period of political and military decline. In the eleventh century, a new enemy, the Seljuk Turks, appeared on the eastern frontier. From the Battle of Manzikert (1071) onward, the Seljuks, then their more dangerous

successors, the Ottoman Turks, slowly but unceasingly stripped territory away from Byzantium. By the 1400s, Constantinople itself was under threat; in 1453, the Ottomans seized it. The Byzantine Empire was destroyed, the Turks made Constantinople their capital, and the Ottoman Empire went on to conquer large parts of southeastern Europe, clashing for centuries with the Holy Roman (Austrian) Empire.

Territories on Europe's eastern and northern fringe tended to be more poorly defined, politically speaking. Much of this had to do with the stress of invasions from the east. Mongol attacks in the mid-1200s and constant pressure from the Ottomans during and after the 1400s took their toll and, in many ways, held back the political development of nations. Countries such as Hungary, Sweden, and Poland were exceptions: they were stable and sophisticated for the time being. More typical were the Russian lands, farther to the east. During most of the medieval era, Russia was a loose confederation of city-states, governed by constantly feuding princes. The Mongol invasions of the 1240s placed the Russians under the domination of the Golden Horde; not until the mid-1400s did Russia become free. Only after that did a Russian nation begin to take shape, under the leadership of the tsars of Moscow.

THE CRUSADES

The Concept and Origin of Crusading

Among the powers of the medieval popes was the ability to request monarchs to provide troops and money for holy wars known as **crusades**. Crusades were fought for a number of reasons: to convert nonbelievers to Catholicism, to crush Christian movements the papacy considered heretical (infamous crusades of this type were fought in southern France during the early 1200s), and to resist attacks by foreigners who were not Christian (especially Muslims).

Many underlying factors motivated the Crusades:

- Genuine religious fervor on the part of both Muslims and Christians
- Geopolitical conflict between Europe and the Middle East
- The Europeans' desire to become more involved in the international trade network stretching from the Mediterranean to China
- Personal ambitions of Europeans hoping to gain wealth and land in the Middle East
- Racial and religious prejudice

The Crusading Experience

The spark of the **First Crusade** (1096–1099) came in 1095, when the Byzantine Empire asked fellow Christians in Europe for military assistance against the Seljuk Turks, who had recently captured Jerusalem. To increase their chances of receiving aid, the Byzantines exaggerated rumors of Turkish atrocities in the Holy Land. Pope Urban II responded by summoning the **Council of Clermont** and calling upon the knights of Catholic Europe to retake the Holy Land from the Turks. In 1096, a massive army of Crusaders traveled to Constantinople, then through the Middle East,

NOTE

The best-known crusades, and the ones generally referred to when the term "the Crusades" is used, are those fought by European Catholics against the Muslims of the Middle East and North Africa from 1095 to 1291.

fighting Muslim forces along the way. In the summer of 1099, they reached Jerusalem and placed it under siege. After taking the city, the Crusaders, in one of the bloodiest episodes in military history, butchered almost every Muslim and Jew within its walls (as well as a number of native Christians whom they mistook for Muslims). A key reason for the First Crusade's success was lack of unity among Turks, Arabs, and other Muslim peoples.

After the First Crusade, the Europeans established four Christian states known as the Latin Kingdoms. While they lasted, these served as a military and political foothold in the Middle East. They also enabled Europeans to become involved in the lucrative commercial economy that made the region so wealthy.

The Christians maintained their presence in the Middle East for two centuries. However, the Muslims united their efforts in order to expel the Europeans. The many crusades that followed were generally responses to successful Muslim campaigns. Jerusalem, for example, fell under Muslim control again in 1187. Especially after 1200, European crusades lost their focus (the Fourth Crusade of 1202–1204 turned into a sack of Christian Constantinople) or failed miserably (like the ill-fated Children's Crusades). In 1291, the Europeans abandoned their last major outpost in the Middle East.

Effects of the Crusades

Long-term effects of the Crusades include the worsening of the relationship between the Muslim and Christian worlds. Also important was the greater awareness of the wider world, especially the lands of the east, that the Crusades stimulated among the Europeans. Along with this came an increased knowledge of—and desire for—the economic wealth to be gained by greater interaction with the Middle and Far East. Moreover, the crusading ideal—the notion that Christian warriors were fighting a holy war on behalf of a sacred cause—contributed to the powerful myth of knighthood and chivalry that emerged in Europe during the Middle Ages. There was also technology transfer, as Europeans learned much about castle architecture from their experience in the Middle East.

URBANIZATION, TRADE, AND SOCIETY

While the early medieval era was a time of social and economic backwardness, significant gains were made between 1000 and 1500. However, the period after 1300 was a time of social crisis as well.

Population Growth, Trade, and Commerce

From 1000 to 1300, population growth in Europe was considerable. Advanced agricultural techniques—such as the three-field system of crop rotation and the invention of better plows—caused the food supply to increase.

Trade and commerce became a larger part of the European economy. Political stability made **banking**, the movement of goods, and the creation of **markets** safer and more convenient. Because the movement of goods was easier by water than by land, **trade routes** tended to follow rivers and coastlines. One major network, centered on

Italy, sprang up throughout the Mediterranean, and did much to connect Europe with the commerce of the Middle and Far East. The Crusades did much to stimulate this. Other important networks formed along the Rhine River, in the North Sea and English Channel, and throughout the Baltic Sea. Trade in the Baltic was dominated by the **Hanseatic League**, a group whose influence stretched from England in the west to Russia in the east. The relatively new practice of banking made trade more feasible and dependable. Powerful banking houses were run by the Medicis in Italy and the Fuggers in central Europe.

European Trade Routes During the Late Medieval Period and the Renaissance.
European desire for more direct access to the goods of East and South Asia prompted the great wave of exploration that began during the 1400s and continued during the 1500s and 1600s.

Urbanization

Another social trend was **urbanization**. Although the majority of people in medieval Europe remained in the countryside, working as peasants and serfs, an increasingly large number were moving to cities. Existing cities grew larger, and new cities were founded at a great rate. Some parts of Europe, particularly Italy and Flanders, urbanized more quickly than others.

Cities were excellent sites for trade. They attracted artists, writers, and scholars. The growth of cities also encouraged specialization of labor. Most skilled trades in medieval cities were organized according to the **guild system**. Guilds were labor groups that maintained a monopoly on their respective trades. They restricted membership, established prices, set standards of quality and fair practice, and provided pensions.

Cities were often overcrowded and polluted, and many people lived in poverty. There were benefits to city life, however, including cultural opportunities and the chance to gain greater wealth. A key advantage was immunity from feudal obligations, especially serfdom: typically, if a person left the countryside and lived in a city for a year and a day, he or she was released from status as a serf, as reflected in the popular saying, "city air makes you free."

Social Stress and Black Death in the Late Medieval Period

Although trade and urbanization continued to expand, social stress increased after 1300. A wave of uprisings swept Europe from the early 1300s through the early 1500s, including the peasant Jacquerie of 1358 in France, the Wool Carders' Revolt in Florence, in 1378, and, in 1381, Wat Tyler's Rebellion in England. The causes of such disturbances were many. A general cooling of the climate, referred to by environmental historians as the Little Ice Age, affected harvests and made life in the countryside difficult. More wars were being fought, armies were growing larger, and the new gunpowder weaponry of the day was extremely expensive. More peasants were forced into military service (especially during the Hundred Years' War). The taxes of common people also increased. During the last half of the 1400s, religious disagreements and dissatisfaction with the Church sometimes led to rebellion.

Another manifestation of social stress was a sharp rise in the persecution of people thought to be witches. Catholic authorities sought to root out suspected **witchcraft**, issuing a manual in the late 1400s, *The Hammer of Witchcraft*, to aid in spotting and trying witches. Ordinary people were caught up in the hysteria as well. Most of the victims of witch hunts were women.

Social trauma also came in the form of the **Black Death**, the popular name for the bubonic plague. The arrival of bubonic plague in the mid-fourteenth century ranks as one of the greatest medical disasters in Eurasian history. After killing millions of people in China, the disease traveled westward to the Middle East. It reached Europe in 1347 on a ship landing in Sicily.

In 1347 and 1348, the plague ravaged southern Europe. By 1349 and 1350, it spread to central Europe and the British Isles; it was felt in Russia and Scandinavia from 1351 to 1353. The disease's deadliness and rapid spread caused tremendous panic throughout Europe. This initial bout of the plague killed 25 to 30 million people, roughly one-third the population of Europe. For centuries afterward, the plague recurred periodically in Europe (although no attack was as bad as the first).

Women in Medieval Europe

As a rule, women were subservient to men in all parts of Europe during these years. How much freedom or how many rights a woman enjoyed depended mainly on her social status.

Women of lower classes cared for the household and assisted with farmwork. They bore children and raised them. Women of low birth also worked as servants for upper-class families. One of the few peasant women to leave an individual mark on medieval Europe was the French war leader **Joan of Arc** (ca. 1410–1431).

In most parts of medieval Europe, women had some property rights. They could own and inherit land and property. They often received dowries (although in some places and times, it was the woman's family that had to provide a dowry to the husband-to-be). Women could separate from their husbands, although obtaining divorces and annulments was difficult, especially for women of the upper classes. Women had protection, but not equality, before the law.

Women could enter religious life; they could not become priests in either the Catholic or Orthodox Church, but they could become nuns. The majority of nuns

NOTE

Many people saw the plague as a sign that the world was coming to an end; others accused Jews of poisoning or bewitching Christians and persecuted them harshly.

NOTE

In this era of poor hygiene and limited medical knowledge, many women—as many as 10 to 15 percent—died in childbirth.

were from the landed aristocracy. To marry off daughters, noble families had to provide potential husbands with land, money, or a title; an aristocratic family with many daughters was often unable to pay for all of them to get married, and a common solution was to place younger daughters in convents. Women who preferred intellectual pursuits sometimes found safe haven as nuns. For example, **Hildegard of Bingen** (1098–1179), celebrated for her mystical writings and songs, became abbess of a German convent.

Aristocratic women, while not legally the equal of men, could exert informal political and cultural influence. If an aristocratic woman was heir to rich property or a kingdom, she was a desirable match. Noblewomen often managed their husbands' estates and financial accounts. Frequently, the mothers of young kings whose fathers died early served as regents and advisers until their sons came of age.

Some women ruled in their own right, as queens. This situation was not common, and countries whose legal systems were based on tribal Germanic (Salic) law, such as France and the Holy Roman Empire, did not allow women to inherit thrones. However, women would come to rule England, parts of Spain, Russia, and elsewhere. The most famous example of a politically important woman during the Middle Ages was **Eleanor of Aquitaine** (ca. 1122–1204). A dynamic, intelligent woman, Eleanor married Louis VII of France and then Henry II of England. She had much influence over politics in both countries. She was also a great patron of art and music.

MEDIEVAL CULTURE

For many years, it was traditional to view the medieval period as the Dark Ages, an era lacking in culture or sophistication. More recently, it has become standard to recognize the richness of medieval culture, especially during the High and Late Middle Ages. Even so, medieval Europe lagged behind Byzantium and the Islamic world in terms of cultural attainment.

Catholicism and Classicism as Influences on Medieval Culture

The most important factor shaping medieval culture was the Catholic Church, which administered institutions of learning (monasteries, then universities) and was the largest employer of artists, architects, and musicians. Art and ideas that were not in line with church doctrine could be banned—and could lead to severe punishment.

Another influence on medieval culture was the classical learning and literature preserved from ancient Greece and Rome. During the Middle Ages (and long afterward), **Latin** was Europe's language of learning and culture. (Europeans had much less knowledge of Greek until later, when Arab and Jewish translators made materials in that language more accessible.) Medieval scientific thought was dominated by the theories of the ancient Greeks, mainly through Latin translations. Of special importance was **Aristotle**, whose writings on science, philosophy, ethics, and politics were adapted by Christian scholars and placed at the center of the medieval worldview. Greek science taught the Europeans much, but it also encouraged some mistaken ideas, especially the **geocentric theory**, which argues that the sun revolves around the earth.

NOTE

Ironically, Aristotle had written about **the scientific method** (in which hypotheses have to be tested by observation and experiment), but medieval Europeans tended to ignore this part of his thinking and accepted most Greek science, errors included, as unquestioned fact.

Eventually, increased familiarity of European artists and scholars with Greek and Roman texts helped give birth to the Renaissance.

Art, Architecture, and Literature

Most medieval art was religious in nature. Icons, or religious paintings, were largely inspired by Byzantine styles, even in Catholic Europe. Early church music was mainly plainsong (also known as Gregorian chant): human voices unaccompanied by instruments. Over time, arrangements became more complex, and instruments were used by the end of the Middle Ages. The greatest achievement of medieval architecture was the cathedral, which required skill, money, and decades to build.

In the secular sphere, the medieval Europeans were great builders of castles, although many were modeled on Byzantine and Middle Eastern designs. Troubadours and minstrels appeared in the eleventh and twelfth centuries and popularized nonreligious music. Favorite songs were about love, as well as legends of King Arthur, Charlemagne's knight Roland, and El Cid of Spain.

One trend encouraged by troubadours and minstrels—then later authors like Dante Alighieri of Italy (1265–1321), the English poet Geoffrey Chaucer (1340–1401), and Christine de Pisan (1364–1410), who wrote in French and Italian—was the increased use of native, or **vernacular**, languages. Although Latin remained the language of the educated elite, it became more acceptable to write serious poetic and literary works in the vernacular. This stimulated a growth in literacy and made literature available to a wider range of people.

Cathedral of Notre Dame, Paris, France.
One of the best-known landmarks of Paris, the Cathedral of Notre Dame provides a quintessential example of the Gothic style of church architecture.

The Printing Press

In the late 1430s, a new invention revolutionized European culture and the intellectual life of the entire world. This was the printing press developed by German inventor **Johannes Gutenberg**. The concept of printing by carving images and words into blocks of wood had originated in China (perhaps Korea) centuries before, and was known to the Europeans. However, block printing was costly and unwieldy. Gutenberg created a **movable-type printing press**, in which individual, reusable metal characters could be placed in a frame to form text. The printing press raised literacy rates, spread information, increased the impact of new ideas and scientific theories, and encouraged the expansion of libraries and universities. It played an indispensable role in the Renaissance, the Protestant Reformation, and a general explosion of knowledge that transformed Europe and the West for centuries.

THE RENAISSANCE

The Concept of the Renaissance

During the early 1300s, an important cultural and intellectual revival began in parts of southern Europe, especially the city-states of the Italian peninsula. This revival became known as the **Renaissance**, or "rebirth." By the end of the 1400s, it was spreading from Italy to the rest of Europe. It is considered to have lasted until approximately 1600.

As noted previously, it was common until recently to think of the medieval era as a time of minimal cultural advancement. Consequently, the Renaissance was often viewed as a revolution, a sudden explosion of new ideas and learning. Because historians now have a better appreciation of medieval culture, it has become standard to see the Renaissance more as a gradual cultural and intellectual evolution. Nonetheless, it represented a significant change.

The Cultural Outlook of the Renaissance

One of the hallmarks of Renaissance culture was **classicism**: a greater understanding of and admiration for Greco-Roman literature and learning. Of course, medieval Europeans were familiar with this heritage. What changed during the Renaissance was that a greater number of people probed more deeply into Latin sources and, thanks largely to translations provided by Jews and Arabs, the learning of the Greeks.

Renaissance thought was more secular than that of the medieval era. The authors and artists of the Renaissance did not ignore religion; even if they had wanted to, doing so would have been dangerous, thanks to the church's influence. Still, Renaissance writings and artworks placed a greater emphasis on worldly matters.

Similarly, another feature of Renaissance culture was **humanism**, a Greco-Roman concept that went hand-in-hand with the classical revival and Renaissance secularism. Humanism, the conviction that to be human is something to celebrate, ran counter to the church-dominated medieval view that to be human was to be tainted with sin and that worldly life was less important than heavenly afterlife.

Causes of the Renaissance

Why did the Renaissance occur first in Italy? One cause was the urban sophistication of the Italian city-states. Another was the commercial strength of the Italian cities, which generated excess wealth sufficient to support a sustained cultural revival. Italy's success in trade and commerce also gave birth to a class of patrons who, though not always of noble blood, were rich, educated, and eager to improve their status by sponsoring artists and writers. Italy's position as a naval and economic crossroads in the Mediterranean brought it into contact with new ideas and advanced knowledge from the outside world more quickly than the rest of Europe.

Major Figures and Trends of the Renaissance

Important figures in the early Italian Renaissance were the poet Petrarch (1304–1374), the author Giovanni Boccaccio (1313–1375), and the painter Giotto (ca. 1267–1337). As the Renaissance matured, key individuals included the political philosopher Niccolò Machiavelli (1469–1527), the artist and scientist **Leonardo da Vinci** (1452–1519), and the painter and sculptor **Michelangelo** (1472–1564).

Renaissance architects attained a high degree of engineering skill, boosted by a better understanding of mathematics and a deeper knowledge of the techniques of the Greeks and Romans, who had been master builders. Renaissance painters achieved an astonishing level of realism in their work, compared with the art of the medieval era. In painting, as in architecture, increased familiarity with mathematics enabled painters to work out the **laws of perspective**. The result was a convincing depiction of a three-dimensional subject on a two-dimensional surface. Better paints and equipment, the technique of foreshortening, and the effective use of light and shadowing also increased the quality of Renaissance paintings.

The Spread of Renaissance Culture

By the 1400s, the Italian Renaissance was exerting its influence on the rest of Europe. Travelers, especially northern students attending Italian universities, carried with them techniques drawn from the art and literature of the south. The invention of the movable-type printing press in the 1430s dramatically increased the speed and scope by which information could be produced and transmitted throughout Europe, and the printing press deserves much of the credit for spreading the ideals of the Renaissance beyond Italy. The Renaissance took hold in southern France, and then all of France, as well as England, Spain, the Holy Roman Empire, Poland, Hungary, and elsewhere. By the late 1400s, it was possible to speak of a northern Renaissance. This northern Renaissance had a profound impact on the rest of Europe, especially with regard to the religious controversies of the 1500s that led to the Protestant Reformation.

Islam in the Middle East and Africa

- Mohammed
- The Qur'an
- The Sunni-Shiite split
- The Abbasid Caliphate
- Trans-Saharan caravan routes
- The Arab slave trade
- Mali and Timbuktu
- The Seljuk and Ottoman Turks
- The conquest of Constantinople
- Ibn Battuta

Prior to 600 C.E., the dominant civilizations in the Middle East were the Byzantine Empire and Persia. Suddenly, the political and religious landscape of the Middle East was transformed by the appearance of Islam.

During the 600s and 700s, military conquest carried the new faith out of Arabia, where it was born, to Spain and Morocco in the west, and the borderlands of India in the east. The Islamic caliphate aspired to unite all worshippers into a single political community called dar al-Islam (much as popes strove to do in Christian Europe). The golden age of classical Islam lasted from the middle of the 900s to about 1000, and is associated with the Abbasid Caliphate.

Although the Abbasids retained theoretical control over the Islamic world until the Mongol conquest of 1258, their power started to wane before that. Islamic culture remained advanced, but, politically speaking, the years after 1000 were a period of decline.

Another characteristic of these years was political confusion. From 1000 to the 1400s, many Islamic states rose and fell. Other Middle Eastern peoples, such as the Persians and Turks, rivaled the Arabs as forces in the Islamic community. Outside enemies and invaders added to the chaos. Finally, by the end of the fifteenth century and beginning of the sixteenth, the Islamic world—at least the Middle East and North Africa—was reconsolidated under the Ottoman Turks. However, even under the Ottomans, Islam was never again united as it had been under the Abbasids.

MOHAMMED AND THE ORIGINS OF ISLAM

The youngest of the world's major religions, **Islam** transformed itself with amazing speed from a local faith into a cultural and political force of global dimensions. A monotheistic form of worship that originated in the Middle East, Islam is linked with Judaism and Christianity in many ways, and their relationships have frequently been stormy, even tragic. Nonetheless, the three faiths contain many similarities and possess an eventful shared history.

Islam arose in the Arabian Peninsula during the 600s C.E., a time when Arabia was sparsely populated and its desert interior largely unexplored. Arabia's few major settlements were built up around oases and coastal towns serving as centers of the caravan trade that linked the region with the rest of the Middle East. From Arabia, the new religion spread rapidly throughout the eastern Mediterranean. By 1000 C.E., its influence stretched from Spain and Africa's Atlantic coast to the borderlands of India in the east.

The founder of Islam was **Mohammed** (also Muhammad), a merchant from the Arabian town of Mecca. Born in 570 C.E., Mohammed began to meditate in the mountains near Mecca when he turned forty. In 610 C.E., he experienced a profound vision, in which the archangel Jibril (Gabriel to Jews and Christians) is said to have delivered the word of Allah (Arabic for "God") to him. With the help of family members such as Ali (his cousin and son-in-law), Aisha (his favorite wife), and Abu Bakr (Aisha's father), Mohammed preached and gathered a religious community. In 622, he and his followers were forced out of Mecca by local religious authorities and fled to the city of Medina. This flight—the Hegira—marks the beginning of the Islamic calendar. In 630, Mohammed and his followers returned to Mecca and converted the city. In 632, he died, but the religion he had founded grew.

Mohammed taught that there is one god, Allah, but Islam also pays respect to figures from Jewish and Christian faith and instructs Muslims to acknowledge Jews and Christians as "**people of the book**." Submission to Allah involves living by the **Five Pillars of Faith**, which are to declare that "there is no god but Allah"; to pray daily, facing in the direction of Mecca; to fast during the holiday of Ramadan; to give alms to the poor; and to make a pilgrimage (hajj) to Mecca at least once in one's lifetime. Other traditions include abstinence from alcohol and pork, avoiding the portrayal of human or animal images in art, and polygamy (Muslim men were allowed to take up to four wives). There were also restrictions on women's conduct; a strictly observant Muslim woman was to guard her modesty and veil herself when in public—although many modern Muslims have secularized and allow a less-stringent observance of these practices. Patriarchalism was somewhat offset by the command that men treat women with respect. Women also enjoyed the right to inherit, have dowries, and own property. The teachings of Mohammed are contained in the **Qur'an** (Koran), and the holy language of Islam is **Arabic**. **Sharia** is the codification of traditional Islamic law.

The expansion of Islam during the 600s–800s C.E. went hand-in-hand with military conquest and political domination. Early Islam made no distinction between political allegiance and religious affiliation: to be a Muslim meant also to belong to a political and social community, or **umma**, linked by religious belief. After Mohammed's death, the umma was goverened by a **caliph**, or "successor," who was both a religious and political leader. The first caliph was Mohammed's father-in-law, Abu Bakr.

Before Mohammed's death, most of Arabia had converted to Islam. The first three caliphs broke out of Arabia and brought Islam to the rest of the Middle East and beyond. By the end of the 700s C.E., Muslim forces had destroyed the Persian Empire, were threatening Byzantium, and were converting Iraq, Syria, Palestine, Egypt, most of

TIP

Islamic theology divides the world into two states: dar al-Islam ("house of peace") and dar al-Harb ("house of war"). The former includes those lands where Islam is the dominant faith. In early times, the expansion of dar al-Islam was encouraged. Many moderate Muslims now consider dar al-Islam to be a wider community including all places where their religion can be practiced freely.

North Africa, present-day Pakistan, Spain, and parts of Italy. From the 600s to the 1200s C.E., this vast territory was ruled over by two caliphates: the Umayyad (661–750) and Abbasid (750–1258). The zenith of Islamic civilization as a single political and religious entity came during the first 300 years of the Abbasid Caliphate.

Triumph and expansion did not prevent major splits. From 656 to 661 C.E., disputes among Mohammed's family led to civil war. The final result was the establishment of the Umayyad Caliphate. The majority of Muslims accept this line of successors as legitimate and refer to themselves as **Sunni**, the "people of tradition and community." More than 80 percent of Muslims are Sunni. The followers of Mohammed's son-in-law Ali (who was killed in the war) considered the Umayyads to be usurpers and formed a minority denomination known as the **Shiites**. Another Islamic movement is **Sufism**, a mystical tradition that appeared during the 700s and 800s C.E. as a reaction to the growing worldliness of the caliphs. It places a premium on fasting, prayer, and meditation. Islam is most famously associated with the Middle East, where the vast majority of the population is Muslim. But due to the wide expansion of the religion, countries with Islamic majorities include most of those in North Africa, Pakistan, Indonesia (the country with the largest Muslim population), and others.

THE FIRST CALIPHATES

After the **Sunni-Shiite split** (656–661), power passed to the Umayyad Caliphate (661–750), which governed from Damascus, in Syria, and continued Islam's military expansion. The Umayyad caliphs made Arabic the official language of the Muslim world and imposed a tax on those who did not convert to Islam. A series of rebellions led to the Umayyads' decline.

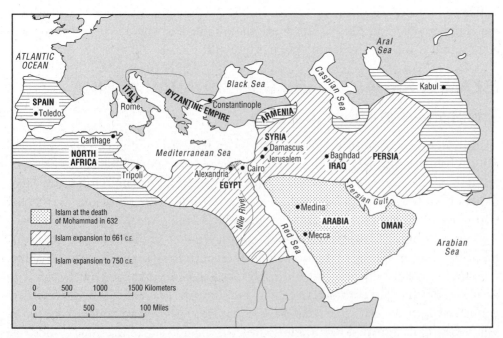

The Birth and Expansion of Islam, 632–750.
Born in Arabia, the dynamic new faith of Islam triumphed throughout the Middle East, where it is still dominant. It then continued to expand, both eastward and westward.

The Abbasid Caliphate

Following the Umayyad dynasty was the **Abbasid Caliphate** (750–1258), which established a great capital at Baghdad and presided over the golden age of classical Islamic culture.

The caliphs were strong and provided peace and stability throughout the Islamic empire. Economic unity prevailed (as it had throughout the empires of Persia, Rome, and Han China), and Abbasid trade networks linked the Middle East with Europe, Africa, the Indian Ocean, and Asia. Just as European bankers facilitated trade there, the concepts of credit and a single currency made possible by Abbasid stability stimulated commerce in the Islamic Empire. Muslim manufacturers were among the most skilled in the world (especially at the production of steel), and, as described at the end of this chapter, the level of cultural advancement was high. The most famous and best loved of the Abbasid caliphs was **Haroun al-Rashid** (776–809).

Abbasid political unity began to disintegrate during and after the 900s. Geographic overextension, the difficulty of ruling millions of people of such diverse ethnicities, and the Sunni-Shiite split all contributed to the caliphate's gradual breakup. Nomadic movements in North Africa, Syria, and Iraq destabilized it as well. As early as 875, Persia and Central Asia came under control of a non-Arabic dynasty (the Samanid). In 909, a Shiite caliphate (the Fatimids) rose up in Egypt and ruled there till 1171. Spain achieved independence briefly from 929 to 976.

At the same time, Baghdad itself was under military threat. It fell to several conquerors, including the Seljuk Turks, who kept the Abbasid caliph in place as a figurehead. Military stress continued, tearing the caliphate apart. (Abbasid weakness largely accounts for the European crusaders' success in seizing Middle Eastern territory.)

The final blow came from the Mongols, who invaded the Middle East in the mid-1200s (for more, see Chapter 11). In 1258, the Mongols captured Baghdad and killed the last Abbasid caliph. Afterward, the Middle East splintered into many separate states. It was reunited, but only partly, by the Turks.

ISLAM IN SAHARAN AND SUB-SAHARAN AFRICA

The Spread of Islam to Africa

Islam reached the eastern parts of North Africa (especially Egypt) in the 600s and 700s. Over the next few hundred years, it spread through the Sahara and to sub-Saharan Africa. Some of northeastern Africa remained Christian: the Nubian kingdoms of Kush and Axum (until the 1300s and 1400s), Ethiopia, and the Coptic Christians of Egypt. However, most converted to Islam.

Islam was brought to Africa by **Arab traders**—either overland (along the **trans-Saharan caravan routes** or by sea, along the continent's Indian Ocean coastline. Conversion was mostly peaceful, although it was sometimes carried out by force. In addition, much of the commercial activity that brought Islam to southern Africa was connected with the extensive **Arab slave trade**. Trade northward consisted of slaves, salt, ivory, and animal skins. Trade southward included manufactured goods like glass, metalwork, and pottery.

As for the west, Islam took root not just in the Sahara, but also sub-Saharan Africa, during the eleventh century. Here, the most dedicated converts were the **Berbers**,

NOTE

Many of the Swahili city-states of Africa's east coast were home to large Muslim communities. After the 1100s, Middle Eastern culture was one of the many elements contributing to the incredible diversity of East African civilizations.

desert nomads and hardened warriors. From Marrakesh, in present-day Morocco, Berber clans extended Muslim authority far to the south.

Mali

By the 1300s and 1400s, Islamic states in western sub-Saharan Africa included Songhai, Kanem-Bornu, and many Hausa city-states. The biggest and most powerful was **Mali** (ca. 1250–1460), along the Niger River basin, an important north–south trade route for centuries. Founded in the mid-1200s by the conqueror Sundiata, and blessed with sizable deposits of gold and metal ore, Mali became a key center for trade in western and northern Africa.

Conversion to Islam proved beneficial. Politically, it enabled good trade relations with Arab states to the north. It also created a group of educated scholars who acted as public servants.

Mali's products were highly valued. They included gold, salt, ivory, animal skins, and slaves. The chief commercial outpost (though not the capital) was **Timbuktu**, a stopping point for caravans and traders traveling in all directions. The main commodity here was salt. Timbuktu was also a renowned center of religious studies and Islamic scholarship.

Mali's most powerful ruler was **Mansa Musa** (1312–1337), famous throughout Europe and Africa as one of the world's wealthiest monarchs (a Spanish map of 1375 referred to Mali as home to the "richest and noblest king in all lands"). Mansa Musa more fully systematized the government. By the early 1400s, Mali was under foreign attack, and its territory was steadily shrinking. Its might collapsed by the end of the century.

Culturally speaking, Mali (like most parts of Africa) was home to a strong tradition of oral storytelling and song making. One of Africa's most famous epic poems from this period comes from Mali, the *Son-Jara* (also known as the *Sundiata*). It dates from the 1200s, and it tells of the many exploits of the chieftain Son-Jara (Sundiata), founder of the Mali state.

THE RISE OF THE TURKS

Originating on the open steppes of Central Asia, the nomadic tribes known collectively as the Turks began to exert a signficant influence on the Middle East, starting around 1000 c.e. By the 1400s, the Ottoman Turks would be the dominant political force there.

Mamluks and Seljuks

Most Turkish tribes were adept at horse combat, and many Turks were brought to the Middle East to serve in Arab armies. These cavalry warriors were called **Mamluks**. They became dedicated converts to Islam and were among the best soldiers in the Middle East. By the eleventh century, there were many Mamluks in Asia Minor (present-day Turkey). In 1250, a large group of them migrated to Egypt and established a kingdom there.

In the eleventh century, the **Seljuk Turks** moved westward. They captured Baghdad in 1055 (but kept the Abbasid caliph in place as a figurehead). In 1071,

the Seljuks defeated the Byzantine Empire at the Battle of Manzikert. They then took most of Asia Minor, Syria, Lebanon, and Palestine (including Jerusalem). Seljuk successes crippled the Byzantine Empire and ushered in its long period of decline. However, Turkish victories prompted European Christians to begin the Crusades in 1095.

Crusaders and Mongol Assaults

The early **Crusades** and the establishment of the Latin Kingdoms (see Chapter 7) threw the Middle East into political confusion. Until the mid-1100s, neither the weakened Abbasids nor their many political rivals proved capable of organizing effective resistance. One of the Middle East's great leaders during this time was the Kurdish general **Saladin**, who recaptured Jerusalem in 1187 and drove back the Third Crusade (1189–1192).

By the 1200s, the Mamluks, Arabs, and Seljuks had gotten better at fighting the crusaders. The Latin Kingdoms shrank steadily, and the Europeans were expelled by the end of the century.

However, an even greater crisis emerged in the form of the **Mongols** (see Chapter 11), who moved into the Middle East in the mid-1200s, seizing Baghdad in 1258 and destroying the Abbasid Caliphate. Only in 1260 was the Mongol advance halted, as a Mamluk army defeated the Mongols at the Battle of Ain Jalut (Goliath Springs) in Syria. The Mongols took no more territory but established a state (the Il-Khan Empire) that lasted until 1349. For a long time, no single state—Mamluk, Seljuk, or Mongol—was strong enough to centralize the Middle East.

The Ottomans

The group that eventually dominated the Middle East, the **Ottoman Turks**, rose to prominence in the 1300s and 1400s. As early as the 1200s, the Ottomans, who served the Seljuks as vassals, settled northwestern Asia Minor. By the century's end, they had their own independent state, founded by the sultan Osman I (1280–1326).

The Ottomans conquered southeastern Europe and what remained of the Byzantine Empire. Attacks on the Balkans began in the late 1300s, and the Ottoman fleet of galleys (oared warships, often rowed by prisoners or slaves) captured many ports and islands in the eastern Mediterranean. Finally, in 1453, Ottoman armies under Sultan Mehmet II, using the world's largest and most advanced gunpowder artillery, captured Constantinople. The **fall of Constantinople** ended the 1,100-year history of the Byzantine Empire and set the stage for a long, intense struggle against Christian Europe during the late 1400s and 1500s.

ISLAMIC CULTURE

For all its political failures, the Abbasid Caliphate presided over the golden era of Islamic culture. Compared with its neighbors—Europe, sub-Saharan Africa, the steppes of Central Asia—the Islamic world was far more culturally advanced during the 700s through the 1200s. Its only cultural and intellectual rivals during these years were India and China.

Mathematics and Science

The mathematical and scientific aptitude of the Muslims was great. Under the Abbasids, the use of so-called Arabic numerals (which actually originated in India) became widespread. Islamic scholars were also adept at medicine. In the 900s, the physician Razi compiled the *Hawi*, the most thorough medical encyclopedia of its time. Even more famous was the Persian scientist Ibn Sina, known to the West as **Avicenna** (980–1037), whose *Canon of Medicine* remained in wide use until the 1600s, both in Europe and the Middle East. The fact that many stars in the night sky bear Arabic names attests to the skill of Muslim astronomers. One reason for the Ottomans' great military successes was a high degree of expertise with gunpowder weaponry, which required a good working knowledge of metallurgy and chemistry. Cultural and technological interchange between the Abbasids and Tang China was extensive.

Philosophy

The Islamic world produced many philosophers: some Muslim, some Jewish (but accepted as citizens and recognized for their accomplishments). Like the Scholastics of medieval Europe, Islamic philosophers investigated the relationship between human reason and religious faith.

The two most famous thinkers came from Muslim Spain. Ibn Rushd, better known as **Averroës** (1126–1198), played an indispensable role in Islamic and European cultural life. A celebrated doctor, Averroës translated and analyzed the works of the Greek philosopher Aristotle, reintroducing his ideas to Europe. A second philosopher was **Maimonides** (1135–1204), a Spanish rabbi. Maimonides wrote commentaries on Jewish scripture and, like Averroës, encouraged the dissemination of Aristotle's ideas throughout Europe. His most famous work, *Guide to the Perplexed*, attempted to reconcile the rationality of Greco-Roman thought with Jewish theology (as Thomas Aquinas would do with Christian thought).

Islam's Influence Over Culture

As in Christian Europe, religion played a large cultural role. Muslim authorities controlled what was acceptable art or literature. Because the **Qur'an** forbids the worship of graven images, Islamic art during these years tended to feature geometric patterns and shapes rather than human or animal figures (although this was not a hard-and-fast rule). Religious colleges (madrasas) provided centers of learning. Much intellectual activity in the Islamic world involved debates and commentaries on the Qur'an, the sayings of Mohammed, and Islamic law (**Sharia**).

Islamic Literature

Among the classics of Islamic literature from the Abbasid years is *The Thousand Nights and a Night*, known in the West as ***The Arabian Nights***. The work includes the tales of Sindbad the Sailor, Ali Baba, and Aladdin. Also important is the *Rubaiyat* of **Omar Khayyám** (ca. 1038–1131). Famous as a mathematician and

astronomer, Khayyám composed this collection of bittersweet, meditative poems in the early 1100s.

Another masterpiece was *Travels*, the journal of **Ibn Battuta** (1304–1368), the Islamic world's greatest explorer. Born in Morocco, Ibn Battuta spent 30 years visiting Mecca, Persia, Mesopotamia, Turkey, Central Asia, Spain, Timbuktu, India, China, and Sumatra, a journey covering more than 75,000 miles.

From Persia came **Sufism**, a mystical strain of Islam that places an emphasis on attaining union with Allah by means of ritual disciplines and spiritual exercises (especially chanting and dancing). The best example of Sufi thought and belief can be found in the poetry of Rumi (1207–1273).

China, Japan, and East Asia

CHAPTER 9

- The Tang dynasty and Song Empire
- The silk industry
- The Silk Road and the Indian Ocean trade network
- The Grand Canal
- Canton and Chinese urbanization
- The invention of gunpowder
- Neo-Confucianism
- Foot binding
- Kublai Khan and the Yuan Empire
- Marco Polo
- The Ming dynasty
- Zheng He
- Nara and Heian Japan
- The shogunates and the samurai class
- Rice-paddy farming
- Block printing

After the Han dynasty's fall in 220 C.E., China alternated between periods of political unity and fragmentation. Imperial collapse in China tended not to be as traumatic as the fall of Rome was for Europe, but it did cause turmoil. Between 589 and 906, China enjoyed a political revival under the Sui and Tang dynasties. However, after the fall of the Tang, it once again split into various empires and states. This disunity lasted for several centuries, until the late 1200s.

During the 1200s, China, like the rest of Eurasia, was rocked by the explosive military expansion of the Mongols. It was conquered by the Mongols, who played a significant part in the country's reunification. After the mid-1300s, China underwent even greater centralization under the Ming dynasty. Whatever the political situation, the growth of China's cities—among the largest and wealthiest in the world—continued.

Other countries of East Asia, especially Japan, Korea, and Vietnam, passed in and out of the Chinese political orbit. At times they were under China's direct control, at others they were free. China also exerted a strong artistic and religious pull on them. As time passed, all three became more independent politically and culturally.

THE SUI AND TANG DYNASTIES

The first strong dynasty to emerge after the fall of the Han was the Sui (589–618). Despite its short life, the Sui reunified China and expanded its borders in a burst of military conquest.

Even stronger was the **Tang dynasty** (618–906). Under the Tang, China became larger than ever before. Emperors like Xuanzong (712–755) extended China's rule to

parts of Central Asia, Mongolia, Manchuria, Tibet, and the Pacific coast. Like the Han Dynasty, Tang China forced many of its neighbors into a **tributary system**, in which Korea, Vietnam, Japan, and others had to make regular monetary payments to avoid punishment.

The Tang economy grew strong thanks to an advanced infrastructure (good roads, waterways, and canals—especially the **Grand Canal**, which the Sui dynasty created to link the Yellow and Yangzi rivers, and the Tang rulers expanded). Increased trade stimulated the Tang economy. In particular, the **silk industry** made the Chinese (who kept the secret of silk production to themselves for centuries) exceptionally wealthy. Greater control over the southern coast allowed China to take greater part in the **Indian Ocean trade network**. The Chinese also traded with the Middle East and the Mediterranean by means of the 5,000-mile **Silk Road**.

The Tang rulers were cultural patrons. Emperor Xuanzong sponsored the creation of the Han Lin Academy of Letters, a key institution of learning. The Tang exerted a strong artistic and religious influence over its neighbors, including Korea and Japan.

During the 800s, a series of peasant rebellions and military disasters weakened the Tang. In 906, the dynasty collapsed completely, and several centuries of disunity followed.

SONG (SUNG) CHINA

The Song Empire and Its Rivals

Following the Tang breakdown, China fragmented into separate states until the late 1200s. The largest and longest lasting was the **Song (Sung) Empire**, which ruled east-central China, from the Yellow River in the north to the Vietnamese border in the south. The Song lasted until 1279 but lost land steadily, because of war with its neighbors.

Until 1121, the primary threat to the Song was the Liao Empire to the north. The Song paid a tribute of silk and cash to the Liao, but then destroyed them with help from the Jurchen, who lived even farther to the north. Unfortunately for the Song, the Jurchen proclaimed their own empire (the Jin) and turned on the Song. The Song gave up much territory, withdrawing to the south. This smaller Song state survived until the Mongol conquest of the 1270s.

Song Society and Economics

Despite its political troubles, the Song Empire was culturally and economically impressive. It enjoyed steady population growth and **urbanization**, becoming the world's most heavily urbanized society—home to the largest cities on earth, several of them with a million or more inhabitants. Although its economic ties with Central Asia and the Middle East lessened, Song China was still connected with the trade routes (such as the Silk Road) that extended to those regions.

If contact with the Middle East lessened, the Song became more involved with the Pacific coast and Southeast Asia. The port of **Canton** (now **Guangzhou**) became one of the world's busiest and most cosmopolitan trading centers. Song China's large

trading vessels, known as junks, cruised the eastern seas and Indian Ocean, carrying silk and manufactured goods.

Song Culture and Religion

Song China was the most scientifically and technologically advanced society of its time, with the possible exception of the Abbasid Caliphate. The Song Chinese were excellent mathematicians and astronomers. Song scientists developed accurate clocks, as well as a working **compass** (first used for navigation at sea in 1090). Also during the Song period, the Chinese invented **gunpowder**, pioneered the use of paper currency (which they called "flying money"), and made use of **block printing** (a practice they may have adopted from the Koreans).

Concerning religion, a great revival of Confucius's teachings—**Neo-Confucianism**—took place during the Song period. Neo-Confucianism was an important unifying factor in a politically divided China. It reinforced Chinese culture's tendency toward hierarchy and obedience, and put a premium on education and cultured behavior. Most governmental officials gained their posts by scoring well on rigorous civil service examinations, a Confucian practice. A new form of Buddhism emerged as well: **Chan** (known as Son in Korea and **Zen** in Japan). Chan stressed simplicity and meditation, and became very popular, both in China and abroad.

TIP

The most striking example of Song China's scientific and technological expertise was the celestial clock of Su Song (built in 1088), an eighty-foot-tall structure that told the time of day, the day of the month, and the positions of the sun, moon, planets, and major stars. It was the first device in world history to use a chain-driven mechanism (powered by flowing water).

Women in Chinese Society

Neo-Confucianism, along with Chinese tradition, was used to justify the greater subordination of women, especially upper-class women, whose families were most likely to follow Confucian dictates. Earlier, a husband's family had to produce a dowry for a new bride; now the reverse became the norm. Marriages were arranged, mainly to the groom's benefit.

The best-known aspect of Chinese subjugation of women was **foot binding**. This painful practice, which kept women's feet tiny and dainty but in the process crippled them, was firmly established by 1200, and it continued into the early 1900s.

Women of the lower classes were generally freer than those of the upper classes, but still occupied a secondary status compared with men. On the other hand, women of all classes had inheritance and property rights, and retained control over their dowry after divorce or a husband's death. Still, the social position of Chinese women was decidedly second-class. (One dramatic exception was Empress Wu Zhao, the only woman ever to rule China in her own right. However, even she was forced off her throne in 705.)

THE MONGOL CONQUEST AND YUAN CHINA

As discussed in Chapter 10, almost all of Eurasia was affected in the 1200s by the sudden and successful military expansion of the Mongols. As **Genghis Khan** and his sons began their conquests, the Chinese states were among their first targets.

The Mongols attacked the Chinese states in 1211. They steadily accumulated territory, even after Genghis Khan's death in 1227. By 1234, the Mongols had captured almost all of western and northern China, and they threatened what remained of the Song Empire. The Song continued to resist for several decades.

In the 1260s, Genghis Khan's grandsons quarreled among themselves and began to divide the Mongol Empire. China and Southeast Asia fell to **Kublai (Khubilai) Khan**, who moved his capital from Mongolia to the Chinese city of Beijing and proclaimed the **Yuan Empire** (1271–1368). Kublai Khan conquered the rest of China, including the Song state, which fell in 1279.

Although Kublai Khan called himself the Great Khan of the Mongols, he and the Mongol leadership adapted themselves to Chinese ways: they adopted Buddhism and made Mandarin Chinese their official language. Indeed, Kublai Khan can be considered the reunifier of China as a single state.

Kublai Khan reigned until 1294 and made Yuan China rich and powerful. Most of his military campaigns succeeded, although he was unable to conquer Japan (which he tried to take in 1274 and 1281) or Java (which he fought in 1293). He forced most of China's neighbors to pay tribute, and the Yuan Empire resisted attacks from other Mongol states in Central Asia.

Kublai Khan rebuilt China's bureaucracy and economy. He repaired roads and canals and built new cities (including the resort of Shangdu, famous in the West as Xanadu). Kublai Khan also restored trade with the west. The **Silk Road**, which had fallen into inactivity, emerged again as a vital trade route. The Venetian merchant **Marco Polo** visited Kublai Khan's China in the 1270s.

The Yuan state was not so fortunate after Kublai Khan's death. During the early 1300s, China suffered tremendous population loss (estimated at 30 to 40 percent), owing to the appearance of **bubonic plague** (which traveled west to the Middle East and Europe, where it was known as the Black Death). Economic decline resulted from the population loss. A series of civil wars broke out in the 1340s, and a final rebellion overthrew the Yuan in 1368.

THE EARLY MING DYNASTY

Triumph of the Ming

The rebel who brought down the Yuan Empire, Zhu Yuanzhang, had been a soldier, a bandit, and a priest. After becoming emperor in 1368, he took the name **Hongwu** (1368–1403) and established the **Ming dynasty** (1368–1644), one of the longest-lasting and most famous in Chinese history. His son **Yongle** (1403–1424) was also a strong ruler.

At home, Hongwu and Yongle recentralized the country and repaired the damage done by the wars of the 1300s. Once again, the population grew, and the economy recovered. To restore imperial legitamacy, Yongle transformed Beijing into a magnificent capital by building the **Forbidden City**, which served for centuries as the imperial residence and seat of government—and still stands at the heart of Beijing.

Abroad, the early Ming rulers expanded China's borders. Like earlier dynasties, they maintained a tributary system. They forged alliances with kingdoms in Vietnam (Annam and Champa) and Korea (the Yi). When the Mongol warlord Timur, who defeated the Delhi Sultanate, attacked China, the Ming drove him away.

Not only was Ming China's army large and effective, its navy was for a time a potent instrument of diplomacy and intimidation. From 1405 to 1433, the admiral and explorer **Zheng He** (Chang Ho) made seven long voyages to Southeast Asia, India, the Middle East, and East Africa. He expanded Chinese trade, gained much knowledge about the outside world, and forced fifty states and cities to pay tribute. After Yongle's death, however, the Ming rulers—distracted by the land-based threat of nomads to the north—lost interest in exploration and naval expansion. This can be seen as a global turning point: had the Ming continued to exploit their power at sea, China might have started a wave of worldwide exploration and colonization, as the nations of Europe were on the verge of doing.

The Voyages of Zheng He, 1405–1433.
China's greatest mariner, Zheng He, sailed several times from China to Arabia and East Africa. He explored, established diplomatic relations, and exacted monetary tribute from weaker states.

Ming Art and Culture

Culturally, the Ming years remain famous as a time of artistic grandeur and intellectual dynamism. Chinese art, religion, and literature continued to exert an influence on countries such as Korea, Vietnam, and Japan (although China's cultural sway over Japan had lessened since the eleventh century).

Confucianism was restored to its place of prominence, rejoining Buddhism as a guiding force in Chinese philosophy and religion. Great works of classical Chinese literature appeared, including a new form of writing, the novel (one example is *The Golden Lotus*, a story about a wicked landowner). Ming artisans produced some of the most exquisite glassware, ceramics, and, especially, **porcelain** that the world has ever seen (it is no accident that the word *china* is synonymous with fine dishware). Another major art form was scroll painting, which depicted landscapes and other scenes on long, vertical rolls of silk and paper.

HEIAN JAPAN

In the 600s C.E., the Japanese imperial family, the Yamato, still ruled from the city of Nara. By the late 700s, however, the emperors wished to escape the political influence of Nara's Buddhist priesthood and shifted their capital to Heian (present-day Kyoto). The classical **Heian period** (794–1185) is a golden age in premodern Japanese history.

The Heian era gave rise to an unusual and complex form of government: the emperor—considered to be the descendant of Japan's Shinto gods, and therefore sacred—lost political power but remained important as a symbolic figurehead. Real power rested with whatever noble family gained the position of chancellor (*kwampaku*) and, with it, the duty of "protecting" the emperor. The chancellor kept the emperor in seclusion and ruled in his name.

Heian Jingu Shrine, Kyoto, Japan.
Kyoto, the old capital of Japan, still contains many of the architectural masterpieces from the Heian era (794–1185), when the city was known by that name. Heian was a major center of Buddhist worship and scholarship, and hundreds of shrines (like the one above) and temples were built there.

From 858 onward, the ruling family in Heian Japan was the **Fujiwara clan**, which gained permanent custody over the chancellorship and imperial family. During the 1000s and early 1100s, the Fujiwara presided over a peaceful, prosperous, and culturally brilliant nation. Japanese painting reached a high level of skill, and one of the classics of world literature, **Lady Murasaki's** *The Tale of Genji*, an epic about love and Japanese court life, dates to this period. Many of Japan's classical prose writers were women. Men considered poetry to be a more elevated art form.

Early in the Heian period, Japanese culture was influenced in many ways by China. Japanese religious life was shaped by the importation of Buddhism and, to a

lesser extent, Confucianism and Daoism, all of which coexisted with Japan's native faith, Shinto. China's system of ideograms influenced the Japanese alphabet, and the poetry, painting, and architecture of Tang China had a great impact on Japanese style. After about 1000, the Japanese began to develop a more independent cultural tradition.

Unfortunately for the Fujiwara, their pursuit of cultural refinement and preoccupation with court life led them to neglect military affairs. For decades, the Fujiwara delegated military responsibilities to various warrior clans (from whom the samurai class would emerge). By the 1100s, these clans were quarreling among themselves and, at the same time, with the Fujiwara.

The Heian regime was destroyed by the **Taira-Minamoto war** (1156–1185), fought by two warrior clans who supported rival claimants to the emperor's throne. The Fujiwara were driven from power by 1160. The Taira gained the upper hand at first, but were eventually defeated by the Minamoto, who created a new government known as the shogunate. The conflict marked Japan's transition from classical age to medieval period (as the fall of Rome did for Europe). It also inspired one of Japan's epic works of literature, *Tales of the Heike.*

FEUDAL JAPAN AND THE FIRST SHOGUNATES

Upon defeating the Taira, the Minamoto moved the capital to Kamakura, far from Heian, and established a decentralized military government. As before, the emperor was a symbolically important figurehead, but real power belonged to the **shogun** ("great general").

Two shogunates governed Japan before the country's breakup in the 1500s: the Kamakura (1185–1333) and the Ashikaga (1336–1573), which, after a short civil war, moved the capital back to Kyoto (formerly Heian). The shogunates were feudal systems, in which the shogun shared power with landowning warlords called **daimyo**. Like the knightly aristocracy of medieval Europe, the shogun and daimyo came from a warrior class known as the **samurai** ("one who serves"). To belong to the samurai class was a great privilege. Just as European knights (in theory) lived by the ideals of chivalry, the samurai followed a strict code of loyalty, honor, and bravery called **Bushido** ("way of the warrior"). Bushido was even more stringent and hierarchical than European chivalry; the most extreme penalty for violating it was ritual suicide (seppuku, or hara-kiri).

The change in government affected the status of upper-class women in Japan. The Heian court had placed great emphasis on cultural brilliance and elaborate manners, and women had a certain social and political influence. The rougher warrior ethic of the shogunates allowed women fewer opportunities. Unlike European chivalry, the code of Bushido did little to encourage respectful treatment of women.

During the 1200s and early 1300s, the Kamakura shoguns kept order in Japan. They even repelled Kublai Khan's two attempts to invade from China (1279 and 1281). The Ashikaga shoguns were politically weaker and allowed greater decentralization. Starting in the mid-1400s, a series of civil wars began tearing Japan apart; by the 1500s, the country was almost completely disunified, with most daimyo ruling their lands independently. Only in the very late 1500s and early 1600s would Japan be reunified.

Under the Ashikaga, trade and commerce flourished in Japan, and an important merchant class emerged. As in China, urbanization proceeded rapidly. New forms of Buddhism arrived, especially **Zen (Chan)**, which proved popular among the samurai class. Pure Land (Jo Do) Buddhism, which promised a heavenly afterlife, gained a large following among the lower classes. The philosophical simplicity of Zen affected several important cultural practices, such as the *cha-no-yu* tea ceremony, landscaping (rock gardens and bonsai trees), and haiku poetry.

KOREA AND VIETNAM

Like Japan, Korea and Vietnam fell under the cultural and religious (and, at times, political) influence of China. As in China, agricultural production in Korea and Vietnam mainly involved rice cultivation. As with Japan, Korea's and Vietnam's art, literature, and architecture were shaped by China. The writing systems of all three countries—*hiragana* and *kanji* in Japan, *hangul* in Korea, and *chu nom* in Vietnam—were based at least somewhat on Chinese ideograms. From China came Confucianism and various forms of Buddhism.

Korean kingdoms, among them the Gojoseon (Old Choson), formed as early as the 2000s B.C.E. By the 500s C.E., they had developed a long, tangled relationship with China. Silla, for example, the first kingdom to unite the entire peninsula, was a close ally of Tang China and collapsed when the Tang fell. Koryo, the next state, had ties with the Song, then was invaded by the Mongols. It won its freedom by the mid-1300s but collapsed soon after. The kingdom of Joseon, known more commonly in the West as Yi (1392–1910), enjoyed close ties with Ming China. Many scholars speculate that **block printing** was invented in the Koryo state and then passed on to the Chinese. It was also through Korea that much of China's influence on Japanese culture was transmitted.

The Vietnamese had contact with the Chinese as early as the 200s B.C.E. Close ties formed between Tang China and the Vietnamese states of Annam and Champa. At various points after 1000, Annam and Champa were under Chinese rule, paid tribute to China, or allied with China.

The widespread practice of **rice-paddy farming**, or growing rice by means of wet cultivation, originated in Southeast Asia—most likely in Vietnam—around 500 B.C.E. Before this, rice had been grown dry. Wet cultivation led to increased crop yields and spread to other parts of Asia, including China and Japan. In this way, the Vietnamese kingdoms had a profound agricultural and environmental impact on a vast portion of Asia.

South and Southeast Asia

CHAPTER 10

- The Delhi Sultanate
- The importation of Islam to India
- The Indian Ocean trade network (Calicut, Malacca)
- Burma, Thailand, and Annam
- The Khmer Empire and Angkor Wat
- Hinduism, Buddhism, and Islam in Southeast Asia
- Borobudur
- The Polynesian migration

South and Southeast Asia are regions of remarkable ethnic and cultural diversity. India and the lands that surround it are environmentally and geographically diverse as well. India measures 2,000 miles east to west and 2,000 miles north to south. In the north are mountains and forest. The center is cut by the Ganges and Indus river basins. The southern third is more tropical. The entire climate of the Indian Ocean region is affected twice per year by huge seasonal rainstorms called **monsoons** (which occur in June–July and December–January). Most of Southeast Asia is tropical in climate.

Until the modern era, Southeast and South Asia were often politically fragmented. India in particular was seldom unified as a single state. In other parts of South Asia, kingdoms and states tended to rise and fall rapidly. Culture, tradition, language, and religion served more than politics as unifying factors.

NOTE

By itself, the Indian subcontinent is home to people of several races, dozens of different languages, and many minor and major religions.

INDIA AND THE DELHI SULTANATE

Between 600 C.E. and 1200 C.E., India was disunified. The Gupta Empire, the last state to provide any sort of unity, collapsed in 550 C.E.

The next group to unite a large part of India were Muslim invaders, who reached the northwest frontier (the Indus valley and Afghanistan) in the 700s and converted it to Islam. By the 900s, Muslims were escalating their attacks on the Indian border.

In 1022, Muslim armies, led by Afghan warlords, began the conquest of northern India, a process that continued for the next two hundred years. In 1206, the Muslims captured the city of Delhi, and most of northern India fell into their hands. Muslim generals established the **Delhi Sultanate** (1206–1520s).

The major impact of the Muslim invasions and the sultanate's establishment was to introduce Islam into India. Islam did not displace earlier faiths like Hinduism and Buddhism, but joined them as one of the country's major religions. (One interesting development is that, in India, Muslim women tended to enjoy more property rights

NOTE

Technically, the Delhi Sultanate was part of the Abbasid Caliphate (see Chapter 8), but only until the caliphate's destruction in 1258.

157

than Hindu women, especially those of low caste; it was also possible for Muslim women in India to divorce and to remarry after their husbands died.)

There were religious conflicts under the Delhi Sultanate. At first, the sultans imposed their new faith harshly. They became less severe over time, but Hindu and Muslim populations did not tend to mix, and tensions—sometimes outright violence and persecution—characterized the relationship. Islam's influence was greatest in the north and along the west coast.

Politically, the Delhi Sultanate grew from the mid-1200s to the mid-1300s, by which point it controlled most of India. Afterward, the sultanate shrank. Many regions in the south broke away. In 1398, the Central Asian warlord **Timur** (see Chapter 11) attacked and captured Delhi itself. When he departed, after a year of plundering, the city was in ruins. The Delhi Sultanate survived, but barely. It grew steadily smaller, then, in the 1520s, succumbed to new invaders from the north.

OTHER INDIAN STATES

Although India's ethnic complexity makes it hard to generalize, for many years, the northern parts of the country were populated by Indo-Europeans (largely descended from the Aryans who invaded ca. 1500 B.C.E.). The south was inhabited by darker-skinned peoples of Dravidian origin.

Independent Southern States

Various states and kingdoms emerged in the south of India, independent of the larger governments in the north. Among them were the Tamil kingdoms on the Indian Ocean coast: they formed around the 100s B.C.E. and survived for 2,000 years.

In the 1300s, even more states emerged in the south, most of them breakaways from the Delhi Sultanate. Bengal became an independent Muslim state in 1338. Gujarat, a Muslim state on the western coast, declared independence from the sultanate in 1390 and flourished as a trading center in the Indian Ocean network. The Vijayanagara Empire (1336–1565) and the Malibar city-states formed Hindu enclaves on the Indian coast. The former controlled many southern ports and the island of Sri Lanka. The latter ruled much of the southwestern coast. The most important of the Malibar cities was **Calicut**.

Indian Ocean Trade

One of the world's most vibrant commercial economies centered on the **Indian Ocean trade network**, which joined East Africa, Arabia, the Persian Gulf, India, the Malay peninsula, Indonesia, China, and Japan. From west to east, this exchange network covered an expanse greater than 6,000 miles.

In the west, a zone controlled largely by Arab traders, goods came from Africa and the Middle East. Africa provided ivory, animal hides, timber, gold, and slaves. From the Middle East came textiles, carpets, glass, and Arabian horses. The middle zone was dominated by Indian cities and kingdoms. India offered precious gems, elephants, salt, and cotton cloth. From Sri Lanka (Ceylon) came cinnamon. Other spices, as well as exotic woods, came from Indonesia. In the east, China traded silk, porcelain, and paper. Japan was a major source of silver.

Major ports in the Indian Ocean network included Sofala, **Mombasa**, and Mogadishu in East Africa; Jidda, Mecca, and Ormuz in Arabia and Persia; the great Malibar metropolis of **Calicut** in western India; and **Canton** (**Guangzhou**) and Hangzhou in China. By means of the Red Sea and Suez isthmus, the Indian Ocean trade network connected to the Mediterranean and the trade networks flourishing there.

The Indian Ocean Trade Network Before 1500 C.E.
The arrival of Portuguese traders just before 1500, then the massive influx of other Europeans, changed the economic patterns of this region forever.

SOUTHEAST ASIA

Geographically, Southeast Asia consists of three zones: the mainland; the Malay Peninsula; and the island chains of the Indian Ocean and South China Sea. The climate is tropical, and much of the terrain is mountainous or blanketed by rain forest.

Between 3000 B.C.E. and 2000 B.C.E., Malays and other peoples arrived, from China, India, and elsewhere. Local inhabitants practiced agriculture by around 2000 B.C.E. The early peoples of Southeast Asia were also skilled bronze workers and navigators (the island peoples traveled great distances in sophisticated outrigger canoes).

Southeast Asian States

Major states emerged in Southeast Asia before and around 500 C.E. These included Burma, the Thai kingdom, and the Vietnamese states of Champa and Annam. Most of these states were culturally and economically influenced by China, India, or both. They traded spices (cinnamon, nutmeg, cloves, and pepper), especially for silk from China, and took part in the vast Indian Ocean and Pacific trade networks.

The Khmer and Srivijayan Empires

For years, the two most developed states in Southeast Asia were the Khmer Empire (500s–1454 C.E.) in Cambodia and the Srivijayan Empire (500s–1100s C.E.) of Sumatra.

The **Khmer** civilization emerged in Cambodia and Laos by the 500s C.E. and reached its peak during the Angkor period (889–1454). The Angkor rulers were militarily aggressive, expanding the Khmer state into parts of Burma and the Malay Peninsula. Culturally and religiously, the Khmer were influenced primarily by India. They adopted both Hinduism and Buddhism, building more than 21,000 temples. The Khmer state collapsed in the 1400s, when Cambodia was conquered by neighboring Thailand.

In the Indonesian islands to the south, the **Srivijayan Empire** took shape. From the island of Sumatra, the Srivijayans expanded, gaining control of the maritime trade routes between Indonesia and the Malay Peninsula by the 600s. They then took over parts of the Malay Peninsula, as well as the Indonesian island of Java. Like the Khmer

NOTE

Thanks to contact with India and China, most Southeast Asian states adopted Hinduism, Buddhism, and sometimes both. Before 1000 C.E., Islam also appeared in Southeast Asia.

NOTE

The city complex of **Angkor Wat**, with its ornate palaces and pagodas, covers forty square miles.

NOTE

The Srivijayan Empire declined in the 1000s and 1100s, weakened by outside enemies, then displaced by a new empire. In the 1200s, Islam arrived in the Indonesian islands. It remains a dominant faith there to this day.

Empire in Cambodia, the Srivijayan Empire was influenced by India and accepted both Hinduism and Buddhism (although Buddhism was dominant). The Srivijayans' greatest architectural legacy is the Buddhist temple complex of **Borobudur**, built on the island of Java from 770 to 825. Borobudur is in the shape of a mountain over 100 feet high; every level represents a stage on the path to enlightenment.

Political Changes, 1200s–1400s

Political change came to Southeast Asia from the 1200s through the 1400s. The Chinese and Mongols made repeated attacks from the north. Thailand expanded, conquering the Khmer state in Cambodia. The Vietnamese state of Annam became a military power after the early 1400s, as did Burma in the 1500s.

After 1400, the economic powerhouse of Southeast Asia was the city of **Malacca (Melaka)**, located on the narrow waterway separating the Malay Peninsula from Sumatra. It connected the Indian Ocean with the South China Sea and was a crucial nexus in the Indian Ocean trade network. Founded in 1400, Malacca was controlled by China, then the Thais. It enjoyed a brief period of freedom before being conquered by European colonists—the Portuguese—in 1511.

THE POLYNESIAN MIGRATIONS

One of history's most epic journeys was the **Polynesian migration** across the Pacific from approximately 2500 B.C.E. to 900 C.E. Originally from Southeast Asia, the Polynesians left their homes in the Philippine and Indonesian islands around 4,500 years ago.

Early Polynesian Culture

NOTE

In a process lasting over 3,000 years, the Polynesians spread eastward across a 20,000-mile expanse, settling thousands of islands. The region known as Oceania is populated mainly by their descendants.

The original Polynesians were root farmers, growing taro and sweet potatoes and supplementing their diet with pigs, chickens, and fish. Their social organization was hierarchical. Tribes were led by powerful chiefs. Polynesian religion was animistic and concerned with avoiding improper behavior, or **taboo** (*tabu* or *kapu* in Polynesia).

Because so much of their life was based on the sea, the Polynesians were expert sailors and navigators. Their **outrigger canoes**, which could sail more than 120 miles per day, allowed them to travel vast distances over open water. Not only could the Polynesians navigate by the sun, moon, and stars, they possessed an intimate knowledge of tides, currents, and wave patterns (creating maps woven from twigs and grasses to represent the ocean's rhythms).

The Migrations

Why the Polynesians began their long migrations is unknown; most scholars speculate that ecological crisis drove them from their homes. Certainly environmental necessity kept them going once they started. When the Polynesians settled an island, the population would grow to such a point that part of the tribe (sometimes all of it) would have to move onward to keep from depleting all the resources.

The first wave of migration took the Polynesians to the island chain of Micronesia, east of the Philippines. Then, around 2000 to 1300 B.C.E., some Polynesians moved to Melanesia, east of New Guinea and Australia and including Fiji.

Another major migration took the Polynesians to the oceanic expanse that now bears the name Polynesia. Polynesia is bounded by an imaginary triangle, with Hawaii at the north, New Zealand to the southwest, and Easter Island to the southeast. By 300 to 400 C.E., Polynesians had settled **Easter Island**, building their famous statues of human heads. By the 1500s, environmental stress and tribal war destroyed the Easter Island civilization. More successful was Polynesian settlement of New Zealand, where the **Maori** culture, established around 800 C.E., survived and prospered. A warrior society, the Maori became the largest single Polynesian subculture by the 1700s.

The Mongol Empires

CHAPTER 11

- Genghis Khan
- The Mongol Empire and the Pax Mongolica
- The Silk Road (Samarkand)
- The breakup of the Mongol Empire
- Kublai Khan
- Timur

During the 1200s, almost all of Eurasia was swept by a whirlwind from Central Asia: the Mongols. United for the first time in their history by Genghis Khan, the Mongols burst out of their homeland in the 1210s, beginning one of the most successful military campaigns of all time. At its peak, the Mongol Empire was the largest conquest state that has ever existed, stretching across most of Asia, parts of the Middle East, and Europe.

By the late 1200s and early 1300s, the Mongol state broke apart into smaller units. The nomadic Mongols were adept at warfare but less so at nation building. This makes for an interesting contrast between their empire and states like Rome and Han China.

Nonetheless, the Mongols had a tremendous impact on Europe and Asia during the 1200s and 1300s. They destroyed and created nations. They shaped the social and political development of many civilizations. Also, for a time, the Mongol states provided a degree of unity—or at least connectedness—to a huge part of the Eurasian landmass. It is increasingly common for historians to speak of the thirteenth century as a period of **Pax Mongolica** (or Pax Tatarica): the "Mongol (or Tatar) Peace." Although the notion of peacefulness may be exaggerated, there is no denying that the Mongols temporarily tamed the vast spaces of Eurasia, affecting many of its great civilizations.

GENGHIS KHAN AND THE RISE OF THE MONGOLS

The Mongols (also Tartars or Tatars) were a group of nomadic tribes from the steppes, or open plains, of Central Asia. They herded livestock. They were excellent horsemen and archers.

The Mongols are frequently perceived as barbaric, even bloodthirsty. This is a stereotype. While they did not have a sophisticated society before their great wave of expansion, they proved adept at **cultural borrowing**. From their neighbors and the people they conquered, the Mongols adoped a law code, a written script, new religious practices, and better technology.

Before 1200, the Mongols, who numbered between 1.5 and 3 million, were divided into more than thirty disunited, often warring tribes. In 1206, the Mongols

were united by the warlord Temujin, better known as **Genghis Khan** (also Chingiz, Jenghiz, or Chinggis), which means "ruler of limitless strength." Genghis Khan reorganized the Mongol armies and, shortly after seizing power, led them on their great campaign of conquest.

The Mongol Empires, 1294 C.E.
By 1294, the Mongols, a nomadic people, had conquered most of Asia and key portions of Europe and the Middle East. Mongol control over these territories had a major and lasting effect on many parts of Eurasia.

THE FIRST WAVE OF CONQUEST

Mongol conquests began in 1211. The first target was northern China; by 1215, the Mongols had breached the Great Wall and seized the city of Beijing. The Mongols also moved against Central Asia, capturing the great Silk Road trading center of Samarkand. By Genghis Khan's death in 1227, the Mongols controlled a large state encompassing present-day Mongolia, much of Central Asia, and northern and western China. His heirs would enlarge the empire even further.

What accounted for the Mongols' success? It used to be thought—incorrectly—that the main reason was great numbers. The early Mongol armies were large (about 80,000 to 100,000 troops) but not so large that they could have easily overwhelmed such a large territory. Mongol warriors were talented cavalrymen and archers, and they could fire from horseback, galloping at full speed, forward or backward. The Mongols (and their horses) were possessed of great endurance and hardiness. They organized their armies efficiently into tightly knit military units based on groups of ten. The Mongols were also quick to adopt advanced military technology and techniques from their more advanced neighbors. This was especially the case with siege warfare, which the Mongols learned from the Chinese and Central Asian states.

THE SECOND WAVE OF CONQUEST AND THE PAX MONGOLICA

Genghis Khan's heirs continued the wars of conquest. Genghis's third son, Ögödei, ruled the Mongols as Great Khan till 1241. He greatly expanded the empire and built a new capital, Karakorum, for it.

In the east, Ögödei's armies moved farther into China, threatening the Song Empire (which the Mongols defeated in the 1260s). Ögödei also forced Koryo, or Korea, into tributary status.

Ögödei had even more ambitious goals in the west. In 1236, he sent a large invasion force to seize as much of Europe as possible. From 1237 to 1240, the Mongols conquered most of Russia and Ukraine. From 1240 to 1242, they took over parts of Bulgaria, Romania, and Hungary. When they tried to push into Poland and Germany, however, they overextended themselves. Also, Ögödei died in 1241, and succession struggles ended the invasion effort. Russian and Ukraine remained under Mongol rule as tributary states for two centuries.

Commanded by Hulegu, Mongol forces invaded the Middle East in the 1250s, toppling the Abbasid Caliphate in 1258 and advancing until 1260, when they were stopped by a Mamluk army at Ain Jalut.

At their zenith, the Mongols ruled an empire that stretched from Poland in the west to Korea in the east, and from Siberia in the north to Vietnam in the south. Over this massive expanse, the Mongols imposed a single political authority, encouraged economic exchange, made travel conditions safer, and imposed legal order. **Silk Road** trade, which had fallen off, now revived and flourished, and cities like **Samarkand** became crucial economic centers, with merchants, missionaries, and travelers of all professions and ethnicities passing through. Among these was the Venetian merchant and explorer Marco Polo.

Many historians refer to this brief semi-unification of Eurasia as the Pax Mongolica, or "Mongol Peace." It was maintained not just by force but by a surprisingly high level of administrative skill. Helped by their habit of cultural adaptation, the Mongols borrowed a written language (Uighur, a Turkic dialect); their law code (the *yasa*, from China); paper currency (from China); and new religious beliefs (Buddhism and Islam). The Mongols used their own skill with horses to create one of the premodern world's fastest and most efficient postal systems (the *yam*).

Breakup of the Mongol Empire

A Chinese proverb is often quoted to describe the Mongol Empire: "One can conquer an empire on horseback, but one cannot govern it from there." Even recognizing their underappreciated political strengths, it must be said that the Mongols were better at conquest than they were at governing. Soon after its size and power peaked, the Mongol Empire, spread too thin, began to break apart.

In 1260, the last khan to rule over a united Mongol empire (Mongke) died. Civil war broke out, and the empire's four largest units became independent states. The homeland, which went to **Kublai Khan**, included Mongolia, China, and territories

to the east and southeast. The Golden Horde ruled over Russia and parts of eastern Europe until the mid-1400s. The Il-Khan Mongols converted to Islam and ruled much of the Middle East until the rise of the Ottoman Turks in the late 1300s. A Mongol state, the Jagadai Khanate, governed Central Asia well into the 1400s. Like the Il-Khans (with whom they often struggled), the Jagadai became Muslims.

A later Mongol warlord was the Jagadai khan **Timur** (also known as Tamerlane). From 1370 to 1405, Timur rose up and attempted to repeat the military triumph of Genghis Khan. Quickly, he conquered Central Asia, Persia, northern India (including Delhi), southern Russia, and parts of the Middle East. The expansion ended with Timur's death, but his descendants ruled over Central Asia—and the Silk Road cities of Samarkand and Bukhara—until the 1500s.

Sub-Saharan Africa

CHAPTER 12

- The Sahara Desert and Africa's sub-Saharan regions
- The Bantu
- Matrilinear societies
- The Arab slave trade
- Trans-Saharan caravan routes
- Ghana and the gold trade
- Great Zimbabwe
- The Indian Ocean trade network (Mombasa and Zanzibar)
- Swahili as a lingua franca

Not just physically, but culturally and politically, Africa is divided by the Sahara Desert. As described in Chapter 8, most of Saharan Africa and the northern continent fell into the orbit of the Islamic world. The story of sub-Saharan Africa is more complex.

INTRODUCTION TO SUB-SAHARAN AFRICA

Factors Restricting the Growth of Major Sub-Saharan States

In sub-Saharan Africa, the development of strong, sizable political units occurred later and more slowly than in other parts of the world. Much of this had to do with the tremendous ethnolinguistic variety there, where more than 2,000 languages and dialects are spoken.

One of the few common threads shared by many—but not all—peoples of sub-Saharan Africa is descent from the **Bantu** tribes. Around 1000 B.C.E., the Bantu began to move out of their homeland in west central Africa. Their descendants settled in almost all parts of the continent south of the Sahara. With the passage of time, each smaller group developed its own distinct language and cultural tradition.

Environmental factors also limited the growth of major states. The fluctuating climate of sub-Saharan Africa and human susceptibility to insect- and animal-borne diseases (especially malaria and sleeping sickness) in sub-Saharan regions were obstacles to population growth.

Basic Features of Sub-Saharan Societies

Most sub-Saharan communities were small. Social life revolved around the village. Food was provided by means of a combination of hunting, herding, and limited agriculture. It appears that most African societies gained the skill of **metalworking** on their own, rather than having it taught to them by outsiders, as was commonly thought until recently.

As in most early civilizations, women in sub-Saharan Africa tended to be subservient to men. Women were often valued, though, for their labor as fieldworkers (while men tended cattle) and for producing heirs. Women also were respected for storytelling abilities and their role in educating young people about moral values and religious beliefs. Interestingly, in Africa, lineage was sometimes **matrilinear**, rather than patrilinear. Women often inherited property, and the husband was required to move into his wife's house. Rules of behavior between the sexes tended to be more informal than in the Middle East, China, or India.

Art and Culture

African tribes possessed a high degree of skill in carving and sculpture, especially in wood and ivory. Metal sculpture became more common over time. By the thirteenth and fourteenth centuries, West African artists were creating masterpieces out of bronze and iron. In Ife, in present-day Nigeria, metalworkers formed bronze and iron statues by first designing molds with melted wax. These sculptures may have influenced the work of metalworkers from the West African state of Benin. Such artists are famous for their sophisticated and detailed bronze, brass, and copper sculptures of heads, ornaments, animal figures, and reliefs depicting court life.

Architecture in Africa varied across regions owing to diverse cultural influences. In sub-Saharan Africa, Great Zimbabwe stood out for its impressive stone buildings and walls. The stones were carefully cut, then set in place without mortar. In Mali, fourteenth-century builders used timber as skeletons in reinforcing mud mosques that still stand today. The architecture of Zanzibar is distinguished by the use of coral to decorate buildings.

African literature of this period was preserved by **oral tradition**. Professional storytellers chronicled history and social custom. They also acted as entertainers and served as advisers to kings. The most famous epic of sub-Saharan Africa from these years is *Son-Jara* (or *Sundiata*), from Mali (see Chapter 8).

Most native African religions were animistic based on the worship of the spirits of animals and ancestors.

Islam and Contacts with North Africa

As time passed, the increased interaction between North Africa and sub-Saharan Africa included trade. Unfortunately, it also included slavery: for hundreds of years, **Arab slavers** penetrated to the south, forcing Africans into bondage. By the eleventh century, some traders in the Sahara owned more than a thousand slaves apiece.

Islam became part of sub-Saharan life, sometimes by force (as in Ghana), sometimes peacefully (as in Mali). Mali's great city of Timbuktu was an important center of Islamic scholarship. Muslims brought religion and trade to the cities of the eastern coast and previously isolated parts of southern Africa. Still, in comparison to North Africa, which became almost completely Muslim, sub-Saharan Africa was less heavily influenced by Islam.

WEST AND CENTRAL AFRICA

Ghana

In West Africa, the state of **Ghana**, founded in the 500s C.E., continued to be strong and prosperous. When Europe began minting coins during the 1200s, Ghana's gold gained in value, and it became a major supplier of gold to the world economy. Koumbi Saleh, one of Ghana's capitals, hosted a prosperous Muslim community of merchants linked to the **trans-Saharan trade route**. Ironically, iron and copper were more useful, and thus more valuable, to Africans than gold was. So caravans carried iron and copper across the Sahara as well.

Over time, Ghana's ecological and demographic conditions weakened its society. As its population grew, food production failed to meet demand in what was by then an extremely arid environment. All of this left Ghana vulnerable to Muslim conquest, the immediate cause of its downfall in 1076.

Central African States and Great Zimbabwe

In Central Africa, a few large city-states became home to advanced civilizations. Among them were Kongo and Benin.

From the 1250s to the 1450s, the most powerful of these states was the one that emerged around the cities of Mutapa and Great Zimbabwe. Politically linked, the two cities controlled seven hundred miles of the Zambezi river basin.

The larger and more important city was **Great Zimbabwe** (ca. 1000–1400). Its name means "sacred graves of the chiefs," and it was crucial as a political and religious center. It was a great walled city, encircling 193 acres and home to approximately 20,000 people.

Great Zimbabwe was immensely wealthy, thanks to large deposits of gold and diamonds. Gold was shipped east to Sofala, where it became part of the East African–Indian Ocean coastal trade complex. Archaeologists have found in the ruins of the city gold, jewelry, copper ornaments, birds carved out of soapstone, iron tools, Chinese ceramics, and Persian artworks. Such an assortment shows how extensive trade was in the area at the time.

Rumors of Great Zimbabwe's wealth—and of lost treasures and hidden mines—persisted for hundreds of years, long after the city itself collapsed in the mid-to-late 1400s.

THE EASTERN COAST

East Africa and the Indian Ocean Trade Network

As part of the large **Indian Ocean trade network**, the East African coast was open to a remarkable variety of cultural and economic influences. East Africa gained its wealth from a diverse selection of desirable goods like ivory. Slaves were part of the economy as well. Through trade, African societies had an impact on the outside world. As early as the Roman era, East Africa had commercial ties with India and the Mediterranean. By the tenth and eleventh centuries, African-made goods were reaching China by way of the Indian Ocean trade network. Chinese maritime trade expanded during the early Ming dynasty and many Chinese vessels made their way to the East African coast.

The Diversity of East African City-States

City-states flourished on the East African shore between 1000 and 1500. Nearly forty urban centers were sprinkled along the 1,500-mile stretch of coast running from Mogadishu (in today's Somalia) to the south. They were all multiethnic. Beginning in the 1100s, Persians and Arabs migrated to Mogadishu and pressed southward, mixing with the local Africans. The East African city-states were politically independent. Many were ruled by Arab sheiks, who led rich mercantile families. Key cities included **Mombasa**, Sofala, and **Zanzibar**.

East African cities were also diverse in terms of their populations, which included native Africans; Arabs, Turks, and other Middle Easterners; and Indians and others from South and Southeast Asia. A tremendous amount of ethnic, religious, cultural, and linguistic mixing occurred along the East African coast. Muslims moved in large numbers to the area, starting in the mid-to-late 600s. Islam became important but did not displace local religions. The region's most widespread language was **Swahili**, which became the lingua franca, or common tongue, for much of the entire coast. East Africa was a vibrant area with a booming economy from approximately 1200 to 1500. Even Indonesians, in search of better economic opportunities, crossed the Indian Ocean to settle on Madagascar, an island off the southeast coast of Africa.

By the early 1500s, the arrival of European colonists and explorers would change everything, not just for East Africa but the entire Indian Ocean basin.

TRANSNATIONAL LANGUAGES

Throughout history, certain languages have risen up to allow communication between cultures whose native tongues are very different. The term *lingua franca* is often used to describe them. Examples include Latin; Arabic; Swahili; the sign language used by Native American tribes on the Great Plains; and, increasingly in our own time, English. A language achieves the status of lingua franca for various reasons. In some cases, it is the shared religious language of people who are ethnically different; in others, it is the tongue that most effectively facilitates trade in a multilingual region. Sometimes it is imposed from above by a military or imperial power (like Spanish in Latin America or English in India).

Christianity in East Africa

Christianity existed as a dominant, even official, religion in two parts of northeastern Africa. The Copts, a Christian minority, formed communities in Egypt and Sudan.

Ethiopia (also known then as Abyssinia) was not only the oldest African state but, for many centuries, a Christian kingdom. Rumors about the wealth and Christianity of the Ethiopian monarchs gave rise in Europe to the legends of Prester John: a mythical Christian king in Africa who possessed fabulous wealth. These legends were among the factors that spurred on the age of exploration.

The Americas

CHAPTER 13

- The pre-Columbian era
- The Anasazi
- Cahokia and the Mississippian civilization
- The Olmecs, the Maya, and the Aztecs
- Pyramids and human sacrifice
- Tenochtitlán and Mesoamerican urbanization
- Terrace farming and llama herding in the Andes
- The Incas and Machu Picchu
- Ayllu clans and mit'a labor obligations

Unlike the peoples of Eurasia and Africa, who interacted with and influenced each other, the early societies of North and South America developed in isolation. Settled by the descendants of Stone Age travelers who crossed from Asia over a land bridge that joined Alaska with Siberia—then disappeared with a rise in ocean levels—North and South America remained geographically separated from other continents for thousands of years.

By about 9000 B.C.E., the entire length of the Americas, north to south, had been settled. The passage of time, geographical spread, and environmental diversity caused the social groups scattered through the Americas to develop unique cultural, social, and linguistic characteristics.

Major areas of settlement included North America's eastern woodlands, desert Southwest, and open plains; the deserts and jungles of Mexico and Central America; and the Andes Mountains of South America. Before 600 C.E., advanced civilizations emerged in all these areas. Many of these societies are unusual in that they reached an advanced state without developing systems of writing (such as the Incas and the Mississippians) or inventing the wheel.

The geographical isolation of the Americas continued until the end of the 1400s. Only with the voyages of Christopher Columbus did the societies of North and South America come into sustained contact with outsiders. (In the historiography of the Americas, the period before 1492 is referred to as the **pre-Columbian era**.) The arrival of the Europeans changed the Americas beyond recognition. In the meantime, between 1000 and 1450, several major civilizations emerged or reached their peak of development.

NORTH AMERICA

In North America, most Native Americans (known popularly by the erroneous term "Indians") were nomadic or seminomadic hunter-gatherers divided into tribes. Around 1000 C.E., the number of tribes—and the differences between them—increased dramatically and grew until about the 1500s.

The role of women in most North American tribes seems to have been defined relatively loosely. Because most of these groups were not yet fully agricultural, the gender division of labor was not as sharply formed as in the more developed empires of Central and South America. Women tended to gather berries and roots, weave, make pottery, and raise children. However, their status was not necessarily secondary to that of men, at least not formally.

Not counting what is today Mexico, two regions of North America became home to advanced societies. One was the Southwest, where settlement seems to have begun in the 300s B.C.E. Unusually for pre-Columbian North America, many Southwestern cultures were agricultural (learning the practice from more sophisticated societies in Mexico). The most famous Southwestern people were the **Anasazi**, who inhabited the region from about 400 (perhaps earlier) to 1300. They lived in complex dwellings known as pueblos—sometimes built on the open flatland, sometimes high up in the caves of canyons. The Anasazi believed that humans emerged from the earth, so they held religious ceremonies in underground chambers called kivas. This practice was passed on to tribes that later settled in the Southwest. Women in Anasazi communities may have had the right to own property.

To the north and east, sophisticated societies emerged in the Ohio and Mississippi river valleys. These groups built large **earth mounds**, presumably for religious and ceremonial purposes. The first was the Adena culture (ca. 500 B.C.E.–100 C.E.), followed by the larger Hopewell culture (ca. 100–400). After 600, the region's most advanced culture was the **Mississippian civilization** (ca. 700–1500). Like their predecessors, the Mississippians built great mounds. They also built cities, the largest of which was **Cahokia**, located in what is now western Illinois; by 1200, it had a population of over 30,000.

Between 1250 and 1500, the Mississippian culture was in decline (for unknown reasons, Cahokia was abandoned around 1250). At the same time, Native Americans began to organize themselves into smaller hunter-gatherer groups. These evolved into the major Native American tribes that remain familiar today. The arrival of European settlers and explorers in the late 1400s and 1500s forever changed the lives of all Native Americans.

MEXICO AND MESOAMERICA

It was in Mexico and Mesoamerica (or Central America) that major civilizations in the Americas first developed. Agriculture, in the form of maize (corn) and potato cultivation, was practiced there as early as 5000 to 3000 B.C.E. As described earlier, the region's first dominant society was the **Olmecs** (ca. 1200 B.C.E.–400 B.C.E.), who, like the Sumerians in Mesopotamia, left behind a religious and cultural tradition that profoundly influenced later Central American peoples. These included the **Teotihuacán** and **Mayan** cultures. Following the Maya were the Toltecs (ca. 968–1156), an aggressive warrior society that conquered central Mexico until civil war and external invasion finished off their civilization.

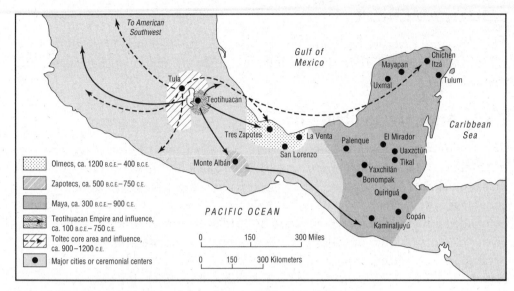

States in Pre-Columbian Central America, ca. 1200 B.C.E.–1200 C.E.
This map demonstrates that, in Central America, many civilizations developed, rose, and fell in succession. The Olmecs set the pattern for cultural development here, followed by the Maya, Toltecs, and Aztecs.

The Aztecs

The next major group in Central America—and the last before the arrival of the Europeans—were the Mexica, better known as the **Aztecs** (ca. 1300–1520). Their chief city was the metropolis of **Tenochtitlán**, on the site of what is today Mexico City. At the height of Aztec power, Tenochtitlán had a population of half a million, and its marketplace could hold more than 60,000 people.

The Aztecs were even more warlike than the Toltecs before them. During the 1300s, they conquered an empire of more than 125,000 square miles, ruling a population of 5 to 10 million in a tributary system that provided them with foodstuffs and gold.

The Aztecs' religion remains their most famous cultural feature. They built pyramids to serve as temples and worshipped many of the same gods as the Mesoamerican peoples before them. Key deities included the jaguar god and the feathered serpent (Quetzalcoátl, who also appeared as a light-skinned, bearded man). Most important was the sun god, Huitzilopochtli, who took the form of a giant hummingbird. The Aztecs believed that the reappearance of the sun every morning depended on their devotion to Huitzilopochtli. They also believed the sun drew its energy from human blood, so they practiced human sacrifice on an extremely large scale. Victims included prisoners of war but also ordinary Aztec citizens. Historians estimate that, by the end of the 1400s, as many as 20,000 people per year were ritually slain.

The Aztecs thrived in Central America until the early 1500s, when the Spanish arrived. The defeat of the Aztecs led to Spanish domination of Mexico and Central America until the 1800s. The Spanish conquest is described in Chapter 20.

SOUTH AMERICA

The ecological diversity of South America is staggering. Climates range from tropical to cool and arid. Terrain types include jungle, desert, mountains, grassland, and the vast Amazon river basin.

Early Andean Civilizations

The environment in which complex South American societies first developed was mountainous. It was on the west coast, in the **Andes Mountains**, that civilizations first took shape. At first glance, the rugged terrain might seem too inhospitable to encourage the growth of advanced societies. However, that very ruggedness demanded a high degree of cooperation and efficient coordination of human labor, giving rise to a number of major cultures, both before and after 600 C.E.

Most of these societies appeared in the northwest Andes, in what is today Ecuador, Bolivia, and Peru. Among the earliest was the **Chavín** (ca. 850–250 B.C.E.). Later civilizations include the Nazca (100–800 C.E.), the **Moche** (200–700 C.E.), the Huari (ca. 500–1000), and the Chimu (ca. 800–1465).

Features of Andean Civilizations

Most Andean societies had certain features in common. Most were organized into clans called **ayllu**. Smaller groups cooperated by taking on rotational labor obligations (**mit'a**) for the entire clan. The Andean peoples practiced animal husbandry, breeding **llamas**, alpacas, and vicuñas for transport, food, and wool. Those living on the coast fished and traded with their neighbors in the mountain valleys. Trade also took place between Andean societies and tribes in the Amazon basin to the east.

Women in Andean societies were greatly constrained in their rights and freedoms. Wives were considered little more than domestic servants. Lower-class women worked as weavers, farmers, and child rearers. One alternative was to become involved in religious life. Especially in Incan society, many young girls were chosen to serve in temples.

Andean cultures also grew crops, but cultivating land was difficult in such a mountainous region. To overcome this difficulty, Andean peoples used a method of **terrace farming**, in which flat surfaces were carved, staircase fashion, out of the mountains' sloped sides. Terrace farming was labor-intensive, but allowed farmers to work in environments not naturally favorable for agriculture.

Another noteworthy feature of Andean societies is that most of them accomplished a high level of cultural sophistication without developing a system of writing. To keep financial records and accounts, Andean civilizations used an elaborate system, called **quipu**, of knots tied in cords.

The Incas

All these features were passed on to the most famous Andean civilization, the **Incas** (ca. 1300s–1536). The Incas rose quickly during the 1300s to build a huge empire in the Andes, subduing many of the peoples already mentioned. In less than a hundred years, Incan territory grew into a massive expanse covering 3,000 miles north

Andean Civilizations, ca. 850 B.C.E.–1532 C.E.

The earliest major civilizations of South America emerged in the Andes Mountains, on the continent's western coast. The last and greatest was the Incan Empire.

to south, from Chile to Ecuador, and stretching from the Pacific coast to the upper Amazon.

Even in such mountainous terrain, the Incas created an elaborate system of transport and communications, including more than 13,000 miles of roads. The Incas constructed large cities, including the capital, Cuzco, and the fortress and temple complex of **Machu Picchu**. The ruler was known as the Great Inca. He was considered the sacred descendant of the sun god, and to look at him directly was an offense punishable by death.

The Incas worshipped a number of deities, but chief among them was the sun god. The Temple of the Sun in Cuzco was the largest place of worship. It was laid out in the shape of a puma, and the interior was lined with gold. The temple was staffed by thousands of *acllas*, or "virgins of the sun." These were young women chosen each year from throughout the empire to serve as acolytes.

The Incan rulers stratified Andean society much more than it had been. They also increased and centralized the mit'a labor obligations, transforming it into something more reminiscent of serfdom or *corvée* labor.

The Incan civilization enjoyed its heyday during the 1400s and early 1500s. After that point, the Incas—like the Aztecs in Mexico—were brought down by the Spanish, as detailed in Chapter 20.

Unit Three: Review Questions

SAMPLE ESSAY QUESTIONS (CCOT AND COMPARATIVE)

CCOT 1

Analyze continuities and changes in the cultural and intellectual traditions of ONE of the following regions between 600 and 1450.

the Middle East
China

CCOT 2

Analyze continuities and changes in the economic development of ONE of the following regions between 600 and 1450.

Central Asia
Europe

COMP 1

Analyze similarities and differences in how TWO of the following expanded and administered their empires.

the Mongols
the Byzantines
the Caliphates

COMP 2

Analyze similarities and differences in the roles played by cities in TWO of the following places between 600 and 1450.

Europe
East Africa
Mesoamerica and Andean America

MULTIPLE-CHOICE QUESTIONS

1. Which of the following is true of the Japanese shogunates?

   (A) Samurai were not subject to a personal code of obedience or loyalty.
   (B) The merchant class dominated Japanese society during this time.
   (C) Land was held by powerful lords called daimyo.
   (D) The status of women improved relative to what it had been during the Heian period.

2. The Aztecs and Chinese dynasties such as the Tang and the Ming resembled each other in that they

   (A) imposed tributary systems upon neighboring peoples.
   (B) made extensive use of gunpowder weaponry.
   (C) practiced human sacrifice on a huge scale.
   (D) cultivated high-yield crops such as corn and the potato.

3. What fate did Russia experience at the hands of the Mongols?

   (A) It was conquered, but only for a short time.
   (B) It allied with the Mongols and joined with them in conquering Central Asia.
   (C) It was bypassed by the Mongols in favor of richer lands in the Middle East.
   (D) It was ruled by the Mongols for more than two centuries.

4. The Hanseatic League

   (A) dominated regional commerce in the Baltic and North seas.
   (B) traded in diamonds and slaves.
   (C) was a powerful banking house in the Holy Roman Empire.
   (D) competed with Italy for trade in the Mediterranean.

5. Timbuktu was renowned for its

   (A) gold and its role in opposing the Arab slave trade.
   (B) salt reserves and Islamic scholarship.
   (C) large harbor.
   (D) glass and ceramic wares.

6. What did Swahili and Latin have in common during the period between 1000 and 1500?

   (A) They were banned by conquering rulers eager to impose their own languages.
   (B) They were the most widely spoken Indo-European languages of the period.
   (C) They allowed communication between diverse populations inhabiting large regions.
   (D) They both died out in favor of vernacular languages during these years.

7. What health-related crisis gravely affected China, the Middle East, and Europe during the fourteenth century?

   (A) the spread of bubonic plague
   (B) crop blights that killed wheat as well as rice
   (C) the outbreak of Spanish flu
   (D) the global cooling known as the Little Ice Age

8. Which of the following was NOT a consequence of the Moorish occupation of Spain?

   (A) The Moors brought advanced knowledge of medicine and science.
   (B) The Moors left behind a distinct artistic and architectural style.
   (C) The Moors persecuted Jewish scholars and professionals.
   (D) The Moors' presence caused other European states to develop feudal defenses more effectively.

9. Which of the following characterized urban life in medieval Europe?

   (A) Urbanization did little to stimulate the revival of trade.
   (B) City governments fought poverty by creating extensive welfare systems.
   (C) Most professions were organized according to the guild system.
   (D) The urban poor shouldered the same labor obligations as serfs in the surrounding countryside.

10. The photo above most likely exemplifies

    (A) the blending of Hindu and Buddhist architectural styles.
    (B) palace-building as practiced in the Incan Empire.
    (C) regal display on the part of a West African monarch.
    (D) the diffusion of Chinese architectural forms throughout Buddhist Asia.

11. Which of the following can most directly be attributed to the Crusades?

    (A) widespread adoption of gunpowder weaponry throughout Eurasia
    (B) European colonization of East African and Southeast Asian ports
    (C) heightened European desire to trade with or control parts of Asia
    (D) the accelerated eastward spread of diseases such as cholera and smallpox

12. The early Ming emperors

    (A) were culturally brilliant but politically decadent.
    (B) surrendered control over much of their territory to European powers.
    (C) overthrew Mongol rule and reconquered much neighboring territory.
    (D) ignored naval power and the usefulness of overseas exploration.

13. Which of the following did the Maya and the Aztecs NOT have in common?

    (A) a religion that practiced human sacrifice
    (B) the architectural capability of building large pyramids
    (C) the veneration of similar deities
    (D) strong, centralized rule from a single capital

14. Which of the following is true of the Abbasid Caliphate?

    (A) It presided over the golden age of Islamic culture.
    (B) It forbade Jews and Christians to practice their own religions.
    (C) It provided skilled and firm leadership against the European crusades.
    (D) It imposed sanctions on China and refused to trade with the Far East.

15. Which of the following is an example of China being influenced by its neighbors, rather than the reverse?

    (A) its openness to Buddhist missionaries from Korea
    (B) its borrowing of the compass from Burma
    (C) its adoption of rice-paddy cultivation from Vietnam
    (D) its adaptation of Japanese ship design in creating the junk

16. A key similarity between women in medieval Europe and in Heian Japan is that

    (A) they could gain educations and respect for their intellectual accomplishments.
    (B) patriarchal discrimination barred them from any role in religious life.
    (C) they frequently ascended to the throne, ruling as queens and empresses.
    (D) medical advances kept them from dying in childbirth as often as women elsewhere did.

17. Which of the following is true about Islam in India?

    (A) Muslim women were as restricted in their behavior as Hindu women.
    (B) After violent introduction, Islam came to coexist with Hinduism as one of the country's major faiths.
    (C) Islam's influence over India faded away after the Delhi Sultanate's collapse.
    (D) Islam displaced Hinduism and Buddhism almost completely by 1400.

18. One example of the Mongols' skill at cultural adaptation is

    (A) promoting Christianity as a common religion to unite their subject peoples.
    (B) imitating the Europeans' expertise at horseback archery.
    (C) adopting Persian as a written script for their native language.
    (D) borrowing their law code from the Chinese.

19. The immediate cause of Ghana's eleventh-century downfall was

    (A) environmental calamity.
    (B) the Crusades.
    (C) Muslim conquest.
    (D) takeover by the Portuguese.

20. In what way did Islamic and medieval European philosophers think alike?

    (A) They attempted to reconcile reason and religious faith.
    (B) They considered astrology to be the unfolding of the divine will.
    (C) They saw monarchy as an illegitimate form of government.
    (D) They concluded that religious belief was superior to empirical observation.

ANSWERS

1. **(C)** Answer A is false; samurai followed the code of bushido. The merchant class gained more importance over time, but was never dominant even in later years, and the cultural attainments of women, highly celebrated at the Heian court, were not valued by the shogunates.

2. **(A)** Although the Chinese invented gunpowder, their armies were slow to adopt it, and the Aztecs knew nothing of it until the Europeans' arrival. Answer C is true only of the Aztecs. Corn and potatoes were unknown outside the Americas until the voyages of Columbus. Both civilizations exacted tribute from nearby tribes and nations.

3. **(D)** The development of the Russian state under Mongol rule (the 1240s through the mid-1400s), during which the city of Moscow rose to prominence, is one of many examples of the Mongol conquests' profound long-term impact on the history of Eurasia.

4. **(A)** The Hanseatic League included cities from England, the Low Countries, the German coast, Scandinavia, and even Russia, and is an excellent example of how wide-ranging trade networks revived in Europe during the high middle ages. It operated in northern Europe.

5. **(B)** Today a synonym for "the middle of nowhere," Timbuktu in Mali was a thriving center of commerce. It was landlocked, making C incorrect. Choosing among A, B, and D requires knowledge of what the city's chief commodities were, but remembering that few African states actively opposed slavery eliminates A, and remembering its fame in the sphere of religious education points to B.

6. **(C)** Latin and Swahili are lingua francas, or common languages spoken by different peoples living or trading in a large region. In Europe, Latin served for centuries as the language of the educated elite, even as vernacular languages grew in importance. Swahili (not an Indo-European tongue) facilitated trade and communication among the diverse communities of East Africa—and still does so.

7. **(A)** Answer C is a modern disease, one of the twentieth century's greatest killers. The Little Ice Age came later and did not have as direct a demographic impact as bubonic plague, the correct answer, which is thought to have killed up to a third of the populations it struck in the 1300s.

8. **(C)** During the medieval period, the Muslims were more advanced than the Europeans, making A and B incorrect choices. Likewise, the Moorish threat caused states like the Frankish kingdom to adapt militarily, as at the Battle of Tours. Spain's Jews were treated far more harshly by Catholic monarchs after the Moors' expulsion than by the Moors themselves.

9. **(C)** The growth of cities had everything to do with trade, and state-sponsored welfare is generally a modern phenomenon, making A and B false. Even the poorest of city people shed serf status ("city air makes you free," as the saying went). D is untrue as well.

10. **(A)** Angkor Wat in Cambodia fuses Hindu and Buddhist traditions. Similar syncretism can be found in India's cave temples; as with most image-based questions, basic familiarity with such styles is the key to success.

11. **(C)** The only plausible alternative to C is B, which one could argue resulted in the long term from the exploring impulse stirred up partly by the Crusades. But C is more relevant in the short term.

12. **(C)** Answers A and D apply to the later Ming dynasty, and B describes Qing weakness during the 1800s. The early Ming rulers were robust conquerers (and sponsored the overseas voyages of Zheng He).

13. **(D)** As Mesoamerican civilizations influenced by the Olmec legacy, the Maya and the Aztecs shared many common features. The former, however, were governed by a variety of independent city-states, while the Aztecs ruled from Tenochtitlán.

14. **(A)** Politically weak by the time the Crusades began (eliminating C), the Abbasid caliphs traded widely (making D false) and presided over cultural brilliance. Jews and Christians were not forced to convert to Islam (as in B), but were taxed if they did not.

15. **(C)** The development of wet rice cultivation led to higher yields and profoundly affected huge parts of East and South Asia. China invented the junk and the compass on its own. Buddhism arrived there from India.

16. **(A)** Upper-class individuals such as Hildegard von Bingen and Lady Murasaki received excellent educations and gained cultural fame. Women in both places could become nuns (though not priests). Answer C applies to Europe, but not Japan; deaths in childbirth were quite high in both.

17. **(B)** The Delhi Sultanate converted large parts of India to Islam by means of violence; long after the sultans passed away, the religion remained. Muslim women were not governed by the caste system as Hindu women were.

18. **(D)** Although a few Mongols became Christians, most converted to Islam or Buddhism, and they adopted Uighur, not Persian, as their written script. Their skill at horseback warfare was their own.

19. **(C)** Long-term environmental changes weakened Ghana and left it vulnerable, but the direct cause of its downfall was Muslim invasion from the north.

20. **(A)** Astrology was widely practiced in the medieval world, but not as part of formal theology. Monarchy was seen as the norm in Europe and the Middle East, and although religion was important to both cultures' intellectual traditions, empiricism was given its due as well. The attempt to strike a balance between reason and faith preoccupied thinkers in both worlds.

UNIT FOUR

GLOBAL INTERACTIONS
(1450–1750)

Unit Overview

GENERAL REMARKS

Between 1450 and 1750, the world's civilizations became truly connected for the first time in history. The most significant trend of this era was the emergence of fully **globalized networks of communication and exchange**. Regrettably, much of this interaction consisted of warfare, exploitation, and slavery. Nonetheless, trade, discovery, cultural interchange, and the faster and easier movement of peoples brought the world's societies into greater proximity.

One of the primary causes of this greater interaction was the massive and sustained **European campaign of exploration and colonization**. Driven by scientific curiosity, the quest for power, the hope of spreading Christianity, and a desire for wealth, European explorers during the 1400s and 1500s sought out oceanic trade routes that would link them directly with China, India, Japan, and elsewhere in Asia. They also encountered the Americas: a "New World" that had, for thousands of years, lain outside the bounds of knowledge of the peoples of Eurasia and Europe.

Within decades, European traders, missionaries, and conquerors had spread throughout the world. The Europeans were the first in history to sail around the globe, and they established a presence in many parts of coastal Africa, Southeast Asia, and East Asia. Most dramatically, European colonizers conquered and transformed the Americas. The opening of the Americas to the rest of the world was done brutally and out of greed, but also played a tremendous role in shifting the world's economic, linguistic, religious, and cultural patterns. It changed forever the environments of the Americas, Africa, and Europe, as new animals, new foods, and new diseases were brought back and forth in a development known as the **Columbian Exchange**.

Another trend of this era was that **state rivalries** and **imperial expansion** led to the **rise of Europe**. Until the 1400s, Europe had been relatively weak and backward, compared with civilizations such as China and the Ottoman Empire. During the 1500s and 1600s, however, Europe pulled even with China and the **gunpowder empires** of the Islamic east (Ottoman Turkey, Safavid Persia, and Mughal India) in terms of scientific advancement, global power, and wealth. During the 1700s, Europe overtook these other cultures, becoming the strongest, most technologically adept, and richest civilization in the world. By the middle of the 1700s, Europe was well situated to dominate the vast majority of the globe, militarily and economically—and did so in the 1800s.

Technological development and scientific knowledge increased in many parts of the world during this time. Many societies' economies became increasingly based on **commerce**. In some places by the 1600s, **proto-industrial** practices were laying the foundation for the fuller industrialization of many societies during the late 1700s and 1800s.

In addition, **peasant labor intensified**. In most societies, agricultural production increased, leading to a huge rise in population worldwide—from 350 million in 1400 to 610 million in 1700, the fastest rate of growth seen to that date. It should be noted that the bulk of this era's economic growth depended on **coerced labor** in many forms.

BROAD TRENDS

Humans and the Environment

- The European age of exploration brought the Americas into contact with Afro-Eurasia at the end of the 1400s. The transmission of foodstuffs, animal species, and disease pathogens, among other things, between both geographical areas is known as the Columbian Exchange.
- The introduction of Afro-Eurasian diseases (especially smallpox and measles) into the Americas caused a massive demographic crisis, killing at least one-fourth to one-half of the indigenous population.
- The importation of corn and potatoes dramatically altered the diets and agricultural practices of Europe and Africa.
- To the Americas, the Europeans brought the horse, domesticated pigs and cattle, okra, and rice.
- The introduction of European modes of economic production into the Americas, especially plantation agriculture and the cultivation of cash crops like sugar and tobacco, radically altered the environment of the Americas.
- After a gradual cooling trend during the 1300s and 1400s, the Little Ice Age began in the early 1500s and persisted until the early- to mid-1800s.

Development and Interaction of Cultures

- After the European encounter with the Americas, networks of communication and exchange moved beyond the level of transregional and became truly global. The Atlantic basin itself became a gigantic cauldron of economic, cultural, religious, ethnic, political, and military interaction.
- Most major societies had well-defined artistic and literary traditions. Increased technological aptitude enabled the production of arts and crafts of high quality.
- The level of scientific knowledge and technological achievement was especially high in civilizations such as China, Ottoman Turkey, Mughal India, and Safavid Persia.
- Europe made exceptional strides in terms of scientific knowledge and technological achievement. The Renaissance, Scientific Revolution, and Enlightenment all furthered the intellectual growth of Europe, to the point that, during the late 1600s and 1700s, it overtook the civilizations listed above.
- The steadily increasing influence of the printing press led to the rapid spread of information, scientific knowledge, religious debates, and new ideas. By creating

more materials to read—and more incentive to read—the printing press helped to boost literacy rates.

- Art, literature, and drama became more accessible to wider segments of society, not just to elite classes. Shakespearean plays in Europe and kabuki theater in Japan are examples of art catering to middle-class tastes as well as upper-class preferences. The same is true of novels like Cervantes's *Don Quixote* and China's *Journey to the West* and *Dream of the Red Chamber*, or the paintings like the Dutch masters commissioned by Dutch merchants or the *ukiyo-e* woodblock prints in Japan.
- New and syncretic religions appeared during this era, including Vodun (voodoo) in the Caribbean, the cult of saints in Latin America, and Sikhism in India.
- Within established religions, schisms appeared or widened. The Sunni-Shiite split in Islam grew more pronounced during this era. Europe experienced a religious earthquake, the Protestant Reformation, that profoundly affected not just matters of faith, but cultural life, military and political affairs, and the way Europeans spread Christianity to other parts of the world.
- The movement of Europeans and Africans (mainly slaves) altered the patterns of North and South American ethnicity, religion, language, art, and music.
- Buddhism and Christianity spread particularly far during these years, thanks to missionary activity, trade, and colonization.

State-Building, Expansion, and Conflict

- During the first centuries of this era (the 1500s and 1600s), global might was concentrated in China and the Islamic world's gunpowder empires (Ottoman Turkey, Safavid Persia, and Mughal India).
- The nations of Europe grew steadily more powerful. By the early 1700s, they were overtaking the civilizations listed previously in terms of military, scientific, and technological aptitude.
- The most dramatic development of the era was the European campaign to explore (and, where possible, colonize) the rest of the world.
- European colonization of the Americas, the African coast, and parts of Southeast Asia set the stage for a massive burst of imperial activity during the 1800s. It also created a worldwide system of military competition among European powers for global dominance. Some of the European wars of the 1700s—especially the Seven Years' War (1756–1763), which raged not only in Europe, but also North America and India—can be considered history's first "world wars."
- In many parts of the world, political organization became more centralized and sophisticated. Features of modern government, such as bureaucracies, admiralties, general staffs, treasuries, and state banks were more commonplace.
- Nation-states in the contemporary sense of the word emerged. These were political units with relatively fixed borders, a sense of national unity, and populations that were largely (though never completely) homogeneous in terms of language and ethnicity.
- Most monarchies remained traditionally autocratic, but some nations experimented with representative and parliamentary forms of monarchy.

- The increased importance of gunpowder weaponry meant that, from this time forward, military strength depended even more on technological aptitude than it had before.

Economic Systems

- The incorporation of the Americas into existing networks of exchange led to the emergence of a truly global economic system.
- Diasporic communities and foreign enclaves continued to form in many towns and ports.
- The rise in global productivity and wealth rested on the foundation of coerced labor. The Atlantic and Arab slave trades were extensive. Serfdom was common in Europe (especially Russia) and other parts of the world. Plantation and cash-crop agriculture in the Americas was based on unfree labor, and other examples abound.
- Mercantilism became the dominant economic approach of colonizing powers. Joint-stock companies like the Dutch East India Company, the Hudson's Bay Company, the Company of New France, and the British East India Company helped to finance much of the exploration and colonization of this era.
- During the 1500s and 1600s, Spanish and Portuguese extraction of precious metals (especially silver) from the Americas affected economies around the world. This huge and sudden influx of gold and silver coinage into so many economies created a glut of precious metals. Many societies, from Europe to China, experienced severe inflation as a result of this trend during the 1600s.
- In several civilizations, primarily Europe, proto-industrial modes of production began to appear, especially during the 1700s. By the late 1700s, the concept of capitalism was emerging as well. Both these trends would have a profound impact on the 1800s.
- Interregional trade was facilitated by the warmer weather of the medieval climatic optimum, and then affected by the global cooling that led to the Little Ice Age.

Social Structures

- Social diversification resulted from the growing importance of nonagricultural ways of making a living. Banking, commerce, trade, shopkeeping, and artisanry all led to the creation of middle and urban working classes. These classes were small to begin with, but steadily grew in numbers and cultural and social influence.
- Urbanization continued, even if most people continued to live in the countryside and farm.
- More economic importance began to be placed on trade, commerce, and money, rather than on land, which had been the traditional source and measure of wealth.
- In more societies, merit became more important as a criterion for social advancement and even entering elite classes.

- In most parts of the world, women continued to occupy a secondary status in terms of social roles, economic opportunities, and political influence. In parts of Europe, a limited sense that the treatment of women was unjust began to develop gradually.
- Individual women of small but important segments of society (from the aristocracy or emerging middle class, for example), gained educations, became active in business, made scientific discoveries, and became artists and writers.
- Colonization, particularly in the Americas, created mixed populations, such as mulattos, mestizos, and creoles. New hierarchies emerged in Europe's New World colonies.

QUESTIONS AND COMPARISONS TO CONSIDER

- Compare one or more major European monarchies from this period with an Asian empire (such as Ottoman Turkey, Ming China, Tokugawa Japan, or Mughal India).
- How were the states of Africa and the Americas similar to and different from those in Europe and Asia?
- Consider various forms of monarchy during this era and how they were legitimated (divine right, constitutionality, mandate of heaven, impressive displays of art and architecture).
- Compare the growing Atlantic slave trade with other systems of coerced labor (for example, serfdom in Russia, the Arab slave network in Africa, the encomienda and hacienda systems in Latin America, and the Ottoman devshirme).
- What technologies facilitated exploration? Imperial expansion of all kinds?
- What made European exploration different from earlier campaigns of exploration?
- Examine the emergence of gunpowder weaponry, the way it spread, and the consequences of its invention.
- Compare existing elites, such as Europe's noble class, zamindars in Mughal India, and the daimyo in Japan. What other elites existed or emerged? What were the criteria for elite status? Wealth? Birthright? Merit?
- How did elites in various regions interact with European traders and colonizers?
- What were the environmental effects of the European encounter with the Americas? The economic effects? What were the cultural and social consequences? What mixed populations came into being as a result (mestizos, mulattos, creoles)?
- What were the social and political consequences of the rise of commerce in various societies?
- Examine the development of popular and more easily accessible forms of culture, such as drama (Shakespeare, kabuki) or poetry and the novel (Cervantes, the Sundiata epic, Ming China's *Journey to the West*, Qing China's *Dream of the Red Chamber*) or painting (Dutch Masters, *ukiyo-e* woodblock prints).
- Consider key state rivalries during this period. Also consider the way competition over trade affected the global balance of power and patterns of international commerce.

Europe: Reformation, Absolutism, and Enlightenment

- The Protestant Reformation and Catholic Counter-Reformation
- Absolute monarchies versus parliamentary monarchies
- The movable-type (Gutenberg) printing press
- The scientific revolution and the heliocentric theory
- The Enlightenment (Age of Reason)

- The agricultural revolution and the Columbian exchange
- Urbanization and the appearance of a middle class
- Mercantilism, capitalism, and proto-industrialization
- The Atlantic slave trade

For Europe, the years between the mid-1400s and late 1700s were a time of political, religious, intellectual, and socioeconomic transformation. European nations grew stronger and more stable. The Protestant churches were born. Until approximately 1600, the Renaissance spread northward from Italy, affecting all of Europe. Afterward, the scientific awareness and intellectual sophistication of Europe (at least its upper classes) increased by leaps and bounds. The continent's population grew and diversified. Europeans improved their agricultural techniques, their technological aptitude increased, and they took the first steps in building modern industrial and commercial economies.

In addition, Europe's global power skyrocketed. The Europeans did not invent gunpowder weaponry, but in the long term, they used it most efficiently. Also, as described in Chapter 15, it was during these years that Europe, unlike any other civilization, explored most of the globe, then colonized a vast portion of it. In the 1400s, Europe was simply one of many major civilizations, and a relatively weak one. By the end of the 1700s, it was among the most powerful, and its military, diplomatic, and economic might would only increase in the 1800s.

THE PROTESTANT REFORMATION AND ITS AFTERMATH

The Crisis of European Catholicism

For more than a thousand years, there had been only one major Christian denomination in most of Europe: Roman Catholicism. (Eastern Orthodoxy was important in Byzantium and eastern Europe.) As described in Chapter 7, the Catholic Church enjoyed an immense amount of power and wealth during most of the medieval era.

During the 1300s and 1400s, the church entered a period of long-term crisis. For most of the 1300s, the papacy was transferred by force to the French city of Avignon, making the church look weak. In the late 1300s and early 1400s, there were rival popes, each claiming allegiance from all Catholics, causing great confusion. The church hierarchy grew corrupt in the 1400s, selling church offices and granting certificates of forgiveness for sins (indulgences) in exchange for money. As years passed, more people came to see the church as hypocritical and too concerned with money and power. Until the early 1500s, though, the church was able to crush any opposition.

The Protestant Churches

Real change began in 1517, when a German monk, **Martin Luther**, protested the sale of indulgences in his hometown. In his Ninety-five Theses, Luther launched a general attack against church abuses and certain parts of Catholic doctrine. When the church ordered him to retract his criticisms, he refused and was excommunicated. Quickly, what started as a simple dispute grew into a complete rupture of the Catholic Church. In the 1520s, Luther, now a fugitive, founded a new church, Lutheranism, the first of Europe's Protestant denominations.

With the **Protestant Reformation** under way, other movements soon emerged. The French scholar **John Calvin** established a theocratic community in the Swiss city of Geneva and preached an even more extreme form of Protestantism. Calvinism caught on in France (the Huguenots, an oppressed minority), the Dutch Republic (the Reformed Church), parts of England (the Puritans), and Scotland (the Presbyterians). In England, Henry VIII formed the Protestant **Church of England**, also known as the **Anglican Church**.

Many beliefs and practices separated Protestants from Catholics. In the beginning, Lutheran and Calvinist churches favored institutional simplicity, in contrast to the bureaucracy of the Catholic Church. Protestants did not venerate the saints or the Virgin Mary the way Catholics did. Rituals and sacraments were less important to them. Priests were allowed to marry. Most important was the concept of **salvation by grace**, the belief that only God's grace—not good works, observance of rituals, or the power of the pope—could bring a worshipper to heaven. (Calvin's doctrine of **predestination** took the idea further, arguing that whether a person would be saved or not was known to God from the beginning of time.) Lutherans and Calvinists were encouraged to read the Bible for themselves (unlike Catholics), making education and literacy important to them.

The Catholic Counter-Reformation and Religious War

In response to the Protestant Reformation, the Catholic Church underwent change in the mid-to-late 1500s, a process known as the **Catholic Counter-Reformation**. At the Council of Trent (1545–1563), the church worked to eliminate the worst of its corruption. To compete with Protestant churches for worshippers, the church sponsored the creation of impressive religious art and architecture, helping give birth to the Baroque movement. The church also reaffirmed the authority of the pope, gave new powers to the Holy Inquisition, and created an Index of Forbidden Books. It formed a new religious order, the Jesuits (Society of Jesus), which

produced missionaries, teachers, and diplomats to combat Protestantism.

From the 1520s through the 1640s, Europe was plagued by a series of **religious wars**, as the papacy and Catholic monarchs attempted to halt the Protestant tide and, where possible, force Protestants to return to the Catholic fold. The first serious conflicts were in Switzerland and the Holy Roman Empire (Catholic forces won in the 1540s and 1550s, but were forced by political factors to compromise and allow some German states to remain Protestant). Religious violence rocked England and Scotland from the 1530s through the first half of the 1600s. The Dutch war of independence from Spain, which began in the 1560s and lasted eighty years, was motivated largely by the desire of the Dutch to remain Calvinist. During the last half of the 1500s, France tore itself apart in a series of bloody civil wars between the Catholic majority and Calvinist (Huguenot) minority. The failed attack of the Armada in 1588 was part of Spain's attempt to defeat Elizabeth I and destroy English Protestantism. The last and deadliest of the religious wars was the **Thirty Years' War** (1618–1648), which pitted Spain, the Holy Roman Empire, and Catholic German states against the Dutch, the Danes, the Swedes, and Protestant German states (England lent financial support but did not fight). For political reasons, Catholic France sided with the Protestant powers, who won in the end.

FACT

Europe's religious wars were particularly brutal. All sides felt justified by their beliefs in committing horrible atrocities. These wars tended to last a long time and frequently involved women, children, and other civilians. They took place when Europe's armies were growing larger and starting to use **gunpowder weaponry** full-scale, a fact that made them even deadlier. After the Thirty Years' War came to its close in 1648, religious strife did not end, but major wars were no longer primarily about religion.

Religious Divisions in Europe, ca. 1600.
For centuries, Christianity had been divided into two large denominations, Eastern Orthodoxy and Roman Catholicism. In most of Europe, the latter had predominated. Starting with the Protestant Reformation in 1517, new religious rifts began to appear. By the end of the 1500s, western and northern Europe were divided into Catholic and Protestant camps, as shown in this map.

ABSOLUTE AND PARLIAMENTARY MONARCHIES

The Fading of Feudalism and the Emergence of European Nation-States

Although traces of feudalism survived, European countries in the early modern period became more like **nation-states** in the contemporary sense: solid political units with fixed borders, a sense of national unity, and mostly (though never completely) homogenous populations in terms of language and ethnicity.

Much of this had to do with the strengthening of central state institutions. During the Middle Ages, institutions had been weak, forcing monarchs to resort to the feudal system. By the 1500s onward, this power structure was changing. Especially by the 1600s and 1700s, European states were developing **bureaucracies**, such as tax-collecting bodies, central banks, general staffs (for the army), admiralties (for the navy), and various ministries and cabinets. Although monarchs and aristocrats still controlled most positions of power, governments were becoming more rational and bureaucratic. Combined with advancements in communications and transport, the development of stronger state institutions allowed monarchs to centralize in a way they had not been able to during the Middle Ages.

Centralizing Rulers

During the late 1400s and 1500s, many rulers went to great lengths to centralize political power. Frequently, this meant competing with the noble (aristocratic) class, which was anxious to keep for itself the feudal privileges it had been granted during the medieval era.

By the 1600s and 1700s, two major forms of monarchy emerged. The more centralized form was absolutism, the less centralized was parliamentarism.

Absolute Monarchy

In **absolute monarchies**, there were no legal limitations to the monarch's power (in real life, even absolute monarchs were restricted by informal factors, such as a weak personality, uncooperative nobles, or an unreliable army). Absolutism in Europe was typically justified by the doctrine of **divine right**, according to which the monarch reigns by the will of God. (This is similar to the Mandate of Heaven in China, although divine right theory places no obligation on the monarch to rule justly.)

Europe's archetypal absolute monarch was **Louis XIV** of France, the Sun King who ruled from 1661 to 1715 (he ascended the throne in 1638, but was only five years old at the time). Louis XIV created a highly centralized bureaucracy and national economy. He broke the power of his aristocracy and made it obey him. He built the largest army and navy that Europe had seen in centuries. He turned Paris and his palace of Versailles into grand, impressive centers of power. In many ways, Louis illustrated the strengths and weaknesses of absolute monarchy. He was an intelligent, forceful man who used his extensive powers to make France better-organized, better-run, and mighty. On the other hand, he involved France in too many wars, damaging the economy he had worked so hard to improve. Near the end of his reign, he persecuted French Protestants, to whom his grandfather had guaranteed religious freedom.

France remained an absolute monarchy until the French Revolution of 1789. Other countries created similar regimes. In the late 1600s, the Austrian Habsburgs brought absolutism to the Holy Roman Empire as they fought wars against the Turks. (In 1683, the Turks nearly destroyed Austria in the **Siege of Vienna** but were turned back; afterward, the Austrians and their allies pushed the Turks steadily to the east.) The constant Turkish pressure on Austria's eastern frontier provided a good excuse for greater imperial control.

The small but militarily powerful German state of Prussia became an absolute monarchy during the late 1600s and 1700s. **Frederick the Great** (1740–1786)—a great general as well as a skilled ruler—was one of the most effective monarchs of his time. His victory over Austria, France, and Russia during the Seven Years' War (1756–1763) is considered one of the greatest military triumphs in European history. However, the price Prussia paid for Frederick's talents was greater dictatorship and decreased freedoms.

The largest nation in the world, Russia, also emerged as an absolute monarchy. Thanks to Moscow's tsars, Russia already possessed a tradition of strong central authority. It was, however, economically, culturally, and scientifically backward compared with the West. (One effect of Mongol rule had been to cut Russia off from Europe during the Renaissance.) During the late 1600s and early 1700s, **Peter the Great** not only centralized political power but forced rapid, Western-style modernization on Russia. He also turned Russia into Europe's great power of the east. Much longer than other European states, Russia kept in place an oppressive system of **serfdom**.

Parliamentary Monarchy

Other governments, such as those in England and the Dutch Republic, took another direction. Even as these states centralized and modernized, the rulers became less powerful. These regimes were known as **parliamentary monarchies**, because the ruler governed in conjunction with some kind of lawmaking body appointed by the aristocracy, elected by some or all of the people, or some combination of both.

During and after their war of independence from Spain, the Dutch wavered back and forth between centralized and decentralized rule. Either way, the *stadholder*—an executive leader who was not quite a king—had to share power with a larger council called the States General.

Even more famous was the system that emerged in England (which joined with Wales, Scotland, and Ireland to form Great Britain in the early 1700s). Since the 1200s, England's monarchs had been compelled to share power with the legislative body known as Parliament. Parliament gradually assumed greater powers until, in the 1600s, the balance of power shifted in its favor. The English Civil War (1640–1649) was partly about religion (Anglican vs. Puritan) but more about power (king vs. Parliament). The forces of Parliament won the civil war, killed the king (Charles I), and established the Commonwealth, ruled by Parliament (then by the general Oliver Cromwell).

When the royal family returned to England in the Restoration of 1660, the rivalry between monarch and Parliament remained. Another uprising—the Glorious Revolution of 1688—followed, and another king, William I, also the ruler of the

Dutch Republic, was invited to take the throne. The invitation, however, was conditional: William I had to agree to a **Bill of Rights**, which curtailed the powers of the monarch and made Parliament the dominant partner in English politics. From 1688 onward, Parliament grew steadily stronger, while the monarchy grew weaker and more symbolic.

The advantages of parliamentary monarchy are clear from the English and Dutch examples. Both nations developed strong economies, powerful navies, urbanized societies, and intellectual and cultural outlooks that were relatively open and free from religious persecution. Although poverty and inequality existed in both countries, society was more flexible, and social advancement was more feasible than in absolute monarchies.

THE PRINTING PRESS, THE SCIENTIFIC REVOLUTION, AND ENLIGHTENMENT PHILOSOPHY

The Northern Renaissance and the Baroque

Europe's level of intellectual sophistication rose during these years. The Renaissance, which had begun in Italy during the 1300s, spread to the rest of Europe and continued till approximately 1600. Important figures in this later, **northern Renaissance** included the Dutch philosopher Desiderius Erasmus (known for his debates with Luther, as well as his satirical novel *In Praise of Folly*), the Spanish novelist **Miguel de Cervantes** (author of *Don Quixote*), the English cleric Thomas More (who invented the term *utopia* in his book of the same name), and, also from England, the poet and playwright **William Shakespeare**.

The cultural style that followed the Renaissance was the **baroque**, which dominated painting and architecture from the early 1600s through the early 1700s. In music, it lasted longer, until the mid-to-late 1700s. Baroque culture emphasized the bold, dynamic, and colorful and was used by religious (especially Catholic) and political elites to impress the public and legitimize their policies. On the other hand, much art and literature was aimed at middle-class audiences, such as the portraits commissioned by merchants from the Dutch Masters. Shakespearean drama appealed to and was performed for all classes.

The Movable-Type Printing Press and Its Effect on European Culture

A prime cause of Europe's remarkable cultural growth was Johannes Gutenberg's movable-type printing press, invented in Germany in the 1430s.

The spread of Renaissance ideas from Italy to the rest of Europe was due largely to the printing press. The press had even more of an impact on the religious debates that preceded, then caused, the Protestant Reformation. Because an increasing number of people could read the Bible itself, not to mention the hundreds of essays and articles written for and against church reform, religious ideas had a much wider impact than they could have had before.

Renaissance Science and the Heliocentric Theory

Europe's scientific and technological aptitude increased during the early modern period. During the late Renaissance, certain thinkers and scholars were moving away from the intellectual orthodoxy of the Middle Ages, in which a fixed set of ideas from ancient Greece and Rome (especially selected theories from the writings of Aristotle) were combined with Catholic doctrine.

During the mid-1500s, despite the Catholic Church's continued control over European intellectual life, individuals such as the Flemish doctor Andreas Vesalius and the Polish astronomer **Nicolaus Copernicus** began to cross important scientific boundaries. Vesalius did pioneering work in the field of human anatomy. Copernicus provided mathematical proof for the **heliocentric theory**, according to which the earth and other planets revolve around the sun. The Catholic Church favored the geocentric theory, in which the earth—home to what the church considered God's greatest creation, human beings—was at the center of the universe. It took more than another century before the heliocentric theory was accepted as fact throughout Europe.

The Scientific Revolution

The pace of scientific discovery accelerated during the 1600s and early 1700s, which are commonly spoken of as a time of **Scientific Revolution**. Early in the 1600s, thinkers such as René Descartes of France and Roger Bacon of England laid the groundwork for modern formal logic and revitalized the ancient concept of the **scientific method**.

Also in the 1600s, the German astronomer Johannes Kepler and the Italian physicist **Galileo** confirmed and popularized Copernicus's theories. In doing so, they ran afoul of the Catholic Church; Galileo was tried by the Inquisition and forced to reject his own scientific conclusions in public. (Protestant nations such as England and the Dutch Republic were safer havens for scientific pioneers; only in the 1700s did it become less risky for those in Catholic countries to challenge church doctrine.)

Many of the ideas behind the modern understanding of science were discovered or proven during the Scientific Revolution. They include the states of matter (liquid, gas, or solid), the question of whether light consists of waves or particles, the fact that living creatures are made of cells, the concept of the vacuum, and the science of statistics. Among the scientific instruments invented or perfected during these years were the telescope, the microscope, the pendulum clock, the thermometer, and the barometer.

Isaac Newton (1642–1727) of England represents the Scientific Revolution at its peak. Newton is famous for the laws of motion, his thoughts on the concept of gravity, and his role in inventing the mathematical system of calculus. Just as important, however, is the fact that Newton, more than any other figure of the Scientific Revolution, understood scientific thought as a totality. He took the discoveries of his day and tied them together into a single system of thought—Newtonian physics—backed up by mathematical proof. Not until Einstein's theory of relativity in the early 1900s would Newton's fundamental principles be seriously challenged or altered.

The Age of Reason (The Enlightenment)

During the 1700s, the educated public of Europe felt it was living in a culturally and intellectually advanced era. They put great faith in the power of human logic, as well as the recent discoveries of the Scientific Revolution, to solve problems and understand the world around them. Accordingly, it was common to refer to the 1700s as the **Age of Reason** or the **Age of Enlightenment**.

Enlightenment culture valued not just science but also philosophy and ideas about how to make society and government more efficient and humane. Philosophical societies and literary circles appeared in all the major cities of the Western world during the 1700s, but especially Edinburgh, London, and Paris.

Women played a significant role in the Enlightenment. A number became renowned for important Enlightenment writings and activities, including **Mary Wollstonecraft** of England (author of *A Vindication of the Rights of Women*) and Catherine the Great, Empress of Russia. Upper-class women, particularly in France, played a key part in organizing and hosting the salons at which much Enlightenment discussion and debate took place.

Among the most prominent Enlightenment philosophers were John Locke of England, and **Voltaire** of France. A later Enlightenment figure was Jean-Jacques Rousseau, also of France. All these thinkers, as well as others, shared a faith in order and logic. Beyond that, not all had the same ideas about politics and society. All believed that government should be rationally organized and fairly regulated. Most believed in freedom of expression, opinion, and religion. Some, however, were monarchists (they simply felt that the monarch should govern according to law, not tyranny). Others, such as Rousseau, believed in granting more political power to ordinary people, although Rousseau viewed women as inferior to men.

Some Enlightenment philosophers remained Christian, while others, especially Voltaire, opposed organized religion as a flawed institution, and some became atheists. Nonetheless, their common emphasis on reason and progress bound them together. Enlightenment ideas played a crucial role in motivating several revolutions at the end of the 1700s, including those in America and France.

SOCIETY AND ECONOMICS

Population Growth and Class Diversification

The 1500s and 1600s were a time of demographic and economic crisis in Europe. Ecologically, Europe experienced a cooling period referred to by historians as the **Little Ice Age**, and famines were common. The wars of religion not only caused combat deaths but spread disease and caused mass starvation. Agricultural techniques remained relatively primitive. Populations declined or stayed level, depending on year and region.

Many changes came during the 1700s. Environmental conditions improved. New foods from the Americas, especially corn and the potato, revitalized European agriculture (on this **Columbian Exchange**, see Chapters 15 and 20). New methods for effective food production also emerged; this **agricultural revolution** included the

adoption of iron plows instead of wooden ones, and the scientific rotation of crops. The number and severity of famines decreased, and crop yields grew larger.

As a result, Europe's population grew during the 1700s. In addition, it began to diversify. The vast majority were peasants. At the top, royal families and noble classes made up a tiny but powerful segment of society. However, an increasing percentage of Europeans made their living as craftsmen and shopkeepers—or even merchants, bankers, and professionals, such as doctors and lawyers. Such people formed a growing **middle class**. A related development was **urbanization**. All these trends would accelerate in the 1800s.

Mercantilism, Capitalism, and Proto-Industrialization

The economic philosophy that prevailed during most of the early modern period was **mercantilism**, which advocated strict state control over economic activity and the exploitation of colonies (as sources of raw materials and as markets for the home country's manufactured goods).

As part of the Enlightenment, a new economic theory appeared, based on the concept of free trade, competition, and the market forces of supply and demand: **capitalism**. The most famous of capitalism's early supporters was the Scottish economist **Adam Smith**, who made a case for it in *The Wealth of Nations* (1776). Capitalism became the Western world's dominant approach to economics in the modern era.

Although full-scale industrialization did not occur in Europe until the end of the 1700s, a growing number of people became involved in manufacturing during the early and mid-1700s (and even the late 1600s). They also made use of machines and methods like cottage industry. This **proto-industrialization** was the immediate precursor to the Industrial Revolution of the late 1700s and early 1800s.

A final note about early modern European economics: because of the Age of Exploration, international trade became a key part of European economic activity. A great deal of Europe's wealth during these years was directly or indirectly connected with the **Atlantic slave trade**.

Women in Early Modern Europe

The status and rights of women changed considerably in early modern Europe. On the whole, women of the upper class gained greater access to education and participated more actively in intellectual life. Many women in the emerging middle class became more educated and assumed a greater economic role as business partners, bookkeepers, and operators of various enterprises. Women of all classes gained more control over when and whom they married, as well as divorce, childbirth, inheritance, and similar issues.

In no sense, however, were women considered equal to men, intellectually or economically. Nor did they have equal status or rights. Rates of death during childbirth were still high. Women made up the majority of victims—approximately 75 percent—in the witch hunts of the 1500s and 1600s. Both Catholicism and the new Protestant faiths maintained that women were inferior to and more sinful than men, and both used arguments based on scripture to reinforce these notions.

Women made significant progress in cultural life. Many Catholic nuns maintained a high level of education. Protestantism's emphasis on literacy led upper- and middle-class women to gain at least some degree of learning.

A number of painters were women. Women took part in scientific work, although they were not allowed to become university faculty (except on extremely rare occasions) or join scientific societies. Women also turned to writing and philosophy, especially during the eighteenth century. Like Mary Wollstonecraft and others, they played a crucial part in the Enlightenment.

Some of the most important monarchs of early modern Europe were women. Among them were Isabella of Castile, Elizabeth I of England, Maria Theresa of Austria, and Catherine the Great of Russia.

The Western Campaign of Exploration and Colonization

- Exploration, colonization, and the rise of the West
- The compass and improved naval technology
- Gunpowder weaponry
- Trade and missionary activity
- Slavery and resource extraction
- Major explorers and conquistadors
- Trading companies

Between the early-to-mid 1400s and the mid-to-late 1700s, the nations of Europe accomplished what no other civilization had done: they explored the wider world around them, discovered how to sail around the globe, and mapped the planet's major oceans and landmasses.

With this knowledge came might and wealth. The nations of Europe conquered, colonized, and forced open foreign markets. European explorers and generals were aided by superior technology, the vulnerability of many non-Europeans to European diseases, and, in many cases, sheer ruthlessness.

The legacy is mixed. On one hand, exploration gave Europe's nations an unprecedented amount of geographical and scientific knowledge. Colonization made Europe rich and powerful. It was during the years of exploration—and largely *because* of exploration—that Europe started to become the dominant civilization on the planet.

On the other hand, Europe paid a moral and ethical price for the knowledge and power it gained. Exploration and colonization went hand-in-hand with war, greed, prejudice, religious intolerance, and slavery. Many parts of the world remained under European rule for hundreds of years. Even now, the long-standing tensions left over between Western nations and their former colonies continue to have an impact on international relations.

ECONOMIC MOTIVATIONS AND TECHNOLOGICAL CAPABILITIES

Why and how did the Europeans become the first to explore the world? For many centuries, the peoples of Europe had been less technologically and scientifically advanced than their neighbors in the Middle East or countries such as China. Any observer during the medieval era would have thought it unlikely that Europe, only a short time later, would emerge as the leader in world exploration.

Until the 1400s, Europeans' geographic knowledge was limited. They knew the Mediterranean, Baltic, and North seas well. Africa, the Middle East, Asia, and even Russia were poorly known, inaccessible, or impassable. For the time being, the only outlet was the Atlantic Ocean, which was frighteningly unfamiliar.

Economic Motives for Exploration

The Europeans' primary motivation for exploring was economic. During the Middle Ages, the nations of Europe had become aware of the fabulous wealth of other parts of the world, especially to the east. Europeans also knew how desirable many eastern goods were.

By the 1400s, Europeans were dreaming of silk, metal goods, spices, fruit, jewels and precious metals, and other items unknown or in short supply in their own lands. If they could reach the Far East directly, rather than trading with middlemen in the Middle East, they would be able to make tremendous profits.

New Navigational and Maritime Technology

If Europeans were interested in exploring by the 1400s, they needed the technology and knowledge to do so. Already by the 1300s, Europeans had learned the secret of the **compass** from the Chinese. Better knowledge of the stars (gained largely from the Arabs) and better navigational instruments, such as the astrolabe and sextant, made it possible for European sailors to venture farther from shore without getting lost.

Naval technology improved as well. During the 1300s and 1400s, the Europeans began to build large, long ships, allowing them to sail faster, carry larger food supplies, and cover greater distances. Larger ships were able to crest the huge waves of the open ocean without capsizing or breaking apart. Finally, stern rudders and advanced systems of sails and rigging allowed ships to travel in almost any direction the captain wanted to go, even if the wind was not favorable.

Finally, European nations were beginning to use **gunpowder weapons** by the 1300s and 1400s. Although it was not until the 1500s and 1600s that Europeans invented the huge gunships that let them carry massive firepower to every part of the globe, European sailors and soldiers came equipped with muskets, pistols, and small artillery pieces. Not only could they use gunpowder weapons at sea, but they would be able to use them against less technologically advanced native populations when they reached new lands.

THE IBERIAN WAVE OF EXPLORATION: SPAIN AND PORTUGAL

The first European nations to explore the wider Atlantic world were Portugal and Spain. Both were on Europe's Atlantic frontier. They also had a great deal of maritime experience in the Mediterranean, thanks to trade and a long series of naval wars against the Ottoman Turks.

Portuguese and Spanish exploration during the 1400s and early 1500s proceeded in two ways. First, the Portuguese attempted to reach the lands of the Far East by inching their way down the coast of Africa, rounding the continent, and then sailing

NOTE

Mediterranean trade, greater knowledge about the Middle East gained during the Crusades, and the tales of Marco Polo all whetted European appetites for the wealth of far-off places such as China, the Indies, and Japan.

across the Indian Ocean to Asia. In the meantime, the Spanish, competing with the Portuguese, attempted to find their own route to Asia by sailing west, around the world. Famously, they found the continents of North and South America instead, as well as an ocean previously unknown to them: the Pacific. Quickly, both countries figured out the relationship between the Atlantic and Pacific.

Henry the Navigator and Portugal's Exploration of West Africa

The Portuguese began Europe's age of exploration thanks mainly to their prince, known popularly as **Henry the Navigator** (1394–1460). He and his successors sent out many voyages to the west and south, attempting to find a sea route to India and the Far East. The Portuguese claimed several Atlantic island groups, including the Madeiras and Azores, and traveled down Africa's western coast, conquering and exploring. They seized the Moroccan port of Ceuta in 1411, and soon afterward, the Cape Verde Islands. The Portuguese continued to expand along Africa's western shore, taking over or domineering areas like Kongo (see Chapter 19). In 1488, Bartholomeu Díaz reached the southern tip of Africa. In honor of the completion of his first leg of the journey to India, the Portuguese named the tip of Africa the Cape of Good Hope.

Spain, Christopher Columbus, and the New World

The Spanish, distracted by the Reconquista (see Chapter 7), were not as quick as the Portuguese to start exploring. Falling behind meant that, if the Spanish wanted their own sea route to Asia, they would have to try something different. The result was the famous voyage of the Italian captain **Christopher Columbus** in 1492, sponsored by King Ferdinand and Queen Isabella.

What Columbus proposed was to sail west to reach China and India. The boldness of his plan lay not in the idea that the world was round, because that was well known to educated Europeans. What made his proposal striking was his belief that the world was small enough that an expedition would be able to sail from Spain to Asia without getting lost or running out of food and water. He set sail in August 1492, and his ships reached the islands of the Caribbean on October 12.

Columbus was convinced that he had found the Indies (hence the mistaken term Indians for Native Americans), but the Spanish and Portuguese realized quickly that what he had found were lands completely unknown to them. The two countries turned to the pope to determine who would be allowed to claim which parts of the New World. In **lines of demarcation** agreed to in 1494 and 1529, the pope gave jurisdiction over most of South America and all of North America to the Spanish. The Portuguese received Brazil.

Reaching India and Circumnavigating the Globe

By the end of the 1490s, the Spanish and Portuguese had two worlds to explore and conquer. The Portuguese continued to sail eastward to India from the southern tip of

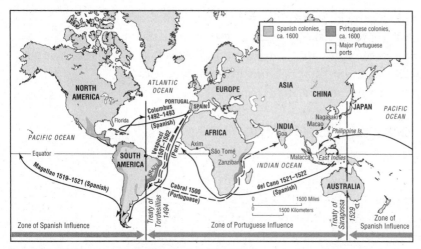

Spanish and Portuguese Exploration, 1492–1529.
The first European nations to colonize the wider world were Spain and Portugal. Their successes are attested to in this map. The north–south lines of demarcation were established by the papacy, to whose authority both nations, being Catholic, submitted.

Africa. In 1498, Vasco da Gama became the first European to reach India by sea, and the profit from his voyage equaled sixty times the original investment.

Shortly thereafter, the Portuguese captain **Ferdinand Magellan** (sailing for Spain) led an expedition that tied together all of Spain's and Portugal's previous efforts. Magellan was inspired by the 1513 discovery of Panama by Spanish explorer Vasco de Balboa, the first European to sight the Pacific Ocean from the New World. Hoping to cross both oceans, Magellan's ships left Europe in 1519 and traversed the Atlantic. They rounded South America and made their way through the Pacific, returning to Europe in 1522 (although Magellan himself died along the way).

Spanish and Portuguese Colonization

Having reached Africa, Southeast Asia, and the Far East on one hand and the New World on the other, the Spanish and Portuguese established a colonial presence in all these areas. In the Far East and Southeast Asia, many countries were too strong or too advanced for the Portuguese to conquer, and for the most part they settled for trade. Still, the Portuguese seized some areas, including the Indian port of Goa (1510), the thriving commercial center of Malacca (1511), and the island of Sri Lanka. As they had in West Africa, the Portuguese took over much of the East African coast, setting up strongholds in cities such as Mombasa and Zanzibar.

In the New World, the Portuguese moved into Brazil during the early 1500s. The Spanish built up their power in the Caribbean, using islands such as Cuba, Puerto Rico, and Hispaniola (today Haiti and the Dominican Republic) as bases.

The North and South American mainland fell to the **conquistadores**—generals who brought huge parts of both continents under Spanish control. Florida fell to Juan Ponce de León after 1513. From 1519 to 1521, **Hernán Cortés** waged an effective and brutal campaign against the Aztecs. The Aztec capital, Tenochtitlán, became Mexico City, headquarters of what the Spanish now called New Spain. Later, California, Arizona, New Mexico, Colorado, Texas, Missouri, Louisiana, and Alabama were taken over by other conquistadores, such as Hernando de Soto, Francisco de Coronado, and Álvar Cabeza de Vaca. Farther to the south, in the 1530s, **Francisco Pizarro** destroyed the mighty Incan Empire.

Both in Africa and the New World, Portuguese and Spanish colonies were originally intended to boost their home countries' power and wealth through the exploitation of raw materials. From the start, the Spanish and Portuguese attempted

to use Native Americans as slaves. When that effort failed, they brought slaves to the New World from Africa.

THE NORTHERN WAVE: FRANCE, THE DUTCH REPUBLIC, AND ENGLAND

During the 1500s, other European nations began to explore and colonize. The most important were France, the Dutch Republic, and England.

For decades, the Spanish and Portuguese jealously guarded their geographic knowledge and navigational techniques, and were anxious to lock the countries of northern Europe out of Atlantic exploration. At stake were military power, immense wealth, and Catholic-Protestant rivalry.

Only after the mid-1500s were the French, Dutch, and English able to steal enough information, shadow enough Spanish and Portuguese ships, and gain enough knowledge about sea routes to begin their own exploration and colonization. During the 1500s and 1600s, for the French, English, and Dutch to explore and colonize typically meant also fighting the Spanish and Portuguese—either at sea or on land—as the new arrivals tried to take colonial territories away from the older powers.

French Exploration and Colonization

In the 1520s, the Italian captain Giovanni da Verrazano, commissioned by the French, surveyed North America's Atlantic coast. From 1534 to 1541, Jacques Cartier traced the course of the St. Lawrence River, the first step in France's settlement of Canada. France established its first cities in Canada in the early 1600s: Port Royal in Nova Scotia (1605) and Quebec, founded by Samuel Champlain (1608).

Later in the 1600s, the French moved southward, exploring the Great Lakes and major rivers. In 1673, Louis Joliet and Father Jacques Marquette, traveling west from the Great Lakes, discovered the Mississippi River and mapped its northern reaches. In 1682, René Robert de la Salle sailed down the entire length of the Mississippi, claiming land for France, even though much of this territory was already under Spanish control. During the late 1600s and 1700s, the French took much of the Mississippi basin and some of the coast of the Gulf of Mexico away from the Spanish. This large expanse was called Louisiana (different from the state of the same name).

NOTE

During the early 1500s, the only area that France, the Dutch Republic, and England were able to settle was the northern coast of North America, which the Spanish saw as less desirable. One reason these countries explored here was their hope of finding an alternative route (a "northwest passage") to Asia through the Arctic.

French, English, and Dutch Colonization by 1700.
By 1700, France, England, and the Netherlands had gained many imperial footholds in the Americas, the Caribbean, Africa, and Asia.

Dutch Exploration and Colonization

Dutch exploration was closely tied to the war of independence against Spain. Dutch strategy in the late 1500s and early 1600s was to fight the Spanish at sea and, if possible, disrupt connections with their colonies. The Dutch did the same to the Portuguese and, by the 1590s, were seizing colonies from them: the Spice Islands in 1595, the Southeast Asian port of Malacca in 1641, the island of Sri Lanka, much of West Africa, and a number of Caribbean islands. To manage their colonies in Asia, the Dutch formed the **Dutch East India Company** (1602). The Dutch also invaded Indonesia, where they maintained a colonial presence for hundreds of years. They ran pepper and spice plantations on the island of Sumatra. On Java, they established the colonial capital of Batavia (1619), now the Indonesian capital, Jakarta.

The Dutch colonized North America as well. In 1609, they commissioned the English sailor Henry Hudson to explore the bay and river that now bear his name.

English Exploration and Colonization

Although England did not begin a major campaign of exploration until after the mid-1500s, it claimed parts of North America as early as the 1490s, thanks to the voyages of John Cabot, who attempted to find an Arctic passage to Asia through Canadian waters. During the mid-to-late 1500s, the English fought a series of naval wars with the Spanish. The English gained much navigational knowledge from these conflicts. Francis Drake, raiding Spanish ports, became the first Englishman to sail around the world (1577–1580).

In the 1600s, the English established their own colonies in North America, from the Carolinas to the Canadian border. Two colonies failed during the 1580s, but the English settlement of Jamestown, led by John Smith, gave the English a foothold in the New World. English Puritans, the so-called Pilgrims, came to America as well, seeking religious freedom. They sailed across on the *Mayflower*, which landed at Plymouth Rock in 1620. Later, the **Hudson's Bay Company**, in search of furs, began to move into French Canada.

The English made incursions into South Asia as well. Their first expedition to the Indies came in 1591. Shortly afterward, they founded the **British East India Company** (1600) to manage economic—and, later, military—relations with South and Southeast Asia. The English were in northwestern India by 1608 and would gradually take over more of the subcontinent. The English seized the Southeast Asian port of Malacca from the Dutch in 1795.

As with the Spanish and Portuguese, the countries of the northern wave were eager to gain military strength and, especially, economic wealth from their colonies. Exploitation of natural resources—and of the native populations—was the norm. Like the Spanish and Portuguese, the French and English brought slaves to the New World from Africa (see Chapters 19 and 20).

Islamic Empires in the Middle East and North Africa

- The gunpowder empires
- The Ottoman Empire and the sultan
- The capture of Constantinople (Istanbul)
- The janissaries
- Suleiman's conquests
- The siege of Vienna
- The millet system
- The harem

The unity of the single Islamic state, the Abbasid Caliphate, stretching from Spain to India, vanished during the 1200s. Decades of chaos and confusion followed, as Mongol warriors invaded and the Seljuk and Ottoman Turks rose up as regional powers.

Afterward, strong Islamic empires emerged in place of the fallen caliphate: the Ottoman Empire, the Safavid Empire in Persia, and the Mughal Empire in India (the last is described in Chapter 18). All three were highly centralized, technologically advanced, and militarily powerful. They are commonly referred to as the **gunpowder empires**, because of their mastery of new weaponry and their effective use of it in accumulating regional might.

The grandest and most influential of the Islamic states was the Ottoman Empire. It was also the longest lasting, with a geopolitical role to play on three continents: Africa, Asia, and Europe. Its neighbor to the east, Persia's Safavid Empire, was impressive, but not as strong as the Ottoman state, and it did not survive nearly as long.

THE OTTOMAN EMPIRE

The Ottoman State

The Ottoman Turks, originally nomads from Central Asia, established their own state in 1280. They rose in the late 1300s and 1400s to gain hegemony over most of the Middle East, restoring central authority to the region.

Centralized authority was provided by the **sultan**. He ruled with the help of an elaborate bureaucracy, run by ministers called viziers (*wazirs*), headed by the grand vizier, and provincial governors (beys and pashas). In the early 1500s, Selim I (1512–1520) claimed religious as well as political authority for the sultan, equating the Ottomans' right to rule the Islamic world with that of the Arab caliphates of bygone years.

The sultan's position was hereditary, although the eldest son did not always inherit, largely because the sultan typically did not marry but fathered heirs with a number of

The Islamic World's Gunpowder Empires, ca. 1629–1707.

The Blue Mosque, Istanbul, Turkey.
Officially the Sultan Ahmed Mosque, this seventeenth-century masterpiece is popularly known as the Blue Mosque. One of the great landmarks of Istanbul, the Blue Mosque is unusual in having six minarets, rather than the usual four.

concubines. A concubine whose son became the sultan's heir was known as the queen mother and generally enjoyed influence as an adviser to the sultan and her son. When a new sultan came to power, he often killed his brothers to eliminate potential competition.

The Ottoman Military

The Ottoman Empire was a mighty conquest state. Under a series of militarily active sultans, it moved into southeastern Europe, and its navies gained sway over the eastern Mediterranean. One of the Ottomans' great triumphs was the destruction of the Byzantine Empire in 1453. That year, the army of Mehmet II **captured the city of Constantinople**, after bombarding it with 26-foot-long cannons that fired ammunition weighing 1,200 pounds. Mehmet turned Constantinople into his new capital, **Istanbul**.

Further conquests followed. Selim I moved into North Africa. Ottoman forces pushed farther into Europe, along the Danube River. They seized the Romanian province of Wallachia in 1476, then paused for the next four and a half decades.

A larger and more successful thrust into Europe came under **Suleiman I the Magnificent** (1520–1566), greatest of the Ottoman sultans. Suleiman resumed the Ottoman assault on the Danube and Romania, Hungary, and the Holy Roman Empire. By 1529, the Ottomans had reached the outskirts of Vienna, where Christian armies finally stopped them. The Turks were pushed back somewhat, but they now controlled a vast part of southeastern Europe. Moreover, the Turkish fleet enjoyed almost complete superiority in the Mediterranean until the end of the 1500s—and remained a deadly enemy even afterward. The Ottoman presence in Europe lingered into the early 1900s.

During the 1500s and first two-thirds of the 1600s, the Ottoman Empire was at its military and organizational peak. As one of the Islamic world's three gunpowder empires, Ottoman Turkey was for a time innovative in its adoption of military technology and capable in administering its armies and navies.

The sultans supplemented the traditional cavalry (outdated and not entirely trustworthy) with elite soldiers called **janissaries** (from *yeni cheri*, or "new troops"). They were taken from their families as boys as part of the devshirme system, but given many privileges. The infantrymen were equipped with muskets, and they received advanced training. For many years, the janissary system, although harsh, kept Ottoman Turkey at the forefront of world military affairs.

Diversity and Religious Policy

Also during the 1500s and early 1600s, the Ottomans were efficient at governing their large territory as well as the diverse population that lived there. The Ottomans ruled not only Sunni Muslims, but members of the Shiite minority, Jews, and Christians of the Orthodox, Catholic, and Protestant denominations. Many tongues—especially Turkish, Arabic, and Persian—were spoken in the empire.

Both for political and economic reasons, the sultans practiced relative religious tolerance: non-Muslims were allowed to convert to Islam if they wished but were not forced to do so. They did not have equal rights, they were not permitted to serve in the military, and they had to pay a special head tax. There were occasional abuses, and one form of labor organization caused particular resentment. This was the **devshirme** system, designed to create members of state institutions loyal to the sultan and without (hopefully) too many ambitions of their own. Boys were taken from Christian families, converted to Islam, and raised in one of four professions: the palace (civil servants), scribes, religious, and military (the janissaries). Some families saw this as an opportunity for their sons, but none had a choice in the matter. Still, most non-Muslims were not treated badly. Ottoman policy kept the peace, and the extra tax revenue was economically beneficial. Each religious group (Muslims included) was grouped into an administrative unit called a **millet** ("nation"): there was one for Jews, another for Orthodox Christians, and so on.

Women in the Ottoman Empire

Among the Ottoman elite, women played influential but informal roles. The sultan's mother (the queen mother) ran the household, controlled marriage alliances, and was sometimes involved in diplomatic relations with foreign officials.

Despite its popular reputation, the **harem** ("sacred place") was not simply a collection of concubines for the sultan's pleasure. It was a complex elite social network. Male members of the harem (mostly eunuchs) were trained for military or administrative positions, while concubines were educated to read the Qur'an, to sew, and to perform music. Members of the harem were ranked by status, and some could leave the harem to marry officials. Few of the women in the imperial harem were used for sexual purposes; most were members of the sultan's extended family. These women also gained influence over male rulers by raising them as boys and training them to respect their guidance.

Outside the imperial family, women on the whole were not seen in public. However, they had the right to own property, retain it after marriage, and could buy, sell, and inherit real estate. They could also testify for themselves in court.

NOTE

Janissaries were recruited at childhood from conquered Christian communities, converted to Islam, and raised to be loyal to the sultan.

The Long Decline of the Ottoman Empire

The last truly gifted Ottoman sultan was Suleiman the Magnificent. In addition to being a talented commander, he was an excellent domestic ruler. Because of his gift for governance, he is often referred to as Suleiman the Lawgiver. Few of the sultans who followed had Suleiman's qualities, and many were mediocre or worse.

In the late 1600s, the Ottomans made one last attempt at a major European offensive. The attack almost succeeded but was turned back in 1683. That year, the Turks, as they had in 1529, reached Vienna, capital of the Holy Roman Empire. The **siege of Vienna** was seen at the time as a great turning point; had the city fallen, even more of Europe would have been open to Muslim conquest. At the last minute, Vienna was saved by a massive Austrian counteroffensive (greatly assisted by other Catholic allies, especially the Poles, whose cavalry played a key role in the battle). Afterward, the Europeans pushed the Ottomans back to the east. The Turks were not expelled from Europe, but lost much territory from 1683 to 1718.

During the 1700s, the Ottomans fought the Europeans—especially the Austrians and Russians—frequently. However, they never again seriously threatened Europe, and their power declined steadily during the 1700s and 1800s.

Ottoman Culture

The culture of the Ottoman Empire was sophisticated. Its level of intellectual advancement was high. However, after the 1500s and early 1600s, complacency caused the Ottomans to lose the scientific and technological advantages they had enjoyed over the Europeans, who were experiencing their own scientific revolution.

Nonetheless, the Ottomans were skilled at art, literature, music, and architecture. The best-known Ottoman architect is Sinan: during the mid-1500s, he designed eighty-one mosques with large domes and tall, thin minarets. The Turks were also renowned for their mosaics.

NORTH AFRICA UNDER THE OTTOMAN EMPIRE

Just as North Africa had converted to Islam from the late 600s onward, much of the region fell to the Ottomans. In the early 1500s, Selim I conquered Egypt and claimed authority over all Muslims in North Africa.

The Turkish presence in North Africa was mainly restricted to the coast. To the south, the Ottomans gained control over the trade routes crossing the Sahara. They also supervised trading towns along the Niger River and other waterways. Beyond that, the Turks ruled relatively lightly, leaving day-to-day government to local governors called pashas.

THE SAFAVID EMPIRE IN PERSIA

Since Islam's early days, the land of Persia (now Iran) had been an important part of the Muslim world. It had been absorbed by the Arab caliphates and, from the 1200s to the 1400s, controlled by various Mongol and Turkic warlords. At the beginning of the 1500s, under a new empire, it regained its independence.

In 1501, a fifteen-year-old boy rose to power in Persia, took the ancient title of shah, and proclaimed the Safavid Empire. Devoted Shiites, the Safavid shahs converted the majority of the Persian population to that denomination. Safavid Persia was commercially vibrant; the beautiful city of Isfahan was a great center of trade for silk, ceramic tile, and Persian rugs.

Militarily, the early Safavids were innovative and well organized. Like Ottoman Turkey and Mughal India, Safavid Persia was one of the Islamic world's gunpowder empires. Abbas I the Great (1587–1628) added gunpowder infantry (similar to the Ottoman janissaries) to his army.

Like the Ottoman Empire, Safavid Persia declined in the late 1600s and 1700s. The dynasty fell in 1723.

CHAPTER 17

China, Japan, and East Asia

- The Ming dynasty
- The Manchu conquest and the Qing dynasty
- The European arrival in East Asia
- Silk and tea production
- Canton and trade protectionism
- Daimyo, samurai, and Japanese feudalism
- The reunification of Japan
- The Tokugawa Shogunate
- Social stratification versus urbanization and the merchant class
- Nagasaki and Japanese isolationism

Between the 1400s and 1700s, China and Japan consolidated their position as the dominant powers of East Asia. Under the Ming dynasty, established in 1368, China reached a peak of cultural grandeur and elegance. After 1644, when a younger dynasty, the Qing (Manchu), arose, the Chinese continued to enjoy a high level of artistic and intellectual sophistication and even greater military and political prominence in Asia.

Japan began this period disunited and divided. For more than two centuries—the mid-1300s through the late 1500s—it tore itself apart in feudal wars and civil conflicts. Finally, during the late 1500s and early 1600s, Japan reunified. The regime that completed the reunification, the Tokugawa Shogunate, established strict control over Japanese politics and society, and ruled till the mid-1800s.

In the international context, the Chinese and Japanese remained only dimly aware of a major change: despite their cultural advancement and political consolidation at home, both countries slipped in terms of global power, losing the scientific and technological advantages they had possessed during the period between 1000 and 1450. This power shift, resulting from a certain stagnation, left both countries, especially China, vulnerable to foreign influence and domination during the 1800s.

MING CHINA

In 1450, the **Ming dynasty** was almost a century old. From its foundation in 1368 to the early 1400s, Ming China had been a politically dynamic and militarily active state, conquering neighbors and exploring faraway lands. It was economically prosperous. Its population grew steadily during the late 1300s and 1400s, recovering from the wars and diseases of the late Yuan period.

Although Ming China remained powerful during the 1500s and early 1600s, its principal strengths during these years were cultural. As described in Chapter 9, the artistic and intellectual achievements of the Ming were impressive: literary master-pieces (including the novel *Journey to the West*, a fictionalized depiction of the Silk Road journey taken by the seventh-century monk Xuanzang and his companion—in the novel—the Monkey King), fine porcelain ("china"), architecture, and the revival of Confucianism.

During the Ming period, the first European explorers began to arrive. As Portuguese traders and captains arrived in Asia, they established commercial ties with the Ming. The Spanish and Dutch arrived later. Because China was too large and powerful for the Europeans to conquer, they established embassies and trading houses there. Catholic (particularly Jesuit) missionaries were important as well.

The 1600s were a time of rapid decline. The late Ming rulers were weak and allowed the government to decentralize and then unravel. The Portuguese and Spanish traded with silver from North and South America, and the sudden, massive influx of precious metal triggered inflation, then economic breakdown. At the same time, agriculture yields shrank (perhaps because of a worsening of soil quality or a general cooling of the climate). The population grew more quickly than the land's ability to support it, and famines occurred regularly.

Finally, revolution and war drove the Ming to collapse. Serious military threats came from nomads and other invaders from Central Asia, Mongolia, and Manchuria. The huge cost of defending China's borders drained the economy. A massive peasant revolt, lasting from 1636 to 1644, toppled the dynasty. The last Ming emperor committed suicide, after first trying to kill his family.

The peasants' victory, however, was short-lived. Within weeks, enemies from the north, the Manchus, swept into northern China, took Beijing, and established a new dynasty.

THE QING (MANCHU) CONQUEST OF CHINA

The Manchus and the Establishment of the Qing Empire

The **Manchus** were from Manchuria, the large region northeast of China. Although related to the Chinese, the Manchus were ethnically distinct. For many years, the Manchus (who made up less than 5 percent of the population) created an ethnically based system of social stratification, in which the Chinese, as subjects, had to wear certain clothing and tie their hair in long braids, or queues. Males had to shave their foreheads, as reflected in a proverb of the time: "lose your hair or lose your head."

The empire established by the Manchus was called the **Qing** (or Ch'ing, 1644–1911). It included Manchuria and, after 1644, northern China. Skilled warlords, the Manchus continued their conquests. By 1683, they had taken southern China and the island of Formosa (now Taiwan).

The Manchus also controlled or added to their tributary system areas such as Mongolia, Tibet, Nepal, Burma, Vietnam, and much of Central Asia. Qing expansion to the north brought the Chinese into contact with Russia, which was moving deeper into Siberia by the 1600s and 1700s. It took much negotiation for the Chinese and Russians to arrive at a mutually acceptable boundary.

Qing Economics and Foreign Contacts

Full-scale trade with European nations began under the Qing, during the 1690s. Foreign trade was closely regulated by the state, and by the 1750s, most of it was allowed to take place only in one city, the port of **Canton**. Along with silk and porcelain, China's most important commodity was **tea**. While the Qing Empire sent a high volume of exports to other nations, it allowed few imports. This policy of **trade protection** gave China a highly favorable balance of trade.

The Qing regime sharply limited foreign contacts, economic or cultural, with ordinary Chinese, and strove to prevent the population from developing an appetite for foreign goods. Also suspicious of outside influences (and because of their strong support of Confucian ideals), the Qing banned Christianity in 1724. Another reason for limiting foreign contacts was cultural arrogance: like the Ming before them, the Qing considered China to be the center of the world and superior to all nations. In their eyes, Europeans were barbarians.

Emperors Kangxi and Qianlong

During the late 1600s and early 1700s, the Qing emperors were capable rulers, good administrators, and strong centralizers. The Emperor **Kangxi** (1662–1722) is widely considered one of the greatest monarchs in Chinese history: a skilled general, a just lawgiver, and a sponsor of culture and learning. Kangxi bolstered the imperial authority of the Qing by patronizing Confucianism, with its emphasis on respect for authority. Unlike many of the rulers who followed, he appreciated the importance of the West's growing technological aptitude. A later ruler, Qianlong (1735–1796), was the last dynamic ruler the Qing had. He strengthened China's borders, fostered economic growth, and promoted scholarship and art.

After Qianlong, the quality of the Qing rulers declined. They grew more complacent and less active. Also, as during the late Ming period, the Chinese population grew much faster than the economy, partly because of the introduction of New World crops like corn and the potato (population surpassed 300 million by 1799). Over time, national wealth was barely sufficient to support the population. For all but the upper classes, poverty worsened. Despite its strength as a regional power, Qing China was slipping backward in terms of technological innovation, scientific advancement, and global power—a danger the emperors succeeding Kangxi and Qianlong failed to perceive properly. By the 1800s, China would be increasingly open to European and American influence, then domination.

FEUDAL WAR AND REUNIFICATION IN JAPAN

As discussed in Chapter 9, Japan was governed after 1185 by military rulers called **shoguns**, who held power on behalf of the emperor, whose position was essentially symbolic. Although the shoguns preserved order and kept the country relatively unified in the late 1200s and early 1300s, decentralization became an increasingly serious problem in the late 1300s and 1400s. In theory, the Ashikaga Shogunate (1336–1573) ruled the country. In reality, Japan was becoming steadily more feudal, breaking down into semi- or wholly independent states ruled by the landed

aristocracy, or **daimyo**. As most feudal nobles in Europe had been knights, most Japanese daimyo belonged to the **samurai** elite.

In the 1460s, Japan descended into an even more chaotic period of anarchy and civil war that lasted till the late 1500s. During this **Era of Independent Lords**, the shogun was weak, daimyo fought daimyo, and samurai who lost or left their masters (*ronin*) became mercenaries or turned to banditry. The economy suffered, and crime rates rose. Starting in the 1540s, Portuguese, Spanish, and Dutch traders, as well as Catholic missionaries (including the Jesuit **Francis Xavier**, who did much to promote his faith in Asia), arrived. The shoguns' political weakness allowed foreigners and their Christian beliefs to gain substantial influence. The Europeans also introduced gunpowder weaponry.

The **reunification of Japan** took more than fifty years (1560 to 1615) and involved the military and diplomatic efforts of three warlords. Oda Nobunaga, one of the first Japanese generals to use gunpowder weapons (especially at Nagashino in 1573), conquered east and central Japan but was assassinated in 1582. Following him was Toyotomi Hideyoshi, who rose from humble origins to reunify almost the entire country. A clever politician, he centralized power from his capital, Osaka, and restored order (at the cost of harsh social stratification). In 1598, when he died, his son was only a child, and civil war broke out once again. The victor was **Tokugawa Ieyasu**, a brilliant, ruthless commander. He appointed himself shogun in 1603 and completed the full unification of Japan in 1615 (a process that included forcing Hideyoshi's son to kill himself). The Tokugawa shoguns would rule Japan for two and a half centuries.

THE TOKUGAWA SHOGUNATE AND THE CONSOLIDATION OF JAPAN

The Tokugawa Shogunate lasted from 1603 to 1868. After so many years of disunity, order and stability were its main priorities. The Tokugawa era is also known as the Great Peace (or the Pax Tokugawa).

Centralization, Dictatorship, and Social Stratification

As Hideyoshi had done before him, Ieyasu centralized the country. He established a new capital at the city of Edo (modern-day Tokyo). As before, the emperor remained a figurehead. Peace came at the price of dictatorship, as well as increased **social stratification**. Japan's class system became more rigid than ever before, and until the mid-1700s, it was almost impossible for a person to move from one class or profession to another. One tool the Tokugawa used to enforce this policy was a renewed emphasis on Confucianism. Ordinary citizens were forbidden to own weapons; the samurai retained the privilege of owning swords. The Tokugawa maintained a strict monopoly on gunpowder technology and kept the number of guns in Japan as small as possible.

Under the Tokugawa, women lived under increased restrictions, particularly if they belonged to the samurai class. Wives had to obey their husbands or face death. They had little authority over property and received less education than men, although they were encouraged to follow artistic and cultural pursuits. Among the

lower classes, gender relations were more egalitarian. Peasant men and women both worked in the fields, and women gained respect as homemakers and mothers. Even so, as in earlier eras, girl children were less valued and sometimes either put to death or sold into prostitution. Some women gained status as **geishas**, special courtesans who were highly valued for their musical, artistic, and conversational skills.

Japanese Isolationism

Many Portuguese, Spanish, and Dutch traders and missionaries entered Japan in the late 1500s, and Christianity became quite popular. However, many Japanese, like the Chinese, considered Europeans barbaric. More important, Japanese authorities suspected foreign ideas, including religious ones, and feared the possible effects of uncontrolled importation of gunpowder weaponry. Both Nobunaga and Hideyoshi started the process of restricting foreign access to Japan, even persecuting (and crucifying) Christians on several occasions.

The Tokugawa shoguns continued this policy of **isolationism**. Christianity was officially discouraged. A national seclusion policy was instituted in the 1630s, and from 1649 until the 1720s, foreign traders were allowed entry only into one city, the port of **Nagasaki**. A brief period of openness followed, and then Japan sealed itself off again until the 1850s.

Economics, Society, and Culture

Despite the Tokugawa regime's oppressive nature, it had many accomplishments to its credit. It restored and kept the peace. The population grew rapidly. Rice and grain production more than doubled between 1600 and 1720. Tokugawa Japan became highly urbanized (Edo was one of the world's largest cities), and the shoguns built an elaborate network of roads and canals. Economic growth was impressive: the Japanese became great producers of lacquerware, pottery, steel, and quality weapons.

During the 1600s, and especially the 1700s, the **merchant class** became increasingly wealthy and powerful (an exception to the general rule of social stratification). As for the samurai class, peace brought with it difficult transitions. At the price of obedience, samurai kept their social prestige, but in a modernizing society not at war, there was little need for a warrior elite with traditional combat skills. Some samurai were released from service by their daimyo lords; others found that the value of their land decreased as the country's economic center of gravity shifted to the cities. Masterless samurai (ronin) sometimes turned to crime, and there were occasional samurai uprisings. Most samurai, however, remained loyal, even if their traditionalist mindset kept many of them from embracing social and economic change.

In the cultural sphere, the samurai class maintained many of the traditions and styles mentioned in Chapter 9. There was some European influence on architecture (especially castle building, which had to adapt to the introduction of gunpowder) and painting (more emphasis on the laws of perspective). Among the urban classes, a new form of drama, **kabuki theater**—which featured acrobatics, swordplay, and scenes of city life—became popular. It was very different from the older, more refined Noh drama favored by the upper classes. Thanks to woodblock printing, **ukiyo-e** painting became affordable and, like kabuki, was driven largely by urban, middle-class tastes.

South and Southeast Asia

- Gunpowder empires
- The Mughal Empire
- The Indian cotton trade
- The Indian Ocean trade network
- Sati
- The rise of Sikhism
- The European arrival in South and Southeast Asia
- The British East India Company
- The Maori and the Aborigines

Between 1450 and 1750, South and Southeast Asia experienced, on the whole, greater political centralization. These areas were also confronted by the sudden appearance of European explorers and merchants in the late 1400s and early 1500s. Both developments changed the region considerably.

The largest and most powerful states in the region were in India. In 1450, India was ruled by the Delhi Sultanate, which was declining rapidly. In the 1520s, invaders from the north destroyed the sultanate and established in its place the even stronger state: the Mughal Empire, which survived into the mid-1700s.

As before, India and the rest of South and Southeast Asia were characterized by an incredible diversity of ethnicity, language, and religion (major faiths included Hinduism, several forms of Buddhism, Islam, and more). In many ways, this diversity enriched India and its neighbors. However, it also created deep social and cultural divisions, which often caused conflict and strife.

MUGHAL INDIA

As detailed in Chapter 10, the Delhi Sultanate had been weakening steadily during the 1300s and 1400s. The final blows against it came in the early 1500s.

Babur the Tiger and the Mughal Empire

Starting in 1520, **Babur**—a Mongol warlord in the tradition of Genghis Khan and Timur—launched a full-scale invasion of India from the north. Known as the Tiger, he quickly defeated the Delhi Sultanate.

In 1526, after the battle of Panipat, Babur established his own government, the **Mughal Empire**, which he ruled until his death in 1530. His successors conquered most of the rest of India, and the empire continued for the next 200 years. Its name comes from the Persian word for *Mongol* (the word *mughal* is often spelled *mogul*, which, in English, still refers to any rich or powerful individual).

Like the Delhi sultans, the Mughals were Muslims, making their state one of the three great Islamic empires of the era, along with the Ottoman Empire and Safavid Persia (see Chapter 16). Like the Ottoman and Safavid states, Mughal India was a **gunpowder empire**, using military force and advanced weaponry to maintain power, both at home and abroad.

In its prime, the Mughals expanded steadily southward, ruling India from their famous Peacock Throne. Their first capital was Agra; later, the capital moved to Delhi, which was restored to its former glory. The Mughal rulers centralized India. The economy thrived thanks to a boom in the Indian **cotton trade**. The early Mughals were religiously flexible, allowing Hindus and Buddhists to practice their own faiths, even under Muslim rule. Only during the last years of the empire did this approach change.

NOTE

Mughal India was similar to other Islamic empires of the day in that, while it was more technologically and scientifically advanced than most parts of the world during the 1500s and first half of the 1600s, it lost ground, especially to the nations of Europe, during the late 1600s and afterward.

Mughal India was culturally vibrant. Its architectural brilliance is illustrated by India's most famous landmark, the **Taj Mahal**, the white marble mausoleum built in Agra by Shah Jahan in memory of his wife. In painting and literature, there was a fusion of Persian and Indian styles.

Women in Mughal India

The effect of Mughal rule on women was mixed. On one hand, the Mughals allowed women certain rights. Female aristocrats were awarded titles, earned salaries, owned land, and ran businesses. Some received an education and expressed their creative talents openly. Women of all castes were permitted to sell their woven products. They could inherit land.

However, the Mughals restricted women's rights through **Sharia**, or Islamic law. These practices tended to coincide with restrictions that Indian society had already placed on women, such as cloistering women inside the home, as in the case of Hindu upper-class women. The Hindu practice of **sati** remained legal (although Akbar the Great attempted to outlaw it), and women were instructed to serve their husbands.

Akbar the Great

Mughal rule reached its peak under **Akbar the Great** (1556–1605), grandson of Babur. Akbar completed the conquest of India. A great commander, he used gunpowder weapons to gain control over most of the subcontinent.

Akbar created an efficient nationwide bureaucracy. The tax codes and legal system operated fairly. His reign was one of prosperity.

Akbar was also famed for religious tolerance. He allowed non-Muslims to worship as they wished, abolished the tax paid by non-Muslims, and encouraged friendly relations among Muslims, Buddhists, and Hindus. He even sought advice from the Catholic priests who arrived with European traders. Akbar ensured that a specific percentage of government officials were Hindu, and he married a Hindu princess.

Decline of the Mughal Empire

The Mughals' fortunes took a downward turn during the late 1600s and early 1700s. Akbar's great-grandson, **Aurangzeb** (1658–1707), a militant Muslim who abandoned the policy of religious tolerance, reimposed the tax on non-Muslims and forced thousands to convert to Islam against their will. His policy caused tremendous civil strife which, in turn, adversely affected the economy. Aurangzeb's intolerance also turned one religious minority, the **Sikhs**, into a rebellious and warlike group. The Sikhs' religion, which stressed the power of prayer and meditation, had been founded in the 1400s by the teacher Nanak. During the 1500s and early 1600s, the Sikhs had been peaceful. When Aurangzeb killed their leader in 1675, they revolted, founded their own state in Punjab, and developed a strong warrior tradition.

The Mughal state declined during the 1700s. The social and economic effects of religious struggle continued. Provinces broke away and became independent. In 1739, an Iranian marauder sacked Delhi and carried away the Peacock Throne, the symbol of Mughal glory.

Arrival of the Europeans

European interference in Indian affairs increased. The Portuguese trader Vasco da Gama arrived in 1498. More Portuguese, then Spanish, came to South Asia. They were followed by the Dutch, the French, and the English, who arrived in the 1600s. During the 1500s and early 1600s, the gunpowder empire of the Mughals was strong and technologically advanced enough to keep the Europeans in their place.

During the 1600s, however, the balance of power shifted. The English built textile factories at Fort William (near Calcutta, in the northeast) and Madras. The western gateway port of Bombay (now Mumbai) was ceded to the **British East India Company** (one of the most politically powerful corporations in world history) in 1661. The Dutch East India Company established bases in Ceylon (now Sri Lanka). The French created a great garrison and trading center at Pondicherry, on the east coast. The Europeans profited by gaining control over the trade of Indian cotton for spices from the East Indies.

European, particularly English, control over India increased during the 1700s. Until after the 1750s, the European presence was concentrated mainly on the coastline. Starting in the 1740s, though, large numbers of French and British troops were fighting each other in India, for the "right" to colonize the entire subcontinent. By the 1750s, the English had defeated the French; they then turned to the conquest of India itself. They triumphed over the Mughal state easily, although they kept Mughal rulers in charge of certain parts of India as puppets. In a short time, one of the world's mightiest empires had been transformed into a weak colonial possession.

SOUTHEAST ASIA

Kingdoms of Southeast Asia

Like India, the nations of Southeast Asia solidified politically. They also faced the arrival and constant encroachments of European explorers and colonizers.

Strong states in the region during these years included Thailand (which conquered the neighboring Khmer state in Cambodia), the Vietnamese nation of Annam, and Burma (which maintained the largest army in Southeast Asia). Vietnam and Burma became tributary states of Qing China. The islands of Indonesia were politically and economically important, until they submitted to Dutch colonial control.

Buddhism and Hinduism were dominant religions. Islam was important as well, especially in Indonesia, where it became the majority faith.

The European Presence in Southeast Asia

Europeans arrived in Southeast Asia after 1498, when Vasco da Gama reached India. The Portuguese quickly took over whatever parts of Southeast Asia they could: Malacca, Goa, Sri Lanka, and more. Where they could not conquer, they traded. The same was true for the Europeans who followed: the Spanish, Dutch (who took over Indonesia), French, and English. Because they were smaller and less advanced than India, it was harder for the nations of Southeast Asia to remain free from European colonization—although many managed to do so, at least until the 1800s, when European imperialism became even harder to resist. The Jesuit priest **Francis Xavier** came to Southeast Asia in the 1540s and spent the rest of his life cementing a Catholic foothold throughout Asia.

Australia and Its Neighbors

Farther to the south, the English encountered the continent of Australia. In 1770, the British mariner and explorer **James Cook** charted the east coast of Australia and claimed the continent for his country. The nearby islands of New Zealand (home to the Polynesian **Maori**) and Tasmania came under English control as well.

Full-scale settlement of Australia began in 1788. For years, the population consisted mainly of soldiers, government officials, and criminals "transported" to the colony as punishment. In 1830, Britain claimed the entire continent of Australia. The rate of settlement increased, as free settlers joined the colony seeking their fortunes. Mainly sheep farmers, Australians pushed into the interior and displaced the original inhabitants, the **Aborigines**, who had lived there for tens of thousands of years. The confrontations between colonists and Aborigines were often violent and one-sided, ending with the dispossession and ill treatment of the natives.

Sub-Saharan Africa

CHAPTER 19

- The Songhai state
- The kingdom of Kongo
- The Asante (Ashanti) kingdom
- The Zulu
- The gold and ivory trades
- The Indian Ocean trade network
- The Boers (Afrikaners) and the apartheid system
- Abstraction in African art
- The Arab slave trade
- European exploitation of Africa
- The Atlantic slave trade, the Middle Passage, and triangular trade

Starting in the early 1400s, Africa came under the increased influence of the exploring powers of Europe. Along the western and eastern coasts, Portugal, then other European nations, seized cities, built fortresses, and established permanent colonies. For centuries, Europeans exploited Africa economically, taking gold, spices, ivory, and other resources through trade and by force. Most shameful was the **Atlantic slave trade**, which began in the 1400s, as Portugal started transporting Africans overseas for use as forced labor. Quickly, more nations became involved, and the size and number of slave shipments grew astronomically, with the slave trade persisting well into the 1800s. Its effect on Africa, the Americas, and the economies of Europe was profound.

For the time being, however, the interior of Africa remained largely free from European control. Not till after the mid-1800s would Europeans penetrate much beyond the coasts. Certain African nations grew strong and thrived. On occasion, Africans were able to defeat European forces and stop colonists and slavers from moving deeper into the continent. Nonetheless, the economic impact of European imperialism was felt even in the interior, as were the effects of the slave trade.

INTRODUCTION TO WEST AND CENTRAL AFRICA

The Songhai State and Kongo

By the mid-1400s, the previously dominant power in West Africa, Mali, was fading. In its place, the Muslim kingdom of **Songhai** (previously a part of the Mali Empire), rose up. The first of its powerful kings, Sunni Ali, conquered neighboring territory in the 1460s and asserted control over many trade routes and the key city of Timbuktu. Songhai's most famous ruler, **Askia Mohammed** (1493–1528), came to the throne by deposing the last Sunni ruler (the name *askia*, which he adopted after coming to power, means "usurper"). A skilled general, Askia Mohammed continued to expand Songhai's boundaries. He centralized power by creating a complex bureaucracy, and he sponsored art, scholarship, and the building of many mosques. He encouraged

trade, and the growing merchant class generated wealth by exchanging salt for gold. A fictionalized account of his reign, *The Epic of Askia Mohammed*, is one of the classics of the West African oral tradition. Songhai prospered until the late 1500s. Civil war followed the peaceful reign of Askia Daoud, and Morocco conquered the divided kingdom in 1590.

Taking shape around 1400, the kingdom of **Kongo** grew out of Bantu-descended communities that had existed since 1000 B.C.E. The state extended from the Atlantic coast to the western edge of what is now the modern state of Congo. Prior to European contact, its economy was based on ivory, cloth, pottery, and metal.

In 1483, the Portuguese arrived in force, and although they did not conquer Kongo outright, they compelled it—largely by taking hostages—to enter into a long and complex relationship with Portugal. The king converted to Catholicism and took the name João I. Later monarchs followed the same example, adopting European names and the Christian faith. For many years, Kongo existed not as a colony, but as a state forced into economic and political partnership with an outside power. This relationship cost Kongo some of its autonomy, but also helped make it powerful. (Much the same is true of the Asante kingdom, discussed below.) During most of the 1500s, Kongo expanded and centralized, establishing an elaborate system of provinces and duchies to govern its population of approximately 500,000. Its large army acquired modern weaponry—and many mercenaries—from Portugal. Kongo helped to satisfy Portugal's growing appetite for African slaves, mainly by using its army to fight its neighbors and enslave thousands of prisoners of war.

Internal disputes and succession struggles weakened Kongo in the late 1500s and early 1600s, and again in the mid-1600s. Even so, Kongo managed to reduce Portuguese dominance: in 1622, with help from the Dutch, it expelled the official Portuguese presence. Periodic conflicts followed until Kongo's decisive defeat of Portuguese armies in 1670. The country went through various phases of unity and disunity throughout the 1700s and most of the 1800s, until, near the end of the century, it was fully colonized.

The Europeans and West and Central Africa

All of West Africa was affected by the arrival of the Europeans in the 1400s. First the Portuguese and then the Dutch, English, and French landed on the African coast, began trading, and built permanent outposts. The original purpose of the Portuguese had been to find their way south and east to India. As they became interested in Africa for its own sake, the Europeans sought to gain control over the **gold** and **ivory trades** that extended throughout West and Central Africa and the upper Zambezi River.

Women in West and Central Africa

As mentioned in Chapter 12, several African groups, particularly in West Africa, were **matrilineal** in organization, and women took part in leadership. In some instances, women became rulers. For example, **Queen Nzinga** (1582–1663) ruled the Mbundu peoples in what is now Angola. She was respected for defending her people against the Portuguese.

In West African trading villages, women took part in market activities. Sometimes women's councils administered the markets.

In North African cities, where Islam dominated, upper-class women were more likely to be cloistered and made to wear veils. However, economic necessity compelled lower-class women to work outside the home.

The Emergence of the Slave Trade

From the late 1400s onward, the development of African nations, the patterns of African trade, and the history of entire tribes were shaped by the growing European presence. The strongest states in West Africa—Oyo, Benin, Dahomey, Kongo, and Asante—were those that cooperated with the European slave trade, by warring on and imprisoning other African tribes, and then selling the captives to European slavers.

In particular, the **Asante (Ashanti)** kingdom, founded by Osei Tutu in 1680, became immensely powerful because its leaders sold gold and slaves to Europeans in exchange for muskets and gunpowder. West Africa was nicknamed the Gold Coast in recognition of the lucrative exchange of gold for slaves. Asante was one of the few parts of Africa where both minerals and agricultural resources were found in abundance.

Even states and tribes in Equatorial Africa, beyond the direct impact of Europeans on the coast, were affected. The trade networks connecting Equatorial Africa with the west coast were redirected or destroyed by the Europeans. Some West Africans began to raid Equatorial Africa for goods to trade with Europeans. Worst of all, the Europeans' desire for slaves frequently led West Africans to fight their neighbors in Equatorial Africa in search of prisoners to sell into slavery.

SOUTHERN AFRICA

Before the arrival of the Europeans, the southern tip of Africa had been settled by various tribes, mainly descended from the Bantu. The Portuguese rounded the tip of Africa in 1488, establishing an outpost on what they called the Cape of Good Hope.

During the 1600s, control of the region passed from the Portuguese to the Dutch. Dutch settlers known as **Boers** (also Afrikaners) arrived in 1652 and became firmly established as farmers and traders; their language evolved into a dialect called Afrikaans. Even more so than most white Europeans, the Boers possessed a strong sense of racial superiority and looked upon Africans and other peoples of color as inferior. Over the centuries, the Boers' harsh treatment of native Africans developed into the infamous system of **apartheid**.

The Boers enslaved the nearest African tribe, the Xhosa, a peaceful herding people. As the Boers expanded to the north, they encountered a stronger and more warlike people, the **Zulu**. Many wars broke out between the Boers and the Zulu. By the

WOMEN IN POWER

Many women throughout history have held political power on an individual basis. Examples include Cleopatra, Elizabeth I, Catherine the Great, Nzinga, Cixi, Golda Meir, Indira Gandhi, and Margaret Thatcher. Matrilineal societies, like those found in parts of West Africa, often afforded women more respect and authority than elsewhere. An interesting question, however, is whether this means that women are treated *equally*. Many queens and empresses came to power only because male alternatives were not available, and it did not necessarily follow that they could (or even wanted to) use their position to improve the overall condition of women. Even in modern democracies, women tend to be underrepresented as elected officials. In discussing how women have influenced historical developments, be sure not to overgeneralize from the often atypical experiences of powerful individuals. Until very recently, sexism and inequality have been the norms in most times and places.

early 1800s, the entire region came under British control, although the Boers continued to live there. This awkward, three-way situation caused much conflict during the 1800s.

EAST AFRICA

As discussed in Chapter 12, the towns and states of East Africa were part of the vibrant, cosmopolitan **Indian Ocean trade network**. From the 1400s onward, this system continued to exist, although the arrival of European merchants and conquerors changed conditions considerably.

The Portuguese, the first to arrive, originally viewed East Africa as a platform for reaching the Indies. For example, in 1498, the East African port of Malindi was Vasco da Gama's jumping-off point to Calicut, in India. Soon, however, the Portuguese realized the advantages of having permanent bases in East Africa. Not only would this allow them to reach India more efficiently, it would give them tighter control over trade in the Indian Ocean basin, especially in spices.

In the early 1500s, the Portuguese conquered a chain of cities along the East African coast, turning them into colonies. These included Malindi, Sofala, Mozambique, and Mombasa. Arabs expelled the Portuguese from Mombasa in 1728, but Portugal's presence in the region remained strong for hundreds of years. Others, including the English, later colonized East Africa as well.

AFRICAN CULTURE

Africa did not have a unified approach to art, although it is possible to make some generalizations. **Sculpture** was its most dominant medium. African art was also concerned with human adornment, as in masks and elaborate beadwork. Moreover, much of African art has been **abstract**, or not made to recreate visual reality (long before abstract art became a popular concept in the West).

Between 1450 and 1750, artists continued to produce wood carvings, sculptures, metalwork, and paintings. European traders brought home with them carved **ivory** pieces and textiles, which were admired by distinguished art patrons. **Textile arts** were prevalent in places like the West Congo basin. While textiles were considered prestige objects, owned by the elite, they were also sold to people of the lower classes.

Finely woven **basketry**, often done in intersecting geometric patterns, was treasured by royal families in East Africa. Basketry of high value was produced in Rwanda and Burundi. In the seventeenth and eighteenth centuries in Christian Ethiopia, kings commissioned artists to produce churches with brightly colored wall paintings of holy events. One of the most famous of these churches is the Church of Debre Berhan Selassie in Gondar, Ethiopia.

African architecture was influenced by Arabs and European colonists, who built fortresses and residences in East and West Africa.

THE ATLANTIC SLAVE TRADE

As in most parts of the world, slavery had existed in Africa for many years. African tribes often enslaved members of other tribes. In addition, the large **Arab slave trade** had for a long time extended throughout the Sahara and southward.

The Origins of the Atlantic Slave Trade

The arrival of the Europeans changed the character of slave trading in Africa. The Portuguese began this process, but other European nations followed suit. Over time, the Atlantic slave trade became a central part of the European economy and a primary factor in Europe's ability to generate such great wealth from the 1500s onward.

Starting in 1441, the Portuguese began to enslave Africans, taking them to Portugal and selling them in Europe. The number of slaves brought directly to Europe was relatively small. During the 1500s, however, slaves began to be taken to the Americas, and the numbers grew.

This new slave trade involved important changes. It took Africans farther from home. It became far greater in scale. Also, while unjust, earlier forms of slavery had not always involved hard labor, and owners took some care of slaves, at least as pieces of property. The Atlantic slave trade involved a greater degree of manual labor, and treatment of slaves tended to be harsher.

Reasons for the Expansion of the Atlantic Slave Trade

Several factors increased the demand for African slaves. One was the labor-intensive nature of planting, harvesting, and refining sugar. During the 1500s, Portuguese and Spanish colonies in Brazil and the Caribbean became major centers of **sugar production**, and the desire for slave labor there became more intense.

Also during the early 1500s, it became clear to the Spanish and Portuguese that, in the New World, Native Americans were not well suited as slaves. In addition, by 1542, the Catholic Church had abolished the encomienda system that allowed the Spanish to enslave Native Americans (see Chapter 20). If the Spanish and Portuguese wanted a source of slave labor—not just for sugar cultivation but also for **mining**, agricultural work, and menial labor—they had to turn elsewhere. Africa seemed an ideal source.

The Growing Scope of the Atlantic Slave Trade

Roughly 1,000 slaves per year were taken from Africa in the late 1400s, and more than 2,000 per year in the 1500s. It is estimated that at least 325,000 Africans were enslaved by Europeans in the 1400s and 1500s.

The Atlantic slave trade mushroomed in scale during the 1600s and 1700s. More than a million slaves were transported from Africa in the 1600s, and at least 6 million were taken in the 1700s. It is thought that, in total, no fewer than 12 million Africans became slaves in the New World between the mid-1400s and the late 1800s. Thirty-seven percent went to Brazil (the largest slaveholding country), 15 percent to Spanish America, 41 percent to non-Spanish parts of the Caribbean, and 5 percent to the southern colonies of British North America, where they grew crops such as cotton and tobacco.

The Middle Passage

Slaves were captured and shipped to the Americas under notoriously appalling conditions. Many were captives or prisoners of war, herded like animals to the coast and sold to European slavers by other Africans. Most were separated from their families;

many were mixed in with members of other tribes, who spoke different languages and followed different customs.

On the West African coast, slaves were loaded onto ships to make the infamous **Middle Passage** across the Atlantic. The more slaves a ship could carry, the greater its profits, so slaves were packed into boats as tightly as possible. Chained, lying on their backs, surrounded by hundreds of other bodies, all in darkness, slaves endured a nightmarish sea journey for weeks. Upon arrival in the New World, they would be taken to slave markets and sold. In the early years, up to 25 percent of slaves perished during the Middle Passage. During the 1700s and 1800s, slavers cut the average death rate to 10 percent or less—not for humane reasons but because each dead slave was a financial loss.

Atlantic Slavery, the Triangular Trade, and the World Economy

By the 1700s, African slavery had become a crucial element in European economic life and global trade. Until the early 1800s, no major nation made slavery or the slave trade illegal. Moreover, slaves were an integral part of the economic system known as **triangular trade**. European manufactured goods (metalware, cotton textiles, processed alcohol such as gin and rum, firearms) would be brought to Africa and exchanged for gold, ivory, timber, and slaves. The gold, ivory, and timber would be brought back to Europe, while slaves were sold in the Americas.

The Middle Passage therefore comprised the second leg of this triangular trade. In the Americas, slaves would be traded for furs and other materials, such as tobacco, raw cotton, sugar, and silver (typically grown or mined by slaves—and thus, slaves were not only commodities in the triangular trade network but unwilling producers in it as well). These materials would be brought back to Europe. This system was paramount in the growth of European wealth.

The Americas as "New World"

CHAPTER 20

- The conquistadors and New Spain
- Gunpowder weaponry and horse warfare
- The importation of smallpox and measles
- Seville's House of Trade and the viceregal system
- The encomienda system
- Silver mining and sugarcane cultivation
- Plantation monoculture
- The Atlantic slave trade
- The North American fur trade
- The French and Indian Wars
- Indentured servitude and "transportation"
- The Columbian Exchange

As described in Chapter 15, North and South America, which had existed in a state of isolation for thousands of years, came into contact with the rest of the world after the middle of the 1400s. European explorers arrived, considering themselves to have discovered what they thought of as the New World. Of course, the concepts of "discovery" and "New World" were meaningless to the Americas' original inhabitants. Equally meaningless was the name given to them by the Europeans: "Indians" reflected Columbus's mistaken belief that he had reached Asia during his voyages of the 1490s.

During the 1500s and afterward, the Spanish and Portuguese, then other Europeans, turned the Americas into their own spheres of influence. The Europeans also brought the Americas into contact with the rest of the world, economically, culturally, ecologically, and politically.

Most notably, the Europeans made North and South America part of a network of trade and exchange that was expanding literally around the world. Traders, settlers, explorers, and slaves came to the Americas, as did new technology, knowledge, and cultural traditions. The environment of the Americas changed forever, thanks to the Europeans' exploitation of the continents' resources—and their introduction of new diseases, plants, and animals. Conversely, the new foods and natural resources (especially precious metals) extracted from the New World had a significant impact on civilization worldwide—not just in Europe but also Asia and Africa. This so-called **Columbian Exchange** proved to be one of the most significant global developments during the period from 1450 to 1750.

NEW SPAIN

After the 1492 voyage of Columbus, the papal **lines of demarcation** granted jurisdiction over the entire New World to Spain, with the exception of Brazil, which went to Portugal.

The Spanish first established themselves on the islands of the Caribbean. Military expeditions led by **conquistadores** led to the creation of New Spain on the mainland of North and South America. The conquistadores took over Florida and most of what is today the southern and southwestern United States, including Texas and California. Their most striking victories were the conquest of Montezuma (Moctezuma) II and the Aztecs by **Hernán Cortés**, from 1519 to 1522, and the destruction of the Incan Empire between 1531 and 1536 by **Francisco Pizarro**. The former allowed the Spanish to turn Mexico City (built on the site of the Aztec capital, Tenochtitlán) into New Spain's principal headquarters. The latter opened up South America for future conquests.

☞ ——————

NOTE

Starting in 1535, New Spain was governed as a viceroyalty (*viceroy* means "in place of the king"). By the 1700s, three new viceroyalties—Peru, New Granada (northern South America), and La Plata (southern South America)—had been added.

Reasons for Spanish Success

Even with very small forces, the Spanish defeated large and powerful cultures in the Americas quickly and decisively. With their **horses** and **gunpowder weapons**, conquistadores such as Cortés and Pizarro enjoyed a military advantage that outweighed their lack of numbers. The Spanish (especially Cortés) were also adept at **divide-and-conquer tactics**, whereby they stirred up rivalries among native tribes and allied with some against others.

What most enabled the Spanish conquest was disease, particularly **smallpox** and **measles** (the same was true of the Portuguese in Brazil). Having no immunity to these new illnesses, native peoples died in massive numbers. Anywhere from one-quarter to one-half of the original population perished—some historians think even more—and the survivors were even more vulnerable to Spanish invasion.

Exploitation, Forced Labor, and Slavery

The conquistador Cortés famously stated that he had come to the Americas for "God, gold, and glory." Although converting Native Americans to Catholicism was considered important (especially to offset the loss of worshippers to Protestant churches in Europe), Cortés's second motivation—economic exploitation—was Spain's highest priority in the New World.

At first, the conquistadores governed the territory they conquered, sending one-fifth (*la quinta*) of their profits back to Spain. The viceregal system placed the New World colonies under Madrid's direct control. All colonial economic activity was run by the **House of Trade** in Seville.

Above all, the Spanish extracted precious metals from the Americas: gold and, even more important, **silver**. The largest silver mines were dug near Mexico City and at **Potosí**, Bolivia's "mountain of silver." Agriculture was important as well. Chief crops included coffee, bananas, tomatoes, corn, potatoes, and most crucial, the cash crop of **sugarcane**, which was turned into rum and molasses. The Spanish (and Portuguese) made use of **plantation monoculture**: the intensive cultivation of a single crop on large estates (known as haciendas, estancias, or latifundia).

Mining, labor-intensive sugarcane farming, and plantation monoculture required large numbers of manual laborers. At first, conquistadores resorted to the **encomienda** system (which declared all peoples in the Americas Spanish subjects) as a way of forcing Native Americans to work as slaves. This practice ended by the 1530s and 1540s, not only because Native Americans proved unable and unwilling to work as slaves but also because the Catholic clergy protested the cruelty resulting from the encomienda system. The book *Tears of the Indians,* by the monk Bartolomé de las Casas, did much to sway Spanish opinion about the plight of Native Americans. The encomienda was abolished in 1542. The result was to persuade the Spanish (like the Portuguese) to turn to Africa as a source of forced labor, leading to the escalation of the **Atlantic slave trade**.

NOTE

Plantation monoculture is environmentally damaging (it wears out soil); it leads to long-term economic backwardness (by discouraging countries from diversifying their resource base) and, worst of all, encourages unfair labor practices (including slavery).

Ethnic Diversity and Social Stratification

The arrival of the Spanish increased racial diversity in the Americas. Pure-bred Spanish who settled in the New World were known as *peninsulares.* Those of Spanish descent born in the colonies were criollos (better known as creoles). When Spanish and Native Americans intermarried, their families were known as mestizos, or "mixed." Other mixed races were mulattos (Europeans and African blacks) and *zambos* (Native Americans and African blacks). This intermixing of ethnicities and traditions has made Latin American culture very rich.

Unfortunately, during the centuries of Spanish rule, these groups were organized into a rigid social hierarchy, with European Spaniards at the top and those of mixed blood and native ancestry near the bottom. Slaves were on the lowest rung of the social ladder. (Compare this arrangement with India's caste system.)

PORTUGUESE BRAZIL

Brazil, the one major territory in the New World allotted to Portugal rather than Spain, was discovered by accident in 1500 by Pedro Cabral, whose ship blew off course in a storm. At first, the Portuguese considered Brazil unimportant and established an outpost there only in 1532. By the mid-1500s, the Portuguese came to recognize Brazil's economic potential.

Native populations were decimated by Portuguese conquerors, falling victim to superior technology and new diseases. Portugal's treatment of the natives, a mixture of labor exploitation and mass conversion to Catholicism, was similar to Spain's. Various ethnic mixes of European, Native American, and African emerged. **Plantation monoculture** was dominant.

Mining was important in Portuguese Brazil, as were the forest industries of the Amazon basin. For years, however, the most important resource was the cash crop of **sugarcane**. The labor-intensive nature of sugarcane cultivation prompted the Portuguese to use African slaves, first on their islands off the African coast and then Brazil. The first boatload of slaves to be brought directly from Africa to the New World arrived in 1518 (although African slaves had been brought there indirectly before then). Brazil was the largest importer of African slaves, and it was the last country in the Americas to outlaw slavery—not until 1888.

NOTE

Many of the same trends found in New Spain applied to Brazil.

DUTCH AND ENGLISH NORTH AMERICA

The Dutch in the Americas

In the late 1500s, the Netherlands and England started breaking the Portuguese and Spanish monopoly on global trade routes and overseas colonization. They began to settle in the New World.

The Dutch took over a number of islands in the Caribbean and seized part of northwestern Brazil from the Portuguese. In 1621, the Netherlands established the Dutch West India Company, twin to the older Dutch East India Company.

Farther to the north, the Dutch founded New Netherlands, in the region explored and claimed by Henry Hudson on their behalf. In 1624, Peter Minuit purchased the island of Manhattan from a local Native American tribe. Here, the city of **New Amsterdam**, capital of the new colony, grew into a thriving commercial center. The colony's leader was Peter Stuyvesant. In 1664, the Dutch lost New Netherlands to the English, who gave New Amsterdam another name: New York.

English Colonies and Permanent Settlement in the New World

Like the Dutch, the English moved into the New World as part of their commercial and military rivalry with Spain. They established a presence in the Caribbean, particularly on the islands of Barbados, Trinidad, and Jamaica.

Successful colonization of North America began at Jamestown, Virginia, in 1606. Economic activity was important, although many colonies were established by religious minorities, especially Puritans and Quakers, fleeing persecution at home. The *Mayflower* Pilgrims' Plymouth colony was founded in 1620; the nearby Massachusetts Bay Colony followed in 1628, and Boston was founded in 1630. The English seized New Amsterdam in 1664, renaming it New York. The colony of Pennsylvania, organized in 1682 by William Penn, was home to the English New World's largest city, Philadelphia.

The English took raw materials from the New World: sugarcane from the Caribbean; timber, corn, and potatoes (which caught on in England's oldest and closest colony, Ireland); and in the southern colonies, tobacco, which proved remarkably profitable. In addition, England, more so than other European nations, viewed the New World as a place to encourage large-scale **permanent settlement**. English colonies in the Americas became politically sophisticated, developed strong systems of local government, and, by the 1700s, felt a deep sense of local, even independent, identity.

Slaves were used by English colonists in the New World, especially in the Caribbean and the southern mainland. English criminals were often punished by "transportation," or exile, to the Americas. One institution that brought labor to the English New World was **indentured servitude**: would-be colonists who could not afford passage across the Atlantic would agree to work for a period of time for the families that paid their way. This was more common in the northern colonies.

NOTE

After the American Revolution, England deported its criminals to Australia.

FRENCH CANADA AND LOUISIANA

The French colonial presence in the New World began in **Canada**, in the 1500s and early 1600s, as Jacques Cartier, Samuel Champlain and other explorers charted the St. Lawrence River and established outposts like Quebec and Montreal. In the 1600s,

the French and their joint-stock company, the **Company of New France**, laid claim to the vast **Louisiana** territory, which included the Great Lakes and the Mississippi basin. In the south and along the Gulf of Mexico, they challenged the Spanish. The main priority of the French in North America was the **fur trade**: French colonists were great hunters, trappers, and woodsmen (*voyageurs*).

The French maintained island bases in the Caribbean, including Martinique, Guadeloupe, and Saint Domingue (today Haiti). Sugarcane production was the economic mainstay here.

By the mid-1700s, France had lost much of its territory in the New World. Its principal enemy was England and the **Hudson's Bay Company**, although Spain was a foe as well. Despite allying with Native American tribes, French colonists lost several conflicts with English settlers, including Queen Anne's War (1701–1714), King George's War (1740–1748), and the **French and Indian Wars** (1756–1763), an offshoot of the Seven Years' War in Europe.

As a result of the third conflict, the English took over Canada (the province of Quebec retained its French heritage). The Louisiana region was handed over to Spain, although the French got it back briefly in the late 1700s. French culture remains important in eastern Canada, the northern fringe of the United States, and the state of Louisiana. There, the Cajuns are descendants of the Canada's Acadians, who were expelled and forced southward by the English after the French and Indian Wars.

NOTE

The French were more adept than other Europeans at cooperating with Native Americans (especially the Hurons and Algonquins), learning their ways, and adapting themselves to local customs and environments.

THE RUSSIAN-AMERICAN COMPANY

Europe's least famous colony in North America was Russia's. After conquering Siberia in the 1500s and reaching the Pacific coast in the 1600s, the Russians set their sights on Alaska and other areas. In the 1730s and 1740s, the **Bering expedition**, organized by the Russian government, surveyed the waters separating Siberia from North America. Afterward, Russian hunters and soldiers moved into the Aleutian Islands and Alaska.

The **fur trade** stimulated Russian settlement of North America. The Russians established a colony in Alaska in 1784. They created the **Russian-American Company** and moved down the Pacific coast, building fortresses as far south as northern California. They sold Alaska to America in 1867.

NOTE

At least 80 percent of the Aleutians' native population is said to have perished due to Russian colonization, thanks to violence, the spread of disease, and alcoholism.

THE COLUMBIAN EXCHANGE

Europe's encounter with the Americas led to one of the greatest demographic and ecological transformations in world history, known commonly as the **Columbian Exchange**.

The exchange of foods, plants, and animals shaped the environments of Old World and New World alike. From Europe came sheep, goats, cattle, and pigs, which increased the meat and milk supply in the Americas. The Europeans also brought the **horse**, which provided labor and transport and radically changed the lifestyle of Native Americans who lived on plains and grasslands. **Coffee**, which came from Arabia and Turkey and had already been transplanted to Africa, was found to flourish in South America. The southeastern part of North America joined Egypt and India

NOTE

Among the effects of this exchange was the mass transfer of populations. Millions of slaves and hundreds of thousands of colonists came from Africa and Europe to the New World. Once in the Americas, their interaction with the indigenous peoples led to complex and rich ethnic and cultural mixing.

as one of the world's great sources of **cotton**. Wheat, olives, and grapevines were brought to the Americas as well.

From the Americas came manioc (which became a staple in Africa), squash, sweet potatoes, peppers, beans, peanuts, and vitamin-rich tomatoes. Caribbean **sugarcane** displaced the Old World's sugar beet as a primary source of sugar and became central to the world economy (and the Atlantic slave trade). **Tobacco** and cacao (for making chocolate) became eagerly sought luxury goods in Europe. Because they were easy to grow and yielded many calories per acre, **corn** (maize) and **potatoes** were the New World crops that most affected Eurasia and Africa.

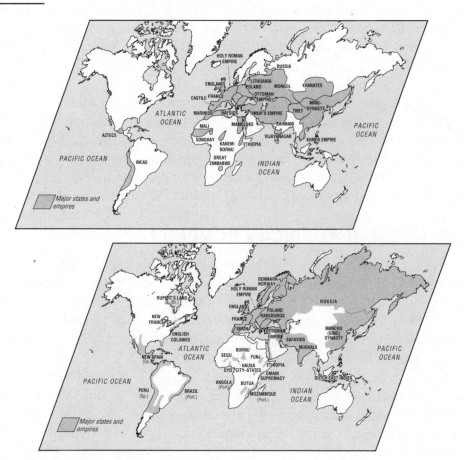

World Boundaries in 1453 and 1700.
In 1453, major states and empires were concentrated in Eurasia and small territories in Africa and the Americas. By 1700, large civilizations had spread into Russia, more portions of the Americas, and deeper into Africa.

NOTE

The death rate caused by European diseases is thought to have been at least 25 percent of the Americas' pre-Columbian population; some estimates run higher than 50 percent.

Tragically, the transfer of diseases, such as **smallpox** and **measles** from Europe—and malaria and yellow fever from Africa—was part of the Columbian Exchange. Environmentally isolated from Eurasia and Africa for so many centuries, the inhabitants of the Americas had no immunity to these new illnesses. The one disease Europeans may have brought back from the New World is the sexually transmitted disease syphilis (although there is much scholarly debate about the origins of this disease).

Unit Four: Review Questions

SAMPLE ESSAY QUESTIONS (CCOT and COMPARATIVE)

CCOT 1

Analyze the changes and continuities in the development of science and technology in ONE of the following between 1450 and 1750.

China
Ottoman Turkey

CCOT 2

Analyze the changes and continuities in how ONE of the following states consolidated between 1450 and 1750.

India
Japan

COMP 1

Compare and contrast the experience of TWO of the following civilizations as they encountered the Europeans between 1450 and 1750.

Kongo
Mughal India
the Aztecs

COMP 2

Compare and contrast the characteristics of TWO of the following labor systems.

the *encomienda* system
Russian serfdom
the Atlantic slave trade

MULTIPLE-CHOICE QUESTIONS

1. The encomienda system most resembled Russian serfdom in that

   (A) both used laborers to work agriculturally and on other projects.
   (B) both legally enslaved their labor force.
   (C) both were imposed by foreign conquerors.
   (D) both drew their labor force from prisoners of war.

2. Which of the following is MOST true of eighteenth-century European society?

   (A) A majority of the population moved into the relatively new middle class.
   (B) The majority of people continued to live in the countryside and work as peasants.
   (C) The rate of population growth fell off sharply.
   (D) The cause of women's suffrage gained great momentum in western Europe.

3. The tendency of the Muslim gunpowder empires to innovate technologically in the 1500s and 1600s, and then stagnate, is best illustrated by

   (A) a decline in the quality of goods manufactured in Safavid Persia after the mid-1600s.
   (B) the transformation of the janissaries into a pampered but obsolete musketeer corps.
   (C) the Ottoman Empire's failure in the 1700s to create a steamship navy.
   (D) Mughal India's decision to abandon railway construction projects begun around 1750.

4. This commodity played the chief role in motivating French exploration of Canada and Russian exploration of Siberia:

   (A) coffee
   (B) gold
   (C) fur
   (D) tobacco

5. Which of the following negatively affected economic life in Ming China during the early 1600s?

   (A) a decrease in the supply of precious metals, especially silver
   (B) a failure of its economic productivity to keep up with population growth
   (C) a decline in productivity caused by the addiction of Chinese workers to opium
   (D) a series of wars with Russia on the Siberian frontier

6. Which of the following can be considered true of Japanese geishas and the women of the Ottoman harem?

   (A) In both cases, they were not expected to display musical or artistic talents.
   (B) In both cases, their services could be purchased by members of any social class.
   (C) In both cases, they often advised rulers and served as regents.
   (D) In neither case was their exclusive role to provide sexual pleasure.

7. What resulted from Portuguese exploration of West Africa in the 1400s?

    (A) The Portuguese gained control over trade in gold and ivory.
    (B) The Portuguese destroyed existing states like the Asante kingdom.
    (C) The Portuguese used the region as a base from which to conquer Egypt.
    (D) The Portuguese expelled nearly all the Muslims living in the region.

8. Which is an example of the changes brought about by the Columbian Exchange?

    (A) the importation of coffee to Africa from South America
    (B) the European encounter with the horse in the plains of North America
    (C) the introduction of corn and potatoes to Europe from the Americas
    (D) the spread of smallpox from North America to Europe

9. What did Europe's Scientific Revolution accomplish?

    (A) It successfully promoted the geocentric theory.
    (B) It reconfirmed the teachings of Galen and Aristotle.
    (C) It put into practice Descartes's and Bacon's revival of the scientific method.
    (D) It immediately swept away the Catholic Church's authority over intellectual affairs.

10. The map on page 204 (without looking at the caption) relates to

    (A) patterns of large-scale migration from Spain and Portugal to other parts of the world.
    (B) the Papal Lines of Demarcation that assigned claims to new lands to Spain and Portugal.
    (C) Spanish and Portuguese shipments of tobacco and silver from Africa to Asia and the Americas.
    (D) epidemiological vectors showing how New World diseases affected Spain and Portugal.

11. This New World region imported the largest percentage of African slaves:

    (A) the Carolinas
    (B) Haiti
    (C) Brazil
    (D) Cuba

12. Forced migration in the form of "transportation"—a punishment often handed down by British courts in the 1700s and 1800s—was the primary cause of population growth in which colony?

    (A) Barbados
    (B) India
    (C) Australia
    (D) Jamaica

13. How is the religious policy of the Ottoman sultans best described?

    (A) They expelled Catholics and Protestants, but not Orthodox Christians.
    (B) They allowed a degree of toleration but taxed religious minorities.
    (C) They gave full equality to all worshippers, regardless of faith.
    (D) They ruthlessly suppressed Jews and Christians.

14. What was a major consequence of plantation monoculture?

    (A) It created fewer incentives to rely on slave labor.
    (B) It tended to enrich the lower and middle classes.
    (C) It encouraged the harvesting of a larger variety of crops.
    (D) It led to severe environmental degradation.

15. Which art forms were most prominent in sub-Saharan Africa before 1750?

    (A) sculpture and basketry
    (B) written literature and painting
    (C) basketry and written literature
    (D) sculpture and orchestral music

16. In what way did Qing China's social policies resemble those of the Tokugawa Shogunate?

    (A) Both relied on systems of rigid social stratification.
    (B) Both wished their populations to have greater exposure to foreign goods and ideas.
    (C) Both boosted the rights and privileges of the growing merchant class.
    (D) Both persecuted ethnic and religious minorities.

17. How does capitalism differ from mercantilism?

    (A) Capitalism emphasizes state-controlled accumulation of wealth, whereas mercantilism gives greater commercial power to merchants.
    (B) Capitalism shows greater sympathy to socialist ideals than mercantilism does.
    (C) Capitalism places a premium on free trade and market forces, whereas mercantilism favors state control over economic activity.
    (D) Capitalism is more concerned with land-based economic activity, whereas mercantilism is more associated with maritime trade.

18. What effect did the Portuguese presence have on the kingdom of Kongo between the late 1400s and early 1600s?

    (A) The Portuguese forced Kongo's rulers to convert to Catholicism.
    (B) The Portuguese persuaded the people of Kongo to stop enslaving their neighbors.
    (C) The Portuguese protected Kongo from Dutch encroachment.
    (D) The Portuguese enslaved most of Kongo's population by 1600.

19. Russia's colonization of the Aleutian Islands and Spain's conquest of its American territories are similar in that

    (A) large armies were required in both cases to outnumber huge native forces.
    (B) both nations were motivated principally by the desire to convert the natives to Christianity.
    (C) the economic commodity most sought in both cases was gold.
    (D) a large percentage of both native populations died because of exposure to new diseases.

20. The Mughal Empire grew wealthy in the 1600s and 1700s because of a boom in the global demand for this commodity:

    (A) nutmeg
    (B) cotton
    (C) coffee
    (D) wool

ANSWERS

1. **(A)** Answers B and C are true of the encomienda system, but not of Russian serfdom. D is true of neither. Although most famously associated with farming, Russia's serfs were put to work in many ways.

2. **(B)** Answers A and D apply to the nineteenth century, not the eighteenth. Answer C is exactly opposite to the truth; population grew steadily in the 1700s. Not until well into the 1800s did the majority in any European nation leave agricultural work behind.

3. **(B)** Industrial efforts like the ones described in C and D were not feasible until the 1800s. The janissaries began as one of the world's most effective gunpowder forces, but became corrupt and disobedient over time.

4. **(C)** Each of these commodities motivated some sort of colonial effort. Expansion into Canada and Siberia, however, was driven above all by Europe's ever-growing appetite for fur.

5. **(B)** Like many parts of the world, Ming China suffered a glut, not a shortage, of silver during this time, because of Spanish exploitation of New World precious metals. Defense costs were a heavy burden during these years, and China was wary of Russia, but it was not the main foe compared with nomads, warlords, and bandits. Opium was not introduced until the 1700s. Several times over, the pressures of population growth strained China's economy.

6. **(D)** A great deal of myth surrounds the popular understanding of harems and geishas. Harems were complex sub-societies, many of whose members had nothing to do with the ruler's sexual pleasure, and geishas were entertainers and culturally sophisticated companions more than they were courtesans. A key difference is that the harem existed solely for the benefit of the royal family.

7. **(A)** The Portuguese did none of the things described in B through D. They also began the practice of enslaving Africans, a fact not touched on by this question.

8. **(C)** Corn and potatoes, with their high-calorie yields, changed the diets of people around the world forever. The other answers were all involved in the Columbian Exchange, but the direction in which they exerted their influence is reversed or mistaken.

9. **(C)** Answers A and B involve ideas done away with or modified by the Scientific Revolution. Not only did the Scientific Revolution last many years, but Catholicism's influence over intellectual life never disappeared altogether, so D is false as well. Descartes and Bacon resurrected the logic behind scientific problem-solving that Aristotle had spoken of long ago, but that had tended to be ignored by the medieval Europeans who accepted his often flawed empirical observations as fact.

10. **(B)** The names of explorers and the map's discussion of spheres of influence should be enough to exclude the false clues, even without much historical knowledge of the expeditions depicted by the map.

11. **(C)** Although African slaves were first used in large numbers in the Caribbean, and although the slaveholding experience in the U.S. South is the one most familiar to American readers, the largest proportion of slaves brought to the New World went to Brazil—which was also the last country in the hemisphere to ban slavery.

12. **(C)** Until the American Revolution, many of those sentenced to "transportation" were sent to North America.

13. **(B)** Like many empires—Rome's, Alexander's, and Akbar the Great's, for example—the Ottoman state found it useful to show some respect for religious minorities. It made subject peoples easier to govern, and if one taxed them if they refused to convert (as the Ottomans did), the practice was profitable as well. People of the same religion were grouped into social units called millets, an institution worth comparing with the Indian caste system.

14. **(D)** Lack of variety makes areas under cultivation more susceptible to having all their crops wiped out by one plant disease. Plantation monoculture favors rich landowners and not the middle or lower classes, and it lends itself readily to unfair labor practices, slavery included. It tends to wear out soil and cause massive deforestation.

15. **(A)** Oral traditions tended to be stronger than written ones in sub-Saharan Africa. Painting was not unknown, but textiles, basketry, carving, and sculpture were much more common. The abstract nature of many of these works was discovered and eagerly appropriated by Western artists in the late 1800s and early 1900s.

16. **(A)** Although Japan's social system was arguably more stratified than China's, both were extremely hierarchal—with Confucianism providing justification, especially in China. Merchant classes grew in importance, but were not particularly respected by either state.

17. **(C)** Capitalism emerged after (and partly as a reaction against) mercantilism. Socialism, in turn, is largely a reaction against capitalism. Capitalism favors free trade above state control.

18. **(A)** During these years, Kongo was a puppet state under Portugal's control, adopting Catholicism, accepting weapons and new technology from Portugal, and taking prisoners from neighboring tribes for the Portuguese to use as slaves.

19. **(D)** European conquerors tended to have much smaller armies than those they defeated. Although military violence and other forms of abuse led to many native deaths at the hands of European imperialists, disease did the most damage by far. Most scholars estimate that 25 to 50 percent of the pre-Columbian population of the Americas died, mainly because of disease—but some argue that the percentage was much higher still. The Russians were principally interested in territorial acquisition and seal pelts.

20. **(B)** India, Central Asia, Egypt, and the U.S. South were among the world's great producers of cotton. Great Britain especially desired to control India (and, later, Egypt) in order to supply its rapidly growing textile industry.

UNIT FIVE

INDUSTRIALIZATION
AND GLOBAL INTEGRATION
(1750–1900)

Unit Overview

GENERAL REMARKS

During the 1750–1914 period, the world entered the modern age. In this, it was led by the nations of the West, consisting of Europe and the United States.

Exactly what defines **modernity** is a question of debate among historians. In popular terms, the word *modern* is used as a synonym for "contemporary" or as a way to describe one's own times. In historical terms, it describes an era characterized by certain features. Different scholars outline modernity's features in different ways, but most agree on the following:

- In politics, there is a move from traditional monarchy toward greater political representation. The end result in most societies is some form of democracy or at least the appearance of democracy.
- In economics, industrialization becomes a driving force. There is a shift from feudalism and mercantilism to capitalism. Rather than being based primarily on agriculture, economies are based increasingly on industry and commerce.
- In society, there is class transformation, as old aristocracies fade away in favor of new elites whose status derives from wealth. New classes expand or emerge, especially the middle class and industrial working class. As agriculture gives way to industry, societies urbanize. Population growth accelerates.
- In culture, a scientific, secular worldview becomes dominant. Artistic and literary styles change more rapidly and radically than ever before.

In all these things, Europe, with the United States, moved forward first. Great political upheavals such as the **American Revolution** and the **French Revolution** began the long process of expanding political representation and giving more people a greater voice in politics. It was in Europe that the **Industrial Revolution** began, and it was there that **capitalism** emerged (as well as visions alternative to it, such as **socialism**). These changes transformed the economies of the world. Population growth, class diversification, and urbanization were hallmarks of Western social development during the late 1700s and throughout the 1800s. The foundations for modern culture and intellectual life had been laid in Europe during the 1700s, during the Scientific Revolution and the Enlightenment.

To varying degrees, modernization reached the rest of the world in the nineteenth and early twentieth centuries. A few non-Western nations adapted quickly, such as Japan. Some, including the Ottoman Empire, China, and the nations of Latin America, modernized slowly or partially. Other civilizations, most notably those of Africa and Southeast Asia, lagged farther behind. No matter the pace, however, change came to all these regions. **Coerced** and **semi-coerced labor** remained common worldwide.

Another overarching development between 1750 and 1914 was the **rise of the West** as the world's dominant civilization. Not only did industrialization and modernization make the West prosperous and technologically advanced, they made it powerful as well. European (and American) imperialism resulted in control over most of the world's habitable territory. Many areas that had originally been colonized during the Age of Exploration—such as North and South America—became free during the late 1700s and early 1800s. However, a **new imperialism** swept over Asia, the Middle East, the Pacific, and Africa during the 1800s and early 1900s. Seeking markets and raw materials, armed with industrial-era weaponry, the nations of the West established control over a vast portion of the globe. Never before in history had a single civilization become so powerful. But as impressive as imperialism was practically, it carried a steep moral and ethical price. Imperialism was inextricably bound up with warfare, racial prejudice, economic rapacity, and slavery. Many of the harmful effects of Western imperialism are still felt to this day.

By the end of the nineteenth century, Europe had reached the peak of its power, but would soon fall from that pinnacle. The young United States was overtaking Europe in economic and military strength. New philosophies, scientific theories, and cultural movements were calling into question the traditional certainties and values of the Western world. Most important, Europe was moving toward war. The conflict resulting from the diplomatic tensions of the late 1800s and early 1900s—World War I—was the worst ever fought to that date. It did much to start and then speed up the process of European decline.

BROAD TRENDS

Humans and the Environment

- Industrialization vastly increased humanity's impact on the environment. Rising levels of pollution were one result.
- The hunger of industrializing economies for natural resources (such as metals, minerals, guano for fertilizer, oil, rubber, foodstuffs, and cotton) led to extractive practices that placed huge strains on the environment. Mining and single- and cash-crop agriculture were tremendously damaging to ecosystems.
- Industrialization permitted major earth-shaping engineering projects such as the Suez Canal (and the Panama Canal, early in the 1900s).
- Industrial-era forms of transportation contributed to the widespread distribution of diseases.
- Diseases such as tuberculosis and cholera also spread easily amid the overcrowded living conditions created by industrialization and rapid urbanization.
- The Little Ice Age came to an end during the early to mid-1800s.

Development and Interaction of Cultures

- Starting in the West, a scientific, secular worldview became paramount. Enlightenment thinking and the technological and scientific advancements of the Industrial Revolution, as well as the theories of scholars such as Charles Darwin, accelerated this process.
- Greater access to public education became a normal part of life in North America and northern and western Europe throughout the 1800s. Literacy rates rose as a result. The same is true for many other parts of the world during the late 1800s.
- Nationalism became a powerful political and cultural force in Europe and then elsewhere. By the end of the 1800s, nationalist and national-liberation movements became prevalent in non-Western parts of the world dominated by foreign colonial rule.
- The non-Western world began to adopt many of the artistic and literary forms of the West, especially print culture and writing styles, as well as architecture. Conversely, styles from Asia, Africa, and the Middle East had an influence on Western culture, particularly in painting, sculpture, and decor.
- In Europe and the Americas, the pace of cultural change sped up. By the end of the 1800s and the beginning of the 1900s, new artistic and literary trends were emerging at a rapid rate. Increasingly, these were about breaking rules and defying conventions.

State-Building, Expansion, and Conflict

- The hallmark of modern political life is greater popular representation. This trend first got underway in the West. It began in the late 1700s, primarily with the American and French Revolutions (also see "Social Structures" below).
- Other parts of the world tended to be slower in moving away from traditional autocracies or monarchies. A few, such as Japan and the Ottoman Empire, did so, developing parliamentary forms of monarchy by the start of the twentieth century. The nations of Latin America developed parliamentary governments in theory, but many of those slipped into dictatorship or military rule.
- The technological, economic, and military rise of the West—Europe and the United States—completely altered the balance of global power. World affairs were increasingly determined by foreign-policy and military developments in Europe, especially as the 1800s progressed.
- The United States broke away from English rule during the late 1700s. During the 1800s, it dominated the North American continent and became a world power.
- The Spanish and Portuguese colonies of Latin America freed themselves from European rule during the early 1800s.
- In North Africa, the eastern Mediterranean, and the Middle East, the gradual collapse of the Ottoman Empire presented the nations of Europe with a troubling and destabilizing diplomatic issue known as the Eastern Question.
- European (and U.S.) imperialism—the "new imperialism" of the mid- to late 1800s—gave the nations of the West unprecedented global dominance.

In 1815, the nations of the West controlled 35 percent of the world's habitable territory. In 1914, they controlled 85 percent.

- The one non-Western nation that developed a modern colonial empire in the late 1800s and early 1900s was Japan.
- By the end of the 1800s, diplomatic tensions, nationalism, and competition over colonies made it increasingly likely that the nations of Europe would go to war. An alliance system formed. The level of aggression rose steadily. World War I resulted in 1914.

Economic Systems

- Economic life was transformed by the phenomenon of industrialization, which displaced agriculture as the largest and most important sector of the economy. Industrialization began in England and spread to parts of Europe during the late 1700s and early 1800s (the Industrial Revolution). It matured and spread further throughout Europe, also expanding to include steel, electricity, chemical industries, and petroleum (the Second Industrial Revolution) in the late 1800s. Gradually and to varying extents, industrialization spread to other parts of the world.
- The non-Western world adopted industrialization at varying speeds and in different ways. Sometimes, European imperial powers introduced it to their colonies. In other cases, rulers of free non-Western nations imposed industrialization from above.
- The dominant mode of economic organization in the West became free-market capitalism. Along with industry, commerce, and banking—the foundations of a money-based economy (as opposed to a land-based one)—grew in importance. Banks, stock markets, and other modern financial instruments became more common and more solidly established.
- See "Social Structures" below for the relationship between economic growth during this era and reliance on coerced and semi-coerced forms of labor.

Social Structures

- During the 1800s, especially after the 1848 revolution, politics in Europe and the West became increasingly representative. By the end of the century, Great Britain, France, and the United States, along with a few smaller countries, had become democracies (although women could not yet vote). Even in nondemocratic states, bureaucracies and parliamentary bodies became an increasingly important part of government, even more so than the will of individual rulers and monarchs.
- Industrialization transformed class structures. The traditional aristocracy, with its status based on land and family prestige, faded. Among the lower classes, the proportion of peasants and farmers shrank. The middle class (bourgeoisie) expanded, gained great wealth, and diversified. A new lower class, the industrial working class (proletariat), was born.
- Industrialization led to urbanization. Cities grew in size, and more cities were established.
- For any society, the first decades of industrialization were typically painful for the lower classes. Working conditions were poor, and wages were low. Over

time, industrialization raised the average prosperity of a society's population, and even the lower classes benefited after some time.

- Coerced and semi-coerced forms of labor persisted. Along with slavery, indentured servitude (common in India and China) and migrant labor (technically free, but poorly paid) were common. Africa was the primary victim of slave trading. The East African and Atlantic slave trades continued well into the late 1800s.
- There was a tremendous movement of peoples during this period. In particular, there were massive waves of emigration from Europe and China to the Americas during the mid- to late 1800s and early 1900s. The United States was the preferred destination, but Canada, Australia, Argentina, and Chile took in many immigrants as well. Anti-immigration sentiment was common in these places, both on a popular and an official level (see the Chinese Exclusion Acts and the White Australia Policy, or the slogan "no Irish need apply").
- Diasporic communities and foreign enclaves (Chinese in Southeast Asia, for example, or Indians in East and South Africa) remained common, thanks to expanding commercial ties or overcrowding at home.
- Although in most societies, the status of women remained secondary, the 1750–1914 period saw great changes in gender relations. In the West, a greater awareness of the unequal treatment of women began to spread, starting around the late 1700s. This was stimulated partly by the theories of Enlightenment philosophy, as well as the active role played by women in the American and French Revolutions.
- During the late 1700s and early 1800s, the Industrial Revolution profoundly altered the conditions under which women worked. It shifted the workplace away from the farm, where men and women both lived and worked, to mines, factories, and other spaces away from the home. This shift created a domestic sphere and a separate working sphere away from the home. In Europe and the United States, women of the lower classes were generally compelled to enter the workplace (most frequently textile factories). These women also bore the double burden of serving as the primary homemakers and caregivers for their families.
- After the mid-1800s, the number of working women in Europe and North America declined. Women of the middle and upper classes had rarely worked to begin with. As wages for industrial workers rose (making those jobs more desirable to men) and as laws restricting the number of hours women and children could work were passed, the number of lower-class working women fell. A cult of domesticity, stressing that a woman's place was in the home and a man's in the workplace, dominated Western culture—especially among the middle and upper classes—during the mid- to late nineteenth century. Certain occupations were open to women, such as child care (governesses), teaching, domestic household work (servants and maids), nursing, and artisanry.
- Strong and vigorous women's movements appeared in Europe, Canada, and the United States. They agitated for suffrage (the right to vote), equal opportunity to work, equal pay, temperance, and other causes. A handful of European nations—but no major ones—gave women the right to vote before World War I.
- The move toward women's equality tended to be slower in non-Western societies. In some, however, the educational level of women rose, as did the extent of property rights. As in the West, women worked, especially in certain

occupations, such as agricultural labor, domestic service, and nursing. As non-Western parts of the world industrialized, lower-class women tended to enter the workplace, as in the industrial West.

QUESTIONS AND COMPARISONS TO CONSIDER

- What factors contributed to the rise of industrial production? Consider Europe's Atlantic location; the global distribution of resources like coal, iron, and timber; demographic changes in Europe; urbanization; the general rise in agricultural productivity; changes in property laws, such as the Enclosure Acts; infrastructural advantages, such as networks of canals, rivers, and roads; easy access to natural resources from abroad, especially from within one's own empire; and economic practices that allowed many parties to accumulate capital.
- What distinguished the initial Industrial Revolution from the second one of the late 1800s?
- What role did the exploitation and export of raw materials play in world trade? In international politics?
- What socio-economic visions alternative to capitalism appeared during this era?
- How were gender and family dynamics affected by industrialization? Or by the way non-industrial societies did or did not change during this era?
- Compare the nature and content of key revolutionary documents, such as the Declaration of Independence, the Declaration of the Rights of Man and the Citizen, and the Jamaica Letter.
- Compare various acts of resistance against Western imperialism. Examples include Japanese modernization, the Indian Mutiny, the Boxer Rebellion, the Filipino war against U.S. occupation, and Wounded Knee.
- Compare revolutions in two or more of the following countries: America, Haiti, France, Mexico, and China.
- Discuss the response of non-Western parts of the world such as China, India, Japan, and the Ottoman Empire to imperial encroachments and foreign pressures (especially from Europe and the United States) during this period.
- Compare the status of women in the West and that of women in other parts of the world. Compare the roles and conditions of upper- and middle-class women with those of the peasant and working classes.
- Describe the various approaches taken by various Western powers to colonization. Also, how did the late-nineteenth-century wave of imperialism (the "new" imperialism) compare to earlier waves of colonization?
- Discuss various ways in which non-Western states attempted to modernize and adopt industrial practices. How important is the question of whether industrialization was imposed on a society from above, by the ruler, or emerged from below?
- Compare Japanese industrialization and European industrialization.
- Compare Western intervention in Latin America with Western intervention in Africa during the 1750–1900 period.
- Examine nationalist and anticolonial movements in non-Western parts of the world. Compare and contrast their methods and their successes and/or failures.

The Europeans at Home: Revolution, Reaction, and Reform

- The Atlantic revolutions and the French Revolution
- The Napoleonic wars, the Congress of Vienna, and reaction
- The Industrial Revolution
- Increased representation (reform versus revolution)
- Women's movements and female suffrage
- Nationalism and the unifications of Italy and Germany
- Anti-Semitism (pogroms; the Dreyfus Affair)
- Romanticism, realism, and artistic modernism
- Charles Darwin and the theory of natural selection
- Albert Einstein and the theory of relativity
- Sigmund Freud and psychology

From 1750 to 1914, the European political order changed dramatically. In the mid-1700s, all of Europe's major nations were monarchies. Although a handful were parliamentary, allowing for some level of popular representation, most were absolute—meaning that, in theory, the monarch had few if any restrictions on his or her power. In general, monarchs shared power only with aristocratic noble classes. In any given country, the nobility made up an extremely small proportion of the overall population but controlled most of the country's wealth, owned most of the nation's land, and enjoyed virtually all influence over politics.

From the 1770s through the 1810s, this state of affairs was shaken apart by a wave of **Atlantic revolutions**. The most famous took place in Britain's North American colonies (see Chapter 28) and France, but there were others as well. Although not all their goals were met, the revolutions dealt a death blow to absolute monarchy in most of Europe. Another effect was that an ever-increasing number of people began to dream of—and fight for—social and political systems that treated them fairly and gave them more voice in government. Another factor that changed ordinary Europeans' social and economic aspirations was the **Industrial Revolution**, which happened at the same time as the political revolutions in America and France and is described in Chapter 22.

Although a conservative backlash, known as **reaction**, settled over Europe in the decades following the French Revolution and its Napoleonic aftermath, the desire for more representative government never died. Each nation, its rulers and its people, struggled with this issue in different ways and at different paces. The general trend, however, was for governments to liberalize and democratize over time. This was especially the case after the **revolutions of 1848**. During the second half of the century, reform movements helped to accelerate political change, as well as social and economic progress.

By the late 1800s and early 1900s, most countries in Europe were more or less representative, and a few were, by the day's standards, democratic. Most European economies were fully or partially industrialized. As described in Chapter 23, European powers, thanks to their imperial successes, dominated a vast amount of the rest of the world. These years marked the peak of Europe's global might. Underlying diplomatic and strategic tensions, however, gave rise to World War I (1914–1918): the huge cataclysm that began the process by which Europe toppled from its position of world power.

THE FRENCH REVOLUTION AND THE NAPOLEONIC ERA

Long-term Causes of the French Revolution

The causes of the **French Revolution** (1789–1799) are many and complex. Long-term factors included

- The wide social and economic gap between ordinary citizens (the Third Estate) and the country's elite, the Catholic clergy (First Estate) and the aristocracy (Second Estate)
- The unfair tax system, from which the wealthy First and Second Estates were exempt
- The frustrated ambitions of the middle class, who had wealth and education but, because they belonged to the Third Estate, were barred from social advancement
- The influence of the Enlightenment (see Chapter 14), whose philosophers, many of whom were French, made powerful arguments in favor of fair government, equal treatment of citizens, and civil rights

Added to these causes were the political ineptitude of the last two absolute monarchs of France, Louis XV and Louis XVI, and a long-standing financial crisis in France. Another ingredient was the American Revolution (1775–1783), which France supported (adding to its financial troubles). Little did the French government realize that by helping the Americans, it would encourage revolution in its own country.

The Estates General and the Early French Revolution

The immediate cause of the French Revolution was the impending bankruptcy of the government. Saddled with debts, unable to tax the rich First and Second Estates, and burdened with a wife, Marie Antoinette, who spent lavishly, **Louis XVI** (1774–1792)

could not solve France's financial crisis. By 1787 and 1788, inflation, unemployment, and food shortages were tormenting the entire country.

In May 1789, desperate for a solution, Louis XVI summoned the **Estates General:** a national assembly of delegates from each estate. The delegates of the Third Estate—mainly middle-class lawyers—came to Versailles expecting to negotiate seriously about changing the tax system and granting equal rights to all classes. By June, however, it was clear that neither Louis XVI nor the other Estates were prepared to compromise. This clash of wills sparked ten years of revolution.

In late June, the delegates of the Third Estate, with liberal members of the First and Second Estates, formed a new governmental body, the National Assembly, and vowed not to leave Versailles until the king granted them a constitution. In July, the people of Paris and other cities rose up in support of the assembly, as did peasants in the countryside. Over the summer, the assembly assumed power in Paris.

The first two years of the revolution were a relatively moderate time. Louis XVI was allowed to remain king, but with the reduced powers of a parliamentary monarch. Guided by Enlightenment ideals and the American Declaration of Independence, the assembly guaranteed civil liberties in the **Declaration of the Rights of Man and the Citizen.** Future assemblies were to be elected by popular vote. Aristocratic status and privileges (especially exemption from taxes) were done away with, and church and state were separated. Policy was guided by the motto Liberty, Equality, and Fraternity.

There were, however, problems. At first, the rights proclaimed by the revolution, including the vote, applied only to white, Catholic, adult males. Only with time did Jews, Protestants, and blacks gain those rights, and women never did. Slavery was not ended in France's colonies until 1794. Also, the assembly failed to solve worsening economic problems. Louis XVI, encouraged by Marie Antoinette, secretly plotted **counterrevolution**, as did many former aristocrats. Other countries, fearing that their people would follow the French example if the revolution succeeded, threatened war.

Moreover, the victorious revolutionaries could not agree on how to change France. Liberal nobles and clergy, with much of the middle class, were satisfied with parliamentary monarchy and moderate change. The rural population, happy to have equal rights and to limit the power of the king, wanted economic relief but not deeper social change. The urban lower classes (known as sans-culottes) and certain middle-class idealists were more radical. They wanted to end the monarchy altogether, drive out or persecute former aristocrats (even liberal nobles), change society more thoroughly (some favored abolishing Catholicism), and export the revolution to other countries by force. Resolving all these desires would prove impossible.

Radicalism, the Reign of Terror, and the Directory

From the spring of 1792 through the summer of 1794, the French Revolution took a sharply radical turn. In April 1792, France went to war with Austria and Prussia; other countries, including Britain, joined in, and France would remain at war for almost the entirety of the next quarter century. The economy worsened, and early military failures caused mass hysteria. Remaining aristocrats and political moderates fell under suspicion, as did the royal family. Radical parties became more influential.

In the fall of 1792, a new constitution created a new legislature, stripped the king of all powers, and proclaimed the French Republic. Elections brought the radical parties to power. Most important were the **Jacobins**, led by Maximilien Robespierre, a fanatically idealistic lawyer. In January 1793, Louis XVI was executed for treason; Marie Antoinette was killed in October. The Jacobins created an executive body, the **Committee of Public Safety**, which assumed dictatorial powers, persecuted enemies, and attempted the radical transformation of French society. It expanded the war effort, mobilized the economy for combat, and carried out the modern world's first national draft. Civil war erupted in the countryside (especially the Vendee), as peasants rebelled against conscription and the radicals' efforts to eradicate Catholicism.

Between the summer of 1793 and the summer of 1794, Robespierre and the Committee, supported by the urban sans-culottes, carried out a **Reign of Terror**, searching for counterrevolutionaries and traitors. In this panicked, witch-hunt atmosphere, civil liberties were largely ignored. More than 300,000 people were arrested without warrant and tried without jury or appeal. Between 30,000 and 50,000 were killed, many beheaded by the guillotine. In July 1794, a coup within the committee overthrew Robespierre, who was guillotined, and ended the Terror.

For the next five years, a more moderate government called the Directory ruled France. The military situation stabilized, and the Directory attempted to restore order after the chaos caused by the Terror. However, the Directory was unpopular, and it was overthrown in 1799, bringing an end to the revolution.

Napoleon Bonaparte

Among those who ousted the Directory was a talented and popular general, **Napoleon Bonaparte**, who quickly seized power for himself. Napoleon claimed to follow the ideals of the French Revolution, but, in reality, created a new dictatorship. Indeed, in 1804, Napoleon crowned himself emperor of France.

Evaluating Napoleon's reign is difficult. He was arrogant and autocratic. His wars lasted for years, cost untold amounts of money, and killed millions. On the other hand, he modernized France, creating institutions that still exist today, such as the **Bank of France** and the **Civil Law Code** (known then as the **Napoleonic Code**, still the foundation of modern French law). Until his wars went badly in 1812, his military skills made France rich and powerful.

Napoleon is best known for his military career. After coming to power, he continued the wars France had begun during the revolution. His chief enemies were Britain, Austria, Prussia, and Russia. From 1805 through 1811, his victories made France the most powerful nation in Europe: the only major nations not under his control were Britain and Russia.

Several factors brought about Napoleon's downfall: his inability to counter British naval power, a guerrilla war in Spain and Portugal, and, finally, an overambitious invasion of Russia in 1812. He was defeated, captured, and exiled in 1814. In 1815, he escaped and had to be beaten again at the Battle of Waterloo. After years of captivity, he died in 1821.

Successes, Failures, and Long-term Effects of the French Revolution

What made the French Revolution and its Napoleonic aftermath so important? In many ways, the revolution failed. The dream of a popularly elected government faded, only to be replaced by the harsh Committee of Public Safety and then the unmistakably dictatorial Napoleon. After Napoleon's defeat, the old royal family was restored to power. Moreover, it is hard to argue that liberty, equality, and fraternity were achieved by means of Jacobin terror and the guillotine.

On the other hand, the French Revolution did away with absolute monarchy. Kings, queens, and emperors continued to sit on European thrones, but in no major country, with the exception of Russia, were they all-powerful. As time passed, monarchs yielded more of their power to ministries, parliaments, and legislatures.

Also, the French Revolution, like the American Revolution before it, sparked other **Atlantic revolutions**. Uprisings in Ireland, Belgium, the Netherlands, and Poland followed the American and French examples. They failed, but revolutions in Haiti and Latin America succeeded (see Chapter 28). Even Napoleon spread revolutionary ideals through Europe by writing constitutions for the countries he conquered. Much later, the Mexican (1910), Chinese (1911), and Russian (1917) revolutions were inspired in large part by France's.

In the end, the greatest legacy of the American and French revolutions was to cause people to demand greater popular participation in government and to force nineteenth-century governments to be more attentive to those demands. The rulers of the 1800s might not give into all of their subjects' desires, but they could no longer ignore them as they had before. As time passed, ordinary people became more successful in getting their voices heard and their demands met. The story of European politics during the 1800s and early 1900s is primarily *this* story.

REACTION AND REFORM: POLITICS IN EUROPE, 1815–1914

The Congress of Vienna and the Principle of Reaction, 1815–1848

After the defeat of Napoleon, the leaders of Europe gathered at the **Congress of Vienna** (1814–1815) to settle the peace. Not only did they redraw the map of Europe, they restored prerevolutionary governments wherever possible (including in France) and agreed to cooperate in preserving the **diplomatic balance of power**. The experience of the French Revolution and the Napoleonic wars convinced most politicians that any kind of liberalism led automatically to political chaos and war; to them, the best way to maintain order was to oppose any kind of democratic change. This arch-conservative stance was called **reaction**.

The resulting Congress System helped to keep the peace in Europe until the early 1850s. However, stability came at the price of stifling political change and civil liberties. Although monarchies were no longer absolute, freedom of expression and freedom of the press were restricted, secret police forces became common, and censorship was heavy. Trade unions and workers' associations were illegal (just as the

industrial working class was expanding), and political parties were outlawed in many countries.

Even in western nations such as Britain and France, political controls tightened. Change in both countries was slow. In Britain, it took place by means of gradual reform. In 1832, the First Reform Act slightly expanded the vote. France lurched forward by means of periodic revolution (in 1830, 1848, and 1871).

In central and eastern Europe, the level of repression was much greater. Austria was ruled with an iron hand. Prussia, now a leading German state, was militaristic and authoritarian. Russia remained an absolute monarchy; there were no meaningful checks on the tsar's power. In addition, Russia continued the practice of **serfdom**, the system of unfree agricultural labor that had died away elsewhere in Europe decades, if not centuries, before. In addition to being inherently unjust, serfdom was inefficient and kept Russia socially and economically backward.

The Revolution of 1848

The **Revolution of 1848**, which shook almost every country on the continent to its political roots, is a dividing point in nineteenth-century European history. Underlying causes include popular impatience with reactionary rule, social and economic pressures caused by the **Industrial Revolution**, and a long series of economic downturns and bad harvests (like the Irish Potato Famine) that caused the decade to be known as the "hungry forties."

The 1848 revolution began in France, where the king was deposed, and Napoleon's nephew (Louis Napoleon, later Napoleon III) became president. It spread to the rest of Europe, prompting a famous quote about revolution: "Every time France sneezes, Europe catches cold." Only Britain, which was flexible enough to avoid revolution, and Russia, which punished liberals and radicals harshly enough to make revolution too dangerous, remained immune.

By early 1849, all the revolts were crushed or faded away. Historians often speak of 1848 as "the turning point that did not quite turn." Still, the revolutions had their effects. They compelled Prussia and Austria to grant constitutions. They demonstrated the growing political importance of nationalism and laid the foundation for the later unifications of Italy and Germany. They inspired **Karl Marx** to write *The Communist Manifesto*. Most of all, they hammered home for good the lesson of the French Revolution: that the political, social, and economic demands of ordinary people had to be taken seriously, if not met.

Representative Government and Unifications, 1848–1914

During the second half of the century, most European countries moved closer to representative forms of government. Britain and France became democracies (defined by **universal male suffrage**, or a politically meaningful vote for all adult males). Even in less representative regimes, political power spread outward to larger numbers of governmental advisers, ministries, and agencies.

Britain under Queen Victoria gradually extended the vote to the middle and lower classes by means of the **Second** (1867) and **Third** (1885) **Reform Acts**. It also granted economic concessions and fairer labor laws to the lower classes. By the early 1900s, the working class had enough political influence that a new party, Labour,

was founded to serve its interests. Britain in the late 1800s had the world's greatest empire and was extremely prosperous. It wrestled, however, with the questions of women's suffrage and Irish nationalism.

France's progress toward democracy was less gentle than Britain's. In the republic that existed for a short time after 1848, all adult males could vote. In 1851, however, the president, Louis Napoleon, staged a coup and crowned himself Napoleon III. He was not an absolute dictator, and he helped to modernize Paris and industrialize the country. He abdicated after losing the bitter **Franco-Prussian War** (1870–1871). From that time, France remained a democratic republic, although democracy did not solve all of its problems. France was rocked by corruption and financial scandals, and worst of all was the **Dreyfus Affair** (1894–1906), in which the army and government falsely blamed a Jewish officer for the leaking of military secrets to Germany. The controversy divided the left (which maintained Dreyfus's innocence) from the right (which was convinced of his guilt) and exposed the ugly streak of **anti-Semitism** in modern European society.

Nationalism profoundly affected politics in Italy, Germany, and Austria. The **unification of Italy** as a constitutional monarchy took place in the 1860s.

The **unification of Germany** was spearheaded by Prussia in a series of short, decisive wars against Denmark (1864), Austria (1866), and especially France (1870–1871). The new German state had a parliament (the Reichstag), and all adult males technically had the vote, although the electoral system was heavily stacked in favor of the upper classes. Germany rapidly became a strong, modern, industrialized state, but it was very conservative politically. Craftily, the government offered the lower classes generous economic concessions (pensions, insurance, shorter workdays) to keep them from being attracted to trade unions or socialism.

After 1848, the Austrian emperor was forced to liberalize somewhat, and a parliament was established in 1861. A multinational empire, Austria had to confront many ethnic tensions throughout the late 1800s and early 1900s, as the nationalist aspirations of minority populations such as Czechs, Poles, Slovaks, Croats, Serbs, Hungarians, and others mounted. In the **Ausgleich** ("Compromise") of 1867, the Hungarian minority, Austria's largest, won equal status, and the country was renamed the Austro-Hungarian Empire. As in other parts of Europe, **anti-Semitism** became an ugly part of political life here.

Even autocratic Russia was forced to change somewhat. Alexander II, a moderate liberal, modernized the country with a series of "great reforms." The most important of these was the **emancipation of the serfs** (1861), which ended a morally reprehensible practice and allowed some economic progress. Alexander, however, was assassinated by terrorists, and the extremely conservative rulers who succeeded him undid many of his reforms. A serious uprising in 1905 almost overthrew the tsar; he survived but was forced to create and share power with an elected, semiparliamentary body called the Duma. However, he kept the Duma weak and took every opportunity to avoid cooperating with it. Anti-Semitic persecution escalated in Russia, and **pogroms** (violent raids on Jewish settlements) became increasingly common.

Women's Movements

The English author **Mary Wollstonecraft** is considered the founder of modern European feminism. Her 1792 treatise, *A Vindication of the Rights of Women,* insisted

that women, like men, possessed reason and were therefore entitled to equal rights. During the French Revolution, the playwright **Olympe de Gouges** argued in her "Declaration of the Rights of Woman and the Citizeness" that women should have the same rights as men. The government dismissed her proposal, and she died during the Reign of Terror.

Larger women's rights movements emerged in the 1830s in Europe and the United States. Early on, they focused on reforming laws to allow women to own property and file for divorce. This initial effort did not reap quick results, as women did not gain full property rights in Britain until 1870, Germany until 1900, and France until 1907.

Soon, feminists were seeking better access to higher education and jobs. The first professions open to women (beyond domestic servitude, already dominated by women) were teaching and nursing. Women also led the way in campaigning for temperance, the abolition of slavery, and aid for orphans and the poor.

By the middle of the nineteenth century, women began to seek political rights, most notably suffrage, the right to vote. As a rule, European and American **suffragette movements** were led by women of the middle and upper classes. The most vocal women's movement was Britain's, led by Emmeline Pankhurst. Major figures in the U.S. movement were Susan B. Anthony and Elizabeth Cady Stanton. American and Canadian women not only called for the right to vote notably at the 1848 **Seneca Falls Convention**, which based its Declaration of Sentiments on the U.S. Declaration of Independence, they agitated for better working conditions for women, child welfare, and temperance. Almost no countries gave women the vote until late in World War I or afterward. Exceptions include Norway, Finland, and a handful of U.S. states.

INTELLECTUAL AND CULTURAL CURRENTS

TIP

Around the 1840s, romanticism, while it did not die away, yielded its place of prominence to **realism**. Realists were concerned with everyday life, social problems (such as poverty), and the psychology of their characters.

In contrast to long-lasting cultural and intellectual movements such as the Renaissance and the Enlightenment, trends and styles in the 1800s and 1900s changed constantly. Such rapid evolution has been a hallmark of modern Western culture.

The principal cultural movement of the late 1700s and early 1800s was **romanticism**. A backlash against the rational Enlightenment, romanticism emphasized emotion, heroism, individuality, and the imagination.

In the mid-1800s came numerous scientific discoveries that changed the outlook of the Western world. The most important was the work of English naturalist **Charles Darwin**, who explained the biological process of evolution with his **theory of natural selection**. In *On the Origin of Species* (1859), Darwin caused a scientific and cultural storm by arguing that evolution is a random process in which physical changes that increase an animal's chance for survival are passed on to that animal's offspring. In *The Descent of Man* (1871), he applied the principles of natural selection to human beings and postulated that humans and apes share a common evolutionary ancestry. Darwin's ideas, along with discoveries in other sciences, including geology and archaeology, did much to erode faith in traditional religion and encourage a more secular worldview in the West.

The culture of the late 1800s and early 1900s was characterized by diversity and innovation. Turning away from realism in the 1870s, **modernist** artists and writers

(including Vincent van Gogh, and a young Pablo Picasso) broke the rules of traditional culture and experimented with a dazzling array of new styles: impressionism, post-impressionism, cubism, and abstraction. Asian and African art powerfully influenced this generation of artists.

During most of the 1800s, Western culture was characterized by faith in progress and excitement about new technology and science. For the most part, especially among the general public, this sense of optimism continued until the eve of World War I. In some ways, however, this was a time of intellectual crisis and uncertainty. German philosopher Friedrich Nietzsche proclaimed famously that "God is dead," and argued that all systems of morality were valueless in the materialistic modern age. Quantum theory and **Albert Einstein's theory of relativity**, elaborated in 1905, opened up new (and unsettling) questions in the field of physics for the first time since the days of Isaac Newton. The early theories of the Austrian physician **Sigmund Freud** about dreams and the subconscious advanced the new science of psychology, but his insights made many people uneasy, both before and after World War I.

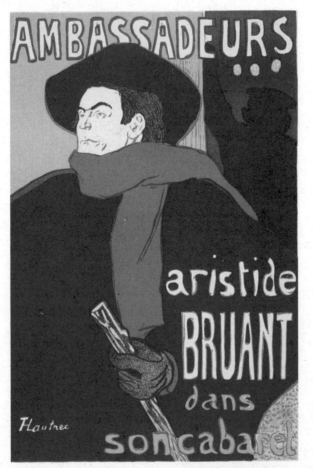

Aristide Bruant at Les Ambassadeurs (1892), by Henri de Toulouse-Lautrec.
French painter and poster artist Henri de Toulouse-Lautrec (1864–1901) was one of many artists who, during the late 1800s, departed from the strictly realist styles of the early and middle nineteenth century. Like many of France's impressionist and post-impressionist painters, Toulouse-Lautrec was influenced by foreign art, most particularly Japanese prints.

Industrialization and Worldwide Economic Trends

CHAPTER 22

- Industrialization and the Industrial Revolution
- Proto-industrialization versus traditional artisanry
- The steam engine and the mining and textile industries
- Steamships, railroads, and the telegraph
- The gradual application of electric and petroleum power (the Second Industrial Revolution)
- The factory system and interchangeable parts

- Rise of the middle (bourgeois) and working (proletariat) classes
- The stimulation of population growth and urbanization
- Effects on women
- Capitalism (Adam Smith)
- Trade unionism
- Socialism and communism (Karl Marx)
- Global ramifications of Western industrialization
- The cotton gin's impact on the Atlantic slave trade

Until the end of the 1700s, the economies of the world's major civilizations were principally agricultural, and their societies rural. Over the centuries, trade and commerce, as well as arts and crafts, had become increasingly important—but compared with agriculture, remained relatively minor.

In Europe and the United States, this state of affairs changed dramatically during the end of the 1700s and the 1800s. The mass production of goods by means of machine power—industrialization—became a key part of Western economies. The importance of trade and commerce skyrocketed, and a growing number of people moved from rural areas to the city. Capitalism became the dominant economic system. Taken together, these changes form what is commonly known as the **Industrial Revolution**, whose first stage coincided roughly with the political revolutions taking place in America, France, and the Atlantic world. Although industrialization was a "revolution" only in a metaphorical sense—it lasted decades and had no clear-cut beginning or end—it changed life in Europe and the rest of the world as thoroughly as the political revolutions did. It placed new machines and inventions at the disposal of ordinary people. It affected old social classes and created new ones. It changed the way millions worked, where they lived, and how they understood political problems. By 1900, the United States and northern and western Europe had industrialized and urbanized. Many other parts of the world were starting to follow suit.

THE INDUSTRIAL REVOLUTION

Background to Industrialization

The Industrial Revolution is considered to have begun in England in the 1780s with the successful application of the **steam engine** to two sectors of the economy: **mining** and **textiles**.

Many things combined to spark industrialization in England. Already from the late 1600s, proto-industrial practices (methods more productive than traditional artisanry and craftsmanship) had been in place. Machines such as the flying shuttle and the spinning jenny, which sped up the manufacture of cotton, were invented as early as 1733 and 1764. England was already relatively urbanized, and a set of harsh agricultural laws, the **Enclosure Acts**—which, in favor of wealthy landowners, fenced off large amounts of farmland that had once been common property— impoverished many farmers and forced them to relocate to the cities, creating a large pool of available labor. Environmental change played a role as well: the depletion of forests in England and Ireland (timber was used both for fuel and to build ships for the Royal Navy) increased dependency on coal, and efficient coal mining required machine power, especially to pump water out of mine shafts. Other factors working in England's favor were its location in the Atlantic, an excellent system of roads and canals, large supplies of iron and coal, and a strong tradition of trade and commerce, which allowed investors to accumulate capital.

Steam Power and Beyond: The Industrial Era Begins and Matures

What was needed by the end of the 1700s was a power source greater and more reliable than wind, water, or muscle to drive new machines in factories and mines. In 1782, the Scottish inventor **James Watt** patented a steam engine that was both powerful and cost-effective. The first stage of the Industrial Revolution involved the integration of Watt's steam engine into the textile and coal-mining industries.

The next stage of the Industrial Revolution, which lasted roughly until the middle of the 1800s, involved the universal application of steam power—and, more slowly, electricity—to all areas of economic activity. Industrialization also spread to other parts of Europe, as well as to North America. Key trends include

- The modernization of transport, thanks to **steamships** (1807) and **railroads** (the 1820s)
- The modernization of communications, beginning with the **telegraph** (1837)
- The **factory system**, which systematized, mechanized, and increased the scale of production
- The concept of **interchangeable parts**, pioneered by two Americans, the inventor Eli Whitney and a gunsmith, Samuel Colt

Although the Industrial Revolution is considered to have ended around the mid-1800s, the **industrial era** (often referred to as a **Second Industrial Revolution**) continued throughout the rest of the century and gave birth to a huge wave of invention. Crucial innovations include the vulcanization of rubber (1839); the **Bessemer process** (the 1850s), which made steel production cheaper and easier; the

wider use of **electricity** (Thomas Edison's lightbulb came in 1879); the commercial use of **petroleum** (starting in 1859); the birth of chemical industries; the **internal combustion engine** (1866–1885), which led to the automobile; the **telephone** (1876–1879); the **radio** (1895–1901); and the **airplane** (1903). Warfare industrialized as well, with modern rifles, better artillery, and the machine gun. In the countryside, the **tractor** helped cause an agricultural boom.

Industrialization occurred first and most thoroughly in western Europe (especially Britain, the Low Countries, France, and Germany), as well as the United States. Southern and eastern Europe lagged behind. Britain led the world in industrial production for most of the 1800s. By the end of the century, Germany and the United States were catching up to, then surpassing, Britain.

The Social and Environmental Effects of Industrialization

The Industrial Revolution and its aftermath vastly transformed Western society. Especially between the 1780s and 1840s, the effects were as traumatic as they were important. For the lower classes, the industrial era's birth pangs were extremely painful.

The economic clout of the traditional aristocracy, whose wealth had been based primarily on land, was diminished by industrialization. The class that benefited most was the **middle class** (or bourgeoisie), especially bankers, merchants, and factory owners who drew direct profits from industrial growth.

The Industrial Revolution astronomically expanded the size of the **working class** (or proletariat). During the first decades of industrialization, this class bore the heaviest economic burden. Their labor allowed the Industrial Revolution to move forward, but until the second half of the 1800s, they were badly treated and barely compensated. Workers received low wages, lived in squalid and crowded housing, worked long shifts (fourteen hours a day, six days a week, was not unusual), coped with unsafe working conditions (risk of fire, dangerous machines, exposure to poisonous or harmful substances), and had no pensions, safety laws, or insurance. Child labor was common.

In the countryside, industrialization caused new social divisions. More land came to be owned by well-off farmers and homesteaders who were essentially middle class. Under them were poor agricultural laborers who formed a rural working class of sorts. (In Russia until 1861, the system of **serfdom** still prevailed, and **slavery** persisted until 1865 in the southern United States.)

Only after the 1840s is industrialization considered to have brought about meaningful improvements for large numbers of Americans and Europeans. Especially after the **1848 Revolutions** (caused partly by the socioeconomic stress of early industrialization), various laws and measures began to give relief to the working class—although completely fair treatment and full political equality were still distant goals, achieved only after hard effort and not until the late 1800s or even 1900s. The overall standard of living rose during the second half of the 1800s, even for the lower classes. At least in major cities, many features of modern life became available after mid-century, including bus service, streetlights (gas, then electric), citywide sewage systems, icebox refrigeration, indoor plumbing, steam heating, canned food, and medical advances (vaccination, germ theory, antiseptic surgery, anesthesia).

Related social trends are massive **population growth** and **urbanization**. Europe's population grew from 175 million (187 million, by some estimates) in 1800 to 266

million in 1850 and 423 million by 1900. Similar growth took place in the United States. Such growth was not the product of higher birth rates, but declining death rates caused by gradual improvements. European cities that existed grew larger; in 1800, London reached the 1 million mark, as did Paris in the 1830s. Many new cities sprang up, such as Liverpool and Manchester, precisely because of the Industrial Revolution. By the mid-1800s, England and Wales were urban societies, meaning that 50 percent or more of the population lived in cities. At that time, the level of urbanization had reached 25 percent in France and the German states, and it continued to grow, as in the Low Countries and the United States. Urbanization is generally associated with social advancement, but it had its seamier side during the industrial era: cities were typically polluted and crowded, and the lower classes lived in slums or shantytowns where sewage was primitive or nonexistent. Diseases such as **cholera**, **tuberculosis**, and typhoid ran rampant in such conditions.

Population growth and urban concentration affected the environment, as did the industrialized nations' voracious appetite for resources and raw materials (wood, coal, metals, and petroleum). **Pollution** reached unprecedented levels, and, unlike today, there were few laws to combat it. **Resource extraction** (such as mining) on a large scale harmed the environment, as did the **large-scale agriculture** needed to produce cotton and similar crops. As non-Western parts of the world industrialized, they repeated this pattern. The early stages of human-caused climate change (global warming) are thought to date to the nineteenth-century industrial takeoff.

Women and Industrialization

Before the Industrial Revolution, European women of the lower (and sometimes middle) class worked with men on the farm or in the family business, so motherhood and homemaking were not full-time pursuits. The Industrial Revolution altered that reality, turning husbands into wage earners and wives into homemakers. By the late 1800s, it had created a sharply defined **domestic sphere** for women.

This evolution took time. In the early 1800s, husbands and wives (and often children) in working-class families had to labor in factories or mines to make ends meet. Before 1870, women made up 50 percent of the textile workforce. Ironically, this meant that lower-class women had more opportunity to work than those of the middle and upper classes, but this was not a matter of privilege or right. It was economic necessity, and working women earned much lower pay than men.

Throughout the 1800s, most working women remained in traditional types of female labor, such as domestic service or agricultural work. Most were single, not married. Some single women, desperate for jobs, left Europe for Australia, the United States, or Canada. By the late 1800s, large numbers of poor women worked outside the home.

Increasingly, though, as salaries improved in industry (making these jobs more desirable to men) and laws restricted the number of hours women could work, more working-class women stayed at home. Fewer middle-class (and almost no upper-class) women worked.

Around the turn of the century, with the rising standard of living, a mass consumer society began to emerge. Products such as sewing machines and cast-iron stoves freed up time for women of all classes to pursue activities outside the home. Medical advances reduced infant mortality and the number of women who died in childbirth.

ECONOMIC THEORIES AND MOVEMENTS

Industrialization coincided with the rise of **capitalism** in the West. **Adam Smith's** *The Wealth of Nations* appeared in 1776, just before the Industrial Revolution began. Capitalism encouraged free trade and political liberalism (at least for the middle classes), and it led to the creation of great wealth in the Western world. On the other hand, it was based on competition and, left unregulated, could be cruel to those who lost (like the early working class).

Smith and the other classical economists who favored capitalism argued that the laws of supply and demand—the **"invisible hand,"** to use Smith's metaphor—should operate freely, with minimal government intervention. (Germany, where state control of the economy was pronounced, broke this rule and still became an industrial powerhouse.) Smith himself insisted that governments should take measures to fight extreme poverty, a point often forgotten today. Other economic thinkers of the day maintained that little could be done about poverty. Thomas Malthus of England wrote in his influential *Essay on Population* (1799) that poverty was one of the inevitable consequences of population growth. David Ricardo's **"iron law of wages"** was even more pessimistic: employers, he said, will naturally pay workers no more than what is needed to allow them to survive. To force them to pay higher wages, Ricardo predicted, would cause them to fire workers, who would then starve. Such theories caused economics to be nicknamed the "dismal science" and were used for a long time by middle- and upper-class industrialists to justify oppressive labor practices.

After the **1848 Revolutions**, it was clear that pure, dog-eat-dog capitalism could not remain as it was without causing severe social and economic stress. But how should it be changed? Liberals and reformers sought to soften capitalism's hard edge by agreeing to fairer labor laws and social welfare measures. For workers, a more radical option (by the standards of the day) was the **trade union** movement. In the early 1800s, unions were illegal in Europe and the United States, and workers risked injury and arrest if they joined unions or went on strike. Still, the union movement gave them a way to struggle for political rights and better treatment in the workplace (higher wages, five-day work week, shorter hours, safety regulations, pensions, and employee insurance). In the late 1800s and early 1900s, unions earned legal status in most countries and gained greater economic and political strength. Political parties dedicated to the needs of workers, such as Labour in Britain, formed.

Even more extreme were **socialism**, which rejected capitalism and denied the validity of private property, and anarchism, which rejected all forms of government. Many varieties of socialism appeared in the 1800s, all sharing the belief that economic competition is inherently unfair and leads to injustice and inequality. The most influential form of socialism is **communism**, originated by the German philosophers **Karl Marx** and Friedrich Engels and most famously outlined in *The Communist Manifesto* (1848) and *Das Kapital* (1867–1894). Marx and Engels argued that all historical development was driven by a **class struggle** between the upper class (which controls capital, or the means of economic production) and the lower class (which is forced to labor for the upper class). They predicted that the age of industrial capitalism, with its struggle between bourgeoisie and proletariat, was the final stage of human history before the realization of socialism. Society would then move on to communism, an

economic state of perfect justice, equality, and prosperity. To achieve socialism, however, Marx and Engels believed that revolution would be needed, so they advocated the overthrow of capitalism, by force if need be.

THE GLOBAL IMPACT OF INDUSTRIALIZATION

Industrialization and Imperialism

Western industrialization and imperialism (see Chapter 23) were intimately connected in several ways. First, industrialization gave Western nations the wealth, technological aptitude, and scientific knowledge to conquer and colonize other parts of the world. Particularly, it placed new weapons in the hands of Westerners: gunboats, artillery, quick-firing and accurate rifles, and machine guns, all of which made Western imperialism difficult for poorly armed native forces to resist.

Second, if industrialization gave the West greater ability to conquer and colonize, it also provided more motivation. Industrialization required ever-greater amounts of raw materials: iron ore, coal, rubber, metals, timber, and chemicals, all of which could be stripped from other parts of the world. The growing importance of steamships made it necessary for Western nations to maintain naval bases and refueling stations around the globe. Moreover, as Europe and America produced more manufactured goods, they needed overseas markets to sell them to. All these needs spurred the Western nations' intense burst of imperial activity during the 1800s, especially the second half.

The Influence of Industrial Nations over Nonindustrial Nations

Even in parts of the world that Europe and America did not conquer or colonize, industrialization had a profound effect. In Africa, Asia, and Latin America, Western businessmen and industrialists struck deals with aristocrats or the political elite to exploit local resources. These bargains typically involved the large-scale growth or extraction of a small set of crops or natural resources. This kind of **monoculture** generally damages the environment and retards the development of a healthy, diverse economy. It also exploits these countries' native workers: foreign payments or investments end up in the pockets of a small number of local elites, rather than adding to the national well-being.

In the long term, most non-Western parts of the world came to imitate industrial methods of production. Western colonizing powers exported industrial practices to their imperial possessions. Political leaders in free nations came to see industrialization as a way to gain wealth and power. In such cases, industrialization was typically imposed from above by the ruler. The worldwide adoption of industrialization worldwide continued through the twentieth century and continues today.

Industrialization and the Atlantic Slave Trade

Another global effect of early industrialization concerns the **Atlantic slave trade**. The 1793 invention of the **cotton gin** by the American engineer Eli Whitney transformed the international textile trade. One of the factors limiting growth in the textile trade

NOTE

In the tropics, the derogatory slang for countries with mono-culture economies is "banana republic."

was the fact that raw cotton still had to be cleaned by hand. The cotton gin changed this situation, enabling the industry to be fully mechanized, which phenomenally boosted England's demand for raw cotton. Although Egypt was a major source of cotton, an equally important supplier was the American South, where cotton was grown and harvested mainly by slaves. Most economic historians argue that, before the 1790s, slavery was becoming less profitable in the American South and might have died away relatively quickly and easily. The advent of the cotton gin, combined with increased English demand, revived the profitability of slave-based production. Therefore, slavery in America was prolonged for decades—necessitating civil war to end it—largely because of the textile trade's industrialization.

The Europeans Abroad: Imperialism, Nationalism, and Foreign Policy

CHAPTER 23

- The new imperialism
- Social Darwinism and the "white man's burden" concept
- The Monroe Doctrine and manifest destiny
- The British East India Company and the Indian Mutiny
- Foreign concessions in China and the Boxer Rebellion
- Japanese imperialism and the Russo-Japanese War
- The Great Game
- The Eastern Question
- The Scramble for Africa and the Berlin Conference
- Nationalism, competition for empire, and the European alliance system

One of the most astounding facts of the nineteenth century is that, while, in 1815, the nations of the West—Europe and America—controlled 35 percent of the world's habitable territory, they controlled 85 percent by 1914. The nineteenth century was an age of empire, in which the West came to achieve dominance over a larger portion of the globe than any civilization had before.

Western imperialism was nothing new. European powers had been conquering other parts of the world since the 1400s. From the 1700s onward, the United States had grown "from sea to shining sea" by means of warfare and subjugation of the native population. From the mid-1800s to the early 1900s, however, imperialism took on a more aggressive and systematic character, and many historians refer to this as the **new imperialism**.

Imperialism remains one of the Western world's longest-lasting and most controversial legacies. As a practical undertaking and a military enterprise, the West's domination of the world was impressive, and it made Europe and America powerful and rich. On the other hand, imperialism was inseparable from bloodshed, racial prejudice, and slavery. As the English-Polish author Joseph Conrad wrote in the novel *Heart of Darkness*—one of the classic literary depictions of European imperialism—"The conquest of the earth, which mostly means the taking it away from those who have a different complexion or slightly flatter noses than ourselves, is not a pretty thing when you look into it too much." Moreover, Europe's and America's campaigns

of colonization left deep political scars around the globe, many of which have not yet healed even in the twenty-first century.

Whether abroad or at home, European foreign policy became increasingly aggressive. During the first half of the 1800s, the balance of power achieved by the Congress of Vienna largely kept the peace. After 1850, however, several wars broke out among the European powers: the Crimean War (1853–1856), in which Russia fought France and Britain; the wars of Italian unification, which entangled France, Austria, and several Italian states; and the three wars Prussia fought to unify the German states, especially the Franco-Prussian War (1870–1871).

Much of this aggression was caused by the growing intensity of **nationalism**, a relatively new cultural phenomenon that placed a premium on patriotic sentiment. Another cause was competition over imperial possessions, especially as the century drew to a close and the amount of desirable territory left to be conquered shrank. On the surface, relative stability was maintained from 1871 to 1914, a period in European history known as the Long Peace. But underneath, the potential for conflict grew with every passing year. The **European alliance system** emerged during the 1890s and early 1900s as a result of this growing sense of foreign policy crisis. It was a principal factor in the complex background of World War I.

CAUSES OF IMPERIALISM

A variety of interrelated factors enabled and motivated the new imperialism of the 1800s. They apply to the nations of Europe and, to a degree, the United States.

One set of factors was economic. Industrialization gave the West the ability to conquer and more reasons to do so. It made Western economies hungry for **raw materials**, many of which could be seized from less powerful nations by force. Also, Western nations needed **markets** for the goods they produced and thought colonies would serve well (in retrospect, economic historians have determined that this was a mistaken belief and that colonies were less suitable as markets than other industrialized countries).

A second factor was **military superiority**. Industrialization gave Western armies and navies ocean-going fleets powered by steam (and, later, petroleum), modern rifles, machine guns, rapid-fire and long-range artillery, and more. Only rarely could native populations resist Western military forces. Also, because modern ships required elaborate repair bases and fueling facilities, Western navies needed control over islands and ports around the world to maintain **sea power**.

A social factor prompting imperialism was Europe's rapid **population growth** during the 1800s. One outlet for excess population growth was emigration to the Americas, and millions of Europeans made that choice. Another option was to leave the homeland and go to the colonies.

Scientific and technological aptitude were also instrumental. In this case, knowledge was power. A new wave of exploration during the 1700s and early 1800s added to Western nations' understanding of Africa, Asia, the polar regions, and the Amazon basin. Better maps and geographical familiarity made it easier for Westerners to conquer these areas. Medical advances made it possible to penetrate tropical regions more deeply. Previously, diseases such as sleeping sickness, yellow fever, and **malaria**

had prevented Westerners from controlling the interior of Africa and Southeast Asia. The development of effective treatments for these illnesses (especially **quinine**, which relieved the symptoms of malaria) changed this situation.

Finally, a complex set of cultural factors motivated the West to build empires. A sense of racial superiority was widespread among white Europeans and Americans, who believed they were entitled to conquer and colonize "backward" or "primitive" peoples. Cecil Rhodes, who did much to colonize Africa, said famously of his British homeland, "I contend that we are the finest race in the world, and the more of it we inhabit, the better it is." In some cases, this belief was "justified" by crude prejudice. A more sophisticated but still misguided doctrine of **social Darwinism** was also used to argue in favor of imperialism. Social Darwinists implied that it was natural for technologically advanced peoples to conquer those who were less so. (Darwin himself denounced this idea as a perversion of his theories.)

Yet another cultural impulse behind imperialism was a conviction that white Westerners had a duty to teach and modernize the darker-skinned, supposedly primitive peoples of Africa and Asia. The English poet Rudyard Kipling gave this sentiment its most famous label: the **White Man's Burden**. The French spoke of their civilizing mission (*la mission civilisatrice*). This attitude was well-meaning and heartfelt, but also condescending. European and American missionaries, doctors, scientists, and colonial officials sometimes did much good in the places they visited. However, they did so out of at least a subconscious sense of racial superiority, and they often trampled on or eradicated native cultural practices and beliefs.

EUROPE'S OVERSEAS EMPIRES

Western Approaches to Imperialism

Almost the entire non-Western world was colonized during the nineteenth century or fell under the influence of Western nations. By far the largest and most widespread empire was Britain's. (A famous motto of the time: "The sun never sets on the British Empire.") France had a sizable empire, as did Belgium and the Netherlands. Although Austria is not commonly thought of as a colonizing power, its empire was in eastern and southeastern Europe. Russia conquered Siberia, much of Central Asia, and for a time, parts of North America. After 1870, new countries such as Germany and Italy began to build overseas empires, in an attempt to catch up with older imperial powers like Britain and France.

Different powers treated their empires differently. The British are considered to have had the most enlightened approach, relatively speaking. Although they took their colonies by force and exploited them economically—and were prone to the same sense of racial superiority as other Westerners—they interfered less with local customs than other colonizers. In keeping with their sense of the White Man's Burden, they introduced positive social reforms and useful scientific and technological knowledge. Likewise, the French subscribed to the notion of *la mission civilisatrice*, but were less consistent about it. The Portuguese and Belgians were known to be especially harsh masters, particularly in Africa, and Germany and Italy (which used poison gas in parts of North Africa) were arguably more brutal yet.

The Americas

North America fell mainly under the sway of the United States, which conquered the entire Western frontier during the nineteenth century. Motivated by the doctrine of **manifest destiny**—the belief that it was entitled to the entire landmass between the Atlantic and Pacific—the United States fought Mexico, negotiated borders with British Canada, and warred on Native Americans, driving them to defeat and onto reservations. This was no less an imperial campaign than what European nations did in Africa or Asia. The Spanish lost their empire in North America when Mexico launched a revolution in the 1810s and 1820s. The Russians gave up their North American possession, Alaska, to the United States in 1867.

The **Latin American wars of independence** freed Mexico, Mesoamerica, and South America from Spain and Portugal in the early 1800s. However, much of Latin America came under the sway of the United States, which did not conquer the region but considered it part of the U.S. sphere of influence. The **Monroe Doctrine**, issued in 1823, formally stated that the United States would not permit European interference in the Western Hemisphere. U.S. economic and political influence over Central and South America increased throughout the 1800s. At the end of the century, in 1898, the **Spanish-American War** gave the United States control over Cuba, Puerto Rico, and the Virgin Islands, making it an imperial power in Latin America.

Southeast Asia

The vast expanse of Asia was colonized and influenced by a variety of powers. The region that had been longest under European control was Southeast Asia. The Dutch tightened their grasp over Indonesia. France took over Indochina, the area that is today Laos, Cambodia, and Vietnam. By the mid-1880s, the British controlled Burma, the Malay Peninsula (with the trading center of Singapore), and northern Borneo. Farther to the south, Britain reigned over the continent of Australia. The Philippines had belonged to Spain since Magellan's voyage of 1521, but the United States took them in 1898, following the Spanish-American War. Later in the century, Germany seized a number of Pacific islands for use as naval posts.

India

The heart of the British Empire was India. Britain and France quarreled with each other over hegemony in India during the 1700s. At the battle of **Plassey**, in 1757, the British won a major victory over the Mughal Empire, enabling them to consolidate their military presence in India and leading to a decline of French influence. Over the next decades, the British went on to conquer most of the subcontinent. Until the late 1850s, India was not administered directly by the British government but by the semiprivate **British East India Company**, one of the richest and most powerful business ventures in world history. In 1857, however, the **Indian Mutiny** (also known as the **Sepoy Rebellion**)—which failed but shocked the British badly—persuaded the government to assume full control over the colony. India was exceptionally important to Britain, in terms of national pride, strategic position, and

economic benefit. During the late 1800s, one-quarter of the wealth generated by the British Empire came from India.

China

Qing China, despite its vast size and immense population, fell victim to almost every European nation, as well as to the United States. China was not technically colonized. However, thanks to military defeat at the hands of the British and other foreigners during the middle of the 1800s, it was compelled to open its borders and trade with other countries at highly disadvantageous terms. It gave up pieces of territory such as **Hong Kong** (a British colony from 1842 until 1997, when it returned to Chinese rule), as well as Manchuria and Korea. The British, French, Americans, Germans, Russians, and others were allowed to establish **foreign concessions**: large districts in coastal cities where Western, not Chinese law, prevailed. Foreign ships were allowed to sail as far up Chinese rivers as they pleased. The balance of trade was lopsidedly in favor of the foreigners. The Chinese rose up to resist foreign domination in the failed **Boxer Rebellion** of 1900. In 1911, the Qing dynasty collapsed, its weakness due in large part to foreign meddling.

Japan Resists Western Imperialism

Unlike most Asian nations, Japan resisted Western imperialism, becoming an imperial power itself. Isolated until 1853, when the U.S. Navy forced it to resume diplomatic and economic relations with the wider world, Japan chose to adopt the science, technology, and military know-how of the West, especially under **Emperor Meiji**. Not only did Japan avoid foreign takeover, it began to build its own Asian empire. It defeated China in 1895, taking the island of Taiwan and occupying Korea. More shockingly, Japan dealt Russia a humiliating defeat in the **Russo-Japanese War** (1904–1905), gaining control over more of the Asian mainland, as well as a number of islands.

Central Asia and the Great Game

Much of Central Asia—the wide expanse of desert and mountains through which the Silk Road had run—fell to Russia, which felt the need to protect its southern frontier. Because Russia lacked **warm-water ports**, it hoped to drive to the Indian Ocean and gain an outlet to the sea. The Islamic khanates and cities of Turkestan, Bukhara, Samarkand, and the Afghan border were taken by the Russians between the 1820s and 1880s. Russian imperialism in this region greatly disturbed Britain because it placed the Russians within striking distance of the Middle East, much of which was in the British sphere of influence. More important, Russian encroachments on Central Asia threatened the lines of communication between Europe and India, which the British were determined to protect at all costs.

For most of the 1800s, Britain and Russia were locked in an intense campaign of espionage and diplomatic intrigue known as the **Great Game**, a term coined by the poet Rudyard Kipling (Russians called it the Tournament of Shadows). The Great Game never resulted in outright war, but created a deep rivalry between Britain and Russia until shortly before World War I.

The Middle East and the Eastern Question

For centuries, the Middle East and most of North Africa had been in the hands of the Ottoman Empire. However, the Ottoman Empire was collapsing, and the **Eastern Question**—how to fill the power vacuum caused by the Ottomans' decline—became a central issue in global politics. During the last half of the 1800s, large portions of this region were seized by Europeans, especially the French and British. Algeria, Tunisia, and most of Morocco became French. Part of Morocco fell to Spain, while Italy captured Libya.

The most important territory was Egypt, which became a British protectorate in the 1880s. During the 1870s, Egypt, an autonomous part of the Ottoman Empire, had fallen under French and British influence. Both countries financed the construction of the **Suez Canal**, which opened in 1869. Control over the canal—a vital link between Europe and the Mediterranean on one hand and the Red Sea and the Indian Ocean on the other—was crucial, and the British used economic pressure to gain political control over Egypt. They also established control over the Sudan, and both countries became part of the Anglo-Egyptian Administration. To the east, Persia, which had remained independent of Ottoman rule, was divided into two spheres of influence by Russia and Britain.

The Scramble for Africa

Africa experienced the most intense burst of European imperialism near the end of the century. Until the 1880s, only Africa's coastlines had been directly colonized or exploited. Gold, ivory, foodstuffs, and especially slaves had been wrested from Africa, either by military force or economic pressure. Although slavery and the slave trade had been made illegal by most Western nations following the French Revolution and Napoleonic Wars, both institutions continued throughout the 1800s. Slavery was practiced in the United States until the Civil War of the 1860s, and even afterward, it continued in parts of the Caribbean and South America. Not until Brazil outlawed slavery in 1888 did the **Atlantic slave trade** end completely. More than 2 million slaves were transported from Africa during the 1800s, bringing the likely total of African slaves captured from the late 1400s to the late 1800s to at least 12 million.

The character of African colonization changed remarkably after 1880. From then until the 1910s, European nations raced to take over territory in Africa. Thanks to better maps, industrial-era weapons, and effective tropical medicines, European colonizers penetrated every part of what the West thought of as the "dark continent." This so-called **Scramble for Africa** became so intense that, several times, it almost sparked war in Europe. The **Berlin Conference** (1884–1885), presided over by Otto von Bismarck, laid down guidelines for African expansion and, for a time, preserved peace. Still, competition over African territory caused diplomatic crises among the European powers during the early 1900s, especially the **Boer War** (1899–1902). For the Africans, the sudden and overwhelming influx of Europeans spelled disaster. By 1914, only two nations in Africa remained free: Liberia, whose independence was guaranteed by the United States because it had been founded by freed American slaves, and Abyssinia (Ethiopia), which armed itself with modern weapons and drove

off Italian efforts to conquer it. Within three decades, the rest of the continent had been brought under Europe's imperial sway.

The Balkans

Even parts of Europe were vulnerable to imperial predation. Southeastern Europe—the **Balkans**—lay at the crossroads of several empires. Although this area was the most economically and culturally backward of Europe, the imperial ambitions of Russia, Austria, Italy, and the deteriorating Ottoman Empire all centered on it. The level of competition among these powers steadily escalated. Complicating the situation was the intense wave of **nationalism** that swept most of southeastern Europe during the nineteenth century. Starting with the **Greek War of Independence** in the 1820s, the various minorities ruled by the Ottomans, Austrians, and Russians constantly agitated for greater independence—and, if they had independence, they craved more territory. To realize their goals, many of these peoples were willing to risk war. By the early 1900s, the nationalist ambitions of many Balkan peoples, especially the Serbs, had become a destabilizing force in European politics. Not only were two Balkan wars fought in 1912 and 1913, but the events that triggered World War I took place there.

AGGRESSION AT HOME: NATIONALISM, WARFARE, AND ALLIANCE SYSTEMS

The Balance of Power in Nineteenth-Century Europe

As noted above, the European **balance of power** had been maintained during the first half of the 1800s. Even the wars of the mid-1800s were short and limited in intensity. Ironically, it was during the Long Peace of 1871 to 1914 that tensions worsened. Although this era gave birth to the modern Olympic Games (starting in 1896) and the Nobel Peace Prize (first awarded in 1901), the turn of the century was marked by saber-rattling, **jingoism** (a British nickname for belligerent patriotism), and **brinksmanship** (a diplomatic term referring to a country's willingness to risk war in order to get its way).

Factors Destabilizing the European Balance of Power

Several factors upset Europe's diplomatic stability in the late 1800s and early 1900s. One was the force of **nationalism**, which in most countries transformed patriotic sentiment into aggressive tendencies. Another was **competition over empire**: as the 1800s came to an end, there were fewer places for European nations to expand. Especially in Africa, the jostling for new conquests came close to starting war several times in the early 1900s. A third destabilizing force was the ambitious nature of German foreign policy. An economic and military powerhouse, despite having been united only in 1871, Germany came to believe that it deserved what it called "a place in the sun": equal military and imperial status with older nations such as Britain and France. This was the case especially under **Wilhelm II**, who came to the throne in 1888 and dismissed the skilled and cautious diplomat **Otto von Bismarck** in 1890. Under

Wilhelm II, Germany became openly aggressive and forceful, unnerving the rest of Europe.

The Creation of Europe's Turn-of-the-Century Alliance System

From the 1880s to the 1910s, the **European alliance system** took shape, dividing Europe into two armed camps. Germany and Austria formed an alliance in 1879; joined by Italy in 1881, they formed the Triple Alliance. (Italy dropped out of this coalition in World War I, but the Austro-German partnership held firm.) In response, France, bitter about defeat in the **Franco-Prussian War** (and the resulting loss to Germany of the border provinces Alsace and Lorraine), allied in 1894 with Russia, which viewed Austria as a threat in the Balkans. Geographically, France and Russia had their rivals surrounded.

Until 1907, Britain remained unaligned. Thanks to the **Great Game**, it viewed Russia as an enemy, and it had little affection for France. After 1890, though, it felt increasingly alarmed by Germany. Wilhelm II's aggressive imperialism and his expansion of the navy (which menaced the root of Britain's global power, control of the seas) soured Anglo-German relations and shifted British strategy. In 1907, the British informally joined the Franco-Russian alliance, forming the Triple Entente ("understanding").

At this point, any crisis between two countries could potentially involve all of Europe's major powers, the likelihood of war increased. Worsening the problem was Germany's strategy in case of war, the **Schlieffen Plan**. Facing the dilemma of a two-front war, German generals planned a rapid, massive attack against France. Once France was defeated, the Germans and Austrians could deal with Russia at their leisure. To work, the Schlieffen Plan would have to be executed with lightning speed. In the event of a crisis, Germany would have little time to make decisions or resort to diplomacy, and thus, the outbreak of war became even more probable.

The Middle East

CHAPTER 24

- Decline of the Ottoman Empire
- The janissaries
- The Tanzimat Reforms
- The Greek War of Independence and Balkan nationalism
- Muhammed Ali's uprising
- The Eastern Question
- The Suez Canal
- The Balkan Crisis and the Congress of Berlin
- Enver Pasha and the Young Turks
- The Madhi
- The Great Game

The Middle East, with Islamic North Africa and Central Asia, underwent a fundamental transformation between the early 1700s and early 1900s. Before 1700, the Ottoman Empire, feared and respected throughout Eurasia as a great power, reigned supreme over most of this region. Where it did not, states such as Persia and the khanates of Central Asia stood strong and free.

After 1700, military setbacks at the hands of European enemies weakened the Ottoman Empire. Its European possessions gradually slipped away. Internal decay allowed outlying territories in North Africa to gain autonomy. Those territories were then taken into British, French, and Italian empires, further eroding Ottoman power. By the nineteenth century, the failing Ottoman Empire had earned an unflattering nickname: the "sick man of Europe." Periodic reform efforts kept the state alive during the 1800s but did not stave off decline. More reform came at the beginning of the 1900s, but World War I destroyed the Ottoman Empire, which was then transformed into the modern Turkish state.

In the meantime, how to deal with the steady collapse of the Ottoman state and still maintain the European balance of power became one of the crucial foreign policy issues of the 1800s. This Eastern Question perplexed diplomats for decades.

European imperialism also dealt blows to other states in the Middle East and neighboring regions. Egypt, the Caucasus, Persia, and Central Asia came under European—mainly British and Russian—control during the 1800s.

THE DECLINE OF THE OTTOMAN EMPIRE

The Ottoman Empire sustained a heavy set of blows in the late 1600s and early 1700s. In 1683, the Turks nearly succeeded in capturing Vienna, capital of the Austrian Habsburgs. They failed and, in the next three and a half decades of fighting, lost battle after battle and much territory, including Hungary and Transylvania. The treaties of Karlowitz (1699) and Passarowitz (1718) left the Turks greatly diminished in Europe.

Occasional conflicts with Austria continued to sap Ottoman strength. Even worse were the periodic wars the Turks fought with Russia, especially against Peter the

Great in the 1710s and Catherine the Great in the late 1700s. With each new struggle, the Turks lost more territory.

Internal Decay and Attempted Reform

Internal troubles also damaged the Ottoman state. Mediocre rulers and governmental corruption had weakened the political system during the 1600s and continued to do so in the 1700s. The dilemma was that sultans who wished to improve or modernize the system met with opposition from influential groups and officials with vested interests in the traditional way of doing things.

This was especially the case with the armed forces. The **janissaries**, who had been so innovative and effective in the 1500s and 1600s, became backward and complacent in the 1700s and early 1800s, refusing to adapt to new technology and tactics. Unfortunately for the empire, the janissaries were, until the 1820s, powerful enough to prevent any change for the better. For example, when Selim III tried to reform the bureaucracy and modernize the army and navy, the janissaries, fearing the loss of their privileged position, assassinated him in 1807.

Later sultans were more effective at changing the system. From the 1820s onward, the Ottoman leadership made some progress in modernizing the political system, the economy, and the military. The sultans boosted Western educational principles, scientific knowledge, and technological expertise. To a degree, they also secularized, against the protests of the traditional Islamic clergy. In the late 1820s, Mehmet III created a professional, European-style army and navy and then subdued the janissaries.

From 1839 through 1876, the Ottoman government introduced a wide-ranging set of changes known as the **Tanzimat reforms**. These reforms emphasized greater religious tolerance for the non-Muslims **millets** (social groups categorized by religion) living in the empire, reform of the legal system, the creation of schools that would teach Western science and technology, the establishment of national telegraph and postal systems, and more. The Tanzimat reforms even included discussing the possibility of a constitution. Another effect of the reforms was to give women greater access to education. Public schools were founded for women, and more of them (although still a small number) began to enter public life in the late 1800s.

Still, such limited change was not enough to solve the empire's deep-seated internal and external problems. The Tanzimat reforms and other such measures alienated conservatives and traditionalists, who found them too extreme. Yet they did not do enough to satisfy the growing numbers of forward-looking politicians and military officers who wanted more change than the sultan was willing to make. By the early 1900s, this generation of modernizers, known as the **Young Turks**, would, from within the regime, play a decisive role in ending the sultan's rule.

Revolts, Rebellions, and the Gradual Disintegration of the Ottoman Empire

Long before this, external problems such as rebellion and war were disintegrating the Ottoman Empire. In the early 1800s, an upsurge of nationalism, combined with

political turmoil caused by the Napoleonic Wars, led to many uprisings in Turkish-controlled Europe. Serbia revolted in 1807, and even though the revolt failed, the Serbs remained restless.

More seriously, the **Greek War of Independence** began in 1821. By 1827, France and Britain, responding to Christian Europe's outpouring of sympathy for the Greeks, aided the rebels (earlier, the poet Lord Byron had helped turn the war into an international cause by leaving England to fight and die on the side of the Greeks). Russia, sharing Greece's Eastern Orthodox faith, also joined the war. Defeated by this coalition, the Ottomans were forced to recognize Greek independence in 1832. At the same time, the Ottoman government had to cope with the rebellion of **Muhammad Ali** in Egypt and the growing autonomy of possessions in western North Africa.

The Eastern Question

From the 1820s onward, the steady collapse of the Ottoman state presented the nations of Europe with a geopolitical challenge known as the **Eastern Question**. Although the Turks had been Europe's enemies since the 1300s, the Ottoman Empire was now seen as a satisfactory regime to have in place in the Middle East. It was no longer a real threat, it was predictable, and, for the time being, it held together many volatile parts of Asia and Europe. To destroy it or allow it to fall apart quickly might cause chaos or give birth to a new state that was strong and hostile.

Another aspect of the Eastern Question was that the nations of Europe did not wholly trust each other. The Ottoman Empire sat at a geographically crucial juncture: the crossroads of Europe and Asia, the joining of the Black and Mediterranean seas, and the Suez isthmus, which linked the Mediterranean with the Indian Ocean and Asia. If one European country seized too much territory from the Ottomans at one time, it would upset Europe's fragile **balance of power**. Informally, the nations of Europe agreed to solve this part of the Eastern Question by not acting too suddenly or decisively in the region. The Ottomans' decline was to be managed carefully and slowly. If necessary, the European powers would prop up the empire if it seemed in danger of immediate collapse.

The complexity of the Eastern Question was illustrated many times. The Europeans took so long to help Greece in the 1820s because they feared causing too much damage to the Ottoman Empire at once. Soon after joining the Greeks *against* the Turks, Britain and France gave aid *to* the Turks by helping contain Muhammad Ali's revolt in Egypt; they worried that he would be too formidable an enemy if he toppled the Ottoman sultan. Sometimes the Eastern Question pitted the Europeans against each other; when Russia annexed Ottoman territory in the early 1850s, Britain and France fought alongside the Turks in the Crimean War (1853–1856), the first time since Napoleon's defeat that European powers clashed with each other.

Tensions worsened after 1870. The construction of the **Suez Canal** in 1869 increased the strategic and economic importance of Egypt, as well as Britain's and France's interest in the region. Italy's unification in the 1860s meant yet another European power with ambitions in the eastern Mediterranean. Moreover, Balkan **nationalism** intensified in the late 1800s. The **Balkan Crisis** (1876–1878) nearly destroyed the Ottoman Empire: when Romania, Bulgaria, Serbia, and Montenegro

revolted against the Ottomans, Russia went to war on their behalf, beat the Turks, and imposed a harsh treaty. The rest of Europe, not wanting Russia to defeat the Turks too decisively, intervened. At the Congress of Berlin (1878), the four rebel nations gained their freedom, but the European powers compelled Russia to offer a more generous treaty to the Turks. Once again, the Eastern Question was dealt with through a combination of opportunistic land-grabbing and balanced management.

The Ottoman Empire's Final Years

Domestically, the Ottoman Empire, steadily losing territory and constantly interfered with by the powers of Europe, suffered great difficulties as the 1800s came to an end. As the twentieth century began, the sultan's days were numbered. A group of pro-Western army officers, with a modern, secular outlook, began to form. They called themselves the **Young Turks**, and they were deeply dissatisfied with the sultan's failures to reform and strengthen the Empire. Led by Enver Pasha, the Young Turks seized control in 1908, neutralizing the last sultan and establishing a parliamentary government. The Young Turks modernized the military, aligned themselves with Germany, and began a series of social, economic, and political reforms.

However, they could not save the Ottoman Empire. Between 1911 and 1913, the Italians seized the Ottomans' last provinces in North Africa, and a coalition of Serbia, Greece, and Bulgaria defeated the Ottomans in two Balkan Wars. Finally, during World War I, the Young Turk government sided with the Germans. Defeated by the Allies in 1918, the Ottoman Empire collapsed altogether, and its Middle Eastern possessions rebelled or were stripped away by the French and British. The empire was replaced by the modern Turkish state during the 1920s.

EGYPT AND NORTH AFRICA

At its peak, the Ottoman Empire ruled most of Islamic North Africa. Even before the late 1700s, the empire's grip here was weakening owing to distance and the desire of cities such as Tripoli, Algiers, and Tunis for greater autonomy.

Things worsened with the Napoleonic Wars. In 1798, France sent Napoleon to capture Egypt and the Suez isthmus. He easily defeated Egyptian and Turkish armies, temporarily deposing the Mamluks who ruled Egypt on the Ottomans' behalf. Although the English restored the regime, Ottoman authority in Egypt was badly damaged.

The Revolt of Muhammad Ali

In 1805, the rebellion of **Muhammad Ali** freed Egypt from Ottoman rule. An officer in the Turkish forces, Muhammad Ali seized power and began to modernize Egypt until his death in 1839. He created a Western-style military, modernized agriculture (especially cotton), boosted industrialization, and recruited large numbers of European professionals to work for him and teach his people new skills. Muhammad Ali transformed Egypt into one of the world's greatest suppliers of cotton, industrializing that sector of the economy, although he worked his growers oppressively to do so.

Muhammad Ali threatened the Ottomans even more seriously when he tried to expand his borders. He took the Sudan, then went east, capturing the Sinai, Syria, parts of Arabia, and northern Iraq. He threatened the Ottoman capital, Istanbul. Afraid that he would topple the Ottomans completely, France and Britain stepped in. Recognizing Muhammad Ali as the hereditary prince (khedive) of an autonomous Egypt, the Europeans convinced him not to expand further—and in so doing, saved the Ottoman Empire. Even so, the empire had been badly injured.

European Imperialism in North Africa

As the 1800s passed, the western parts of North Africa, now cut off from the Ottoman Empire by Egypt, fell out of the Ottomans' hands and into those of European imperialists. The French seized Algeria in 1830; more than 150,000 French settled there by the mid-1850s, and France considered Algeria to be as important to it as India was to Britain. Later, the French established a protectorate over neighboring Tunisia. Morocco fell to the French and Spanish late in the century. Libya was conquered by Italy during the Italo-Turkish War (1911–1912). This was the first war in which airplanes flew in combat, and the Italians used poison gas as well.

The Suez Canal and English Dominance over Egypt and Sudan

Egypt fell out of the Ottoman orbit only to be sucked into the European sphere of influence. Muhammad Ali's grandson Ismail, also a reformer, decided to build a canal across the Suez land bridge that linked the Mediterranean with the Red Sea. Ismail's other modernizing efforts, which included building schools and hospitals, were helpful to Egypt. In the short term, building the Suez Canal led to European domination. A French engineer, Ferdinand de Lesseps, designed the canal, and British and French companies supervised the construction, which lasted from 1854 to 1869. The **Suez Canal** was a marvel of modern construction, and it revolutionized international shipping. However, thousands of Egyptians died during the construction, and the French and British held most of the shares in the company that owned the canal. The British bought up many French shares and, in 1875, all of Egypt's. This gave Britain an excuse to interfere in local politics. In 1881, the Egyptian military revolted against the khedive. Under the pretext of protecting their investment in the canal, the British assumed control over the region, establishing a protectorate called the Anglo-Egyptian Administration. Although the khedive technically ruled Egypt, the British controlled the government. (For other examples of Western economic dominance over regions that were not technically colonies, see Latin America and China during the late 1800s and early 1900s.)

The British extended the Anglo-Egyptian Administration southward, bringing the Sudan under its control. In the 1880s and 1890s, British authority was opposed by a religious leader and Islamic rebel known as the **Mahdi** (Arabic for "one who is rightly guided"). In 1885, the Mahdi's army massacred a British force at Khartoum, one of Britain's most stunning imperial defeats. In 1898, the British beat the Mahdi at Omdurman in a classic imperial battle in which a small European army, armed

with modern rifles and machine guns, mowed down a much larger but poorly armed indigenous force.

From the late 1800s until after the end of World War II, Egypt and North Africa remained in European hands.

PERSIA, THE CAUCASUS, AND CENTRAL ASIA

Much the same pattern that applied to the Ottoman Empire and North Africa was repeated in the rest of the Middle East.

The Decline and Partition of Persia

Like the Ottomans, the Persians had created a mighty gunpowder empire, the Safavid state. It remained strong through the early 1700s, but then found itself at the mercy of outside powers. To the north was Russia, which, as it modernized and Westernized, seized Persian territory in a number of wars. In the late 1700s and 1800s, Russia took portions of the Caucasus Mountains, which lay between the two countries, absorbing Armenia, Georgia, and Azerbaijan. The first two, Christian states living under the Islamic Persians, had asked Russia for help (but had not wanted to become part of the Russian Empire as they did).

The Qajar Dynasty, which ruled Persia from 1794 to 1925, was unable to resist foreign control, even though it technically ruled the country. (In this, its situation resembled China during these years.) In the 1800s, Britain and Russia cynically divided Persia into spheres of influence, allowing them to balance their rivalry in the region and flank the Ottomans. The northern zone went to Russia, the southern zone to Britain. This arrangement lasted until after World War II. British investment in Persia was heavy, especially after the discovery of oil reserves 1908.

The Russian Conquest of the Caucasus and Central Asia

From the 1820s through the 1880s, the Russians waged long, intense campaigns of conquest and colonization in the Caucasus and Central Asia, home to the Silk Road khanates. The Russians conquered these regions for several reasons: nationalistic pride, natural resources (Central Asia is a great cotton-producing region), strategy (the Russians feared having a long, open southern frontier), and the hope, never realized, of driving to the Indian Ocean to establish warm-water ports. In long, bloody wars of pacification, the Russians crushed Islamic tribes in the Caucasus. Further to the east, they took Tashkent (1865), Samarkand (1868), and Bukhara (1868), driving all the way to the Afghan border.

As discussed in Chapter 23, Russian ambitions here distressed the British: Russia threatened Britain's lines of communication to India and drew near to India itself. The resulting **Great Game** of espionage and diplomatic maneuver caused much Anglo-Russian rivalry until the early 1900s.

China and Japan

- The decline of Qing China
- The tea and opium trades
- The Opium Wars, the concessions system, and the Open Door Policy
- The Taiping Rebellion
- The Dowager Empress Cixi and the Boxer Rebellion
- Sun Yat-sen and the Nationalist Party
- The Tokugawa Shogunate
- Matthew Perry and the opening of Japan
- The Meiji Restoration and Japan's industrial modernization
- The Russo-Japanese War

As with the rest of the globe, the European presence in East Asia increased dramatically from the late 1700s through the early 1900s. The major states there, China and Japan, reacted to this development in different ways.

Famously, Napoleon Bonaparte referred to China as a sleeping dragon. By that, he meant that with its huge population, vast size, and rich resources, China had the potential to become one of the world's mightiest nations. However, under the rule of the Qing (Manchu) emperors, China continued to slumber, and its power decreased rather than increased. Deluded by a sense of its own grandeur, based on past accomplishments and old traditions, the Qing leadership did little to modernize or industrialize. This backwardness left it vulnerable, and, during the 1800s, China suffered repeated defeats at the hands of Western powers. Although China was not actually conquered and colonized, it was forced to grant so many privileges and economic concessions to outside powers that its integrity as an independent nation was compromised. The Qing state weakened internally in the late 1800s and collapsed in 1911.

By contrast, Japan responded effectively to the challenge posed by the West. When the United States and the nations of Europe forced its markets open to the world in the 1850s, Japan chose to learn from them. From 1868 onward, under new leadership, the Japanese modernized, industrialized, and militarized. They preserved their independence. By the 1890s and early 1900s, Japan was itself an imperial power, expanding its sphere of influence in East Asia. As several wars during these years proved, Japan became the first non-Western nation in the modern era capable of rivaling Europe and America in military ability and strength.

QING (MANCHU) CHINA IN DECLINE

The Peak of the Qing Dynasty

The Qing, or Manchu, rulers who had conquered China from the north in 1644 had been mighty, ruthless leaders. The dynasty's peak, however, had been the long reign of Kangxi (1662–1722). Emperor **Qianlong** (1736–1795) was the Qing's last strong, competent ruler.

During the last half of the 1700s, Qianlong defended China's long borders, kept the empire's far-flung regions under control, improved economic growth, and sponsored art and learning. During his reign, one of the greatest novels in Chinese literary history appeared: Cao Xuequin's *Dream of the Red Chamber* (1791), which narrates the tragedy of two young lovers caught up in the decline of a wealthy and powerful clan.

Internal Decline of the Qing

Unfortunately for the Qing, several negative trends weakened China after Qianlong's death. The quality of leadership steeply declined, as weak, incompetent emperors took the throne.

More widely, the government became riddled with corruption. The cost of maintaining border defenses along the northern and western frontiers became increasingly burdensome. The economy worsened, and population growth was too rapid (China had 300 million people at the beginning of the century, and 400 million by the end). Popular discontent with the Qing and bad economic conditions broke out into open revolt several times. One such occasion was the White Lotus Rebellion (1796–1804), which took years for the authorities to suppress.

Chinese Foreign Trade Before the 1830s

At the same time, an external problem made itself felt: increased economic and diplomatic pressure from the West, particularly from Britain. As late as the 1810s, the Chinese had the upper hand in their relationship with the West. China was too strong to conquer, and it enjoyed an enormous advantage in its balance of trade.

Europeans could trade with China only in a small number of designated ports and cities (including Kiakhta in the north and **Canton** on the southern coast). The Chinese accepted only a tiny selection of Western goods in trade. In return, they sold the nations of the West silk and porcelain. The most profitable commodity was **tea**, which the Chinese sold in immense quantities to the outside world, especially Russia and Britain. In exchange, the West paid China vast amounts of silver bullion.

For years, Westerners complained about these conditions and requested the Chinese to let them sell more goods in China. In 1793, a British delegation led by Lord Macartney made such a request, but it was denied. Famously, Macartney, in order to meet the Emperor Qianlong, was compelled to lower himself onto one knee, and he was referred to by the Chinese not as an ambassador, but as a tribute-bearer. When Macartney asked that the British be allowed to sell more of their goods to China, Qianlong replied, "Your country has nothing we need." In 1816, a similar mission under Lord Amherst received much the same response.

Tea Harvesting in China.
For hundreds of years, silk, then porcelain, had been China's chief trade commodities. During the 1600s and 1700s, however, tea overtook both in importance. The tea trade played a great role in global economics during the 1700s and 1800s. During those centuries, "all the tea in China" became the most popular slang phrase to describe unimaginable wealth. Shown here is the traditional method of harvesting and processing tea in China.

The Qing's refusal to bargain was partly tough business sense. However, it also had to do with feelings of superiority: the Qing believed that the emperor was the Son of Heaven, that China was the **Middle Kingdom** and the center of the universe, and that all outsiders were barbarians. What the Qing failed to realize, however, was that the Western "barbarians" were, by this point, much more scientifically and technologically advanced than the Chinese—and had stronger navies, better weapons, and more effective armies. The days when the Chinese could intimidate foreigners into accepting such an embarrassing and unprofitable imbalance of trade were about to end.

The Opium Wars and Foreign Domination of Qing China

Meanwhile, the British, followed by other Europeans, found a clever, if unethical, way to break into Chinese markets: the **opium trade**. Opium was known in China, but not widely available, in the 1700s. In the early 1800s, the British began flooding China with opium grown in northeastern India. With lightning speed, opium became the drug of choice among Chinese of all classes. The British made fantastic profits, and the balance of trade swung suddenly in their favor. Over time, other countries—including France, Portugal, and the United States—sold opium to China, but Britain controlled 80 percent of the trade.

The Chinese government was outraged. The trade was illegal. It reversed the balance of trade, and silver bullion, instead of flowing into China, flowed out at an alarming rate. Moreover, opium addiction was so widespread that it affected economic productivity: on any given day, millions of farmers and workers were so incapacitated by the drug that they could not work. The Chinese protested to the West. One official lamented, "The foreigners have brought us a disease which will dry up our bones, a worm that gnaws at our hearts, a ruin to our families and persons. It means the destruction of the soul of our nation."

The Qing government tried to strike back by arresting dealers, seizing opium supplies, and intercepting boats carrying the drug. The problem for the Chinese was that

aggressive action risked giving the foreigners an excuse for war. This happened in 1839, when the Chinese navy blockaded Canton, one of the few ports where foreigners were allowed to trade, sparking the first **Opium War** (1839–1842). The British won easily, then forced the humiliating Treaty of Nanking on the Chinese. The Qing government had to open five more ports to foreign trade, lower tariffs on British goods, and grant extraterritorial rights to areas in China where the British lived and worked (British, not Chinese, law prevailed in these areas). In addition, China surrendered **Hong Kong** to Britain.

Further trade conflicts, including a second Opium War (the so-called Arrow War) and a Franco-British expedition to Beijing, took place between 1856 and 1860. New treaties legalized the opium trade, opened more ports to foreign trade, and granted greater powers to the Portuguese, French, British, Americans, and Russians, who set up **economic concessions** on Chinese territory. Later in the 1800s, China grew weaker and had to give more privileges to foreign traders. Japan, Germany, and Italy gained concessions as well. Much territory along the Chinese coast was extraterritorial: legally under foreign, not Chinese, control. By 1898, foreign vessels were allowed unrestricted travel up the rivers of China.

The Taiping Rebellion

Serious internal problems dogged the Qing at the same time. The worst was the **Taiping Rebellion** (1850–1864), the costliest and most devastating civil war in world history. The Taiping Rebellion lasted almost a decade and a half and claimed between 20 to 30 million lives, making it the second deadliest war in history, next to World War II.

MILLENARIAN REBELLIONS

A number of millenarian rebellions during the 1800s were motivated in part by religious and apocalyptic thought. In addition to the Taiping Rebellion discussed in this chapter and the revolt of the Mahdi described in Chapter 24, examples include the Xhosa Cattle-Killing Movement of the mid-1850s and the Ghost Dance frenzy that led to an 1890 massacre of Sioux. In the former, a female prophet foretold in 1856 that, if the Xhosa of South Africa slaughtered their cattle, spirits would wipe out the British settlers. With many of their animals already dying from a sickness probably brought to Africa by European cattle, the Xhosa began killing their cattle in early 1857, leading to a vast famine. In the case of the Ghost Dance, the Paiute visionary Wovoka—ironically a preacher of peace—popularized the ritual among many western Native Americans. It became a rallying point for the Sioux, many of whom were killed by U.S. forces at Wounded Knee.

The uprising was started by Hong Xiuquan, a Cantonese clerk educated partly by Protestant missionaries. An aspiring government official, Hong failed his civil service examination. The shock caused him to have visions, in which he became convinced that he was Jesus Christ's younger brother, destined to establish a "heavenly kingdom of supreme peace"—the meaning of the word *taiping*—in China.

Hong's rebellion began in 1850. An extraordinarily magnetic leader, Hong attracted several followers capable of organizing an effective modern army. His vision of a new China also appealed to millions of ordinary Chinese who resented the Qing's high taxes, its arbitrary and oppressive rule, and the fact that the Manchu emperors were essentially foreign rulers. At their peak, Hong and the Taiping leaders controlled one-third of China.

The Taiping Rebellion waned after 1860. Competent generals took over the Qing war effort, and the government was assisted by a foreign force—the Ever-Victorious Army—commanded by an American soldier of fortune, Frederick Townsend Ward, and then the English general Charles "Chinese" Gordon. Quarrels among the Taiping leadership hurt the movement as well. By the early 1860s, the Taiping forces were in retreat. Hong committed suicide by taking poison in 1864, and the remaining Taiping leaders were captured and executed.

The Leadership of Dowager Empress Cixi

The Taiping Rebellion left China in ruins, and the Qing government was thrown into chaos. A reform campaign—the **self-strengthening movement**—was begun in the 1860s, but was confined to economic and military, not social, modernization. It was also of limited impact, because of opposition from the strongest figure in Chinese politics—the dowager empress **Cixi**, who "ruled" China from 1878 to her death in 1908. A concubine to the emperor in the 1850s, Cixi became a major figure at the Qing court. In 1878, she placed her nephew Guangxu on the imperial throne and gained the position of regent. She did not rule China in her own right, but controlled her nephew—and the government—long after Guangxu became an adult.

Under Cixi's highly conservative influence, Qing rule became more oppressive. China's outlying possessions—Tibet, Mongolia, Chinese Turkestan—began to slip away, gain greater autonomy, or fall into foreign hands. At home, Cixi opposed all reform, which she regarded as pro-Western treason. In 1898, when her nephew, the emperor, began listening seriously to reform-minded advisers, she acted harshly. When Guangxu launched his short-lived Hundred Days' Reform, Cixi placed him under house arrest and executed the reformers.

Western Spheres of Influence in China, 1910.
Starting in the early-to-mid-1800s, Great Britain, then other Western nations, pressured China into opening its markets and yielding up economic and political control over much of its coast. These concessions grew in size and number during the 1800s and early 1900s, reaching their peak just before the Qing dynasty's collapse in 1911.

The Sino-Japanese War and the Open Door Policy

All this time, foreign domination of China increased, especially as the new nations of Germany and Italy pushed for a greater share of Chinese trade. Germany took the major port of Tsingtao. Japan defeated China in the Sino-Japanese War (1894–1895). In 1898, the United States, with its **Open Door Policy**, arranged for all Western nations to have equal access to Chinese markets. Such a policy reduced much of the pressure that European nations were placing on China to open up further, but it also meant that foreign control continued.

Missionaries in China

Another result of increased foreign influence in China was a rise in the level of missionary activity there. From the late 1800s through the mid-1900s, it became more common for Protestant and Catholic clergy and volunteers to travel from Europe and the United States to China in order to spread Christianity and teach Western languages. In this way, they interfered with and even eroded traditional Chinese culture.

However, missionaries also brought scientific and technological knowledge, treated diseases and ailments with modern medicine, and helped eliminate oppressive cultural practices, such as female **foot binding**. Missionary activity serves to illustrate imperialism's mixed legacy of positive and negative impact.

The Boxer Rebellion and Last-Ditch Attempts at Reform

In 1900, Chinese anger at foreign influence burst out of control. Making things worse were a severe drought, which damaged agriculture and hurt farmers, and widespread unemployment in the cities. What followed during the summer was the **Boxer Rebellion**, so called because many of the rebels were Chinese "boxers," or martial-arts experts.

Most of their rage was directed at foreigners, especially in the capital, Beijing, where rebels attacked foreign residents and besieged foreign legations. In the end, the rebellion was put down, mainly by foreign troops. In revenge, the foreign communities in China burned a number of temples. They also forced the Qing government to pay a heavy financial penalty.

Even Cixi now recognized the need for at least some reform. In 1905, she formed a committee to investigate the possibility of writing a constitution. She and Guangxi both died in 1908, but the reform effort continued under China's last emperor, Henry Puyi. Local assemblies were formed, and elections for a national assembly were planned for 1910.

Sun Yat-Sen, the Collapse of the Qing, and the Chinese Republic

However, reform came too late, and was too weak and feeble, to save the Qing dynasty. Opposition groups of many types had formed in China, especially among younger Chinese who opposed Manchu domination of their race and favored Western-style modernization. The most important of these revolutionaries was **Sun Yat-sen** (1866–1925), who lived and traveled widely in America and Europe. Sun

united a number of opposition groups into a movement called the Revolutionary Alliance and promoted three "people's principles": nationalism (opposition to Manchu rule and Western imperialism), democracy, and livelihood (a semi-socialist, but not Marxist, concern for people's welfare). Although he supported using force to remove the Qing, Sun hoped to unite all of China's people in equality under a constitutional democracy. In many respects, his ideals were similar to those of France's revolutionaries in 1789. Unlike them, however, he supported universal suffrage for women as well as men.

The Qing regime collapsed in the fall of 1911, because of a major uprising in the Chinese region of Wuhan. Although Sun was in the United States at the time, his movement was at the rebellion's forefront, and as the revolution spread, he returned from America. A Chinese Republic was founded in early 1912, with Sun as its president. His party now called itself the **Nationalist Party** (**Kuomintang**). For the first time in recorded history, China was ruled not by an imperial dynasty or foreign conqueror, but a politician brought to office by popular action.

But as in revolutionary France, political idealism was no match for ideological disagreements between left and right (with Sun in the middle), economic crisis, and the breakaway of frontier provinces. Shortly after coming to power, Sun was forced to step aside as president in favor of military officers who governed more from the right (a point of similarity between China's revolution and Mexico's, which began in 1910). Decentralization and civil war characterized the 1910s through the 1940s. Sun died in 1925, with China still in chaos. In 1949, his successor, Chiang Kai-shek, was defeated, and a communist government seized power.

ISOLATION AND PARTIAL MODERNIZATION IN TOKUGAWA JAPAN

The Tokugawa Shogunate in the Eighteenth Century

In the 1750s, Japan was ruled by the **Tokugawa Shogunate**, which had taken power in the early 1600s. As before, supreme authority technically rested with the emperor, but real power belonged to the shogun, who ran the country in the emperor's name. Under the shogun were the remnants of the **samurai** class, the warrior aristocracy from Japan's feudal era.

In the 1600s and early 1700s, the Tokugawa shoguns were dynamic rulers. They had centralized Japan and transformed it from a constantly warring collection of disunified states into a single country at peace. The Tokugawa shoguns were highly dictatorial, creating a rigidly stratified society that restricted social mobility, kept ordinary citizens out of politics, and allowed few personal freedoms. Tokugawa Japan also isolated itself from the rest of the world. By the 1720s, the only country Japan had formal relations with was Korea. Informal ties were maintained with China, and the government allowed some foreign trade at the port of **Nagasaki**.

Partial Modernization in Tokugawa Japan

In the late 1700s and early 1800s, Tokugawa Japan partially modernized, both economically and socially. Population growth was steady. Japan, already a society of

cities, experienced even more urban growth. Kyoto and Osaka were major centers, and the capital, Edo (present-day Tokyo), had a population of well over a million. Agriculture practice was rationalized, allowing fewer people to grow more food. This reform led to further urbanization and freed up a labor force just as proto-industrialization began in Japan.

Trade, commerce, and manufacturing became increasingly important. A national infrastructure—more roads, canals, and ports—began to emerge. The **merchant class**, soon to be a modernizing middle class, grew in number, wealth, and influence. Despite the country's international isolation, some Japanese gained an awareness of Western science and technology.

Partial modernization placed the shogun and the samurai in a dilemma. It made Japan more prosperous and more advanced. On the other hand, the spread of new foreign learning, the movement of people from countryside to city, and the increased social and economic clout of the merchant class undermined the power and land-based wealth of the traditional aristocracy.

Therefore, the regime allowed some modernization, but not as much as Japan was capable of. In particular, members of the samurai class—whose military prowess was based on skill with traditional weapons, such as swords—were anxious to preserve the state's monopoly on gunpowder weaponry. How long the Tokugawa leadership would have kept up this approach is impossible to say. In the early 1850s, however, external forces compelled Japan to change.

The Opening of Japan and the Overthrow of the Shogunate

In 1853, American gunships appeared off the Japanese coast. Their commander, **Commodore Matthew Perry**, requested Japan to open its economy to foreign trade. Although the Americans' words were friendly, the threat of naval bombardment lay behind them. After some debate, the shogun agreed to end his country's decades-long isolation. Over the next five years, European nations persuaded the Japanese to open up to them as well. For a time, it appeared that Japan might fall victim to the same kind of Western economic pressure that was crippling China.

Painfully aware of what was happening to China, certain samurai leaders, particularly from the southern provinces of Satsuma and Choshu, urged the shogun to stand up to foreign intimidation. This Sat-Cho Alliance gained a following at the Edo court and pressed for the severance of all ties with the West. It also took matters into its own hands. In 1867, a Choshu coastal fortress fired on Western ships, and the ships fired back. The resulting scandal gave the Sat-Cho Alliance the pretext it needed to move against the last shogun, who had just come to power. In January 1868, the Sat-Cho staged a military uprising and overthrew the shogunate. Meiji, who had ascended to the throne only in 1867, and was the first emperor in nearly a thousand years to enjoy full imperial powers.

THE MEIJI RESTORATION AND JAPANESE ASCENDANCY

The **Meiji Restoration** of 1868 began Japan's modern age. Although the rebellion that brought Meiji to power was initially anti-Western, even the most xenophobic

members of the new government realized that, in order to avoid Western domination, Japan would have to adopt Western learning, economics, and military methods. In addition, the emperor himself was personally inclined toward Westernization. What followed was a revolution from above, in which Meiji's government radically altered Japanese politics, economics, and social organization.

From Feudalism to Constitutional Monarchy

In 1871, Meiji abolished feudalism. Although individual samurai continued to serve in positions of power, hereditary privileges were done away with. Government stipends to the samurai, a privilege of the past, were eliminated. Former samurai were forbidden to wear swords, their traditional symbols of authority, in public.

The rigid social hierarchy of the Tokugawa regime ended. Modern laws (the Civil Code of 1898) were drawn up. The Constitution of 1890 created an elected parliament, the Diet. Owing to property qualifications and other restrictions, suffrage was quite low, around 5 percent, and the emperor had a great deal of power over the Diet. The civil code and constitution also made little room for the rights of women, who were largely confined to a secondary status (industrialization gave many lower-class women jobs, but these were low-paying, low-status positions). In effect, Meiji and his successors created an oligarchy (rule by the few) that was less repressive and restrictive than the Tokugawa regime but hardly representative.

Industrialization and Economic Modernization

Meiji and the emperors who followed him altered the economy beyond recognition. Agricultural productivity increased. The major change, however, involved industrialization. Meiji sent young members of the upper class to visit or study in Europe and America, to learn engineering, economics, and military science. He created a Ministry of Industry in 1870 as well as state banks to finance his industrialization campaign. New railroads, steamships, ports, and canals were constructed every year. Huge corporations called **zaibatsu**, sponsored largely by the state, came to dominate the economic landscape. The government encouraged not just large-scale industry but also private enterprise, spurring the growth of a larger middle class.

Economic growth came at a price. For farmers, taxes increased. Working conditions for the industrial lower classes were oppressive, just as they had been during the first decades of Europe's Industrial Revolution. Sweatshop environments, low wages, and unsafe labor practices prevailed, especially in textile mills and coal mines. In one mine near Nagasaki, workers toiled in temperatures of up to 130 degrees Fahrenheit, and were shot if they tried to escape. Unions of any type were forbidden.

Social and Class Transformation in Japan

Social transformation was a major part of the Meiji Restoration. The traditional privileges of the samurai class were taken away. Access to political positions was increasingly dependent on merit, competence, and civil service examinations. Meiji's reforms and Japanese industrialization increased the size and power of the merchant and middle classes, much as industrialization did in the West. The feudal prejudice against trade and artisanship faded away.

Things changed for the lower classes as well. The farming population decreased, while the industrial working class grew. Taxes increased considerably for both, and the lower classes were barred from full political participation by the Constitution of 1890. However, they also benefited in some ways from the Meiji reforms. The new tax system of 1872 funded a national educational system. Commoners, who previously had not been allowed to handle or learn how to use weapons, were now allowed to serve in the military. Overall, Japanese society adopted Western dress, fashions and manners, the Western calendar, and the metric system. The population boomed, growing from 35 million in 1873 to 55 million in 1918—although this badly strained the economy.

Japanese Militarism and the Russo-Japanese War

Meiji Japan became increasingly militaristic. Nationalist sentiment ran high during the late 1800s and 1900s, spurring the desire for empire building. The government-sponsored religion of **State Shintoism**, a modern revival of Japan's ancient faith, emphasized Japanese superiority and veneration of the emperor as a descendant of the gods. Japan wanted markets for its manufactured goods. A resource-poor island, Japan also needed raw materials to continue industrial growth.

Japan's expansion began in the 1870s. It forced Korean ports open to trade, much as the West had done with China and Japan itself. From China, it took the Ryukyu Islands, which include Okinawa, the most cherished of Japan's overseas possessions. In the 1880s and early 1890s, Japan modernized its navy and drafted a well-drilled and well-equipped army.

More military successes followed. The Sino-Japanese War (1894–1895) resulted in Japan's occupation of Taiwan and Korea (annexed in 1910). An even more impressive triumph was the **Russo-Japanese War** (1904–1905). Competition over influence in Manchuria caused great tension between the two countries. Russia's rapid expansion and its construction of the Trans-Siberian Railroad, the longest in the world, interfered with Japanese ambitions. The Japanese opened the war with a surprise attack on Russia's Pacific naval base at Port Arthur. Tiny compared to Russia, Japan was nonetheless better prepared for war and had the advantage of fighting close to home. When the war ended, Japan was victorious. It annexed land near Korea, the southern half of Sakhalin Island, and the Kurile Islands.

The Russo-Japanese War (which helped cause Russia's 1905 Revolution) marked the first time in the modern era that a non-Western nation had defeated a European power in a full-scale military conflict. It was an early warning signal that, before too long, Europe's peak as the world's dominant civilization would eventually pass—and that its empires would slip away. As for Japan, it entered the new century as a modern, industrial nation and a regional power with a growing empire. Japan would continue to modernize. Unfortunately, its militaristic, nationalistic streak would widen as well, and its imperial ambitions would spin out of control.

India and Southeast Asia

- The decline of Mughal India
- The British East India Company and the battle of Plassey
- The Indian cotton industry
- The zamindar system
- Sepoys and the Indian Mutiny
- National liberation movements and the Indian National Congress

- The Dutch East India Company and Indonesia
- Singapore and Hong Kong
- French Indochina and *la mission civilisatrice*
- Thailand's continued independence
- The Spanish-American War and U.S. annexation of the Philippines

The proverbial jewel in the crown of the British Empire was India. The conquest and ownership of this country, one of the largest and most populous regions on earth, by a small island nation 5,000 miles away was one of the central facts of nineteenth- and early-twentieth-century life. Throughout the 1800s, British control over India affected global economics, the movement of navies, international relations, and the balance of world power. It gave Britain immense wealth and prestige, and it affected the course of Indian history, changing politics, economic development, social practices, language, and virtually every aspect of Indian culture.

Likewise, the great arc of Southeast Asian nations and islands that stretched between British India and China came under increased Western control in the 1800s. By the end of the century, only a tiny portion of Southeast Asia remained free of foreign domination.

On the other hand, **national liberation movements** were beginning to form by the late 1800s, both in India and the rest of Southeast Asia. For the time being, they were unable to dislodge their foreign masters, but they lay the foundation for the movements that successfully expelled European colonists after World War II.

FROM FOOTHOLD TO MASTERY: THE BRITISH IN LATE-EIGHTEENTH-CENTURY INDIA

During the last half of the eighteenth century, most of India was technically ruled by the once-mighty **Mughal Empire**. However, the Mughals' political fortunes had declined badly since the glory days of the 1500s and 1600s. Many parts of the subcontinent had slipped out from under Mughal rule, becoming independent kingdoms or city-states. Also by the 1700s, increased pressure from European outsiders destabilized what was left of Mughal power.

Anglo-French Competition over India

In the early 1700s, the Portuguese and Dutch still maintained small settlements along India's coasts. The Europeans most intent on controlling India, however, were Britain and France, who took advantage of growing Mughal weakness. For the time being, Britain's interests were represented by the **British East India Company**, which financed the military takeover and economic development of India.

From the southeastern ports of Pondicherry and Madras, which they captured temporarily from the British, the French tried until the late 1750s to grapple with the British East India Company for hegemony over India. However, French colonial administrators did not get adequate support from the home government in Paris.

At the end of the decade, the British East India Company, under Sir Robert Clive, enlarged its power by scoring key military successes against the Mughals. When Indians attacked the British population of Bengal and jailed soldiers and civilians alike in a horrible underground prison known as the **Black Hole of Calcutta**, the British used the event as a pretext for military action. In 1757, at the crucial battle of **Plassey**, Clive defeated a Mughal force more than ten times the size of his own. By 1764, all of Bengal was in Clive's hands, and the Mughals granted such extensive military and economic concessions that British superiority on the subcontinent was permanently ensured. The French zone of control shrank to the coastal territory surrounding the port of Pondicherry.

Britain's Gradual Conquest of India

Even in 1800, the British held only a comparatively small part of India. Major centers of control were Bombay, the gateway port of the west coast; Madras, a cloth-making center on the southeast shore; and Fort William, near Calcutta, in the Bengal region of the northeast.

The British East India Company used military and economic power to expand its control and pressure the Mughals to grant it ever-widening tax-collecting rights and administrative powers. At first, the British had footholds only on the coasts, but they gradually extended their reach into the interior, especially up the Ganges River in the north. In some regions, the company governed directly. In others, it ruled through the authority of local Mughal officials or friendly natives.

Between the 1760s and 1810s, the company fought a number of campaigns. Major foes included Haidar Ali, who led guerrilla armies in the south; Tipu Sultan, who fought on central India's Deccan Plateau; and the Maharatta princes. Many British generals who became famous in other conflicts—such as Cornwallis, who lost to the Americans at Yorktown, and Wellington, who defeated Napoleon at Waterloo—saw service in these wars.

By 1810, the company controlled almost one-fourth of India, and most of Ceylon (now Sri Lanka).

British Administration of India Before 1800

Before 1800, the British East India Company's administration of British India was heavy-handed, even clumsy. Initially, the main goal was to create a local **cotton industry**. The British would process the cotton into cloth and sell it to the East Indies for spices, which were sent back to Britain.

In the beginning, British rule harmed the local population in several ways. Profits generated by Indian raw materials went to Britain, rather than benefiting the local economy. The size and efficiency of British-built textile mills drove local textile enterprises, often run by women, out of business. Also, British tax law allowed local authorities to confiscate land from peasants who could not pay their taxes. The British thought they had created a fair taxation system by leaving collection to native officials called **zamindars**. However, the zamindars lost no time in overtaxing their countrymen and then making themselves rich by using British law to seize land from peasants. Such confiscations became so common in the 1770s that famines struck the countryside, killing approximately one-third of the Indians—mainly peasants—living under British control.

INDIA UNDER BRITISH RULE: THE 1800s

During the first half of the 1800s, the British extended their control over India. They moved from the coastline and the Ganges River valley into the interior, gaining authority—whether direct or indirect—over the entire country. The British also took outlying northwestern areas, such as Punjab and parts of Afghanistan, after a series of conflicts with skilled warriors like the **Sikhs** and mountain peoples like the Pathans.

Methods of British Control

British colonial authority—referred to popularly as the **Raj**—was complex. Although the British crown became more involved, the British East India Company still assumed primary responsibility for administering and exploiting the expanding colony. Cities such as Bombay and Calcutta were directly governed by the Raj, as were the coasts and large swathes of the interior. In some parts of the interior, the British ruled indirectly, allowing obedient rajas and maharajas to stay on their thrones. In this way, the British ruled some areas at less cost and effort.

Positive and Negative Effects of British Colonial Rule

The British got better at colonial administration than they had been during the 1700s. They were guided by a combination of selfishness, a desire for efficiency, and the well-meaning but condescending sense of superiority that poet Rudyard Kipling later called the **White Man's Burden**. British economic interests in India, formerly restricted to cotton, now became multifaceted. A wide variety of resources was now sought and exploited. To make their own lives in India more comfortable and because they felt it would be better for the native Indians, British colonizers modernized the country in many ways. They created roads and railroads (which reduced the number of famines by improving food distribution), a telegraph system, and a postal service.

The British also affected India's cultural life. They put into place a quality educational system, partly to raise the level of scientific and technological knowledge, partly to create a group of Western-educated natives who would be loyal to Britain and assist in governing a pro-British India. In the words of the historian Thomas Macauley, who helped create this system, the goal was to educate a native elite that was "Indian in blood and color, but English in taste, in opinion, in morals, and in intellect." For the same reasons, the British created a civil service examination system

for Indians who wished to work in the government. The Raj officially discouraged the conversion of Indians to Christianity (although individual British officials sometimes violated this policy). Still, the British sometimes eliminated cultural and religious (particularly Hindu) practices they felt were inhumane, including **sati** (or suttee) the practice of burning a widow alive at her husband's funeral; **thuggee** (the ritual assassination of travelers in the name of the goddess Kali); and the **caste system's** harsh treatment of so-called untouchables.

Native Officials and Sepoy Troops

The British went to great lengths to instill loyalty within their native subjects. Their comparatively light touch in religious and cultural practices helped greatly. Whenever possible, the British delegated local political authority to Indians. The British East India Company also trained large numbers of native troops called **sepoys**. Using native troops made it easier for Indians to accept foreign rule; as well, it saved the British a great deal of money and kept them from having to draft large numbers of their own citizens to serve far from home. The number of actual British soldiers and officers in India was quite low.

The British Approach to Colonial Rule

The British method of imperialism in India—which they tended to follow in other colonies in Asia and Africa—is difficult to evaluate. British rule brought many benefits and new learning to the non-Western world, and compared with other imperial nations, British colonial practice was relatively humane. However, British rule was established by conquest, supported by military might, preserved by divide-and-conquer politics, and done for the purpose of economic exploitation. Even when they did good, it was out of a belief that they were civilizing a "lesser" race.

The Indian Mutiny (The Sepoy Rebellion)

Tensions between the British and Indians were present throughout the 1800s. On one occasion, those tensions exploded suddenly and violently: the **Indian Mutiny** (1857–1858), also known as the **Sepoy Rebellion**, ranks as one of the most traumatic events in modern Indian and British history.

Within many sepoy regiments, underlying resentment of British rule broke out into open revolt, owing to rumors that British officers were deliberately trying to undermine Hindu and Muslim religious practices. Legally, the Raj was allowed to require sepoys to serve overseas. In the case of Hindus, crossing large bodies of water would break their caste. Hindu sepoys were not, in fact, sent overseas, but fear that they might be stirred up trouble. The perceived violation of Muslim and Hindu dietary restrictions actually triggered the rebellion. New rifles with greased cartridges were issued to sepoys in 1857. The false rumor that the grease was made from pig and cow fat—unclean to devout Muslims and Hindus, respectively—caused great outrage.

With lightning speed, the initial disturbances became a massive wave of nationwide revolt. Hundreds of thousands were killed: British soldiers, British civilians, loyal Indian troops, rebels, and Indian civilians. Massacres and atrocities were committed by both sides.

By 1858, after great effort and a tremendous amount of anxiety that India would be lost altogether, British troops, along with natives who continued to serve the Raj, put down the rebellion.

The British Crown Assumes Control

For the rest of the century, British rule over India remained solid. One important change was that the British crown took from the British East India Company all authority over the subcontinent. The British government now oversaw politics, ran the army, and supervised the colonial economy. In 1877, Victoria, queen of England, took the title empress of India.

Nationalist Movements in Turn-of-the-Century India

Even though British control grew more secure, problems simmered under the surface. The British strategy of educating a native elite in the Western style was generally successful, but in some cases backfired. Larger numbers of these educated young people used their knowledge to agitate for freedom. Education exposed many of them to liberal or radical ideas and convinced them that it was hypocritical of the British—with their long tradition of civil liberties and representative government—not to apply those liberties to nonwhite races.

Eventually, the most famous and influential member of Congress was **Mohandas K. Gandhi**. Trained as a lawyer in London, he lived in South Africa from 1893 to 1915, defending the rights of Indian workers living under the system of apartheid. After returning to India in 1915, he started to preach nonviolent resistance to British rule.

SOUTHEAST ASIA

Like India, Southeast Asia found itself increasingly in foreign hands during the late 1700s and 1800s. Before 1800, the only large areas firmly under European control were **Indonesia**, or the Dutch East Indies, and the Philippines, which belonged to Spain. By 1786, the British also had a presence in the Malay Peninsula. The Portuguese retained parts of the island of Timor, a tiny remnant of the Indonesian colony the Dutch had taken from them. Dutch rule over Indonesia was the responsibility of the **Dutch East India Company**, which handed much responsibility over to upper-class natives, trained and educated in the Western style.

Malaya and Singapore

As the British tightened their grip on India during the early 1800s, they made parallel advances into nearby Southeast Asia. In exchange for giving up claims on Indonesian territory, the British were allowed by the Dutch to absorb the Malay Peninsula, which was rich in rubber, tin, oil, copper, iron, and aluminum ore (bauxite). In 1819, British official Stamford Raffles established a British outpost on **Singapore**, an island at the peninsula's tip. Quickly, Singapore became an important trading center and fortress; with the advent of steamships, it became a key naval base and one of Britain's prized possessions in Asia.

NOTE

The British were fortunate that the rebels had no clear plan or single leader. Moreover, Hindu and Muslim rebels often failed to cooperate with each other—and sometimes fought each other.

FACT

The most important of the new nationalist groups was the **Indian National Congress**, formed in 1885. Most members were English-speaking, educated members of the native upper classes.

NOTE

The French placed more emphasis on religious conversion than the British.

The French Conquest of Indochina

The European incursion into Southeast Asia never ceased. Britain took over Burma, formerly a major power, in 1826. To prevent the British from having an unbroken chain of colonies stretching from India to the South China coast, France moved into **Indochina**, the territory that now encompasses Vietnam, Cambodia, and Laos.

From 1857 to 1859, France pressured Vietnam into accepting foreign rule. Cambodia followed in 1863, and Laos in 1893. Indochina was the source of many raw materials, but most profitable to the French were chrome, oil, bauxite, tin, and rubber.

The French model of imperialism was similar but not identical to that of Britain's. The French exploited the economy, but in accordance with their ideal of *la mission civilisatrice*, they also brought modern science and technology to their colonies in Southeast Asia. They educated—and often converted to Catholicism—a local elite of upper-class, Westernized natives. On average, the French resorted more readily to repression and violence to maintain order and carry out policy.

Modernization and Freedom in Thailand

The only state on the Southeast Asian mainland that remained independent throughout the 1800s was Thailand, owing to good leadership and good luck. Like Emperor Meiji in Japan, King Mongkut and his successor, King Chulalongkorn (both made famous in Anna Leonowens's memoir, *Anna and the King of Siam*, grossly distorted by Broadway and Hollywood), were modernizing monarchs, introducing industrialization and Western-style reform into their country. Thailand's geographic setting was also fortunate. The country lay between British-controlled Burma and French-dominated Indochina, and both European powers agreed informally to let it serve as a buffer zone between their colonies.

U.S. Annexation of the Philippines

The last major colonial takeover in Southeast Asia was the 1898 **annexation of the Philippines** by the United States, as a result of victory in the **Spanish-American War**. Although the conflict centered on Cuba, the United States sent a fleet under George Dewey to neutralize the Spanish naval forces based at Manila Bay. Then, with the assistance of native Filipinos (who, at first, saw the Americans as liberators), U.S. troops landed, defeated Spanish ground forces, and occupied the islands.

FACT

The English poet Rudyard Kipling wrote the poem *White Man's Burden* to commemorate the U.S. victory over the Spanish.

American victory resulted in Spain's being stripped of its colonies. This action raised the question of what to do with the Philippines. After great debate, the U.S., wishing to keep the Philippines from falling into the hands of the Japanese, chose to take possession. The islands also provided the United States with a superb naval base in the Pacific and a way station for trade with China. Moreover, the Americans felt a "moral" obligation, similar to the **White Man's Burden**, to civilize the Filipinos. The tragedy was that American colonization had to be imposed by means of a savage jungle war, as a Filipino guerrilla force led by **Emilio Aguinaldo** resisted the American takeover until 1901.

Sub-Saharan Africa

CHAPTER 27

- Kongo
- The Asante (Ashanti) kingdom
- The Boers (Afrikaners) and the Great Trek
- The Xhosa cattle-killing movement
- The Zulu
- The diamond industry in South Africa
- Zanzibar and the Arab-East African slave trade
- The Atlantic slave trade
- The Scramble for Africa and the Berlin Conference
- The Belgian Congo and the rubber industry
- The Herero Wars
- The Boer War

Like most of the non-Western world, sub-Saharan Africa fell under the increased sway of European imperialism from 1750 to 1914. Already for several centuries, Africa had been victimized by the **Atlantic slave trade**. Europeans had plundered gold, ivory, and countless other goods. They had established outposts, naval bases, and small colonies on the east and west coasts of the continent.

Nonetheless, Europe's direct influence, especially south of the Sahara, was comparatively limited until late in the 1800s. After the Napoleonic Wars, the slave trade was made illegal in most Western countries. Although it continued for decades unlawfully, the Atlantic traffic in slaves tapered off and faded away. Moreover, strong African states resisted foreign domination for much of this period (in a sad irony, much of this strength was due to profits made by cooperating with the slave trade). Although the Europeans found it relatively easy to take control of North Africa and parts of the coastline, the central and southern interior remained for a long time difficult to penetrate.

Great changes came after 1880. Before then, outside powers controlled approximately 10 percent of Africa. Less than three and a half decades later, in 1914, foreigners controlled the entire continent, with the exception of two small countries. By the middle of the 1800s, explorers and missionaries had gained precise geographical knowledge of the African interior. Better medicines enabled larger numbers of soldiers and settlers to travel to and live in Africa's tropical zones. Industrial-era weaponry increased the Europeans' military superiority. During the 1880s and 1890s, they voraciously carved up African territory while there was still room to expand. This **Scramble for Africa** subjugated virtually the entire continent. It also stirred up the combative passions of the Europeans and contributed to the diplomatic tensions behind World War I.

FREEDOM'S TWILIGHT: AFRICAN STATES FROM THE LATE 1700s TO THE MID-1800s

European hegemony over Africa was a long time in coming. During the late 1700s and early 1800s, a number of states were strong enough to resist foreign domination. Others were useful and cooperative enough that it was worthwhile for the Europeans to work with them rather than fight them. Some of these states, such as Benin, Oyo, Dahomey, **Kongo** (see Chapter 19), and Asante (Ashanti), played large roles in the Atlantic slave trade. They helped European traders and slavers capture and transport their fellow Africans.

In the west, a number of states remained independent well into the 1800s. These included the Hausa, Fulani, and Yoruba states. These Muslim theocracies formed, broke apart, and reformed, constantly fighting each other in costly civil wars.

The Asante (Ashanti) Kingdom

The strongest and most unified of the West African states was the **Asante** (**Ashanti**) kingdom, one of the last to survive as an independent state. Founded in the late 1600s, Asante took part in the flourishing trade in gold and slaves on Africa's west coast. Using profits to buy guns, it became a strong military power.

Asante's might increased dramatically during the late 1700s and early 1800s, especially as its African neighbors fought each other or came under foreign control. A large military buildup began under Osei Kojo (1764–1777). During the early 1800s, the Asante threatened European outposts and trade routes along the Gold Coast. They also resisted British, French, and American attempts to destroy the slave trade in the 1820s. By 1823, Britain found itself locked in a series of Asante wars that lasted until the end of the century, when it finally subdued the kingdom.

South Africa, the Boers, and the Zulu

South Africa had been colonized by the Dutch in the mid-1600s. For a century and a half, these Afrikaner **Boers**, as they called themselves, displaced or conquered native Africans. When the British assumed control over South Africa during the Napoleonic Wars, the Boers were themselves displaced. In the 1830s, they made their **Great Trek** to the north and east and, in the 1850s, founded the Orange Free State and the South African Republic (Transvaal), both of which bordered British South Africa. In the meantime, they and the recently arrived British came into contact with a new native power: the Zulu tribe.

The **Zulu**, a Bantu-speaking people, were relatively quiet and peaceful before 1800. But around 1816, a new chieftain, **Shaka**, seized power and united Zulu clans into a single tribe. A gifted military leader, Shaka has been called the Black Napoleon, and even after his death in 1828, the Zulu remained warlike.

The Zulu defeated neighbor after neighbor, causing a significant wave of tribal migration throughout the southern part of the continent. The Zulu also fought the Boers and British, and it took several wars for the Europeans to pacify them. The last major conflict, in 1879, was provoked by British officials who hoped to move into the Zulu lands because diamonds had recently been found there.

The discovery of these **diamond fields** heightened tensions in South Africa. Gold deposits were also found. The sudden emergence of such great potential wealth destabilized things by making parties more willing to fight over territory. The British began annexing diamond fields in 1871. Diamond mines cruelly exploited African labor. Workers were rigidly segregated by race.

Also subjected to foreign rule were South Africa's **Xhosa**, whose **cattle-killing movement** of 1856–1857 was a form of resistance spurred by the belief that, if the Xhosa killed their own livestock, the spirits would expel the British from their lands.

East Africa

The East African coast, which had come under Portuguese domination between the late 1400s and late 1600s, enjoyed a period of strength and independence, at least from European control, during the late 1700s and early-to-mid 1800s. For the time being, the large island of Madagascar remained free, as did the Batutsi state in what is today Rwanda.

The Coptic Christian kingdom of Ethiopia, which earlier had allied with Portugal against Muslim conquerors, expelled the Portuguese, largely over questions of religious doctrine, in 1632. For the next two and a half centuries, Ethiopia went into isolation, then modernized under Theodore II, who came to the throne in 1855. As for the rest of the coast, the new power was not European but Arab. In 1728, Arabs drove the Portuguese from the port of Mombasa. Portugal's strength in the region then waned, although it retained footholds along the coast.

By the early 1800s, Omani Arabs had gained tremendous political influence in East Africa, and also controlled the flourishing trade between the East African coast and India. The most important East African port was **Zanzibar**, on a small island off the coast of Tanganyika. Its role as an economic powerhouse was demonstrated by the fact that the Omani sultan made it his capital in 1840. Zanzibar's primary trading partner was Bombay. This fusion of Arab, African, and Indian stimulated not just economic interaction but cultural interchange as well. Zanzibar's Arab masters extended their economic influence into Africa's interior, to the west and north.

Among the principal resources that flowed through Zanzibar were cloves, spices, sugar, and ivory. An even more important part of Zanzibar's economy was slavery. Ironically, just as the demand for slaves in the Atlantic was finally withering away, there was a major resurgence in the **Arab–East African slave market**. This had much to do with the growth of plantation agriculture in the area, fueled by the increased demand for sugar and spices. Between 1875 and 1884, the peak of the East African plantation economy, 44 percent of the total population was made up of slaves.

THE END OF THE ATLANTIC SLAVE TRADE
The Atlantic Slave Trade Becomes Illegal

One of the great changes coming to Africa during the 1800s was the gradual end of the **Atlantic slave trade**. Its demise resulted

NOTE

Zulu armies, led by Cetewayo, eventually lost the **Zulu War of 1879**. This took eight months for the British to win, and one of the early battles, Isandhlwana, in which a British force was massacred to the last soldier, was one of the worst military defeats suffered by a European force in Africa.

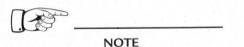

NOTE

It took decades for the Western powers to eliminate the East African slave trade. Abolition came about as a result of popular outrage, missionary activity (a key figure was the Scottish explorer and humanitarian **David Livingstone**), and military action. The great slave market in the center of Zanzibar was shut down in 1873. The British took over the city later in the century.

partly from economic and practical considerations. It was becoming more difficult and therefore more expensive to obtain slaves. Equally important was the growing revulsion that slavery caused in many Western countries. For moral, ethical, and religious reasons, an ever-greater number of citizens and politicians were unwilling to continue basing their nations' economies so squarely on slavery. Countries like revolutionary France, the Netherlands (1795), and Denmark (1803) began to make slavery illegal.

The major turning point came when Great Britain, in 1808, resolved to make the slave trade illegal (slavery was banned in all parts of the British Empire in 1834). During the peace settlements that followed the Napoleonic Wars, the British convinced almost all of Europe and the Americas to outlaw slavery and the slave trade. With the exception of Spain and Portugal, Europe agreed (Russia relied on **serfdom** till 1861, but this was a different question). For the most part, the Americas went along as well. Canada (still part of the British Empire) and most of Latin America outlawed slavery. The holdouts were Cuba and Brazil, which did not end slavery until 1883 and 1888. The United States, split between the slaveholding South and the nonslave North, agreed to make the slave trade illegal. The government also worked to restrict the spread of slavery within the United States as the country expanded. Not until after the U.S. Civil War (1861–1865) was slavery made illegal throughout the country.

The Atlantic Slave Trade Continues Illegally

The continued survival of slavery in the Americas meant that the Atlantic slave trade, illegal or not, went on during a good part of the 1800s. It has been calculated that 2 million Africans were transported to Brazil, Cuba, and the Caribbean during the 1800s. A small percentage of these were smuggled into the United States. The best estimate of the number of Africans enslaved by the Atlantic slave trade between the late 1400s and the 1800s is approximately 12 million.

As noted above, a market in African slaves flourished in Zanzibar during the 1800s, not ending until 1873. According to some sources, at the end of the nineteenth century, the number of slaves in the Islamic states of West Africa stood at nearly 5 million.

Foreign powers did more than legislate against the slave trade. **Abolition movements**, especially in Britain and the northern United States, pressured their governments to fight slavery actively. Canada served as a haven for slaves escaping from the southern United States. **Missionaries** in Africa, especially those from Britain, campaigned against slave raids and slave markets—both on the Atlantic coast and in East Africa and Zanzibar.

The British founded special colonies in Sierra Leone and the Gold Coast for freed blacks. Similarly, a group of American blacks and freed slaves settled the nation of Liberia, on the West African coast, with sponsorship from the U.S. government.

In the early 1800s, the British government dispatched the Royal Navy to blockade the West African shoreline, hunt down slave ships, and bombard the coastal forts of African states that continued to support the slave trade. Less enthusiastically, France and the United States joined in these expeditions.

Effects of the Slave Trade on Africa

The slave trade took an immense toll on Africa. Obvious effects included human suffering, population loss, dependence on foreign goods (as opposed to indigenous production), the stirring up of tribal warfare, and the disruption of traditional trade networks and economic practices.

It is equally obvious how the ending of the slave trade benefited Africa. However, there were also unforeseen, less positive consequences. One was a sharp economic slump—because, however heinous, the slave trade had been extremely lucrative. Economic weakness left African states more vulnerable to foreign takeover in the late 1800s. Moreover, the antislavery intervention of Great Britain and other nations, however well-intentioned, gave Europeans a pretext for involving themselves in Africa's affairs and thinking of military action as legitimate. This helped pave the way for the rush to conquer all of Africa at the end of the century.

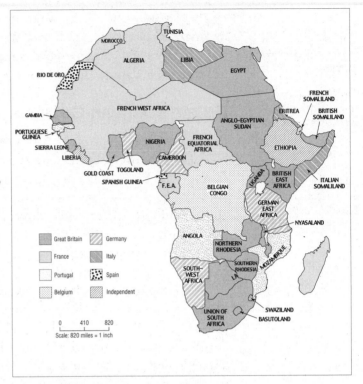

European Imperialism in Africa, 1914.

EUROPEAN IMPERIALISM AND THE "SCRAMBLE FOR AFRICA"

Approximately 10 percent of Africa was under foreign control before 1880. Most of this territory lay north of the Sahara or along the coastlines. Suddenly, between 1880 and 1914, the states of Europe were caught up in a breathlessly rapid "**Scramble for Africa.**" On the eve of World War I, only two countries—Ethiopia and Liberia—remained free.

Reasons for Europe's Late-Nineteenth-Century Domination of Africa

Many factors motivated and enabled the Scramble for Africa. First, a series of geographic expeditions from the 1770s through the 1860s gave the Western world an unprecedented amount of information about the African interior. Mungo Park of Scotland traced the entire Niger River from 1795 to 1805. The missionary David Livingstone, who arrived from Scotland in 1841 and fought the East African slave trade, also found time to explore the Zambezi basin and discover the Victoria Falls (1855). Anglo-American adventurer Henry Stanley explored the Congo, while England's John Speke unraveled one of Africa's greatest geographical mysteries by locating the source of the Nile in 1863.

The development of effective treatments for tropical diseases—such as **quinine** for malaria—enabled large numbers of Westerners to move into the African interior. With modern rifles and machine guns, small numbers of European soldiers were able to inflict horrible damage on native warriors, even when outnumbered.

Britain's African Colonies

Britain's zone of control in Africa included the Gold Coast, Sierra Leone, and Nigeria in the west. Even more extensive was its collection of colonies in northeastern and East Africa, an almost unbroken chain that included South Africa, Bechuanaland (now Botswana), Rhodesia (now Zimbabwe), Kenya, Uganda, the Sudan, and Egypt. The British dreamed of building a continental railway stretching from South Africa to Egypt ("from **Cape to Cairo**," as the imperialist Cecil Rhodes put it), but they were blocked by the German acquisition of territory on the eastern coast.

Late in the century, Britain gained influence over the rich port of Zanzibar, partly in connection with its efforts to end slavery there. Zanzibar had been claimed by Germany, but Britain received control over it as part of a swap of colonial territories.

Britain's method of African colonial administration was similar to the one it followed in India: a comparatively enlightened **White Man's Burden** approach that made use of an educated native elite, deployed native troops trained in the Western style, and brought new science and industrial technology to the colonies.

The French in Africa

France's African empire was restricted mainly to the Saharan north: Morocco, Algeria, Tunisia, West Africa, and Equatorial Africa. However, it had territories elsewhere, such as Djibouti, part of the Somali coast, and the island of Madagascar. As in Southeast Asia, France acted in accordance with its "civilizing mission" and, for the most part, treated its colonial subjects responsibly.

The Portuguese

Portugal retained control over its longtime possession in West Africa, Angola. On the eastern coast, where it had once reigned supreme, it took Mozambique. Unlike the French and British, the Portuguese were quite harsh with their African colonies.

Belgium and the Congo

Tiny Belgium gained control over one of the largest African colonies: the vast **Congo** basin. In 1876, **Leopold II** of Belgium, with the Anglo-American explorer Henry Stanley as his manager, established a private company for the economic development of the Congo. By 1884, the Congo was fully under the company's control. In his will, Leopold left the colony to Belgium.

Leopold's exploitation of the Congo was brutal, and Belgium's record as a colonizing power was among the worst in Africa. Belgian-owned **rubber plantations** overexploited rubber trees and, worse, brutally forced Congolese villagers to meet production quotas. One vile practice was the policy of some overseers to chop off the

right hands of Congolese workers who did not harvest enough rubber. Some workers were simply massacred. Belgian occupation led to massive depopulation. Elephant ivory was overexploited as well.

Italian and German Colonization of Africa

The new nation of Italy had poor luck in Africa. In 1911 and 1912, it seized Libya from the Ottoman Empire in a short war that involved the use of aircraft and poison gas. Before that, in 1896, the Italians had attempted to conquer Ethiopia. King Menelik II, however, had prepared well by purchasing modern rifles for his army and hiring Western mercenaries to train his troops. The Italians were prevented from taking Ethiopia by their humiliating defeat at the Battle of **Adowa**, which ranks as one of the most embarrassing setbacks in the history of European imperialism.

Also new to the world stage was Germany. In keeping with the military prowess they had shown in Europe, the Germans quickly assembled a sizable empire in Africa. Their possessions included Togoland, the Cameroons, Southwest Africa, and German East Africa (Tanganyika, off of which the island of Zanzibar lay).

Unfortunately, the colonies left for the Germans were those no one else had wanted. Rather than turning a profit, they lost money. The Germans also had to deal with several major uprisings, including the Maji Maji revolt in Tanganyika (1905–1907) and the infamous **Herero Wars** in Southwest Africa (1904–1908). The latter were especially savage, to the point of genocide.

NOTE

Historians estimate that the Germans killed almost 80 percent of the Herero—64,000 of 80,000—by the time they quelled the rebellion.

African Women and European Imperialism

One of the major consequences of colonial rule was that many African families were broken up. Husbands went to work in mines or on plantations, while wives and children stayed behind in villages and on reserves. Women were left to grow food for their families for mere survival and to care for the sick and aged. Long separations between spouses led to a rise in the level of prostitution and the spread of sexually transmitted diseases.

In general, African men benefited more than women from the economic changes brought by colonial rule. In regions where colonial officials introduced private property rights, property was given to male heads of households, not women. Most jobs, even those in teaching, were reserved for men, and women were discouraged from running family businesses or selling goods in markets.

Imperialism in Africa and Its Effects on European Diplomacy

The Scramble for Africa stirred up aggression among the Europeans, bringing them numerous times to the brink of conflict.

The German diplomat Otto von Bismarck attempted to cool tensions at the **Berlin Conference** (1884–1885), whose purpose was to agree on boundary lines and set down rules for further expansion into Africa. The lines on the resulting map reflected European desires and had little relation to the traditional territorial boundaries of African tribes or ethnic groups, none of whom were invited to take part.

The Berlin Conference temporarily helped to prevent war over Africa, but tensions rose in the 1890s and 1900s. In 1896, France and Britain almost came to blows as a result of the Fashoda Incident, in which French troops moving eastward into the Nile Valley encountered British soldiers who regarded the region as belonging to them. The French withdrew, but not before a short war scare. In the early 1900s, Germany's naked ambitions in Africa caused more trouble. Its interference with French and Spanish plans for northwestern Africa led to a Morocco Crisis in 1906 and another one in 1911.

Even worse was Germany's public support of the Dutch Afrikaners in the **Boer War** (1899–1902). Here, fighting had broken out between the British and Boers in South Africa. Although the British had a larger, better-equipped army, the Boers were skilled guerrilla soldiers and excellent sharpshooters, fighting on their home territory. The war was a painful one, with the British forced to pacify the Boer civilian population. More than 120,000 women, children, and male noncombatants, many of them black Africans, were placed in **concentration camps** (the twentieth century's first) by the British. Between 26,000 and 28,000 died, causing an international outcry. The Germans made no secret of their sympathy for the Boers. This public favoritism had the result of worsening Anglo-German relations, already strained because of the two countries' naval race and Britain's anxieties about German imperialism elsewhere in Africa (especially German East Africa, which kept Britain from building a continental railroad from Egypt to South Africa). These tensions had profound effects on the alliance system that emerged in the years before World War I.

In this way, the Scramble for Africa backfired on the Europeans. Imperial successes led to diplomatic problems, which, taken together, helped bring about World War I—the conflict that began breaking down European world power.

Revolution and Consolidation in North and South America

- The Atlantic revolutions
- The American Revolution
- The Monroe Doctrine, the Louisiana Purchase, and manifest destiny
- Slavery in America and the Atlantic slave trade
- Immigration to the United States and the Americas
- The Haitian Rebellion
- The Latin American wars of independence and the Jamaica Letter
- The Mexican-American War
- Caudillos, monoculture, and dollar diplomacy
- The Spanish-American War
- The Panama Canal
- The Mexican Revolution

During the late 1700s and early 1800s, the colonies of the New World—the possessions of European powers for three centuries—threw off the ties that bound them politically and economically to their home countries. The **American Revolution**, the **Haitian Rebellion**, and the **Latin American wars of independence** were all part of the great wave of revolutions, including the French Revolution, that struck the Atlantic world during this era.

However, their results differed greatly. In the north, the American Revolution created an economic and political powerhouse: the United States, the modern world's first major nation to become a democracy, steadily expanded across the continent. Despite internal troubles, even wars, concerning slavery and the suppression of Native Americans, it grew in size and might. Like the nations of Europe, it industrialized. Already by the early 1800s, the United States was the dominant power in the Western Hemisphere. By the end of the century, it had acquired overseas territories of its own and was on the threshold of becoming a world power.

As for Latin America, revolution brought freedom, but did not create nations as well equipped to deal with freedom as the United States was. Despite high ideals, most of the new Latin American nations were plagued by dictatorial politics, economic backwardness, poverty, racial prejudice, and frequent revolutions and civil conflicts. In addition, the great power to the north, the United States, became increasingly involved in Latin American economics and politics, and not always for the better.

THE AMERICAN REVOLUTION AND THE BIRTH OF THE UNITED STATES

Causes of the American Revolution

The **American Revolution** (1775–1783) resulted from the combination of several trends in the thirteen British colonies in New England and the mid-Atlantic coast:

- A growing sense of patriotism and national identity. In this sense, the "revolution" was less a revolution and more a war of independence.
- Increased resentment of Great Britain's economic mastery. The taxes Britain levied to pay for the army it maintained in North America angered many colonists, especially because they lacked representation in the British Parliament.
- The desire of the colonial merchant (that is, middle) class to better itself. Economic freedom from Britain would allow American merchants to become wealthier, thanks to free trade and the new spirit of capitalism.
- The influence of Enlightenment philosophy. Most of the leaders who carried out the American Revolution and shaped the government afterward had read the works of Enlightenment thinkers such as Locke, Montesquieu, and Voltaire. The **Declaration of Independence** (1776), by Thomas Jefferson, is considered a classic Enlightenment text.

The American Revolution

Whatever the causes, the American Revolution broke out in 1775, with the twin battles of Lexington and Concord. At first, the poorly trained and poorly armed American forces, led by George Washington, struggled against Britain's professional armies. By 1777, however, the tide was turning. Although some colonists, nick-named Tories, remained loyal to the British, popular support for the revolution was high; most members of all classes—lower, middle, and upper—united behind it. The Americans were fighting on their home territory. Not only did European mercenaries and freedom fighters with military experience arrive to train American troops, the Americans used unconventional tactics and guerrilla warfare to counter the British soldiers' training. The British were fighting far from home, at the end of extremely long supply lines.

After America's victory at Saratoga in late 1777, France, Britain's mortal enemy, lent military and naval aid to the American colonists. The assistance of the French fleet against Britain's Royal Navy was particularly helpful.

By 1781, the British war effort was failing. When the main British force was surrounded at Yorktown, the war was effectively over, although peace talks dragged on until 1783. The Americans were victorious—and had won themselves a new country.

The U.S. Constitution and the Formation of the American Government

The next step was to determine a form of government. There was much disagreement over how closely bound the thirteen colonies would be. Also, who should have

power? Should the government be elected? If so, who should be allowed to vote? What should be done about slavery? These questions and others were decided at the Constitutional Convention of 1787. By 1789, the **United States Constitution** had been accepted by all thirteen states.

The system that resulted was a democratic republic, in which a federal government shared powers with governments in each state. To prevent a dictatorship, power at the federal level was shared among three branches (a concept borrowed from the Enlightenment philosopher Montesquieu): executive (president), legislative (Congress), and judicial (Supreme Court). State governments, as well as the president and members of Congress, were to be elected. However, democracy in this case—as in all cases before the twentieth century—was not all-inclusive. Elections were indirect. Women and Native Americans could not vote; nor could men who failed to fulfill certain property requirements. Moreover, the U.S. Constitution did not outlaw slavery.

Despite its initial flaws, the U.S. Constitution has remained one of the most successful political documents in world history. It is also the product and cause of an international philosophical exchange. Most of the Constitution's ideals and political principles came from England and France, thanks to the influence of Locke, Voltaire, Montesquieu, Rousseau, and others. In turn, the Constitution (and the Declaration of Independence) had an enormous impact on the **Atlantic revolutions** that followed in the 1780s, 1790s, and early 1800s. France's **Declaration of the Rights of Man and the Citizen** drew heavily upon both documents, as did the failed Dutch rebellion of the 1780s. In the early 1800s, the revolutionaries of Latin America tried to adapt the American Revolution's methods and ideals.

The Growing Global Importance of the United States

The domestic history of the United States is beyond the scope of the AP World History examination. A few points, however, should be made about the new country's effect on global affairs during the 1800s and early 1900s:

- *Inspiring freedom*: America's example of representative government and respect for civil liberties (in spite of flaws such as slavery) stood out as an example to people in other countries who wished to bring about similar changes.
- *Sphere of influence*: The **Monroe Doctrine** (1823), in which the U.S. government warned the nations of Europe against intervening in the Western Hemisphere's political affairs, was the first step in creating a sphere of influence. The United States quickly became the dominant power in the Americas. By the end of the 1800s, especially after the **Spanish-American War** (1898), its economic and political influence over Latin America was considerable—and, in some cases, imperial.
- *Expansion*: The rapid growth of the United States, from the east coast to the Pacific, greatly altered the balance of world power. This growth began with the **Louisiana Purchase** (1803) and continued with the **Mexican-American War** (1846–1848). The United States became a huge nation, incredibly rich in natural resources. It was motivated by the ideology of **manifest destiny**, the belief that continental expansion was a natural right.

- *Slavery.* The persistence of **slavery in the American South** was a key factor in allowing the Atlantic slave trade to continue for so long. It was the underlying cause of the U.S. Civil War (1861–1865).
- *Industrial growth.* During the last two thirds of the 1800s, the United States not only followed Europe in industrializing but surpassed it. Many of the era's key innovations and inventions came from the United States. Also, by the end of the 1800s, America was poised to become the greatest economic power in the world. It was overtaking Europe's strongest industrial powers, Britain and Germany, in many economic sectors.
- *Immigration.* America's reputation as a land of freedom and economic opportunity drew millions of **immigrants** from Europe and Asia during the 1800s. Between the 1830s and 1890s, an estimated 17 million people came to settle in the United States. Immigrants continued to arrive during the early 1900s. Combined with the large numbers of Europeans and Asians who emigrated to Latin America during these years, this development had a tremendous demographic effect on the geographic balance of world population. **Anti-immigration sentiment** was common, especially against non-whites.

Developments in Canada

Canada, the other British colony in North America, underwent changes during the 1800s. Although Canada remained loyal during the American Revolution, a desire for greater autonomy made itself felt not long afterward. Armed uprisings took place in 1837 and 1838. Although they failed, they convinced the British that flexibility was called for. In 1840, Upper Canada (now Ontario) and Lower Canada (now Quebec), along with other territories in the east, joined together as the United Provinces of Canada. However, they were not self-governing.

More independence came in the 1860s. Canadian politician John Macdonald became the leader of the country's freedom movement. Thanks largely to his efforts, not to mention British fears that a disgruntled Canada might grow closer to the United States, Britain's government, in 1867, conferred upon Canada **dominion status**, entitling Canada to its own constitution and parliament. The constitution created a confederation of Upper and Lower Canada, Nova Scotia, and New Brunswick.

The British monarch was still the head of state, and, for the time being, foreign affairs were still controlled by Britain. Still, in most respects, Canada was self-governing. John Macdonald became the first prime minister. Later, Great Britain used the scheme of dominion status to give similar autonomy to Australia and New Zealand.

THE HAITIAN REBELLION

A key moment in the spread of the Atlantic revolutions to Latin America and the Caribbean was the **Haitian Rebellion** (1791–1804), the only large-scale slave revolt to succeed in the New World. The Haitian Rebellion was inspired in large part by the American Revolution and caused directly by events related to the French Revolution.

The island of Haiti, known then as Saint Domingue, had been colonized by the Spanish and French. Each ruled half of the island, whose economy was based on sugar and coffee. The French half was populated by a mix of French colonists, Creoles (those of French descent but born in the colonies), free blacks (known as *gens de coleur*), mulattos, and half a million black slaves. When the French Revolution began in 1789, it threw French Haiti into chaos, mainly because the white colonists and free blacks, who competed over Haiti's sugar economy, quarreled. Free blacks and mulattos received equal rights in May 1791 (losing them temporarily between September 1791 and March 1792), but slaves, who remained unfree, rebelled in August 1791.

By 1793, **François Toussaint L'Ouverture**, often referred to as the Black Washington, was leading the revolt. L'Ouverture was literate, well-read, and a talented commander. The French government ended slavery in 1794, but L'Ouverture's goal was now full independence and the liberation of slaves on the Spanish side of the island, which he crossed into in 1798. At this point, L'Ouverture hoped to make Haiti a country for free blacks that would be friendly to France but self-governing.

Unfortunately for L'Ouverture, the French had no intention of letting Haiti go free. Over the next four years, the French debated the Haitian question. Then, in 1802, Napoleon Bonaparte decided to send troops to retake Haiti for France. Ironically, while a young officer in France's revolutionary army, Napoleon had been an admirer of L'Ouverture, but now the two men were enemies.

The French captured L'Ouverture and sent him back to France, where he died in prison. However, the French, unused to tropical warfare, failed to conquer the Haitian rebels. Yellow fever killed over 40,000 French troops. In 1804, the French went home in disgrace, and the independent nation of Haiti was born.

The Haitian Rebellion inspired rebellion elsewhere in Latin America and had one other far-reaching effect. Because of his frustration with the fighting in Haiti, Napoleon decided not to maintain major colonies in the New World. To this point, France had been the master of central North America: the large Louisiana territory, stretching from the Great Lakes to the Mississippi Delta. In 1803, Napoleon sold it at a bargain price to the United States President Thomas Jefferson, who, unlike Napoleon, recognized that the **Louisiana Purchase** would allow the United States to control the North American continent. By helping to convince Napoleon to sell Louisiana, the Haitian Rebellion brought about a major shift in global power.

THE LATIN AMERICAN WARS OF INDEPENDENCE

From 1810 to 1825, Mexico, Central America, and South America gained their independence from Spain and Portugal. As with the American Revolution, reasons for the **Latin American wars of independence** included a growing sense of national identity and local resentment of Spanish and Portuguese economic policies. Also important was the frustration that the European-descended, or *criollo* ("creole"), upper and middle classes felt toward the rigid social hierarchy of Latin American societies, which prevented them from realizing their goal of upward social and economic mobility. Even before the revolutions began, tensions were brewing.

The spark that set off the Latin American revolutions was lit by Napoleon back in Europe. Between 1807 and 1809, Napoleon invaded Spain and Portugal, toppling

THE CAUSES OF REVOLUTION

Understanding how and why revolutions take place is a daunting task for any historian. Social stress and class differences, economic inequality and poverty, incompetent or oppressive political leadership, and intellectual and cultural forces (religion, nationalism, doctrines, ideologies) are almost always at the root of any major revolution. Studying and comparing revolutions involves trying to figure out which of these is more or less important in any given case. Another important distinction has to do with whether forces causing revolution come *from above* (top-down), *from below* (bottom-up), or, as is often the case, both. Who are the actual revolutionaries? Do they continue to cooperate after the initial seizure of power, or do they disagree and quarrel among themselves, leading to further struggle?

the royal governments there. The Spanish king was placed under house arrest, while the Portuguese royal family fled to Brazil. These sudden blows to the monarchies had a swift and profound impact on Latin American politics. Brazil's transition to independence was relatively smooth. Spain's possessions, however, rose up in rebellion.

Simón Bolívar and the Liberation of Spanish South America

The most influential revolutionary was **Simón Bolívar** (1783–1830), known throughout Latin America as the Liberator. A member of the creole upper class in Venezuela, Bolívar was inspired by the ideals of the Enlightenment, frustrated by the inefficiency and injustice of Spanish rule, and personally ambitious.

In 1810, Bolívar took control of the independence movement sweeping across northern South America: Venezuela, Colombia, Bolivia, and Ecuador. Unlike many members of the creole elite, who rebelled against Spain for the sake of their narrow class interests, Bolívar realized that no revolt could succeed unless it attracted all classes. In a bold stroke, he promised to fight for the rights of mixed-race Latin Americans, as well as the emancipation of slaves. These principles, elaborated in documents like Bolívar's 1815 **Jamaica Letter**, turned a small and unsuccessful upper- and middle-class rebellion into a mass war of independence. The military turning point of Bolívar's wars came from 1819 to 1821, when he gained control over Venezuela and Colombia.

At this juncture, Bolívar joined forces with another freedom fighter, José de San Martín, a general turned revolutionary. Between 1816 and 1820, San Martín had freed Argentina, Chile, Uruguay, and Paraguay. Despite political differences—San Martín was more conservative—the two men decided to cooperate, with Bolívar as leader. By 1825, royalists had been cleared out of Bolivia, Ecuador, and Peru, and Spanish South America was now free.

Brazilian Independence

In the meantime, Brazil also became independent. Here, the move toward freedom came from above, rather than below. In 1820, the king of Portugal went back to Europe to reclaim his throne. He left his son, Prince Pedro, as regent. However, he also gave Pedro this advice: "My son, if Brazil starts to demand independence, make sure you are the one to proclaim it. Then put the crown on your own head." Indeed, in 1822, when Brazilians began to agitate for freedom, Pedro declared independence, created a constitutional monarchy, and proclaimed himself Pedro I.

Mexico's War of Independence

Mexico and Central America liberated themselves as well. The **Mexican War of Independence** (1810–1823) was complicated by the inability of various social classes

to cooperate. It began in September 1810, when the priest **Miguel Hidalgo**, unfurling the flag of the Virgin of Guadalupe, called for independence from Spain. Hidalgo was killed in 1811, but his fight was carried on by another priest, **José Maria Morelos**. Hidalgo and Morelos fought not just for freedom from Spain but also social justice. They wanted equal rights for Indians, mestizos, and slaves (whom they planned to set free). They wanted constitutional rule. Hidalgo and Morelos's platform gained mass support from the lower classes. Unfortunately, they were opposed not just by the Spanish but many upper-class Mexicans, even those who wanted independence. Like Hidalgo, Morelos was killed, in 1815, by conservative Mexicans, not the Spanish.

Therefore, Mexico's revolt was completed by the elite, not the lower classes. A conservative colonel, Agustín Iturbide, overthrew Spanish rule in 1820–1821. He tried to establish a dictatorship, with himself as emperor, but was quickly overthrown. A Mexican republic was proclaimed in 1823, the same year that the nations of Central America, south of Mexico, established the United Provinces of Central America.

The Caribbean

Only in the Caribbean did Spain retain American colonies. Until its defeat by the United States in the Spanish-American War of 1898, it kept islands such as Cuba and Puerto Rico. Other European countries also held onto Caribbean colonies.

POLITICAL CONSOLIDATION IN LATIN AMERICA
Political Difficulties in Nineteenth-Century Latin America

Before his death in 1830, Simón Bolívar commented pessimistically about the revolutions he had helped to make: "We have achieved our independence…at the expense of everything else." In and of itself, freedom did not bring about good government, social justice, or healthy economies. Throughout the 1800s and early 1900s, Latin America suffered from a number of fundamental problems.

First and most immediate was political breakdown. Bolívar divided Latin America into a handful of sizable states. Almost right away, though, Bolívar's mega-confederations—such as Gran Colombia and the United Provinces of the Río de la Plata—split apart into smaller states.

Second was the failure of constitutional rule in many of these states. Bolívar drafted constitutions for more than a dozen nations. These were influenced by the Napoleonic law code and the ideals of the American and French revolutions (although they favored indirect over direct democracy). But there was little tradition of constitutional rule in Latin America, so civil liberties and political rights had little meaning.

This failing led to a third problem: the prevalence of dictatorial rule. Military or political strongmen, known as **caudillos**, often gained control of Latin American governments. They ruled by means of personal charisma, military force, or oppression. Despite the efforts of reformers and liberals, such as Mexico's Benito Juárez, who led the country from 1867 to 1872, conservative dictatorship, rather than representative government, was the rule in nineteenth-century Latin America.

Economic Backwardness

Another difficulty was economic backwardness. Hundreds of years of Spanish and Portuguese rule had geared Latin American economies to extract raw materials. They generally emphasized **monoculture** or, at best, the development of only a small set of resources. They required large reserves of slaves or cheap labor. These practices continued, as did plantation agriculture. Latin American leaders failed to diversify their economies. Profits benefited only the elite (or foreign investors), while the labor was carried out by large numbers of extremely poor peasants and workers. Latin American economies were comparatively slow to modernize and industrialize.

Social and Racial Divisions

Social inequality persisted. Although constitutions theoretically did away with the rigid social hierarchies put into place by the Spanish and Portuguese, people of mixed race, Indians, and blacks still experienced much prejudice. In many areas, such as Mexico's Yucatán Peninsula, the Argentinian pampas, southern Chile, and Brazil's Amazon basin, racial tensions led to uprisings and guerrilla wars. Another social problem was economic inequality: the gap between rich and poor had always been wide, and it remained so or grew even wider during the 1800s. In Brazil and Cuba, slavery continued to be legal until the 1880s.

Foreign Influence over Latin America

Yet another problem was the increased influence of foreign countries over Latin American economics and even politics. This was especially the case with the United States. During the Texas rebellion of the 1830s and the **Mexican-American War** (1846–1848), the United States took vast amounts of territory from Mexico, including Texas, New Mexico, Arizona, and California.

During the 1860s, Napoleon III of France attempted to install a Habsburg emperor, Maximilian, as the ruler of Mexico.

Slavery in Brazil.
From the mid-1500s to the end of the 1800s, Brazil was the largest single importer of slaves from Africa. In particular, the sugar industry depended on slave labor. Not until the 1800s did Brazil's government make slavery illegal. Shown here are scenes of the sale and punishment of slaves in Brazil.

Less dramatically, foreign investors, especially from Britain and the United States, worked hand-in-hand with Latin American elites to control Latin American economies, then pocket the profits. This "**dollar diplomacy**" gave Britain and, later, the United States a tremendous amount of influence in the region.

Until late in the 1800s, Spain maintained a presence in the Caribbean, retaining control over islands such as Puerto Rico and Cuba. Spanish treatment of these colonies was harsh. Slavery persisted in Cuba until the 1880s. Cuban freedom movements began to appear. The most famous voice for Cuban independence was the poet José Martí. Spain responded by placing political agitators in **concentration camps**, the modern world's first such prisons (borrowed by the British in the early 1900s, during the Boer War). Spain's influence here ended in 1898, with the Spanish-American War.

The United States also exercised political power in the region, viewing the Americas as its sphere of influence. The **Spanish-American War** (1898) gave the United States an empire of sorts in Latin America, by placing Cuba and Puerto Rico under its protection. The United States built the **Panama Canal** in the early 1900s, another sign of its regional dominance.

TIP

When the Pan-American Union formed in 1889 to promote cooperation among Latin American nations, cynics referred to it as the "Colonial Division of the U.S. State Department."

Limited Modernization and Industrialization

Despite all these problems, Latin America modernized somewhat in the late 1800s and early 1900s. Industrialization came late, but it did come, especially in countries like Mexico and Argentina. Countries such as Argentina, Uruguay, and Chile made it possible for women to gain educations (even, in Chile, law and medical degrees), and extended greater rights to them.

Immigration from Europe and Asia swelled the populations of Latin American nations. Although countries like Argentina, Brazil, and Chile did not receive the same numbers as the United States, millions settled there during the last half of the 1800s, adding to what was already a diverse social and ethnic mix.

The Mexican Revolution

From 1910 to 1920, at roughly the same time as China and Russia, Mexico experienced one of the early twentieth century's most significant political uprisings. The **Mexican Revolution** deposed **Porfirio Díaz**, president of Mexico between 1876 and 1910. Díaz did much to modernize and industrialize the country, but, over the years, grew corrupt and abusive. He rigged elections and hired armed thugs (known as *rurales*) to intimidate people into voting for him. When **Francisco Madero** ran against him in 1910, he put Madero in jail.

However, Madero escaped, gathered supporters, and started a mass uprising by pledging to carry out meaningful agrarian reform. In 1911, he defeated the federal armies and forced Díaz to abdicate. He attempted to create a liberal democracy, but as with the moderates in revolutionary France and Sun Yat-sen in China, he was not destined to govern for long. He found himself caught between conservative counterrevolutionaries and radicals like **Francisco "Pancho" Villa**, **Emiliano Zapata**, and Pascual Orozco, who had initially supported him, but wanted him to reform more rapidly than he was willing to. These leaders, with much of the rural population, rose up against Madero. From the right, the military plotted against him as well,

and General Victoriano Huerta staged a coup d'etat in 1913. Within a week, Madero was murdered.

Huerta (whose government U.S. President Woodrow Wilson refused to recognize) was replaced in 1914 by Venustiano Carranza, who served off and on again as president until 1920. Although he tried to accommodate many of the radicals' demands, rebels such as Villa and Zapata continued to agitate against him. (Zapata, whose movement included many women, was killed in 1919. Villa, whose incursions into U.S. territory provoked an American military response in 1916, survived till 1923.) Carranza devised the populist Constitution of 1917, which embraced socialist principles, but had little chance to enforce it. Villa's and Zapata's rebellions sapped his strength, and his officers betrayed him. In 1920, Carranza, like Madero, was removed and killed by one of his generals, Álvaro Obregón.

In practical, if not ideological, terms, this moment is generally considered to have ended the revolution. Violence continued into the early 1930s, but order was restored, and the leaders—much like Napoleon or France's Directory—claimed to act in the revolution's name. In 1929, they created a **National Revolutionary Party** (renamed the PRI, or **Institutional Revolutionary Party**, in 1946). Between 1934 and 1940, Lázaro Cárdenas made the first genuine attempt to govern according to the Constitution of 1917, but the PRI regime gradually degenerated into mild authoritarianism.

Unit Five: Review Questions

SAMPLE ESSAY QUESTIONS (CCOT AND COMPARATIVE)

CCOT 1

Analyze changes and continuities in the economic practices of ONE of the following areas between 1750 and 1914.

Ottoman Turkey
Latin America

CCOT 2

Analyze changes and continuities in the status of women in ONE of the following areas between 1750 and 1914.

Western Europe
the Middle East

COMP 1

Compare and contrast the way TWO of the following regions experienced European imperialism between 1750 and 1914.

Japan
sub-Saharan Africa
India

COMP 2

Compare and contrast forms of labor organization in TWO of the following regions between 1750 and 1914.

China
Southeast Asia
Latin America

MULTIPLE-CHOICE QUESTIONS

1. Charles Darwin's contribution to nineteenth-century intellectual life is best summed up as follows:

   (A) His theory of natural selection satisfactorily explained how the process of evolution works.
   (B) His cultural relativism cast doubt on Christianity and other traditional value systems.
   (C) He was the first to propose the theory of evolution.
   (D) His understanding of genetic theory unlocked the secret of how evolution worked.

2. How did the leaders of China's Taiping Rebellion and the Madhist revolt in the Sudan resemble each other?

   (A) Both supported a program of rapid industrialization.
   (B) Both redistributed land to impoverished peasants.
   (C) Both successfully expelled Western imperialists.
   (D) Both leaders claimed to be divinely inspired.

3. How did industrialization in the early 1800s affect the Atlantic slave trade?

   (A) It increased demand for U.S. cotton and revived the slave trade for several decades.
   (B) Its emphasis on machine production caused the slave trade to experience a rapid downturn.
   (C) It had little or no effect on the slave trade.
   (D) It brought an immediate end to the slave trade.

4. The discovery of what resource caused great turmoil in South Africa during the late 1800s and early 1900s?

   (A) bauxite
   (B) silver
   (C) diamonds
   (D) rubber

5. Which of the following is NOT true of the Meiji Restoration?

   (A) The middle class expanded and gained influence.
   (B) The regime allowed labor unions to form.
   (C) An industrial working class grew rapidly.
   (D) Commoners were allowed to serve in the military.

6. Which of the following is true of BOTH the French and Mexican revolutions?

   (A) Centrally organized reigns of terror were carried out by each revolutionary regime.
   (B) Rural populations gave wholehearted support to both revolutionary regimes.
   (C) After long struggle, radical social and economic platforms triumphed in the end.
   (D) Early leaders proved unable to keep moderate and radical revolutionaries united.

7. Which of the following accurately describes the Tanzimat Reforms and Qing China's self-strengthening policy?

   (A) Both embarked on a quick transition to free-market capitalism.
   (B) Both argued that traditional religious belief was superior to Western materialism.
   (C) Both set incremental changes into motion, but achieved only limited improvements.
   (D) Both favored rapid industrialization as long as the state controlled economic policy.

8. The map on page 301 illustrates that

   (A) Britain controlled Madagascar and Mali.
   (B) Belgium was the only European nation to colonize Central Africa.
   (C) Germany controlled the largest amount of territory in Africa, followed by France.
   (D) The only African states not colonized by outside powers in 1914 were Liberia and Ethiopia.

9. "Every time Paris sneezes, the rest of Europe catches cold."

   This observation, offered by Prince Klemens von Metternich, most likely refers to

   (A) the intellectual influence exerted over the continent by the French Enlightenment.
   (B) the tendency of French revolutionary impulses to catch on elsewhere in Europe.
   (C) the frequency with which European epidemics originated in France.
   (D) France's habit of violating the treaties signed at the Congress of Vienna.

10. What political strategy contributed most to the success of the Latin American wars of independence?

    (A) promising freedom to slaves and equal rights to all
    (B) attracting lower-class support by calling for a socialist revolution
    (C) appealing to the middle classes by promising the vote only to those with property
    (D) securing aristocratic support by pledging to keep slavery legal

11. Who were the zamindars?

    (A) the pro-British merchant class of eastern India
    (B) Hindu priests who called for a holy war against British rule
    (C) native officials who administered parts of India for the British
    (D) native troops who rebelled against the British occupation of India

12. Great Britain's First Reform Act resembled the Meiji Constitution in that

    (A) both established a system of universal military service.
    (B) both extended the vote to all adult males.
    (C) both allowed trade unions to function legally.
    (D) both permitted only a small fraction of the population to vote.

13. Which of the following did NOT encourage the "new" imperialism of the late 1800s?

    (A) a sense of racial and cultural superiority on the part of Western societies
    (B) a perceived need to compete against the rising industrial economies of Africa and Asia
    (C) the strategic necessity of maintaining naval bases and refueling stations overseas
    (D) new medical treatments for tropical diseases

14. How did Japanese industrialization differ from industrialization in Europe?

(A) The middle class was less important to Japan's industrial growth than in Europe.
(B) Japanese industrialization was directed more by the government than in most of Europe.
(C) Industrial growth in Japan was not accompanied by as much urban growth as in Europe.
(D) Living and working conditions for Japan's working class were much better than in Europe.

15. Which of the following statements would a Marxist most likely oppose?

(A) Employers should not be compelled to pay workers higher wages.
(B) Throughout history, the upper classes exploit the labor of the lower classes.
(C) Free-market capitalism leads to social inequality.
(D) Violent revolution may be necessary to achieve socialism.

16. During the early 1800s, what aspect of their trade relations with Qing China most upset Western nations?

(A) China's insistence on selling rice at exorbitantly high prices
(B) China's refusal to import large amounts of foreign goods
(C) China's sponsorship of the illegal opium trade
(D) China's use of slave labor to harvest tea

17. Which of the following best describes patterns of immigration during the 1800s?

(A) Large numbers of Europeans and Asians emigrated to North and South America.
(B) Many Europeans emigrated to North America, but few Asians did so.
(C) Immigration had little effect on the demographic profile of the United States.
(D) Thousands of North Americans emigrated to western Europe.

18. The artwork reproduced on page 257 is best described (without looking at the caption) as

(A) a portrait inspired by the French Romantics' idealization of heroic individuality.
(B) an excellent example of the influence of African art on French painting and design.
(C) a typically Realist critique of social inequities in nineteenth-century France.
(D) a French post-impressionist's blurring of the lines between art and advertising.

19. Who were the caudillos in the context of Latin American history?

(A) cattle ranchers who developed the southern pampas
(B) wealthy plantation owners who dominated agricultural production
(C) conservative strongmen who established authoritarian regimes
(D) native warriors who rebelled against several post-independence regimes

20. Which of the following is true of Western missionaries in the 1800s?

(A) They eliminated the sati ritual in India.
(B) They combated the East African slave trade.
(C) They encouraged the Chinese practice of foot binding.
(D) They converted much of Indochina's population to Protestantism.

ANSWERS

1. **(A)** Theories of evolution arose as early as the 1700s; the difficulty lay in finding a scientifically convincing way to explain the process. Darwin's concept of natural selection did, although he had no awareness of genetic theory, which was pioneered by Gregor Mendel. Although Darwinian theory played a role in destabilizing literal interpretations of Christian doctrine, answer C applies more to figures such as Friedrich Nietzsche.

2. **(D)** Whereas the Taiping redistributed wealth in certain ways and claimed to support certain aspects of modernization, as in answers B and C, the Madhi did not. Both failed to expel foreign forces. The Madhi claimed to be a messiah figure from Sufi tradition, and Hong Xiuquan claimed to be Jesus Christ's younger brother.

3. **(A)** By mechanizing the way cotton bolls were cleaned, Eli Whitney's cotton gin allowed cotton suppliers to satisfy demand from the thread-spinning and cloth-weaving sectors of the textile industry, which were already mechanized. The industry's capacity exploded in the 1790s, and hunger for raw cotton boosted cotton production in the slaveholding U.S. South—prolonging slavery much longer than most historians believe it would otherwise have lasted.

4. **(C)** All of the commodities listed here inspired imperial efforts on the part of European powers, and rubber is produced elsewhere in Africa. It was diamonds, however, that provoked intense competition among the British, the Boers, and the Zulu over mineral-rich territories.

5. **(B)** The Meiji regime liberalized as much as was necessary to spur modernization, but no more. Industrialization and class change led to the developments listed in A, C, and D. However, industrial working conditions were extremely hard in nineteenth-century Japan, and, as in Europe earlier in the 1800s, trade unions were forbidden.

6. **(D)** Answer A applies to France, not Mexico. Both revolutions were opposed by peasant uprisings (Zapatistas and Villa supporters in Mexico, the Vendée rebels in France), but enjoyed the support of liberal and centrist military officers. Neither achieved all their aims, and the problem described in answer D is the main reason.

7. **(C)** These programs exemplify the failure of Ottoman Turkey and Qing China to keep up with a rapidly modernizing and industrializing West, a problem reflected in answer C. Ottoman rulers made a better effort, but were hindered by anti-reformist forces such as the janissaries.

8. **(D)** Choosing the right response is a function of simple map-reading skills. All the information needed to answer this question is contained in the map's legend. Some map questions require you to rely on outside knowledge.

9. **(B)** Answer A is a reasonably plausible answer, but knowing about Metternich's role at the Congress of Vienna and his reactionary opposition to political change of any sort should call to mind how French revolutions in 1789, 1830, and 1848 were imitated throughout Europe.

10. **(A)** Early independence efforts in Latin America tended to stall because they were seen as benefiting merely the interests of the upper classes. Once leaders such as Simón Bolívar began to appeal to a larger cross section of society, independence movements gained the strength needed to throw off Spanish rule.

11. **(C)** Answer D refers to the sepoys. Zamindars did not always act in the interest of their own people (sometimes overtaxing native Indians and skimming revenues off the top before passing the correct amount on to the British). In general, the British made the task of imperial governance easier and cheaper by relying on native troops and administrators whenever feasible.

12. **(D)** The British Parliament and Japanese Diet are examples of how, in the 1800s, elected law-making bodies were not necessarily democratic by contemporary standards. In these cases, restrictions on who could vote meant that less than 10 percent of the population could take part in the electoral process. All adult males voted for Germany's Reichstag, but, there, not all votes counted equally.

13. **(B)** All these factors contributed to the "new" imperialism except B. Apart from Japan, no country in Africa or Asia was industrializing to the extent that it could have competed with Europe or North America.

14. **(B)** Although Japan industrialized later and more quickly than Europe, its social and economic experience of industrialization greatly resembled Europe's. One chief difference lay in how Japan's imperial government closely directed the industrialization process, whereas laissez-faire, noninterventionist economics were the rule in Europe. (Bear in mind, though, that in Germany and especially in Russia, industrialization was firmly guided by the hand of the state, a fact that did not prevent Germany, at least, from becoming an industrial power.)

15. **(A)** All of these are standard Marxist principles, except for A, which is a restatement of David Ricardo's "iron law of wages"—an axiom Marx himself was familiar with but did not recognize as a naturally desirable state of affairs. (Ricardo saw it as an unavoidable evil in economic life.)

16. **(B)** As it does today, China in the 1700s and 1800s went to great lengths to maintain a positive balance of trade, or to export more than it imported. China was happy to sell whatever the Europeans wanted to buy, including silk, porcelain, and especially tea. The British responded by selling opium to the Chinese, who quickly became addicted to the drug.

17. **(A)** Nineteenth-century immigration resulted in one of the largest population transfers in world history. The Americas attracted a great number of immigrants from Europe and Asia—whose populations still grew tremendously, despite losing millions to emigration. Although many traveled to the United States, Argentina, Chile, and Canada were important destinations as well, and remain multicultural societies as a result.

18. **(D)** Basic familiarity with nineteenth-century artistic styles is the best tool for answering this question. The presence of text (even without being able to read the French) helps narrow the likeliest alternative to D.

19. **(C)** The categories described in the other answers existed, but went by different names.

20. **(B)** Sati was eliminated in India, but by the authorities, and the British East India Company, which had no wish to offend natives on religious grounds, actively restricted missionary efforts. Missionaries discouraged foot binding in China; in Indochina, missionary activity was carried out mainly by French Catholics, not Protestants. Missionaries such as David Livingstone were instrumental in ending the slave trade in East Africa.

UNIT SIX

ACCELERATING GLOBAL CHANGE AND REALIGNMENTS
(1900 to Present)

Unit Overview

GENERAL REMARKS

The twentieth century ranks as one of the most tumultuous eras ever. It was a time of paradox and contradiction, leading one historian to refer to it as the "age of extremes." The largest part of the world to date adopted democratic forms of government (and allowed women to vote), but history's most oppressive dictatorships appeared as well. The 1900s were a time of unprecedented prosperity, but also of striking socioeconomic polarity, as the gap between rich and poor widened. There were tremendous cultural and scientific advancements, but also the worst wars and the greatest arms buildup in human history.

The first half of the century was dominated by two great military conflicts: **World War I** and **World War II**, both of which were characterized by improved military technology and new tactics, and therefore caused immense devastation. The latter was the bloodiest and costliest conflict humanity has ever experienced, and both led to profound changes in the world balance of power. World War I destroyed several of the nineteenth century's great empires and sapped Europe's strength. World War II completed the weakening of Europe, dislodging it from its position of global mastery.

The interwar years were marked by economic crisis, resulting from the **Great Depression**, which emanated outward from the United States. This period also saw the emergence of powerful dictatorial regimes, such as Soviet Russia, Fascist Italy, and Nazi Germany, and it appeared for a time that **totalitarianism**, not democracy, might be the wave of the future. Starting with the establishment of the Soviet state, **communism** became an influential—although, in the end, seemingly unworkable—alternative to **capitalism** as a form of economic organization.

During the century's second half, sweeping trends affected the entire world. One, following the collapse of Europe's global dominance, was **decolonization** (or **national liberation**). From the 1940s through the 1970s, parts of Africa, Asia, and the Pacific that had been under European (and U.S.) imperial control became free. This wave of national liberation created dozens of new nations. In some cases, decolonization proceeded peacefully. In others, it was attained by force or disintegrated into violence and political chaos.

Another effect of World War II and Europe's decline as a global power was a new diplomatic alignment, the **Cold War**. In the previous century and a half, world affairs had been determined by the workings of the European balance of power.

After World War II, political and economic power might was concentrated in the hands of two evenly matched superpowers: the United States and the Soviet Union. This situation of bipolar equilibrium persisted for four and a half decades, dividing most of the globe into two hostile camps.

The twentieth century was an era of modernization. Societies already industrialized when the 1900s began—such as the United States, Canada, western Europe, and Japan—became even more adept at scientific and technological innovation, until, after the 1940s and 1950s, they moved into postindustrial modes of economic organization. Such societies are generally referred to as the **developed world**. A number of other countries, especially in Asia, have similarly modernized. The majority of the world's nations, known as the **developing** or **nondeveloped world** (or, in Cold War terms, the **Third World**), remain in a less advanced stage of economic and technological progress. The gap between poverty and prosperity is perhaps wider today than at any other time in history. All modern soicieties, developed or nondeveloped, have had an immensely greater impact on the environment. The most noticeable effect today is **climate change** (popularly known as global warming).

The 1980s and 1990s saw the collapse of communism in Europe and the USSR, and with that, the end of the Cold War. The same decades witnessed a wave of democratization in many parts of the world, as well as the increased **globalization** of the world economy. The greater ease with which ethnicities and traditions meet and mix has stimulated a high degree of **multiculturalism**, and mass communications have made the world, metaphorically speaking, a much smaller and more connected place. This is especially due to the sudden proliferation of computer technology, which has caused an **information** (or **digital**) **revolution**. Entities other than **nation-states**—such **multinational corporations**, **non-governmental organizations**, and **regional trade alliances**—have had an increasingly large impact on world affairs.

The world's general direction in the early twenty-first century remains unclear. Many trends, such as the end of the nuclear arms race, economic globalization, the worldwide prevalence of American popular culture, and the spread of mass communications and computer technology, seem to be drawing the world closer together. On the other hand, ethnic violence and **genocide**, extreme forms of nationalism, religious fundamentalism, proliferation of **weapons of mass destruction**, potential tensions between China and the West, and ongoing tensions between the West and the Islamic world all threaten to pull the world farther apart. The same is true of the terrorist attacks of **September 11, 2001**, on the World Trade Center and Pentagon—the symbolic beginning of the new century—and the resulting **war on terror**.

BROAD TRENDS

Humans and the Environment

- Escalating industrialization, increased energy and resource consumption, massive engineering projects, and the production of toxic, chemical, and nuclear waste have exponentially increased humanity's impact on the environment.

- Diseases associated with poverty, such as malaria, tuberculosis, and cholera persisted in many parts of the world.
- New epidemic diseases, their global spread made easier by better and faster transportation, emerged, such as ebola, HIV/AIDS, and many new strains of influenza, starting with the "Spanish flu," which killed millions at the end of World War I. Diseases associated with sedentary lifestyles and new dietary habits, such as heart disease, diabetes, and obesity, became more common.
- Between the late 1940s and the 1970s, a "Green Revolution" spread advanced agricultural techniques around the world, leading to a huge rise in the production of food. Mexico and India played important roles in this development. The environmental impact of agriculture increased as a result, especially thanks to greater water consumption, more reliance on monoculture, and the extensive use of pesticides.
- Environmental awareness in the West grew slowly during the early 1900s and then expanded after World War II. Green movements have grown in size and influence.
- Climate change, or global warming, increased throughout the twentieth century and is thought by most scientists to have been caused by the human-produced emission of greenhouse gases (especially carbon dioxide). It began to reach a new peak in the 1990s and early 2000s. The best known international effort to cooperate in understanding and reversing this trend is the Kyoto Protocol (1997).
- Warfare in the twentieth and twenty-first centuries has had a growing impact on the environment. Examples include radiation from nuclear-weapons testing, biological and chemical warfare between Iran and Iraq during the 1970s, the napalming of forests during the Vietnam War, and the destruction of oil wells during times of armed conflict.
- Natural disasters (Hurricane Katrina, the Southeast Asian tsunami) and energy-related crises (Chernobyl, Three Mile Island, the Bhopal Incident, Exxon Valdez, Fukushima nuclear disaster, the Gulf of Mexico oil spill) demonstrate how contemporary societies can still be affected by the environment, and how technology now allows them to affect the environment far more deeply than before.

Development and Interaction of Cultures

- Mass media and mass communications technology transformed the cultural sphere. Cinema, radio, television, and other electronic media have been used to create high art.
- Mass media have also been used to create popular (or mass) culture: music, literature, and so forth aimed at a popular audience for purposes of entertainment.
- The art of the twentieth century was characterized by bold experimentation and the distortion, even abandonment, of traditional norms and conventions.
- During the first two-thirds of the 1900s, largely because of the demoralizing effects of Europe's decline and the world wars, Western high art tended to be

marked by uncertainty and pessimism (in contrast to the exuberance and energy of popular, or mass, culture).

- Scientific advancement proceeded at a breathtaking pace and scale. Especially innovative fields were physics, biotechnology and genetics, rocketry, electronics, and computers.
- After World War II, Western culture began to move beyond the "modern" period into a newer "postmodern" era.
- Global cultures have mixed, interacted, and blended to an unprecedented degree. This celebration and acknowledgment of different traditions and styles is generally referred to as multiculturalism.
- Since the 1990s, the proliferation of personal computer technology, particularly access to the Internet and World Wide Web, has led to an information (or digital revolution).

State-Building, Expansion, and Conflict

- During the first half of the 1900s, two world wars profoundly reshaped global affairs. After 1914, Europe's position of world dominance was weakened by World War I, and the United States became the world's richest and most powerful nation. World War II completed the dismantling of Europe's global dominance.
- For four and a half decades after World War II, most of the world was divided into hostile camps, led by two superpowers, the United States and the USSR, in a geopolitical struggle known as the Cold War. This involved a nuclear arms race, the largest and most expensive weapons buildup in world history.
- The nations of the so-called Third World, which joined neither the U.S. alliance nor the Soviet bloc during the Cold War, experimented with a variety of political and economic systems.
- From the 1940s through the 1970s, a mass wave of decolonization deprived the European powers of their empires. Sometimes through peaceful negotiation, sometimes through violent separation, former colonies in Asia, Africa, the Pacific, and elsewhere became free. Dozens of new nations were formed.
- During the late 1980s and 1990s, communism in Eastern Europe and the USSR collapsed. This dramatic development ended the Cold War. The only remaining superpower since has been the United States, with China as a rising power.
- The terrorist attacks of September 11, 2001, by al-Qaeda began a new global struggle, the U.S.-led war on terror. This sharpened tensions between the West and the Islamic world, and sparked wars in Iraq and Afghanistan. Terrorism in general (carried out by groups such as ETA, the IRA, the PLO, Hamas, and others) has played a significant role in international politics in the 1900s and 2000s.
- New weapons and tactics were constantly developed throughout this period. Wars caused greater numbers of casualties, especially among civilian populations. By the 1990s and early 2000s, the gap between high-tech and low-level warfare had grown wider than ever before in history. The most advanced armed forces possess weapons of mass destruction, precision-guided ("smart") weapons,

and—thanks to what strategists call the "revolution in military affairs"—digitally integrated systems. Much of the rest of the world fights low-intensity or guerrilla wars, using only small arms and hand-to-hand weapons.

- Domestically, the level of popular representation in national governments grew in many countries, especially the Western democracies. Women gained the vote in most Western countries in the early twentieth century, and later in most other countries.
- Between the world wars, democracies tended to be politically weak and economically depressed. The most dynamic governments of the interwar period were the totalitarian dictatorships, which aimed to control as many aspects of their subjects' lives as possible.
- After World War II, the primary form of political and economic organization in the West (Canada, the United States, and Western Europe) was the democratic state with a capitalist system, although capitalism was modified to varying degrees by social welfare systems.
- A number of regimes, led by the Soviet Union and China, adopted communist economic systems. Their political systems tended to be dictatorial.
- Entities other than nation-states, including regional trade organizations (such as the European Union and NAFTA), non-governmental organizations (such as Amnesty International and the Red Cross), and multinational corporations (such as Coca-Cola and Shell Oil), began to exert greater influence over world affairs.

Economic Systems

- During the first half of the twentieth century, the West (Europe, Canada, and the United States) fully industrialized. Certain other parts of the world achieved significant degrees of modernization and industrialization (such as Japan, parts of Latin America, and China).
- A number of countries experimented with communist economies (the Soviet Union, Eastern Europe, China, North Korea, Cuba, Vietnam, and others).
- During the 1930s, the Great Depression, emanating from the United States, negatively affected the economies of most of Europe and Latin America, as well as Asia and Africa to a lesser degree.
- After World War II, a great split between the capitalist West and the communist Soviet bloc (and China) emerged. This split prevailed until the end of the Cold War.
- Also after World War II, a different split emerged between the developed world, whose prosperity steadily grew (with a few minor regressions, such as the economic crisis of the 1970s), and the nondeveloped and developing (or Third) world, which lagged behind. Because so many nondeveloped and developing nations are located near or south of the equator, this disparity is sometimes referred to as the north-south split.
- After the 1950s and 1960s, Western economies began to move from industrial economies to postindustrial economies, based less on manufacturing and more on service, information, and advanced technology (especially computers). This trend continues.

- During the 1970s, a general economic crisis, characterized by energy (particularly oil) shortages, recession, and unemployment struck the capitalist West. A general rise in prosperity—associated with an emphasis on free-market economics, but not necessarily equitably distributed throughout society—took place in Western economies during the 1980s and 1990s. The same was true in China. The Soviet bloc experienced a severe economic downturn.
- 1980s and 1990s were an era of greater economic globalization, as international trade, economic regionalization, and the clout of multinational corporations became increasingly important. This trend continues.
- A worldwide financial crisis, arguably the worst since the Great Depression, struck in 2007. Its effects still linger.

Social Structures

- In the West, labor unions grew in power during the first half of the century. During the 1920s, and especially during the Great Depression of the 1930s, many capitalist societies adopted social welfare policies (the British "dole," the U.S. New Deal, Scandinavia's "third way") to provide a social safety net.
- The middle class became the dominant and most numerous class in most developed societies by World War II, and this trend deepened during the postwar era. In the communist societies, class divisions were minimized, at least in theory. In the developing world, class divisions between the elite and the rest of society were very wide.
- Gender equality made great strides during the twentieth century in the developed world. Most women in these countries received the right to vote after World War I. Job opportunities increased, partly due to the world wars, and especially World War II.
- The postwar development of reliable contraception (especially birth-control pills) gave women with access to it unprecedented control over pregnancy and sexuality.
- During the 1960s and 1970s, a great feminist movement, agitating for women's liberation and equal rights, swept Canada, the United States, and most of Europe. Since then, women's movements have sought to achieve more than simple legal equality and the right to vote. Their goals have been full cultural and economic equality, changing social norms and behaviors to create a more positive climate for equal gender relations.
- Progress toward equal treatment of women has been uneven in other parts of the world.
- The collapse of communism in Eastern Europe and the USSR forced a number of countries to make a painful social and economic transition from communism to free-market economies. Most of these places continue to wrestle with this transition in the twenty-first century.
- Many parts of the West, including the United States, experienced a general rise in prosperity from the 1980s up through the financial collapse of 2007. However, this was accompanied by a growing split between rich and poor, and increased burdens on the middle class.

- Globally, the world still struggles with a north-south split, meaning that economic prosperity and access to cutting-edge technology, medical care, and social stability tend to be concentrated in the developed world, with many parts of the developing world lagging behind and still impoverished.

QUESTIONS AND COMPARISONS TO CONSIDER

- Discuss the ways different nations and regions modernized during the twentieth century. Were they industrialized before the 1900s? Did modernization efforts come from the population at large, or were they instituted by the government? Did they have to be put into place by force? Has modernization by force proven effective?
- In what ways did war evolve during this period? Consider tactics, weapons technology, and impact on population.
- What impact did the world wars have on the non-Western world? Compare different regions, such as Africa and Asia. How did the wars affect women?
- Compare two or more of the twentieth century's major revolutions, such as the Russian, Chinese, Mexican, Cuban, or Iranian. Alternatively, compare one or more of these with revolutions in previous centuries. Compare how each affected women and/or ethnic minorities.
- Examine the process of decolonization as it played out in various parts of the world. Be sure to address cases that involved negotiation (India, the Gold Coast) and those that involved violent separation (Vietnam, Algeria, Angola).
- Focus on specific national liberation movements and independence struggles during the period of decolonization. What obstacles did various movements face? What role did nationalism play? Were groups or individuals more important in a given movement? To what degree did Cold War dynamics affect a given movement? What role if any did force play?
- How has the legacy of colonialism affected cultural identity and/or patterns of economic development in Africa, Asia, and Latin America?
- How has nationalism in Europe differed from nationalism in decolonizing or decolonized parts of the world, both in character and in its political effects? Be sure to consider xenophobia, anti-immigration sentiment, and Christian-Muslim tension since 9/11.
- How has the rise of Western consumer society and economic globalization affected different civilizations outside Europe?
- How have twentieth- and twenty-first-century technologies and agricultural techniques affected the environment?
- How have epidemics and other medical crises affected states and societies during this era?
- How does ethnic violence in the 1990s and early 2000s compare with the Holocaust?
- What effects have major scientific breakthroughs (genetics, quantum physics, the digital revolution) had on society, politics, and culture during this era? How have certain scientific programs (the space race, for example) interacted with global political affairs?

World War I

- World War I (Allies versus Central Powers)
- Nationalism and competition over empire
- The European alliance system
- Trench warfare and the Western Front
- naval blockade and submarine (U-boat) warfare
- The Armenian genocide
- Total war
- The home front (rationing, conscription, restriction of civil liberties)
- Women's roles and female suffrage
- The Paris Peace Conference, Treaty of Versailles, and the Fourteen Points
- The League of Nations
- The Balfour Declaration
- The Spanish flu

In the late summer of 1914, the nations of Europe went to war. All of them expected that the conflict would be short and decisive. As the British press proclaimed, "the boys" would be "home by Christmas."

Instead, **World War I** (1914–1918), known to the people who experienced it as the Great War, lasted more than four years. More than thirty nations joined in the fighting. The war killed up to 10 million soldiers. Between 3 to 5 million civilians perished as well, mainly of disease and starvation caused by the war but also as a result of direct military action. Approximately 28 to 30 million people were wounded or disabled. At war's end, Europe's economies lay in ruins, even those of the countries that had won. The treaties that ended the war completely redrew the map of the world.

World War I shattered Europe politically and culturally. Four great empires—the German Reich, Russia's tsarist regime, Austria-Hungary's Habsburg dynasty, and Ottoman Turkey—were destroyed. Russia's suffering led directly to communist revolution; Germany's defeat inspired Adolf Hitler to follow the path of fascism. Even victorious nations like Britain, France, and Italy were exhausted and demoralized. The optimistic faith in progress so prevalent in the nineteenth century vanished, to be replaced by gloom and anxiety, and the Europeans' view of themselves as models of civilized behavior and cultural superiority was exposed as a foolish illusion. The only major nation in the West to escape this malaise was the United States, which remained comparatively undamaged by the war—and profited from it economically.

Far-reaching social changes resulted from or were sped up by the war. These included the final decline of the aristocracy, the rise of the middle and lower classes, the greater democratization of European politics, the complete industrialization and modernization of European economies, and the granting of suffrage to women.

In global terms, World War I caused a fundamental shift in power. Europe had gained tremendous global might during the last half of the 1700s. In the nineteenth century, it had become the dominant civilization on the planet, and it reached the zenith of its power from 1870 to 1914. After World War I, it was clear that Europe would not be able to continue in this position of preeminence for much longer. The United States was becoming the world's military and economic powerhouse. Europe's imperial possessions were increasingly restless, and although countries such as Britain and France held on to their empires for a while longer, the process of decolonization was unavoidable—the question was when, not whether, it would happen.

For all these reasons and more, World War I, rather than the calendar year 1900, is considered metaphorically to be the true beginning of the twentieth century.

BACKGROUND AND BEGINNING

As discussed in Chapter 23, long-term causes of World War I include a potent cocktail of **nationalism**, **competition over empire**, and an unstable **European alliance system** (France and Russia, informally aligned with Britain, against Germany, Austria, and Italy) with the potential to draw all the continent's powers into conflict in the event of crisis.

That crisis came in the Balkans, in Sarajevo, capital of Bosnia: a Slavic province under Austrian authority but with a large Serb population and, therefore, coveted by the young and intensely nationalistic nation of Serbia. On June 28, 1914, a Bosnian Serb student assassinated the heir to Austria's throne, Franz Ferdinand, and his wife.

The assassination caused outrage worldwide but especially in Austria, which blamed Serbia and decided to use the murders as a pretext to humble its troublesome neighbor. In July, Austria issued Serbia an ultimatum, a list of humiliating demands, and threatened war if Serbia did not agree to them. Because of the alliance system and a general sense of nationalist belligerence, this regional quarrel rapidly escalated into a continental conflict. Russia, protective of its fellow Slavs (and unfriendly to Austria) supported Serbia. Germany assured Austria of its support (the infamous "blank check"), even if Russia intervened. France was pledged to aid Russia in the event of hostilities.

On July 28, Austria declared war on Serbia. Russia responded by mobilizing its troops. Like clockwork, the alliance system went into operation (Germany's plan for avoiding a long two-front war required immediate action, a factor that sped up the process). Between July 28 and August 4, Serbia, Austria, Russia, Germany, France, and Britain entered the war. Although guilt for the the war was later assigned principally to Germany, many factors contributed to its beginning, and a number of countries share at least some blame.

COMBAT

The Combatants: The Allies and the Central Powers

The war expanded beyond the original alliance system. The **Allies**, as the Triple Entente now called itself, consisted of Great Britain, France, and Russia. Britain's imperial dominions, including Canada, Australia, New Zealand, and South Africa, also took part. Italy abandoned its former partners and joined the Allies in 1915, because Britain and France promised it Austrian territory. In 1917, the United

States would join the Allied war effort; later that year, Russia would drop out of the war. On the other side were the **Central Powers**. These were Germany and Austria, the nations of the Triple Alliance, minus Italy. They were joined by Bulgaria and the Ottoman Empire. Other nations took part in the war, but these were the major combatants.

The Schlieffen Plan, the Invasion of Belgium, and the Battle of the Marne

Germany's **Schlieffen Plan** and its failure shaped the first phase of World War I. Faced with a two-front ground war against France and Russia, as well as the long-term threat of the British navy, Germany made a daring gamble: the Schlieffen Plan sent 75 percent of the German army against France, with the goal of taking Paris in six weeks. The rest

World War I in Europe, 1914–1918.
In Western Europe, the basic dynamic of the conflict was determined quite early. Then, thanks to the stalemate of trench warfare, it changed very little until the last months of war. In the east, fighting conditions were much more fluid.

of the army, with the Austrians, would defend against Russia. To catch the French off guard, the main attack force would move through Belgium, which was neutral.

The illegal invasion of Belgium, which killed many civilians, stained Germany's reputation badly. It enabled Allied propaganda to argue convincingly that the Germans were aggressors, "barbarians," and "Huns."

By early September, the Schlieffen Plan had failed. Belgium resisted more stoutly than Germany had anticipated. The Russians mobilized more quickly than expected. Although German troops came within sight of Paris, the French army made a heroic stand at the Marne River. The battle there saved Paris, foiled the Schlieffen Plan, and dashed any hope of a quick end to the war.

Trench Warfare, the Western Front, and the Eastern Front

In late 1914, two European fronts, the Western Front and Eastern Front, took shape. They were very different. In the west, stalemate prevailed. Both sides were evenly matched and armed with the latest in industrial-era weaponry. Artillery, machine guns, and modern rifles had made the battlefield so deadly that traditional tactics, which involved charging the enemy, were no longer feasible. Military technology disproportionately favored the defensive. The result was **trench warfare**, one of the most horrific styles of combat in human history. For the next three years, fighting on the **Western Front**, while exceptionally bloody, resulted in almost no movement at all. Actions such as the Verdun Offensive and the Battle of the Somme, both in 1916, rank among the most futile operations of all time, resulting in hundreds of thousands of casualties but no useful outcome.

NOTE

By the end of 1914, 500 miles of trenches, bunkers, and barbed wire, separating the Germans from the Allied forces, stretched from the English Channel to the Swiss border.

NOTE

Not until 1917 and 1918 did tactical changes and new weaponry (such as tanks and airplanes) start to end the painful stalemate of trench warfare.

Ordinary life in the trenches could be almost as miserable as combat. Mud, lice, rats, disease, and the smell of dead bodies combined to make the trench experience maddeningly terrible. Eloquent descriptions of trench warfare can be found in literary works such as Erich Maria Remarque's novel *All Quiet on the Western Front*, Robert Graves's autobiographical *Goodbye to All That*, and the work of Britain's so-called "war poets" (Robert Owen, Siegfried Sassoon, Stephen Spender, and others).

Fighting on the Eastern Front was very different. This front was much longer, extending well over a thousand miles, and less entrenched. Serbia fell to the Austrians. After initial setbacks, the Germans and Austrians moved quickly and efficiently against the Russians, killing, wounding, and capturing millions. They also took hundreds of thousands of square miles of Russian territory. From the beginning, the Russians found themselves in terrible trouble. Bulgaria and the Ottoman Empire joined the war on the side of the Central Powers, cutting Russia off from its allies. By 1917, Russia was nearing the end of its capacity to fight.

Naval Warfare and the Use of Submarines

Considering that the naval race between Britain and Germany had been an underlying cause of the war, it was ironic that there were few traditional ship-to-ship battles in World War I. Britain's Royal Navy imposed a blockade on Germany and Austria, causing the starvation of thousands. In response, Germany deployed its most effective naval weapon: the **submarine** (or **U-boat**), which enabled the German navy to do tremendous economic damage to Britain. However, submarine warfare carried with it the danger of destroying neutral ships or killing civilians from neutral countries, so it was diplomatically risky. Over time, Germany's success with submarine warfare would backfire, bringing the United States into the war in 1917.

The Global Dimensions of World War I

The war also took on a global dimension. The war had begun largely because of empire, and its effects spread to Europe's colonies. Britain's imperial dominions, including Canada, Australia, New Zealand, and South Africa, declared war on the Central Powers and took an active part in European and Middle Eastern combat.

France and Britain mobilized native troops in Africa. Although most played a support role, performing construction and garrison duties, some saw combat in Africa against German colonial troops. The French also brought African troops to the Western Front (in a classic instance of prejudice, the Germans feared these soldiers as cannibals). More than 2.5 million Africans (almost 2 percent of the total population) were involved in the war effort in some way. Britain mobilized Indian sepoys, Sikhs, and Nepalese Gurkhas for combat in the Middle East.

The fighting spread beyond Europe. There were clashes in Africa. Japan joined the Allied war effort, then took over Germany's island colonies in the Pacific. Australia seized German New Guinea. The most important non-European theater of war was the Middle East. In 1915, the British, using Australian and New Zealander troops, tried to knock Ottoman Turkey out of the war by landing at Gallipoli, southwest of Istanbul. This campaign proved an utter disaster, resulting in 50 percent casualties.

More successful was the effort of T. E. Lawrence, better known as Lawrence of Arabia, who persuaded Arab princes to rise up against their Ottoman masters. By 1917 and 1918, the British, with their Arab allies, dismantled what was left of the Ottomans' Middle Eastern empire. Before that, however, in 1915, the Ottomans carried out the **Armenian genocide**, using the excuse of potential pro-Russian disloyalty to massacre somewhere between 500,000 to 2 million victims.

The War's Last Stages: 1917 and 1918

The year 1917 was a crucial turning point in several ways. The original European combatants were exhausted by the fighting. Frustrated by the stalemate and its ability to win surface battles at sea, the German navy turned to unrestricted submarine warfare, hoping to starve Britain out of the war. Economically, the U-boat campaign worked: by the spring of 1917, Britain was reduced to a six-week food supply. Diplomatically, however, submarine warfare was a disaster, as it provoked the United States to declare war in April.

On the other hand, Russia was collapsing. The tsarist regime fell in March, and although the new government attempted to continue the war effort, the Russian army was in full retreat and suffering mass desertions. When Vladimir Lenin and the Bolsheviks staged their Communist revolution in October–November 1917, they took immediate steps to pull Russia out of the war. Germany was now free to send large numbers of troops to the Western Front, where the balance of force was already razor-thin.

The last year of World War I—late 1917 to late 1918—was a great military race. The Allies' goal was to get American soldiers across the Atlantic (with German U-boats sinking troop ships) and ready for combat. The German goal was to transfer soldiers from the Eastern Front to the west and use them to knock the weary French and British out of the war before the Americans arrived in large numbers. Whichever side accomplished its goal first would win, and it was not clear until the summer of 1918 who would prevail.

Realizing that time was against them, the Germans launched a massive offensive against Paris in the spring of 1918. As in 1914, this attack was halted by a determined stand at the Marne River. During the summer, American, Canadian, British, and French troops pushed the Germans back. By the fall, the Germans were in full retreat, and strikes and mutinies convinced the Austrian and German governments to surrender. World War I ended on November 11, 1918.

THE HOME FRONT

World War I was a **total war**, requiring nations to involve their populations and mobilize their resources completely in order to carry on the fight. The last such war in the Western world had been the U.S. Civil War (1861–1865). Europe itself had not experienced such a conflict since the days of Napoleon. Against their expectations, the nations of Europe—and, to a lesser extent, the United States—found that World War I affected their civilian populations deeply and directly. The **home front** became a crucial part of every combatant's war effort.

Conscription

The war required mass **conscription**. Already before the war, most European powers had armies of 1 to 2 million men, larger than ever before in history, but those numbers did not suffice. Even in Britain, which had a long tradition of maintaining an all-volunteer army, substantial conscription was called for. Eventually, the belligerent nations of World War I drafted more than 70 million men. Small numbers of women volunteered to serve in Anglo-American forces but did not take active part in combat. Many women served on the front as nurses.

Economic Mobilization and Rationing

Entire economies had to be geared for war. Industrial wartime production required enormous amounts of raw material: iron, steel, petroleum, rubber, cloth, and more. The need for uniforms, weapons, tanks, aircraft, ships, and other wartime necessities was immense. Agricultural production had to be stepped up in order to feed armies and civilians. With so many able-bodied men gone to fight, the strain put on civilians—especially women—to keep national economies functioning was incredible. All major combatants centralized their economies, placing even private enterprise at least somewhat under state control. Food, strategic materials, and consumer goods were rationed, and the **rationing** grew stricter as time passed.

By late 1916 and early 1917, all European nations were suffering terrible shortages. Britain's food supply was almost depleted by Germany's campaign of unrestricted submarine warfare. Germany and Austria experienced the so-called turnip winter in 1916–1917. Russia, cut off from outside help and supplies by Germany and the Ottoman Empire, was so lacking in food and equipment that, by the end of 1916, its soldiers were sent to the front barefoot and unarmed. They were told to scavenge boots and rifles from soldiers who had died in battle.

Restrictions on Civil Liberties

Another domestic effect was the **restriction of civil liberties**, even in democracies such as Britain, France, and America. All countries imposed censorship on the press, the mass media, and the mail. Those suspected of espionage or treason could be arrested, tried, and sentenced without due process. In most countries, political parties agreed to unite behind the war effort and refrain from criticizing the government. Socialist parties and trade unions were supervised and their activities curtailed. Even pessimism or an insufficient display of patriotism could bring a person under suspicion; men who attempted to gain conscientious objector status were often denied, and even if they succeeded, they were harassed or ridiculed. German-speaking immigrants in Allied nations sometimes suffered persecution.

Women and the War Effort

Perhaps the most striking effect on the home front involved the **role of women**. With so many men serving in the armed forces, farms, factories, and workplaces were left understaffed, just as wartime economic pressures required greater production. In all major countries, women stepped up to take the place of men in the

workplace, serving as truck drivers, farmhands, factory workers, and munitions workers.

The economic contribution of women to their countries' war efforts was considerable. In Britain, over 1.35 million women who had never worked before took jobs. In the factories of Germany's most important arms producer, Krupp, women made up 38 percent of the workforce. Even France, highly resistant to the notion of giving women equal rights, granted a minimum wage to female textile workers producing uniforms.

NOTE

Once the war was over, many of the jobs that had gone to women were given back to the men who returned.

THE PARIS PEACE CONFERENCE

After the war, peace terms were decided at the **Paris Peace Conference**, which lasted from 1919 to 1920. All decisions were made by the leaders of the victorious Allied nations. Delegates from the defeated Central Powers were excluded. The major players were Woodrow Wilson of the United States, David Lloyd George of Britain, Georges Clemenceau of France, and Vittorio Orlando of Italy. The Allies drew up five treaties, one for each defeated power: Germany, Austria, Hungary, Bulgaria, and the Ottoman Empire. The most important was the **Treaty of Versailles**, the agreement reached with Germany and signed on June 28, 1919.

Diplomatic Disagreements Among the Allied Leaders

The Conference was characterized by a clash between American idealism and the European Allies' thirst for revenge. In his words, Wilson's desire was "to make the world safe for democracy" and prevent war in the future. These goals were reflected in his **Fourteen Points**, which called for freedom of the seas, an end to secret treaties, free trade, arms reduction, **decolonization**, the rearrangement of European borders according to the "self-determination" of national groups, and the establishment of an international dispute-resolution body called the **League of Nations**.

By contrast, Lloyd George and Clemenceau focused on making Germany pay for the war and keeping it weak in the future. Italy wanted the Austrian land and German colonies it had been promised by Britain and France.

NOTE

All the European victors were opposed to Wilson's goal of decolonization.

The Terms of the Treaties

The treaties that resulted were the product of bitter negotiation and compromise. As Wilson wished, the League of Nations was formed. Ironically, since the U.S. Congress did not ratify the Treaty of Versailles, America never joined the League, a fact that weakened it from the start. Many of the other Fourteen Points were discarded or watered down. Taken together, the main points laid out in the five treaties included

- *Dismantling of Austria-Hungary.* The Habsburg Empire was destroyed. Austria and Hungary became two separate states, and each lost territory.
- *New nations.* Out of Habsburg territory, and out of lands lost by Germany and Russia, new countries were created, including Yugoslavia, Czechoslovakia, Poland, Finland, Latvia, Lithuania, and Estonia. This was done in accordance with Wilson's principle of **self-determination**.

- *Italy and Austria*: Italy received some of the Austrian territory it was promised, but not all.
- *Population transfer in the Balkans*: Thousands of Turks living in southeastern Europe were expelled and sent to the Ottoman Empire. Likewise, large numbers of Greeks living in the Ottoman Empire were forced to move to Greece.
- *The Middle East*: The Ottoman Empire was stripped of its Middle Eastern possessions, especially the Arab lands. These were placed under temporary French and British control, according to a **mandate system** (the League of Nations would help supervise these areas, which were to be prepared for eventual independence). This stipulation disappointed the Arabs, who had expected freedom in exchange for their military assistance against the Ottomans. Britain also assumed control over Palestine. In the **Balfour Declaration** of 1917, Britain agreed in principle to the creation of a Jewish homeland in Palestine, but delayed on this question, to avoid antagonizing Arabs throughout the Middle East.

Germany and the Treaty of Versailles

The most important provisions pertained to Germany. The Treaty of Versailles imposed the following terms:

NOTE

Article 231 was used to justify the heavy punishments that the Treaty of Versailles imposed on Germany.

- *War guilt*: Article 231, the **war-guilt clause**, laid chief blame for World War I on Germany (although Germany deserved a good part of the blame, other nations, such as Austria, did much to start it as well).
- *Loss of territory*: Germany lost approximately 13 percent of its territory. The provinces of Alsace and Lorraine went to France, and other lands went to Denmark, Belgium, and Poland. France and Belgium occupied the resource-rich Saar until 1935. The Rhineland, the borderland between France and Germany, was to be occupied till 1935 and maintained as a demilitarized zone in perpetuity.
- *Loss of colonies*: Germany's colonies were placed under Allied trusteeship. Only Wilson prevented France and Britain from colonizing them outright.
- *Disarmament*: France and Britain feared a resurgent Germany and disarmed it. The army was allowed a token force of 100,000 soldiers. It was not permitted any military aircraft, submarines, battleships, or heavy artillery.
- *War payments*: Against Wilson's wishes, France and Britain insisted that Germany pay the full cost of the war, calculated to be $32 billion. According to the initial repayment schedule (which was changed several times), Germany was to make war payments until 1961.

The Paris Peace Conference is considered to have produced a flawed peace. Greed and revenge determined many of the terms. Ignorance, especially regarding Eastern Europe and the Balkans, where new regimes tended to be unstable and weak, played a large role in redrawing the world map. Justified or not, the harsh treatment of Germany made the peace unacceptable to most Germans and would be a significant factor in the rise of Hitler and the beginning of World War II. (On the other hand, it cannot be said that the Treaty of Versailles *directly* caused either of these events.)

LONG-TERM CONSEQUENCES

The grim immediate consequences of World War I were obvious: 10 million soldiers killed, somewhere between 3 to 5 million civilians killed, and 28 to 30 million people wounded. Financially, the cost was assessed at $32 billion. Countless people, particularly in eastern Europe, where borders shifted constantly, were made homeless or stateless. As a final injury, a global epidemic of **Spanish flu** struck during the closing months of World War I, killing 20 million people (perhaps more) worldwide.

Long-term consequences were as follows:

- *Destruction of Eastern and Central European empires*: The German, Austro-Hungarian, Russian, and Ottoman empires all fell.
- *Instability in Eastern Europe*: The new nations of Eastern Europe were inexperienced and weak. Nationalist tensions within them ran high. During the 1920s and 1930s, only Czechoslovakia would prosper and remain democratic. The others experienced economic difficulties, became politically authoritarian, and suffered from ethnic strife.
- *Social and political transformation*: World War I did not cause this trend, but helped to accelerate it. Even before the war, the political power and socioeconomic influence of the traditional aristocracy had been vanishing, while that of the middle and lower classes had been rising. In almost all countries of Europe—and elsewhere—World War I did much to complete this transformation.
- *Further industrialization and modernization of Western economies*: War mobilization spurred further industrialization in Europe and North America.
- *Women's suffrage*: Thanks largely to the economic role they played during the war, women gained greater respect not just in the workplace but the public sphere overall. The most important result was **women's suffrage** in most Western nations, during or just after World War I. Scandinavia, the Low Countries, Russia, Britain, Canada, the United States, and others gave women the vote. France and Italy were alone among the major Western powers in resisting this trend; not until the 1940s did women there get the vote.
- *German resentment*: Almost all Germans regarded the Treaty of Versailles as unfair. Many saw it as illegitimate. Anger about the war payments was universal. Years later, this attitude played an important role in the rise of Hitler and the outbreak of World War II.
- *General decline in European economic and global power*: Although the nations of Europe still maintained the appearance of great powers, they had been badly drained. Even the victors' economies were in sad shape, and those of the losers were in shambles. France, Britain, Belgium, Portugal, and the Netherlands still

DISEASE AND WORLD HISTORY

From humanity's earliest days, disease has played an enormous role in how societies interact with each other. Pandemics in the form of bubonic plague (which swept from China to Europe in the 1300s and plagued Eurasia for centuries) devastated numerous societies. The demographic impact of the spread of smallpox and measles to the Americas by European explorers and conquerors in the 1400s and 1500s was nightmarish. Rampant urbanization and overcrowding in the 1700s and 1800s caused massive outbreaks in cholera and tuberculosis. Until the mid-1800s, illnesses like malaria and sleeping sickness prevented European imperial powers from penetrating too deeply into the interiors of Southeast Asia and especially Africa. The modern age has brought with it a better understanding of disease, but it has also given rise to much greater global mobility, a factor that makes the widespread outbreak of epidemics and pandemics faster and more likely than before. The Spanish influenza after World War I, the emergence of AIDS (acquired immune deficiency syndrome), and the recent appearance of SARS (severe acute respiratory syndrome) and avian flu are good examples.

possessed their overseas empires, but maintaining control over them would become increasingly difficult during the 1920s and 1930s and even more so after World War II.

- *Sense of uncertainty and anxiety in European culture.* Even before World War I, the prevailing faith in progress that had characterized Europe's cultural life during most of the 1800s had been waning (see Chapter 21). Despair caused by the war, plus the gloom surrounding Europe's political and economic comedown, brought this sense of uncertainty and anxiety to the forefront of European culture.

The Twenty Years' Crisis: The World During the Interwar Period

- The League of Nations
- Democratic weakness in Europe and U.S. isolationism
- The Great Depression and its global impact
- Totalitarianism
- Soviet communism (Vladimir Lenin and Joseph Stalin)
- Italian fascism (Benito Mussolini)
- Nazi Germany (Adolf Hitler) and anti-Semitic policy
- State capitalism (syndicalism)
- Modernization from above in Turkey and Persia
- Oil in the Middle East
- Nationalists vs. Communists in China (Chiang Kai-shek versus Mao Zedong)
- Japanese militarism, war in China, and the Rape of Nanjing
- The Indian National Congress and *satyagraha*
- Latin America, U.S. influence, and dictatorship

Many historians have argued that World War I and World War II were simply two halves of the same conflict, separated by twenty years of temporary peace. Whatever the truth of that observation, it is undeniable that the peace of the 1920s and 1930s rested on a shaky foundation.

This was certainly the case in Europe, where many of the problems stirred up by World War I were not solved by the treaty settlements that followed. Also, the social, economic, and political forces unleashed by twentieth-century modernization were too strong to handle for many governments, especially those that had been damaged badly by the war or newly created by the Paris Peace Conference. Another factor that affected the fortunes of interwar Europe was the **Great Depression**. Starting in the United States in October 1929, the Depression began to affect the economies of Europe (and elsewhere) by 1930 and 1931. It damaged beyond repair many economies that had already been struggling during the 1920s. As a result, dictatorship, often in its most extreme form, **totalitarianism**, became the rule, not the exception, in European politics during the 1930s.

Elsewhere in the world, powerful political developments were underway. Revolution, modernization, and industrialization caught up with many countries that had not experienced those trends during the 1800s. European possessions in

Africa, Asia, and the Middle East began to agitate more actively for **decolonization** and **national liberation**. Nationalism, dictatorship, and militarism became part of political life in much of the non-Western world.

Finally, by the mid-to-late 1930s, the storm clouds of war gathered. Japanese aggression in Asia, along with German and Italian belligerence in Europe and elsewhere (see Chapter 31), made it more likely with every passing year that a major conflict would break out. The failure of the Western democracies to prevent such a conflict demonstrates the weakness of the interwar peace.

POLITICAL EXTREMISM AND ECONOMIC DEPRESSION IN EUROPE

Fragile Peace and the Crisis of Democracy

During the 1920s, peace prevailed in Europe, but it was fragile. Also, at the beginning of the decade, it was incomplete. From 1919 through 1922, there were revolutions, civil wars, and military clashes in Germany, Russia, Poland, Hungary, and the Balkans. Even afterward, peace was preserved mainly by the fact that European nations were too exhausted to fight. The new **League of Nations** provided what little political leadership there was. It was well-meaning and accomplished a great deal of humanitarian work, but it was largely ineffective. It had few powers of enforcement. Also, the United States, now the world's strongest and richest country, refused to join.

Despite treaties during the 1920s intended to outlaw war (such as the Treaty of Locarno and the Kellogg–Briand Pact), there was little political will on the part of liberal democracies to ensure long-term peace. During the 1920s, the absence of any real threat created an illusion that permanent peace had been achieved. That illusion would be shattered during the 1930s.

European democracy did not flourish during the 1920s or 1930s. In 1920, there were twenty-three governments in Europe that could be considered democratic. By 1939, there were only twelve. Most of the new states of Central and Eastern Europe fell victim to political extremism, especially during the 1930s, when inflation and, especially, mass unemployment caused by the Great Depression made it difficult to maintain a healthy form of government. Right-wing dictatorship, as well as ethnic discrimination and class tensions, plagued this part of Europe during these years. As described below, the most famous of these dictatorships emerged in Italy and Germany.

Even in stronger and better-established democracies such as France and Great Britain, times were troubled. During the comparatively easier 1920s, both economies, especially Britain's, were sluggish as a result of World War I's draining effect. Both had borrowed a great deal of money from the United States, and each relied on German war reparations to keep up its own payments. Unemployment, strikes, and deficits became the norm in France during the early 1920s and in Britain during the entire decade.

The 1930s were even worse because of the Depression. By 1932, one British worker in four was out of work. France was not as badly hurt as Britain, but it went through hard times. Particularly during the 1930s, both democracies suffered from

a lack of firm political leadership. In Britain, a shaky coalition, the National Government ran Parliament with caution and compromise. Some relief came with the creation of a **modern welfare state**, as social security, pensions, unemployment insurance, and so on, were put into place. In France, elections were frequent, and leadership passed from left to right and back again on a regular basis. During the 1930s, economic weakness and political mediocrity made it difficult for France and Britain to cope with the growing threat of Hitler's Germany.

Communism in the Soviet Union

The general crisis of democracy in interwar Europe meant that the most dynamic regimes tended to be the dictatorships, which grew in number and power during the 1920s and especially the 1930s. The first of the new dictatorships was the Union of Soviet Socialist Republics (USSR), or the Soviet Union, the communist regime that rose to power during World War I, in October–November 1917.

When the tsarist regime of Nicholas II fell in February–March 1917, its place was taken briefly by a moderate Provisional Government that attempted to continue the war against Germany, solve Russia's dismal economic problems, and establish a democratic government. In that its first stage was relatively liberal, the Russian Revolution resembled the French Revolution of 1789.

However, the Provisional Government did not satisfy the desire of the vast majority of the Russian population (80–85 percent of whom were peasants) for economic stability, land reform, and peace. The party that benefited most from popular discontent were the Communists, or Bolsheviks, led by **Vladimir Lenin** and his second-in-command, Leon Trotsky.

In the fall of 1917, Lenin and Trotsky overthrew the Provisional Government. From then until 1921, they pulled out of World War I, formed the Soviet government, and fought and won the terrible Russian Civil War (which pitted the Bolshevik Red Army against their anticommunist enemies, called Whites). From 1921 till his death in 1924, Lenin tightened his grip on power and attempted to modernize the Soviet Union along Marxist lines. One of his major challenges was that, while Marx had predicted that communist revolution would first take place in a mature capitalist society with a large industrial working class, Russia was a backward, barely capitalist nation with a huge peasantry and an extremely small working class. A compromise in 1921, Lenin's New Economic Plan (NEP) took a more gradual approach to socialist development, allowing for limited private trade. It lasted until 1927–1928.

Lenin died in 1924. A half-decade succession struggle followed, during which **Joseph Stalin** defeated Trotsky for control over the Soviet government. Stalin became one of the most oppressive dictators of all time. Overturning the NEP, Stalin rapidly modernized the USSR, starting in 1928. His **Five-Year Plans** were intended to transform the Soviet Union from an agricultural society into a modern industrial state. The **collectivization of agriculture**—the placement of all peasants on state-run farms—was meant to rationalize farming, increase governmental control over the countryside, and harness the labor of the peasants (profits generated by agriculture were used to pay for the Five-Year Plans).

Although the USSR modernized under Stalin, the price was steep. The Five-Year Plans amounted to a state-sponsored industrial revolution, with the same social and economic trauma, but applied with ruthlessness and police brutality. Collectivization resulted in a **Great Famine** in southern Russia, Ukraine, and Kazakhstan that killed approximately 4 million to 6 million people. Later in the 1930s, Stalin carried out a huge campaign of terror, the **Purges**, which resulted in the execution of approximately a million people and the arrest and exile to labor camps (**gulags**) of at least 5 to 7 million. Like most modern dictators, Stalin used propaganda to indoctrinate his subjects and instituted an extravagant cult of personality to glorify himself. The Stalinist experience is an extreme example of rapid modernization, directed from above by dictatorial leadership. In Stalin's case, this approach brought the country far more torment then benefit.

Fascism in Italy

In Italy, dictatorship came from the right. After World War I, Italy was rocked by economic depression and political turmoil. Strikes, communist agitation, and constant governmental turnover brought the country to the edge of chaos. The middle and upper classes, frightened of social breakdown and left-wing revolution, looked for a strong leader to restore stability. They turned to **Benito Mussolini**, the right-wing, anticommunist leader of the Fascist Party.

Fascism, Mussolini's invention, is a difficult political concept to define. It can best be described as right-wing radicalism or revolution from the right, unlike ordinary right-wing conservatism, which seeks to prevent change. Fascism seeks to bring about change. It is anticommunist but also anticapitalist and antidemocratic. Fascism is also often characterized by hypernationalism and a state-sponsored campaign of racial and ethnic bigotry.

In October 1922, Mussolini was placed in charge of the government by the king, who feared the communists. For the next twenty-one years, governing Italy, he became increasingly dictatorial. He coined a new term to describe his style of rule: **totalitarianism**, a twentieth-century form of dictatorship in which the regime, using modern technology and bureaucracy, attempts to control every aspect of its subjects' lives. Compared with other totalitarian rulers, such as Stalin and Hitler, Mussolini was actually mild. Still, he imposed censorship over culture, imprisoned (and sometimes killed) political enemies and dissidents, and used propaganda to create a cult of personality.

On the other hand, Mussolini modernized Italy. He built new highways, sponsored literacy campaigns, fought the Mafia, and brought medicine and technology to backward parts of his country. His chief claim to fame was to have made Italy's notoriously inefficient trains run on time. His economic policy was based on the principle of syndicalism (a form of **corporatism** or **state capitalism**, common in right-wing dictatorships). In fascist economies, corporate leaders, rather than practicing free trade, are required to cooperate directly with the government, and labor unions are suppressed. During the 1920s, Mussolini was considered by many to be an effective, even admirable, leader despite his dictatorial tendencies. During the 1930s, however, the Depression undercut his modernizing efforts. He became more dictatorial and,

in foreign policy, more aggressive (see Chapter 31). Also during the 1930s, Mussolini drew closer to the newer fascist regime of Nazi Germany.

Nazism in Germany

Germany's road to dictatorship was longer than Italy's, and the results were infinitely worse. From 1919 to 1933, Germany was governed by a democratic regime, the **Weimar Republic,** which was dogged by economic trouble (hyperinflation during the early 1920s wiped out the value of the German mark), the burden of war payments, widespread resentment of the Treaty of Versailles (which the Weimar regime had been forced to sign), and the rise of extremist political parties.

From the left, the German Communist Party became a powerful threat. From the right appeared **Adolf Hitler** and the **Nazi Party**: an anticommunist, antidemocratic group that, after Mussolini's rise to power in Italy, consciously imitated fascism in many ways. The Nazi Party, also obsessed with the notion of racial purity, hated all minorities, but especially Jews, whom the Nazis viewed as "subhuman" and the source of all of Germany's troubles. In 1923, Hitler and the Nazis made a failed attempt to take over the German government. During the short time he spent in prison, Hitler wrote his infamous memoir, *Mein Kampf* (*My Struggle*).

By the late 1920s, the Weimar Republic appeared to have established a reasonably solid democracy. The Depression, however, ended the calm. Its effects reached Germany in 1930. The economic pain, destroying the Weimar Republic's ability to govern democratically, boosted Germany's extremist parties, the Communists and the Nazis. A series of elections in 1932 made the Nazi Party the largest in Germany. In January 1933, Hitler was appointed chancellor of Germany.

Having risen to power by legal means, Hitler established himself as an absolute dictator within months. In February 1933, the Reichstag building, seat of the German government, was burned down. Hitler took advantage of the resulting panic to declare a state of emergency and pass the Enabling Act (March 1933), which suspended the Weimar constitution and gave Hitler the power to rule by decree for four years (a limit Hitler had no intention of obeying).

With blinding speed, Hitler outlawed all other political parties (especially his archenemies, the Communists), took control of the press and mass media, banned labor unions, imposed a system of state capitalism similar to Mussolini's, built **concentration camps**, such as Dachau, for political opponents and dissidents, and established a secret police, the Gestapo. He managed to end German unemployment by means of a giant program of public works and highway building, as well as a massive increase in arms production.

The Nazi regime also instituted **anti-Semitic policies** (it targeted other racial "undesirables" as well). Jews were forced out of various professions (such as law, civil service, and university teaching), their businesses were boycotted, and they were physically harassed. Before World War II, the most drastic official measures taken against the Jews were the **Nuremberg Laws** of 1935. These laws stripped German Jews of their citizenship and forbade Jews and German non-Jews to marry or have sexual relations of any kind.

TIP

By 1932, 6 million Germans—almost 40 percent of the workforce—were unemployed.

In terms of foreign policy, Hitler pursued a highly aggressive diplomatic line. As described in Chapter 31, Hitler's belligerence was the principal reason that the fragile peace of the 1920s began to shatter in the 1930s.

NATIONALISM AND MODERNIZATION IN THE MIDDLE EAST

Even before World War I, the Middle East had been on the threshold of great change. Modernization was coming gradually to the Ottoman Empire. In those parts of the Middle East controlled by outside powers, the force of nationalism was rising. By toppling the Ottoman Empire, World War I brought even greater changes to the region.

The Birth of Modern Turkey

The transformation of the Ottoman Empire into the modern Turkish state had its roots in the efforts of the **Young Turks**, who had seized power in 1908 (see Chapter 24). These pro-Western, modernizing officers and politicians had already started to carry out reform before World War I. During the war, the Turks joined the Central Powers and shared defeat with them. The Ottoman Empire suffered more than 300,000 casualties and saw their Middle Eastern possessions rise up in revolt. It surrendered in October 1918.

After the war, the Turks lost most of their Middle Eastern territories to France and Britain. Greece, with Allied permission, was threatening to seize Turkey's western provinces. In the midst of this crisis, a new leader emerged: **Mustafa Kemal**, a colonel who had fought bravely against the British landing at Gallipoli in 1915. Kemal formed a new government in the city of Ankara, drove the Greeks from the Turkish mainland, and negotiated a new treaty with the Allies. In 1923, the last sultan fled the country, and the Ottoman Empire was no more. In its place, Kemal established the Turkish Republic, becoming its first president. He took the title **Ataturk**, meaning "father of the Turks."

From 1923 till his death in 1938, Ataturk labored to create a modern, secular state in Turkey. He wrote a constitution and, despite the fact that he was quite authoritarian, made the pretense of acting like a democratic ruler. Industrialization, Western dress, and Western education were encouraged. Turkish was written in the Roman alphabet. Church and state were separated, and Islamic law (Sharia) was replaced by a European law code. Women were no longer required to wear the veil. They received the right to vote in 1934, and they were encouraged to become educated and join the workforce.

Persian Independence and Modernization

Persia went through a change similar to that of Turkey, becoming the modern state of Iran. From 1794 to 1925, Persia was ruled by the Qajar dynasty. In reality, however, the country had been divided into two spheres of influence: Russian in the north, British in the south. After World War I, the British presence in Persia increased, largely because of the oil reserves there. Resentment of foreign domination

TIP

To this day, Turkey's status as the most Westernized and most secular state in the Middle East, next to Israel, is a direct legacy of Ataturk's policies.

grew steadily, and a nationalist backlash was inevitable. In 1921, an officer named Reza Khan mutinied against the Qajar rulers and expelled the British. By 1925, he had gained control of the country. He called himself **Reza Shah Pahlavi** and established a new royal dynasty. Like Ataturk in Turkey, Reza reformed his country, which he renamed Iran. Although he was not as much a foe of the Islamic clergy as Ataturk was, he Westernized Iran, boosted education, did away with the veil for women, and, in general, secularized the nation. Like Ataturk, he tended toward authoritarianism.

Egypt, North Africa, and Arabia

The political fate of the rest of the Middle East was mixed. Egypt and North Africa remained in British, French, and Italian hands, although nationalist sentiment there was growing. For the time being, the Arabian Peninsula remained under Turkish control. The other Arab states formerly under Ottoman rulership were now placed under French and British control and divided into **mandates**, to be supervised partially by the League of Nations. Syria and Lebanon were assigned to France, while Iraq, Jordan, and Palestine fell to Britain.

This arrangement angered most Arabs, who had thought that, by helping the British fight the Turks, they would gain full independence. Another thing enraging the Arabs was the **Balfour Declaration** of 1917, which publicly stated the British government's intention to create a Jewish homeland in Palestine—whose population, in the late 1910s, was 90 percent Arab.

Change came to all these areas during the 1920s and 1930s. Despite the fact that the British allowed only limited Jewish emigration to Palestine to keep from provoking the Arabs, thousands of Jews flooded into the region, many of them illegally. By 1939, the Jewish proportion of the population had risen from 10 to 30 percent.

In the early 1920s, an Arab prince named **Ibn Saud** drove the Ottomans out of the Arabian Peninsula and then united Arabia's many tribes. In 1932, he founded the kingdom of Saudi Arabia. As the only major Arab state to enjoy full independence, Saudi Arabia was important in and of itself. After 1938, it became even more important, with the discovery of huge oil reserves. Overnight, Saudi Arabia became wealthy and strategically vital.

MILITARISM AND REVOLUTION IN ASIA

The Chinese Republic

In 1911, revolution in China had overthrown the Qing imperial dynasty. Taking its place was the Chinese Republic, governed by the **Nationalist Party (Kuomintang)**. **Sun Yat-sen**, often regarded as the father of modern China, was president.

Quickly, however, the republic disintegrated. In 1912, Sun was forced to give up the presidency to General Yuan Shikai, in order to gain the support of the armed forces. In the face of Yuan's growing traditionalism and dictatorialism, Sun and the Kuomintang found themselves in opposition to the government. In 1913, Yuan disbanded the parliament. In response, the Kuomintang began a revolution. It failed, and Sun fled to Japan. Yuan ruled until his death in 1916. Military officers continued to govern in Beijing until the early 1920s.

The rest of China slipped into anarchy. Warlords and bandits took control of vast stretches of the country. In 1920, Sun and the Nationalists returned to the mainland, establishing a base at Canton and throughout southern China. The **Chinese Communist Party** (CCP), founded by radicals at Beijing University in 1921, became a major force. A deadly external threat came from Japan, whose imperial ambitions grew during and after World War I. Japan already controlled Korea and had a sphere of influence in southern Manchuria. Because it had aided the Allies in World War I, Japan also had their blessing to expand that sphere after the war.

Political control was not the only issue over which Chinese parties struggled. During these years, there was a great clash between traditional values and the desire for modernization. The military government in Beijing attempted to revive Confucian principles, while younger students and intellectuals embraced progressive concepts such as democracy, technology, and science. The clearest example of popular activism came on May 4, 1919, when thousands of students came to **Tiananmen Square** in Beijing to protest against the military government. The immediate cause of the May Fourth Movement was the government's willingness to allow Japan to annex Shantung Province. Underlying that specific issue, however, was the desire for political and social reform. As for China's other major political actors, the CCP was progressive in its outlook, while the Kuomintang was torn between the past and the future.

The Chinese Civil War: Nationalists Versus Communists

By the mid-1920s, the main political forces in China were the Nationalists and Communists. From 1923 to early 1927, both parties cooperated to drive warlords and foreign powers out of China. Sun Yat-sen died of cancer, leaving the leadership of the Kuomintang to **Chiang Kai-shek**, a Western-educated officer who leaned farther to the right than Sun had. By early 1927, the Nationalist-Communist alliance had gained control of all China south of the Yangtze River, including the major cities of Shanghai and Nanjing.

TIP

Mao's central strategy was to make communism appealing to China's vast peasant masses, rather than concentrate on the small industrial working class in the cities.

In April, Chiang turned against the Communists, murdering thousands of them in Shanghai. Most of the rest of the party was driven far to the north, under the revolutionary **Mao Tse-tung (Mao Zedong)**. Chiang took Beijing in 1928 and founded a Kuomintang regime that combined Westernization with mild authoritarianism. Chiang proclaimed his allegiance to Sun's principles and made some attempts to create a constitutional government and an industrial economy. However, corruption, backwardness, the threat of Japanese imperialism, and warlord anarchy hampered his efforts.

Full-scale civil war against the Communists would soon resume. Against incredible odds, Mao Tse-tung kept the CCP alive, leading it on the Long March (1934–1935), far to the north. At Yenan, the Communists established a base from which to launch military operations against the Nationalists.

Starting in 1931, Japan seized all of Manchuria from China. In 1937, Japanese forces attacked China itself, starting a three-way conflict among the Nationalists, Mao's Communists, and the invading Japanese.

Japan During the 1920s

In the early 1900s, Japan evolved in some ways toward a democratic parliamentary monarchy. The powers of the Diet increased, and a bill of rights guaranteeing universal male suffrage and other civil liberties was granted in 1925. Freedom of the press expanded. The emperor, Taisho, supported democratic reform. The economy continued to industrialize and modernize.

On the other hand, traditional forces remained in place. The upper class retained its oligarchical outlook. Most of Japan's industrial might was concentrated in the hands of a small number of corporate conglomerates called *zaibatsu*. The effect of this system was to keep wealth in the hands of a tiny number of rich and powerful industrialists and capitalists. Also, because the *zaibatsu* enjoyed such a close relationship with the government, economic policy was largely under state influence, in a way not unlike the system of state capitalism practiced in Fascist Italy and Nazi Germany. There was little economic liberalization to match political democratization; trade unions remained weak, working conditions remained dreadful, and strikes and riots were common. Even before the Depression, social stress was building to a dangerous level. Japan's new emperor, Hirohito, who took the throne in 1926, was easily influenced and poorly equipped to cope with the growing crisis.

Japanese Militarism and the Invasion of Mainland Asia

Imperial aggression and the effects of the Great Depression derailed Japanese democratization during the 1930s. Japan's exports plummeted more than 50 percent. Farmers and workers were badly hurt. Nationalism, bolstered by state Shintoism (a bigoted and politicized perversion of Japan's indigenous faith), skyrocketed, and anti-Western feelings sharpened. The slogan "Asia for the Asians" called for the expulsion of colonizing powers such as Britain and France.

In September 1931, Japan took Manchuria from China, turning it into a puppet kingdom, Manchukuo. Shortly afterward, Japan withdrew from the League of Nations. At home, two prime ministers were assassinated, one in 1930 by left-wing extremists, the other in 1932 by radical rightists. By 1941, the Japanese military, under Hideki Tojo, had gained control of the parliamentary government and dominated Emperor Hirohito.

In July 1937, the Japanese invaded China, committing dreadful atrocities against the civilian population. The **Rape of Nanjing** in December climaxed with the massacre of 200,000 to 300,000 noncombatants, including women and children. Japan's war against China continued throughout the 1930s and World War II. In 1938 and 1939, the Japanese clashed with the Soviets on the Siberian borderland but were turned back. The war then spread to Southeast Asia, as Japan took over French and British colonies and established its own empire, which it referred to as the **Greater East Asian Co-Prosperity Sphere**.

Nationalist Movements in South and Southeast Asia

In South and Southeast Asia, most of which remained under British and French colonial rule, nationalism became widespread. In Vietnam, Burma, Indonesia, and elsewhere, anticolonial agitation escalated. Typically, such efforts involved an uneasy

alliance of Western-educated, middle-class modernizers with intellectuals and students inspired by the communist ideals of Marx and Lenin. It was similar to the temporary joining of the Nationalists and Communists in China—and, as in China, these alliances typically broke apart.

Gandhi, Nehru, and the Indian National Congress

The most successful freedom movement appeared in British-controlled India. The moving force here was the **Indian National Congress** (later the Congress Party), founded in 1885. After World War I, the movement's dominant figure was **Mohandas K. Gandhi**. Because it had loyally supported Britain in World War I, India hoped it would gain greater autonomy after the war, perhaps even dominion status, as Canada, Australia, and New Zealand had. However, demonstrations and protests, organized largely by Gandhi, led to clashes with the British. In 1919, at Amritsar, British troops fired on unarmed protestors, killing 379 and wounding 1,137. This massacre led to chaos. The British imposed a strict crackdown, and Gandhi went to prison.

For the rest of the 1920s, India balanced on a political knife-edge. The British began to make concessions, such as the Government of India Act (1921), which allowed 5 million Indians to vote and created a new parliament, two-thirds of whose members would be Indian. However, the earlier repression of the British prompted the Congress Party to demand more. India could easily have erupted into bloody revolution. That it did not was due mainly to Gandhi's political and spiritual guidance.

Whether free or in prison, Gandhi—now known increasingly as Mahatma, which means "great soul"—preached the policy of nonviolent resistance. Based partly on Hindu religious principles, this policy was called *satyagraha* ("hold to the truth"). An example of *satyagraha* in action came when the British imposed a high tax on salt. Rather than protest violently, Gandhi led 50,000 people on a 200-mile march to the seashore, where they began to make salt illegally by drying out seawater. When the British arrived, Gandhi allowed himself to be arrested peacefully.

Gandhi was freed in 1931. He continued to work with the Congress Party but as a guiding force rather than as a politician. The political leader, also Gandhi's working partner, was a younger lawyer and intellectual, **Jawaharlal Nehru**. The spiritual, traditional Gandhi and the modern, secular Nehru pressed the British for greater reform. In 1935, the British granted a constitution that was a long step forward on the path to eventual self-rule. In 1937, Gandhi and Nehru began their Quit India campaign, trying to convince the British to leave altogether. The advent of World War II delayed British withdrawal, but India gained its freedom in 1947, soon after the war.

Muhammad Ali Jinnah and the Muslim League

The Congress Party was not the only force pressing for Indian independence. India's Muslims had their own freedom movement. During World War I, Muslims and Hindus had pledged to work together for greater autonomy from the British, but they went their separate ways during the 1920s. In 1930, the **Muslim League**, led by **Muhammad Ali Jinnah**, formed. It paralleled the Congress Party's independence efforts, but its aims were different. The Muslim League called for the creation of a separate Muslim state called Pakistan ("land of the pure"). The failure of the Muslim League and the Congress Party to resolve their differences peacefully led to great

bloodshed when independence was finally achieved in 1947. It also lay the foundation for the bitter Indo-Pakistani rivalry that still persists.

DICTATORSHIP IN LATIN AMERICA

Outside Influences on Latin America

Before World War I, modern nations in Latin America, while politically independent, had been economically dominated by outside influences. British and U.S. investors exercised great control over enterprises in Latin America. Most Latin American nations relied on the export of one or two raw materials or agricultural products. Chile was a source of fertilizer and copper; Peru mined copper as well. Chile and Brazil sold steel. Oil was taken out of Mexico, Bolivia, Argentina, and Peru. Argentina produced wheat and beef. Central America grew bananas and other fruit. As it had for centuries, sugar came from the Caribbean and Brazil. Brazil was the source of 75 percent of the world's coffee supply.

In exchange for foreign capital and industrial know-how, political elites in Latin American countries allowed foreigners much influence over local politics. The great mass of the population did the work and saw very few of the resulting profits.

The U.S. Sphere of Influence in Latin America

World War I increased the U.S. role in Latin America's political and economic life. With their economies weakened by the war, countries such as France and Britain no longer had the funds to invest in Latin America. The United Fruit Company and other U.S. corporations became major forces in Latin America.

Strategically, the United States viewed Latin America as its sphere of influence and had done so since the late 1800s. The United States had gained possessions such as Puerto Rico and the Virgin Islands, as well as a protectorate over Cuba, after the Spanish-American War of 1898. U.S. Marines had occupied Haiti. Just as the British had taken control of the Suez Canal, America established a military presence after constructing the **Panama Canal**. Instability in Mexico convinced the United States to militarize the border. The United States sponsored dictators, such as Vicente Gómez of Venezuela and Fulgencio Batista of Cuba, in order to preserve stability. A sense grew among Latin Americans that the people of the United States—the *yanquis*, or "yankees"—were imperialists.

In the mid-1930s, Franklin Roosevelt attempted to reduce U.S. influence over Latin America. His **Good Neighbor Policy** (1935) was intended to accomplish this goal and thereby improve relations with the region. As a token of goodwill, Roosevelt withdrew U.S. Marines from Haiti. For the first time in three decades, the United States had no troops in Latin America.

The Great Depression's Effects on Latin America

Unfortunately, the United States affected Latin America in yet another way during the 1930s. The effects of the Great Depression on the region were devastating. Since Latin American economies were so dependent on exports to the United States, the inability of the United States to purchase Latin American goods caused tremendous damage. Exports were cut almost in half. As in many parts of Europe, the economic

pain caused by the Depression had a negative effect on politics, inclining Latin American governments toward extremism and dictatorship.

As discussed in Chapter 28, there was a long-standing tradition of authoritarian rule in Latin America. This trend continued into the 1920s and 1930s, when there were few if any genuine democracies in Latin America. The three largest and wealthiest nations—Mexico, Brazil, and Argentina—all became dictatorial, to one degree or another, during these years.

Dictatorship in Mexico, Brazil, and Argentina

The revolution Mexico began in 1910 was declared to have ended in 1920, when military officers took charge of the regime. Violence continued till 1929, when power passed to the National Revolutionary Party, which renamed itself the **Institutional Revolutionary Party** (PRI) in 1946 and ruled until the late 1980s. Governed in theory by the Constitution of 1917—which guaranteed universal suffrage (including for women) and the right to strike—Mexico tended in reality toward oligarchy, in which the PRI chose a president every six years and then arranged an election that guaranteed victory to its candidate.

Under this mild form of authoritarianism, the upper classes prospered and the country modernized. But the middle class was small and narrow, while the large lower classes—workers and peasants—lagged far behind the elite. Things improved under **Lázaro Cárdenas**, who became president in 1934. His land reform, in which 40 million acres were taken from the upper class and distributed among the peasantry, made him popular with the lower classes. He also stood up to the United States by nationalizing the oil industry. Roosevelt lived up to his Good Neighbor promises and refrained from intervention. In exchange, Cárdenas compensated U.S. companies for their losses, then formed PEMEX, Mexico's state-run oil enterprise. He transferred power legally to his successor, Manuel Camacho, in 1940.

Brazil became more genuinely dictatorial. Before 1930, the government was dominated by wealthy landowners, most of whom owed their power and riches to the **coffee trade**. The Depression, however, plunged the country into crisis. In 1930, Getúlio Vargas, a cattle rancher, became president and ruled as dictator until 1945. He governed from the far right, imitating Fascist Italy and Nazi Germany. He censored the press and authorized his secret police to torture political opponents. On the other hand, he modernized the economy, diversifying it and freeing it from its dependence on coffee. Under Vargas, Brazil became Latin America's most industrialized nation. He was forced out of office by his army in 1945.

Argentina became a military dictatorship during the 1930s. In 1916, Hipólito Irigoyen of the Radical Party was elected president. His reform measures were intended to improve the lot of the lower and middle classes, and labor unions became more active. However, landowners and the upper class sabotaged Irigoyen's efforts and, in 1930, supported the army as it ousted him. The military government lasted throughout World War II, but its efforts to return to the old export-based economy failed. Labor unrest increased, and the radical lower classes, the *descamisados* ("shirtless ones"), grew louder and more belligerent. Shortly after World War II, in 1946, General **Juan Perón**, with his charismatic wife, Eva, appealed to the lower classes to come to power, then established his own dictatorship.

World War II and the Holocaust

CHAPTER 31

- World War II (Allies versus the Axis)
- Aggression versus appeasement before the war
- Blitzkrieg warfare and the effects of tanks and aircraft
- The Lend-Lease program
- The Greater East Asian Co-Prosperity Sphere

- Pivotal battles (Midway, El Alamein, Stalingrad, the D-Day landings)
- Submarines and the war at sea
- Strategic bombing and the atomic bomb
- War crimes, crimes against humanity, and genocide
- The Holocaust (Final Solution)
- The Cold War

World War II (1939–1945) was and remains the biggest, costliest, and deadliest armed conflict in human history. Beyond that, its long-term global impact continued to be felt in world politics, economics, and diplomacy for five decades.

Before the war ended, sixty-one nations joined the fighting. They were divided into two coalitions, the **Axis Powers** and the **Allied Powers**. The major combatants were

- The Axis Powers: Nazi Germany, Fascist Italy (joined the war in June 1940; left the war in July 1943), and Japan
- The Allied Powers: Great Britain, France (left the war in June 1940), Canada, Australia, New Zealand, the Soviet Union (joined the war in June 1941), and the United States (joined the war in December 1941).

The war was waged over two-thirds of the entire planet. Economically, it has been calculated to have cost $1.6 trillion in 1940s dollars ($4 trillion to $5 trillion in contemporary terms). By the war's midpoint, somewhere between one-quarter and one-third of the world's productive capacity was directly dedicated to war production.

Concerning the grimmest statistic of all, somewhere between 55 to 60 million people were killed during the war. Almost half of those who died were civilians. World War II involved **genocide** as well. Millions of victims—6 million of them Jewish—perished in the German campaign of racial extermination known as the **Holocaust**.

World War II also shifted the balance of global strength completely. World War I had begun the process of toppling the powers of Europe from their position of dominance; World War II finished it. When World War II was over, only two

nations, the United States and the Soviet Union, had the military and economic might to affect the course of world events. The great geopolitical struggle between these two new superpowers, the **Cold War**, was the dominant factor shaping global diplomacy, military affairs, and international trade for four and a half decades. World War II also destroyed the imperial might of the European powers. From the 1940s through the 1970s, a massive wave of **decolonization** swept through the non-Western world, and dozens of nations in Africa and Asia became free.

In addition, World War II changed the patterns of international trade, shifted global wealth to the superpowers (especially the United States), spurred a boom in technological and scientific innovation that would be put to civilian use long after the war was over, brought women into the workplace, and had countless other social, economic, and cultural effects. For these and many other reasons, World War II can be considered not only the largest military enterprise in world history but also the most influential.

THE ROAD TO WAR

Unlike World War I, whose origins were quite complex, World War II resulted from a straightforward pattern of aggression on the part of Nazi Germany, Fascist Italy, and Japan. Especially in Europe, major democracies responded weakly and passively. Hamstrung by the Great Depression, anxious to avoid another global conflict, and simply hoping that each aggressive move would be the last, countries such as France, Britain, and the United States did little to stand up to the dictatorships. This policy of letting aggressors have what they want in the hope they will demand no more is known as **appeasement**. The **League of Nations** proved almost useless in dealing with foreign-policy crises. Here is a timetable of what is often referred to as the road to war:

- 1933:
  —Hitler withdrew from the League of Nations.

- 1935:
  —Hitler openly began to rebuild the German army and navy, violating the disarmament clauses of the Treaty of Versailles.
  —Mussolini invaded Ethiopia, causing international outrage. The League of Nations imposed weak sanctions. They did not prevent Italy from taking Ethiopia; their effect was to anger Mussolini and draw him closer to Hitler.
  —The Soviet Union, fearful of Germany, concluded an alliance with France. Both countries agreed to protect Czechoslovakia. France also signed a treaty to protect Poland. This policy of antifascist cooperation was known as **collective security**.

- 1936:
  —Again violating the Treaty of Versailles, Hitler sent troops into the Rhineland, a demilitarized zone. France and Britain protested but took no action. This lack of response set a precedent, in which Hitler would act and the democracies would appease him.

—Mussolini completed his conquest of Ethiopia.

—The Spanish Civil War (1936–1939) began with Francisco Franco's military uprising against the leftist government. Because Franco was allied with Spanish fascists, Mussolini and Hitler assisted him (the Germans took the opportunity to test tanks, airplanes, and new tactics, including terror bombing). Stalin attempted to aid the Spanish government and expected France and Britain to help him do so. He was disappointed when they did not, and his trust in the Western democracies eroded. Aside from the USSR, only a contingent of volunteers, the International Brigades, joined against the rebels. Franco won, became dictator of Spain, and ruled till his death in 1975.

- 1937:

—In Japan, the military gained control of the government.

—Germany, Italy, and Japan formed their alliance.

—Japan invaded mainland China, where the Japanese committed terrible atrocities, including the **Rape of Nanjing**.

- 1938:

—Germany annexed Austria in the **Anschluss** ("union").

—Hitler announced plans to seize the Sudetenland, formerly German territory, given to Czechoslovakia after World War I. Mussolini and Hitler met with Neville Chamberlain, Britain's prime minister, and the French premier at the German city of Munich. The Czechoslovaks were not invited; neither were the Soviets, who, with France, had promised to protect Czechoslovakia from aggression. Britain and France let Germany have the Sudetenland in exchange for Hitler's promise to expand no further. Chamberlain claimed to have guaranteed "peace in our time," but the **Munich Agreement** was **appeasement** at its worst. It also destroyed collective security: Stalin, angry and betrayed, chose not to trust Britain and France any further.

—Japanese and Soviet troops clashed on the Siberian border.

- 1939:

—Germany took the rest of Czechoslovakia. By doing so Hitler showed the world how foolish France and Britain had been to believe his promises.

—Germany took western Lithuania.

—Italy invaded Albania.

—The Japanese and Soviets fought again in Siberia.

—Hitler began to make claims on Polish territory that had formerly belonged to Germany. Realizing that this was where Hitler would act next, France and Britain promised to guarantee Poland's safety.

—Wishing to avoid a two-front war, Hitler sought to reach an agreement with Stalin before invading Poland. In August, Stalin, no longer trusting Britain and France, agreed to sign a nonaggression pact with Hitler. This **Nazi-Soviet Pact** kept the USSR neutral and opened the way for Hitler to invade Poland.

—On September 1, 1939, Germany invaded Poland and thus World War II began.

THE AXIS ASCENDANT, 1939–1941

During the first half of the war, the Axis powers were triumphant. In Europe, the only major powers opposing Germany were France and Britain. The USSR had agreed to remain neutral, and the United States, sunk into isolationism, stayed out of the fighting as well. In Asia, Japan expanded its war against China to include a greater war of conquest against British, Dutch, and French colonies in Southeast Asia.

New Technology and World War II

In terms of combat and technology, World War II was very different from World War I. In the latter, military technology had favored the defensive, resulting in the hellish stalemate of trench warfare. By the time World War II began, military technology had developed in such a way as to make warfare more rapid and more dynamic.

At sea, naval aircraft, aircraft carriers, new landing craft that allowed marine troops to invade faraway islands and beachheads, and long-range submarines gave the combatants a truly global reach. On the ground, new artillery and, especially, tanks gave armies tremendous offensive punch, as well as the ability to move quickly. In the air, giant strategic bombers were able to fly thousands of miles and drop unheard-of quantities of explosives, further increasing offensive capacity.

This new technology helped make World War II a fast-paced, decisive conflict. It also had the unfortunate effect of making warfare deadlier and involving civilians to a degree never before imagined.

The need to develop better and more effective military technology had a tremendous effect on civilian technology long after the war was over. Among the many wartime innovations that played a large role in postwar life were radar, sonar; jet aircraft, synthetic materials (such as nylon), rocketry, atomic energy, and computer science.

Blitzkrieg, the Invasion of Poland, and Sitzkrieg

The war began with Germany's invasion of Poland, in September 1939 (although it must be remembered that Japan had been fighting China since 1937). The new offensive character of war could be seen right away in Germany's innovative method of **Blitzkrieg** ("lightning war"), which used tanks and airplanes to penetrate deeply and quickly into enemy territory. Within weeks, the fighting in Poland was over—especially because the USSR invaded the eastern half of the country, in accordance with the Nazi-Soviet Pact.

In contrast to Germany's fast action, Britain and France, although they declared war, did very little. With an outdated World War I mentality, the Allies waited for Germany to attack them, believing that, as in 1914, the defense would prevail. While Britain and France marked time, Germany prepared its attack. The winter of 1939–1940 was nicknamed Sitzkrieg ("phony war").

Germany's Invasion of Western Europe and the Fall of France

In April 1940, Hitler launched his assault on Western Europe. The next several months were stunningly successful. Denmark, Norway, Luxembourg, Belgium, and the Netherlands were defeated in weeks, if not days.

Most amazing of all was the fall of France. The Germans attacked France on May 10. By June 22, the largest and most powerful democracy on the European continent had surrendered. The French had been confident that their great chain of border fortifications, the Maginot Line, would protect them. The German Blitzkrieg sidestepped the Maginot Line and sent tanks streaming into northern France. The defeat of France shocked the world. It also left Great Britain in the seemingly hopeless position of fighting Germany and Italy (which joined the war in June) by itself.

The Battle of Britain

From the summer of 1940 to the spring of 1941, Germany concentrated its attention on Britain. Meanwhile, Italy launched attacks in the Mediterranean, trying to take Greece, Yugoslavia, and Egypt (still under British protection). Hitler's attempt to knock Britain out of the war failed. The Royal Navy protected the British Isles from invasion. When Hitler tried to win the war from the air, the Royal Air Force defended England's skies in the **Battle of Britain**.

Britain held out thanks to the skill of its air force, its use of radar, and economic aid from Canada and the United States (although the United States was neutral, the government of Franklin Roosevelt was sympathetic, and its **Lend-Lease program** of economic assistance kept Britain and, later, the USSR well-supplied throughout the war).

Invasions in the East and Operation Barbarossa

In the spring and summer of 1941, Hitler shifted his focus from Britain to Eastern Europe. Mussolini's wars in Greece, Yugoslavia, and North Africa had gone wrong, and Germany had to assist him. One of Hitler's most skilled tank commanders, Erwin Rommel, was sent to Africa to fight the British in Egypt.

Hitler also had a larger plan in mind: the invasion of the Soviet Union, code-named **Operation Barbarossa**. Although the USSR and Germany had carefully observed their pact of neutrality since August 1939, Hitler, having eliminated France from the war, felt confident enough to fight the USSR, even though Britain had not yet been defeated.

On June 22, 1941, Germany invaded the Soviet Union, starting the largest ground war in history. From this point onward, 60 to 75 percent of the German armed forces would fight on this eastern front. At first, it looked as though the USSR would fall as quickly as France had. German forces surrounded Leningrad, the USSR's second largest city, placing it under the worst siege in modern times. They drove deep into Ukraine and southern Russia. They also reached the outskirts of Moscow, the capital. A last-ditch defensive effort in December halted the German advance, but only barely.

Japanese Aggression in Southeast Asia

In the Pacific, fighting between China and Japan continued. Japan's war effort widened in 1940 and 1941, as French, Dutch, and British misfortunes in Europe made their Asian empires vulnerable. When France fell in 1940, Japan began to

threaten its colony in Indochina. Japan's eventual goal was to establish its **Greater East Asian Co-Prosperity Sphere** over the entire Chinese coast, all of Southeast Asia, India, Indonesia, and perhaps Australia and New Zealand.

By the summer of 1941, Japan's takeover of Indochina and increased aggression toward Southeast Asia compelled the United States, already upset at Japanese atrocities in China, to impose economic sanctions. Without steel, oil, and other raw materials from the United States, the Japanese war effort on the Asian mainland would be badly damaged. Japan viewed the embargo as an act of war and in late 1941 began to plan a military assault against the United States.

Pearl Harbor and Japan's Assault on the South Pacific

On December 7, 1941, just as the Soviets were halting the Germans outside Moscow, Japan launched its surprise attack on the U.S. naval installation at **Pearl Harbor**, Hawaii. At the same time, the Japanese bombed and invaded U.S. bases throughout the Pacific and on the Philippines.

By the spring of 1942, the Japanese were masters of the South Pacific and Southeast Asia, having captured Hong Kong, Indochina, Thailand, part of Burma, the Malaysian Peninsula (including the great British base of Singapore), the Philippines, Indonesia (the Dutch East Indies), and hundreds of small Pacific islands. However, the effect of the Japanese attack was to bring the United States into World War II, both in the Pacific and in Europe (several days after Pearl Harbor, Germany joined Japan in declaring war on the United States).

Because Pearl Harbor, however devastating, was not a knockout blow, what the Japanese had managed to do was to rouse one of the world's largest countries—with great humanpower resources and the most productive economy on earth—and involve it in the war. In the long term, neither Japan nor Germany would be able to match America's capacity for military industrialization or mass conscription of troops.

THE ALLIED QUEST FOR VICTORY, 1942–1945

The Shifting Balance of World War II

The second half of the war, 1942 through 1945, was very different in character from the first. Most obviously, a different set of countries was involved. France had dropped out, but the USSR and the United States had joined in. Just as important, a different set of factors came into play. The Axis Powers' advantage lay in the skill and quality of Germany's and Japan's armed forces. Allied advantages, especially once the Soviets and Americans became involved, were geographic size, huge reserves of humanpower, large economies, and abundant natural resources.

This distribution of advantages meant that the longer the war lasted, the more likely it was that the Allies would win. Realizing that time was against them, Germany and Japan had been trying to gain decisive victories between 1939 and the end of 1941. Germany's failure to take Moscow and Japan's failure to cripple America permanently with its initial sweep through the Pacific ended the Axis's chances of ending the war quickly. Although Germany and Japan still held the advantage when 1942 began, all the long-term trends were against them.

The Turning Point: 1942

A handful of battles during the summer and fall of 1942 completely changed the tide of the war. If the Axis had won these encounters, they might have been able to force a favorable end to the war. By losing all three, Japan and Germany wasted vast amounts of irreplaceable troops, weapons, and equipment—and lost the strategic initiative they had enjoyed since 1939. These battles were

- **Midway** (June 1942), a naval battle in which the United States destroyed much of the Japanese aircraft-carrier fleet;
- **El Alamein** (July–November 1942), where the British turned back the drive of German tanks toward Egypt and the Suez Canal;
- **Stalingrad** (August 1942–February 1943), a savage clash on the Volga, where the Soviets prevented Germany from capturing south Russia and oil reserves in the east.

With these victories, the Allies had held on long enough for their advantages—larger populations and larger economies—to become decisive.

The European and Mediterranean Theaters of Combat, World War II, 1942.
From September 1939 until the autumn of 1942, the Axis Powers—Germany, Italy, and Japan—succeeded in seizing the military initiative and keeping it. By the middle of 1942, Nazi Germany had reached the height of its power. The areas shaded in gray mark territory that was controlled directly by Germany before the war, belonged to its allies, or had been conquered by it during the war. Not long after this point, primarily because of defeats at El Alamein and Stalingrad, the tide of war turned against the Germans and their partners.

The Shifting Tide: 1943 and 1944

In 1943 and 1944, the Allies determined the direction and pace of the war effort. In the Pacific, the Americans pushed the Japanese steadily westward. Australia, India, Burma, and large parts of China remained free and joined in the fighting. Guerrilla uprisings in Thailand, Vietnam, Indonesia, and the Philippines hurt the Japanese badly.

On the European and Mediterranean fronts, Britain and America took control of North Africa and then used it as a platform from which to invade Italy, depose Mussolini's Fascist government, and knock Italy out of the war. From the east, the Soviets pushed the Germans out of their country, into Eastern Europe, and toward Berlin.

In June 1944, in the **D-Day invasion** (technically known as Operation Overlord, or the Normandy Invasion), British, Canadian, and American troops, ships, and aircraft crossed the English Channel and landed on the coast of France. On land, Hitler now faced Allied threats from three directions: the eastern front, the Italian peninsula, and Western Europe.

War at Sea and in the Air

At sea, the Allies neutralized the last weapon with which Germany had any real chance of threatening them: the **submarine fleet**, which became ineffective by mid-1943.

In the air, the Allies had complete control of the skies by late 1943. From that point forward, British and American aircraft were able to bomb German-held Europe with impunity. After the summer of 1944, American forces had gone far enough across the Pacific that U.S. bombers were able to pound Japan from the air constantly. This practice of **strategic bombing** caused immense damage and killed tens of thousands of civilians. It remains one of the most controversial aspects of the Allied war effort.

The End of World War II

In 1945, the Axis surrendered. Germany gave up the fight first. Caught between the Anglo-American Allies in the west and the Soviet advance from the east, Hitler chose to commit suicide on April 30. Germany stopped fighting in early May.

Despite the fact that it had no hope of winning, Japan continued its struggle against the Allies. The U.S. Navy and Marines closed in on the Japanese home islands, while U.S. bombers continued their assault from the skies.

America's new president, Harry Truman (who came to the Oval Office in April 1945, when Franklin Roosevelt died), greatly feared that an invasion of the Japanese islands would cost tens of thousands of American and Japanese lives. He hoped to win from the air, but conventional bombardment did not seem to be forcing the Japanese to surrender. In July, an international team of scientists working for the Allies tested the first operational atomic bomb in New Mexico. Truman chose to use the A-bomb against the Japanese.

After warning Japan's government that the United States had a new weapon of terrible power, Truman acted. On August 6, 1945, a B-29 bomber named *Enola Gay* dropped an atomic bomb on **Hiroshima**. The initial blast killed at least 78,000 people and destroyed the entire city center; tens of thousands more died later, of

burns or radioactive fallout. When the Japanese government ignored Truman's next request for surrender, the Americans dropped a second bomb on August 9, on the port of Nagasaki. The following week, the Japanese agreed to a cease-fire. They surrendered officially on September 2.

THE HOLOCAUST AND OTHER WAR CRIMES
War Crimes and Crimes Against Humanity

The most grisly aspect of World War II involved the many war crimes committed during the seventy-three months of fighting. Of the 55 to 60 million people who died during the war, approximately half were civilians. A good number were killed by means that fell outside the bounds established by international law or acceptable military behavior. Many of these atrocities were horrendous enough that the phrase "war crime" seemed inadequate to describe them. It was after World War II, therefore, that the phrase **"crime against humanity"** entered the world's legal vocabularies.

The Axis Powers were not the only nations to kill civilians. The Red Army committed many crimes—rape, plunder, wanton destruction of civilian property—as the Soviets advanced through Eastern Europe and Germany. The American and British policy of strategic bombing, both over Japan and German-held Europe, caused tremendous civilian suffering. Some commentators, including many Germans and Japanese, have argued that strategic bombing can be considered a war crime (it should be noted that this is a minority opinion). America remains the only nation that has ever used an atomic or nuclear weapon in wartime, and the question of whether it was necessary to use it against Japan continues to be a matter of controversy.

Japanese War Crimes

Nonetheless, it was the Axis that committed war crimes and crimes against humanity systematically and on a large scale. In Asia, Japan was guilty of a wide variety of atrocities. Even before World War II, Japanese forces had raped, pillaged, and butchered civilian populations in many Chinese cities, most notably Nanjing in December 1937.

As the Greater East Asian Co-Prosperity Sphere widened during World War II, Japanese soldiers continued to terrorize civilian populations, not just in China but in all of Southeast Asia. On many occasions, Japanese armies killed American, British, and Asian prisoners of war, against all legal conventions pertaining to military conduct. Prisoners of war were also used as subjects for Japanese scientific experiments, especially for testing biological and chemical weapons. Finally, the Japanese military rounded up women from Korea and Southeast Asia and forced them to serve as prostitutes, or "comfort women," for Japanese soldiers. After the war, the U.S. military authorities held a series of Tokyo Trials, during which Japanese civilian and military officials were tried for these crimes.

Nazi Atrocities

More infamous were the crimes against humanity committed by the Germans. Prior to the war, the Nazis operated an extensive apparatus of terror, which included a

secret police (the Gestapo) and concentration camps (such as Dachau). Dissidents (including Protestant and, especially, Catholic religious leaders who protested Nazi policy) had been imprisoned, even executed, since the early 1930s.

As the war began and then progressed, the Nazis began to "euthanize" medical patients with incurable diseases, venereal diseases, or tuberculosis. They killed homosexuals, people with mental disabilities, and political dissidents. They performed medical and scientific experiments on human subjects, typically to the point of mutilation and death (Jews and Soviet prisoners of war were used most often).

Nazi Racial Policy and Genocide

Most heinous were the Nazi campaigns of **genocide** (a term devised in the 1940s, by a Jewish lawyer, to reflect the special, premeditated nature of the crime). The Nazis targeted a number of ethnic and cultural groups. Roma (Gypsies) and Slavs were among those they considered to be "subhuman" or "undesirable."

Most of all, the Nazis hated the Jews. After Hitler's rise to power in 1933, the Nazis passed a number of anti-Semitic policies that grew worse over time. The worst had been the **Nuremberg Laws** (1935), which deprived German Jews of their civil rights. Before the war, however, violence against Jews was not yet official policy, even though, in reality, thousands of Jews were harassed and beaten and their homes and businesses vandalized during the late 1930s. In November 1938, on Kristallnacht ("Night of Broken Glass"), thousands of Jewish shops, synagogues, and homes throughout Germany and Austria were attacked or burned in a single night.

It was during the war that Nazi anti-Semitic policy escalated to the point of genocide. There were 11 million Jews in Europe before the beginning of the war. In 1939 and 1940, as the Germans brought more of Europe under their control, Nazi authorities began to round up Jews and detain them, either in **ghettos** or in existing concentration camps, such as Dachau. It was sometime in 1941 that the order for genocide came down from above. Although no written orders survive, it is certain that, ultimately, the command was issued by Hitler himself.

The Holocaust

Nazi genocidal policy is popularly referred to by the name given it by the Jews: the **Holocaust**. The Nazis referred to it as the **Final Solution**. Whatever its name, it evolved as follows:

- 1939–1940:
  —Jews were forced to wear the yellow star to identify themselves.
  —Polish Jews were rounded up and placed in ghettos.
  —Other European Jews were imprisoned in concentration and transit camps.
  —Some Jews were sporadically executed or died by random violence.

- 1941:
  —In July, an order "to make preparations for the general final solution of the Jewish problem within the German sphere of influence in Europe" was handed down to the SS (the Nazi security forces).

—The Nazis organized **special action squads** (*Einsatzgruppen*) to follow the German army into the Soviet Union, round up Jews, and execute them by shooting.

—Dissatisfaction with the special action squads grew. This method of execution was considered to be too slow, too wasteful of ammunition, and too hard on the morale of the executioners. Because the squads only buried the bodies instead of destroying them, the danger remained that the victims could later be found.

—Experiments with carbon monoxide and other gases were carried out at various concentration camps in an attempt to find an "efficient" way to kill large numbers of victims. Experimental cremation methods were tested.

—Late in the year, construction of special camps for execution and cremation began.

—A cyanide-based insecticide, Zyklon-B, was chosen as the means of extermination.

- 1942:
  —In January, fifteen Nazi officials met in the suburbs of Berlin. Here, at the **Wannsee Conference**, it was decided to use special **extermination camps**, already under construction in German-held Poland, to eliminate Jews and other undesirables. Among these were Majdanek, Chelmno, Belzec, Sobibor, and Treblinka. The largest and most infamous was **Auschwitz-Birkenau**.

  —The special extermination camps went into operation.

- 1943–1945:
  —Jews from all over Europe were shipped to the extermination camps. Other victims were also taken there. Victims were gassed, their bodies processed, their remains cremated.

  —Soviet liberation of camps in Poland began in 1944. Auschwitz-Birkenau was liberated in early 1945.

  —Camps in the west were liberated by the British and Americans.

In the end, the Final Solution resulted in millions of deaths. Of Europe's 11 million Jews, approximately 6 million were killed. In addition, many non-Jewish victims (especially Roma) perished.

It was mainly to punish these crimes that the Americans, British, and Soviets organized the Nuremberg Trials (1946), which prosecuted Nazi leaders. During these trials, the term *crime against humanity* was codified as law. In 1948, in a collective effort to avoid such atrocities in the future, the United Nations adopted the Universal Declaration of Human Rights.

The Cold War

CHAPTER 32

- The Cold War
- The Yalta Conference
- The United Nations
- The containment strategy (the Truman Doctrine and the Marshall Plan)
- NATO versus the Warsaw Pact
- Chinese communism and the Sino-Soviet split
- The domino principle
- The Korean and Vietnam wars
- The Soviet invasions of Hungary and Czechoslovakia
- National liberation and decolonization
- Nonalignment, the third world, and proxy wars
- The Berlin Wall and the Cuban Missile Crisis
- The nuclear arms race, deterrence, and MAD
- Détente
- Solidarity and unrest in Eastern Europe
- Perestroika and glasnost
- The fall of the Berlin Wall
- The collapse of the USSR

The end of World War II fundamentally shifted global power. For over 200 years, the constantly shifting balance of power among six or seven European nations had determined the course of world events. With Europe devastated by the war, only two nations possessed true global strength: the United States and the Soviet Union. Because these two nations were orders of magnitude stronger and wealthier than any great power had been before them, they were referred to as **superpowers**.

The popular name given to the state of rivalry that existed between the United States and the USSR from 1945 to 1991 is the **Cold War**. It divided the world into hostile camps—although its bipolar nature was complicated by the eventual breakup of the alliance between Communist China and the Soviet Union. The Cold War gave birth to a nuclear arms race that brought into the world the deadliest weapons ever seen. The great wave of **decolonization** that took place after World War II (see Chapter 33) was deeply affected by the Cold War, because newly free nations often had to choose between allying with one superpower or another. Although the United States and USSR never went to war with each other, dozens of small and medium-size conflicts were fought worldwide between 1945 and the end of the Cold War, killing an estimated total of 50 million people, more than half of them civilian.

The Cold War finally ended in the late 1980s and early 1990s, with the collapse of communism in Eastern Europe and the breakup of the Soviet Union.

WARTIME DIPLOMACY

The wartime alliance between the United States, Great Britain, and the Soviet Union had been a marriage of convenience. Although the United States and Britain were mutually sympathetic, they cooperated with the USSR and its dictator, Joseph Stalin, only because they needed Soviet help to defeat Hitler. Even during the war effort, many tensions arose between Franklin Roosevelt and Winston Churchill on one hand and Stalin on the other. It was clear to all that things would only get worse after the war ended.

The issues concerning the wartime allies were discussed at three summit meetings: the Teheran Conference (November 1943), the Yalta Conference (February 1945), and the Potsdam Conference (July 1945). The questions dealt with included the following:

- *Second front*: The USSR, which fought the vast bulk of the German army, desperately wanted its allies to open up a second front in western Europe as soon as possible. At Teheran, it was decided to invade France in June 1944.
- *Japan*: In exchange for Asian territory, the Soviets agreed to help fight Japan after Germany was defeated. The Americans struck this deal before the atomic bomb was tested.
- *Division and denazification of Germany and Austria*: Germany was to be occupied and divided into four sectors: British, French, U.S., and Soviet. Berlin, which fell into the Soviet zone, was likewise divided, and the western parts of the city were guaranteed highway, air, and rail access to the other zones. Austria was similarly partitioned. Both countries were to undergo a process of denazification, in which former Nazis would be removed from public offices and positions of authority. Germany was to repay $20 billion in reparations. The division of Germany lasted until the end of the Cold War. Austria was allowed to reunify in 1955.
- *United Nations*: Just as Woodrow Wilson had created the League of Nations after World War I, Franklin Roosevelt hoped to establish a new international body, stronger and more effective than the League had been. This body was to be called the **United Nations**.
- *Fate of Eastern Europe*: By far, this was the most sensitive issue. As they defeated Germany, Soviet troops occupied Eastern Europe. It was clear that Stalin hoped to turn this territory into a Soviet sphere of influence. Roosevelt and Churchill were deeply concerned, but Stalin had millions of troops in the region and to press him too hard on this question was to risk having him drop out of the war before Germany was defeated. At Yalta, Roosevelt and Churchill came up with an awkward compromise. They agreed that the USSR would have informal influence in certain East European nations. In exchange, they asked the Soviets to promise to allow free elections throughout Eastern Europe. Stalin agreed and then broke his promises. Some historians see Roosevelt and Churchill as having betrayed Eastern Europe; others argue that there was little they could have done, considering the situation's military realities.

THE COLD WAR BEGINS, 1945–1949

The first stage of the Cold War can be considered to have lasted from 1945 to 1949. Although there were concerns about other parts of the world, such as Japan, Korea, and China, the focus of the Cold War during these early years was primarily European and Mediterranean. For Europe itself, of course, this was a bitter comedown. From being the shaper of world events, Europe—reduced to the superpowers' battleground—was now shaped by them.

The Cold War Division of Europe, 1957.
From 1945 until 1989, the Cold War divided the nations of Europe—with only a few exceptions—into two camps, one dominated by the Soviet Union, the other led by the United States and its European allies. By the mid-1950s, the so-called Iron Curtain had descended over Europe. The nations of the West were joined by the North Atlantic Treaty Organization, a military alliance, and many also joined in the European Economic Community. The Eastern bloc was held together by the Soviet-imposed military alliance known as the Warsaw Pact, as well as COMECON, an economic union led by the USSR.

The Soviet Absorption of Eastern Europe

From 1945 through 1948, the USSR took over Eastern Europe, installing pro-Soviet, communist governments in the eastern half of Germany and in Poland, Czechoslovakia, Hungary, Romania, and Bulgaria. Yugoslavia became communist as well, but under its stubbornly independent leader, Josip Tito, Yugoslavia broke

with the USSR in 1948. Albania, also communist, allied with the Soviets until Stalin's death; the mid-1950s, it isolated itself from both superpowers. In March 1946, Winston Churchill warned of the permanent division of the continent in his famous "**iron curtain**" speech.

All of this was a violation of the Soviets' promises at Yalta. In addition, the USSR was threatening Iran and Turkey in 1945 and 1946. The Yugoslavs were sponsoring a communist rebellion in Greece. This brought the Soviet bloc perilously close to the oil fields of the Middle East, as well as the important waterways of the eastern Mediterranean.

Stalin's policy during these years was simple: to gain as much territory as possible without a fight. Although they kept it as secret as possible, the Soviets had been hurt badly by World War II. They had lost 25 million to 28 million dead. One-third of their entire economy had been destroyed. The USSR could not afford to fight the West. On the other hand, Stalin wanted a buffer zone in Eastern Europe, in order to protect his country from suffering again as it had in World War II. Also, because the United States had atomic weaponry and the USSR did not, Stalin felt even more vulnerable. His goal was to push the Americans as hard as he could, up to the point where they pushed back. The clearest example of this came in 1948, during the **Berlin Blockade**. In March, the Soviets suddenly cut off highway and railroad traffic between West Berlin and the western zones of Germany. It was easy to do this without provoking an actual war. When the United States began to fly airplanes to West Berlin, however, Stalin was faced with a choice: allow the flights to continue or shoot the aircraft out of the skies, an act that would certainly start a war. Stalin backed down, having reached the limit of what the United States would allow.

The U.S. Response: Containment

Until 1947, the United States had no coherent strategy for the emerging Cold War. That year, however, as communist takeover threatened Greece and Turkey, President Harry Truman acted. In March, the United States assisted Greece and Turkey, proclaiming the **Truman Doctrine**, which promised "moral and material aid to any and all countries whose political stability is threatened by communism."

Later in 1947, the United States unveiled the European Recovery Plan (or **Marshall Plan**), brainchild of the secretary of state, General George Marshall. Remembering how, during the Depression, economic suffering had driven many European nations to political extremism, Marshall argued that poverty and homelessness in post-World War II Europe might drive governments to communism. The Marshall Plan pumped over $13 billion into Europe for purposes of economic reconstruction. Even the nations of Eastern Europe were invited to take part in the Marshall Plan, but the USSR forbade them to do so.

Finally, in 1949, the Truman Administration made a military commitment to the Cold War with the formation of the **North Atlantic Treaty Organization** (NATO), which bound the United States, Canada, Britain, and nine other Western European states into a formal strategic alliance (the number of NATO members has grown steadily over time).

All these initiatives were elements in the United States's overarching strategy for dealing with the USSR: **containment**. This term was coined by the diplomat George Kennan, who argued that the USSR would expand as far as it could, as long as it did not have to fight. Soviet expansion, therefore, could be halted by "long-term, patient, but firm and vigilant containment."

Containment did not necessarily mean war but could also consist of economic and diplomatic support for countries targeted by the USSR. The advantage was that Soviet expansion could be kept in check without risking combat. There were, however, drawbacks. Containment gave the initiative to the Soviet Union: it acted, then the United States reacted. There was no end in sight, meaning that containment would have to be pursued for years, if not decades. It would cost immense amounts of money, especially as the arms race between the two countries escalated. Moreover, as described below and in Chapter 33, the containment strategy affected—and not for the better—how America chose its allies in the developing (or "third") world of Africa, Asia, and Latin America.

The Soviets resisted containment. In response to the Marshall Plan, the USSR formed its own economic union, the Council for Mutual Economic Assistance (COMECON). It also developed its own military bloc, the **Warsaw Pact**, to oppose NATO.

By the end of the 1940s, Europe was sharply divided between noncommunist and communist camps, with only a few nations remaining neutral. By 1949, however, Europe ceased to be the only battleground—or even the primary battleground—of the Cold War.

THE COLD WAR GLOBALIZES, 1949–1968

Nineteen forty-nine was a key year in the history of the Cold War. NATO was established. That summer witnessed the **first Soviet atomic test**, which eliminated America's edge in military technology and started a four-decade nuclear arms race.

The Cold War in Asia and the Third World

Also in 1949, after years of civil war, **Mao Tse-tung** defeated Chiang Kai-shek's Nationalists, completing the **communist revolution in China**. The Nationalists fled to Taiwan. On the mainland, Mao established the People's Republic of China (PRC) and allied with the USSR (on Mao's domestic policies, see Chapter 33). In a matter of months, the Cold War had expanded dramatically: The two largest nations on the Eurasian landmass were now together under the banner of communism, and one of them possessed atomic weapons.

With the situation in Europe largely stalemated, the Cold War's focus shifted increasingly to Asia, as well as Africa and Latin America. The first sign of this shift was the **Korean War** (1950–1953), which began with an invasion of the noncommunist South by the communist North (with support from Stalin and, especially, Mao). The United States led a United Nations army to defend South Korea. After three years of combat and more than a million deaths, the war ended with the country still divided, exactly where it had been before.

As the Cold War took on a more global dimension, the U.S. policy of containment became more difficult. In Asia, Africa, and Latin America, there was already a so-called **Third World** of nonaligned nations, most of them less economically developed than the West or the USSR, and if the Soviets attempted to win influence there, the Americans had to compete. The post-World War II wave of **decolonization** and **national liberation** added new regimes to the Third World, and because they had just freed themselves from Western imperialism or overthrown dictators supported by Western powers, many were inclined to stay unaligned (like India and Egypt) or seek ties with the USSR (for example, Cuba after 1959). As the Soviets, Chinese, and Cuba tried to spread communism throughout the Third World, the United States responded with its own interventions. Unfortunately, America came to choose its Third World allies based mainly on how anticommunist they were, not how democratic—and thus, it supported many dictatorial and authoritarian regimes.

After Korea, key Cold War events in the Third World include the **Cuban Revolution** (1959), which heightened tensions by placing a communist regime and Soviet ally only miles off the U.S. coast. The **Vietnam War** (1954–1975) began with the liberation of Vietnam from French colonization and continued with America's attempt to prop up an unpopular government in South Vietnam against revolution and invasion from the communist north. This was classic domino-principle strategy on the part of the United States, which feared the spread of communism throughout all of Southeast Asia. However, the war took a turn for the worse in 1968, and America withdrew in defeat in 1973. For more on Cuba and Vietnam, see Chapter 33.

Superpower Rivalry and the Sino-Soviet Split

In the United States, presidents of both political parties pursued firm and active foreign policies and followed the policy of containment. In the USSR, Stalin died in 1953, and new leadership caused more noticeable changes. Nikita Khrushchev (1953–1964) was less brutal than Stalin. He denounced the crimes of Stalin and (within strict limits) allowed some liberalization at home and in the Eastern bloc. He declared his willingness to be friendlier to the West and even visited the United States. Leonid Brezhnev (1964–1982), who forced Khrushchev into retirement, was more of a hard-liner but still not as harsh as Stalin.

Even so, Cold War tensions and the arms race continued. During the 1950s and early 1960s, Khrushchev showed that liberalization had its limits. In 1956, when Hungary reformed more than the USSR wished, then tried to leave the Soviet bloc, Khrushchev suppressed the **Hungarian uprising** by force. His foreign policy became unpredictable. Encouraged by the Cuban Revolution and angered by the flight of American U-2 spy planes over the USSR (in May 1960, the Soviets shot down a U-2 and captured the pilot, causing an international crisis), Khrushchev pursued a boldly aggressive course in East Germany and in Cuba. In August 1961, the Soviets built the **Berlin Wall**. To demonstrate U.S. determination, the U.S. president John F. Kennedy visited the city and declared in a rousing speech, "I am a Berliner." A bigger and more dangerous showdown came in 1962, when Khrushchev attempted to install nuclear missiles in Cuba. In October, U.S. spy

TIP

American anxieties about the possible global expansion of communism were based on what was popularly known as the **domino principle** (if one country in a region "falls" to communism, the rest will too).

planes uncovered what the Soviets were doing, and Kennedy answered with a naval blockade of Cuba. The resulting **Cuban Missile Crisis** is generally considered to be the moment that brought the world closest to nuclear war. The Soviets backed down and withdrew the missiles; the failed gamble and the resulting loss of prestige played a major role in the ouster of Khrushchev in 1964. (Another factor was the USSR's worsening relationship with China, discussed below.)

Tensions cooled somewhat during the rest of the 1960s, although relations were not friendly. When Brezhnev came to power, he proved more authoritarian than Khrushchev, but also more predictable. In 1968, when Czechoslovakia began a major reform program, the "Prague Spring," Brezhnev cracked down hard, sending in a Warsaw Pact army to restore Soviet control. He justified the intervention by stating that the USSR had the right to "protect communism" in Eastern Europe (in other words, to control the Soviet bloc as it pleased), a stance that became known as the **Brezhnev Doctrine**. However, Brezhnev seemed less likely to threaten Europe outside the USSR's declared sphere of influence. Of course, proxy struggles in the Third World continued, and the U.S. involvement in Vietnam escalated.

Cold War geopolitics grew more complex with the **Sino-Soviet split**, which began in the 1960s and continued till the collapse of the USSR. Even though both nations were communist, the Chinese resented the Soviets' patronizing "older brother" attitude (they also felt that many Russians, being white, treated them as racial inferiors). The Soviets did not give the Chinese the secret of nuclear weapons. (China finally developed its own atomic bomb in 1964.) Mao was upset with what he saw as the softer line of Stalin's successors. By the early 1960s, tensions between China and the USSR were serious (but not yet understood in the West). As the decade ended, the Sino-Soviet border became a militarized zone, and occasional episodes of violence broke out. The United States would exploit this split in the 1970s.

The Arms Race and Space Race

When the USSR ended the American monopoly on atomic weapons in 1949, a long **nuclear arms race** began. During the 1950s and early 1960s, the United States had more weapons, but its advantage narrowed as time passed. By the mid-to-late 1960s, the superpowers reached a state of nuclear parity: they each had roughly the same quantity of weapons, and they each had the ability to drop nuclear bombs from airplanes, fire nuclear missiles from submarines, and launch nuclear warheads on intercontinental ballistic missiles (ICBMs) directly at each other's countries. Britain, France, and China also possessed small nuclear arsenals.

Nuclear weapons made traditional military thinking obsolete and greatly heightened international tensions. Any quarrel that got out of control (as, for example, the assassination of Franz Ferdinand did in 1914) could result not just in a world war but global devastation. Over time, nuclear weapons became most important for how they were *not* used: their **deterrence** value was seen as a way of preventing war between the superpowers. In theory, as long as each side remained convinced that rash or aggressive action would destroy it as well as its enemy, both sides would avoid doing anything that might trigger a serious crisis. This logic was referred to as **Mutually Assured Destruction**, with the appropriate abbreviation MAD.

Because rocket technology was so intimately connected with the development of nuclear missiles, the arms race had much to do with another form of superpower competition: the **space race**. Ostensibly a peaceful scientific venture, the exploration of space became associated with hyperpatriotic pride and military rivalry. At the start, the Soviets had the advantage: they launched the first human-made object into space, the satellite *Sputnik*, in 1957, and they sent the first human into space, Yuri Gagarin, in 1961. However, the United States pulled ahead, becoming, in 1969, the first (and, so far, only) nation to land a crewed spacecraft on the moon.

THE LATE STAGES OF THE COLD WAR, 1968–1991

Détente During the 1970s

Between 1969 and 1979, the Cold War entered a more peaceful phase known as *détente* (a French diplomatic term referring to the relaxation of tensions). The United States, wearied by the Vietnam conflict and plagued by economic recession at home, was relieved to scale back hostilities. The USSR was motivated by the need for U.S. and Canadian grain shipments, as well as fears that America was growing closer to China—President Richard Nixon skillfully exploited the Sino-Soviet split by visiting China in 1972.

Détente did not mean tensions disappeared completely. Conflicts in Africa, Asia, and Latin America raged, with the United States and USSR sponsoring opposing sides. The arms race continued, and nuclear arsenals grew larger. Still, for almost a decade, the Soviets and Americans established a working relationship and, at times, genuinely cooperated. The United States sold grain to the USSR. Both powers cooperated in the enforcement of the **Nuclear Non-Proliferation Treaty** (1968–1969), whose purpose has been to prevent the spread of nuclear weaponry. The United States and USSR signed the first arms-control treaties, such as SALT (1972) and the Anti-Ballistic Missile Treaty (1972). In the Helsinki Accords of 1975, the Soviet government agreed to guarantee its people basic human rights. The superpowers even cooperated in space, during the Apollo-Soyuz mission (1975).

The Early- to Mid-1980s: The Cold War Resumes

The spirit of détente ended in 1979. That year, the **Soviet invasion of Afghanistan**, which threatened the oil supplies of the Middle East as well as the Indian Ocean coastline, damaged relations between the superpowers. Another point of tension was the **Sandinista revolution in Nicaragua** (1979), which the Soviets supported. The latest arms-control treaty, SALT II (1979), went unratified. In 1980 U.S. President Ronald Reagan swung American foreign policy far to the right.

In terms of the arms race and the risk of nuclear war, the period between 1979 and 1985 was the Cold War's most dangerous time, with the exception of the Cuban Missile Crisis of 1962. The arms race escalated. Third World brushfire wars, terrorist campaigns sponsored by the USSR and its allies, and covert operations carried out by the CIA or the KGB increased in number. Both superpowers publicly expressed hostility. Each boycotted Olympic Games hosted by the other (Moscow in 1980,

Los Angeles in 1984). Reagan referred to the Soviet Union explicitly as the Evil Empire. Because the nuclear weaponry of the 1980s was faster, more accurate, and more destructive than ever before, the chances that a diplomatic crisis could result in a full-scale, civilization-destroying exchange mounted.

Unrest and Reform in the Soviet Bloc

In the meantime, the USSR experienced political stagnation and economic slow-down at home (especially because of the arms race and the cost of the war in Afghanistan). In Eastern Europe, there was growing unrest, especially in Poland, where the 1980 creation of the trade union **Solidarity**, led by Lech Walesa, sparked a decade-long protest movement that united workers, intellectuals, and Catholic clergy (Pope John Paul II, originally from Poland, did much to support anti-Soviet agitation in Eastern Europe). Other important dissidents included the playwright Vaclav Havel of Czechoslovakia and, in the USSR, the physicist Andrei Sakharov, as well as his wife, Elena Bonner.

Real change was impossible under the aging Brezhnev and his immediate successors. In 1985, however, a younger, reform-minded leader rose to power in the Soviet Union: **Mikhail Gorbachev**. Gorbachev understood that inefficency, corruption, and economic weakness were undermining his country. He also knew that the USSR could no longer afford to continue fighting in Afghanistan, keep up with America in the arms race, or even maintain control over Eastern Europe.

During the late 1980s, Gorbachev launched two interrelated reform efforts: *perestroika* ("restructuring") and *glasnost* ("openness"). **Perestroika** involved economic changes similar to the reforms of **Deng Xiaoping** in China (see Chapter 33). Within limits, it reduced central state control over the economy, allowing for some free enterprise and expansion of private property. Such changes worked better in China than in the USSR, partly because of long-ingrained inefficiency in the Soviet system, partly because Deng fought conservative opposition in his government more effectively than Gorbachev did. Another difference was Gorbachev's policy of **glasnost**, which allowed greater freedom of the press, public criticism of political corruption and workplace abuses, and frankness about the USSR's clouded past (especially the Stalin era). He allowed competitive voting, created an elective parliament, and legalized non-Communist political parties. Gorbachev hoped that such freedoms would motivate the Soviet people to work harder to make perestroika succeed. Instead, glasnost made people feel freer to ask for even more change—and to criticize Gorbachev himself when things began to go wrong. (Deng did not permit such social and cultural freedoms in China.)

The Walls Come Down: The Cooling of the Arms Race and the Liberation of Eastern Europe

Gorbachev, hoping to reduce superpower tensions, turned a friendlier face to the West. Although tough discussions lay ahead, the terrible nuclear fears of the previous half decade began to fade. By 1987, Gorbachev and Reagan were negotiating arms-reduction agreements and cooling tensions even further.

Gorbachev also started to loosen the USSR's grip on Eastern Europe. He began economic reform and called for greater observance of human rights. Gorbachev's press secretary joked about the "Sinatra Doctrine," hinting that, instead of upholding the Brezhnev Doctrine, the Soviets would allow East European governments to do things "their way."

In the end, Eastern Europe went free. The key year was 1989. Poland, where Lech Walesa and the Solidarity movement won free nationwide elections, led the way. Hungary followed suit by opening its borders to the West. In Czechoslovakia, Vaclav Havel's dissident movement came to power in the so-called Velvet Revolution. Bulgaria's communist regime resigned. In November, the East German Communist Party collapsed, bringing about the freedom movement's most celebrated, most euphoric event, the **fall of the Berlin Wall**. In December, the deeply repressive regime in Romania was overthrown (in one of the freedom movement's rare moments of violence, the dictator, Nicolae Ceausescu, and his wife were executed). Soon, in October 1990, the map of Europe would be dramatically redrawn by the **reunification of Germany**.

Parallel Freedom Movements

The freedom movement in Eastern Europe inspired or paralleled other freedom movements worldwide in 1989 and 1990. Not all succeeded. In May 1989, the seventieth anniversary of the May Fourth Movement that had demanded progressive reform from the Chinese Republic, Chinese students gathered at **Tiananmen Square** in Beijing. They, too, wanted greater freedoms. The Deng regime refused to grant any concessions and, when the students disobeyed orders to disperse, crushed the demonstrations by sending in tanks. Economic change was allowed but not political change.

The nations of Latin America were luckier. Starting in the late 1980s, they began a wave of democratization that continued into the 1990s. In South Africa, in 1990, **Nelson Mandela**, leader of the African National Congress, was released from prison, where he had been held since 1964. Free elections and the **end of apartheid** soon followed.

The Fall of the Soviet Union, 1989–1991

While Eastern Europe rejoiced, trouble brewed in the USSR. Gorbachev faced two major problems after 1989. At home, perestroika was failing, and discontent with his leadership was rising. Liberals and moderates who had originally supported Gorbachev wanted more change than he was willing to give. On the other hand, he had made enough changes to alienate hard-liners and conservative communists. Abroad, the East European freedom movement encouraged an upsurge of **anti-Soviet nationalism** in the USSR itself. In 1990 and 1991, non-Russian parts of the country (especially the Baltic republics, Georgia, and Ukraine) pushed for greater autonomy or declared independence outright. In one instance, Gorbachev resorted to violence (he sent tanks into Lithuania in 1990), but overall, he did not have the heart to crush independence movements by force. As 1991 progressed, the continued existence of the Soviet nation was in doubt.

A sudden blow came in August 1991, when hard-line members of the regime staged a three-day coup against Gorbachev. Thanks to popular resistance and bold leadership by politicians, including Boris Yeltsin, who rallied people against the coup, the takeover failed. Gorbachev returned to power, but he had been fatally weakened. The breakup of the USSR continued; various republics, including Russia itself, went their own way in the fall and early winter, and Gorbachev was powerless to stop them. In December 1991, Yeltsin (now president of the Russian Republic) and the leaders of Ukraine and Belarus declared the formation of a new, post-Soviet confederation, the Commonwealth of Independent States, which made the USSR irrelevant. Bowing to the inevitable, on December 25, Gorbachev resigned as Soviet leader and declared an end to the USSR itself. Soviet Communism, whose birth in 1917 had been one of the major events of the early twentieth century, did not live to see the twenty-first.

The Fall of the Soviet Union and Formation of the Commonwealth of Independent States, January 1992.
In late 1991, Mikhail Gorbachev was forced to dissolve the USSR. At that time, leaders of the former republics of the Soviet Union, with the exception of Estonia, Latvia, Lithuania, and Georgia, chose to form the Commonwealth of Independent States as a way to maintain ties and attempt a smooth transition from Soviet rule.

Divergent Forms of Development in the Postwar World, 1945–1991

- The developed world and postindustrial (service) economies
- Sovietization versus Westernization in postwar Europe
- European economic union (the European Union)
- The 1968 protests
- The economic slump of the 1970s
- National liberation and decolonization
- The developing (third) world and the north-south split
- The Organization of Petroleum Exporting Countries (OPEC)
- The Arab-Israeli conflict
- The Iranian Revolution
- Apartheid
- Indian and Indonesian independence and nonalignment
- Japan, the "little tigers," and economic growth in Asia
- Communism in Vietnam, Cambodia, and North Korea
- Maoist radicalism versus Deng Xiaoping's reformism in China
- The Cuban and Nicaraguan revolutions
- Dictatorship and democratization in Latin America

While the postwar decades were dominated diplomatically by the Cold War (see Chapter 32), individual parts of the world underwent a variety of political and social changes.

One preeminent trend was economic and technological modernization. However, this trend applied unevenly to different parts of the world. The societies of the West, the United States, Canada, and Western Europe, were already the most developed and industrialized in the world and therefore had the capacity to keep modernizing quickly and thoroughly. They became immensely prosperous and advanced, moving into a **postindustrial stage** by the end of the twentieth century. As for regions such as the Middle East, Africa, Asia, and Latin America, modernization, in most cases, was slower. The labels typically given to these regions—the **developing world**, less developed countries, or nondeveloped world—indicate how they lagged behind the nations of the West.

The postwar world was also an era of **decolonization**. World War II completed the process of weakening the grasp that several European nations still had on their empires. From the 1940s through the 1970s, countries such as Britain, France, Belgium, and the Netherlands were convinced or forced to free their colonies in the Middle East, Africa, and Asia. Moreover, many regions that had not been colonized per se but had been economically and/or politically dominated by outside powers began to assert themselves in the postwar era. This made the so-called **Third World**—the developing or newly liberated nations of Asia, Africa, the Mideast, and Latin America—increasingly important in global politics and economics. Unfortunately for many of these states, decolonization has sometimes caused as many problems as it has solved. Not all newly liberated countries were able to develop healthy forms of government and economic organization. Also, many of them were caught up on one side or the other in the politics of the Cold War, as the United States and Soviet Union dueled for global influence.

To this day, many imbalances and inequities between the West and the developing world still persist from the Cold War era. In particular, the great disparity in technological development and the vast gap between the West's affluence and the ghastly poverty of many parts of the developing world remain in place and continue to cause political and economic tension. The geographical placement of most of the developed or developing world has made it common to refer to their divide as the **north–south split**.

RECOVERY IN POSTWAR EUROPE

Europe found itself in a paradoxical situation during the postwar era. On one hand, World War II had ended its global dominance. It had been divided by the superpowers into a Cold War battleground. It lost its remaining colonies. On the other hand, after repairing the damage caused by World War II, most of Europe came to enjoy an unprecedented level of prosperity. This was certainly the case in Western Europe, which became one of the wealthiest and most technologically advanced societies on earth. Even communist-controlled Eastern Europe, which remained more backward, overcame the devastation caused by the war. Albeit more crudely and more slowly than in Western Europe, Eastern Europe's standard of living and level of modernization rose from the 1950s onward.

World War II's Effects on Europe

Wartime damage had been extensive. Millions were dead. A third of the Soviet economy had been destroyed. German cities lay in ruins. At least 50 million people were homeless, and more than 16 million were refugees displaced persons (DPs) without a country. The migration and dislocation caused by World War II was tremendous. Horrendous poverty, marked by shortages of food, clothing, consumer goods, and housing, threatened to plunge Europe into chaos.

In another blow to European prestige, colonies worldwide began to agitate for and win their freedom during the late 1940s and afterward. These national liberation movements and wars of decolonization caused European governments great stress and strain.

Sovietization in Eastern Europe

Despite these effects of war, economic recovery began surprisingly quickly. In the east, owing to the sheer political will of Stalin and the plundering of its new East European satellites (especially the Soviet-controlled zone of Germany), the USSR recovered to prewar economic levels within a decade. The USSR went on to create Soviet-style economies throughout the Eastern bloc. Economies were nationalized and centrally planned. Massive industrialization campaigns began. Collectivization, while not as brutally implemented as in the USSR during the 1930s, brought agriculture under state control.

In both the USSR and Eastern Europe, there was substantial economic growth after the 1940s and early 1950s. **Social welfare systems**, which provided education, medical care, pensions, and other basic services to all citizens, were put in place. However, East European economic production was characterized by poor quality. Consumer goods were constantly in short supply because so much emphasis was placed on weapons production during the arms race against the United States. Because Soviet and East European production was carried out without any regard for the environment, the ecological damage caused by a half century of East European industrialization was nothing short of catastrophic—and remains a problematic legacy. Moreover, the entire system was maintained by means of political repression. Especially under Stalin, Soviet control over Eastern Europe was harsh. There were periods of liberalization, but they were sporadic and temporary. The price of going beyond what the Soviets were willing to allow was demonstrated by the Soviet invasions of Hungary (1956) and Czechoslovakia (1968). Not until the end of the 1980s would the Eastern bloc experience real freedom.

Recovery in Western Europe

Economic recovery was more dramatic in Western Europe. As a first step, the European Recovery Plan (better known as the **Marshall Plan**) infused more than $13 billion into the economies of Western Europe. This infusion helped to rebuild the war-torn nations of Europe. It helped prevent the spread of communism. It also rewarded the United States, because this first dose of economic aid created healthy markets eager to buy U.S. goods.

Growth continued throughout the next two decades. A particular star was West Germany, which rose from the ruins of war to become Europe's economic powerhouse. Ironically, Great Britain, one of the victors of World War II, took a longer time than most European nations to recover (mainly because it had spent so much money fighting World War II). Industrial growth was high. Technological innovation allowed West European economies to move beyond industrial production to service, or postindustrial, modes of economic activity (the same was true in the United States).

As in Eastern Europe, most West European nations put into place social welfare systems or improved on the ones created during the 1920s and 1930s. Although they were not socialist or communist, many West European nations began to experiment with economic systems that were not purely capitalist either. This blend of capitalist and social-welfare (even mildly socialist) practice began to be called the "**third way.**"

Not all developments in Western Europe were positive. Europe was caught in the crossfire of the superpowers' nuclear arms race. For a long time, Germany refused to come to grips with the Holocaust or its Nazi past. Democracies such as France and Italy, mired for decades in widespread official corruption, experienced frequent government turnover. France was rocked by the worldwide wave of **1968 protests** that struck not only Paris but also Mexico City, Prague, and universities throughout the United States. Mild authoritarianism and antiunionism persisted in countries such as Spain, Portugal, and Greece until after the mid-1970s. Great Britain wrestled with nationalist aspirations and, after the late 1960s, terrorism in Northern Ireland.

Economic Union in Western Europe

One way the West Europeans made up for their loss of global might was to devise various forms of union. Over time, the principle of union has enabled Europe to boost its economic strength, increase its diplomatic clout, and (less successfully) work together to prevent the outbreak of war or political extremism.

At first, efforts to unite were economic. In 1952, six nations (Belgium, Luxembourg, the Netherlands, Italy, France, and West Germany) formed the European Coal and Steel Community. In 1957, the same countries agreed to even stronger ties by establishing the European Economic Community, also known as the Common Market. The goal of the EEC was to eliminate internal tariffs and encourage the free movement of money, goods, services, and labor. Eventually renamed the **European Union**, the group expanded (Britain, Ireland, and Denmark joined in 1973, while others were admitted later) and strengthened its ties. By the mid-1990s, it included fifteen members and was moving toward monetary union (see Chapter 35).

Other regional organizations binding Western Europe together include the **North Atlantic Treaty Organization** (NATO, formed in 1949) and the Council of Europe (also 1949).

Economic Crisis During the 1970s

Economic crisis struck the Western world—the United States as well as Europe—in the early 1970s. In 1971, the United States was forced to detach the dollar from the gold standard. This move led to monetary instability across Western Europe, whose trade was so dependent on the U.S. currency. The **oil embargo** of 1973, imposed by the nations of the Middle East (from which Western Europe bought 70 percent of its oil), badly damaged the economies of Europe and the United States.

Both Western Europe and the United States suffered from inflation, recession, and unemployment.

Western Europe During the 1980s and 1990s

During the 1980s, many West European nations moved to the right, in an effort to escape the malaise of the 1970s. The elections of leaders such as Margaret Thatcher in Great Britain and Helmut Kohl in West Germany were part of this general trend. The

same is true of the election of Ronald Reagan in the United States. Even France's first socialist president, François Mitterand, was forced to make concessions to the right.

In many West European countries, there was a partial retreat from the social-welfare systems of the past, as Thatcher and other leaders carried out **privatization** of state-run sectors of the economy. Overall, West Europe economies recovered during the 1980s and 1990s. To be sure, unemployment, poverty, socioeconomic inequality, and racial prejudice (stirred up by the large influx of non-European and East European immigration into Western Europe) were problems. Still, by the end of the Cold War, Western Europe was a region in which economic prosperity, healthy democratic government, and technological advancement could be taken largely— although not universally—for granted.

Major leaders of postwar Europe include Charles de Gaulle, president of France during the late 1950s and 1960s. France's most decorated World War II hero, de Gaulle was fiercely independent and resisted American domination of European affairs. Konrad Adenauer, chancellor of West Germany (1949–1963), restored Germany's place in the international community. Willy Brandt (1969–1974), also of West Germany, became famous for his policy of *Ostpolitik* (détente with Eastern Europe). Margaret Thatcher, the first female prime minister of Great Britain (1979–1990), moved British politics and economics to the right, dismantled and privatized much of Britain's nationalized social-welfare apparatus, and worked with Ronald Reagan (and later President George Bush) of the United States in opposing Soviet communism. In France, president François Mitterand (1981–1995) made the socialists, rather than the communists, the respectable voices of the French left wing. Helmut Kohl (1982–1998) of West Germany led his country to economic dominance during the 1980s. His enduring mark on German history is his reunification of East and West Germany in October 1990 after the collapse of communism in Eastern Europe.

DECOLONIZATION AND THE EMERGENCE OF THE DEVELOPING WORLD

One of the most powerful trends of the postwar era was the surge in importance of the **developing world** (also referred to in Cold War terms as the **Third World**). It consisted of nations in Latin America, Asia, Africa, and the Middle East that had lagged behind the countries of the West in economic and political development, had been kept under the political and economic thumb of foreign powers, or had been directly colonized.

Decolonization and National Liberation

Even before World War II, some steps had been taken to decolonize. Britain gave home rule to Ireland in 1922 thanks largely to an armed uprising there in 1916. In 1931, the Statute of Westminster transformed the British Empire into the British Commonwealth, whose members were entitled to varying degrees of autonomy. France and Britain began to allow some of their Middle Eastern mandates and protectorates greater freedom, if not actual independence, during the 1930s.

After World War II, **decolonization** and **national liberation** became major agents of change in Asia, the Middle East, and Africa. World War II pried loose the grip that countries such as Britain and France had kept on their empires even after World War I. From the 1940s through the 1970s, dozens of new nations came into being, having attained freedom from their imperial masters.

Another change in the developing world during the Cold War era was the overthrow (or attempted overthrow) of dictators and oligarchies, many of whom had been installed or supported by foreign governments or economic interests. This was especially the case in Latin America, the countries of which were nominally free but often influenced heavily by the United States. These political conflicts were often referred to as struggles for national liberation, just as actual decolonization campaigns were.

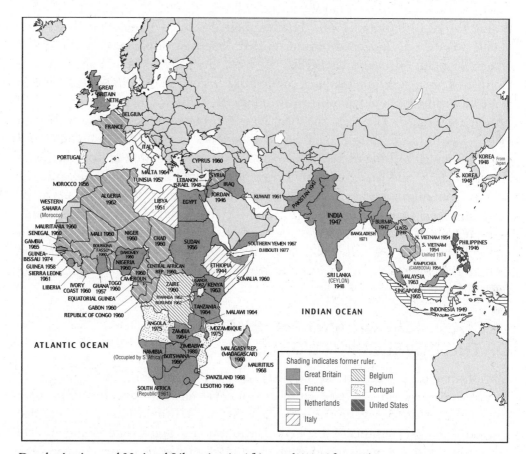

Decolonization and National Liberation in Africa and Asia After 1945.
World War II dealt the final blow to Europe's ability to maintain control over colonial empires. From the 1940s through the 1970s, a great wave of decolonization and national liberation swept Africa and Asia. Freedom was attained in a variety of ways—sometimes peacefully, sometimes by force.

Patterns of Decolonization

The means and results of decolonization varied from country to country. Specific cases are discussed in the geographical sections that follow. There was no set pattern to decolonization. Whether or not a newly liberated nation succeeded in building a healthy political and economic system depended on, among other things, the following questions:

- Did a newly decolonized nation have to fight a war to become free?
- How enlightened had the colonizing power been? Had it educated a native elite, leaving behind politicians, economists, and trained personnel with practical skills? Did the colonizing power assist actively with the transition to freedom? As a rule, Britain had a good record in this respect. To a lesser degree, France did as well.
- Were there serious ethnic, cultural, or religious divisions? In some countries, the colonizing power kept such tensions under control. Decolonization sometimes released them, leading to violence.
- Did a country have natural resources to exploit? Did the government exploit them efficiently? Former colonies that could not compete on the international market often suffered economic difficulties. Also, a newly liberated nation that did not diversify its economy but continued to rely on monoculture or the extraction of a small set of resources tended to recreate the same problems—a gap between rich and poor, economic backwardness, and environmental damage—that colonialism had caused.
- Did a newly liberated country take sides in the Cold War? Often, former colonies turned to one of the superpowers for economic and political support. Because their former masters were typically aligned with the United States and because the Marxist rhetoric of the Soviet Union (and as time passed, China) sounded appealing, many newly liberated countries turned at least for a while to the USSR (or less frequently, China). Superpowers often intervened in the affairs of decolonized nations.

THE MIDDLE EAST

General Patterns in the Postwar Middle East

Developments in the postwar Middle East were dominated mainly by the following factors:

- *The region's strategic and economic importance as the world's key source of petroleum.* Two-thirds of the world's crude oil is produced in the Middle East. The **Organization of Petroleum Exporting Countries** (OPEC), founded in 1960, is dominated by states from this area. Unfortunately, the wealth derived from oil has not led to the elimination of poverty or socio-economic inequality.
- *Contradictions between the urge to modernize and a desire to preserve Islamic tradition.* Long before the September 11, 2001, bombings, **Islamic fundamentalism** had been a force in the Middle East. One of the difficult questions facing the Middle East is how to balance Islamic heritage and Sharia law with progressive social and political practices such as democracy, civil liberties, secular law codes, and gender equality. In particular, how women are treated depends on how this issue is resolved.
- *The destabilizing effect of the Arab-Israeli conflict since 1948.* This remains an intractable, painful, and divisive issue, even into the twenty-first century.
- *Competition between the United States and the USSR for influence in the region during the Cold War.* The Middle Eastern states firmly in the U.S. camp were

Turkey and Israel. All others switched sides, back and forth, depending on where they thought their advantage lay.

- *Authoritarianism.* Dictatorship and human rights abuses have persisted, even in countries that are technically democratic.

Autonomy and Modernization

Even before World War II, the protectorates and mandates of the Middle East had gained freedom or greater autonomy. Saudi Arabia, Iraq, Jordan, Syria, and Lebanon were all free. Egypt and North Africa became independent during the 1950s and 1960s. Egyptian officers staged a coup against the pro-British king in 1952. Libya, taken from Italy by France and Britain during World War II, was also freed in 1952. Morocco and Tunisia gained freedom from France in 1956. Algeria, the African colony France was most unwilling to set free, fought a bitter war of independence from 1954 to 1962.

Turkey and Iran, already independent, continued on their paths toward modernization. More than any other Islamic state, Turkey has remained dedicated to secularism and Westernization. It has integrated itself into European markets, as well as the NATO alliance. Thus, Turkey has served as a gateway between the Western world and the Middle East. Iran did much the same but to a lesser extent and only until 1979, when its pro-Western government was overthrown.

Egypt Under Gamal Abdel Nasser

Independence, oil-based wealth, and geostrategic importance made the states of the Middle East more assertive in the 1950s and 1960s. The most famous example of this new **Arab nationalism** appeared in Egypt, which became an independent republic in 1952. By 1954, Colonel **Gamal Abdel Nasser** had taken control of the government.

A great booster of modernization, Nasser was a proponent of pan-Arabism and tried create a United Arab Republic joining all Arab nations together. This effort failed, but Nasser succeeded in modernizing his country. He also stood up to the West, nationalizing foreign-owned or foreign-controlled industries and businesses.

In 1956, Nasser took the bold step of declaring **Egyptian ownership of the Suez Canal**. This prompted the Suez Crisis, in which French, British, and Israeli troops tried to seize the canal. The United States and USSR, wishing to avoid serious armed conflict in the region, forced the three armies to withdraw, leaving the canal in Egyptian hands. The end result was a blow to British and French prestige, showing how the Cold War diminished European power.

Because Nasser was anti-British, he chose to strengthen ties with the USSR, at least temporarily. Soviet advisers and engineers brought technology and weaponry to Egypt; they also constructed the **Aswan Dam**, the world's largest. However, when the Soviets tried to control Egyptian politics, Nasser expelled them.

Nasser died in 1970. He was succeeded by Anwar Sadat, who drew Egypt closer to the United States and, in 1978, became the first Arab leader to recognize Israel. Sadat was assassinated by Islamic militants in 1981. Since then, Hosni Mubarak has served as president.

The Establishment of Israel and the Arab-Israeli Conflict

One of the most dramatic developments in the postwar Middle East was the **establishment of the State of Israel** (1948) as a homeland for the world's Jews. In 1917, Britain, which gained control over Palestine at the end of World War I, agreed in principle to create a Jewish state there but delayed this decision during the 1920s and 1930s in order to avoid Arab unrest.

After World War II and the horrors of the Holocaust, international sympathy for the Jews, along with strong U.S. support, led to the creation of Israel. Immediately, this stirred up Arab outrage and plunged the Middle East into war. The Israelis had to fight a war in 1948 simply to keep the state that had been given them. This had the effect of displacing Palestinian Arabs, who scattered to Jordan, Lebanon, and throughout the Middle East.

In 1964, the Palestinians gained a semblance of leadership with the foundation of the Palestinian Liberation Organization (PLO), a terrorist group and political movement led by **Yasser Arafat**.

The Arab states fought several wars against Israel, most notably the Six-Day War in 1967 and the Yom Kippur War in 1973. Each time, Israel, with a supremely trained, highly motivated army and strong backing from the United States, defeated the Arab coalitions, taking territory away from Arab states in the process. PLO terrorism was frequent; most infamously, a PLO squad assassinated members of the Israeli Olympic team in 1972.

Not until 1978, when **Anwar Sadat** of Egypt, encouraged by U.S. President Jimmy Carter, agreed with Israeli Prime Minister **Menachem Begin** to recognize Israel in exchange for the return of the Sinai Peninsula, was there an end to outright war in the region. Following Egypt's lead, a number of moderate Arab states began to recognize Israel during the 1980s.

However, problems remained. Throughout the 1980s, the Palestinian population of Israel staged a continuous uprising called the **intifada**. These demonstrations and protests often led to bloodshed. At the same time, terrorist groups acted against Israel as well. Terrorist attacks placed Israel in a difficult position: To avoid a total breakdown of security, it—despite being a democracy, committed to human rights—felt compelled to use violence against civilian agitators, who, while hostile and sometimes dangerous, were poorly armed and often minors.

In 1993 and 1994, the Israelis and Palestinians signed historic peace agreements, one of which called for Palestinian self-rule in parts of Israel. The United States attempted throughout the 1990s to mediate between the two sides and to keep the peace process alive. Nonetheless, tensions remained high, and the peace effort collapsed in 2001, amid violence from both sides.

Iran and Iraq

The most powerful dictatorships in the Middle East were those of Iran and Iraq. Since the 1920s, Iran had been ruled by the secular, modernizing Pahlavi shahs. The last shah, **Mohammad Reza Pahlavi**, ruled from 1941 to 1979. He used Iran's oil wealth to industrialize and modernize. Like the Turkish government, the shah's regime opposed Islamic traditionalism, encouraging Western dress, Western education, the

unveiling of women, and the eradication of Sharia law. The shah became an ally of the United States.

Unfortunately, the shah relied on repression to carry out modernization: dissidents were ruthlessly suppressed by the secret police, and the regime was decidedly antidemocratic. By 1979, the shah was in poor health, and his popularity had plummeted; he was seen by many as an American puppet and a disrespecter of Islam. He left the country to seek medical treatment and died of cancer in 1980.

In the meantime, in 1979, the Shiite cleric **Ayatollah Ruhollah Khomeini**, an Islamic fundamentalist the shah had exiled years before, returned to Iran and took control of the country. This **Iranian Revolution** transformed the country into an anti-Western (particularly anti-U.S.), theocratic dictatorship. Famously, the new regime held American hostages captive from 1979 to 1981. At the same time, Iran went to war with neighboring Iraq. The Iran-Iraq War lasted from 1980 to 1988, and devastated both countries. Khomeini died in 1989. The theocracy he created remains in place. Compared with other major revolutions of the modern era, the Iranian Revolution is unusual, if not unique, in being antimodern and religiously based.

Iraq came under the control of **Saddam Hussein** and his Baath Party in 1979. Although his title was president, Hussein became one of the Middle East's most powerful dictators. Originally sponsored by the United States because of his opposition to Iran, Hussein turned his brutality against his own people, his neighbors, and the United States. During his war with Iran, he used poison gas, drafted teenaged children to fight, and killed many civilians. He viciously persecuted Iraq's Kurdish minority.

In 1990, Hussein invaded the oil-rich state of Kuwait and appeared ready to move against Saudi Arabia. In the first major conflict of the post–Cold War era, the first **Gulf War** (1991), the United States led a military coalition to push Hussein out of Kuwait. Between 1991 and 2003, the United Nations imposed trade sanctions, backed by U.S. and allied military action, to prevent Iraq's development of weapons of mass destruction (and to compel Hussein to allow weapons inspections). Hussein's regime was overthrown in a U.S.-led war in 2003.

AFRICA

Decolonization began in Africa mainly during the 1950s and 1960s, somewhat later than in the Middle East or Asia. By the late 1990s, Africa would contain forty-six countries. Security and economic stability in most of them are still affected by the legacy of colonialism.

National Liberation in North Africa

The Islamic states of North Africa became free during the 1950s. Egypt declared independence in 1952, as did Libya. Morocco and Tunisia gained freedom from France in 1956. The long and painful **Algerian War of Independence** (1954–1962) against France completed the process of lifting the colonial yoke from North Africa.

North African states had several advantages over sub-Saharan Africa when it came to decolonization. They were largely, although not completely, homogeneous in terms of religion, ethnicity, and language. They had existed as meaningful political units for

a long time, making the transition to nation-state easier. Their colonizing powers also left behind technology and industrial infrastructures (railroads, telegraphs, canals, roads) that proved economically useful, especially in Algeria and Egypt.

Independence in Sub-Saharan Africa

The nations of sub-Saharan Africa had more of a struggle to create successful independent states. Major freedom movements began during the 1940s, in South Africa (the African National Congress); the Gold Coast, or Ghana (Kwame Nkrumah); and Kenya (Jomo Kenyatta).

For the most part, these were nonviolent movements led by intellectuals and labor activists. There were, however, exceptions. The Mau Mau movement in Kenya departed from Kenyatta's approach and killed almost 2,000 people in the 1950s. Violence played a substantial part in the decolonization of Zimbabwe (Rhodesia), South Africa, Rwanda, Zaire (the Belgian Congo), Angola, and Mozambique.

Varying Transitions to Freedom

For the most part, decolonization in the parts of Africa that had been British and French went smoothly. Both Britain and France prepared their colonies for freedom by educating native elites, allowing greater native representation in transitional governments, and minimizing the possibility of interethnic conflict.

Not all went well, however. In Rhodesia, a white-controlled government declared independence from Britain in 1965. It harshly repressed black natives, who responded with violence. Only after a savage conflict was Rhodesia placed under native rule, in 1980, when the country renamed itself Zimbabwe. South African independence from Britain involved serious problems as well.

The worst transitions to independence were made by Belgian and Portuguese colonies. Here, the imperial masters had been particularly exploitative, and neither country took steps to prepare its colonies for independence. Guinea-Bissau gained freedom from Portugal in 1974 but only after a vicious guerrilla war. Angola fought a war of liberation against Portugal from 1961 to 1975. After achieving independence, Angola suffered years of civil war. Likewise, Mozambique fought Portugal from 1965 to 1975, only to descend into a long civil conflict.

Belgium pulled out of Rwanda in 1962, having artificially exacerbated differences between two tribes, the Hutu and Tutsi, who came to hate each other deeply. When the Belgians freed the Congo, postindependence violence was so pervasive from 1960 to 1964 that the United Nations had to intervene. The prime mover in the Congolese independence movement, the Marxist Patrice Lumumba, was assassinated by political rivals (almost certainly with U.S. knowledge, if not complicity) in late 1965.

South Africa and the Experience of Apartheid

As in Rhodesia/Zimbabwe, but for much longer, decolonization in South Africa was tainted by the clash between white and black citizens of the newly free country. The government that declared freedom from Britain was controlled by the white

minority, largely descended from Dutch Boers. These Afrikaners practiced the policy of **apartheid** (extreme racial segregation). South Africa is one of the world's richest sources of gold and diamonds. Between the 1960s and the 1990s, the white government of South Africa turned the country into the wealthiest, most modern, and most industrialized on the continent.

However, South Africa became one of Africa's most repressive nations as well. By the 1980s, internal unrest, economic problems, and international revulsion were placing pressure on the South African government to abandon apartheid. The Zulu Confederation, the African National Congress (ANC), and other such groups opposed the white government. The ANC's leader, **Nelson Mandela**, gained the status of sympathetic dissident during his long imprisonment (1964–1990) by the white authorities. His wife, Winnie Mandela, continued the struggle on his behalf. Another moral figure in the antiapartheid movement was Bishop **Desmond Tutu**, a black clergyman in the Anglican Church and a Nobel Peace Prize recipient. In 1990, the government released Nelson Mandela. In 1994, free elections resulted in the ANC's victory. Mandela became the country's president.

Problems Facing Independent Africa

Unfortunately, many of Africa's original aspirations proved difficult if not impossible to attain. Few nations managed to achieve democratic governments, open societies, and economies that led to prosperity for all (or even many) citizens. Some of the problems that have interfered with African modernization include the following:

- *Dictatorship*: Despite beginning as democratic systems, many of Africa's governments degenerated into strongman regimes. Among the most notorious were Idi Amin of Uganda (1971–1979) and Mobutu Sese Seko of Zaire (1965–1997).
- *Corruption*: Dictatorial or not, many African regimes tended to function according to unlawful systems of patronage, nepotism, and graft.
- *Failure to modernize and diversify economies*: Rather than industrialize and diversify, many African regimes generated wealth by continuing to export the natural resources their former colonial masters took from them. This enabled foreign investors great control over African politics. It also kept profits in the hands of political rulers, rather than spreading wealth among the population at large.
- *The Cold War*: As with the rest of the developing world, many African nations became pawns in the global chess game between the United States and USSR.
- *Rapid population growth and food shortages*: The rate of African population growth has outstripped the rate of economic growth. Systems of food distribution are often inadequate, leading to food shortages and famine. The worst famines have been in Somalia and Ethiopia.
- *The HIV/AIDS pandemic*: From the 1980s onward, the HIV virus, which seems to have originated in Africa, has caused millions of deaths. Containing the virus has proven impossible, and African nations are too poor to afford large quantities of the medicines needed to treat it.

- *Lack of cultural or linguistic unity:* In Africa, the lines determining a nation's political borders often do not match where people of certain ethnicities or languages live. Most borders were drawn by European colonizers for their own benefit and convenience, leaving behind confusing varieties of ethnicities, languages, cultural practices, and religions in each country. This makes it difficult for a single state to govern all its people fairly.
- *Intertribal and interethnic conflict:* Frequently, the above problem becomes serious enough that it breaks out into violence. Since the colonial period, most of the wars in Africa have been fought within national borders, not between different countries.
- *Uncontrolled flow of small arms and light weapons:* Although this is a problem throughout the developing world, it is particularly dire in Africa. Small arms feature prominently in armed conflicts, postconflict situations, and everyday life. Thousands of children have been forcibly drafted into militias and paramilitaries.
- *Treatment of women:* In Africa's more developed countries and especially in the cities, women have attained a certain degree of economic and social equality: the right to an education, the right to work, the right to legal divorce and birth control, and so on. However, progress has been slow, and women are still dominated by men, especially in rural areas. In some regions, polygamy is still permitted. One infamous custom, clitoridectomy (female circumcision), is still practiced in some parts of Africa.

ASIA

Among the nations of the developing world, those of Asia have been the most successful in building stable governments and attaining economic prosperity. Regional organizations, notably the Association of Southeast Asian Nations (ASEAN, formed in 1967), have boosted economic, social, and cultural developments and cooperation among their members. Nonetheless, political repression, interethnic and interreligious strife, socioeconomic inequality, and periodic economic crises have caused problems as well. The Cold War also played a role in creating tensions.

The Philippines

In South and Southeast Asia, decolonization campaigns began immediately after World War II. Some were ended quickly, others dragged on. Almost all involved some degree of violence. The first colony in the region to be freed was the Philippines, which, during World War II, had been promised independence from the United States. Freedom was granted voluntarily in 1946. The United States hoped that this would provide an example to colonial powers such as France and Britain.

Indian and Pakistani Independence

India and Pakistan gained their independence next. In this case, Britain handed over power freely. In 1945, the British viceroy, Lord Louis Mountbatten, was ordered to prepare to transfer government to "responsible Indian hands" by 1948. Riots and

disturbances, mainly consisting of clashes between Muslims and Hindus, sped up the British timetable.

Indian and Pakistani independence was granted on August 15, 1947. Although the British did not have to be expelled by force, independence still led to violence. Hindu-Muslim conflict cost at least a million lives. In January 1948, **Mohandas (Mahatma) Gandhi**, spiritual leader of the Indian freedom movement, was assassinated by a Hindu extremist who opposed his rhetoric of tolerance between the two faiths.

Despite their difficult beginnings, both nations survived. Pakistan became a modern Islamic republic and a major regional power. However, the original goal of its founder, **Muhammad Ali Jinnah**, has not been attained. Jinnah dreamed of a democratic, modernizing republic that could also remain true to Muslim traditions. Instead, Pakistan has been plagued by corruption, political repression, and military rule. It has also been caught up in a costly and dangerous diplomatic rivalry with its neighbor India. Both India and Pakistan developed nuclear-weapons capability during the 1990s, making their conflict even tenser.

Modern India

India has turned itself into the world's largest democracy. On the other hand, it has also suffered from sprawling inefficiency, an inability to balance population growth with economic growth, and interethnic and interfaith strife. The dominant political force in free India was the Congress Party, led by **Jawaharlal Nehru**, who served as India's prime minister from 1947 until his death in 1964. Unlike Gandhi, who had favored traditional Hindu values (although not religious bigotry) and economic simplicity, Nehru wanted to secularize India and turn it into a modern, educated industrial power.

Diplomatically, Nehru negotiated a difficult position: neighbor to a hostile China and an even more hostile Pakistan and not wishing to be a client of the Soviets, the British, or the United States, Nehru maintained a friendly, cooperative relationship with the USSR, without actually falling into the Soviet camp. As Sukarno had done in Indonesia (see below), Nehru preserved his country's status as a nonaligned nation.

From 1966 to 1975 and again from 1977 to 1984, Nehru's daughter, Indira Gandhi, was prime minister. She continued her father's policies of modernization and political **nonalignment**. Religious strife was her downfall. Her government's actions against the Sikh minority of Punjab provoked Sikh soldiers to assassinate her. From 1984 to 1991, her son, Rajiv Gandhi, served as prime minister, before being killed by Sri Lankan separatists. Since 1991, India's democratic government has continued to struggle with the same problems that Nehru and his descendants did—although the country has enjoyed a boom in high-tech industries like computers and film making.

After freeing India, Britain let go of its Southeast Asian colonies. Burma became independent in 1948, Malaysia in 1957, Singapore (which had been attached to Malaysia) in 1965. Hong Kong remained in British hands until 1997, when it was returned to mainland China.

Indonesia

Less willingly than the British, the Dutch and French were forced out of Southeast Asia. After World War II, the Netherlands retained control over the Dutch East Indies, or Indonesia. The charismatic leader of the Indonesian Nationalist Party, **Sukarno**, began to agitate for freedom, and a war of national liberation began in 1945. Afraid that continued combat would lead to a communist takeover of the region, the United States persuaded the Dutch to hand over freedom.

The new nation of Indonesia was born in 1949, with Sukarno as its leader. A huge archipelago, Indonesia is one of the world's largest and most populous nations. It is linguistically and ethnically diverse, although 80 percent of the population is Muslim. At first Sukarno governed democratically, but he became authoritarian over time. Like Nehru, he pursued a nonaligned foreign policy but was far more radical in calling for the Third World to defy the West. Eventually, he drew closer to the Indonesian Communist Party. In 1965, the army, allied with conservative Muslims, staged a coup against Sukarno. It turned into a popular uprising, in which as many as half a million people—mainly Communists—were killed. Sukarno was weakened by the coup, then forced out of office in 1967.

From 1967 to 1998, Indonesia was governed by a military strongman, Suharto. A dictatorial ruler with a record of frequent human-rights abuses, Suharto promoted economic growth, anticommunism, and alliance with the United States.

Vietnam, Laos, and Cambodia

The French attempted for almost a decade to hold on to their colony of Indochina (Vietnam, Laos, and Cambodia). In September 1945, the Vietnamese nationalist and communist **Ho Chi Minh** declared independence. Encouraged by the U.S. promise of freedom to the Philippines and proud of his movement's record of anti-Japanese resistance during World War II, Ho Chi Minh hoped that freedom would be granted without a struggle.

Instead, the French, with U.S. support, tried until 1954 to keep Indochina. Defeated by Vietnamese expertise in guerrilla warfare, the French withdrew. Laos, Cambodia, and Vietnam were given their independence. Vietnam was temporarily divided into a northern communist-dominated zone and a southern noncommunist zone.

Elections were to be held as soon as possible, but the French-educated, Catholic, U.S.-backed leader of South Vietnam, Ngo Dinh Diem, refused to allow elections, knowing that the Buddhist, anti-French peasant masses would vote against him. The North Vietnamese began to fight the south in 1959.

By the early 1960s, the United States was providing substantial military support for South Vietnam; it continued its military intervention for years. In 1968, the United States suffered a serious public-relations setback when the communists staged the Tet Offensive, catching the Americans and South Vietnamese off guard. America scaled back its war effort, withdrawing its troops in 1973. In April 1975, the communists captured the South Vietnamese capital and, with much violence, unified the country under their rule.

Militarism and Authoritarianism in Southeast Asia

Military or authoritarian government became the rule throughout much of Southeast Asia. The Communist **Khmer Rouge** movement in Cambodia took power and carried out a hideous reign of terror that claimed as many as 2 million victims. The U.S.-backed regime of Ferdinand Marcos, which governed the Philippines until the early 1980s, violated civil rights and was extravagantly corrupt. Myanmar (Burma) and Thailand came under military rule. As noted above, Indonesia was heavily authoritarian. Even prosperous and ultramodern Singapore, under prime minister Lee Kuan-yew, emphasized conformity and tradition over freedom and civil liberties.

Japan After World War II

Modernization came to the major nations of East Asia. Japan became the region's surprise powerhouse, just as West Germany, one of the defeated powers of World War II, became the economic dynamo of postwar Europe. At its peak during the 1980s, the Japanese economy was the world's third most productive, after the United States's and West Germany's. Per capita income was among the world's highest, and social services such as education and health care were excellent.

After World War II, Japan was occupied by the U.S. armed forces, which presided over democratic constitutional reform (1947) and the demilitarization of the country. The United States viewed Japan as a strategic anchor of its Cold War policy in Asia and invested in it heavily, both militarily and economically. Politically, Japan became a parliamentary democracy; although the emperor retained his symbolic role, the Diet (parliament) ran the government.

The Liberal Democratic Party came to dominate party politics, and while Japan's democratic system never ceased to function, the Liberal Democrats' influence over the Diet led some commentators to view Japan as slightly oligarchic. Much of Japan's postwar success depended on its population's dedicated work ethic and, through the 1980s, its willingness to place the needs of Japanese society above the desires of the individual.

The 1990s, however, brought not only an economic recession and revelations of deep-seated government corruption but also changes in social attitudes. Younger generations are less willing to conform, to work as selflessly as their parents and grandparents, or to accept traditional social roles. A desire for greater gender equality, in a society where women have generally been expected to play secondary and supporting roles, has also taken hold.

Taiwan, South Korea, and the "Little Tigers"

Like Japan, but to a lesser extent, Taiwan (the Republic of China) and South Korea developed prosperous and free societies. From the 1950s through the 1970s, neither Taiwan nor South Korea was truly democratic. Instead, they were anticommunist regimes that, while parliamentary, concentrated power in the hands of one dominant party. In the case of Taiwan, this was the Nationalist Party (Kuomintang) that had been defeated by Mao's Chinese Communist Party in 1949. Chiang Kai-shek

remained in control of the Kuomintang—and thus Taiwan—until his death in 1975. By the end of the 1970s, Taiwan began to democratize.

South Korea remained authoritarian until 1987, when free elections were held. Despite their less than democratic nature, both Taiwan and South Korea became allies of the United States because of their staunch anticommunism. They also became economic success stories; along with Hong Kong, Singapore, and Thailand, they became known as the **"little tigers"** for their economic strength (as distinct from the great "tiger" of the Japanese economy).

Both Taiwan and South Korea were important to the United States's Cold War strategic posture. In 1950–1953, the United States spearheaded the United Nations coalition that kept South Korea safe from North Korean invasion. In the 1970s, even though the United States was forced to disclaim its formal recognition of Taiwan in order to establish ties with the People's Republic of China, the U.S.-Taiwanese relationship has remained strong, both politically and economically.

North Korea

Communism came to North Korea after World War II, when the country was divided by the Americans and Soviets. From the 1940s onward, North Korea has remained one of the most isolated and rigidly dictatorial societies on earth. Its long-time leader, **Kim Il Sung** (1948–1994), was an uncompromising Stalinist and ruthlessly oppressive. To the present day, North Korea retains its communist system, although economic collapse and its insistence on maintaining a huge military (which now includes a nuclear-missile capacity) have placed the population in danger of mass starvation.

The People's Republic of China

The People's Republic of China, established in 1949 by **Mao Tse-tung** and the Chinese Communist Party (CCP), has been the most populous communist nation on earth for more than five decades. Like the rest of East Asia, China has modernized, although not as consistently.

China was ruled by Mao from 1949 until his death in 1976. At first, Mao seemed to want to carry out pragmatic social and economic reform. His New Democracy of the early 1950s was greeted with some enthusiasm, as were his initial land reforms. His first Five-Year Plan (1953–1958), which imitated the USSR's five-year plans, led to industrial growth. Collectivization of agriculture began in 1955 but was (at first!) carried out more gradually than Stalin's collectivization of the late 1920s and early 1930s.

On the other hand, Mao's radical transformation of society, which included persecution of dissenters and so-called class enemies (members of the bourgeoisie or aristocracy), was harsh. Also, his aspirations became overly ambitious by the end of the 1950s, and he pressed too quickly for further modernization. In 1958, Mao began the **Great Leap Forward**, which included a rapid industrial buildup, even more grandiose than the Five-Year Plan's. In the agricultural sphere, it intensified collectivization and called for an unrealistic increase in food production. The trauma,

stress, and confusion caused by the Great Leap Forward led to chaos and breakdown in industry. Even worse, agriculture collapsed altogether. The famines that resulted in 1959 and 1960 killed millions (the best estimate is 15 to 20 million). The Great Leap Forward was halted in 1960 but not before the damage was done. It caused splits within the CCP leadership, and opposition to Mao grew. (An interesting exercise is to compare Mao's method of rapid modernization to Stalin's.)

In 1966, Mao embarked on another program of radical modernization, the **Great Proletarian Cultural Revolution**, which lasted until 1976. This has been interpreted by historians as a policy used by Mao and his wife, Jiang Qing (the movement's primary architect), to strike at their political enemies, and also to instill absolute revolutionary purity within Chinese society and culture. Censorship was absolute, and indoctrination was crushingly heavy. The one acceptable source of all wisdom was *The Little Red Book*, a collection of Mao's sayings. Young communist activists, known as Red Guards, rampaged throughout the country denouncing and putting on trial any person—university professors, factory foremen, heads of collective farms, writers and journalists, and even politicians—whom they considered to be untrue to revolutionary communist ideals. Victims were demoted, harassed, often arrested and sent to labor camps for "reeducation," and sometimes executed. Even members of the CCP elite were not immune; among those arrested was Deng Xiaoping.

The Cultural Revolution ended with Mao's death in 1976. In 1978, **Deng Xiaoping**, having defeated Mao's widow and her allies (known afterward as the Gang of Four), came to power. Like Mao, Deng was a modernizer. However, while Mao had been inflexible and revolutionary, the pragmatic Deng was more concerned with China's well-being and growing strength than with absolute commitment to abstract Marxist ideals. Famously, he commented that whether a cat is black or white makes no difference, as long as it catches mice.

In contrast to Mao's anticapitalism, Deng allowed limited free-market reform and returned land to the farmers that Mao had communized. As a result, China experienced huge economic growth throughout the 1980s. Wages and standards of living improved. There was, however, a social and cultural effect as well. With greater wealth came the desire for greater freedom, a luxury Deng was not prepared to allow. By the end of the 1980s, China would have to deal with this growing problem. One of this era's most interesting comparisons is the success of Deng's reforms with the failure of Gorbachev's perestroika campaign.

LATIN AMERICA

Dictatorship and Economic Exploitation in Latin America

Latin America had freed itself from colonial domination in the 1800s, so national liberation and modernization here involved the struggle against dictatorship at home and the political and economic influence of the United States.

The Great Depression, despite its generally negative impact, compelled Latin American nations to diversify their economies somewhat. World War II also forced a number of the interwar period's dictators out of power. However, despite some temporary progress toward economic modernization and democratization during the late 1940s and early 1950s, many Latin American countries reverted to exploitative

economies and dictatorial government from the late 1950s through the early 1980s. Moreover, in Latin America, "modernization" often led to a concentration of wealth in the hands of a narrow social stratum and weak social justice for the working classes and indigenous peoples.

Military governments and right-wing dictatorships appeared during these decades. By the mid-1970s, only Colombia, Venezuela, and Costa Rica could be considered democratic.

In 1943, military rule was established in Argentina. By 1946, the charismatic **Juan Perón** had come to dominate the military government by appealing to the poor. His wife, **Eva**, whose appeal among the lower-class *descamisados* ("shirtless ones") was great, helped him in this. During the 1950s, Perón became increasingly right-wing, even fascistic. He was overthrown by the army in 1955 and fled to Spain. Perón's popularity remained so high, however, that he was able to return in 1973 and become president until his death in 1974. A brutal military regime ruled from 1976 to 1983. This regime ruthlessly purged leftists, intellectuals, and dissidents, causing at least 30,000 to "disappear" over a decade and a half.

Brazil and Chile also had military regimes from the mid-1960s through the mid-1980s. In Chile, General **Augusto Pinochet** (backed by the U.S. Central Intelligence Agency) led a 1973 coup against the left-wing government of Salvador Allende—who, in 1970, had become one of the few Marxist politicians to come to power by means of democratic election. Pinochet remained in charge until the late 1980s. Like the military dictators of Argentina, Pinochet held the reins of power tightly, using force and violence to eliminate enemies and dissidents.

Mexico, although nominally democratic, was really an authoritarian oligarchy run by the **Institutional Revolutionary Party** (PRI). Its ability to keep the oil-based Mexican economy healthy during the 1950s and 1960s made the PRI's less than democratic nature acceptable to most Mexicans. By the end of the 1960s, however, economic stress, as well as the rising resentment of Indians, Mayans, and other minorities, who felt they were being treated as second-class citizens, stirred up discontent with the government.

The **1968 protests** shook Mexico City (as they did Paris, Prague, and many U.S. universities), showing how the PRI's democratic facade was wearing thin. By the 1980s, the Mexican government was starting to reform gradually but not completely.

Fidel Castro and the Cuban Revolution

Dictatorship from the left appeared in Cuba. In January 1959, the revolutionary movement led by **Fidel Castro** overthrew the right-wing dictator Fulgencio Batista. Within months, Castro had begun to nationalize industry and carry out land reform. His goals were to modernize, industrialize, increase literacy rates, and eliminate socioeconomic inequality. With his second-in-command, the Argentine radical Ernesto "Che" Guevara, he also wanted to combat what he saw as U.S. imperialism in Latin America. Accordingly, the Cuban revolutionaires declared themselves Marxists and turned to the Soviet Union for assistance.

Because of its proximity to the United States, Cuba became a Cold War hot spot from 1961 onward, as demonstrated by the Bay of Pigs incident (1961) and the **Cuban Missile Crisis** (1962). Domestically, the Castro regime's record is mixed. It is

undeniable that Cuba has modernized under Castro, and the gap between rich and poor that had prevailed under Batista narrowed considerably. Educational levels have improved, and women (at least officially) are treated with greater equality than before. However, Castro's regime has been rigidly dictatorial and has violated human rights for more than four decades.

Latin America as Cold War Battlefield

Many problems plagued Latin America during the 1970s and early 1980s. Almost all of the military dictatorships found themselves heavily in debt, especially to the United States. Latin America had also become a great Cold War battlefield. Cuba, both on its own and on behalf of the USSR, consistently attempted to export Marxist revolution throughout Latin America. The Soviet Union did the same. For its part, the United States, fearing the spread of leftism directly to its south, made a practice of supporting any Latin American regime that opposed communism. Unfortunately, pro-U.S. regimes in Latin America tended to be right-wing and dictatorial.

One of the clearest examples of how Cold War politics were played out in Latin America during these years was the **Nicaraguan Revolution**. In 1979, the Marxist, Soviet-supported Sandinista movement overthrew the right-wing Somoza dictatorship that had ruled (with U.S. support) since 1937. In response, the U.S. government began to support a right-wing, counterrevolutionary guerrilla movement known as the Contras. In essence, the struggle between the Sandinista government and the Contra movement, both of whom were responsible for political abuses, was a proxy war between the Soviets and the Americans.

Democratization in Latin America

During the late 1980s and early 1990s, a wave of democratization swept Latin America. Much of it was tied to economic improvements, but just as much was due to the cooling down of the Cold War, which reduced the superpowers' anxiety about influence in the region. In addition, the Organization of American States (OAS), a regional organization of approximately forty countries, has promoted democratization, peace, and security in the region.

Argentina's dictatorship fell in 1983, and a free election peacefully handed power over in 1989. Brazil's dictatorship collapsed in 1985. Mexican elections in 1988 prompted the PRI to loosen its monopoly on power. The controversial Pinochet lost power in Chile in 1989.

One of the few exceptions to this trend was Cuba, where Castro's communist regime remained in power, despite the fall of communism in Eastern Europe and the USSR. Latin America's transition to democracy is still not complete. Corruption, backsliding toward authoritarian practice, the widespread economic dependence on illicit drug trafficking (especially in Colombia), and economic instability have troubled many of the region's new democracies. Nonetheless, the struggle to move toward democracy—or continue in that direction—continues.

Social Developments, Cultural Changes, and Intellectual Trends

CHAPTER 34

- The modern versus the postmodernist (contemporary) period
- Postindustrial (service and high-tech) economies
- Economic globalization (multinational corporations and international trade agreements)
- Socio-economic features of the developed world
- The green revolution in agriculture
- The developing (third) world and the north-south split
- Population growth and modern migration

- Social activism and nongovernmental organizations (NGOs)
- Women's liberation and feminism
- Multiculturalism versus Americanization
- Mass-media technology, the computer, and the information (digital) revolution
- Scientific advancements (quantum physics, genetics, rocketry, computers, robotics)

The twentieth and twenty-first centuries have witnessed an explosion of social, cultural, and intellectual changes. The pace of scientific and technological advancement is faster than ever before. The world's population has grown with breathtaking speed. The world's economies have become increasingly interconnected.

Different parts of the world experienced these transformations differently. As a general rule, the changes of the twentieth and twenty-first centuries can be said to have proceeded along four basic tracks:

- In Western Europe, the United States, and Canada—the West—and Australia and New Zealand, movement has been toward stable democratization, greater economic prosperity, thorough urbanization, commitment to social equality and individual liberties, and the creation of social welfare systems. Scientific and technological achievement has been tremendous. These nations have developed postindustrial economies that emphasize services, consumerism, and cutting-edge technology (especially biotech and computers).

- Prosperous nations in Asia—the so-called tigers, such as Japan and, to a lesser extent, Taiwan, South Korea, Indonesia, and Singapore—have made great strides toward economic and technological modernization. They have urbanized greatly and developed a variety of social services. Their economies are postindustrial and high-tech. In many respects, Japan has equaled or surpassed the West (even though its phenomenal economic growth slowed during the 1990s). However, these societies, although nominally democratic, have been relatively slow to embrace or even tolerate the diversity and individualism that have been the hallmarks of Western societies during the late 1800s and 1900s.

- The Soviet Union and Eastern Europe modernized economically, especially during the postwar era. They urbanized and developed social welfare services. Technological and scientific advancement was considerable. However, Soviet and East European economies remained industrial rather than postindustrial and, in terms of technological finesse (especially with regard to computers), were cruder than Western economies. Moreover, until the collapse of communism in this region from 1989 to 1991, political systems were dictatorial and repressive. Even after the collapse of communism, it has been difficult for this region to move toward democracy and economic prosperity.

- The developing nations of Asia, Africa, the Middle East, and Latin America are all, to one degree or another, striving to attain advanced economic systems, modern societies, and representative forms of government. Some have made progress, attaining a relatively high level of prosperity or functioning democracies, or both. Others are mired in backwardness, poverty, civil war, and dictatorship. Most are somewhere in between. Perhaps the most distinctive case is the People's Republic of China. Communist China has the geography, population, and military capacity of a major power, and its economic growth has been considerable from the 1980s onward. The government is still authoritarian, however, and social and economic progress remains uneven.

With regard to historical labels, it is common to speak of the **modern period** (ca. 1800–1945) as having come to an end, at least in the more developed West. The postwar era and the early twenty-first century are generally referred to by historians as the **contemporary** or **postmodern era**. The modern era was characterized by industrialization, the formation of the nation-state as the primary form of political organization, and the struggle for representative government and economic equality. The postmodern era is characterized by postindustrial and global forms of economic organization, multiculturalism and the blurring of national lines, and an extreme individualism that takes for granted the political and social equality won during the modern era.

One can argue convincingly that this description suits the Western world well. It is more difficult to fit the label "postmodern" to the less developed nations of Africa, Asia, Latin America, and the Middle East, many of which are still in the process of modernizing. This unevenness of social, political, and economic development is in and of itself a major characteristic of twentieth- and twenty-first-century world history.

ECONOMIC GLOBALIZATION

International Trade Before World War II

Systems of international trade had existed long before the twentieth century, and the scope and volume of that trade grew steadily between World War I and the **Great Depression** of the 1930s. The Depression sparked a wave of **protectionism**, as countries sought to shield their own industries and farms by imposing high tariffs on other nations' goods. The most notorious example of protectionism was the United States' **Smoot-Hawley Tariff Act** (1930). This act is widely considered to have spread the Depression to Europe, Latin America, and Asia by destroying the ability of these regions to export goods to the United States. World War II altered the patterns of international commerce in obvious ways.

Foundations of the Post-World War II Economic System

True globalization of the world economy began after World War II. Franklin Roosevelt, guided by the economic principles of John Maynard Keynes (and the convictions of Woodrow Wilson before him), believed that free trade was the key not only to economic prosperity but also to world peace. Nations whose economies interacted equitably, he felt, would be less likely to go to war.

In July 1944, Roosevelt met with Allied delegates at Bretton Woods, New Hampshire. It was here that the International Bank for Reconstruction and Development (the **World Bank**) and the **International Monetary Fund** (IMF), whose purpose was to rebuild Europe and lend assistance to countries in Asia, Africa, and Latin America, were created. In 1958, the first round of the **General Agreement on Tariffs and Trade** (GATT) was held, to establish the working rules governing imports, exports, and economic interaction among participating nations. The Soviet Union and the Eastern bloc refused to join this **Bretton Woods System**, and so their economies were cut off from much of the rest of the world's. Until the international economic crises of the 1970s, currency exchanges were fixed to the value of the U.S. dollar, the world's strongest. In turn, the U.S. dollar was based on the gold standard.

Varieties of Economic Development, 1940s–1970s

Over time, great prosperity came to the United States, Canada, Japan, and the nations of Western Europe. One way Western Europe staged its economic recovery was through **economic union** (the European Coal and Steel Community, the European Economic Community, the European Union), as described in Chapter 33. The reconstruction of war-torn Western Europe—particularly West Germany—was nothing short of incredible. The same was true of Japan.

The rest of the world developed unevenly. In Latin America and Africa, many governments relied on the export of small sets of natural resources or crops, just as they had done as colonies or economic dependents during the 1800s. The Middle East benefited from its dominance on oil production. The **Organization of Petroleum Exporting Countries** (OPEC), formed in 1960, consists mainly of Mideastern nations. OPEC has been one of the most successful and influential international economic coalitions in history.

The economies of the Soviet Union, its East European allies, and Communist China tended to remain largely but not completely isolated from the Western world.

Many nations in Asia, such as Japan, Taiwan, South Korea, Indonesia, and Singapore, were quick to adapt to global capitalism. As Western Europe had done, many Asian nations joined together in regional economic associations. Although the **Association of Southeast Asian Nations** (ASEAN), formed in 1967, was mainly a diplomatic group, it also tightened economic ties. The Asia-Pacific Economic Cooperation Group (1989) did the same.

A general economic crisis struck most of the world during the 1970s. OPEC's **oil embargo** severely affected the energy-dependent economies of the West. Recession and inflation plagued the United States and Western Europe. Although the USSR had its own oil reserves and was safe from OPEC's embargo, inefficiency, food shortages, the cost of the arms race, and governmental corruption sapped the economies of the Eastern bloc. In 1971, President Richard Nixon rocked the international community by taking the U.S. dollar off the gold standard.

Multinational Corporations

Nevertheless, Western economies recovered during the mid-to-late 1980s. Part of this recovery involved the growing strength of **multinational corporations**: huge conglomerates that, while technically "from" a single country, maintained factories, subsidiaries, and distribution networks all over the world, employing foreign workers and selling directly to foreign markets.

For years, the activities of these multinational corporations had been laying the groundwork for further globalization of the economy during the 1980s and 1990s. Critics say that multinational corporations have hurt indigenous populations by exploiting their labor, harming their environments, and preventing their own economies from producing homegrown industries and manufactured goods.

Economic Globalization During the 1990s

The 1990s brought about a high tide of **economic globalization**, at the same time as (and somewhat related to) the collapse of Soviet and East European communism and the democratization of much of the developing world, especially Latin America. The strength of multinational corporations increased. The explosion of computer technology facilitated the electronic transfer of money. Meetings of the **Group of Seven**, or **G-7** (the **Group of Eight**, or **G-8**, after 1998, when Russia joined), an informal association of the countries with the world's largest economies—the United States, Canada, Great Britain, Japan, Germany, France, and Italy—became more frequent and increasingly influential.

In 1995, the GATT regulations were upgraded and strengthened by the formation of the **World Trade Organization** (WTO), whose purpose is to regulate the economic interaction of the more than 100 nations that belong to it.

Regional economic unions became increasingly important. In 1994, the United States, Mexico, and Canada created a zone of free movement of money, goods, services, and labor by means of the **North American Free Trade Agreement** (NAFTA). Moves are afoot to enlarge this zone to include all of the Americas, through the auspices of the Organization of American States (OAS).

Asian nations have tightened their ties as well. By far the boldest experiment in economic integration, however, is Western Europe's. In 1991, the nations of the **European Union** (EU) agreed to the Maastricht Treaty, which provides for the creation of a single currency (the **euro**), the establishment of a European Central Bank, and common policymaking in the fields of immigration, environmental protection, and even foreign affairs and security issues. It took until the mid-1990s for EU nations to ratify the Maastricht Treaty, and friction between member states regarding the details of integration continues. Still, in 2002, many of the EU states abandoned their own currencies for the euro.

Costs and Benefits of Globalization

The costs and benefits of economic globalization are mixed. On one hand, it has generated great wealth, at least in a broad sense and in certain parts of the world. Proponents of globalization argue, with some justification, that free trade helps to preserve peace.

On the other hand, the fact that the economies of all (or most) nations influence each other so strongly means that negative trends in one region—financial crisis in Mexico in 1994 or Asia in 1997, for example, or Russia and Brazil in 1998—can adversely affect the entire world. In addition, it is questionable whether all nations will be willing to subject their individual economic policies to the dictates of the WTO or other international bodies. There have already been bitter disputes over this issue, especially between developing and developed countries.

Finally, globalization threatens to lead to a constant state of economic change and instability. Seeking profits, multinational corporations tend to move to wherever they can produce more cheaply. This means relocating to whatever city or country will provide them with the least expensive labor force, the most advantageous tax benefits or exemptions, and the most lenient environmental regulations. This can also mean the lowering of wages, the sudden unemployment or layoff of local labor forces, and great social stress. Agriculture has been greatly affected by globalization, as farmers in one country find themselves competing with cheap food being imported from other parts of the world. Some critics of globalization also point to its homogenizing effects on culture and fear that their own indigenous cultures are being crushed under the force of foreign (in particular, American) popular culture and values.

Whether or not economic globalization will continue remains to be seen. It most likely will. What also remains to be seen is whether the benefits will eventually outweigh the costs. This is much harder to predict and will remain a major issue into the twenty-first century.

SOCIAL TRENDS AND MOVEMENTS

Basic Features of Western Societies

Social change during the twentieth century was so rapid and thorough that it is difficult to generalize about it. By and large, Western nations and other developed states can be said to have evolved the following social features (albeit imperfectly and/or gradually in many cases):

- Elimination of legal distinctions between social classes.
- The replacement of aristocratic social elites by a professional, white-collar class that attains its elite status through earned wealth and/or educational status (often referred to as meritocracy or technocracy).
- Creation of a large, stable **middle class**.
- Access to at least a minimum standard of living and adequate level of material well-being, even among lower classes.
- **Urbanization**, as well as **suburbanization**.
- Establishment of a **social welfare system** that includes unemployment insurance, pensions, and health care (at least for the elderly, if not the population as a whole).
- Universal educational system.
- Equal political rights for all adult citizens, including females.
- Equal treatment of all citizens before the law.
- Equal rights for minorities (still an ongoing process).
- The participation of **nongovernmental organizations** (NGOs) in the political process. NGOs, representing the interests of various groups in society, pressure governments to implement policies and provide social services.

Standard-of-Living Disparity Between the West and Developing World

TIP

In 1998, the United States alone consumed 25 percent of the world's energy, while its population makes up only 5 percent of the total world population.

With varying degrees of success, countries in the developing regions of Africa, Asia, Latin America, and the Middle East attempted to bring about many of these same changes. Some managed to do so by the end of the century, others did not. Agricultural productivity rose between the 1940s and 1970s, thanks to the **green revolution**, which spread new technology and techniques throughout the developing world. Still, food shortages in many places are not uncommon.

One of the most pressing issues affecting the globe is the vast standard-of-living disparity between the developed world and the **developing world**. Many political scientists and sociologists refer to this as the **north–south split**, because most of the world's advanced, postindustrial societies are located well above the equator.

The gap between the developed and developing worlds causes diplomatic friction, interferes with the smooth and equitable globalization of the world economy, and perpetuates tremendous socioeconomic inequality. An extremely small number of people in the developed nations possesses the majority of global wealth, uses up the bulk of the world's resources, eats a massive share of the world's food, and is responsible for most of the world's energy consumption and pollution. This trend has been in place during the entire twentieth century and showed no signs of reversing as the century ended.

Major Trends

Other important trends of the 1900s and/or early 2000s:

- *Population growth.* In 1900, the world population was 1.6 billion. At the century's end, that number had risen to 6 billion. Even in the developed world, where birthrates have tended to decline, population has increased. In the developing and less developed worlds, **population growth** has literally exploded.

China and India each have populations of over 1 billion. The rate of growth in Africa has averaged over 3 percent per year. Latin America went from 165 million in 1950 to 400 million in the mid-1980s. Cities such as Mexico City, Shanghai, and Buenos Aires are among the most densely populated in the world. Ironically, the true problems resulting from population growth—over-consumption of food and energy and overproduction of waste and pollution—have more to do with the developed world, where population growth is slower.

- *Migration*: Patterns of **modern migration** date to the last half of the 1800s, when millions of immigrants from Europe (and a smaller number from China) flooded to the United States, Canada, Argentina, and Chile. This trend continued through the early 1900s, until the United States instituted stricter immigration policies. The movement of peoples continued after World War II, however, and even intensified. During the late 1940s and 1950s, European refugees and displaced persons (largely from Eastern Europe, where Nazi genocide and then Soviet occupation led to massive population transfers) moved throughout the continent, mainly to Western Europe. All throughout the postwar period, economic opportunity, violence in the developing world (caused largely by brushfire conflicts related to the Cold War), and political repression have led millions of people to leave Asia, the Middle East, Latin America, and Africa for Western Europe and North America. Even as France and Britain dismantled their empires, many of their former colonial subjects migrated from Algeria, India, sub-Saharan Africa, the Caribbean, and elsewhere. Refugees have fled from Asia and Latin America to the United States and Canada, from Africa and the Middle East to Europe. Guest workers from the Middle East (especially Turkey) and elsewhere began to be admitted to Western Europe; by the 1980s, there were more than 15 million. Most recently, the collapse of communism in the former Soviet bloc, as well as ethnic conflict in the former Yugoslavia, has led to a rush of migration from Eastern to Western Europe. Migration has often provided a much-needed labor force and enriched the cultural diversity of the host nation. However, especially when economic times are tight, it has stirred up xenophobia, typically among right-wing extremists.

- *Rise of the consumer society*: In developed societies, inexpensive, mass-produced goods tend to be available to almost all people, even the lower classes. At the same time, fewer people in these societies earn their living by means of agricultural or even industrial production. Consumer societies therefore tend to be based on service, or postindustrial, economies.

- *Social activism*: Demonstrations, protests, and strikes have brought about social, political, and economic change ever since the French Revolution. During the twentieth century, however, **social activism** and the work of NGOs have become increasingly important. The most famous wave of activism came in the 1960s and early 1970s (especially the various **1968 protests** that broke out in Paris, Prague, Mexico City, and U.S. cities and universities). Social activism has toppled colonial regimes (for example, in India), helped to end wars (as in Vietnam), and achieved civil rights (including in South Africa and the American South). It has also been crucial to women's liberation, campaigns against nuclear weapons, and the environmental movement.

- *Environmentalism*: Ever since the Industrial Revolution, there has been a spirit of environmentalism, striving to prevent the natural world from overdevelopment or destruction. Conservation efforts date back to figures such as Henry Thoreau, Ralph Waldo Emerson, and John Muir. The modern **environmental (or green) movement**, however, is a product of the post-World War II era, when it became clear that pollution, species extinction, and uncontrolled industrialism posed a dire threat to the earth's ecological well-being. Such movements began during the 1960s, both in North America and Western Europe. A major boost came with the publication of Rachel Carson's *Silent Spring* (1962), which warned of the dangers connected with the insecticide DDT. The celebration of Earth Day in 1970 also popularized the environmental movement. NGOs working on behalf of the environment, such as Greenpeace and the World Wildlife Fund, have become globally influential. In some West European countries (particularly Germany), green parties play an important role in national politics. Contemporary environmental efforts, including the Kyoto Protocol are largely focused on the problem of **climate change** (see Chapter 35).

- *Terrorism*: The first major conflict of the twentieth century, World War I, was sparked by a terrorist. Ever since, it has become more common for political movements to achieve their goals by means of violence and assassination. Especially in the post-World War II era, **terrorist activity** has escalated. The first major terrorist act of the twenty-first century and the one that has had the greatest single impact on global affairs is the September 11, 2001 attack on the United States. al-Qaeda terrorists linked to **Osama bin Laden** hijacked several aircraft and flew them into the World Trade Center and Pentagon, killing over 3,000 people.

TIP

Major terrorist groups have included the Palestinian Liberation Organization (PLO), the Irish Republican Army (IRA), the Red Brigades (a communist organization in Italy), a variety of anti-Israeli groups (including Hamas and Hizbollah), Chechen extremists, and al-Qaeda.

- *Rise in extreme nationalism, ethnic hostility, and religious fundamentalism*: The most advanced age in human history has also been the most prone to hyperpatriotic **nationalism**, ethnic and religious violence, and **genocide**. The **Armenian genocide** and the **Holocaust** are instances from the first half of the century. The Arab-Israeli conflict, intertribal violence in Africa, and Hindu-Muslim tensions in South Asia have troubled the postwar era. Similar trends have been even more on the rise in the 1990s and early 2000s, as the end of the Cold War has removed many of the restraints keeping ethnic and religious tensions in check (see Chapter 35).

WOMEN AND THE SHIFT IN GENDER RELATIONS

One of the most important trends of the twentieth century—affecting slightly more than half of the world's entire population—is **women's liberation**. Progress here came mainly in the Western world, although other regions have also moved forward, if slowly and partially.

The Early Twentieth Century

Chapters 21 and 29 have already discussed the progress that women's movements in the West made during the late 1800s and World War I in agitating for **women's suffrage**, entering the workplace, and pushing for social, educational, and political equality.

Between 1917 and 1920, women got the vote in almost all Western nations, France and Italy being the most noteworthy exceptions. Except in the USSR (where rapid industrialization required as large a workforce as possible), the rate of female unemployment decreased in the 1920s, as men returned from World War I, and especially in the 1930s, when, during the mass unemployment of the Great Depression, it was considered "wrong" for women to have jobs if men were out of work.

The interwar dictatorships differed sharply in their treatment of women. In the USSR, Marxist ideology called for gender equality. The Soviets observed this ideal to a degree (but far from perfectly), and women made up a large part of the workforce. By contrast, Italian Fascism, German Nazism, and Japanese traditionalism were explicitly hostile to the notion of gender equality. In all three countries, women were expected to be principally mothers and homemakers.

Women and World War II

Famously, World War II brought women into the workplace in even greater numbers than World War I had. The image of "Rosie the Riveter" became a potent symbol of the role of women in U.S. wartime production. In the Soviet Union, women made up nearly 40 percent of the national workforce. Large numbers of American, Canadian, ANZAC, and British women served as war nurses and military personnel (although not combat troops). In the USSR, women served in the military and, in some limited but important cases, saw active duty in combat (mainly as pilots and snipers).

Although there was a temporary dip in female employment afterward, the war had served the purpose of permanently cementing women's place in the working world. Moreover, France and Italy gave women the vote in 1945.

Western Women and Feminism in the Postwar Era

During the postwar era, as Japan, Western Europe, the United States, and Canada moved on to ever-higher levels of economic advancement, women took an increasingly larger role in the workplace and public life. The same was true—and to an even larger degree—in Eastern Europe and the Soviet Union. However, during the late 1940s and 1950s, it was still generally considered that a woman's main roles were that of homemaker, childbearer, and caregiver to children. Even those women who worked suffered widespread gender discrimination: sexual harassment, unequal wages, lack of access to positions of leadership, and so on. The French philosopher Simone de Beauvoir analyzed women's place in modern society in *The Second Sex* (1949), which investigated the deep-seated cultural and biological reasons for male domination of women.

A great step toward equality was taken by women in the Western world during the 1960s and 1970s. This was the era of **feminism**, or women's liberation. Major figures here were Gloria Steinem and Betty Friedan, whose book *The Feminine Mystique* (1963) joined de Beauvoir's *The Second Sex* in providing the movement with an intellectual foundation.

The goal of the women's movement was not just to achieve legal equality but also to eliminate the cultural stereotype of women as the "weaker sex" and to remove social barriers blocking the way toward true equality. Achievements of the women's movement include better and more varied career opportunities, better pay, equal access to higher education, greater respect for women's athletics, a greater role in political life, and the right to birth control, legal abortion, and divorce.

Contemporary Gender Issues

Problems still remain, however. Informal discrimination and sexual harassment have not been eliminated. Access to the highest levels of business and political life is still not complete (a phenomenon commonly referred to as the "glass ceiling").

Moreover, women are still relegated to traditional and secondary roles in many non-Western societies. Although it is a stereotype to say that women are not treated equally in Asia, Africa, the Middle East, and Latin America, the fact remains that Islamic fundamentalism, conservative Catholicism, machismo, old-fashioned views of women as inferior (or wives as servants, even property) constrain women more commonly in these regions than in the West.

THOUGHT, CULTURE, AND SCIENCE

The hallmarks of twentieth-century thought and culture are rapid change and incredible diversity. Other major trends have included **multiculturalism**—the interaction and fusion of the world's various ethnic, artistic, and intellectual traditions—and the effect of **mass media technology** on culture and the arts. Scientific and technological advancement has proceeded at a breathtaking pace. The **information** (or **digital**) **revolution** caused by the computer has vastly altered life in the 1990s and beyond.

Pessimism and Uncertainty in Western Culture

After World War I, art and literature in the Western world tended to be dominated by the themes of uncertainty and anxiety that had already emerged in the late 1800s and early 1900s (see Chapter 21). The psychological theories of **Sigmund Freud**, as well as the philosophical implications of the theory of relativity and the new field of quantum physics, had dampened the overall optimism of the mid-to-late 1800s.

The demoralization caused by World War I increased the spirit of pessimism and relativism (the belief or attitude that there are no objective standards or truths). The best-selling nonfiction book in interwar Europe was the philosopher Oswald Spengler's *The Decline of the West*. The prose and poetry of T. S. Eliot and Franz Kafka dealt with dehumanization in an industrialized, bureaucratized era. By experimenting with stream-of-consciousness prose, authors such as Virginia Woolf, Marcel Proust, and James Joyce attempted to capture the workings of the human mind on the written page. Abstract painters, such as Pablo Picasso, distorted reality to

demonstrate that things could be seen from a variety of perspectives. Surrealists, Salvador Dalí and others, placed realistic objects in unrealistic situations to confuse the viewer's sense of reality.

After World War II, the philosophical and literary school of **existentialism**, championed by the playwright Samuel Beckett and the philosophers Albert Camus and Jean-Paul Sartre, proposed that humanity was not guided by any deity, special destiny, or objective morality. Alone in the universe, the individual must learn to create a worthwhile, ethical existence for himself or herself without the benefit of religion or the hope of any life beyond the earthly one.

Mass Media

Mass media came to play an increasingly important role in cultural life. Radio, film, television, the inexpensive production of mass quantities of books, and computers have brought music, drama, literature, and information into the lives of a greater variety of people than ever before. In addition, in the hands of creative directors and filmmakers, cinema has been used to create genuinely great art.

On the other hand, critics of such **mass** (or **popular**) **culture** have argued that it tends to cheapen or dumb down culture by catering to the taste of the lowest common denominator. In addition, mass media have been used for political purposes, such as **propaganda** and indoctrination ("brainwashing"), especially in dictatorships. Even in free societies, critics say, mass media have become powerful tools in the hands of corporate entities, brainwashing people not for political purposes but to advertise goods and make a profit.

Another effect of mass media has been the westernization, even **Americanization**, of global popular culture. Before World War II, the lure of American jazz and Hollywood movies was immensely seductive. Afterward, when America dominated world markets and mass-media technology, Disney, McDonald's, and Coca-Cola, among others, became economic and cultural symbols recognizable not just in the United States but almost literally in every part of the globe. Some intellectuals, especially non-Western ones, have expressed concern about the corporatizing and Americanizing effects of mass culture; the Japanese novelist Yukio Mishima angrily condemned it as "coca-colonization." Others, however, have talked about the potential of mass media to draw people closer together. In the 1960s, Canadian sociologist Marshall McLuhan became famous for writing that modern communications would create a **"global village"**—a prediction that seems to have been at least partly realized, thanks to the Internet and World Wide Web.

Arts and Literature in the Non-Western World

The twentieth and twenty-first centuries have seen the literary and artistic traditions of the non-Western world achieve a status equal to—and in some cases surpassing—those of the West. In addition to maintaining their own indigenous traditions, non-Western authors and artists have adopted Western forms of writing, painting, and composing, often adapting, modifying, and adding native elements to them.

The Mexican painter Diego Rivera created powerful murals that vividly expressed the plight of the working poor, as well as that of Mayans and other indigenous peoples in his country. Chinese author Lu Xun (Lu Hsun) wrote hard-hitting stories about his

nation's economic domination by outside powers, as well as the government's inability and unwillingness to care for the lower classes. The Indian poet Rabindranath Tagore, the first non-Westerner to win the Nobel Prize for literature, dazzled readers throughout the world with lyrical, mystical verses based on Hindu concepts.

Non-Western voices in the artistic world grew bolder and more eloquent after World War II. Common themes include the growing pains associated with decolonization, the difficulty of resisting Western (especially U.S.) cultural hegemony, the clash of Western and non-Western culture, and political opposition to one's own politically repressive regime. In *The Interpreters*, the Nobel laureate Wole Soyinka writes about corruption and dictatorship in his native Nigeria. A fellow Nigerian, Chinua Achebe, also takes on themes of decolonization and dictatorship, especially in *Things Fall Apart*. Ama Ata Aidoo describes the place of women in contemporary Ghana in *Changes: A Love Story*.

Cry, the Peacock is Anita Desai's famous treatment of women's lives in India. In Japan, Yukio Mishima, a traditional (but also gay) nationalist, bitterly opposed what he saw as the destruction of Japan's cultural values. His ritual, samurai-style suicide in 1970 elevated him to cult status.

In Latin America, authors such as Gabriel García Márquez and Isabel Allende pioneered magical realism: a richly textured style featuring detailed storytelling.

In the Islamic world, the novelist Naguib Mahfouz won the Nobel Prize for his *Cairo Trilogy*, a vibrant portrait of postwar Egypt. The Indian-born, English-speaking Muslim Salman Rushdie came to world attention in 1988 with *The Satanic Verses*, an irreverent treatment of Islamic orthodoxy. Both Mahfouz and Rushdie fell afoul of Muslim traditionalists. Mahfouz was stabbed by an Islamic extremist in 1984. Rushdie was declared a heretic by Iran's Ayatollah Khomeini, who openly called for Rushdie's assassination and forced him to go into hiding for years.

Science and Technology

Scientific and technological advancement during the twentieth and twenty-first centuries has been constant and spectacular. During the first half of the 1900s, the Western world fully industrialized, moving into a world where petroleum and electricity were the primary sources of energy.

Also in the Western world, great innovation has been made in all fields of science. Progress in certain areas has been most noteworthy. Physics was revolutionized at the beginning of the 1900s. First, **Albert Einstein** developed the **theory of relativity**, making the first major changes to the system of science and mathematics that had been synthesized by Isaac Newton in the late 1600s and early 1700s. Also in the early 1900s came the birth of **quantum physics**. Major figures here included Max Planck, Niels Bohr, Werner Heisenberg, and Enrico Fermi. The work of quantum physicists has completely altered our understanding of astronomy and subatomic particles. It also made atomic weaponry and nuclear energy possible.

Rocketry and space science emerged in the 1900s. Pioneers of rocket science included the American Robert Goddard and Russia's Konstantin Tsiolkovsky. The new science matured during World War II thanks largely to the efforts of German scientists. As discussed in Chapter 32, the nuclear arms race between the United

States and the Soviet Union spurred a parallel space race. The move toward a permanent presence in space was encouraged by the USSR's work in developing orbital laboratories and the United States' invention of the space shuttle. Rocket science has also made satellite communications possible.

Great medical advances have been made, including the polio vaccine, the elimination of smallpox, heart transplants and artificial hearts, and the development of antibiotics. A related field of special significance is **genetics**, which came into being in the late 1800s thanks to the work of an Austrian monk, Gregor Mendel. The field's great breakthrough came when James Watson and Francis Crick deciphered the **molecular structure of DNA** in 1953. Since then, scientists have gained an unprecedented wealth of knowledge about how living organisms work.

Yet another significant advancement was the invention of the **computer**, during and shortly after World War II. Computers caused an information revolution that altered the way people communicate, transact business, entertain themselves, and work. A key innovation was the development of the **Internet**, originally created in the 1960s for U.S. defense research purposes. By the end of the 1990s, a World Wide Web had connected millions of users, and it continues to grow. Although a "digital divide" exists between those people who have better access to computer technology in the northern hemisphere and those who have poorer access south of the equator, the worldwide trend is toward greater access for all.

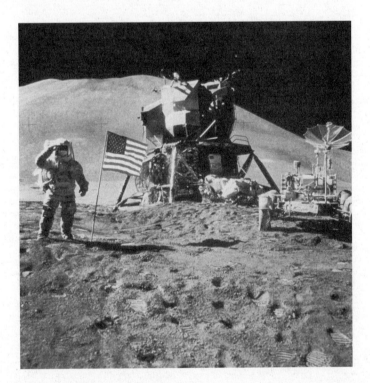

Apollo 15 Mission to the Moon, August 1971.
To this date, the United States is the only nation that has landed crewed spacecraft on the moon. The first moon landing came on July 20, 1969. The Apollo 15 mission, pictured here, was one of the several landings that followed. In recent years, trends in space exploration have included the deployment of crewless probes deep into the solar system (and beyond), long-term space station missions, space shuttle flights, and the use of remote-controlled technology to explore hostile environments, such as the surfaces of other planets.

Integration or Fragmentation? Globalism in the Late Twentieth and Early Twenty-First Centuries

- Global integration vs. global fragmentation
- The end of the Cold War
- The September 11, 2001 attacks and the war on terror
- Asymmetrical warfare (terrorism, guerrilla conflict, and small arms versus WMDs and the revolution in military affairs)
- Nuclear proliferation and weapons of mass destruction (WMDs)
- Nationalist aggression and genocide
- Religious fundamentalism
- Environmentalism, climate change, and the Kyoto Protocol
- The United Nations
- Nongovernmental organizations (NGOs)
- Multiculturalism

Are the nations of the world growing closer together or further apart? Enduring symbols of the late 1900s and early 2000s would include the sight of McDonald's golden arches in cities such as Nairobi and Shanghai, as well as the all-pervasive presence of mass media and the Internet in every corner of the planet. One might argue that these are signs of **global integration**.

However, other images of the recent turn of the century would seem to indicate of **global fragmentation**. Ethnic cleansing in the former Yugoslavia. Genocidal butchery in Rwanda. The breakdown of peace talks between Israelis and Palestinians. The terrorist attacks of September 11, 2001, as well as the tensions caused by the resulting war on terror. All of these would appear to signal that world communities are growing apart, not together.

The fact of the matter is that, globally speaking, centripetal and centrifugal forces are both acting on the nations of the world, simultaneously pushing them together and pulling them apart. Which will prevail as the twenty-first century progresses remains to be seen.

DIPLOMACY AFTER THE COLD WAR

In 1992, U.S. President George Bush stated that the **end of the Cold War** had brought about a "new world order." The U.S.-Soviet arms race halted, as did the bipolar division of most of the world into two hostile camps. In this way, the nations of the world were free to emerge from underneath the nuclear umbrellas of the superpowers and associate with each other as they pleased. The risk of nuclear annihilation decreased dramatically, and as described in Chapter 32, the end of the Cold War coincided with a general rise in the level of democratization worldwide.

On the other hand, the end of the Cold War has left the world without a defining diplomatic framework. Instead of two superpowers, only one, the United States, remains. The fact that other countries are now free to join or clash as they wish has made international relations more unpredictable. New diplomatic alignments appear and disappear. Many old alliances have broken or weakened. Others have had to be redesigned. For instance, what purpose does NATO have in Europe now that the threat of Soviet invasion has been removed?

Furthermore, during the Cold War, any conflict anywhere carried with it the risk of superpower involvement and with it the possibility of nuclear war. In its way, then, the Cold War had something of a restraining effect, which contained certain ethnic and cultural pressures, especially within the superpowers' spheres of influence. With the restraining effect of the Cold War removed, many of those hostilities have emerged, breaking out of control in Yugoslavia, Rwanda, Indonesia, and elsewhere. In addition, the post-Cold War years have witnessed the gradual spread of nuclear-weapons capability.

Another point of tension in the post-Cold War era is the strained relationship between the United States and China, the largest remaining communist power on earth. China is not yet a superpower, but its economic growth has been rapid throughout the 1980s and 1990s, and the wealthy commercial center of Hong Kong returned to Chinese rule in 1997. China possesses the humanpower and geographical size eventually to achieve superpower status. Although the United States pursued a policy of engagement with China during the 1990s, trade disputes and diplomatic disagreements have been frequent. U.S. support for Taiwan, which China regards as a breakaway province, is another potential source of conflict. Although the United States does not officially recognize Taiwanese independence, it would probably help to defend Taiwan if China attempted a reunification by force.

As for Russia, America's briefly friendly relationship with it has cooled. During most of the 1990s, Russia was led by Boris Yeltsin, who was then succeeded by a former KGB operative, Vladimir Putin. Russia is still struggling to build democracy and regain its economic footing. Nationalist forces are building, and Russia wishes to retain its sphere of influence in parts of the former USSR (this desire has embroiled Russia in a war with Chechnya since 1995 and caused it to meddle, often unsuccessfully, in the political affairs of countries such as Ukraine and Georgia). On the other hand, its leaders do not want to seem overly aggressive or remain isolated from other parts of Europe. While Russia is, for the moment, too weak to renew its superpower hostility—or nuclear arms race—with the West, it is still an important force in Europe and Asia.

At the time, the end of the Cold War was thought to have brought about lasting global peace. It has not. It would be too much to say that the result has been global anarchy, the post-Cold War years have called for new and creative ways of thinking about diplomacy. As one U.S. government official said during the mid-1990s, "We have slain the dragon; but we now live in a jungle filled with a bewildering variety of poisonous snakes."

SECURITY CONCERNS

War After the Cold War

The end of the Cold War has by no means brought about an era of peace. One major war—the Iraqi invasion of Kuwait and the resulting Gulf War (1990–1991)—took place soon after. War raged in Yugoslavia during the 1990s. In 1999, NATO bombed Yugoslavia in an effort to stop Serb aggression against the Albanian population of the Serbian province of Kosovo. Russia has fought Chechnya.

Just as important, a large variety of brushfire wars, small armed conflicts, and civil disturbances have raged throughout the decade following the collapse of the Cold War, resulting in the deaths of hundreds of thousands. Many of these have been motivated by ethnic hostilities that the Cold War had helped to keep in check. Finally, the **al-Qaeda attacks on September 11, 2001**, have resulted in a U.S.-led war on terror that spans the globe and has continued to this day, despite the death of al-Qaeda leader Osama bin Laden in May, 2011.

Weapons of Mass Destruction

Other troublesome security issues involve **weapons of mass destruction**. From 1987 onward, the United States and Russia have made progress in restricting, even scaling back, the production and testing of nuclear weapons. (Recent tension between the two countries has slowed this process down.) Beyond that, there have been worries that, given the conditions of extreme economic and political breakdown in Russia, nuclear weapons or weapons-grade atomic material might be stolen or smuggled out of the former Soviet Union and end up in the hands of terrorists or rogue governments.

Even more worrisome is the issue of **nuclear proliferation**. Only five countries belong to the "nuclear club," the group of nations officially acknowledged to possess nuclear-weapons capability: the United States, Russia, China, France, and Great Britain. Most nations of the world have signed the Nuclear Non-Proliferation Treaty. Generally, the treaty's effectiveness and longevity have been remarkable.

Nonetheless, several countries, most notably Israel, developed nuclear arsenals during the 1970s and 1980s. In 1998, India and Pakistan, deadly enemies, each tested nuclear weapons, adding new peril to an already dangerous diplomatic situation. North Korea gained nuclear-weapons capability sometime after 2000, and Iran is actively seeking it. How long nuclear proliferation can be contained is one of the most pressing questions of the new century.

The same can be said for other weapons of mass destruction, such as biological weapons (various germs, viruses, and bacteria packaged in a delivery system) and chemical weapons (such as nerve gas and water-based toxins). These are relatively easy

weapons to manufacture and deliver and extremely difficult to defend against. During the Cold War, both superpowers abided by international agreements banning the use of biological and chemical weapons. Whether or not all states will choose to honor such agreements, now that the Cold War is over, is an open question.

The Proliferation of Small Arms

At the other end of the weapons spectrum are small arms: pistols, rifles, submachine guns, and automatic rifles. During the Cold War, some 50 million people were killed, mainly in the developing world, because of small-scale conflicts of various types. This trend has continued since 1991. Certain parts of the world, such as Africa, Southeast Asia, and Latin America, are awash with small arms. A huge illegal trade in these weapons thrives. Societies in which large numbers of civilians, non-combatants, and members of paramilitary groups—as opposed to regular military forces—have access to heavy weaponry are inherently unstable.

The Revolution in Military Affairs and High-Tech Warfare

One of the most striking features of contemporary military life is the unprecedented disparity between the technological capabilities of the world's most advanced armed forces and those of the least advanced.

The gap between high-tech forces and the lowest level of military capability has always been important, as the West's imperial successes of the 1800s proved. After World War II, however, that gap widened considerably. Nuclear weapons, jet aircraft, third-generation tanks, helicopter gunships, nuclear submarines and aircraft carriers, and global airlift capacity—owned and used by the superpowers and the small group of other nations able to afford them—were a far cry from the assault rifles, grenade launchers, hand-to-hand weapons and other small arms available to most armies or paramilitary groups. On the other hand (as in the nineteenth-century era of imperialism), technological superiority in **asymmetrical wars**—conflicts that pit high-tech adversaries against low-tech enemies—was not always a guarantee of military success. That fact was made painfully clear to the superpowers in Vietnam and Afghanistan, where guerrilla warfare and other irregular forms of combat prevailed.

Computer technology has widened the military gap even further. During the 1990s and early 2000s, the United States and a tiny handful of other nations experienced what generals and strategists refer to as the "**revolution in military affairs**" (RMA). This involved the full integration of computer technology, satellite communications, and precision-guided ("smart") weapons into military operations. Whether such changes will guarantee future victories remains to be seen.

NATIONALIST EXTREMISM, ETHNIC TENSIONS, AND RELIGIOUS FUNDAMENTALISM

One of the forces that the Cold War tended to keep under control was nationalist and ethnic extremism. The collapse of the superpower rivalry has, in many cases, released national, ethnic, and religious pressures, allowing them to boil out of control.

Nationalist Extremism in the West

Even in Western Europe, with its democratic governments and tradition of respecting civil rights, there is a certain level of ethnic tension. Since 1975, the island of Cyprus has been divided between Turks and Greeks, with a United Nations force needed to keep the peace. In countries such as Britain, Germany, France, Switzerland, and Italy, the millions of Turks, Middle Easterners, Africans, Pakistanis, Indians, and Caribbean islanders who live and work there (many of them as **guest workers**) suffer varying degrees of prejudice and discrimination. Right-wing and neo-Nazi groups harass minorities and call for their deportation, especially in times of economic distress. Likewise, much the same applies to the United States, where **anti-immigration sentiment** sometimes rises up in opposition to America's "melting-pot" tradition.

East European Nationalism and the Breakup of Yugoslavia

In Eastern Europe, ethnic tensions are even higher than in the West. Each Eastern European state is home to substantial minority populations, many of which have long histories of conflict. Even the Eastern European states that have made the most progress toward democratization have found it difficult to ensure that the rights of national minorities—Romanians living in Hungary, for example, or Slovaks in the Czech Republic or Russians in the Baltic States—are protected. One group that is heavily discriminated against throughout Eastern Europe is the Roma, better known as Gypsies.

The most striking examples of ethnic hostilities in Eastern Europe are the various wars in the former Yugoslavia. With the collapse of communism in 1989 and 1990, Yugoslavia, an artificial nation created after World War I to unite the southern Slavs—Serbs, Croats, Bosnians, Slovenes, Montenegrins, and Macedonians—began to break apart. Complicating the matter was the fact that these groups practice three religions, Roman Catholicism (Croatians and Slovenes), Eastern Orthodoxy (Serbs, Montenegrins, Macedonians, the Serbian minority in Bosnia), and Islam (the majority of Bosnians). There is also a sizable Albanian minority in Serbia and Macedonia, most of whom are Muslims. All these peoples have a long history of conflict. However, from 1945 until 1980, the communist government of Josip Tito held these conflicts in check and encouraged multicultural coexistence. Even during the 1980s, the various people of Yugoslavia lived together reasonably amicably.

After 1989, **ethnic tensions** began to reemerge. Such tensions were due partly to the stress and strain of communist breakdown but also to the efforts of nationalist politicians (such as the Serbian leader Slobodan Milosevic), who deliberately whipped ethnic hostility out of control for their own purposes. Slovenia, Macedonia, and Croatia declared independence in 1991.

The first Yugoslav war resulted from Serbia's attempt to take territory from Croatia. When Bosnia declared independence in 1992, the Serbian minority there rose up in arms, with assistance from Milosevic and the Serbian government. Their goal was to create a "Greater Serbia."

From 1992 to 1995, while the Serbian-Croatian war came to an end, a second war raged in Bosnia. Serb forces took three-quarters of Bosnia. Even worse, Bosnian Serbs, with full support of Milosevic's Serbian government, carried out

the policy of ethnic cleansing. This form of genocide involved the forced deportation of Bosnian Muslims from territories the Bosnian Serbs wanted for themselves. It also included mass executions and the systematic rape of large numbers of women. The Serbian campaign of ethnic cleansing was the worst military atrocity committed in Europe since the Nazi Holocaust. The failure of the United Nations and European community to deal effectively with the crisis was not only embarrassing but called into doubt the ability of international organizations to cope with international conflict in the post-Cold War era. The war in Bosnia was finally ended by the U.S.-sponsored Dayton Accords, in the fall of 1995, when the Serbs backed down under the pressure of U.S. airstrikes and a renewed Croatian offensive.

Another round of fighting came in 1998 and 1999, when Milosevic and the Serbs began another campaign of ethnic cleansing, this time against the Albanian minority living in the Serbian province of Kosovo. For three months in 1999, NATO, in its first-ever military action, bombed Serbia until Milosevic relented. Although, technically, a state of peace exists in the former Yugoslavia, ethnic resentment and bitterness boils just beneath the surface.

Ethnic Violence in Africa, Asia, and the Middle East

Other notorious examples of ethnic violence include the Hutu-Tutsi conflict in Rwanda. In 1994, these two tribes fought each other. In the process, the Hutu killed approximately 800,000 Tutsi men, women, and children. The long-standing effort of the people of East Timor, a Pacific island illegally annexed by Indonesia in 1975, to free themselves has led to great bloodshed. Indonesian suppression of the East Timorese has verged on the genocidal since the 1970s. In 1999, the reign of terror Indonesia visited upon the tiny island was so bloody that it prompted United Nations intervention. Along with a severe currency crisis, the disturbances and scandals connected with East Timorese independence also played a role in toppling Suharto, the dictator who had ruled Indonesia since 1967.

Perhaps the longest-lasting, and still problematic, ethnic clash is that of the Israelis and the Palestinians. The Oslo Accord of 1993, in which the PLO leader Yasser Arafat and the Israeli prime minister Yitzhak Rabin agreed to pursue peace, led to more than half a decade of relative calm in the Middle East. Negotiations came to a deadlock, however, and tensions began to mount once again. In 2001, those tensions broke out into open conflict, as the Palestinians began a second uprising, or intifada. The balance of power in the entire Middle East has been shifted radically by the **Arab Spring** of 2010–2011, which toppled authoritarian regimes such as Hosni Mubarak's in Egypt and Moammar Gadhafi's in Libya. Whether the rise of new governments will facilitate the keeping of peace or increase the chance of Arab-Israeli or inter-Muslim violence remains to be seen.

Religious Fundamentalism

Religious fundamentalism has experienced a revival during the late 1900s and early 2000s. In India, religious conflict among Hindus, Muslims, and Sikhs continues. Policy in Iran is still shaped largely by Islamic fundamentalism. In Afghanistan,

Islamic fundamentalism led to the creation of a strictly theocratic government under the Taliban, which ruled from 1989 to 2002. Religious differences are at the heart of the Israeli-Arab conflict in the Middle East and largely at the heart of the ethnic tensions plaguing the former Yugoslavia. They played an overwhelming role in the September 11, 2001 bombings, and they have been heightened by the subsequent war on terror.

Ethnic and religious tensions and violence have to be counted among the fragmenting factors threatening to tear the world apart, rather than bring it together.

ENVIRONMENTAL ISSUES

Despite the existence of vibrant and active environmental movements since the 1960s, environmental problems still remain. In several ways, they have become more pressing during the 1990s and early 2000s.

Environmentalism in the Developed World

In the developed world—the United States, Canada, Western Europe, Japan, and others like them—strict environmental regulations have been put into place from the 1970s onward in an attempt to ensure clean air and clean water for all. Recycling has become common practice. Endangered species have received greater protections. Growing concern about the depletion of the ozone layer led to the elimination of chlorofluorocarbons (CFCs). The ongoing debate about the effect of carbon dioxide and other greenhouse gasses on planetary climate patterns—**global warming**—has raised awareness about this issue.

Consumption and Pollution in the Developed World

However, the developed world's economies continue to modernize. With that, the rate of consumption among the populations of these countries continues to escalate. This group—a small segment of the world population—eats more, generates more trash, burns more gasoline, uses more electricity, consumes more wood and paper products, and releases more additives and emissions into the air and water than the rest of the people in the world combined.

Modernization and Environmental Problems in the Developing World

Added to this issue is the modernization of the developing world. As large parts of Asia, Africa, Latin America, and the Middle East industrialize and attempt to catch up with the developing world, their rates of energy use and resource consumption have been

THE ENVIRONMENT

It is common to think of pollution and environmental crisis as modern problems. In fact, societies have affected—and been affected by—the environment from the Stone Age onward. Resource extraction and consumption, as well as pollution, have always been part of the human community. The downfall of civilizations like those of the Indus Valley and Easter Island has been linked directly to environmental disaster or, in the latter case, mismanagement. In countless ways, the industrial era has made humanity's footprint on the environment heavier than ever before: Societies consume more, rely more on machine production and fuel-driven transport, and possess engineering skills that involve the capacity to change the earth in ways unimaginable to preindustrial societies. Currently, climate change (global warming) serves as the clearest demonstration of how profoundly human action has affected the environment.

increasing. These countries also do not have the same clean-air, clean-water, and other regulations in place that nations in the developed world do.

The Failure of International Environmental Regulations

On the whole, international agreements to take greater care of the environment have met with limited success. A prime example of this is the Kyoto Summit (1997), where over 150 nations gathered to discuss environmental issues, especially the potential dangers of global warming. Although a **Kyoto Protocol** was hammered out, it is still contentious, and many countries, including the United States, have not ratified it. A particular point of conflict is the question of whether or not industrializing countries of the less developed world should be compelled to abide by the same clean-air regulations that nations of the developed world do.

Energy Sources

Another failure has been the inability or unwillingness to develop clean, sustainable sources of energy. Continued reliance on fossil fuels such as coal and especially petroleum has led not only to periodic shortages and economic difficulties but also to continued air pollution. Hydroelectric generation of electric power has its limits. Experiments with wind and solar power—potentially the cleanest sources of power possible—have not been supported by governments or corporations (at times, the latter, whose profits are dependent on oil-based technologies, have actively opposed such experiments).

The only alternative source of energy that has met with any success is nuclear power. This, however, carries with it serious risks, as nuclear accidents at Three Mile Island (1979) in Pennsylvania, Chernobyl (1986) in Ukraine—where 8,000 people were killed immediately and hundreds of thousands were made sick or born deformed afterward—and Fukushima (2011) in Japan have demonstrated.

Although a variety of environmental issues will confront the nations of the world in the twenty-first century, perhaps the most dangerous and the one that threatens all countries equally is global warming.

REGIONALISM, GLOBALIZATION, AND MULTICULTURALISM

Trends that would seem to encourage the integration rather than fragmentation of world communities include regionalism, economic globalization, and multicultural interaction. All are prominent features of contemporary life. However, they also have their limits.

The United Nations

Regional and international organizations and agencies serve to unite the efforts of countries around the world or in specific parts of the world. The **United Nations**, despite certain failures and flaws, has provided a forum for dispute resolution among the countries of the world since 1945. It oversees peacekeeping missions, monitors the observance of human rights and international treaties, and organizes humanitarian efforts, cultural preservation, and many other activities.

In terms of punitive measures, such as economic embargos, peacekeeping, and peacemaking, the United Nations' record is mixed. It has many successes to its credit, but events in Bosnia, Rwanda, Central Africa, and Sierra Leone have embarrassed it greatly. Its failure to dissuade the United States from invading Iraq in 2003 has called the United Nations' political effectiveness into some question.

Nongovernmental Organizations

A relatively recent trend has been the proliferation of **nongovernmental organizations** (NGOs). These nonprofit groups harness the effort of volunteers and activists locally, nationally, and around the world to work on various causes. Among the best-known NGOs are Greenpeace, the World Wildlife Fund, Amnesty International, Human Rights Watch, the National Organization for Women, Planned Parenthood, and Medecins sans Frontieres (Doctors Without Borders).

Regional Organizations and Alliances

Regional organizations that have fostered international cooperation include the Organization for Security and Cooperation in Europe, the Association of Southeast Asian Nations, the Organization for African Unity, and the Organization of American States. Western Europe has made the greatest efforts to regionalize its economic, military, and political activities. In addition to the European Union and the OSCE mentioned above, many European nations belong to the NATO alliance and the Council of Europe.

Technology as an Integrating Force

Various cultural and technological factors seem to be bringing nations and regions closer together. Mass media technology has greatly increased people's awareness of other parts of the world. Enhanced means of communication—improved telephone networks, satellite transmissions, and above all the Internet and World Wide Web—have made it more possible than ever before for greater numbers of people to be continually in touch with other people in all parts of the globe. Cheaper and quicker modes of transport have enabled people to travel, work, study, or live abroad in vaster numbers than ever before. The celebration of art, literature, music, and traditions from all parts of the world—**multiculturalism**—has become extremely prominent during the 1990s and early 2000s. Cultural fusion and interaction have given multiculturalism even more of a boost.

Economic Globalization

The **globalization** of the world economy continues. The **European Union**, which, as of 2005, includes twenty-five members, has already removed barriers to the movement of people, goods, money, and services. In 2002, many of its members began to use a single currency, the euro. The North American Free Trade Agreement, in operation since 1994, is likely to serve as a model for similar agreements elsewhere. The **World Trade Organization**, formed in 1995, aims to bring the operations of the global economy under a single set of laws, rules, and practices.

However, economic globalization is not complete, nor is it self-evident that the trend is completely positive. Some of the flaws and potential dangers connected with globalization are discussed in Chapter 34. Not all nations belong to the WTO, and even member states quarrel with each other—and with the WTO's rulings. The great gap between the developed and developing worlds still remains—and, at least in some respects, it is widening.

Unit Six: Review Questions

SAMPLE ESSAY QUESTIONS (CCOT AND COMPARATIVE)

CCOT 1

Analyze the changes and continuities in the role played by non-governmental organizations (NGOs) between 1900 and the present.

CCOT 2

Analyze the changes and continuities in global economic exchange between 1900 and the present.

COMP 1

Compare and contrast the policy directions followed by TWO of the following:

> Communist China
> Soviet Russia
> Cuba under the Castros

COMP 2

Compare and contrast the political and social experiences of women between 1900 and the present in TWO of the following:

> sub-Saharan Africa
> India
> the Middle East

MULTIPLE-CHOICE QUESTIONS

1. How did World War II change the patterns of international trade?

   (A) Most countries refused to trade with Japan or Germany after the war.
   (B) The World Trade Organization was created soon after the war's end.
   (C) The war diminished the European powers' control over world markets.
   (D) The USSR began trading extensively with Western Europe.

2. What caused apartheid to end in South Africa during the 1990s?

   (A) White leaders came to realize how unjust it was.
   (B) Guerrilla violence committed by the African National Congress terrorized whites into ending it.
   (C) Pressure from the Vatican mobilized white opinion against it.
   (D) White leaders saw that it was harming its international reputation and trade ties.

3. During the 1960s and 1970s, the Sino-Soviet alliance

   (A) was strained by Soviet de-Stalinization, but remained intact.
   (B) came to an end, with the two nations agreeing to be friendly neutrals.
   (C) expanded to include India.
   (D) broke apart, with great bitterness on both sides.

4. After the Paris Peace Conference of 1919, Arab leaders

   (A) were frustrated by the limited autonomy granted them as mandate states.
   (B) were content with their newfound independence.
   (C) were overjoyed by the Balfour Declaration.
   (D) were grateful to Turkey's delegation for representing their interests.

5. The image below most likely celebrates which Cold War–related event?

   (A) the first U.S. astronaut flight
   (B) the USSR's launch of the first human-made object into space
   (C) the testing of orbital missiles by the United States
   (D) the European Space Agency's first space mission

6. During the 1990s, nationalist violence in the former Yugoslavia

   (A) was purposely stirred up by opportunistic politicians after communism's collapse.
   (B) was unavoidable because of historically rooted and irrepressible hatred between ethnic groups.
   (C) resulted from covert intervention by radical Islamic fundamentalists.
   (D) was successfully averted by United Nations mediation.

7. Reza Shah Pahlavi of Iran is similar to Mustafa Kemal of Turkey in that both

   (A) democratized their countries.
   (B) introduced communism into their countries.
   (C) secularized their countries.
   (D) granted their countries liberal constitutions.

8. Which of the following is LEAST true of non-Western art and culture in the twentieth century?

   (A) The fusion of indigenous and Western forms and styles was common.
   (B) Multicultural influences grew in importance.
   (C) Most non-Western intellectuals embraced the Americanization of global culture.
   (D) Many non-Western authors dealt with themes related to the legacy of colonialism.

9. Modern environmental movements

   (A) began with the publication of Rachel Carson's *Silent Spring*.
   (B) have not had an impact on national-level politics in any major country.
   (C) have stimulated greater public awareness of species extinction and climate change.
   (D) persuaded the U.S. government to ratify the Kyoto Protocol.

10. What effect did the liberation of Eastern Europe in 1989–1990 have on the USSR itself?

    (A) It stifled freedom movements within the USSR.
    (B) It drained badly needed finances from the Soviet economy.
    (C) It boosted Mikhail Gorbachev's prestige at home.
    (D) It provided an example for non-Russians in the USSR who wanted freedom.

11. What is *satyagraha*?

    (A) a fusion of Marxism and Hindu theology
    (B) a policy of nonviolent resistance, mixed with Hindu theology
    (C) a fusion of Marxism and Muslim radicalism
    (D) an ethical justification for the use of violence to resist Western imperialism

12. Which of the following accurately describes World War II's impact on civilian populations?

    (A) Nearly half of the war's casualties were civilians.
    (B) Only Jewish civilians were killed in great numbers.
    (C) Combat rarely occurred near major population centers.
    (D) Allied naval blockades caused the death of hundreds of thousands of Axis civilians.

13. Which of the following best describes the Communist takeover of Russia in 1917?

    (A) Defeat in World War I caused the masses to overthrow the tsar and vote the Communists into power.
    (B) Recognizing its weakness, the Provisional Government voluntarily handed power to the Communists.
    (C) Taking advantage of popular discontent with the Provisional Government, the Communists staged a successful insurrection.
    (D) The Communists used their majority in the Provisional Government to take power by parliamentary means.

14. Which of the following describes developments in Mexico and Brazil during the 1930s?

    (A) Mexico pursued populist reform and constitutional rule, and Brazil modernized its economy under an authoritarian regime.
    (B) Mexico sympathized with fascist regimes in Europe, and Brazil supported socialist governments there.
    (C) Mexico brutally suppressed peasants seeking land reform, and Brazil disbanded its secret police.
    (D) Mexico experienced political disorder and mass uprisings, and Brazil fought a border war against Peru.

15. Japanese war crimes between 1937 and 1945 did NOT include

    (A) the abuse of Chinese and Southeast Asian civilians.
    (B) the forced prostitution of Korean women.
    (C) the persecution of worshippers who practiced the Shinto faith.
    (D) the use of prisoners in chemical- and biological-weapons experiments.

16. Which of the following is NOT associated with the economic downturn experienced by the Western world during the 1970s?

    (A) the century's highest levels of unemployment
    (B) inflation
    (C) oil shortages
    (D) recession and slowdowns in production

17. Between the world wars, the League of Nations:

    (A) provided strong leadership and kept most of the world at peace.
    (B) proved effective at famine relief and dealing with refugees, but was otherwise weak.
    (C) benefited from U.S. leadership in stopping aggression in China and Spain.
    (D) had lost all its major European member states by the late 1930s.

18. According to the map on page 375, which country did NOT become a member of the Commonwealth of Independent States?

    (A) Belarus
    (B) Moldova
    (C) Russia
    (D) Estonia

19. Which of the following has NOT been a factor interfering with modernization in Africa?

    (A) the HIV/AIDS epidemic
    (B) lack of cultural and linguistic unity in many African states
    (C) negative population growth
    (D) corruption on the part of political elites

20. What ethnic group is generally recognized to have suffered genocide during World War I?

    (A) the Armenians
    (B) the Jews
    (C) the Roma (Gypsies)
    (D) Bosnian Muslims

ANSWERS

1. **(C)** Germany and Japan received a great deal of economic assistance from other nations, allowing it to rebuild, and the United States stepped up its involvement with Asian markets after the war, so A is false. The postwar USSR was not completely cut off from the world economy, but tried to minimize trade with Western Europe—refusing, for example, to allow Eastern Europe to participate in the Marshall Plan. The World Trade Organization was not established until the 1990s. World War II did reduce Europe's global economic clout.

2. **(D)** Although some whites felt ethically uneasy about apartheid, and although clergy of many denominations denounced it (especially Desmond Tutu of the Anglican Church), moral pressures did not suffice to end it. Neither did ANC violence, which convinced many whites that more, not less, control over the black population was necessary. Only when South Africa was reduced to the status of international pariah—and had its wealth threatened by divestiture and sanctions—did the white leadership end apartheid.

3. **(D)** Soviet condescension, the USSR's unwillingness to share nuclear technology, and border disputes helped break the Sino-Soviet alliance. Especially as the USSR de-Stalinized, Mao perceived the Soviet brand of communism as ideologically impure. The split was not amicable, and China began competing with the USSR for influence over communist movements worldwide. India never entered into any kind of Soviet-Chinese alliance.

4. **(A)** The Arabs had rebelled against Ottoman rule, and would not have been represented by Turkey. Like most Middle Eastern Muslims, they were appalled by the Balfour Declaration, which pledged British support for a Jewish homeland in Palestine. On the whole, the Arabs, who had expected to win full independence in exchange for supporting the Allies against Ottoman Turkey, were disappointed by the post–World War I settlement.

5. **(B)** The Cyrillic script indicates that a Russian mission is depicted, eliminating A, C, and D. The date of 1957 should recall the *Sputnik* launch—a major moment in both the "space race" and the Cold War arms race.

6. **(A)** When violence broke out in Yugoslavia, the United Nations and most foreign powers acted slowly and weakly. Although some argued that ethnic hatred in the region was the "natural" state of affairs and therefore irresistible, the record shows that Serb politicians like Slobodan Milosevic deliberately stirred tensions up and exploited them to further their own agendas. Answer C is simply contrary to facts.

7. **(C)** Both of these rulers rapidly modernized their countries. Although Kemal was more ideologically flexible and inclined more toward constitutional governance, neither ruler was a communist or a liberal democrat. Both saw traditional Islam as an obstacle to progress and secularized their countries. Turkey succeeded at this more than Iran, where Islamic fundamentalists swept to power in 1979.

8. **(C)** The twentieth century, like the twenty-first, was an era of multicultural interchange. A number of non-Westerners gained global reputations and won awards like the Nobel Prize. National liberation and decolonization were major themes, as was a sense of unease about—or outright hostility toward—the worldwide influence of American mass culture.

9. **(C)** The United States has not ratified the Kyoto Protocol, and modern environmental awareness, stirred up by figures like John Muir, dates back to the 1800s and early 1900s. "Green" parties have had an impact on national politics in many countries, in several cases gaining seats in parliaments and legislatures.

10. **(D)** The Soviet regime under Gorbachev concluded quickly that it would be better for the USSR's economy and international reputation to allow its East European bloc to go free. What the Soviets did not count on was how the East European example would encourage already-powerful nationalist feelings among non-Russian subject peoples in the USSR. Even at his peak, Gorbachev was always more popular in the West than at home, and "losing" the USSR's East European possessions did not boost his reputation domestically.

11. **(B)** Famously associated with the nonviolent resistance of Mohandas Gandhi, *satyagraha* played a huge role in Indian opposition to British rule by exposing Britain's failure to live up to its own liberal ideals. It blended Hinduism with principles that Gandhi absorbed from other idealists, such as Russian novelist Leo Tolstoy and the American philosophers Emerson and Thoreau. It remains an open question as to how effective nonviolent resistance can be in the face of an illiberal, oppressive authority.

12. **(A)** The unhappiest trend in modern warfare has been the steadily escalating level of civilian involvement. Roughly half of the 55 million to 60 million people who perished in World

War II were noncombatants. Both sides bombed civilian populations, and combat often took place near or in cities and smaller settlements. Deaths by naval blockade were much more numerous in World War I, when the Allies succeeded in blocking shipments to Germany and Austria.

13. **(C)** Russia experienced two revolutions in 1917: the spontaneous February (March) Revolution that deposed the tsar, and the October (November) Revolution that brought the Communists to power. In between, a Provisional Government attempted to govern the country, prepare for national elections, and continue Russia's World War I effort. Its failure to extract Russia from the war and to solve socioeconomic problems turned sentiment against it, leaving it vulnerable. Lenin and Trotsky led the Communists in a successful coup.

14. **(A)** Mexico under Lázaro Cárdenas came as close as it would to realizing the populist ideals of the 1910 revolution, and land reform on behalf of the peasants was a key priority. Brazil experienced authoritarian rule under Getúlio Vargas, who admired Europe's fascist regimes.

15. **(C)** Japan's leaders encouraged belief in Shinto, which they distorted to justify militarist aggression and a sense of racial superiority. All the other atrocities listed here took place and were prosecuted at the Tokyo Trials—the Japanese counterpart to the Nuremberg Trials held in Germany.

16. **(A)** The key clue here is the phrase "the century's highest levels." Unemployment in the 1970s did not surpass the levels reached during the Great Depression of the 1930s. All the other items are true of the 1970s.

17. **(B)** With no formal powers to enforce its rulings, and without America—whose idea the league was—as a member, the League of Nations proved impotent when it came to dealing with serious diplomatic or military crises. Although Germany and Italy left during the 1930s, most European nations still belonged to it on the eve of World War II. Germany either took territories by force during the 1930s or negotiated directly with countries such as France and Britain.

18. **(D)** Simple map-reading skills should suffice to answer this question. All three Baltic countries, highly motivated by nationalism and feeling no sense of unity with the Slavic states to the east, were eager to integrate with the West and wanted nothing to do with the Russian-dominated CIS.

19. **(C)** Many obstacles have stood in the way of African modernization since decolonization. Its population, however, has grown rather than shrunk—and to the point where *overpopulation* has added to the other problems already listed.

20. **(A)** Although the Turkish government continues to deny it, the Ottoman Empire massacred somewhere between half a million and 2 million Armenians on the basis of race during World War I. Turkey maintains that these were "accidental" civilian deaths in uncontrolled military circumstances, but the record shows otherwise. In discussing how extermination of the Jews might be possible, Hitler alluded to how quickly the world public had forgotten the Armenians.

MODEL AP
WORLD HISTORY TESTS

Answer Sheet

MODEL TEST 1

Section I

1 (A) (B) (C) (D)	21 (A) (B) (C) (D)	41 (A) (B) (C) (D)	61 (A) (B) (C) (D)
2 (A) (B) (C) (D)	22 (A) (B) (C) (D)	42 (A) (B) (C) (D)	62 (A) (B) (C) (D)
3 (A) (B) (C) (D)	23 (A) (B) (C) (D)	43 (A) (B) (C) (D)	63 (A) (B) (C) (D)
4 (A) (B) (C) (D)	24 (A) (B) (C) (D)	44 (A) (B) (C) (D)	64 (A) (B) (C) (D)
5 (A) (B) (C) (D)	25 (A) (B) (C) (D)	45 (A) (B) (C) (D)	65 (A) (B) (C) (D)
6 (A) (B) (C) (D)	26 (A) (B) (C) (D)	46 (A) (B) (C) (D)	66 (A) (B) (C) (D)
7 (A) (B) (C) (D)	27 (A) (B) (C) (D)	47 (A) (B) (C) (D)	67 (A) (B) (C) (D)
8 (A) (B) (C) (D)	28 (A) (B) (C) (D)	48 (A) (B) (C) (D)	68 (A) (B) (C) (D)
9 (A) (B) (C) (D)	29 (A) (B) (C) (D)	49 (A) (B) (C) (D)	69 (A) (B) (C) (D)
10 (A) (B) (C) (D)	30 (A) (B) (C) (D)	50 (A) (B) (C) (D)	70 (A) (B) (C) (D)
11 (A) (B) (C) (D)	31 (A) (B) (C) (D)	51 (A) (B) (C) (D)	
12 (A) (B) (C) (D)	32 (A) (B) (C) (D)	52 (A) (B) (C) (D)	
13 (A) (B) (C) (D)	33 (A) (B) (C) (D)	53 (A) (B) (C) (D)	
14 (A) (B) (C) (D)	34 (A) (B) (C) (D)	54 (A) (B) (C) (D)	
15 (A) (B) (C) (D)	35 (A) (B) (C) (D)	55 (A) (B) (C) (D)	
16 (A) (B) (C) (D)	36 (A) (B) (C) (D)	56 (A) (B) (C) (D)	
17 (A) (B) (C) (D)	37 (A) (B) (C) (D)	57 (A) (B) (C) (D)	
18 (A) (B) (C) (D)	38 (A) (B) (C) (D)	58 (A) (B) (C) (D)	
19 (A) (B) (C) (D)	39 (A) (B) (C) (D)	59 (A) (B) (C) (D)	
20 (A) (B) (C) (D)	40 (A) (B) (C) (D)	60 (A) (B) (C) (D)	

Model Test 1

SECTION I: MULTIPLE-CHOICE QUESTIONS

TIME: 55 MINUTES FOR 70 QUESTIONS

Directions: Each of the questions or incomplete statements below is followed by suggested answers or completions. Select the one that is best in each case and then fill in the corresponding oval on the answer sheet.

1. Which of the following correctly illustrates simultaneous occurrences of technological innovation in different regions of the world?

   (A) Chinese and Mesopotamian toolmakers creating bronze between 4000 B.C.E. and 3000 B.C.E.
   (B) European and Olmec engineers inventing the wheel around 2500 B.C.E.
   (C) Sumerian and Celtic scholars devising written scripts between 3500 B.C.E. and 3000 B.C.E.
   (D) Egyptian and Indus River agriculturalists fermenting alcohol around 2000 B.C.E.

2. Before the onset of the Neolithic era, Stone Age societies are NOT believed to have

   (A) buried their dead.
   (B) expressed themselves by means of painting.
   (C) domesticated plants.
   (D) worshipped polytheistically.

3. The effect of the Upanishads on Indian religious thought was to

   (A) provoke the schism that led many Indians to embrace Islam.
   (B) reduce priestly authority in favor of individual responsibility for spiritual evolution.
   (C) elevate the status of the Vedic gods over Hindu deities.
   (D) cause the doctrines of karma and reincarnation to be declared heretical.

4. The pack animal most crucial to economic life in Andean societies was

   (A) the horse.
   (B) the ox.
   (C) the llama.
   (D) the water buffalo.

5. Which of the following is an accurate example of a diasporic community that came into being thanks to transregional trade between 600 B.C.E. and 600 C.E.?

   (A) Roman traders living in East African ports
   (B) Chinese traders living on the Malay Peninsula
   (C) Polynesian traders living along the Persian Gulf
   (D) Ottoman traders living on India's western coast

6. Which of the following BEST describes how Buddhism changed as the religion spread throughout Asia?

   (A) It shed the Buddha's original teachings about a heavenly afterlife.
   (B) It absorbed doctrinal and ritual elements from other Asian religions.
   (C) It rejected the concept of karma in order to appeal to non-Indian worshippers.
   (D) It became more dogmatic as it competed with other faiths.

7. The imperial experiences of Rome and Han China are most alike in that

   (A) both had their resources drained by frontier wars with nomadic enemies.
   (B) both fell primarily due to environmental stress caused by deforestation.
   (C) both suffered internal stability because of schisms within their state religions.
   (D) both failed to develop effective methods of regional administration.

8. Which of the following is a suitable comparison of political systems in China and Europe between 1000 and 1300?

   (A) China was unravelling politically, and in Europe the trend was toward unification.
   (B) Religious doctrine dominated political affairs in Europe, but had little political influence in China.
   (C) Chinese leaders ruled a unified empire, whereas Europe was governed by many monarchies.
   (D) Chinese law instituted civil rights, while European codes focused on preserving the feudal system.

9. What social trauma did China, the Middle East, and Europe experience in common during the 1300s C.E.?

   (A) religious schisms dividing the official church
   (B) peasant revolts caused by rising levels of taxation
   (C) the bubonic plague in pandemic form
   (D) mass hysteria caused by fears of witchcraft

10. What strategy did Mali employ to increase its state power in the 1300s?

   (A) It mobilized large armies and equipped them with gunpowder weapons.
   (B) It profited by cooperating with European slave traders.
   (C) It gained control over the spice trade between East Africa and India.
   (D) It became a center of Islamic instruction and traded in gold.

11. Which of the following best describes the system of feudalism?

   (A) Rulers exchanged land with nobles in exchange for allegiance and military service.
   (B) A sophisticated and multilayered bureaucracy permitted the centralization of authority.
   (C) Peasants tended to live freer lives under feudalism than under absolute monarchies.
   (D) It tended to have a dampening effect on the formation of cities and trade networks.

12. One impact of Islam on India between 600 and 1450 was

   (A) to eradicate Hinduism in most of northern India.
   (B) the outlawing of the traditional caste system.
   (C) an improvement of the status of women where Islam took hold.
   (D) the destruction of a strong centralized state and political fragmentation.

13. Which of the following presents events in their proper order?

   (A) Genghis Khan conquers Central Asia and parts of China; Kublai Khan establishes the Yuan Dynasty; the warlord Timur emerges in Central Asia; Russia falls to the Golden Horde
   (B) Genghis Khan conquers Central Asia and parts of China; the warlord Timur emerges in Central Asia; Russia falls to the Golden Horde; Kublai Khan establishes the Yuan Dynasty
   (C) Genghis Khan conquers Central Asia and parts of China; Russia falls to the Golden Horde; Kublai Khan establishes the Yuan Dynasty; the warlord Timur emerges in Central Asia
   (D) Genghis Khan conquers Central Asia and parts of China; the warlord Timur emerges in Central Asia; Kublai Khan establishes the Yuan Dynasty; Russia falls to the Golden Horde

O ye who believe! Strong drink and games of chance and idols . . . are only an infamy of Satan's handiwork. Leave it aside in order that ye may succeed.

the Qur'an, Sura 5: 89

When once you hear the roses are in bloom,
Then is the time, my love, to pour the wine.

the *Rubáiyát* of Omar Khayyám

14. The second passage does not support the first because the second

    (A) shows a noted Muslim author arguing in favor of gambling.
    (B) shows a noted Muslim author favoring a practice discouraged by the Qur'an.
    (C) shows a noted Muslim author in violation of the Qur'an's injunction against writing verse.
    (D) shows a noted Muslim expressing atheistic sentiments.

15. Which of the following did the MOST to encourage European exploration during the 1400s and 1500s?

    (A) scientific curiosity about world geography
    (B) the desire to trade directly with China and the Indies
    (C) the chance to gain converts to Christianity
    (D) hopes of finding ivory and gold in Africa

16. Russian colonization of Siberia most resembled French colonization of North America in that

    (A) both made extensive use of indentured servitude to provide a labor force.
    (B) both involved the desire of religious minorities to worship as they pleased.
    (C) both were carried out by the deployment of powerful land forces.
    (D) both were motivated largely by the fur trade.

17. Which of the following would best explain why the early 1500s are treated as a turning point in the historiography of East Africa?

    (A) Environmental stress and desertification made much of the region uninhabitable.
    (B) The abolition of the Arab slave trade liberalized society in the coastal cities.
    (C) European traders and colonists first arrived on the scene.
    (D) Invading Berber warriors converted most of the population to Islam.

18. Which of the following seems MOST true of the city depicted below?

(A) It appears to have expanded naturally from its medieval boundaries.
(B) It appears to have been built principally to allow for a high volume of trade.
(C) It appears to have come into being as a center of religious pilgrimage.
(D) It appears to have been erected recently from the ground up as a fortified point.

19. Latin America's encomienda system most resembles agriculture as it was practiced on Caribbean sugar plantations in that

(A) both relied on forced labor.
(B) both diversified the types of crop grown.
(C) both weakened the elite class's hold on land under cultivation.
(D) both reduced the environmental impact on farming.

20. Modernization in Russia during the early 1700s MOST resembled which of the following?

(A) Franklin Roosevelt's New Deal in the 1930s
(B) the Meiji Restoration in Japan during the late 1800s
(C) Ottoman Turkey's Tanzimat Reforms during the 1800s
(D) Louis XIV's strengthening of French absolutism during the 1600s

21. The world's leading producer of cotton textiles around 1700 was

(A) the American South.
(B) India.
(C) China.
(D) Egypt.

22. Which innovation had the greatest impact on the early Industrial Revolution in England?

(A) the cotton gin
(B) the electric motor
(C) the Bessemer process
(D) the steam engine

23. The United States' relationship with Latin America during the nineteenth century was characterized mainly by

    (A) at attempt to colonize as much territory there as possible.
    (B) a program of assisting the region with its social and economic development.
    (C) U.S. corporate influence over political elites in many countries there.
    (D) an almost complete absence of interaction.

24. What do the Tanzimat Reforms and China's self-strengthening movement have in common?

    (A) They were limited modernizations carried out from above with moderate success.
    (B) They focused principally on improving the armed forces.
    (C) They emphasized social liberalization at the expense of industrialization.
    (D) They provided women with a greater range of rights and freedoms.

25. The building of the Suez Canal

    (A) reduced the economic importance of trans-Atlantic shipping.
    (B) illustrated the way non-Western societies emulated industrial practices.
    (C) lessened the diplomatic tensions surrounding the Eastern Question.
    (D) demonstrated humankind's growing capacity to affect its environment.

26. Arab merchants

    (A) contributed little to the spread of Islam to Africa.
    (B) gradually lost control over Saharan caravan routes.
    (C) refused for religious reasons to trade with Hindus across the Indian Ocean.
    (D) dominated the East African slave trade until the late 1800s.

27. How did the Japanese and German styles of industrialization differ from Great Britain's?

    (A) Industrial workers were treated more humanely than in Britain.
    (B) By 1900, levels of industrial output were higher than in Britain.
    (C) The state intervened more heavily in industrial development than in Britain.
    (D) Less emphasis was placed on the production of armaments than in Britain.

28. The photograph below most likely illustrates which late-nineteenth-century trend?

(A) Native hunters pursuing their traditional livelihood.
(B) Native hunters exploiting resources under orders from colonial masters.
(C) Native hunters engaged in trade with Westerners on equal terms.
(D) Native hunters taking charge of ivory harvesting to keep whites from depleting supplies.

29. Which is the best explanation for the global spread of Spanish flu?

(A) the biological warfare program carried out by Germany in World War I
(B) the worldwide movement of large numbers of soldiers and refugees
(C) the failure of governments to attend to public health while distracted by World War I
(D) the weakening of world populations by hunger and wartime exhaustion

30. Which of the following is NOT true of Japan during the 1920s and 1930s?

(A) Universal male suffrage was granted.
(B) Zaibatsu corporations persuaded the government to pass generous labor laws.
(C) A state-sponsored form of Shintoism justified militaristic policies.
(D) Japan pursued aggressive campaigns of imperial expansion in China.

31. The poster shown below is most likely meant to communicate

(A) the Nazis' anti-Semitic ideology.
(B) the Nazis' preoccupation with racial purity.
(C) the Nazis' plans for economic recovery.
(D) the Nazis' opposition to communism.

32. How did decolonization in most British and French colonies differ from that in possessions ruled by Belgium and Portugal?

(A) The British and French better prepared their colonies for freedom and kept violence to a minimum.
(B) The Belgians and Portuguese tended to grant independence more quickly and readily.
(C) The British and French, with their record as abusive colonial masters, had poor relations with their former colonies.
(D) Decolonization proceeded in much the same fashion in all these colonies.

33. In what way did India and Indonesia pursue similar foreign policies during the Cold War?

(A) Both enjoyed cordial relations with their countries' former colonizers.
(B) Both opted to remain unaligned in the Cold War superpower conflict.
(C) Both considered Maoist China to be their most natural ally.
(D) Both established closer ties with the United States than with the USSR.

34. Postindustrial modes of economic activity focus MAINLY on providing

(A) factory-produced goods.
(B) consumer services.
(C) raw materials.
(D) transportational infrastructure.

35. During the 1980s and 1990s, many Latin American nations made transitions to what kind of regime?

    (A) democratic
    (B) anarchist
    (C) communist
    (D) fascist

36. How did pastoralism affect the development of early societies?

    (A) It caused herding clans to become more sedentary.
    (B) It encouraged monotheistic forms of worship.
    (C) It did away with gendered divisions of labor.
    (D) It diversified the types of food available to communities.

37. How did the discovery of agriculture affect Neolithic people?

    (A) The need to find new plots of arable land forced a nomadic lifestyle on agriculturalists.
    (B) Permanent settlement gave rise to the concept of private property.
    (C) The effort involved with agriculture compelled planters to give up animal domestication.
    (D) Labor specialization became less necessary as more people grew food.

38. Which of the following BEST summarizes Confucian thought?

    (A) Power is given to rulers by the gods; therefore, rulers may treat their people as they please.
    (B) Husbands and wives should equally share the responsibility for family leadership.
    (C) Harmony is attained when superiors treat those below them with kindness and inferiors respect those above them.
    (D) Only members of the aristocracy are capable of cultivating the qualities of etiquette and grace.

39. How did rugged terrain affect the formation of Andean societies?

    (A) People were forced to cooperate in working out an effective division of labor.
    (B) The level of cultural sophistication remained quite low.
    (C) Tribal wars regularly broke out over scarce resources.
    (D) Individual clans remained isolated, slowing the development of larger societies.

40. Which of the following state-building techniques did the most to strengthen Persian imperial power between the 500s B.C.E. and 300s B.C.E.?

    (A) suppressing all forms of worship besides Zoroastrianism to foster cultural unity
    (B) creating a free-trade zone within Persia's economic sphere of influence
    (C) forming a regional military alliance with neighboring peoples like the Greeks
    (D) relying on satraps to provide effective regional administration

41. How were Carthage and Rome most alike during the years of their Mediterranean rivalry?

    (A) Both were governed by aristocratic oligarchies.
    (B) Both were theocratically inclined.
    (C) Both were prosperous naval powers.
    (D) Both were loose confederations of city-states.

42. The Silk Road was unusual among major premodern trade routes in that it

    (A) did little to encourage the spread of cultural and religious influences.
    (B) required government support to keep it open.
    (C) succeeded in covering vast distances overland.
    (D) ran through the most violent territory in Eurasia.

43. Which of the following accurately describes socio-economic practice in the Americas and West Africa before 1500?

    (A) Polytheism was a common form of worship.
    (B) Sorghum and rye were the main food supplies.
    (C) Large domesticated animals allowed for large-scale agriculture.
    (D) The most prevalent trade goods were plantains and salt.

44. Which crop dominated Southeast Asian agriculture in the 1400s?

    (A) rice
    (B) ginseng
    (C) soybeans
    (D) millet

45. Viking longboats and Polynesian double-hulled canoes have which of the following in common?

    (A) The building of both required advanced knowledge of metallurgy.
    (B) They both facilitated the effective projection of military force.
    (C) Each of them permitted open-water navigation over great distances.
    (D) The design of the former was inspired by the latter in a process of cultural diffusion.

46. The examples of Timbuktu, Zanzibar, and Great Zimbabwe indicate that, prior to 1450,

    (A) most of Africa was joined together by a great sub-Saharan empire.
    (B) African cultures were capable of developing large and prosperous urban centers.
    (C) networks of trade and communication were limited in Africa.
    (D) the political culture of African cities tended to be democratic.

47. Which of the following is an example of technology transfer resulting from the Crusades?

    (A) Europeans learned castlebuilding techniques from the Muslims.
    (B) Muslims acquired knowledge of the movable-type printing press from the Europeans.
    (C) Europeans gained the formula for gunpowder from the Muslims.
    (D) Muslims borrowed the stirrup from the Europeans.

48. Which innovation did the most to spread new ideas and cultural trends throughout Europe between 1450 and 1750?

    (A) the ability to build large domes
    (B) the appeal of oil-based paints
    (C) the invention of the printing press
    (D) the rediscovery of the laws of perspective

49. The voyages of Zheng He

    (A) had scientific discovery as their main purpose.
    (B) focused principally on Pacific navigation.
    (C) turned China into a naval power for centuries.
    (D) exacted tribute from or traded with many Indian Ocean states.

50. Which of the following best describes how West and Central African states reacted to the arrival of Europeans in the late 1400s and 1500s?

    (A) Roughly half their population fell victim to European diseases such as smallpox.
    (B) They sent fleets across the Mediterranean to raid Spain's and Portugal's southern shores.
    (C) Some remained strong by selling their neighbors as slaves in exchange for European guns.
    (D) Most managed to deny Europeans access to African networks of trade.

51. How did the adoption of parliamentary monarchies in some parts of Europe between 1450 and 1750 change the lives of citizens?

    (A) They tended to enjoy more social mobility and greater freedom of worship.
    (B) They quickly went on to campaign successfully for universal male suffrage.
    (C) Their average rate of literacy dropped.
    (D) They were protected from poverty by stronger social welfare systems.

52. How did trends in New Spain and Brazil resemble each other during European colonization of the Americas?

    (A) The Catholic Church prevented the Spanish and Portuguese from using slaves.
    (B) Diseases carried by Spanish and Portuguese colonizers decimated indigenous populations.
    (C) Copper mining became the chief priority for the Spanish and Portuguese alike.
    (D) The Spanish and Portuguese both treated those of mixed ancestry as equals.

53. Dutch colonization in the 1500s and 1600s

    (A) was carried out in partnership with Spanish allies.
    (B) resulted in the creation of the world's first joint-stock companies.
    (C) aimed principally to convert natives to Protestantism.
    (D) resulted in Dutch rule over Australia until the late 1800s.

54. Which of the following best characterizes Japan's relations with the outside world during the 1600s?

    (A) Japanese merchants persuaded the shoguns to allow free trade with Europe.
    (B) Foreign traders and missionaries turned out to have little interest in Japan.
    (C) The European presence in Japan was restricted extremely tightly.
    (D) Most shoguns actively supported Christian missionary activity.

55. What marked the 1600s and 1700s as a period of scientific revolution in Europe?

    (A) the development of the theory of natural selection
    (B) the development of a cost-effective steam engine
    (C) the development of navigational science and the invention of the compass
    (D) the development of a unified system of mathematics, physics, and chemistry

56. During the 1700s, Ottoman janissaries and the aristocrats of continental Europe both

    (A) frequently opposed reforms carried out by centralizing monarchs.
    (B) rejected gunpowder weaponry in favor of traditional forms of combat.
    (C) tended to be more religiously devout than the population at large.
    (D) invested heavily in joint-stock companies that funded overseas colonization.

57. Which of the following did NOT contribute to worldwide population growth between 1700 and 1800?

    (A) a decline in infant mortality rates
    (B) the rise of state-supported health care systems
    (C) the introduction of American food crops to Afro-Eurasian diets
    (D) a growth in the amount of land under agricultural cultivation

58. Which industrial-era technology did the most to improve land-based transport in the nineteenth century?

    (A) the internal-combustion engine
    (B) paved highways
    (C) the railroad
    (D) improved horse wagons

59. China's Taiping Rebellion most resembles which of the following conflicts?

    (A) the Indian Mutiny
    (B) the Mahdi's uprising in the Sudan
    (C) the Zulu Wars
    (D) the Philippine insurrection

60. Modernization in nineteenth-century Latin America often led to

    (A) greater social and gender equality.
    (B) concentration of wealth in the hands of a small elite.
    (C) the sharp reduction of illegal drug trafficking.
    (D) economic and agricultural diversification.

61. The cartoon shown below depicts which nineteenth-century trend?

    (A) Western fears about growing numbers of Asian immigrants
    (B) Korean protests against the influx of Christian missionaries
    (C) Burmese opposition to the French colonization of Indochina
    (D) China's inability to prevent Western encroachments on its sovereignty

62. How did the French Revolution resemble the Russian Revolution?

    (A) The principal leaders of both came from the peasant class.
    (B) In both, the first stage was more liberal than later stages.
    (C) For both, the initial goal was to found a democratic republic.
    (D) Both respected the right of citizens to worship as they pleased.

63. At the Berlin Conference of 1884–1885,

    (A) socialist parties ratified *The Communist Manifesto.*
    (B) foreign ministers resolved the Eastern Question.
    (C) suffragettes issued their famous Declaration of Sentiments.
    (D) diplomats set the rules and boundary lines for claiming African colonies.

64. Which of the following best describes the effect of World War I on European culture?

    (A) Poetry in the victorious nations reflected triumph and pride.
    (B) Artists quickly put the wartime experience behind them and ignored it.
    (C) Despair and uncertainty came to the forefront of intellectual life.
    (D) Abstract painting, equated with the war's brutality, was rejected in favor of representational realism.

65. Hindu-Muslim tensions in the 1940s

    (A) caused India to postpone its drive for independence.
    (B) persuaded many Hindus to collaborate with Japan during World War II.
    (C) led to the partition of India and Pakistan soon after independence.
    (D) was, in the end, resolved without violence.

66. Among the technological innovations that stemmed from or were perfected during World War II was

    (A) the radio.
    (B) the supersonic airplane.
    (C) the tank.
    (D) radar.

67. The Bretton Woods System was created after World War II to

    (A) protect an increasingly polluted environment.
    (B) promote international free trade.
    (C) provide for military cooperation among Western powers.
    (D) engage the Soviet bloc in arms control talks.

68. A key difference between the Indian National Congress and the African National Congress is that

    (A) the former embraced communism, whereas the latter leaned toward anarchism.
    (B) the former committed to nonviolent resistance, whereas the latter turned more readily to violence.
    (C) the former collaborated with Britain's enemies during World War II, whereas the latter remained loyal.
    (D) the former was content to remain in the British Empire as a dominion, whereas the latter wanted complete freedom.

World Human Population Growth: 1 C.E.–1999	
Year	*Population*
1 C.E.	200 million
1650	500 million
1850	1 billion
1930	2 billion
1975	4 billion
1999	6 billion

69. According to the chart above, during which of the following intervals did world population grow at the fastest rate (people per year)?

(A) 1650–1850
(B) 1850–1930
(C) 1930–1975
(D) 1975–1999

70. The image below is best interpreted as an example of?

(A) U.S. military domination over the Middle East
(B) foreign takeover of U.S. corporations
(C) cultural autonomy on the part of the non-Western world
(D) the global influence of U.S. mass culture

END OF SECTION I

SECTION II: FREE-RESPONSE QUESTIONS

Part A: Document-Based Question

(SUGGESTED WRITING TIME—40 MINUTES)
PERCENT OF SECTION II SCORE—33⅓

Directions: The following question is based on the accompanying Documents 1–8. (The documents have been edited for the purpose of this exercise.) Write your answer on the lined pages of the Section II free-response booklet.

This question is designed to test your ability to work with and understand historical documents.

Write an essay that

- has a relevant thesis and supports that thesis with evidence from the documents.
- uses all of the documents.
- analyzes the documents by grouping them in as many appropriate ways as possible, and does not simply summarize the documents individually.
- takes into account the sources of the documents and analyzes the authors' points of view.
- identifies and explains the need for at least one additional type of document.

You may refer to relevant historical information not mentioned in the documents.

1. Using the documents, analyze the attitudes of Western and non-Western attitudes toward scientific and technological change from the 1500s onward. Identify an additional type of document and explain how it would help in assessing Western or non-Western actions and reactions.

DOCUMENT 1

Source: Charlotte Brontë, English novelist, upon viewing the Crystal Palace at London's Great Exhibition (1851).

> Yesterday I went for the second time to the Crystal Palace. . . . I must say I was more struck with it on this occasion than at my first visit. It is a wonderful place—vast, strange, new, and impossible to describe. . . . Whatever human industry has created you find there, from the great compartments filled with railway engines and boilers, with mill machinery in full work, with splendid carriages of all kinds, with harness of every description, to the glass-covered and velvet-spread stands loaded with the most gorgeous work of the goldsmith and silversmith. . . . It may be called a bazaar or a fair, but it is such a bazaar or fair as Eastern genii might have created. It seems as if only magic could have gathered this mass of wealth from all the ends of the earth.

DOCUMENT 2

Source: Victor Hugo, "This Will Kill That," *The Hunchback of Notre Dame* (1830).

Our readers must excuse us if we stop a moment to investigate the enigmatic words of the archdeacon: "This will kill that. The book will kill the edifice."

First of all, it was the view of a priest. It was the fear of an ecclesiastic before a new force, the printing press. It was the frightened yet dazzled man of the sanctuary confronting the illuminating Gutenberg press. . . . It signified that one great power was following upon the heels of another great power. It meant: The printing press will destroy the Church.

But besides this first thought, there was a second . . . but it no longer belongs to the priest alone, but to the scholar and to the artist as well. Here was a premonition that human thought had advanced, and, in changing, was about to change its mode of expression, that the important ideas of each new generation would be recorded in a new way, that the book of stone, [in which carvings and sculptures had provided the illiterate with a language of images and symbols], so solid and enduring, was about to be supplanted by the paper book, which would become more enduring still. In this respect, the vague formula of the archdeacon had a second meaning: That one art would dethrone another art. It meant: Printing will destroy architecture.

DOCUMENT 3

Source: Ito Hirobumi, young samurai from Japan, in letter to British official (1866).

Hitherto there have been a great number of stupid and ignorant persons in our provinces, who still adhered to the foolish old learning. They were unaware of the daily scientific progress of the Western nations, being like the frog at the bottom of a well. But lately they have learned. The eyes and ears of the stupid having thus been opened, the desirability of opening our country to foreign knowledge has become clear.

DOCUMENT 4

Source: Mohandas K. Gandhi, leader of Indian independence movement, *Gandhi: His Life and Message* (1954).

The incessant search for material comforts and their multiplication is such an evil, and I make bold to say that the Europeans themselves will have to remodel their outlook if they are not to perish under the weight of the comfort to which they are becoming slaves.

DOCUMENT 5

Source: Matteo Ricci, sixteenth-century Jesuit priest, showing a map of the world to the people of Canton during his visit to China (1578).

Of all the great nations, the Chinese have had the least commerce, indeed, one might say that they have had practically no contact whatever with outside nations, and consequently they are grossly ignorant of what the world in general is like. True, they had charts somewhat similar to this one, that were supposed to represent the whole world, but their universe was limited to their own fifteen provinces, and in the sea painted around it, they had placed a few islands to which they gave the names of different kingdoms they had heard of. . . . When they learned that China was only a part of the great east, they considered such an idea, so unlike their own, to be something utterly impossible. . . .

To them the heavens are round but the earth is flat and square, and they firmly believe that their empire is right in the middle of it. They do not like the idea of our geographies pushing their China into one corner of the Orient. They could not comprehend the demonstrations proving that the earth is a globe, made up of land and water, and that a globe of its nature has neither beginning nor end.

DOCUMENT 6

Source: Swiss author Henri Frédéric Amiel, on European industrialization, as seen at London's Great Exhibition (1851).

The useful will take the place of the beautiful, industry will take the place of art, political economy of religion, and arithmetic of poetry.

DOCUMENT 7

Source: Ali Akbar Davar, journalist and Iran's Minister of Public Works, editorial in *The Free Man* (1923).

Until we dedicate ourselves to an economic and technological revolution, nothing will move or change. We shall remain a nation of beggars, hungry and in ragged clothing, and we shall continue to suffer. We have six thousand years of history, but that will not translate into factories, railroads, hospitals, or schools. Schools alone without economic reforms will change nothing, as long as the environment outside the schools continues to reek of poverty. . . . When we have at least 5,000 kilometers of railways, 50 factories, 50 roads linking east and west, dams on the Karun River, and have eradicated locusts, we can then attend to the graduation of 1,000 students from institutions of higher learning.

DOCUMENT 8

Source: William Blake (1757–1827), English romantic poet, *Milton*.

> And did those feet in ancient time
> Walk upon England's mountains green?
> And was the Holy Lamb of God
> On England's pleasant pastures seen?
>
> And did the Countenance Divine
> Shine forth upon our clouded hills?
> And was Jerusalem builded here
> Among these dark Satanic Mills?
>
> Bring me my Bow of burning gold:
> Bring me my Arrows of desire:
> Bring me my Spear: O clouds unfold!
> Bring me my Chariot of fire.
>
> I will not cease from Mental Fight,
> Nor shall my Sword sleep in my hand
> Till we have built Jerusalem
> In England's green and pleasant Land.

Part B: Continuity and Change-Over-Time Question

(SUGGESTED PLANNING AND WRITING TIME—40 MINUTES)
PERCENT OF SECTION II SCORE—33⅓

Directions: You are to answer the following question. You should spend 5 minutes organizing or outlining your essay.

Write an essay that:

- has a relevant thesis and supports that thesis with appropriate historical evidence.
- addresses all parts of the question.
- uses world historical context to show continuities and changes over time.
- analyzes the process of continuity and change over time.

2. Describe the continuities and changes in the impact of religion on politics in China (600–1450) OR in South Asia (1450–1750) and assess the effects of the continuities and changes that you describe.

Part C: Comparative Essay

(SUGGESTED PLANNING AND WRITING TIME—40 MINUTES)
PERCENT OF SECTION II SCORE—33⅓

Directions: You are to answer the following question. You should spend 5 minutes organizing or outlining your essay.

Write an essay that

- has a relevant thesis and supports that thesis with appropriate historical evidence.
- addresses all parts of the question.
- makes direct, relevant comparisons.
- analyzes relevant reasons for similarities and differences.

3. Compare the impact of Western imperialism on Latin America between 1750 and 1900 with the impact it had on sub-Saharan Africa during the same period. Be sure to include similarities and differences.

END OF SECTION II

Answer Key
MODEL TEST 1

Section I

1. A	21. B	41. A	61. D
2. C	22. D	42. C	62. B
3. B	23. C	43. A	63. D
4. C	24. A	44. A	64. C
5. B	25. D	45. C	65. C
6. B	26. D	46. B	66. D
7. A	27. C	47. A	67. B
8. C	28. B	48. C	68. B
9. C	29. B	49. D	69. D
10. D	30. B	50. C	70. D
11. A	31. D	51. A	
12. C	32. A	52. B	
13. C	33. B	53. B	
14. B	34. B	54. C	
15. B	35. A	55. D	
16. D	36. D	56. A	
17. C	37. B	57. B	
18. D	38. C	58. C	
19. A	39. A	59. B	
20. B	40. D	60. B	

ANSWERS EXPLAINED

1. **(A)** Diffusion, or adapting a technology or idea from a neighboring people, played a great role in how early societies learned to do things. Certain innovations, however, arose independently, among them bronze metalworking in China and the Middle East.

2. **(C)** Agriculture, or the domestication of plants, is the key innovation of the Neolithic Revolution. While generalizing about Paleolithic life is difficult, we know that early humans buried their dead, painted, played musical instruments, and tended toward animist and polytheistic faiths.

3. **(B)** The Upanishads revolutionized Indian religious thought by adding new dimensions to the Vedic religion and paving the way for the emergence of Hinduism. They did not deny the doctrines of karma and reincarnation, but emphasized the ability of each person to evolve spiritually without relying so much on priestly guidance or elaborate ritual.

4. **(C)** All of the animals listed played important roles in economic and agricultural life throughout world history. The horse, however, did not reach the Americas until after the Europeans' arrival, and neither were water buffalo or oxen domesticated there. The llama provided labor, wool, and food for the peoples of the Andes.

5. **(B)** The Ottoman Empire did not exist at this time, making D incorrect. While East Africa was not unknown to the Romans, North Africa was as far south as they resided in large numbers, and Polynesians are not known to have moved in the direction of the Middle East. The Chinese presence in Southeast Asia, the Malay Peninsula included, was and continues to be prominent.

6. **(B)** Just as new religions can change the societies that adopt them, they themselves can be changed by the experience of being adopted. Many Asian faiths are highly syncretic, meaning that they share elements easily with one another, as Daoism, Buddhism, and Confucianism have tended to do over time, and as Buddhism and Hinduism have done elsewhere. Answer A reverses what actually happened, and C and D are simply false.

7. **(A)** The Han Chinese and Romans were master administrators, making D false. Answers B and C have posed problems for other states, but were not crucial factors in the decline of Han China or Rome, although some have proposed that Christianity's influence "softened" Rome in its final centuries. Both empires exhausted themselve with constant warfare against nomadic invaders.

8. **(C)** During this period in Europe, a large number of relatively centralized states had emerged and were led by monarchs. In China, centralization was achieved first by Mongol rule in the 1200s and then deepened by the Ming dynasty from the mid-1300s onward.

9. **(C)** Although all these problems troubled all three regions at one time or another, the only one to strike all of them during the time in question was the

bubonic plague, which swept from east to west, killing on average one-third of a given population.

10. **(D)** Between the mid-1200s and mid-1400s, Mali was the largest and most powerful Islamic state in West Africa. It controlled large metal deposits, including gold. Europeans began trading in African slaves somewhat later, and gunpowder weaponry was not yet widely available.

11. **(A)** Feudalism is a response to conditions of political centralization, making B incorrect. It forces monarchs to rely on nobles to protect and govern their land, but it does not restrict trade or urban growth. Most peasants under feudalism were serfs or otherwise coerced for their labor, and so C is false.

12. **(C)** Muslim invaders arrived at a time when India was decentralized, and they created the Delhi Sultanate, making D false. The two religions and their customs coexisted, so A and B are incorrect as well. Muslim women in India tended to have more rights than Hindu women.

13. **(C)** The rise of the Mongol Empire began with Genghis Khan's early victories in the east. Russia was taken during a later wave of conquest begun while Genghis was still alive. Kublai Khan was one of Genghis's successors, and his rise coincided with the gradual breakup of the Mongol Empire. Timur came later, near the end of the 1300s.

14. **(B)** The Qur'an does not forbid the writing of poetry, and there is nothing on Khayyám's verse about games of chance or non-belief in Allah, so A, C, and D are false. In studying world religions and their effect on social and political behavior, it is important to note that not all adherents of a given religion observe every one of its precepts.

15. **(B)** Economic ambitions mainly motivated European exploration, eliminating A and C. While D ended up being an effect of the Europeans' voyages around Africa to the Indian Ocean, it was in hopes of trading with the nations of Asia that prompted them to sail in the first place.

16. **(D)** Answers A and B apply more to North America, whereas C applies more to Siberia, which was physically adjacent to Russia and conquered by land rather than over the sea. The search for furs drove French colonization of Canada and Russia's drive into Siberia.

17. **(C)** The arrival of the Portuguese in this region in the early 1500s hugely transformed the political, social, and economic life not just of East Africa, but the Indian Ocean basin as a whole. The Berbers lived far to the west, and the Arab slave trade persisted into the 1800s.

18. **(D)** The symmetrical layout argues against A and in favor of D. There is no sign of a major church or cathedral, and while there are roads, there are no rivers or sea harbors that would indicate a significant amount of trade, making B and

C unlikely. The presence of thick, bastioned city walls—a new style meant to protect against gunpowder artillery—makes D an even likelier answer.

19. **(A)** The encomienda system involved the enslavement of indigenous Americans, and the cultivation of sugarcane in the Caribbean created a huge demand for slaves from Africa. Both benefited the elite class, harmed the environment, and encouraged monoculture rather than diversification.

20. **(B)** Russia during the early 1700s was modernized rapidly and almost single-handedly by Peter the Great. Answers A and C refer to programs that were more gradual and reformist. Louis XIV, mentioned in D, was an absolutist like Peter, but the top-down, revolutionary nature of Meiji's modernization in Japan is a better match.

21. **(B)** Egypt and the U.S. South developed into large cotton producers in later years, but not around 1700, eliminating A and D. In Mughal India, the economy thrived largely because of a boom in the cotton trade. After the Europeans defeated the Mughal state, they established their own control over cotton production in India.

22. **(D)** Although the cotton gin is associated with increased production during the early industrial period, the emergence of a powerful and cost-effective steam engine made full-scale mechanization possible. Answers B and C came later.

23. **(C)** The United States considered the Western Hemisphere to be its sphere of influence, ever since the proclamation of the Monroe Doctrine in the 1820s. Except for the territories it seized after the Mexican-American and Spanish-American Wars, it exercised that influence informally, and often through corporate ties.

24. **(A)** Both Qing China and Ottoman Turkey attempted to modernize from above during the mid- to late 1800s. The latter had more success, because more of the leadership was committed to change. In China, the self-strengthening movement was about industrial and military improvement; although the Tanzimat reforms spoke somewhat to social and gender issues, they too prioritized military and economic affairs.

25. **(D)** A marvel of industrial-era construction, the Suez Canal was, quite literally, an earth-shaping engineering project. It did not render trans-Atlantic shipping any less crucial, and it was built by the French, making A and B incorrect. By increasing the economic and strategic importance of Egypt, the Suez Canal actually made the Eastern Question more urgent.

26. **(D)** Arab merchants were involved in Saharan trade for many centuries, and they played a crucial role in bringing Islam to many parts of Africa. Their religion did not bar them from trading with those of other faiths.

27. **(C)** Answer B is true of Germany, but not of Japan, and while Germany provided a more generous package of social benefits than Britain, as in A, Japan did not.

Answer D is not true of Japan or Germany. Both in Germany and Japan, industry had a much closer relationship with the government than in *laissez-faire* Britain.

28. **(B)** This scene from the Belgian Congo shows a typical scene of colonial subjects being forced to despoil their own home to benefit their colonizers. In Belgium's case, the level of exploitation was especially brutal; Congolese natives were also forced to labor under terrible conditions on rubber plantations.

29. **(B)** World War I resulted in the deployment of huge numbers of soldiers over vast distances, and also displaced a number of civilians. Their movement, especially as demobilized soldiers returned home, created excellent conditions for the rapid spread of the disease. Even though the Germans began the use of poison gas in World War I, they did not use biological warfare.

30. **(B)** Although Japan liberalized politically to some extent during the 1920s, the zaibatsu corporations, which enjoyed a close relationship with the government, had no interest in social or economic liberalization. Militarism and racial superiority were core elements of State Shintoism, and the Japanese invaded China in the early 1930s, leaving only after their defeat in World War II.

31. **(D)** Nazi propaganda targeted all the topics listed in this question. The snake representing the social evil to be crushed in this poster, however, bears the label "Marxismus," a clear clue, even without knowing German, that communism is its subject.

32. **(A)** Belgium and Portugal, which already had particularly brutal records as colonial masters, did very little to prepare their colonies for independence after World War II. Britain and France tended to train native elites in administration and management and to provide advice and guidance even after independence. Violence and weak states tended to be the norm in former Belgian and Portuguese colonies.

33. **(B)** Many Third World governments, including those of India and Indonesia, did not want to align exclusively with either side during the Cold War. Instead, they thought it was in their best interests to remain neutral or deal with whichever side gave them more economic and military assistance. Indonesia's leader Sukarno attempted to create a worldwide coalition of unaligned states, but with limited success.

34. **(B)** Postindustrial economies emphasize services, consumerism, and cutting-edge technologies. Workforces are employed more in the services, including the biotech and computer fields, and there is a smaller proportion of unionized, blue-collar workers.

35. **(A)** For decades, many regimes in Latin America were dictatorial, but the 1980s and 1990s witnessed a wave of democratization in such countries as Argentina, Chile, Brazil, and Nicaragua. One exception to this trend was Cuba.

36. **(D)** Pastoralism encouraged nomadism, not permanent settlement, eliminating A, and there is no provable connection between modes of economic production and forms of worship, making B false. Although the gendered division of labor became more pronounced in agricultural societies, it was never absent.

37 **(B)** Agriculture discourages nomadism, but does nothing to discourage animal domestication. The shift away from hunter-gatherer and herding economies led to greater, not lesser, specialization of labor.

38. **(C)** Although Confucianism is hierarchical, it expects ethical, graceful, and courteous behavior from all classes, making A and D incorrect. It placed women in a secondary status, eliminating B.

39. **(A)** Cooperative effort gave rise to a number of large and sophisticated societies in the Andes Mountains. Among the earliest were the Chavín and Moche. They traded locally and also with peoples living in the Amazon basin, and were thus not isolated.

40. **(D)** Although later Persian empires made Zoroastrianism their official religion, the first empire was more flexible with respect to religious choice. They conquered or fought the Greeks, and free-trade zones are a more modern innovation. Regional governance and well-developed administrations enabled empires like Persia's, Rome's, and China's to rule over large areas even without modern technology.

41. **(A)** Although both societies took religion seriously, neither was theocratic. Carthage's founders, the Phoenicians, founded city-states throughout the Mediterranean, but Rome was more centralized, and whereas the Phoenicians were sea people from the beginning, it was only by fighting Carthage that Rome developed any kind of navy at all. The Roman Republic was governed by its Senate and two elected consuls, while Carthage was ruled by judges and an aristocratic council; neither was a traditional monarchy.

42. **(C)** Until the modern era, water transport was overwhelmingly easier than overland transport, and trade along rivers and coastlines was far more common. The Silk Road was remarkable in how it enabled overland trade over such a vast expanse. Also impressive were the caravan routes through the Sahara Desert.

43. **(A)** In neither of these places were animals used in large-scale agricultural production, and in neither place were sorghum or rye staple crops, or plantains and salt key commodities, eliminating B, C, and D. Polytheism was common in both areas, although Islam was important in West Africa as well, and persisted even after contact with Europeans.

44. **(A)** Rice-paddy farming probably originated in the Vietnamese states around 500 B.C.E. By the 1400s, the method had spread to other parts of Asia, including China and Japan. However it was cultivated, it became Asia's mainstay crop.

45. **(C)** Both the Vikings and Polynesians were strikingly talented seafarers. They had no known contact, and both built their boats out of wood, making A and D false. Answer B applies to the Vikings, and less to the Polynesians.

46. **(B)** Despite being thought of for a long time as "primitive" by the Western world, Africa developed many complex and sophisticated societies without outside assistance or colonization. There was no great single empire, however, and democracy was not known, making A and D incorrect. African cities traded widely, both throughout the continent and with the Indian Ocean basin, and so C is false as well.

47. **(A)** Answers B and C refer to innovations from a later time, and the stirrup in D traveled east to west at a much earlier date. The Europeans became more proficient at building elaborate stone castles after encountering them in the Middle East.

48. **(C)** Answers A, B, and D correctly list innovations that improved the dissemination of information, but the first two came later, while D came much earlier. It was the printing press's ability to mass-produce information after the 1430s that allowed the philosophies and concepts that animated Renaissance art and literature, as well as the Protestant Reformation, to be disseminated throughout Europe.

49. **(D)** Zheng He sailed as much in the Indian Ocean as he did the Pacific, and the projection of force was more important than science, and so A and B are incorrect. The Ming rulers abandoned long-range naval voyaging soon after Zheng He's navigations, making C false as well.

50. **(C)** Even where they did not conquer or trade directly, Europeans became indirectly involved with trade networks that reached far into the African interior, making D false, and because Africa was not isolated from Eurasia, its populations did not suffer the same vulnerability to European diseases that New World peoples did, making A incorrect. African kingdoms were strong enough at this point to make use of the strategy described in C, but not strong enough to attack Europe as in B.

51. **(A)** In parliamentary monarchies, rulers became less powerful, governing in conjunction with some kind of lawmaking body that had meaningful powers. They tended to allow more social mobility and freedom of worship, but they did not guarantee the right to vote or protection from poverty.

52. **(B)** Both colonies extracted precious metals from South America, but mainly silver. Both used slaves (the Church ended the use of indigenous Americans as slaves, but their place was taken by Africans), and both created rigid racial hierarchies with whites on top. The diseases brought to the New World by European colonizers proved extremely deadly.

53. **(B)** The Dutch were enemies of Spain and for the most part religiously tolerant, so A and C are false. The British, not the Dutch, colonized Australia. To support their exploration efforts, the Dutch formed the Dutch East India Company,

the first of its type (which later included the British East India Company and the Hudson's Bay Company), in the 1500s.

54. **(C)** Japan kept itself extremely isolated, eliminating A and D (although some shoguns did adopt Christianity). Foreigners greatly desired to trade with Japan, making B incorrect, but the shogunate, fearing outside influences, allowed interaction to take place only under highly restricted conditions.

55. **(D)** The other innovations here are misdated. Interest in and understanding of the concept of the scientific method revived in Europe during these years, and figures like Isaac Newton incorporated the age's discoveries into a single system of thought.

56. **(A)** During the early modern period, monarchs who wished to modernize or centralize often met with opposition from aristocratic classes who wished to retain their privileges. Answer D is not relevant to the Ottoman Empire, and while they did not always support the adoption of cutting-edge military technologies, both groups were comfortable with the use of gunpowder weaponry. Neither was on the whole more or less religious than those of lower classes.

57. **(B)** Public health and state-run systems of medical care are modern inventions. All the other factors helped boost population growth during the 1700s.

58. **(C)** One of the key innovations of early-nineteenth-century industrialization was the railroad, the first technology to allow easy movement of large amounts of freight over land. Highways and internal-combustion engines came later, while horse-drawn wagons were gradually phased out.

59. **(B)** As distinct from the other conflicts listed, the Taiping Rebellion and the rising of the Mahdi were both motivated by religious millenarianism.

60. **(B)** As in many non-Western parts of the world, modernization and industrialization were carried out by rulers and/or wealthy elites. In these cases, wealth tended to stay in the hands of the elite, rather than being put to use for the good of the population at large. Economies were typically based on plantation monoculture or the extraction of one or two resources, making D false, and drug trafficking belongs more to the twentieth and twenty-first centuries.

61. **(D)** Facial expressions make it clear that the strong emotions are Asian, not European, making A wrong, and there is nothing to indicate the presence of a religious dispute, eliminating B. The Europeans shown are multinational, arguing against C, even without the hint provided by the French word "Chine," for "China," on the pie being carved up.

62. **(B)** In neither of these cases did peasants play a leading role, and both regimes eventually interfered with the right to worship, and so A and D are incorrect. The French Revolution intended first to establish a constitutional monarchy, not a republic, making C false. The Russian Revolution began with the toppling

of the tsar by a provisional government that intended to create a democratic regime. In both cases, radical groups seized control and instituted reigns of terror.

63. (D) Hosted by Otto von Bismarck, representatives of European nations set down rules for expanding further into Africa. They drew boundary lines and decided that no European state could make new claims without demonstrating "effective occupation." This helped to set off the "scramble for Africa."

64. (C) World War I's cultural impact was so profound and so dispiriting, even for the nations on the winning side, that one can easily eliminate A and B. The leading edge of art and literature did not retreat into the styles of the 1800s, making D wrong as well.

65. (C) India's Muslim League and the Indian Congress both pursued independence during the early 1900s, but the former advocated a separate Muslim state. The two parties' failure to resolve their differences peacefully after World War II and independence led to great bloodshed in 1947 and the two-state partition that separated Pakistan from India. Tensions between the two continue today.

66. (D) Radar was made workable in time to help Great Britain fend off German air attacks in 1940. All the other items listed here were invented or perfected before or after World War II.

67. (B) In 1944, the United States and its allies met in Bretton Woods, New Hampshire, to create new economic institutions that would promote free trade and a stable monetary system. This included the establishment of the International Monetary Fund and the World Bank.

68. (B) Both groups wanted full independence, and the leaders of each were jailed. Although there were pro-Japanese collaborationists in India, Congress did not endorse them. The ANC flirted with Marxism to an extent that Congress did not. Gandhi and others put the Congress firmly on the path of nonviolent resistance.

69. (D) Although world population grew by 2 billion both between 1930 and 1975 and between 1975 and 1999, the second period is shorter, making its rate of growth faster.

70. (D) U.S. brands such as Coca-Cola and McDonald's (which are arguably no longer "American," but multinational), enjoy worldwide recognition, as shown by this sign reading "McDonald's" in Arabic. Their omnipresence demonstrates the symbolic power and appeal of American mass culture.

Answer Sheet

MODEL TEST 2

Section I

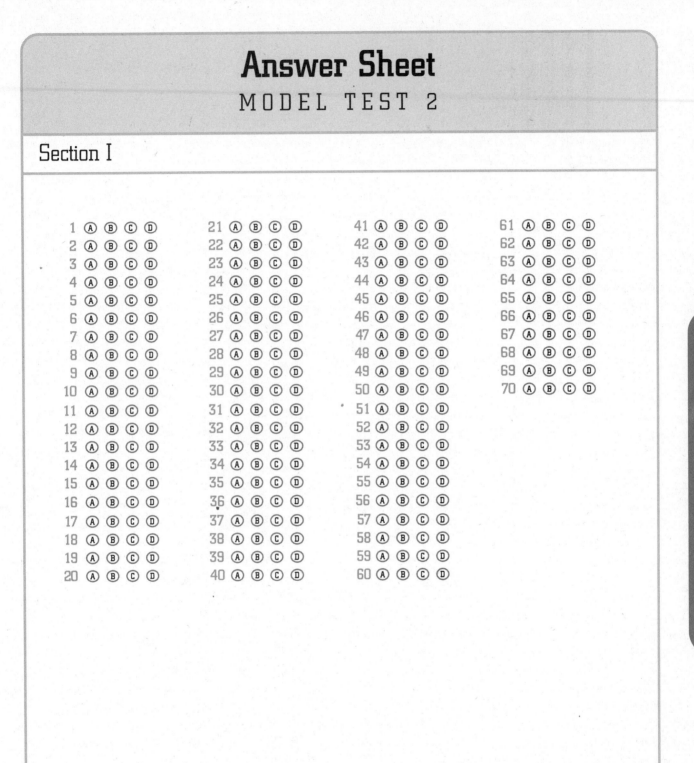

1 Ⓐ Ⓑ Ⓒ Ⓓ	21 Ⓐ Ⓑ Ⓒ Ⓓ	41 Ⓐ Ⓑ Ⓒ Ⓓ	61 Ⓐ Ⓑ Ⓒ Ⓓ
2 Ⓐ Ⓑ Ⓒ Ⓓ	22 Ⓐ Ⓑ Ⓒ Ⓓ	42 Ⓐ Ⓑ Ⓒ Ⓓ	62 Ⓐ Ⓑ Ⓒ Ⓓ
3 Ⓐ Ⓑ Ⓒ Ⓓ	23 Ⓐ Ⓑ Ⓒ Ⓓ	43 Ⓐ Ⓑ Ⓒ Ⓓ	63 Ⓐ Ⓑ Ⓒ Ⓓ
4 Ⓐ Ⓑ Ⓒ Ⓓ	24 Ⓐ Ⓑ Ⓒ Ⓓ	44 Ⓐ Ⓑ Ⓒ Ⓓ	64 Ⓐ Ⓑ Ⓒ Ⓓ
5 Ⓐ Ⓑ Ⓒ Ⓓ	25 Ⓐ Ⓑ Ⓒ Ⓓ	45 Ⓐ Ⓑ Ⓒ Ⓓ	65 Ⓐ Ⓑ Ⓒ Ⓓ
6 Ⓐ Ⓑ Ⓒ Ⓓ	26 Ⓐ Ⓑ Ⓒ Ⓓ	46 Ⓐ Ⓑ Ⓒ Ⓓ	66 Ⓐ Ⓑ Ⓒ Ⓓ
7 Ⓐ Ⓑ Ⓒ Ⓓ	27 Ⓐ Ⓑ Ⓒ Ⓓ	47 Ⓐ Ⓑ Ⓒ Ⓓ	67 Ⓐ Ⓑ Ⓒ Ⓓ
8 Ⓐ Ⓑ Ⓒ Ⓓ	28 Ⓐ Ⓑ Ⓒ Ⓓ	48 Ⓐ Ⓑ Ⓒ Ⓓ	68 Ⓐ Ⓑ Ⓒ Ⓓ
9 Ⓐ Ⓑ Ⓒ Ⓓ	29 Ⓐ Ⓑ Ⓒ Ⓓ	49 Ⓐ Ⓑ Ⓒ Ⓓ	69 Ⓐ Ⓑ Ⓒ Ⓓ
10 Ⓐ Ⓑ Ⓒ Ⓓ	30 Ⓐ Ⓑ Ⓒ Ⓓ	50 Ⓐ Ⓑ Ⓒ Ⓓ	70 Ⓐ Ⓑ Ⓒ Ⓓ
11 Ⓐ Ⓑ Ⓒ Ⓓ	31 Ⓐ Ⓑ Ⓒ Ⓓ	51 Ⓐ Ⓑ Ⓒ Ⓓ	
12 Ⓐ Ⓑ Ⓒ Ⓓ	32 Ⓐ Ⓑ Ⓒ Ⓓ	52 Ⓐ Ⓑ Ⓒ Ⓓ	
13 Ⓐ Ⓑ Ⓒ Ⓓ	33 Ⓐ Ⓑ Ⓒ Ⓓ	53 Ⓐ Ⓑ Ⓒ Ⓓ	
14 Ⓐ Ⓑ Ⓒ Ⓓ	34 Ⓐ Ⓑ Ⓒ Ⓓ	54 Ⓐ Ⓑ Ⓒ Ⓓ	
15 Ⓐ Ⓑ Ⓒ Ⓓ	35 Ⓐ Ⓑ Ⓒ Ⓓ	55 Ⓐ Ⓑ Ⓒ Ⓓ	
16 Ⓐ Ⓑ Ⓒ Ⓓ	36 Ⓐ Ⓑ Ⓒ Ⓓ	56 Ⓐ Ⓑ Ⓒ Ⓓ	
17 Ⓐ Ⓑ Ⓒ Ⓓ	37 Ⓐ Ⓑ Ⓒ Ⓓ	57 Ⓐ Ⓑ Ⓒ Ⓓ	
18 Ⓐ Ⓑ Ⓒ Ⓓ	38 Ⓐ Ⓑ Ⓒ Ⓓ	58 Ⓐ Ⓑ Ⓒ Ⓓ	
19 Ⓐ Ⓑ Ⓒ Ⓓ	39 Ⓐ Ⓑ Ⓒ Ⓓ	59 Ⓐ Ⓑ Ⓒ Ⓓ	
20 Ⓐ Ⓑ Ⓒ Ⓓ	40 Ⓐ Ⓑ Ⓒ Ⓓ	60 Ⓐ Ⓑ Ⓒ Ⓓ	

Answer Sheet

Model Test 2

SECTION I: MULTIPLE-CHOICE QUESTIONS

TIME: 55 MINUTES FOR 70 QUESTIONS

> **Directions:** Each of the questions or incomplete statements below is followed by suggested answers or completions. Select the one that is best in each case and then fill in the corresponding oval on the answer sheet.

1. Why is the period ca. 3500–3000 B.C.E. so often presented as a major threshold in world history?

   (A) The glaciers from the last ice age had receded fully by that point.
   (B) The earliest cities came into being around that time.
   (B) The first civilizations are considered to have take shape then.
   (D) The practice of agriculture first emerged during those years.

2. Which of the following serves as an example of technological innovation in the ancient Middle East?

   (A) the Hittites' use of iron weapons
   (B) the Egyptians' development of the printing press
   (C) the Phoenicians' invention of the first alphabet
   (D) the Lydians' discovery of the wheel

3. The ancient Athenians used the above structure for what purpose?

   (A) as a marketplace
   (B) as a government meeting place
   (C) as a temple
   (D) as a public bathhouse

4. The Hebrew adoption of monotheistic worship had the effect of

   (A) strengthening their sense of cultural unity.
   (B) making them likelier to assimilate fully into other societies.
   (C) weakening them politically.
   (D) turning them into pacifists.

5. Scholars from Gupta India are best known for

   (A) inventing the scientific method.
   (B) rejecting Hinduism in favor of secular thought.
   (C) compiling the text of the *Bhagavad-Gita*.
   (D) devising the concepts of zero and *pi*.

6. The sculpture pictured above most likely depicts

   (A) a subject in awe of the divine power of his king.
   (B) a slave attending upon his noble master.
   (C) an enemy acknowledging defeat before a mighty conqueror.
   (D) a performer taking a bow before a royal patron.

7. What feature typical to most advanced civilizations did Andean societies lack?

   (A) organized religion
   (B) a written script
   (C) the ability to domesticate animals
   (D) agricultural skills

8. The political and social effect of Neo-Confucianism in China was

   (A) to diminish public respect for the emperor.
   (B) to reinforce social hierarchy.
   (C) to elevate the status of women.
   (D) to foster greater individualism.

9. Which of the following is LEAST related to the expansion of trade in medieval Europe?

   (A) the formation of the Hanseatic League
   (B) the emergence of the guild system
   (C) the growth of Europe's urban population
   (D) the rising unpopularity of the Catholic Church

10. Which of the following most encouraged the intellectual attainments of the Muslim world during the Abbasid era?

   (A) artistic influences from Renaissance-era Europe
   (B) the granting of complete equality to all worshippers
   (C) the cultural and ethnic diversity of the population
   (D) strict state control over the production of art and literature

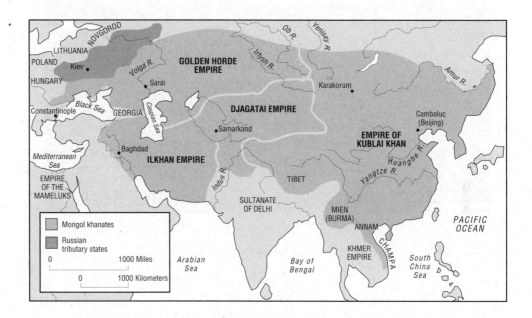

11. What is the central focus of the map above?

   (A) the expansion of Muscovite Russia into Mongol territory
   (B) the breakdown of the Mongol Empire into smaller states
   (C) the decline and fall of the Delhi Sultanate
   (D) the rise of the Khmer Empire

12. The travels of Ibn Battuta and Zheng He have what in common?

   (A) They demonstrate that the West did not have a monopoly on campaigns of exploration.
   (B) They were motivated principally by the desire to gain religious converts.
   (C) Both compelled many of the places they visited to pay tribute to their home countries.
   (D) Both involved the projection of military force.

13. Which of the statements below gives the best assessment of the Renaissance?

 (A) It strengthened the Papacy by emphasizing Catholic dogma.
 (B) It boldly experimented with non-realistic forms of artistic expression.
 (C) It combined Greco-Latin learning with a conviction that worldly life was worthwhile.
 (D) It ignored religious subject matter because of its secular outlook.

14. Which of the following describes patterns of trade in the Indian Ocean between the 1200s and the early 1400s?

 (A) ivory and gold from Africa; salt and cotton from India; porcelain and silk from China
 (B) gold and ivory from Africa; cotton from China; silk from India
 (C) spices from Africa; slaves from India; gold from China
 (D) ivory from India; porcelain and silk from China; tea from Africa

15. Which of the following would help a historian argue that a high degree of social organization prevailed among the people of the Mississippian culture?

 (A) It erected large mounds for ritual purposes and built a large city.
 (B) It was a highly warlike culture, conquering much of North America.
 (C) It was one of pre-Columbian America's first monotheistic civilizations.
 (D) It built complex cliff dwellings in the walls of canyons.

16. Which of the following was caused by the Columbian Exchange?

 (A) the introduction of corn to the Americas
 (B) the introduction of smallpox to Afro-Eurasia
 (C) the introduction of the horse to the Americas
 (D) the introduction of tea to Afro-Eurasia

17. Shakespearean drama and kabuki theater have which of the following in common?

 (A) They catered exclusively to the aesthetic sensibilities of elite classes.
 (B) They rejected poetic forms of storytelling.
 (C) They were considered low forms of entertainment in their own day.
 (D) They appealed to a wider cross-section of society than earlier forms of drama.

18. The devshirme system differed from serfdom in that

 (A) serfs were used only as agricultural laborers.
 (B) those recruited by devshirme received more privileges.
 (C) those using devshirme coerced people of their own kind into service.
 (D) serfs were in a legal sense more free.

19. The image below represents

(A) an agrarian revolution on the brink of victory.
(B) the importation of a new technology into a traditional social order.
(C) the invasion of a less advanced nation by a more advanced one.
(D) the inability of non-Western peoples to adapt to innovative technologies.

20. Copernicus's proof of the heliocentric theory had which of the following effects?

(A) It gave European fleets a navigational advantage over foreign navies.
(B) It led immediately to the discovery of new planets.
(C) It destabilized the scientific orthodoxy supported by Europe's Christian churches.
(D) It boosted humankind's confidence in its existential importance.

21. Safavid Persia, Ottoman Turkey, and Mughal India had which of the following in common?

(A) skill at organizing powerful armies equipped with gunpowder weapons
(B) a tradition of overseas exploration and colonization
(C) limited networks of trade and communication outside their own region
(D) an impoverished cultural and intellectual life

22. Which of the following best describes the effects of the eighteenth-century agricultural revolution in Europe?

    (A) There were fewer famines and better crop yields.
    (B) Serfdom was abolished.
    (C) Peasants revolted and took control of manor estates.
    (D) Poverty was largely eliminated in the countryside.

23. Which of the following trends is associated with the Industrial Revolution in Europe?

    (A) outmigration from the cities to the countryside
    (B) a steep decline in population levels
    (C) a general increase in prosperity after the mid-1800s
    (D) an immediate improvement in the lives of the lower classes

24. Latin America's wars of independence resulted in which of the following?

    (A) the rise of new monarchies
    (B) the full industrialization of the economy
    (C) a tendency toward authoritarian rule
    (D) the emancipation of slaves

25. The worldwide ramifications of the Seven Years' War (1756–1763) included

    (A) Prussia's colonization of the Suez region.
    (B) France's loss of its colony in Canada.
    (C) Britain's takeover of Cuba and Puerto Rico.
    (D) Austria's expansion of its foothold in India.

26. The Declaration of the Rights of Man and the Citizen is most similar in its outlook to

    (A) the Magna Carta.
    (B) the American Declaration of Independence.
    (C) the Seneca Falls Declaration of Sentiments.
    (D) the Atlantic Charter.

27. Which pair of nations abolished systems of coerced labor in the 1860s?

    (A) China and Ethiopia
    (B) Portugal and the Congo
    (C) the United States and Russia
    (D) Brazil and Argentina

28. The photograph below most likely illustrates an instance of

(A) racial tensions breaking out into open conflict.
(B) the West's imperial strategy of training and deploying native troops.
(C) interregional trade involving the sale of military equipment.
(D) technology transfer of gunpowder weaponry from Africa to Europe.

29. The Young Turk movement exemplifies what sort of change?

(A) major change caused by dissatisfied elites
(B) a return to religious fundamentalism
(C) incremental reform
(D) grass roots revolution

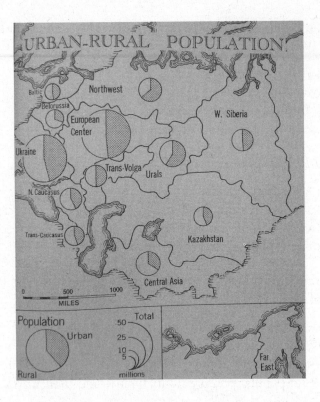

30. Examining the chart above, one can safely reach the conclusion that

    (A) more people in the Northwest live in cities than in the USSR's European Center.
    (B) Western Siberia has a larger agrarian population than the Soviet Ukraine.
    (C) Central Asia is, by percentage, the least urbanized of the Soviet regions shown.
    (D) the Baltic is home to more urban dwellers than the Trans-Caucasus.

31. Which of the following was NOT a major characteristic of Middle Eastern political life in the twentieth century?

    (A) widespread democratization
    (B) tensions between religious fundamentalism and Westernization
    (C) the Arab-Israeli conflict
    (D) the persistence of human-rights abuses

32. Which of the following is NOT associated with religious fundamentalism in the post-1945 era?

    (A) the Iranian Revolution
    (B) the Rwandan genocide
    (C) Sikh-Hindu conflicts in India
    (D) the rise of the Taliban in Afghanistan

33. The Marshall Plan is an example of

    (A) a defensive military alliance.
    (B) the formation of a multinational corporation.
    (C) the effectiveness of non-governmental organizations.
    (D) economic diplomacy in action.

34. Why did the United States support Ferdinand Marcos in the Philippines and the Shah of Iran?

    (A) because they were committed to democratic principles
    (B) because they were strongly anti-communist
    (C) because they observed international human rights standards
    (D) because of popular pressure from Filipino- and Iranian-American voters

World's Major Consumers of Primary Energy (1998) Measured in quadrillions of British thermal units (Btu)	
United States	94.57 quadrillion Btu
China	33.93 quadrillion Btu
Russia	25.99 quadrillion Btu
Japan	21.21 quadrillion Btu
Germany	13.83 quadrillion Btu
India	12.51 quadrillion Btu
Canada	11.85 quadrillion Btu
France	10.00 quadrillion Btu
United Kingdom	9.75 quadrillion Btu
Brazil	8.08 quadrillion Btu

35. Based on the data presented in the above table, which of the following conclusions might one safely make?

    (A) Brazil has a smaller population than China does.
    (B) The top energy-consuming nations are to be found mainly in the developed world.
    (C) Russia is a more efficient consumer of energy than China is.
    (D) Japan has a larger population than India does.

36. Which of the following would provide the BEST evidence for a high degree of political centralization among the Indus River city-states?

    (A) the presence of what appear to be public baths
    (B) the uniform layout of streets and public buildings
    (C) the profusion of statues depicting what seem to be political leaders
    (D) the discovery of trade goods from a variety of faraway lands

37. Which of the following statements accurately describes tool use during the Stone Age?

    (A) Religious rituals were unknown during this era.
    (B) Wheels and metal objects were in common use.
    (C) The chief priority in tool design was ensuring a supply of food.
    (D) Only stone was used to make tools.

38. Which of the following resulted from Alexander the Great's conquests?

    (A) the formation of a Macedonian Empire that lasted several centuries
    (B) the spread of Hellenistic culture through much of Eurasia
    (C) the destruction of the Zoroastrian religion in Persia
    (D) the worsening of relations between Europe and the Muslim world

39. How did Andean and Mesoamerican religious traditions most resemble each other?

    (A) in their tendency toward monotheism
    (B) in the emphasis they placed on building pyramids
    (C) in their practice of human sacrifice
    (D) in the way they mixed religious and political authority

40. Which of the following accurately describes the spread of Buddhism outside of India?

    (A) to Korea, from there to Thailand, and from there to China
    (B) to China, from there to Korea, and from there to Japan
    (C) to Cambodia, from there to China, and from there to Korea
    (D) to China, from there to Thailand, and from there to Cambodia

41. Political characteristics of the Qin Empire included

    (A) a tendency to neglect transportational infrastructure.
    (B) a high degree of decentralization.
    (C) military weakness.
    (D) high levels of taxation and use of forced labor.

42. Maritime technology in the ancient Mediterranean

    (A) was largely nonexistent.
    (B) relied principally on rowed vessels.
    (C) made use of ships with lateen sails.
    (D) routinely involved open-water navigation.

43. The political logic behind the early Islamic caliphates was that

    (A) religious and political authority were to be strictly separated.
    (B) different Muslim communities should govern themselves autonomously.
    (C) unbelievers had no place in Islamic society.
    (D) religious and political leadership should be united in one person.

44. Which of the following pairs of societies enjoyed the most fruitful cultural and economic interchange during the 600–1450 period?

    (A) the Abbasid Caliphate and Tang China
    (B) Gupta India and Heian Japan
    (C) the Aztecs and the Mississippi culture
    (D) Mali and Sassanid Persia

45. In what way are the histories of the Bantu and the Polynesians similar?

    (A) Their migrations dispersed a single cultural group over vast distances.
    (B) They cultivated corn and potatoes before most other peoples.
    (C) They navigated the open ocean with great skill.
    (D) They domesticated the horse and pioneered cavalry warfare.

46. What best describes the relationship between Islamic and medieval European culture?

    (A) Muslim scholars and philosophers borrowed from English and French thinkers.
    (B) Muslim science and translations from Greek were indispensable to Europe's cultural growth.
    (C) Muslims learned much about European art and architecture during the Crusades.
    (D) Muslim and European cultures did not interact, because of intense religious hostility.

47. Zimbabwe and Timbuktu were most alike in what respect?

    (A) They were renowned centers of Islamic scholarship.
    (B) They were key points in trade networks extending beyond Africa's borders.
    (C) They were great repositories of Swahili culture and learning.
    (D) They were successful military powers and built mighty empires.

48. What factor caused Southeast Asia to experience major political change between 1200 and 1400?

    (A) Military pressure was caused by Chinese and Mongol attempts to conquer parts of the region.
    (B) Countries in this region began to adopt Confucianism.
    (C) Invading forces crossed the Indian Ocean from East Africa.
    (D) The peoples of the region started to embrace the Christian faith.

49. What existing labor system in the Americas did Spanish colonizers adapt?

    (A) serfdom
    (B) the mit'a
    (C) the devshirme
    (D) indentured servitude

50. The Kongo kingdom's political strategies during the 1450–1750 period led it to

    (A) avoid outright colonization by ceding some of their powers to Portugal.
    (B) prevent economic entanglement with the Atlantic slave trade.
    (C) fall under Berber rule for three centuries.
    (D) participate heavily in the Indian Ocean trade network.

51. Which of the following is NOT true of the Ottomans' military campaigns between the mid-1400s and the late 1600s?

    (A) They remained at the technological forefront with respect to weaponry.
    (B) They attained naval mastery over the eastern Mediterranean.
    (C) They conquered most of the Balkans and much of Hungary.
    (D) They treated non-Muslims in conquered territories with complete equality.

52. Protestantism and Islam during the 1600s were most alike in that

    (A) they encouraged female literacy so that women could read scripture.
    (B) they subscribed to doctrines of predestination.
    (C) they completely forbade the creation of religious art.
    (D) they justified campaigns of persecution against suspected witches.

53. When the Portuguese arrived in India and Southeast Asia, they

    (A) agreed with local powers not to allow Catholic priests to proselytize.
    (B) quickly conquered India and China, thanks to their naval superiority.
    (C) established control over certain port cities and islands, but not larger nations.
    (D) found that the difficulty of voyaging made trade with these regions unprofitable.

54. Which of the following does NOT accurately describe a major impact of gunpowder on national development?

    (A) Several African states boosted their regional power by acquiring firearms in the 1600s and 1700s.
    (B) Fearful of being made obsolete, Japan's samurai class carefully controlled access to guns.
    (C) The Ottoman Empire and Mughal India proved adept at using gunpowder weaponry in the 1500s and 1600s.
    (D) The appearance of gunpowder led rapidly to Western domination of the world's other major civilizations.

Model Test 2

55. Which of the following is NOT an Enlightenment tenet?

    (A) Organized churches exploit superstitious beliefs to increase their wealth and power.
    (B) Rational thought can achieve a full understanding of the universe.
    (C) Human beings should give free expression to instinct and emotion.
    (D) Freedom from arbitrary governance is a goal worth striving for.

56. Qing China's principal trade commodities were

    (A) spices, porcelain, and cotton.
    (B) tea, gunpowder, and cloves.
    (C) gunpowder, silk, and glassware.
    (D) tea, silk, and porcelain.

57. Radicalism in the French Revolution manifested itself in which of the following ways?

    (A) the decision to allow Louis XVI to reign as a limited monarch
    (B) the peasant uprising in the Vendée
    (C) the Directory's willingness to allow aristocrats to return from exile
    (D) the attempt to replace Catholicism with a "cult of the supreme being"

58. Which of the following accurately describes slavery in the Americas?

    (A) Caribbean slaves worked mainly in cotton fields and silver mines.
    (B) More slaves were brought to Latin America than to the United States.
    (C) The French enslaved entire Native American tribes.
    (D) The outlawing of the slave trade in the early 1800s ended slavery in the Americas.

59. What best explains the Russian conquest of Central Asia in the 1800s?

    (A) the desire to convert the regions' Muslims to Eastern Orthodoxy
    (B) fear that Germany might gain control of Indian Ocean trade
    (C) the need to control the region's vast oil reserves
    (D) anxiety about protecting a long and open southern frontier

60. In what way did China's response to Western colonial pressure differ from Japan's in the 1800s?

    (A) Japan granted economic concessions to foreign powers; China did not.
    (B) China modernized and industrialized; Japan did not.
    (C) China defeated the Western powers in battle; Japan tended to lose to them.
    (D) Japan modernized and industrialized; China did not.

61. Which would most justify historians in calling U.S. conduct "imperial" during and after the Spanish-American War?

    (A) the United States' renunciation of the Monroe Doctrine
    (B) the United States' liberation of Spanish concentration camps in Cuba
    (C) the United States' occupation of Puerto Rico and the Philippines
    (D) the United States' deposition of the Spanish monarchy

62. To deter Germany's workers from embracing radical ideologies, the government

    (A) imprisoned Karl Marx and other prominent socialists.
    (B) stirred up anti-Semitic resentment among German workers.
    (C) gave workers a generous package of social benefits.
    (D) granted universal suffrage, including to women.

63. Why did the European Economic Community form?

    (A) to coordinate economic production during World War II
    (B) to keep U.S. exports from flooding European markets
    (C) to encourage the free movement of goods and labor within Europe
    (D) to increase the number of internal tariffs within Europe

64. How were the decolonization processes in Rhodesia and South Africa similar?

    (A) The post-independence governments were led by whites who controlled black majorities.
    (B) In both cases, mass genocide resulted from decolonization.
    (C) United Nations peacekeepers had to be brought in to maintain order.
    (D) The British tradition of training native elites worked especially well in both cases.

65. The Lend-Lease program affected twentieth-century economic affairs by

    (A) offering U.S. and British economic assistance to recently decolonized states.
    (B) bringing East European economies under tight Soviet control.
    (C) committing the United States to economic support of Britain and the USSR during World War II.
    (D) establishing a regional trade network in East and Southeast Asia.

66. Which of the following is NOT true about the status of women in the twentieth century?

    (A) Fascist Italy and Nazi Germany encouraged the equal treatment of women.
    (B) During World War II, more women worked outside the home than during World War I.
    (C) In theory, Soviet ideology favored the ideal of gender equality.
    (D) Many women's movements won equal access to higher education and political participation.

Model Test 2

67. Existentialists would most likely agree that

(A) a single god exists for the benefit of all humanity.
(B) individuals must act ethically even without the comfort of religion.
(C) the universe is uncaring, making all life meaningless.
(D) with no higher spiritual authority, might makes right.

68. How did the demise of communist regimes in Eastern Europe tend to differ from the collapse of the USSR?

(A) In most East European countries, revolutions were sparked by popular protest, whereas Soviet collapse was caused largely by political elites.
(B) In the USSR, popular uprisings instigated the collapse, whereas in Eastern Europe, political leaders changed the form of government.
(C) The USSR collapsed for economic reasons, whereas East European regimes collapsed due to ethnic conflict.
(D) East European regimes collapsed due to economic exhaustion, whereas the USSR's breakdown was caused by ethnic violence.

69. How have political developments changed in South Korea and Taiwan since the 1980s?

(A) Taiwan has become more authoritarian than South Korea.
(B) Leaders in both countries are actively seeking reunion with their communist counterparts.
(C) Both countries have democratized.
(D) Both countries have allied with the People's Republic of China.

70. The rebuilding of a Sarajevo mosque shelled during the Yugoslav wars of the 1990s is most likely an indication of

(A) hope that reconciliation is possible between Bosnia's Christians and Muslims.
(B) a widespread aesthetic revival of Ottoman architectural forms.
(C) increased social pressure to convert to Islam in the wake of the former conflict.
(D) economic influence applied by non-state organizations like the International Monetary Fund.

SECTION II: FREE-RESPONSE QUESTIONS

Part A: Document-Based Question

TIME: 10 MINUTES TO READ DOCUMENTS; 40 MINUTES
TO COMPLETE ESSAY (RECOMMENDED, NOT OFFICIAL)

Directions: The following question is based on the accompanying Documents 1–7. (The documents have been edited for the purpose of this exercise.) Write your answer on the lined pages of the Section II free-response booklet.

This question is designed to test your ability to work with and understand historical documents.

Write an essay that

- has a relevant thesis and supports that thesis with evidence from the documents.
- uses all of the documents.
- analyzes the documents by grouping them in as many appropriate ways as possible, and does not simply summarize the documents individually.
- takes into account the sources of the documents and analyzes the authors' points of view.
- identifies and explains the need for at least one additional type of document.

You may refer to relevant historical information not mentioned in the documents.

1. Using the documents, compare and contrast European and non-European reactions to encounters with unfamiliar religious beliefs between roughly 1200 and 1900. Identify an additional type of document and explain how it would help in assessing such reactions.

DOCUMENT 1

Source: Thomas Coryate, English traveler in Turkey, on witnessing Sufi dervishes (1613).

There is a College of Turkish Monks in Galata, that are called [Dervishes], . . . who every Tuesday and Friday do perform the strangest exercise of Devotion that ever I saw or heard of. . . .

A little after I came into the room, the Dervishes repaired into the middle void space, sitting Cross-legged, bending their Bodies low toward the floor for Religion['s] sake, even almost flat upon their Faces . . . the whole company of them were about two and fifty. . . .

[A] certain Singing-man sitting apart in an upper room began to sing certain Hymns, but with the most unpleasant and harsh notes that ever I heard, exceedingly differing from our Christian Church singing, for the yelling and disorderly squeaking did even grate mine ears. . . . [T]hree Pipers sitting in the room with the Singer began to play upon certain long Pipes not unlike Tabors, which yielded a very ridiculous and foolish Music . . . whereupon some five and twenty of the two and fifty Dervishes suddenly rose up bare-legged and bare-footed, and casting aside their upper Garments, some of them having their breasts all uncovered, they began by little and little to turn about the Interpreter of the Law. Afterward they redoubled their force and turned with such incredible swiftness, that I could not choose but admire it.

DOCUMENT 2

Source: Council of the Aztec city of Huejotzingo, letter to the king of Spain (1560).

Catholic Royal Majesty!

When your servants the Spaniards reached us and your captain general Don Hernando Cortés arrived, not a single town surpassed us here in New Spain, in that first and earliest we threw ourselves toward you.

. . . we also say and declare before you that [when] your padres, the sons of St. Francis, entered the city of Huejotzingo, of our own free will we honored them and showed them esteem. When they [told us to] abandon the wicked belief in many gods, we did it. Very willingly we destroyed, demolished, and burned the temples. . . .

But now we are taken aback and very afraid, and we ask, have we done something wrong, have we somehow behaved badly, or have we committed some sin against almighty God?

DOCUMENT 3

Source: Jean Bodin, French philosopher (1530–1596), on Ottoman religious policy.

The King of the Turks, who rules over a great part of Europe, safeguards the rites of religion as well as any prince in this world. He constrains no one, but on the contrary permits everyone to live as his conscience dictates. What is more, even in his seraglio at Pera he permits the practice of four diverse religions, that of the Jews, the Christian according to the Roman rite, and according to the Greek rite, and that of Islam.

DOCUMENT 4

Source: Photograph of the Shrine of the Twenty-Six Martyrs, Nagasaki, Japan. Dedicated to twenty-six Japanese converts and Catholic priests crucified in 1597 at the orders of Japanese ruler Toyotomi Hideyoshi.

DOCUMENT 5

Source: Dante Alighieri, Florentine poet, *The Inferno,* Canto XXVIII, 28–36 (ca. 1307).

> I stood and stared at him from the stone shelf;
>   he noticed me and opening his own breast
>   with both hands cried: "See how I rip myself!
>
> See how Mahomet's mangled and split open!
>   Ahead of me walks Ali in his tears
>   his head cleft from the top-knot to the chin.
>
> All the other souls that bleed and mourn
>   along this ditch were sowers of scandal and schism:
>   as they tore others apart, so are they torn."

DOCUMENT 6

Source: The Regulations of the City of Avignon (1243).

> Likewise, we declare that Jews or whores shall not dare to touch with their hands either bread or fruit put out for sale, and that if they should do this they must buy what they have touched.

DOCUMENT 7

Source: Albert Schweitzer, German missionary, doctor, and humanitarian, letter to his sister (April 1913).

Medical knowledge made it possible for me to carry out my intention [of bringing Christ to Africa] in the best and most complete way, wherever the path of service might lead me. . . .

I'm really happy. I feel I've done the right thing in coming here, for the misery is greater than anyone can describe. . . . [T]here are all stages of leprosy. . . . I see a great deal of sleeping sickness. It is very painful for these poor souls. . . . And elephantiasis, that constantly increasing swelling of the limbs. It is dreadful; eventually the legs are so thick that the people can no longer drag them about.

Many heart cases; the people are suffocating. And then the joy when the digitalin works! Evenings I go to bed dead-tired, but in my heart I am profoundly happy that *I am serving at the outpost of the Kingdom of God!*

Part B: Continuity and Change-Over-Time Question

(SUGGESTED PLANNING AND WRITING TIME—40 MINUTES)
PERCENT OF SECTION II SCORE—33⅓

Directions: You are to answer the following question. You should spend 5 minutes organizing or outlining your essay.

Write an essay that:

- has a relevant thesis and supports that thesis with appropriate historical evidence.
- addresses all parts of the question.
- uses world historical context to show continuities and changes over time.
- analyzes the process of continuity and change over time.

2. Describe the continuities and changes in the formation of transregional networks of exchange along the Silk Road between 600 and 1450 OR in the Indian Ocean basin between 600 and 1450. Assess the effects of the continuities and changes that you describe.

Part C: Comparative Essay

(SUGGESTED PLANNING AND WRITING TIME—40 MINUTES)
PERCENT OF SECTION II SCORE—33⅓

Directions: You are to answer the following question. You should spend 5 minutes organizing or outlining your essay.

Write an essay that

- has a relevant thesis and supports that thesis with appropriate historical evidence.
- addresses all parts of the question.
- makes direct, relevant comparisons.
- analyzes relevant reasons for similarities and differences.

3. Compare the aims and results of the French Revolution (1789) with the Russian Revolution (1917). Be sure to include similarities and differences.

END OF SECTION II

Answer Key
MODEL TEST 2

Section I

1. C	21. A	41. D	61. C
2. A	22. A	42. B	62. C
3. C	23. C	43. D	63. C
4. A	24. C	44. A	64. A
5. D	25. B	45. A	65. C
6. C	26. B	46. B	66. A
7. B	27. C	47. B	67. B
8. B	28. B	48. A	68. A
9. D	29. A	49. B	69. C
10. C	30. C	50. A	70. A
11. B	31. A	51. D	
12. A	32. B	52. A	
13. C	33. D	53. C	
14. A	34. B	54. D	
15. A	35. B	55. C	
16. C	36. B	56. D	
17. D	37. C	57. D	
18. B	38. B	58. B	
19. B	39. D	59. D	
20. C	40. B	60. D	

ANSWERS EXPLAINED

1. **(C)** This question tests your sense of historiography, or your understanding of how historians think about history. Answers A, B, and D refer to developments that took place earlier in time.

2. **(A)** Answers B and D are factually wrong. The Phoenicians invented the alphabet, as in C, but it requires a broad definition of "technology" to include a written script.

3. **(C)** Ancient cities tended to contain all these facilities. But this, the Parthenon, on the Acropolis, served as the temple of Athena, the city's patron deity. It is a landmark of Greek architecture.

4. **(A)** Monotheism and Judaic tradition tended to set the Hebrews apart from their neighbors, making B wrong. They fought many wars, so D is incorrect, and when they did suffer military and political setbacks, it was not because of religion.

5. **(D)** Despite being known as "Arabic numerals," the decimal numbering system in use today emerged in Gupta India, along with the concepts of zero and *pi*.

6. **(C)** This carving, of the Persian emperor Shapur II, is clearly intended to convey a sense of the ruler's majesty, and especially his military prowess. Answers A and B are not implausible, but should seem most likely, given the humble posture of the kneeling figure.

7. **(B)** Unusually, the societies of the Andes lacked a written script. For recordkeeping purposes, they relied on a system of knotted strings called *quipu*.

8. **(B)** A revival of Confucian beliefs during the Song dynasty reaffirmed China's cultural commitment to traditional patriarchal values and social and political hierarchy. It also led to a decline in the status of women.

9. **(D)** Trade in medieval Europe was intimately connected with the growth of cities, and the guild system was the most common form of labor organization in medieval cities. The Hanseatic League was a prominent association promoting trade among the cities of northern Europe. Any effect on changing religious attitudes was indirect at best.

10. **(C)** The Islamic world influenced the European Renaissance, not vice versa, and non-Muslims were not treated with complete equality in the caliphates, making A and B incorrect. State control over culture tends to limit creativity, and was not the case in the Abbasid Caliphate. As a cosmopolitan crossroads between the Middle East, Persia, and Central and East Asia, the caliphate drew upon a myriad of cultural traditions.

11. **(B)** After 1260, the Mongol Empire began to split apart into the khanates depicted on the map.

12. **(A)** Although they resemble each other in that they feature non-Westerners engaged in wide-ranging travels, the journeys of Ibn Battuta and Zheng He are in fact quite different. The former was on a private venture, with no military or tribute-gathering purpose. Neither was interested in religious conversion.

13. **(C)** Combining the classical tradition of the Greco-Latin era with Christianity, the culture of the Renaissance was more secular in its outlook than the culture of the medieval period, but did not (and, practically speaking, could not) reject Christian belief altogether.

14. **(A)** Africa contributed gold and ivory to the Indian Ocean trade network. India was a source of salt and cotton. China traded porcelain and silk, among other goods. Southeast Asia took part as well, adding cinnamon and other spices; Japan was a source of silver.

15. **(A)** Not the most warlike civilization in North America, the Mississippian culture is known for building large earth mounds. Cahokia, in what is now Illinois, was a sizable city. No society in the Americas is known to have practiced monotheism in the pre-Columbian era. Cliff dwellings are more typical of the U.S. Southwest.

16. **(C)** Answers A, B, and C all refer to items that crossed the Atlantic as a result of the Columbian Exchange, but A and B reverse the direction. Tea was not part of the Exchange.

17. **(D)** Both of these are examples of art forms driven by demand from a number of social classes, including the early version of what can be thought of as a middle class, making A incorrect. Shakespeare wrote in blank verse and was patronized by England's royal family, invalidating B and C.

18. **(B)** Although most serfs were peasants, they were also used for other kinds of labor, making A wrong, and they were not "freer," as D suggests. Those recruited by the Ottomans under the devshirme system were Christian boys taken from their families and converted to Islam, so C is not correct. They served as elite soldiers, civil servants, scribes, and priests, and were quite well treated, even if their labor was coerced.

19. **(B)** Knowledge of the cultural advancement and inventiveness of many non-Western societies is enough to eliminate D, and there are no clues pointing to agrarian uprising in the image, as in A. Only one side is depicted, so there is no evidence for C. The mix of armor and muskets makes B the likeliest answer. The image depicts Japanese samurai training with firearms and rain-resistant gear.

20. **(C)** By proving mathematically that the earth and other planets revolve around the sun, Polish astronomer Nicolaus Copernicus set into motion an intellectual earthquake, contradicting religious doctrine and scientific orthodoxy, and revealing that humanity did not dwell at the center of the universe.

21. **(A)** Known as the "gunpowder empires," all three of these states were at the fore-front of world power in the 1500s and 1600s. Although Ottoman Turkey had a strong Mediterranean navy and a large empire, none of these states colonized overseas. They traded widely and had vibrant, cosmopolitan cultures.

22. **(A)** By encouraging the use of better technology and more scientific methods of production, the agricultural revolution increased yields in eighteenth-century Europe and caused the rate of population growth to increase. It did not by itself eliminate poverty or serfdom.

23. **(C)** Even during its early stage, when conditions for the lower classes were at their hardest, the Industrial Revolution generated great wealth. Overall prosperity rose in Europe and after mid-century began to become more evenly distributed.

24. **(C)** Constitutional rule did not thrive in Latin America, and rule by caudillos, or strongmen, became common. Except in Brazil, however, these were not monarchs. Latin American economies tended to be based on plantation monoculture and resource extraction, and slavery persisted until near the end of the 1800s.

25. **(B)** Although the Seven Years' War began as a quarrel between Frederick the Great of Prussia and his neighbors, it embroiled France and Britain in a global contest for colonial dominance in several parts of the world, especially India and North America. Colonial authority over Canada was transferred from France to Britain as a result.

26. **(B)** The French Declaration was a product of Enlightenment philosophy and influence from American revolutionaries. The Magna Carta, a medieval document, was more limited in its aims, whereas the Seneca Falls Declaration had to do with women's rights in the 1800s. The Atlantic Charter stated the Allies' war aims during World War II.

27. **(C)** Much of Latin America did not end slavery until the 1880s. The United States abolished slavery as a result of the Civil War, and Russia's Alexander II emancipated the serfs in 1861.

28. **(B)** Answer D can be discarded as contrary to facts. The absence of any sign of violence makes A unlikely, and it does not appear that anything is being bought or sold, calling C into question. These are Senegalese troops trained and armed by the French—a common strategy employed by European imperial powers.

29. **(A)** The Young Turks were Westernizing modernizers impatient with the sultans' cautious, gradual approach to reform and dissatisfied with the influence of Islamic traditionalism in political life.

30. **(C)** When comparing different regions, bear in mind that the size of the circle represents population size, while the balance of light and dark measures percentage. It is possible for a region with a small population to be more heavily

urbanized than another by percentage, and yet still have fewer people living in cities because of the difference in the overall size of population.

31. **(A)** Middle Eastern regimes in the 1900s tended to range from mild authoritarianism to severe dictatorship. Civil liberties and human rights have not been widely observed, and one economic consequence has been a general failure to distribute wealth fairly, even in the region's oil-rich states.

32. **(B)** Religious fundamentalism has been a powerful force in the postwar world, affecting Ireland's "troubles" between Catholics and Protestants, and the Yugoslav wars of the 1990s. The Rwandan genocide, however, was motivated mainly by racial tensions.

33. **(D)** Fearing a repetition of the interwar period, when economic depression drove many European governments to political extremism, Secretary of State George Marshall proposed a large infusion of U.S. funds into the shattered economies of Europe, in order to keep them from becoming attracted to communism.

34. **(B)** During the Cold War, the United States contained Soviet expansion where it seemed to threaten American interests. Therefore, when choosing regimes to support, the United States tended to focus more on whether they were anticommunist rather than on whether they were democratic or observed human rights. Marcos and the Shah of Iran were among the authoritarian leaders who received U.S. backing during this era.

35. **(B)** Without knowing the population of the countries listed on the chart, conclusions about population size or per capita consumption are impossible. What can be determined is that most of the countries on the chart are from the developed world.

36. **(B)** Standardization is generally a sign of centralized authority. Answers A and C refer to common fixtures in ancient urban centers, and city-states governed autonomously were perfectly capable of developing extensive trade networks.

37. **(C)** The need to provide food, clothing, and shelter did the most to spur human invention during the Stone Age. Answer B is false because metalworking was unknown during this era, and the fact that Stone Age people buried their dead indicates that they had religious beliefs. Answer D is false because tools were made of bone, fiber, wood, and other materials that have not survived as well as the stone implements more easily discovered by archaeologists.

38. **(B)** Alexander's empire collapsed very quickly after his death, and Zoroastrianism survived his takeover of Persia, making A and C incorrect. Islam did not exist yet, so D is false. Alexander's great legacy was acquainting a large part of Eurasia with Hellenistic, or Greek-like, culture.

39. **(D)** Both regions were polytheistic, but pyramid-building and human sacrifice were not typical of Andean religious life. Both endowed their rulers with priestly functions or believed that they had divine qualities.

40. **(B)** China became a great center of Buddhist worship, and Korea was an important conduit of Chinese culture to Japan.

41. **(D)** The Qin dynasty, considered to have created China as a nation, was a highly centralized state that mobilized a powerful, modern army and built hundreds of miles of canals, roads, and defensive walls. Its ruthless founder, Shi Huangdi, used countless prisoners as laborers and taxed his people extremely heavily, to the point that social unrest after his death contributed to the dynasty's downfall.

42. **(B)** The Mediterranean hosted a great deal of maritime traffic. The vessels typically operating there during these years were galleys and biremes, propelled by oars and carrying small square sails. They generally did not venture far from the coast, as distinct from the dhows of the Indian Ocean, or the Vikings' longboats, which were capable of crossing large expanses of open ocean.

43. **(D)** Early Islamic doctrine stated that the *umma,* or community of believers, should be united politically and led by a single religious and political authority making A and B incorrect. Although they were not treated as equals, unbelievers were permitted to live under Muslim authority, and Jews and Christians were respected as "people of the book."

44. **(A)** The Middle East and China were among the most culturally and technologically advanced parts of the world, and they interacted with each other regularly during this era.

45. **(A)** Both groups traveled astounding distances, but the Bantu did so over land, while the Polynesians crossed the Pacific, making C and D wrong. Corn (maize) and the potato were New World crops and not available elsewhere until the Columbian Exchange.

46. **(B)** The European debt to Muslim and Jewish scholars, especially concerning the recovery of knowledge about the ancient Greeks, was immense. The less-advanced Europeans had less impact on Islamic culture at this time.

47. **(B)** The people of Mali were not descended from the Bantu, and Zimbabwe at its peak was not Muslim. Neither was part of the Swahili cultural group, and neither built large empires. Both traded widely.

48. **(A)** Mongol and Chinese conquest extended to Southeast Asia during the 1200s, changing political systems and patterns of economic activity. Compared to Hinduism and Buddhism, Confucianism and Christianity—which did not arrive until later—had little influence in the region.

49. **(B)** Common in the Andean societies, the mit'a was co-opted by Spanish conquerors. Answer C belongs to the Ottoman Empire, and A and D were used widely throughout the world.

50. **(A)** Like China in the 1800s, Kongo in the 1500s gave up much of its autonomy to foreign powers, but avoided being conquered outright. Its rulers converted to Catholicism and sold slaves to the Portuguese in exchange for guns and other goods. It was not conquered by the Berbers, and its location in West Africa kept it from participating in Indian Ocean trade.

51. **(D)** The Ottomans were skilled practitioners of gunpowder weaponry until losing their edge in the 1700s. Although they allowed non-Muslims to live under their rule, they taxed them heavily and took many of their children to serve under the devshirme system of labor organization.

52. **(A)** Predestination was a Calvinist doctrine, and witchhunts were a European phenomenon, making B and D incorrect. While Islam strictly discouraged the depiction of human or animal figures in art, Protestantism was split on the question of religious art.

53. **(C)** In the late 1400s and 1500s, most Asian countries were strong enough to resist Western colonial pressures. Portugal gained some footholds in South and Southeast Asia, but, like the other Europeans who followed them, could not conquer or intimidate the larger nations of Asia until the 1700s and 1800s.

54. **(D)** Although Europe eventually used gunpowder more effectively than rival civilizations, it took a number of years for this to happen. In the meantime, other cultures used gunpowder weaponry as well. Several West African states bartered slaves taken from their neighbors in exchange for Western guns.

55. **(C)** Largely a backlash against the Enlightenment, the Romantic movement, which began in the late 1700s and lasted well into the 1800s, stressed instinct and the emotions. All the other answers correctly reflect the ideals of the Enlightenment.

56. **(D)** The Chinese traded silk and porcelain for centuries. In the 1700s and 1800s, tea joined—and surpassed—them as a commodity for export. In particular, the sale of tea to Britain caused such a trade imbalance that the British responded by shipping opium illegally and by force to China.

57. **(D)** Answers A and C are examples of relative moderation, and the Vendée uprising was a response against, not an example of, revolutionary radicalism. Not only did the Revolution separate church and state, but radical leaders attempted to displace or discourage Catholicism by boosting alternatives such as the atheistic "cult of reason" or Robespierre's deistic "cult of the supreme being."

58. **(B)** More slaves went to Spanish and Portuguese colonies than to the United States. Although most European nations outlawed slavery and the slave trade in the early 1800s, slavery itself persisted in the New World until the late 1800s. The French tended to have friendly relations with Native American tribes.

59. **(D)** The Russians worried more about Britain in this region, not Germany, and oil was a concern in the 1900s, making B and C false. Religious conversion was not a priority, but the long, difficult-to-defend border in the south was. The Russians also desired warm-water ports in the south, which they never obtained, and the cotton-growing wealth of the region, which they did.

60. **(D)** Until too late, most Chinese leaders did nothing to modernize, even with a clear threat of foreign domination. Reforms like the self-strengthening movement were limited and not supported by all political elites. By contrast, the Emperor Meiji, rising to power in Japan in 1868, embarked upon a course of rapid Westernization, especially in the industrial and military spheres.

61. **(C)** Spain lost the Spanish-American war decisively, and its status as a colonial power declined as a result. The United States took Puerto Rico, the Philippines, and other colonial possessions, becoming an imperial power itself.

62. **(C)** Although Bismarck governed Germany with an iron hand, he knew how to use positive inducements instead of outright oppression. He put into effect labor laws and a social welfare program appealing enough to keep most workers from feeling that they did not have to join trade unions or socialist parties to improve their lot. All German males could vote, but not women.

63. **(C)** Economic cooperation and the removal of obstacles to free trade were seen as ways to boost European prosperity and economic clout after World War II, which had badly damaged all European economies, even those of the victorious nations.

64. **(A)** In both places, whites controlled the post-independence governments, and so D is incorrect, and in each case racial tensions led to political turmoil. Rhodesia experienced civil war, becoming Zimbabwe after the overthrow of the white regime. The apartheid system was prolonged in South Africa until the 1990s.

65. **(C)** Even before the United States became directly involved in World War II, it supported Britain and the USSR financially. Its assistance was crucial to keeping both war efforts going.

66. **(A)** In the Western democracies, women made many advances. Marxism committed the USSR in principle (not always in reality) to gender equality, whereas the dictatorships in Germany and Italy actively opposed the concept of gender equality. World War II put more women to work than World War I did.

67. **(B)** Made famous after World War II by philosophers such as Sartre and Camus, existentialism continued a trend from earlier in the century by denying that there are any objective moral or religious truths. On their own, people must come to their own understanding of what is right, and then do it for its own sake.

68. **(A)** Mass movements played the decisive role in ending communist rule in Eastern Europe. Although popular discontent and breakaway tendencies on the part of non-Russian populations in the USSR weakened the country, the final collapse came after the attempted coup against Gorbachev in 1991 and the decision later that year by the leaders of Russia and other Soviet republics to form the Commonwealth of Independent States.

69. **(C)** During the Cold War, South Korea and Taiwan, both allies of the United States, were quite authoritarian, but democratized after the Cold War. Taiwan maintains an awkward relationship of undeclared independence from the People's Republic of China, and South and North Korea have remained divided for more than half a century.

70. **(A)** Despite the violence of the 1990s, the states of the former Yugoslavia are at peace. Where multiethnic populations remain, as in Bosnia, the goal is to normalize relations as much as possible among Catholic Croats, Orthodox Serbs, and Bosnian Muslims.

Appendix: Map of Selected World Regions

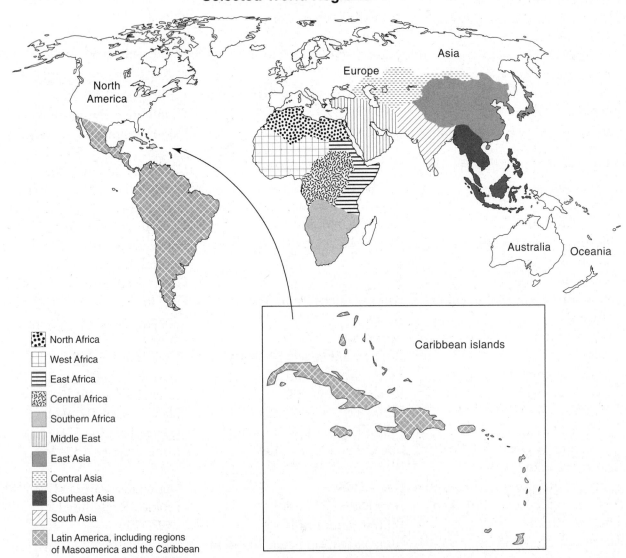

Selected World Regions

North America

Europe

Asia

Australia

Oceania

- North Africa
- West Africa
- East Africa
- Central Africa
- Southern Africa
- Middle East
- East Asia
- Central Asia
- Southeast Asia
- South Asia
- Latin America, including regions of Masoamerica and the Caribbean

Caribbean islands

Index

How to Use the CD-ROM

The software is not installed on your computer; it runs directly from the CD-ROM. Barron's CD-ROM includes an "autorun" feature that automatically launches the application when the CD is inserted into the CD-ROM drive. In the unlikely event that the autorun feature is disabled, follow the manual launching instructions below.

Windows®

1. Click on the Start button and choose "My Computer."
2. Double-click on the CD-ROM drive, which is named **AP_World_History.exe.**
3. Double-click **AP_World_History.exe** to launch the program.

Macintosh®

1. Double-click the CD-ROM icon.
2. Double-click the **AP_World_History** icon to start the program.

<u>SYSTEM REQUIREMENTS</u>

(Flash Player 10.2 is recommended)

Microsoft® Windows®	**MAC OS X**	**Linux® and Solaris™**
Processor: Intel Pentium 4 2.33GHz, Athlon 64 2800+ or faster processor (or equivalent).	Processor: Intel Core™ Duo 1.33GHz or faster processor.	Processor: Intel Pentium 4 2.33GHz, AMD Athlon 64 2800+ or faster processor (or equivalent).
Memory: 128MB of RAM.	Memory: 256MB of RAM.	Memory: 512MB of RAM.
Graphics Memory: 128MB.	Graphics Memory: 128MB.	Graphics Memory: 128MB.
Platforms:	Platforms:	Platforms:
Windows 7, Windows Vista®, Windows XP, Windows Server® 2008, Windows Server 2003.	Mac OS X 10.6, Mac OS X 10.5, Mac OS X 10.4 (Intel) and higher.	Red Hat® Enterprise Linux (RHEL) 5 or later, openSUSE® 11 or later, Ubuntu 9.10 or later. Solaris: Solaris™ 10.

ABOUT THE AUTHOR

John McCannon earned a Ph.D. in history from the University of Chicago in 1994. He has taught Russian history, European history, and world history at several universities in the United States and Canada, and he has worked as an Advanced Placement faculty consultant for the College Board. He is the author of *Red Arctic: Polar Exploration and the Myth of the North in the Soviet Union, 1932–1939.* Professor McCannon is a faculty member in the Department of History at Southern New Hampshire University.

ABOUT THE CONTRIBUTOR

Pamela Jordan received a Ph.D. in political science from the University of Toronto in 1997. In addition to her academic background, she has worked as a news writer for Facts on File News Services, Inc., and as executive director of a nongovernmental organization affiliated with the United Nations. Dr. Jordan is the author of *Defending Rights in Russia: Lawyers, the State and Legal Reform in the Post-Soviet Era.*

ACKNOWLEDGMENTS

This book is dedicated to Pamela Jordan, a co-author in every sense of the word. Without her formidable research skills, her invaluable written contributions to the manuscript, and her sharp editorial eye, this book could never have come into being.

Both the author and contributor would like to thank Jennifer Giammusso, David Rodman, and Anna Damaskos, whose editorial supervision made the preparation of this manuscript a smooth and easy process. We are also grateful to Bill Kuchler for art direction, to Debby Becak and Frank Pasquale for production assistance, and to the anonymous reviewers of this manuscript for their insightful and encouraging comments.

All inquiries should be addressed to:
Barron's Educational Series, Inc.
250 Wireless Boulevard
Hauppauge, New York 11788
www.barronseduc.com

ISBN-13: 978-0-7641-4706-7 (Book)

ISBN-13: 978-1-4380-7134-3 (Book/CD Package)

ISSN: 1937–8874

PRINTED IN THE UNITED STATES OF AMERICA

9 8 7 6 5 4 3

10%
POST-CONSUMER WASTE
Paper contains a minimum of 10% post-consumer waste (PCW). Paper used in this book was derived from certified, sustainable forestlands.

AP*

WORLD HISTORY

5TH EDITION

John McCannon, Ph.D.
Department of History
Southern New Hampshire University
Manchester, New Hampshire

BARRON'S